Gregory E. Samson
1226 E. LaSalle Ave.
Home 335-3954
Business 463-5510

ECONOMICS
FOR MANAGERS

ECONOMICS FOR MANAGERS

CHARLES J. STOKES

Charles Anderson Dana Professor of Economics, University of Bridgeport

McGRAW-HILL BOOK COMPANY

New York   St. Louis   San Francisco   Auckland   Bogotá   Düsseldorf   Johannesburg
London   Madrid   Mexico   Montreal   New Delhi   Panama   Paris   São Paulo   Singapore
Sydney   Tokyo   Toronto

1234567890 FGRFGR 78321098

This book was set in Times Roman by Black Dot, Inc.
The editors were J. S. Dietrich, Bonnie E. Lieberman, and Frances A. Neal;
the designer was Albert M. Cetta;
the production supervisor was Dominick Petrellese.
The drawings were done by ECL Art Associates, Inc.
Fairfield Graphics was printer and binder.

Library of Congress Cataloging in Publication Data

Stokes, Charles J
    Economics for managers.

    Includes bibliographies and index.
    1. Managerial economics. 2. Industrial management—Mathematical models. I. Title.
HD30.22.S8   330'.02'4658   77-16414
ISBN 0-07-061663-9

To Anne who after three decades takes almost anything in stride, including a husband who writes books.

CONTENTS

PREFACE

Managerial Economics, Economics of the Firm, and Business Economics are common titles of courses in applied economics. These courses are often in the core of MBA programs. They are also offered in the upper division or junior-senior sequence in undergraduate business administration throughout North America. I have written this book for students in just such courses. For almost twenty years, I have taught this course at the University of Bridgeport, the University of Colorado, Andrews University, and elsewhere to thousands of both undergraduate and graduate students. Using that wealth of experience, I have focused on a how-to-do-it approach to economics.

I am conscious that few students who take this course will be business economists. Nonetheless, I want them to gain from reading this book an understanding of how they can use what they have learned about economics now and as they advance in their business and government careers. Because in recent years there has been a veritable explosion of both knowledge and application of economic tools in management, this book emphasizes three major principles:

- It is oriented to the firm and to management
- It shows the relevance of economic concepts in actual management situations
- Cases and text are integrated

The presence of thousands of business economists in government and industry, the growth of large corporate economics departments as well as the development of economics management consulting firms have all led to a professionalization of business economics. There is much greater agreement both about what business economists do and about what they should know. Management has a much clearer idea of how to use the results of economic research in making decisions. These important changes mean that although a book on managerial economics is easier to write today, it must meet tougher standards.

As a consulting economist for some large domestic corporations as well as for overseas firms and governments, I have written this book with a good idea of what management wants and needs. I know how the work of economists is judged, and how it is used. Those who read this book will find my treatment of demand, costs, pricing, location decisions, and antitrust matters, among other things, tempered by experience.

Having served at various times as chairman of the board of a bank, corporate director, college trustee, government official, foundation consultant, and senior member of the Brookings Institution, I have had the opportunity to hire economists, to utilize their output, and to present their results to executives and directors. I hope that this experience plus my teaching will provide students with economics relevant to real-life situations.

I have tried to lay a foundation for what mathematics students may need in this book by what I think will be a useful review in Chapter 2 (Numbers, Models and Managerial Economics). For many students there will be no need for such a review, and instructors will, of course, be guided accordingly. For those instructors who wish to present a more intensive analysis of demand and cost theory, Chapters 4 (Statistical and Econometric Analysis of Demand) and 6 (The Production Function and Linear Programming) have been added. For undergraduate courses as well as for those graduate courses in managerial economics with less of a mathematical emphasis, these chapters can be omitted.

Benefit/cost analysis is separated both from capital budgeting and from an analysis of managerial effectiveness. Chapter 12 is intended to give "a state of the art" review of this form of cost and managerial effectiveness evaluation.

Every chapter except Chapter 2 presents at least one case. The cases were selected both for their illustrative value as examples of economics in action and for their teaching effectiveness. Some instructors will want to use them as the focus of their courses. The Instructors' Manual contains both suggested answers for each case and ways to use the case in class discussion. In the Instructors' Manual, too, are other shorter cases as well as batteries of questions, problems, and tests for each chapter.

I owe a heavy debt to those many professors, here in the United States and in Canada as well as overseas, who have used and commented upon my publications over the years. Their suggestions and criticisms have affected, as I think they will see, the form and content of this volume. I am especially indebted to the late Francis X. DiLeo, Dean of the College of Business Administration, a close friend for many years, for his help and inspiration. My colleagues Jerral Nelson, Norman Douglas, and Robert H. Persons, among others, have used various preliminary forms of the current presentation. I must also express my thanks to my other readers and reviewers, H. Marshall Booker (The Christopher Newport College of the College of William and Mary), James F. Crawford (Georgia State University), Erwin Mayer (Western Washington State College), Erwin E. Nemmers (Northwestern University), John Pisciotta (University of Southern Colorado), Franklin E. Robeson (University of Maryland), and Ronald P. Wilder (University of South Carolina), for their help in making this book fit their teaching requirements. Students, among them Fred Prior, Harvey James, Tim Berkel, Otto Densk, Mike Litwinski, and Bob Bialecki, have influenced my thinking greatly. They also helped me to see how to improve my presentation. And what shall I say about Stephen Dietrich, my editor, except thanks for applying the spurs and tightening the reins at the right time.

Charles J. Stokes

1

MANAGERIAL ECONOMICS AND MANAGERIAL ECONOMISTS

Key Concepts

business problem
case analysis
decision relationships
economic tools
management science
management task

managerial economics
managerial economist
operations research
problem formulation
problem solving

What Is Ahead in This Chapter

This chapter begins with a general description of how managerial economics began, who managerial economists are, and how they do what they do. Knowing who these economists are and what they do will help you to see how economics is used in large and small corporations, in government agencies, in policy making, and in consulting.

But don't think that managerial economics is a different kind of economics from principles of economics or from public economics. It isn't. It is neither an easier and less theoretical field nor a more difficult. Managerial economics is a selection from the toolbox of economic principles. It is a collection of those methods and those kinds of analysis that have direct application to management.

Admittedly, there was a tendency some years ago for managerial economics textbooks to "write down." Some authors and even some instructors assumed that business administration students and businessmen really didn't need to know very many economic tools to understand how to use economics in management. Though the feeling was not shared by all economists, there was a perception that much of economic theory actually wasn't relevant to the average business situation. Others, of course, felt that operations research people dominated the management field anyway.

Things have changed dramatically since then. Not only have operations research people and management scientists found it necessary to use ever more complex tools from the economics principles toolbox, but businessmen began to find it essential to have managerial economists on their staffs. Whatever managerial economics was, it became evident that it led to much better management.

Take the case of the president of Brown-Root in Houston who, in some desperation, paused in the middle of an intensive but seemingly directionless planning meeting to call the University of Texas in Austin. He told the head of the economics department he wanted a managerial economist "and soon."

The department head searched among the graduates for such a person and finally found one to send to Houston. When the managerial economist arrived, Brown-Root's president said to him, "I don't know what you do or how you do it, but I do know that I need you. Get in that office and start doing 'managerial economics' and see if you can get us out of this mess."

Contributions of Managerial Economics

One of the special contributions of economics to management is its capacity to identify the key elements in the decision-making process. Out of the welter of facts, economics concentrates upon a few important decision relationships. Managerial economics permits a thorough analysis of these key factors. If a firm's managers want to enlarge their products' share of the market, a knowledge of managerial economics will enable them to determine the dimensions of the market, the kind of competition they face, and the techniques, if any, that will help them to follow the course they propose and to measure the effectiveness of their decision.

In a sense, economics in the United States has always focused on managerial concerns. Very early, American economic writers became interested in the challenges of a fast-growing economy and in the problems of American businessmen who attempted to build enterprises to satisfy the special demands of a new nation. American economists were asked to comment on, to oppose or to support, or, at times, to provide solutions for all kinds of business problems in railroads, steel, oil, sugar, tobacco, and other industries.

Management uses managerial economics to make problem solving easier, improve the quality of decisions, reduce the amount of time required to make good decisions, increase the frequency of correct solutions, or provide some combination of these benefits.

What Do Managerial Economists Do?

Whether they are called "managerial economists," "business economists," "company economists," or just plain economists, managerial economists are now found in every kind of enterprise, regardless of the size of the business, the area of specialization, or the location of company headquarters. There were more than 10,000 managerial economists in the United States by the middle 1970s and the number was growing steadily. Most large firms and commercial banks employ several economists; sometimes there is a large staff of economists as at the Citibank of New York, General Electric, IBM, or Prudential Life. While there is a concentration of managerial economists in New York, Chicago, San Francisco, Boston, Philadelphia, and Los Angeles, regional centers such as Miami, Dayton, Phoenix, Seattle, and Kansas City also have large and growing numbers. Trade associations, business consultants, brokerage houses, and even legal and accounting firms maintain staffs of managerial economists. So do many local, state, and federal agencies as well as the Federal Reserve bank system and the Federal Home Loan bank system. In addition to commercial banks, mutual savings banks, savings and loan associations, and bank holding companies employ managerial economists. The chairman of the Council of Economic Advisers during the presidency of Gerald Ford was a prominent managerial economist, Alan Greenspan, on leave from his position as head of a leading New York economic consulting firm.

The National Association of Business Economists, a professional organization of managerial economists, at various times has prepared case histories of managerial economics careers from which several of the following episodic descriptions are taken. The remainder of the seven reports are derived from interviews with practicing managerial economists.

Seven Managerial Economists and What They Do

Dr. P is an executive vice-president and economist at one of the nation's largest savings banks. He began his career as a professor of economics in a medium-sized Southeastern college. Later he was on the staff of a large trade association prior to coming to his current position.

As a managerial economist, he has had a wide range of duties, including the preparation of business forecasts, position papers on issues facing the industry his trade association served, speeches for corporation executives, testimony before Congressional committees, training programs for analysts and executives, and financial programs for new businesses.

In his savings bank executive position, it is his task to determine the general direction the bank should take, to discover new and possible fields of endeavor, and to assess their costs and benefits for his bank; he is also expected to provide a general set of guidelines for the president and the board of trustees in the continuing management of the bank. Dr. P is both an economist and a manager. He has the pleasure and the responsibility of carrying out his own recommendations. He has come to that stage of his career where he has shifted from adviser to decision maker.

Ms. R directs the economic research activity of a large manufacturing company which produces a broad line of consumer and capital goods and provides consumer services as well. Her job is to provide the senior management of this firm with economic and market forecasts, along with analyses of all pertinent information about the environment in which the various lines of the firm's business are being conducted. She plays a key role in determining the corporate strategy in major markets. The results of her work are relied on in short- and long-range financial, profit, and market planning. She also helps in the evaluation of capital budgets, including proposals to expand into new markets.

As director of economic research and senior economist, she has a staff of six managerial economists to assist in business forecasting, in tracking the indicators of business position, in developing models of business activity, and in speech writing as well as employee, stockholder, and public relations activities.

In her first position with the company, she was concerned with technical model building, which was in line with her mathematical training. She moved up to head of her department as she acquired an ever widening concern with all phases of economic activity. Her functions continue to expand as management learns to rely more and more on its economic staff.

Mr. O is a business economics consultant. He is frequently hired by the economics staffs of major companies and by the managements of smaller firms to provide general forecasts of the national economy. These forecasts serve as the basis for managements' more detailed analyses of internal operations. Mr. O is a specialist in more than forecasting, with interests in petroleum economics, corporate financial planning, and the money market.

On a typical day in his consulting firm, the first activity may be the dictating of a newsletter to his clients. Following that, there is a meeting with the senior officer of a client seeking advice on the proposed construction of a European facility. What the client wants is a way to determine economic feasibility. At lunch, with another client, Mr. O traces the likelihood of important changes in Defense Department procurement policies and their impact on that client firm's sales.

During the afternoon, he meets with his staff to work over a statistical model where there are some thorny problems in theory as well as in data input. Later, he spends time on the development of an input-output model for a multiproduct company. In all that he does he draws upon economics, mathematics, statistics, law, and accounting, as well as political science and sociology. Indeed, he finds it necessary to remain up-to-date and even to learn new techniques constantly so he can be ready to serve his clientele.

Ms. W is an investment economist for one of the larger New York trust companies. Her activities are as diverse as those of her employer; they include stock market forecasting, portfolio selection, money market projection, and watching key business indicators, as well as extensive personal contact within and outside the trust company. She takes an active part in efforts to expand the economic advisory services of the bank and is responsible for planning major seminars to enable clients to understand how to improve the management of their affairs.

Ms. W began as an economist for a Federal Reserve bank and then moved to a small investment company. From there, she went to Washington to work in macroeconomics for a government agency and then back to New York. She has found that a successful managerial economist must be willing to change directions when necessary and must be able to respond to new and varied challenges.

Dr. H is the senior economist and a vice-president on the corporate staff of one of the country's largest communications firms. Because the firm is also involved in many areas of manufacturing, both in the United States and overseas, Dr. H's job involves continual calls on his talents. While his principal task is the preparation of the firm's situation forecast, for which he uses the services of several of the major economic forecasting firms, he must be ready to provide inputs into all phases of a complex planning structure.

The firm has a five-year revolving planning cycle. Each spring, management reviews the accomplishments of the year just ended and extends its plan five years further into the future. While the emphasis is on profitability and assessment of the impact of new technology, evaluation of market competitors as well as changing supply conditions are part of the planning process. Dr. H and his staff are expected to have at hand such necessary information as well as to assist the various divisions in improving their own planning performance.

The firm has sophisticated computer facilities and one of Dr. H's responsibilities is to oversee these activities and to make suggestions for better performance. The various company models of business activity—financial, marketing, and supply models—are subject to his review.

Dr. H has held high positions in the National Association of Business Economists, and as such he has assisted many firms in developing more effective managerial economics departments. He is frequently called upon to help orient other managerial economists.

Dr. L is a managerial economist with a large insurance company, where his function is to provide guidelines for investment as well as for marketing activities. He serves all departments of this company in providing the economic facts and analyses that each department needs to improve its management. In this connection, Dr. L interprets, analyzes, and reports on developments in business, government, and foreign countries, as well as those affecting individuals. His purpose is to provide a basic and continuing understanding of the markets the firm services.

While he operates essentially through his membership on many committees, his function in these committees is to have up-to-date and accurate information available as decisions are being formulated. He and his staff gather economic data, conduct necessary research, and make economic studies and reports. In fulfilling these duties, Dr. L finds his company's computer resources essential to help him retrieve, process, and analyze data. His typical problems involve investing insurance company funds and marketing existing and new insurance policies.

Dr. L entered his company's employment more than two decades ago right after college. While employed there, he obtained master's and doctoral degrees. And now he continues to serve as an adjunct professor in evening classes for the university from which he obtained his advanced degrees.

Mr. A is an economist for a large trade association. Although he entered law, became a candidate in a Ph.D. program where he concentrated on regional economics, and finally began teaching English in college, it was this array of talents and experience that led him to his first managerial economics job in a bank that wanted "an economist who could write."

From the bank, where he spent a number of years in money market analyses, working with financial writers, and writing about financial and economic developments, he returned to teaching as head of the economics department in a select liberal arts college. Next he went into government, serving as a staff economist for a major congressional committee. This led him to his current position. His job requires alertness, quick learning, the ability to work under pressure, and a broad knowledge of economics, government, and the ways of American society.

Mr. A sets the pace for his association's role in a variety of public activities. He analyzes current economic problems, prepares and delivers testimony before congressional committees, writes articles for magazines, newspapers, and newsletters, speaks to many trade groups, makes TV and radio appearances, and acts as informal consultant within the industry his association serves.

Economics, Management, and Decision Making

Before they can apply economic theory to business problems, economists should have some concept of what a business decision is. They should have a framework within which theory can be applied. The emphasis in managerial economics is on recognizing the relevant parts of a problem and organizing them so that, with the aid of economic theory, correct decisions can be made.

Management's task is to manage; the function of the manager is to provide through one strategic decision after another for the needs, requirements, and demands of an enterprise. An enterprise is part of a much larger business environment, however, and this vast complex of firms and organizations of many types and purposes both limits the range of power to decide and imposes many requirements on decisive action.

A business problem is a situation in which a manager must make a choice. The manager must decide between two or more courses of action. This choice is required either because something is preventing a firm from reaching its goal or because a better way to reach that goal is perceived. Sometimes an awareness that a problem exists and that a choice must be made is derived from others. A subordinate asks a question, a superior gives an order, or someone suggests a change. In other cases, the manager sees that a choice exists and has to be made. In any case, someone undertakes to determine which alternatives to implement.

Before it can be solved, a problem must be defined. A clear and precise definition of a problem provides a direction, a basis for control, and the facts on which the entire problem-solving operation rests. If the problem is not correctly defined, time, effort, and money may be wasted no matter how well the rest of the process is accomplished. The correct solution to the wrong problem is of little value.

Problem Formulation

Problem formulation is problem definition. It is the process of determining the question or questions that must and can be answered through the collection and analysis of data. It is the attempt to determine the important issues. However, problem formulation is rarely easy.

Naugatuck Candy Company

The Naugatuck Candy Company sells packaged candy. Profits are adequate and sales are growing at a slow but steady rate. One day the advertising manager suggests that sales and profits could be increased more rapidly by shifting part of the advertising budget from television to the sports pages of newspapers. The newspaper campaign would try to convince men to buy candy as a gift for their families on the way home at night. An alternative course of action—hence a business problem—is recognized.

However, the problem is not whether Naugatuck should shift some of its advertising to newspapers. There are other questions that should be asked. How much profit can be derived from selling candy to men? Will men buy candy if it is advertised in the sports pages of newspapers? Will the shifting of advertising dollars from daytime television to newspapers increase overall profits of the Naugatuck Candy Company? By how much? The problem formulation must ensure that *all* the pertinent questions have been asked. The problem formulation process eliminates the useless study of "nonproblems." Unless there is excess capacity and the ability to produce more candy than is currently being sold, implementations of any plan to increase sales would be a waste of effort.

The problem as presented so far is not in a specific enough form. To be specific in stating a problem so that a relevant decision can be made, it is necessary to determine answers to such questions as

1. What is the sales effect of television advertising?
2. How many men would be exposed to the newspaper ads?
3. What is the profit per item of candy sold?
4. Will appeals of newspaper ads persuade men to buy candy?
5. How many men will be so persuaded?

These are specific questions. The answer to each is usually a specific fact that may be known or can be discovered through research. Good problem formulation, you see, involves breaking down a big problem into manageable segments.

Every problem situation has at least five elements:

1. An objective or a goal the manager is trying to achieve
2. Two or more methods of reaching that objective, each with its own costs and its own expected outcome
3. Uncertainty as to the future, or even, in some cases, the present or the past
4. The need to select which alternative(s) to implement, either because they are mutually exclusive or because limited resources restrict the amount that can be expended
5. Outside constraints or limits, legal or otherwise, that curtail absolute freedom

Problem Solving

There are many ways to solve business problems. Here is one that has the advantage of simplicity. In six steps it answers the question, "Where do we start?"

1. Determine the general area in which the problem lies. Select those tools of theory and practice that should be used. Do not shut the door to other areas that may also be relevant.
2. Determine the objectives.
3. Determine the relevant alternatives, including exactly what each involves as well as what effort or cost each will entail.
4. Determine, for each alternative, the minimum satisfactory results.
5. Determine what chain of cause-and-effect events is required for each alternative to be satisfactory.
6. Assess the impact of the best decision.

To say, for example, that the objective of a firm is to produce more profit will seldom be sufficient. The managerial economist will find it necessary to be more specific, more detailed. Although profit is the goal of the entire enterprise, successful problem solving will require a better understanding of the immediate objective to which the immediate decision must be addressed.

Consider the Naugatuck Candy Company again. It must decide whether to shift part of its advertising dollars from television to newspapers. The long-term reason is to increase profits. But what of the short-term outlook? Will newspaper advertising directly increase profits? The answer is obviously no. The immediate objective of newspaper advertising is to reach men and, having reached them, to persuade them to buy candy. If enough men buy enough candy so that increased revenue exceeds increased costs, then the proposed alternative will increase profits.

In determining immediate objectives, break the problem into its several parts. Be sure that terms are defined precisely. For Naugatuck, exactly what will be given up in television advertising—how many minutes, on what days, sponsoring what program? To be correctly determined an objective must be specific and precise. Often this means that it must be quantified. Vague terms, like "more," "greater," or "increase," are seldom sufficient. By just how much must sales go up to make a profit?

Alternatives

The essence of a managerial decision is the choice among alternatives. But which of the alternatives is best in the short term and in the long term? Are these alternatives logically exclusive, or are they part of the same process so that the company can't have one without the other?

The "bestness" of an alternative is a matter of its advantage over another. The alternative's benefits must exceed the cost of choosing it or the cost of giving up any other alternative. Bestness also relates to how the decision is viewed.

Is a textile firm adding a new product because it has excess capacity or because it wants to complete its product line? In the first case, bestness may involve less clear net advantage than in the second case. If there is space left over on a rug-making machine for a runner, the decision to make the runner can be made in terms of the gain in total sales set against the increase in variable costs. Presumably, machine costs are already covered by the principal product, rugs. However,should the runners become so popular a sales item that they threaten to take the place occupied in the product line by rugs, it will be necessary to rethink the advantages to be obtained from making runners.

By contrast, a new model intended to complete an automobile maker's product line more than likely involves new facilities, new advertising campaigns, in fact, a whole range of new decisions and resources. Deciding what is best in this case requires a different and more complete set of criteria than did the case of runners, though both are new products.

For some decisions the essential question is the order in which they should be made. In what order should a bank establish branches in the suburbs—in terms of the relative populations of the areas, in terms of the income levels and possible rates of saving, in terms of the industrial activity of the communities? How should an expanding machine shop go about obtaining machines—by buying the larger and more efficient units in advance of orders or by allowing the orders to build up and acquiring larger units only as demand requires?

Still other alternatives involve knowing the reactions of other firms. Whether to raise the price of basic copper may involve much more than the relative advantage a higher price may yield over a lower price. One copper producer may be concerned that because of the size of the firm's own refining facilities, any lower price might lead to competition in which the firm would have little chance of coming out ahead. Thus, even though management suspects that a good deal more copper could be sold at lower prices and even though production costs tend to decrease on each additional unit of copper produced, the limits imposed by the capacity of facilities raise the question of what would happen if a large producer were to match the price cut.

Market Organization and Decision Making

Some knowledge of the general organization of the market may be useful in determining the alternatives that a manager must face. A Montana wheat farmer, with large holdings, has a far narrower range of price and production decisions to make than the tractor and farm-supplies dealer. Wheat produced on a farm cannot be distinguished from wheat produced anywhere else. Furthermore, the demand is so widely distributed that the Montana wheat farmer cannot take advantage of market knowledge. By contrast, the farm-supplies dealer has some leeway on the prices charged for the things sold. This leeway depends upon the kind of advertising campaign the manufacturers undertake, the proximity of competitors, and many other factors, all of which characterize a market less competitive than the wheat market.

A New York dressmaker supplying lines for medium-price stores faces a differently organized market from that of a friend across town who makes high-fashion shoes for specialty shops on Fifth Avenue, North Michigan Boulevard, and Wilshire Boulevard. The dressmaker knows that price decisions are limited, whereas the shoemaker is more likely to have some freedom in setting the price of new creations. Thus, even though both make clothing items women will wear—or so they hope—their decisions will not be the same because they operate in differently organized markets.

Management for the Montana wheat farmer requires much less knowledge of prices and much more of costs. The farm-supplies dealer's profit margin is the key factor to be used in setting prices. The dressmaker will be concerned with style, making sure that designers and cutters at least keep up with the market. The dressmaker's product sells in a rapidly changing world where success is not so much determined by the price charged as by the ability to meet the buyers' selling schedules. And the shoemaker is at pains to keep ahead of the vagaries of style and even to set the pace, for shoe profits come from the ability to be continuously ahead of the market in style.

The tools of managerial economics are sometimes different even when they appear superficially alike. There is the danger of assuming that a large oil refining and marketing firm has the same problems in the Atlantic seaboard states as it has in Holland. The stations, the facilities, and even the pricing techniques appear to be similar, but, in the one case, the firm is one among many and, in the second, one of very few.

On the Atlantic seaboard, though the firm's sales are very large, there are so many larger firms in this industry and others of many types and varieties that there is little publicity given to its share of the market, which is, after all, part of a much larger gasoline market. In Holland, though the sales may be smaller, the impact of the firm's prices, profits, and employment policies are nationwide. The outside environment is different. These new dimensions give the decision alternatives a different coloring, and the decisions of the firms about such matters as pricing different grades of gasoline or extending credit to its customers require different approaches.

Management's task differs from market to market, from time to time, from place to place. The economic content of a firm's decisions varies, but there is always the possibility that the firm's problems can be recast. In this form, economic tools can be used to help the firm's managers to make decisions based on economic rationality, that is, maximizing the net gain from business decisions over their cost.

Case Analysis in Managerial Economics

Managerial economics has a strong empirical orientation. It draws heavily upon the results of case analyses of specific situations in individual firms and industries. A case is typically a statement of what happened to a company in a given market. But it is not a complete statement. It is an edited record of experience. Irrelevant materials that do not aid in understanding the key issues in the case are left out. References to persons, firms, and events that might otherwise be identifiable are omitted if there is a question of company security.

A case may not be complete in another more meaningful sense. It goes no further than the record. It may include the actual decision or it may not. It does include most of the facts known to management. But what is missing is the additional information that would have been helpful to management, had it been known. Students can sometimes obtain this information from journals, official records, competitors, and accounting records. But they must remember they cannot fault management for not knowing what it was impossible to know. On the other hand, there may have been available information which management ought to have known.

The purpose of a case is to illustrate the application of managerial economics principles. The illustration may be positive or negative. There will be enough in the illustration to permit the working out of an analysis of the problem contained in the case based on one or more principles.

There are at least three reasons why cases are presented in this book. First, cases lead to a development of understanding of principles. Second, cases provide an appreciation of the connection between a statement in the text and the situation found in a real managerial context. Third, and perhaps most important, cases are an effective means of helping students learn managerial economics. They round out the instructional process.

A case is more than just a problem needing a solution. There is seldom one right answer to a problem. A case is a description of a real situation faced by a firm, a group of consumers, the general public, the courts, a government agency, or an individual. Each case contains several economic issues about which decisions were made or have to be made. It will not always be clear what the key issue is. That is because a case represents a slice of the real world where there is not only uncertainty, but a complex and confusing interrelationship of events. What is more, facts are not always precise.

The recommended approach to case analysis is that each student first decide—from among the several or many possible issues—what the key issue is. Students should be aware that there can be valid differences as to what is the key issue and what key issue should be selected around which to organize an analysis of the facts.

The key issue may be what price to charge, or more accurate cost measurement, or assessment of demand, or profitable alternatives, or measures of competitive structures, or any one of a number of specific identifications of issues on which decisions must be made. Having identified the key issue, the next step is to work out a method for determining what to do or, at least, what to recommend. If a decision has already been made, the next step is to evaluate its effectiveness.

A good case report states the key issue with clarity. It may also state why this issue was recognized as central. Then, there follows a recommendation for action, a statement of a solution, or a critique of actions taken. The purpose of this part of the case report is to provide for management a short summary statement of position. Next comes as thorough an analysis of the case materials as is necessary to back up the recommendation, to prove the validity of the decision, or to assess the actions taken. Thorough analysis means using statistics, accounting data, economic models, research into additional facts and points of view and whatever else—whether or not in the case materials—will strengthen the summary statement. But no more should go into the analysis than is necessary, for it is not its length but its cogency that matters.

Good case analysis calls for good writing, good thinking, and good reporting. Indeed, unless students can report effectively, there is some question as to whether they understand what the case is about. However, good reporting is not an adequate substitute for "correctness" in analysis. For while it is true that good students can and will differ about what the key issue is and while they will differ as to the form of the analysis, there is, in each instance, a way of using managerial economic principles which is "correct." Correctness consists in the application of principles of economics in a cogent and convincing way to the problem being analyzed. The effective writing of case reports has the side effect of making the student a good managerial economist. After all, an economist is a person who thinks and writes about economics.

The Cases Themselves

The cases in this book have been selected from the many available to serve as vehicles for understanding how managerial economics is to be applied. They all represent real situations, though the names may at times be changed. Some come directly from company records, some from interviews, and some from the author's consulting practices. Others are taken from public records, from collections of cases, or from the files of trade associations, banks, or similar agencies. They are not intended to be paragons of good management nor horror stories. They are realistic in that they reflect the state of management in a modern context.

Selected Readings

Fisher, David I.: *The Corporate Economist*, New York, Conference Board, 1975.
Harlan, N. E., C. J. Christenson, and R. F. Vancil: *Managerial Economics: Text and Cases*, Homewood, Ill., Irwin, 1962.
Schmalensee, R.: *Applied Microeconomics: Problems in Estimation, Forecasting and Decision-Making*, San Francisco, Holden-Day, 1973.
Sharpe, W. F.: *Introduction to Managerial Economics*, New York, Columbia, 1973.
Stokes, C. J.: *Managerial Economics: A Casebook*, New York, Random House, 1969.

Questions, Problems, and Projects

1. A recent report on the business research department of the B. F. Goodrich Company noted that the department had had notable success in placing its staff members in higher positions, ranging upward to chief executive officer and board chairman. Is that what business economics is all about? In other words, is managerial economics most successful as a discipline when its practitioners are promoted out of it?
2. Haynes and Henry in their popular managerial economics textbook note that the relation of managerial economics to economic theory is much like that of medicine to biology. Just what does such a comparison imply about the

application of managerial economics? Which area is likely to make greater contributions to knowledge? To society?

3. A Harvard University conference on managerial economics recently examined the role of cases in instruction. Cases were criticized by some as requiring too much inductive reasoning and even experience. Others argued that while deductive reasoning was a good instructional goal, students might know a subject without knowing what they really know. Admittedly, it isn't fair to ask you as you begin this book to advise your fellow students and professors on the case method, but what defense is there for instruction using cases, whether many or few, using all cases, or using lectures plus cases?

4. How do you recognize a problem when you see one? Monroe Bank had been profitable for several years, but management noted that the increase in loans granted was outstripping the growth in deposits by customers. Some directors argued that this high loan/deposit ratio was the result of a good investment policy designed to keep profits high. Others argued that it was a very risky policy since if any loans turned sour, profits would plunge and lending flexibility would be hampered. Management therefore decided to go after a sharp increase in deposits. Comment.

Case 1.1 Economics Function at General Telephone and Electronics Corporation

This is an agenda for a meeting with a corporate consultant reviewing the charter and the performance characteristics of the economics function in one of the nation's largest multiproduct corporations.

I. Introduction—GTE Corporate Approach Re Economics Function
   A. *Background*
      The revenues, sales, and profitability of GTE businesses are directly influenced by economic trends. The analysis and interpretation of these trends, therefore, is an essential element of GTE management. As with most large corporations, GTE is aided in carrying out this function by a staff unit consisting of one or more professional economists. This type of economics function is now present in virtually every major United States corporation (see Conference Board Report No. 655, *The Corporate Economist*).
   B. *History of GTE Economics Function*
      1. An economics function was established within GTE in 1962. It has existed since that time as a unit of the financial organization within the GTE Service Corporation.
      2. There are no direct functional counterparts to the corporate economics unit within the subsidiary companies of GTE. However, the financial, marketing, and planning staffs of the subsidiaries and the counterpart staffs at GTE Service Corporation depend upon and work closely with the corporate economics unit.
   C. *Charter of Corporate Economics Unit*
      1. The economics unit provides professional advice, information, and analytical services to the top management of GTE and to their staffs. This information

flow consists of fulfilling requests from management and from self-initiated analyses based on relevance to the corporation's overall operations.

2. The economics unit works closely with appropriate personnel within the GTE parent company and service corporation to coordinate the use throughout GTE of economic forecasts and econometric forecasting techniques. This includes advice and aid in developing sophisticated forecasting systems for use in production scheduling, market planning, and budgeting.

II. Activities of the Economics Unit within GTE

A. *Develop Short- and Long-Range Forecasts*

The corporate economists develop short-range forecasts covering one to two years and long-range forecasts covering five years for the United States economy, other major industrialized nations, and the American telephone and electronics industries.

These forecasts are developed using sophisticated econometric models. Inputs are drawn from sources both inside and outside the company. Information is obtained from American and foreign publications, professional meetings, and service organizations such as Data Resources, Inc., and Chase Econometrics. Within the company, the corporate economists meet with representatives of the major operating groups for an exchange of views prior to finalizing their forecasts. This is followed by a review with top management prior to release.

B. *Communication of Forecasts to GTE Management*

Economic forecasts and assumptions are communicated to GTE management by means of regular "Economic Outlook" letters issued several times each year. The purpose of these letters is to

1. Provide all GTE subsidiaries with a uniform set of assumptions regarding the outlook for business conditions, inflation, real growth, interest rates, and other economic variables for use in the annual preparation of budgets and five-year plans. This includes an evaluation of the probable impact on GTE businesses of changes in the economic environment.

2. Aside from annual budgets and five-year plans, keep headquarters and subsidiary company management informed of changes in the business outlook for their consideration in decision making throughout the year.

C. *Furnish Supplemental Economic Reports*

The corporate economists issue "Weathervane Reports" or "Economic Highlights" memos to supplement the regular "Economic Outlook" letters. These additional letters are intended to keep GTE management informed on an immediate basis of changes in the outlook for interest rates, inflation, government policy, housing starts, and other significant topics affecting GTE.

D. *Review Budgets and Five-Year Plans*

1. The corporate economists review the budgets and five-year plans submitted by operating groups and subsidiaries to determine reasonableness in light of original economic assumptions and subsequent changes in the economic outlook.

They comment on changes in the outlook and on the reasonableness of subsidiaries' budgets and five-year plans in the consolidated budget book prepared for the GTE executive committee.

2. In conjunction with the evaluation of subsidiary plans, progress is being made toward the development of a GTE corporate model which will interpret the effects of external economic conditions upon the profitability of the corporation and its subsidiaries. This model will also be used to provide GTE management with "what if" analyses of alternate economic conditions.

E. *Participate in Periodic Forecasting Meetings*
1. The corporate economists maintain close liaison with forecasting personnel throughout the corporation and are called upon to participate in selected forecasting meetings of subsidiary companies or groups (examples include the Sylvania home entertainment products industry forecasting meeting or the telephone marketing department meeting).
2. The corporate economists are frequently called upon to make presentations on the economic outlook or on other related topics at various management meetings and training sessions within the company (examples include the management training school held in Tampa, Florida, and briefings at various division or group-level staff meetings).

F. *Provide Specialized Assistance*
The corporate economists are frequently called upon for specialized assistance, covering a wide range of topics, to other departments within the corporation. Most assistance of this type falls into three categories: nonrecurring special projects, econometric forecasting, and assistance in public affairs business-related areas.
1. *Nonrecurring Special Projects* Examples range from an analysis of unique financial or regulatory matters such as "double leverage" to the development of economic forecasts of particular nations such as the Philippines or Mexico.
2. *Econometric Forecasting* Examples include the development of 25-year projections of the United States telephone industry and the development of econometric forecasting models for GTE manufacturing operations.
3. *Public Affairs* Examples include original material and supporting analysis for use in connection with congressional testimony or speeches and articles by senior corporate officials.

G. *Negotiate Contracts with Outside Economic Services*
The corporate economists negotiate and administer contracts with outside economic consulting firms for the purchase of specialized economic source material.

H. *Maintain Outside Communications*
The corporate economists maintain and foster communications with economists at other companies, universities, and government agencies through working with professional associations, by attending occasional outside meetings, and by maintaining memberships on selected professional committees.

III. Future Activities of the Economics Unit
In order to respond to new, specialized needs, the economics unit is developing additional services in the following areas:

A. *Price Trend Forecasting*
Forecasts of inflation can be made more specific to GTE operations. By using "stages of processing models," inflation forecasts will be developed for specific materials inputs into GTE telephone construction programs and manufacturing product lines. Examples include forecasts of price trends for materials such as glass, copper wire and cable, corrugated packaging, communications equipment, and construction labor.

These specific inflation assumptions will be superior to general measures of inflation such as the wholesale price index or the gross national product (GNP) deflator which are provided presently.

B. *International Forecasts*
Additional emphasis will be placed on international economic forecasts, partic-

ularly for the countries of Canada, West Germany, and Italy, where GTE has major operations. Emphasis will be placed on the emerging petroleum and raw materials exporting nations as well, since they represent major markets.

C. *Industry Econometric Models*

Greater emphasis will be placed on the development of econometric forecasting models for particular industries and product lines. The development of a viable color television forecasting model and the use of econometric models within the Lighting Products Group (of GTE Sylvania) are precursors of potentially wider use of these techniques throughout GTE.

DISCUSSION QUESTIONS 1.1

1. Is the economics function at GTE essential to management planning? Try to list the various possible uses management can make of the output of its economists.
2. How do economic inputs become a part of management's decisions?
3. Why do you suppose that GTE economists use the services of outside economic consulting firms? In what areas would these services be helpful?
4. Determine from this review the kinds of knowledge and the backgrounds GTE economists should have.

2

NUMBERS, MODELS, AND MANAGERIAL ECONOMICS

Key Concepts

accounting
aggregation
analytical algebra
Bayesian statistics
cash flows
cobweb theorem
constants
correlation equation
cycle
dynamic stability
economic models
empirical validity
equation
expected value
financial tables
finite difference equation
function
generality
geometry
intercept
interest rate
line
link relatives
microeconomic models
models
monotonic
moving averages

nature's strategy
net present worth
parameter
payoff matrix
prediction
present worth
probability
pure uncertainty
quantifiable patterns
random sample
random variations
rate of return on investment
reciprocal
scientific calculator
seasonality
sign
simultaneous
slope
solution
statistics
testing
time path
time series
trend
trigonometry
variable

What Is Ahead in This Chapter

It just wouldn't be fair to give the impression that managerial economics requires a high level of mathematical competence. That isn't so. Yet there are many numbers that are used and manipulated, and there are all sorts of economic models that relate one set of numbers to other sets and draw or make possible conclusions about management or economic behavior.

There are many ways of presenting and using numbers. There's accounting, with which you probably have more than a nodding acquaintance. And depending on the level of your competence and training in accounting, you will find it possible to use accounting in many of the matters which this book presents.

There's statistics with all its various branches and applications, with which you are probably familiar. But, because it is also likely that there are some areas that you will want to review at least, in this and in later chapters we will spend more time on statistical than on accounting techniques.

Then there's algebra in its many forms. In this book, we deal with simultaneous equation systems such as linear programming, input-output, and econometric models. We also use algebra in some statistical and even in some accounting analyses. What is more, algebra and calculus underlie some of the economic theories that are in the toolbox from which economists draw so many of their models.

There's also geometry, which is used in so many forms and so routinely that sometimes we forget to stop and say, "Oh, that's geometry." We find this especially true of analytical geometry, that combination of algebra and geometry used in many graphs and charts. Close to analytical geometry is trigonometry, dealing with angles, sines, tangents, cosines, and, particularly, with measuring slopes. This book assumes that you can read graphs and that you have some knowledge of the basic ideas of geometry and trigonometry. But every now and then, we also try to explain what a particular form of graphical analysis really means. And why.

The purpose of this chapter is to review—and perhaps for some readers to introduce—basic concepts and techniques that we will be using again and again. The chapter is not intended to be a treatise on mathematics; in its form and in its content, it won't satisfy many mathematicians, but it will help you to understand what you will be doing and why.

Numerical Methods in Managerial Economics

It would be convenient if we could say that what we call managerial economics developed in the following way: Observant economists, pondering the evidence available from the performance of households, individual companies, and governments, put together theories of behavior which explain the way in which business and government policies are made and which help explain in detail how these economic entities perform. Having developed these theories, economists then tested them by a careful analysis of all the facts. They rejected unconfirmed theories and kept those which fitted the facts moderately well. And over the years, economists have improved these theories as more and more evidence has become available.

But, in fact, this is not the way it happened at all. The numbers and data about the behavior of individuals, families, firms, and governments are so massive in detail and so unwieldy that even a straightforward attempt to determine the effect of variations in each of a possible large set of economic variables is so difficult that any theory economists might seek to test for completeness would just be too big to handle. So what really happens?

Economists build models. And this is probably the most important contribution of economics to better management and to the sciences. Model building is an exercise in which highly simplified theories are developed or propounded. They point out the areas which are believed to be the main sources of economic influence on particular economic results. Models deliberately leave out a host of assumed minor influences to permit economists to focus on what they think is important. Models, then, are a slice of reality and their most significant attribute is that they work. But even this pragmatic statement must be considered with caution since what is often meant by a model working is that, even in an "as if" situation, the model gives what seem to be reasonable answers to questions.

The point of these observations on economists and their model building is that we need to know enough mathematics to see what the models mean, how they can be manipulated, and why economists draw certain conclusions from the answers they get from using models. We need mathematics drawn from a variety of mathematical fields to work with economic models. In a sense, that's the frustrating part: It is difficult to acquire a range of mathematical knowledge. Most mathematicians want to tell you all there is to know about calculus or trigonometry or symbolic logic or Bayesian statistics. In effect, you will need to know a little about a lot of mathematics and that is what this chapter introduces. And that is the goal of the teaching technique of this book. The assumption here is that the majority of students in managerial economics are not and will not become economics majors. By the same token, they aren't mathematics majors either. More than likely, if they are undergraduates, they will be in the business administration or management school and they will be majors in such diverse fields as marketing, accounting, industrial relations, quantitative methods, and, of course, economics—though it may be labor economics or business economics. They may be graduate students, MBA candidates, public administration and management students—even some political scientists and sociologists as well as urbanologists. There may even be an occasional student in economic and industrial development, but very few majors in graduate economics. The book and the level of mathematics used have been tailored to this probable range of readers. The author does not mean to imply, however, that it could not be used with some profit by economists, especially practicing business, corporate, and government economists. Or that there isn't something that will interest a Ph.D. candidate in pure economics.

Economic Model Building

One definition of economics is that it is a set of models of behavior. A model of economic behavior is an input-output relationship. Feed into the model inputs (prices, costs, demand states) and as outputs get reaction patterns. Models are deliberately simplified pictures of the real world. The forms a model of economic behavior can take are varied. It can consist of a set of equations, or it can be a chart of time relationships like a flowchart with critical paths. In other instances, it can be a set of computer codes. And in classical economics, it was the practice to spell out models in involved verbal statements. A model— regardless of the form—is developed as follows:

1. Decide what facts and factors are relevant to the questions we want to answer.
2. From these facts and factors select those that are quantifiable, and thus can be described numerically.
3. Cut the list of facts and factors down to manageable size by aggregation.
4. Spell out the relations between the elements of the model quantitatively.

Deciding Which Facts and Factors Are Relevant

Now let us try to make an economic model of the household. About two of every three dollars spent in the United States represents decisions made by members of households. Draw up a list of all the facts and factors that influence these vitally important decisions. It will include income levels, prices, levels of satisfaction, location of households, household sizes, ages of household members, race, education, tastes, available goods and services, styles, debt commitments, asset holdings, weather differences, the likely pattern of income changes in the future, price expectations, and employment and unemployment data.

Simple Economic Model

Take all that we know about the behavior of consumers and try to develop an explanation which can be used both to describe and to forecast what consumers do and will do. Here are some of the elements of a simple consumer behavior model.

1. Consumers buy their food, their housing services, their transportation services, and their health services in regular and predictable patterns. Call a

typical pattern of consumer spending a "market basket"—composed of combinations of a wide but relatively consistent variety of goods and services.

2. Consumers have limited incomes and the available evidence indicates that they attempt with this income to buy their preferred market baskets.
3. The goods and services in the market basket are sold in a marketplace where prices vary.
4. While the size and composition of market baskets reflect the effects of prices and incomes on consumer behavior, the real reason why consumers choose a given market basket is the satisfaction to be obtained from it.

Now put these elements together. Given some basic desires (such as hunger, pleasing the family, maintenance of health), consumers seek to obtain as much satisfaction as possible by using their income at current prices to buy the largest possible market baskets. This simple model, stated in this way, can be presented in mathematical form. Or it can be verbally stated much more elegantly. But you should be aware that it took a long time before economists could agree on the elements and the implications of the model. Even in its present form, there are arguments about whether it is a useful basis for predicting what consumers will do.

For this simple consumer behavior model, the measurable elements are prices, incomes, the quantities of goods and services purchased, as well as the number of consumers, including, of course, the composition of consumer families. But as yet we haven't come up with an effective way of measuring satisfactions. Even if we did have a way of measuring Mrs. Pallotto's satisfactions, would that same measure apply to Mrs. Wojiski? In fact, do the Pallottos, the Wojiskis, and the Schermerhorns actually think and buy in terms of something like a measurable unit of satisfaction? Yet, if we left out satisfaction, all we would have is a model which says that consumers, once the prices of the goods and the services in the market basket are known, make purchases in accordance with their available incomes. And we wouldn't know why.

Of course, if there were a consistent pattern so that, after we had observed the Pallottos, the Wojiskis, and the Schermerhorns several times, we would know enough to predict what they would do, that might be all that we could expect. For managerial economics, it isn't always important to know why consumers behave as they do. But it is important to have consistent, predictable consumer behavior patterns to work with.

Selecting Quantifiable Factors

For many models we can find numbers. For some of them, we can find very good numbers. But, for others, numbers do not exist. The fact that numbers do or do not exist must not be used as an excuse for passing over some hard problems. Yet, economists find themselves forced to leave out nonquantifiable elements, even though some of them might have been quite relevant for the model. In all fairness, it ought to be said that some of these nonquantifiable elements can be handled indirectly. For example, there is the technique of the "dummy variable" by which we can handle race, marriage status, presence or absence of a physically identifying characteristic, or location in the nation or the city (in general terms such as "in city" versus "out of city") and thus provide enough quantification to make the model more descriptive. In this way we can use more effectively what we really know about the economics of the situation.

Aggregation

We can often get a more useful model if, instead of examining a single situation or firm, we look at large groups of situations or firms. For example, in the case of consumer households, aggregation can make it easier for us to build a more useful model. At any one period of time, we can take a cross section of a reading across many households by income. The data would be based on the Survey of Consumer Expenditures, performed every ten years or so by the Bureau of Labor Statistics and the Bureau of the Census. In the most recent survey, completed in the early 1970s, you can take income, family size, household residential location, age of the head of the household, number of cars owned, or education of the head of the household and read across, picking up a wide variety of observations about the behavior of consumer households. What consumer households buy, how much they buy, and even, to some degree, when they buy can be derived from this kind of cross-sectional evidence.

On the other hand, it may be useful to examine groups of households not at a given moment of time but over longer periods. This time-series approach is possible, for example, from the personal consumption expenditures sector of the United States national income accounts. Ever since the first quarter of 1929, there has been, each quarter, a continual recording of consumer spending. With knowledge about prices, consumer incomes, and the composition of consumer households, a time series based on an aggregative model of consumer household behavior can be worked out. We can also compare average spending patterns in different parts of the country or at different times of the year.

Aggregation allows us to derive typical behavior. The costs of model building are much less when we aggregate, if only because we can take advantage of many census and census-type studies and tabulations. And aggregation is frequently the best alternative available to model builders, because data are available only in this form.

Intuition and Model Building

In the analysis of some patterns of economic behavior, the relationships are fairly obvious and often easy to work out. But there are probably as many cases where the relationships are not obvious and interpretation is not easy. Then we may have to turn to intuition. Indeed, without alert intuition, we would hardly have been able to advance as far as we have in economics. What intuition means is that an economist, familiar not only with the numbers and individuals or situations, businesses, or commodities under observation but also with the background, the history, the cultural contexts, and the organizational structure, is able to piece together out of the jigsaw puzzle a relationship that mathematics or statistics alone could not have revealed.

Adam Smith had this kind of genius. And some of the basic economic models of national, firm, consumer household, and individual economic behavior have been developed by him and his followers since 1776 on an intuitive rather than on a deductive basis. There is a problem, though, with intuitively derived models. Sometimes, brilliant as they are and despite the unusually clear explanations they give of economic behavior, they are presented in a form in which it is very difficult to test them. That is, they have to be taken on faith. While managerial economists use intuitive models quite as much as university economists, they have a preference for testable models that can be used for predicting behavior. Management, you see, is likely to want results that can be tested and duplicated. In this book, we will use, whenever it is possible, those kinds of models which are testable. But that doesn't mean that we will never use some very good intuitional models.

Uses of Models in Managerial Economics

Model building fulfills the need to explain particular reaction patterns and to predict the likelihood of occurrence or recurrence of that pattern. A model is adequate if the pattern that we sought to explain can logically be deduced from the working of the model. Furthermore, a model should have empirical validity: It should either be testable or be composed of relations that have been tested satisfactorily. For a model to have general validity, we should find that its output has been confirmed by tests performed again and again under similar conditions. However, we do not always have to have a model of general validity. Or to put the matter another way, models of general validity are harder to derive and may require intensive research.

UFO Model

The kind of model we build depends in part upon the data available and in part upon the questions that it is designed to answer. The Rand Corporation developed various kinds of Martian flying saucers,[1] presumably dispatched for pioneer reconnaissance flights over the United States. In one of these Rand models, the flying saucers appeared as individual serial numbers and Martian worker-hour totals so that a learning curve could predict the rate of construc-

[1] R. D. Specht, "The Why and How of Model Building," in E. S. Quade (ed.), *Analysis for Military Decisions*, Chicago, Rand McNally, 1964.

tion and probable time of appearance on United States radar screens. In another they appeared as point-mass, having velocity and position in the gravitational fields of Mars, the sun, and, of course, the earth. In still another model on early warning radar, they became radar-echoing areas determined by material, size, form, and aspect. Other models tested the UFOs as hostile and they became a profile for range finding, fuel storage, and other vulnerable characteristics. The point is that there were many possible prediction models for UFOs just as there were facts to be measured. Each set of facts and each model comprised another way of representing the UFO. There was no single correct UFO model. Any one model was as good as another. The choice among UFO models depended on the uses to which the model was to be put.

Algebraic Model

Demand and supply are the basic elements of economics. Demand is a functional relationship, expressed by an equation, for example,

$$Q_d = -ap + b$$

where

Q_d = the amount demanded of, say, black-eyed peas at any point in time

p = the price of black-eyed peas, dollars

a,b = the parameters or constants, numbers which will help determine the relationships between a change in the price of black-eyed peas and the effect of that change in price on the quantity of black-eyed peas sold (or bought)

An algebraic function is a sentence carrying a message. In this case, the message is that Q_d (the quantity demanded of black-eyed peas) depends on the price of black-eyed peas (p), the way in which quantity demanded changes as price changes ($-a$), and the quantity of black-eyed peas sold (b) when the price is zero. What is more, this sentence says that you can get the results you want from this function by adding, subtracting, dividing, and multiplying. No more difficult arithmetic manipulations are necessary. The negative sign ($-$) on parameter a says that whenever the price of black-eyed peas is increased (or decreased), that price change will have an opposite effect on the quantity of black-eyed peas demanded. So a price increase leads to a sales (or purchase) decrease.

An algebraic function is always true. You take it as it is and work with it. It is not presented in a form to be challenged or tested. If you know the rules of algebraic manipulation, you go ahead with supreme confidence that life is as the algebraic function says it is. By contrast a statistical function is an estimate; it should be tested, proved to be so—at least to the degree that it is possible to prove it true.

Economists use algebraic functions as illustrations or teaching or explanatory devices. Few economic functions can, in fact, be treated as if they were algebraic. When dealing with real or empirical situations very often economists use statistical functions. Stating economic functions in algebra has the advantages of making it possible to read them with more precision, to work with them, to build complex theories, and to solve problems with them—always provided that we are being theoretical, acting as if what we do and what we say is true.

Black-Eyed-Peas Supply Function

Obviously, if there is a demand function, there must also be a supply function; for example,

$$Q_s = \alpha p + \beta$$

where

Q_s = amount supplied of black-eyed peas, measured in the same units we use for demand

P = price of black-eyed peas, measured in the same way the demand price was measured

α, β = parameters, numbers which will help determine the relationship between a change in the price of black-eyed peas and the effect of that change on the quantities supplied of black-eyed peas

This algebraic function says that Q_s (the quantity of black-eyed peas that holders and/or farmers of black-eyed peas will choose to provide for sale or to supply) depends on the price (p) people are willing to pay for black-eyed peas, the effect of a change in the price of black-eyed peas on the amount supplied of black-eyed peas (α), and the number of black-eyed peas or the amount supplied if the price of black-eyed peas is zero (β). Note that this supply sentence (or function) contains some of the same symbols (or words) as the demand sentence (or function). Even though they may refer to different numbers, because the numbers are going to be treated and manipulated in the same way, we can use the same symbols. We do distinguish, of course, between Q_d as the demand function and Q_s as the supply function.

You will notice that the supply sentence says that when black-eyed pea prices change (upward or downward), the amounts of black-eyed peas suppliers will provide in the marketplace will change in the same direction. So the supply sentence or function describes a positive set of reactions, while the demand sentence (or function) describes a negative (i.e., opposite) reaction. Both sentences are monotonic, that is, they describe a set of behaviors which do not reverse direction (but which can be read up as well as down the scale). The demand sentence is negatively monotonic so that always and forever—as long as the numbers which can be used in this sentence extend in both directions—increases in price lead to decreases in quantity demanded. The supply sentence is positively monotonic and price increases always, but always, lead to supply increases.

Now, once we have two equations, both using the same symbols (though not the same parameters) we have a set of simultaneous equations. The fact that they are simultaneous means that there is one number, in fact, one price, which will solve both equations. Let's see what the words "simultaneous," "system," and "solve" mean. Let's convert these equations by analytical geometry into graphs. Each equation or function has a picture, a trace, of what it means or says. Because we don't know the exact numbers involved in these two (demand and supply) functions, we have to guess where they lie in two-coordinate space. But suppose that Fig. 2.1 is a correct picture of both.

Demand Function

In Fig. 2.1, you will notice that the demand function runs from the northwest to the southeast, that it is a straight line, and that this straight line crosses the vertical axis which measures price of black-eyed peas. This line crosses the quantity axis at b (which is a way of showing what we mean when we say that when the price of black-eyed peas is zero, the amount demanded of black-eyed peas will be b). We call b the intercept for it is the point at which the function crosses the axis of the variable to be explained. In this case, what is to be explained is how the quantity demanded varies as the price of black-eyed peas

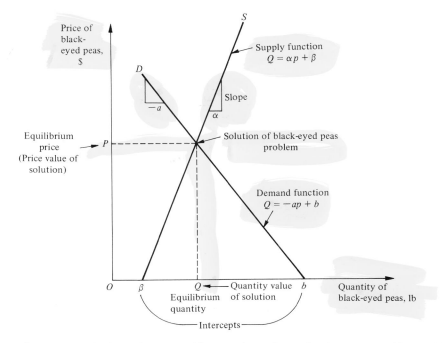

Figure 2.1. Black-eyed peas problem: How to determine how much will be sold and at what price.

varies. We don't name the point at which the demand function crosses the axis of the price of black-eyed peas. We don't need to, because if we know the vertical intercept we know half of what we need to know to describe or picture an algebraic function.

Slope of the Demand Function

The other half is the slope $(-a)$ of the function. What the slope shows is the direction the function takes from the intercept. We know that the direction will be negative, upward to the northwest (or left), because the sign of the slope is $(-)$ and the value of a tells us how much decline in quantity demanded (in a horizontal direction) will take place for each unit change upward in price (in a vertical direction). With an intercept and a slope, we have a straight line. That, by the way, is why the function was written as it was. The algebraic sentence said enough—and no more—to identify the function, to locate it, and to tell its direction, its intercept, and its slope.

By the same token, the supply function rises from an intercept (with the vertical quantity axis) on a positive slope indicated by the value of α, which is the change in the amount of quantity supplied for each unit change in price. Unlike a negative monotonic linear function, this positive monotonic linear function will not cross the vertical axis except at a value below zero (or negative).

Solution of Black-Eyed-Peas Problem

The demand and supply functions are simultaneous in that they use the same variables and intersect somewhere. Thus, there is one set of values of Q and P which will satisfy or be on both lines of functions. That one set of values is the solution. To get the solution in an analytically geometric fashion, we need only extend both functions to find the point of intersection. Then we evaluate that point.

Algebraically, we can proceed as follows. Subtract the supply function from the demand function:

Demand function	$Q = -ap + b$
− Supply function	$Q = \alpha p + \beta$

$$0 = -p\,(\alpha + a) + (b - \beta)$$

so that

$$p = (b - \beta)/(\alpha + a)$$

p is the equilibrium price of black-eyed peas, the price that makes supply of and demand for black-eyed peas equal. Thus, if we know both functions, we can solve either analytically or algebraically for the value of the equilibrium price.

Onions and the Cobweb Theorem

Now let's complicate things a bit. Suppose that while the demand for onions is known as of today, there is a lag in the response of the suppliers to today's demand. In the onion market we will have to wait until after the growing season and the harvest to have a marketable crop. Yet farmers determine how many onions to plant in terms of today's demand for onions. Here, then, are the onion-demand and the onion-supply functions:

Demand function $\quad Q_t = -ap_t + b$

Supply function $\quad Q_t = \alpha p_{t+1} + \beta$

where the subscripts indicate time periods.

To see how this system of simultaneous equations works, we need two initial operational assumptions. One is that $\bar{p}$ will always be the equilibrium price. The other is an assumption about slopes. In this model $|-a| = |\alpha|$. The $|\ |$ means we are comparing absolute values and ignoring signs.

Making the Cobweb Work

Start with Q_1 as the quantity demanded in Fig. 2.2. The price on the demand curve ($Q_d = -a\,p_t + b$) corresponding to the quantity demanded Q_1 is p_t. Unfortunately, onion farmers and suppliers cannot immediately respond to that demand. What these onion suppliers realize, however, is that the market is willing to pay p_t for onions. The supply quantity that a price of p_t will generate is, of course, read off the supply curve ▶ $Q_s = \alpha\,p_{t-1} + \beta$. That quantity is Q_2 but it will be supplied one period later.

You will notice that by the time Q_2 is supplied, the price for Q_2 will not be p_t, but p_{t+1}. That is because of the negative slope of the demand curve. To sell more onions requires a lower price. Demanders will pay only p_{t+1} for Q_2 of onions. That new price message will also be realized by the onion farmers. They will decide that, in accordance with their supply conditions and their supply curve at price p_{t+1} they will supply only Q_1. However, that supply response also comes a period later. We have already noticed that the demand price for onion quantity Q_1 was p_t. So the interaction pattern between supply and demand with this built-in supply response lag of one period is that of a path which goes round and round without ever reaching the equilibrium or solution price and quantity.

Supply is always trying to catch up with demand, with the price fluctuating up and down in search of an equilibrium. The equation of the cobweb model can be derived as follows:

Set the demand for onions equal to the supply of onions

$$-a\,p_t + b = \alpha\,p_{t+1} + \beta$$

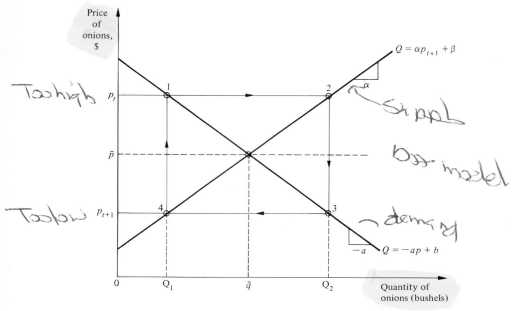

Too high

Too low

Figure 2.2. The onion cobweb: Equilibrium values $= \bar{p}, \bar{q}$.
Start at 1 where demand at price $p_t = Q_1$ but supply at price $p_t = Q_2$. What is more Q_2 won't be supplied until one period later.
So at 2 where at price p_t supply $= Q_2$. But the demand for Q_2 is such that onions will sell only at p_{t+1} ($<p_t$). However this price induces onion sellers to reduce their crop to Q_1 next time around. Note that $|-a| = |\alpha|$.

so that

$$ p_t = \frac{-\alpha}{a} p_{t+1} + \frac{\beta - b}{a} \quad \text{either} \quad +\frac{b-\beta}{a} $$

Now we can state some of the conditions of the behavior of the cobweb model.

1. $|-a| = |\alpha|$.
Here is the interaction pattern as a box with the adjustment between demand and supply always in search of but never reaching an equilibrium or a solution. As before, the $||$ around the $-a$ and α mean that we are comparing absolute values (ignoring signs).
2. $|-a| > |\alpha|$.
With the slope ($-a$) of the demand function larger than the slope (α) of the supply function (Fig. 2.3), the cobweb will turn in upon itself and move inevitably toward the equilibrium price and quantity combination and a final solution.
3. $|-a| < |\alpha|$.
With the slope (a) of the demand function smaller than the slope (α) of the

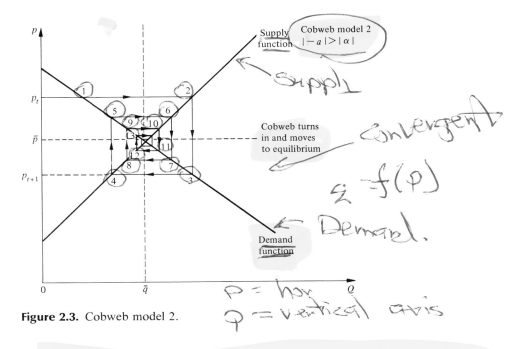

Figure 2.3. Cobweb model 2.

supply function (as in Fig. 2.4), there will never be an equilibrium and the cobweb will expand outward as onion farmers increasingly struggle to catch up with demand but never do so.

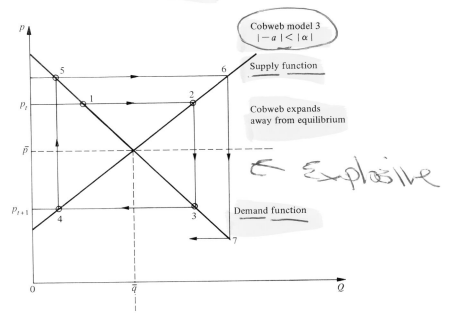

Figure 2.4. Cobweb model 3.

Cobweb with Numbers

Now for some numbers in the onion demand and supply functions. This will help us see more clearly how the cobweb works. Suppose that the onion demand function is

$$Q_t = -5p_t + 200$$

and that the onion supply function is

$$Q_t = 2p_{t-1} + 10$$

Right away you will notice two things about these onion demand and supply functions. First, they have different absolute slopes. Second, the demand function lags behind the supply function.

Solving the Cobweb

We begin with the supply function and with the information that 30 million bushels of onions were supplied in period $t - 1$. That means that the onion price per bushel p_{t-1} must have been $10. Why?
Well, if Q_t in the supply function is 30, then

$$30 = 2p_{t-1} + 10$$
$$20 = 2p_{t-1} \qquad \text{subtract 10 from both sides}$$
$$10 = p_{t-1} \qquad \text{divide both sides by 2}$$

But, for the demand function, if $Q_t = 30$, that must mean a demand price of $34 a bushel in period t since

$$30 = -5p_t + 200$$
$$5p_t = 170 \qquad \text{transfer } -5p_t \text{ to the other side, making it positive. Subtract 30 from both sides.}$$
$$p_t = 34 \qquad \text{divide both sides by 5}$$

Next put $p_t = \$34$ into the supply function,

$$Q_t = 2(34) + 10$$
$$= 78$$

Now, for the demand function,

$$78 = -5p_t + 200$$
$$p_t = \$24.40$$

And so you go round and round.

All these calculations are collected in Table 2.1 where we can observe that the cobweb is fluctuating around a quantity of about 64 million bushels and a price of $27 a bushel. This cobweb is turning in upon itself and will finally after many periods come to rest at about these values. This is therefore an example of cobweb model type 2.

Cobweb Models as Dynamic Models

By introducing this lagged response between demand and supply, we have developed an example of a dynamic model. Dynamic means that time is involved in an important way in the determination of the solution or equilibrium values. What we can get from a dynamic model is a time path of the behavior of the economic elements, in this case, the supply of and demand for onions. What is more, we can picture how quickly or how slowly the time pattern moves toward a final solution. Indeed, the dynamic model will tell us that sometimes there never will be a solution, such as for type 3 cobwebs.

We also get some measure of the stability of the solutions. You could say that a solution is stable in two senses. One is the case of cobweb model 1 where the stability consists of an intersection path which is constant (or, as we shall soon see, a time path which varies in the same way around the equilibrium values for price and quantity). The other is the case of cobweb model 2, where finally an equilibrium solution is arrived at. And that solution is one from which there will be no tendency to move away. These, of course, are not the only examples of stability but they will help you see what can be meant by a stable solution to an economic model.

In addition to giving us finally an equilibrium value for the price and the supply, this dynamic model yields much more.

We have a simple but quite useful microeconomic model which refers to only one market and the participants in that market. From this model, we know the nature of onion supply reaction and the nature of the demand reaction; even more, we know the dynamic stability conditions of the onion market. And

Table 2.1 Onion cobweb searches for a solution

Periods of time, t	Quantities bought and sold, Q_t (in millions)	Price/bushel, p_t
1	30.00	$10.00
2	78.00	34.00
3	58.80	24.40
4	66.48	28.24
5	63.40	36.70
6	64.64	27.32
7	64.14	27.07
8	64.28	27.17
∞	. . .	27.00

without telling you so, we derived a simple finite difference equation with divergences related proportionally by $-\alpha/a$.

Time Path of Onion Prices

Next plot this model's behavior over time. Suppose that what we want to know is how the price of onions behaves, so we (the demanders and suppliers) seek to find an equilibrium. Start with the cobweb model 1 assumption that $|-a| = |\alpha|$ (i.e., that the slopes of the demand and the supply functions are equal but opposite in signs) and what we get is shown in Fig. 2.5. The picture is one of regular oscillations around the equilibrium price for onions. You could say that on the average over time the market tends toward an average price, though it never stays there.

However, if $|-a| > |\alpha|$, then you would get a progressive damping as the market moves unavoidably toward an equilibrium that is cobweb model 2. Then, if $|-a| < |\alpha|$, there is an explosive oscillation as the market goes haywire, cobweb model 3. So learn to look carefully at the differences in the slopes of the demand and the supply functions. They will tell what to expect of price behavior in a dynamic demand model.

Put things a little differently. A market is (dynamically) stable—that is, prices move within a narrow range and always tend toward some average—

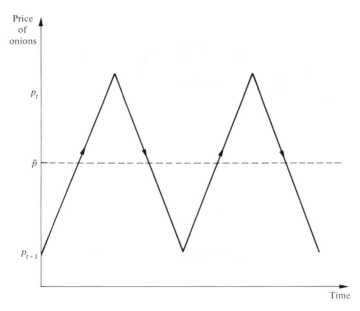

Figure 2.5. Onion prices are volatile. Time path of onion price cobweb with $|-a| = |\alpha|$.

only if the absolute slope of the demand function is equal to or greater than the absolute slope of the supply function. Note that instability in a market is not a matter of oscillations, volatility, or sharp ups and downs, but of whether there is some average price toward which at any moment of time the market seems to be moving.

And that's pretty far to go on a little dose of algebra (plus analytical geometry and even a little theory of difference equations). But this illustrates the approach of managerial economics. The mathematics used is only for the purpose of understanding and predicting behavior. And we pick up as many available mathematical tools as we can without stopping to ask what they are.

Another Economic Model of the Effect of Time: Cash Flows

In many instances a firm has payments owed to it period by period, month by month, or year by year, into the future. Or it may have to pay out a series of amounts over future time. What is needed is a model to evaluate the effect of time on these cash flows. Take the case of a proposed investment in a new restaurant in Boston's Back Bay. The investors find that it is going to cost $200,000 to acquire a good address in the 700s and 800s on Boylston Street. What is more, one of the proposed locations is going to require an outlay of $4,000 just to put the place in shape. Then again it will take a year before the restaurant can start operating.

But, once in business, Table 2.2 shows the estimated gross after tax income year by year. The estimates were put together by a consultant firm which also suggested that at the end of the ninth year, the restaurant ought to be sold to protect the investment. After all, the Back Bay has a fickle clientele.

What kind of annual average rate of return will the restaurateurs get on their money? Or what rate would enable them just to cover their investment? Table 2.3 shows how to calculate the internal rate of return on the Back Bay

Table 2.2 Cash flow from a Boylston Street restaurant

1976	Initial investment	$-$$200,000	
1977	Putting things in shape	$-4,000$	cf_1
1978	Gross after-tax income	$20,000$	cf_2
1979	Gross after-tax income	$27,000$	cf_3
1980	Gross after-tax income	$42,000$	cf_4
1981	Gross after-tax income	$56,000$	cf_5
1982	Gross after-tax income	$50,000$	cf_6
1983	Gross after-tax income	$42,000$	cf_7
1984	Gross after-tax income	$28,000$	cf_8
1985	Sell it	$230,000$	cf_9

Table 2.3   Solution to Back Bay restaurant problem

Year	Cash flow	Discount factor, 14%*	Discounted cash flow, 14%	Discount factor, 15%*	Discounted cash flow, 15%	Discount factor, 14.37%*	Discounted cash flow, 14.37%
1976	−$200,000	1	−$200,000	1	−$200,000	1	−$200,000
1977	— 4,000	.8772	— 3,509	.8696	— 3,478	.8744	— 3,497
1978	20,000	.7695	15,390	.7561	15,122	.7645	15,290
1979	27,000	.6750	18,225	.6575	17,753	.6684	18,047
1980	42,000	.5921	24,868	.5718	24,016	.5845	24,549
1981	56,000	.5194	29,086	.4972	27,843	.5110	28,616
1982	50,000	.4556	22,780	.4323	21,615	.4468	22,340
1983	42,000	.3996	16,783	.3759	15,788	.3907	16,409
1984	28,000	.3506	9,817	.3269	9,153	.3416	9,565
1985	230,000	.3075	70,725	.2843	65,389	.2987	68,701
Net cash flow	$291,000		$ 4,165		−$ 6,799		$ 20 (very close to zero)

*If someone told you to try 14% as the interest rate you would have a cash flow which had a cash value of $4,165. That's too much, since your rate of return should have made the net cash flow zero. Then try 15% and get −$6,779. That's too little. Somewhere between is that correct value which we find by interpolation. That value, 14.37%, makes net cash flow zero.

restaurant. It comes out to 14.37 percent.[2] Since, in 1976, if the would-be restaurateurs had reasonably good credit references, they could get a nine-year loan for an average interest rate around 9.5 percent, our advice was to go ahead. And good luck.

Still Another Time-Cash-Flow Problem

This is the situation facing the Pierpaoli family: They want to buy an old two-apartment condominium on Pacific Heights in San Francisco. The quoted price in 1976 was $65,000. The Pierpaolis don't intend to stay in the city forever. They have set for themselves a deadline seven years ahead when they will be selling their condominium for what they hope will be a 50 percent gain. The mortgage costs are going to be 9.75 percent and they will borrow the entire $65,000. The question is: Is it going to be worth their while?

The Back Bay restaurant problem was to assess the effect of the time pattern of a cash flow on the rate of return. In the Pacific Heights condominium situation, the key question is the present worth of a proposed course of action (Table 2.4). Table 2.5 shows you how to calculate the present worth of the Pacific Heights condominium for the Pierpaolis. It is $3,694. This $3,694 is the net present worth of this course of action. In other words, the Pierpaolis' proposed condominium investment will cover not only the cost of borrowing, the maintenance, and the loss of value of money over time, it will also yield a small after-tax gain.

Algebra of Time Cash Flows

The algebraic form of the Back Bay restaurant or rate-of-return model is the following:

[2]Many of you will have scientific hand calculators programmed to do internal rates of return. Try the calculator out on this problem.

Table 2.4   Cash flows on Pacific Heights condominium

1976	Today's price	−$65,000
1977	After rent, net cost of putting things in shape	−1,000
1978	After-tax rent income	4,900
1979	After-tax rent income	5,300
1980	After-tax rent income	5,700
1981	After-tax rent income	6,500
1982	After-tax rent income	5,000
1983	Sell it	97,500

Table 2.5 Solving the Pierpaolis' problem

Year	(1) Cash flow*	×	(2) Discount factor, 9.75%*	=	(3) Discounted cash flow	(4) Cumulative dis- counted cash flow
1976	−$65,000		1		−$65,000	−$65,000
1977	− 1,000		0.9112		− 911	− 65,911
1978	4,900		0.8302		4,068	− 61,843
1979	5,300		0.7565		4,009	− 57,834
1980	5,700		0.6892		3,928	− 53,906
1981	6,500		0.6280		4,082	− 49,824
1982	5,000		0.5722		2,681	− 47,143
1983	97,500		0.5214		50,837	3,694
Net cash flow = $3,694						

*Just multiply each yearly cash flow times discount factor. For example,

$$4900 \ \times \ \frac{1}{(1.0975)^2}$$

$$4900 \ \times \ \frac{1}{1.0975 \times 1.0975}$$

$$4900 \ \times \ \frac{1}{1.2045}$$

$$\frac{4900}{1.2045} = 4068$$

Solve for i in

$$\begin{aligned}
0 = & - \text{(Initial investment)} + cf_1/(1 + i)^1 + cf_2/(1 + i)^2 \\
& + cf_3/(1 + i)^3 + cf_4/(1 + i)^4 + cf_5/(1 + i)^5 \\
& + cf_6/(1 + i)^6 + cf_7/(1 + i)^7 + cf_8/(1 + i)^8 \\
& + cf_9/(1 + i)^9
\end{aligned}$$

where

cf = cash flow component and the subscript indicates the year or period from the initial investment

i = interest rate which is the best estimate of the yield or rate of return or internal rate of return (or marginal efficiency of capital, mec)

No matter how you go about it, this is not an easy problem to work with if all you have is pencil and paper but no hints.

The algebraic form of the Pacific Heights or net present worth problem is the following:

$$NPW = - \text{(Initial investment)} + cf_1/(1 + i)^1 + cf_2/(1 + i)^2$$
$$+ cf_3/(1 + i)^3 + cf_4/(1 + i)^4 + cf_5/(1 + i)^5$$
$$+ cf_6/(1 + i)^6 + cf_7/(1 + i)^7$$

In this case, the value of i is supplied, 9.75 percent. That makes the paper-and-pencil solution easier than it was for internal rate of return since you could now use a set of financial tables. Find the column of value for the present worth of a dollar at 9.75 percent held for one through seven years. Those values will be the reciprocal of $(1 + i)^j$ or $1/(1 + i)^j$ so that rather than dividing that term into the respective cash-flow component, multiply the cash-flow component by the value in the table. And then sum the values of all the elements in the cash flow (subtracting the negative values, of course). The sum is the net present worth.

Time-Series Analysis

Like dynamic models and cash-flow analysis, time-series analysis is a convenient way of working out relationships among economic variables where time is involved. A time series is a set of values of one or more variables recorded over many periods of time. Ideally, a time series is a set of variables such that the unit of measurement for each variable remains constant with the passage of time. That ideal is seldom met. The time series of prices and quantities in Table 2.6 show the record of behavior of three variables: time, disposable personal

Table 2.6 Two time-series disposable personal income and personal consumption expenditures

Time period, quarter	Disposable personal income	Personal consumption expenditures
1973		
I	$ 866.6	$ 785.7
II	891.7	800.5
III	914.1	818.4
IV	939.9	829.5
1974		
I	953.8	849.5
II	968.2	877.8
III	996.3	907.7
IV	1,015.9	908.4
1975		
I	1,024.0	926.4
II	1,081.7	950.3
III	1,087.1	977.4
IV	1,114.0	1,001.0
1976		
I	1,140.7	1,029.6

income, and personal consumption expenditures in the United States. The time variable serves as a convenient classification.

These time series are not random samples from a large universe of data. The data for each quarter are not independent of the data for other quarters. Putting the data together in this form suggests relationships such that somehow the passage of time affects the data (in a growth rate sense or perhaps in some sort of cycle or seasonality) and that as time passes the behavior of personal disposable income affects the behavior of personal consumption expenditures. If these time series can yield these relationships, then perhaps all we have to do is to work out equations and extrapolate them into the future. The truth of the

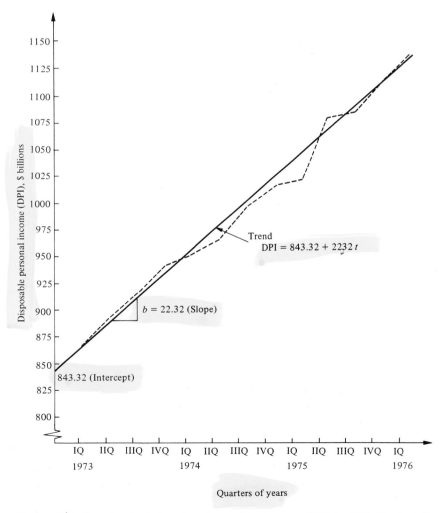

Figure 2.6. Trend calculation for disposable income, I-73 to I-76. Dashed line shows seasonal, cyclical random variations.

matter, however, lies somewhere between extrapolation and random associations among the data.

If we can find a systematic variation in these data, then half the job is done. The systematic variation can be a steady growth or a periodicity in behavior with predictable ups and downs. There does appear to be a growth rate associated with these data and, if so, we can call the growth a secular trend, by which we mean a persistent, long-run tendency to move progressively upward.

A trend is an observable tendency to move in a particular direction over time. Figures 2.6 and 2.7 show the rudiments of how to calculate trend-line equations:

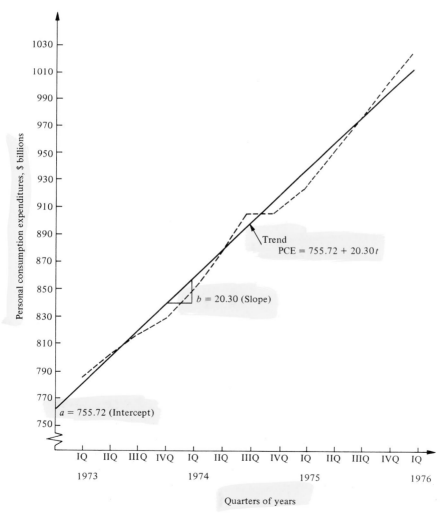

Figure 2.7. Trend calculation for personal consumption expenditure, I-73 to I-76. Dashed line shows seasonal, cyclical random variations.

DPI = 843.32 + 22.32*t*

is the trend equation for disposable personal income, while

PCE = 755.72 + 20.30*t*

is the trend equation for personal consumption expenditures. The DPI equation says that there is a tendency for DPI to increase $22.32 billion each quarter and that the tendency is well established. For PCE, there is a tendency for spending to increase $20.3 billion a quarter over the periods observed and this tendency or trend is as well established as that for DPI.

It is unlikely, however, that time is the only underlying explanation of what is going on. The next step, then, is to attempt a simple linear correlation between the two series. This is done in Fig. 2.8. By estimating intercept and slope the correlation equation becomes

PCE = 5.90 + .89 DPI

Thus, it appears that personal consumption expenditure is closely related to disposable personal income and that for each additional dollar of disposable income, there is a tendency for American households to spend an average of 89 cents. At least, that appears to be true for these thirteen quarters. Of course, the fact that we could get a good relationship among these three variables is subject to the criticism that, despite the complexity of the mathematics involved, we have been quite unsophisticated. Are we really certain that we are any better off with the linear correlation than we were with the trend analysis?

Time-Series Model

Statisticians use a simple model of a time series,

$$A = T \times S \times C \times R$$

where

A = actual values in the time series
T = trend values obtained by a trend equation
S = the magnitude of seasonal forces in the time series
C = the magnitude of cyclical forces in the time series
R = the residual or random variation in the time series

We have already derived the trend component for each of the two series in Figs. 2.6 and 2.7. Our seasonality component can be derived by using link relatives. A link relative is obtained by dividing a value in a time series by the next previous value. The link relative shows the growth in the value from one period to the next. All this is shown in Table 2.7.

Although our observations cover only parts of four years, there is a clear seasonality in the personal consumption expenditure link relatives. The high

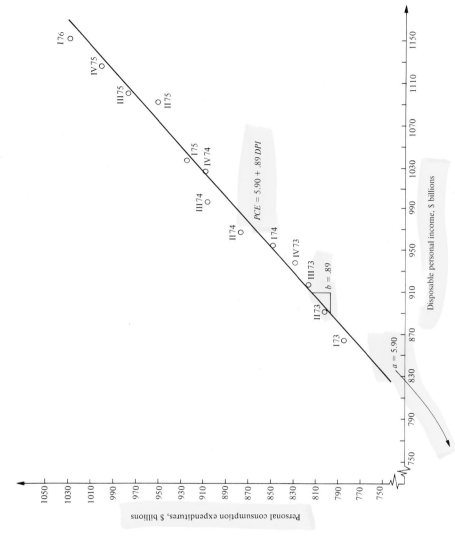

Figure 2.8. Relationship between personal consumption expenditure and disposable personal income, I-73 to I-76.

43

Table 2.7 Comparison of link relatives to determine seasonality

Quarter	I	II	III	IV
Personal 1973		101.9	102.2*	101.3†
consumption 1974	102.4	103.3	103.4*	100.1†
expenditures 1975	102.0†	102.5	102.9*	102.4
1976	102.9			
Disposable 1973		102.9*	102.5†	102.8
personal 1974	101.5†	101.5†	102.9*	102.0
income 1975	100.8	105.6*	100.4†	102.5
1976	102.4			

*High point.
†Low point.

point each year is the third quarter and the low point is the fourth quarter; there is a tendency for the link relatives to build up quarter by quarter to that peak in the third quarter. Seasonality in the disposable personal income series is less obvious.

The cyclical component can be obtained by the technique of moving averages. A three-quarter moving average is the average of the current plus the past two quarters. It is said to move because we advance the calculation each quarter by one quarter. For example, if we use link relatives of three-month moving averages for the PCE time series, it becomes clear that the data build to a peak in the third quarter of 1974. Then they fall steadily to the second quarter of 1975 when a recovery sets in (see Table 2.8).

For DPI, there is less cyclicality. Nonetheless, it appears that the trough came in II-74 and the peak in II-75, whether one uses a two-month or a three-month moving average (see Table 2.9).

Table 2.8 Link relatives of three-quarter moving averages of PCE

Period	Actual value	Moving average	Link relative of moving average
I-73	785.7		
II-73	800.5		
III-73	818.5	801.5	
IV-73	829.5	816.1	101.8
I-74	849.5	832.5	102.0
II-74	877.5	852.2	102.4
III-74	907.4	878.3	103.1 Peak
IV-74	908.4	897.9	102.2
I-75	926.4	914.1	101.8
II-75	950.3	928.4	101.6 Trough
III-75	977.4	951.4	102.5
IV-75	1,001.0	976.2	102.6
I-76	1,029.6	1,002.7	102.7

Table 2.9   Link relatives of three-quarter moving averages of DPI

Period	Actual value	Moving average	Link relative of moving averages
I-73	866.6		
II-73	891.7		
III-73	914.1	890.8	
IV-73	939.9	915.2	102.74
I-74	953.8	935.9	102.26
II-74	968.2	954.0	101.93 Trough
III-74	996.3	972.8	101.97
IV-74	1,015.9	993.5	102.13
I-75	1,024.0	1,012.1	101.87
II-75	1,081.7	1,040.5	102.81 Peak
III-75	1,087.1	1,064.3	102.29
IV-75	1,114.0	1,094.3	102.82*
I-76	1,140.7	1,113.9	101.79

*Do we have a new peak here? It is unlikely in view of other cyclical evidence, but can't be discarded completely. The best thing to do is get more data.

Now put together the parts. Begin by assigning a value to the trend component. For example, in the analysis of the PCE, we could say that for III-74,

$$A = T \times S \times C \times R$$
$$\$907.7 = 894.2 \times 1.03 \times 1.03 \times .995 \quad \text{units in billions}$$

The trend component of \$894.2 billion is, of course, obtained from the trend line. The seasonal component is obtained from the seasonal link relative for PCE in Table 2.7. The decimal point is moved over two places to the left to permit correct multiplication. The cyclical factor is taken from Table 2.9 for III-74. That link relative, too, is reduced by moving the decimal point over two places to the left. The random or residual component is the number or decimal fraction necessary to obtain the actual value.

Statistical Decision Model

Managerial decisions have increased in complexity and in quantity in recent years. Decision analysis is not designed to replace completely the intuitive decision-making approach so many businessmen use. Instead it is intended to sharpen, enrich, and improve the judgment of the decision maker in making the final decision. We have three elements in every decision. First, we have knowledge—all the facts that can be known about a possible decision. Then, we have the uncertainty of the future, the factors that make decision making so chancy. Finally, we have a method for decision making that considers the facts in the context of the uncertainty and provides a way of coming to as correct a decision as possible.

Table 2.10   Profit-payoff matrix for a newsboy

State of nature	Decision					
	Alternative purchases (supply of newspapers)					
Alternative sales (demand)	100	110	120	130	140	150
100	$8.00	$6.30	$4.60	$ 2.90	$ 1.20	$ .50
110	8.00	8.80	7.10	5.40	3.70	2.00
120	8.00	8.80	9.60	7.90	6.20	4.50
130	8.00	8.80	9.60	10.40	8.70	7.00
140	8.00	8.80	9.60	10.40	11.20	9.50
150	8.00	8.80	9.60	10.40	11.20	12.00

Measuring the Consequences of Possible Action

How do we convert knowledge into a usable form, whether we get that knowledge from experience or from a priori distribution? Take the problem of a newsboy who wants to know how many papers to order for tomorrow's sales. Let us say that the *Globe* sells at 25 cents and costs him 17 cents. He has 100 regular customers on the block, but he can carry up to 150 papers if he can find the customers. Obviously, any decision to buy more than 100 papers involves risk. How should he decide?

It will help if he converts what he knows into a profit-payoff matrix like the one presented in Table 2.10. This matrix spells out the alternative results from the range of possible decisions. For each decision to buy a specific number of papers, there is a corresponding set of possible demands and possible profits. If the newsboy were to buy 130 papers just in case but sell only 110, his total daily profit would be $5.40. If he can sell all 130, however, his profit becomes $10.40. Of course, he can get no higher profit than that with his stock of only 130 papers.

Selecting a Decision Strategy

The newsboy's profit-payoff matrix was a good beginning. Now how does he determine which decision strategy is better than another? Here are three possible decision strategies.

Minimax Attempt to avoid the worst possible outcome. For each decision in the payoff matrix, take the worst outcome. From this array of worst outcomes, select the best. This decision will minimize the maximum loss. Table 2.11 illustrates this.

Table 2.11   Minimax criterion

Buy	Decisions					
	100	110	120	130	140	150
Worst outcome for each decision	$8.00	$6.30	$4.60	$2.90	$1.20	$0.50

Select from the worst (mini), the best (max).

Decision   Never buy more than 100 copies of the *Globe*.

Maximax   Attempt to obtain the maximum possible payoff. For each decision, select the best outcome. From this array of best outcomes select the very best. Table 2.12 illustrates this decision strategy or criterion.

Neither the minimax nor the maximax strategy considers the probability or relative likelihood that any state of nature will take place. We need to know how to assign probabilities. And we need a strategy which uses the probability of any state of nature to evaluate each alternative decision.

A probability value is a number assigned to each of the possible events or cells in the payoff matrix. The rule used is that the sum of the probabilities is never greater than 1.0, and the range may be from zero up to 1.0. In the newsboy-payoff matrix, each alternative demands a state of nature. Assign a probability to each state of nature. Now multiply that probability times the profit resulting from each decision. This result will be the expected value for each possible decision.

Optimal expected value criterion   Assume that each state of nature is as likely as any other. Any other assumption could have been made, of course. Since there are six states of nature, each has 16.7 percent chance of occurring. Each then is assigned a probability of 0.167. In the cells are the expected values

Table 2.12   Maximax criterion

Buy	Decisions					
	100	110	120	130	140	150
Best outcome for each decision	$8.00	$8.80	$9.60	$10.40	$11.20	$12.00

Select from best (maxi), the best (max)

Decision   Buy 150 copies of the *Globe*.

Table 2.13 Expected values for alternative supply strategies

State of nature	Probability	Decisions 100	110	120	130	140	150
100	.167	$1.34	$1.05	$0.77	$0.48	$0.20	$0.08
110	.167	1.34	1.47	1.19	0.90	0.62	0.33
120	.167	1.34	1.47	1.60	1.32	1.04	0.75
130	.167	1.34	1.47	1.60	1.74	1.45	1.17
140	.167	1.34	1.47	1.60	1.74	1.87	1.59
150	.167	1.34	1.47	1.60	1.74	1.87	2.00
Expected values →		$8.00	$8.40	$8.37	$7.91	$7.05	$5.92

↑
Maximum expected value

Decision Buy 110 copies of the *Globe*.

for each event associated with each act. In Table 2.13 if the newsboy purchases 110 papers, he will obtain the highest total expected value. Under these assumptions, that is the best decision he can make.

Bayesian Theory of Probability

The word "Bayesian" derives from Thomas Bayes, an English clergyman of the eighteenth century who argued that it was legitimate to quantify our feeling about uncertainty in terms of subjectively assessed numerical probabilities, even if we were confronted by a single unique decision and lacked a past history of events upon which to base the assessment of probabilities.

Assessments could be made, he felt, on the basis of the relative gain or profitability or utility of the alternative decisions available. For example, if actions A and B were to be weighted against each other, we could determine first the relative profitability of each on the basis of the expected value of the utility or profit arising from two possible event sequences. We can present the comparison of A and B in terms of the expected values should events C and D occur in tabular form.

Actions	Expected value of events C	D
A	100	50
B	98	96

The Bayes criterion suggests that if we have absolutely no information about the relative probabilities of success from action A or B, we should assign them equal values and then adopt that action or strategy whose expected value (or payoff or utility) is highest. The criterion evaluated in this case leads to the following answers:

$$\frac{1}{2} \times 100 + \frac{1}{2} \times 50 = 75 \quad \text{for A}$$

$$\frac{1}{2} \times 98 + \frac{1}{2} \times 96 = 97 \quad \text{for B}$$

Therefore, we should rank B ahead of A.

Bayes' rule does have one shortcoming. It is not clear in advance what unknown possibilities ought to be considered equally probable. To illustrate this dilemma, suppose that we are trying to decide whether to sell ice cream (strategy A) or hot dogs (strategy B) at a baseball game. We do not know if it will rain ("nature's strategy C"), if it will be cloudy ("nature's strategy D"), or if the sun will shine ("nature's strategy E"). In the absence of a good weather report, we could assign equal probabilities to C, D, and E.

No longer do we concentrate on the alternative actions to decide among, but upon the strategies available to nature. Although we may consider A and B to be equally likely of success, it is not clear that there is an equal likelihood of rain, sunshine, cloudiness, or something else. If for some intuitive reason our decision maker feels that C, D, and E may reasonably be assigned odds of two-tenths, five-tenths, and three-tenths, then our calculations in the following payoff matrix become:

Actions	Nature's strategies		
	C	D	E
A	100	2	1
B	0	98	99

$$\frac{2}{10} \times 100 + \frac{5}{10} \times 2 + \frac{3}{10} \times 1 = 21.3 \quad \text{for A}$$

$$\frac{2}{10} \times 0 + \frac{5}{10} \times 98 + \frac{3}{10} \times 99 = 59.1 \quad \text{for B}$$

$$78.7$$

We would choose B. In other words, we would sell hot dogs.

In short, Bayes' rule suggests that mathematics plus intuition yields a good decision. But when considering uncertainties under Bayes' rule, we need to evaluate all the economic costs of the alternative courses of action and, with our prior knowledge or current attitudes toward the situation in which the decision is to be made, work out the values of the probabilities.

This approach, of course, is not really new to businessmen. The order of procedure in the Bayesian theory, however, differs from other methods in two significant ways. In the classic probability method, for example, statistical information is gathered, interpreted, and presented to decision makers so that they may see the facts and act on them. In Bayesian theory, executive judgment is translated into mathematical probabilities and combined with statistical data already in hand. The final mathematical analysis is based, then, on data both from statistical sources and from the assignment of probabilities. The executive decides which is the best outcome and acts accordingly. The two differences between the Bayesian method and the classical method are: (1) the use of data based on judgment and intuition at an early stage in the analysis rather than at the end, and (2) the use of data from both sources before interpretation.

Bayesian theory deals with many unknown events and allows the choice of the best action to come out of a many-action situation. Bayesian theory can also systematically and explicitly use opportunity costs to evaluate the worth of actions by assigning weights corresponding to these costs for each different possible action or state of nature. Then, too, Bayesian theory permits sound decisions even when historical information is lacking. It also reduces research cost by allowing smaller samples to be used.

Bayes' Rule and the Value of Sample Information

Suppose our newsboy goes out next Saturday, buys his papers, and tries to sell them. He finds to his and our surprise that he can sell only 100. That bit of information upsets him, as well it should. But now, you see, he has some sample information with which to revise his initial estimates. The original or a priori probabilities were subjective guesses. Bayes' rule tells us and the newsboy how to calculate posterior or conditional probabilities.

Start by reestimating the probabilities
Possibility of all low sales if no days are low   0/5
Possibility of all low sales if one day is low   1/5
Possibility of all low sales if two days are low   2/5
Possibility of all low sales if three days are low   3/5
Possibility of all low sales if four days are low   4/5
Possibility of all low sales if five days are low   5/5
Then multiply each such possibility times a priori probability.

$$(.167) \times (0/5) = 0.0000$$
$$(.167) \times (1/5) = 0.0333$$
$$(.167) \times (2/5) = 0.0666$$
$$(.167) \times (3/5) = 0.0999$$
$$(.167) \times (4/5) = 0.1333$$
$$(.167) \times (5/5) = \underline{0.1666}$$
$$0.5000$$

Thus 0.5000 is the probability that sales will be low. Now using this value, we can convert a priori probabilities into posterior probabilities as shown in Table 2.14.

Table 2.14   Calculation of posterior probabilities

A priori probabilities	States of nature, SON_i	Calculations, $\dfrac{P(SON_i)P(F' \mid SON_i)}{P(F')}$	Posterior probabilities, $P(SON_i \mid F')$
.167	100	$\dfrac{(.167)(0/5)}{.5}$	.000
.167	110	$\dfrac{(.167)(1/5)}{.5}$	.067
.167	120	$\dfrac{(.167)(2/5)}{.5}$	.133
.167	130	$\dfrac{(.167)(3/5)}{.5}$	.200
.167	140	$\dfrac{(.167)(4/5)}{.5}$	.267
.167	150	$\dfrac{(.167)(5/5)}{.5}$	.333 / 1.000

Note: SON stands for state of nature and SON_i means any one of the six states of nature (in this case, the six different estimates of possible sales). The notation $P(SON_i)$ means the "probability of state of nature *i*," i.e., that chance in 100 that this state of nature (or sales estimate) might come true. F' is used to indicate the chance that a sales estimate might be low (in this case, ranging from 0 out of 5 through 5 out of 5 as follows: 0/5, 1/5, 2/5, 3/5, 4/5, 5/5, so that there are six elements corresponding to the six states of nature).

In the calculation of the posterior probabilities in Table 2.14 the formula

$$\frac{P(SON_i)P(F' \mid SON_i)}{P(F')}$$

tells us to multiply the a priori probability $P(SON_i)$ for each state of nature *i* times the chance that a sales estimate as a state of nature might be low (from 0/5 to 5/5). Divide this result by the overall probability that the sales of newspapers might be low.

You will have noticed that just as the sum of the a priori probabilities was one, so the sum of the posterior probabilities will also be one. What we have done is adjust the chance that every given sales outcome might take place by a sample bit of information that the newsboy was able to determine. Note, too, that on the basis of this sample information there has been a considerable revision of the initial guess that one sales outcome was as likely as any other. It turns out that the chance that sales might be 150 papers, for example, becomes one in three against our initial guess that the chance was one in six.

Revised Expected Value

With our posterior probabilities, we can now go back to the profit-payoff matrix (Table 2.10) and calculate a new expected value tableau. The differences between Table 2.13 and Table 2.15 are the following:

Table 2.15 Newsboy Problem: Revised Expected Values for Alternative Supply Strategies

State of nature	Posterior probability	Decisions					
		100	110	120	130	140	150
100	0.	$0.	$0.	$0.	$0.	$0.	$0.
110	0.067	0.54	0.59	0.48	0.36	0.25	0.13
120	0.133	1.06	1.57	1.28	1.05	0.82	0.60
130	0.200	1.60	1.76	1.92	2.02	1.74	1.40
140	0.267	2.14	2.35	2.56	2.78	2.99	2.54
150	0.333	2.66	2.93	3.20	3.46	3.73	4.00
Expected values→		$8.00	$9.20	$9.44	$9.67	$9.53	$8.67

Maximum expected value

1. The expected values for each decision strategy are uniformly higher.
2. The best decision strategy changes from one of buying 110 papers to one of buying 130 papers.
3. The best strategy in the revised expected value tableau is more rewarding than that in the original tableau.

So it pays to sample. The advantage of Bayes' rule is that decisions can be considerably improved even under conditions of inadequate information.

Chapter Summary

A chapter full of mathematical techniques is not the most exciting part of a book on managerial economics. Even if you have found that it wasn't so hard to grasp and that there were some practical applications to what you have learned, it is still true that mathematics is not everybody's cup of tea. Yet if you now understand what an economic model is and how algebra and statistics are used to state and develop models, you are far along the path to making use of the economic tools that managerial economics offers. Cash-flow analysis, time-series models, and decision analysis round out a selection of models and problems that are sure to be useful in what follows this chapter.

Keep in mind that it is not so much the math technique itself that matters, but the awareness that mathematics is a way of stating problems so they can be more readily manipulated. That is, math is used only if it permits economists and managers alike to understand and solve problems. While there is pleasure for math purists simply in solving problems, managerial economics focuses on situations in which better decisions come out of good methods for solving problems. And even more satisfaction can be derived from being able to model reality so that what is important and what can be done stand out.

Selected Readings

Boot, J. C. G., and E. B. Cox: *Statistical Analysis for Managerial Decisions*, 2d ed., New York, McGraw-Hill, 1974.

Champernowne, David Gawen: *Uncertainty and Estimation in Economics*, vols. I and II, San Francisco, Holden-Day, 1969.

Ekeblad, Frederick A.: *The Statistical Method in Business*, New York, Wiley, 1962.

Gupta, Shiv K., and John M. Cozzolino: *Fundamentals of Operations Research for Management*, San Francisco, Holden-Day, 1975.

Harrod, Sir Roy: "What Is a Model," in J. N. Wolfe (ed.), *Value, Capital and Growth*, Chicago, Aldine, 1968.

Hirshleifer, Jack: "The Bayesian Approach to Statistical Decision: An Exposition," *Journal of Business* 34:471–489, October 1961.

Meyer, Donald L., and Raymond O. Collier, Jr.: *Bayesian Statistics*, Itasca, Ill. Peacock Books, 1970.

Miller, David W., and Martin K. Starr: *Executive Decisions and Operations Research*, Englewood Cliffs, N.J., Prentice-Hall, 1961.

Mills, Richard L.: *Statistics for Applied Economics and Business*, New York, McGraw-Hill, 1977.

Willemsen, Eleanor Walker: *Understanding Statistical Reasoning: How to Evaluate Research Literature in the Behavioral Sciences*, San Francisco, Freeman, 1974.

Questions, Problems, and Projects

1. James Turley of the Federal Reserve Bank of St. Louis took a careful look at automobile prices from 1958 through 1975 and found that the relative prices of new cars had been falling steadily. He measured the relative price of new cars by comparing new car prices with the Consumer Price Index. However, he also found that there were temporary pauses in this relative price decline during periods of recession. For example, from late 1973 through mid-1975, this relative price, though much lower than in the previous recession (1969 through 1970), remained steady. In every recession, Turley noticed, automobile sales fell. What do you make of this kind of evidence? Does Turley have the makings of an economic model?

2. What caused the Depression in 1929? Your answer is just about as important as that of anybody else. After all, there is a good deal of disagreement. One group of economists lays all the blame on the shortage of money. Another group puts its finger on sharp cutbacks in investment. Still another group stresses the negative psychology of American consumers in the early 1930s. Why does it matter who is right? Or was this simply an experiment to assist economists to work out a better understanding of how capitalism functions? Treat your explanation of why there was a depression as a model and draw conclusions about what policies ought to be followed to avoid such severe social, economic, and political events.

3. The following are general merchandise sales (in millions of dollars) in a moderate-sized New England city for a recent period:

1970	I	$8.095	1972	I	$ 6.514	1974	I	$ 5.572
	II	7.023		II	7.580		II	7.409
	III	6.780		III	8.526		III	8.097
	IV	9.396		IV	13.599		IV	10.213
1971	I	$ 5.945	1973	I	$7.540	1975	I	$5.904
	II	7.689		II	7.875		II	7.014
	III	10.030		III	8.171			
	IV	17.541		IV	9.413			

What do you make of this time series? Do you see any seasonal behavior? Or trend behavior? Or secular behavior? How can you tell?

4. The Pasadena Chemical Company in Texas has to decide which kind of vinyl chloride plant to build. Here are the data presented to management by the marketing and engineering staffs.

Investment option	Annual capacity (millions of lb)	Rate of return on investment at three forecast demand growth rates*		
		Low growth, 3%/yr	Medium growth, 7%/yr	High growth, 12%/yr
A	50	10%	10%	11%
B	75	5	12	12
C	100	1	8	15

*Forecast probabilities: Low growth, 0.3; medium growth, 0.3; high growth, 0.4.

What is the best decision Pasadena's management can make? Are you sure? A lot of money is riding on your answer.

5. Library of Congress researchers were reported by the *Wall Street Journal* to have estimated the cost of job bias. They did this by examining the unemployment rates and earnings of nonwhite workers as compared with white workers. If both groups had the same job skills and education in 1975, 638,000 more minority workers would have been employed. And if wages had been equal, each minority worker would have earned $1,768 more a year. The Library of Congress study concludes that such changes in labor utilization and training would have generated $22.3 billion more in added gross national product. That would have equaled 3.7 percent of the 1975 gross national product. What kinds of assumptions would have to be made to reach this result? Apart from the fact that most Americans agree that there should be less discrimination, what does the fact that 1975 was largely a recession year imply for this kind of analysis? Is this coming at the matter from a supply or a demand angle?

6. The following are consumer price increases, production changes, and wages for 1975 and early 1976 for ten countries:

Countries	Consumer price increase	Industrial production change	Hourly wage
United Kingdom	21.2	−3.4	$3.20
Italy	11.8	0.6	4.52
Sweden	10.6	0.0	7.12
Japan	10.2	8.6	3.10
Belgium	9.7	−6.3	6.46
Canada	9.7	1.6	6.20
France	9.5	2.6	4.57
Netherlands	8.9	4.3	5.98
United States	6.1	11.5	6.22
Germany	5.4	6.2	6.19

What do you make of this array of numbers from the International Monetary Fund? Do they have a story to tell? What is that story?

3

DEMAND ANALYSIS

Key Concepts

aggregation
complementary
consistency
consumer surplus
cross elasticity
demand
elasticity
Engel
expenditure elasticity
income effect
index numbers
Laspeyres
logarithmic measures

marginal revenue
market basket
market demand
model
own-price
price effect
quantity demanded
rational behavior
revealed preference
substitution
substitution effect
transitivity

What Is Ahead in This Chapter

Is it possible to explain how consumers behave? And, then, is it possible to predict what they will do next? Economists not only think that it is possible to understand and predict consumer behavior, they have developed effective means of analyzing such elements of behavior as

1. How much of any good or service will be bought
2. What happens to consumer spending if consumer incomes increase or decrease

In fact, this is what this chapter on demand is all about.

You have already seen in Chap. 2 how useful models and model building are to managerial economics. Now you are going to examine some of the basic demand models. And, in this examination, the emphasis will be on the practical uses and applications of each model. For example, are there enough data available to permit you or management to use the model to explain why Toyota sells more cars in the United States than Subaru or why Sears Roebuck outsells every other major retailer in the nation?

Let's put the matter a little differently. The purpose of this chapter is to show you what can be done with economic demand models. The intent is to get you to think in operational terms. Ahead in this chapter is an array of the technical knowledge of the world's best economists on the subject of demand. But don't be overwhelmed. Like you, they wanted to understand and to explain the complexities of consumer behavior. You'll find that a good deal of progress in solving a lot of puzzling problems has been made.

What an Operational Approach to Demand Means

There are all sorts of demand models. And there will be more. Because we do not have the space or the time to examine the entire array of demand models, you will find that we have selected in this chapter those models which "work." In a first course in economics, you have already learned the essential characteristics of demand models. The quantity demanded of any commodity, service, or product is examined to see what causes the quantity demanded to vary. Your course probably stressed the relationship between variations in the price of a good and variations in the quantity demanded. In addition, you learned that variations in the income of the buyer have an important influence on quantity demanded.

More than likely, your instructor led you through an analysis which seemed quite theoretical. You didn't study actual sales numbers or real consumers. Instead, you dealt with demand curves, shifts in these curves, and what it all meant. Partly because you will need to review what you have learned, the chapter goes back over these matters in some detail. But the reason for reviewing demand analysis here is to prepare you to work with demand numbers in real situations.

Being operational means, then, that demand analysis in managerial economics is intended to help you see what economists actually do. In this way, you can determine how much confidence to put in one demand analysis compared with another. And you may even learn how to do it yourself.

Demand Models: What Do We Know?

After more than two centuries of intensive research into demand behavior, economists think they know three basic things about consumer behavior:

1. It is rational.
2. It can be measured.
3. It can be predicted.

When economists say that consumer behavior is rational they mean that men and women who buy goods and services do so because they are making choices between more or less, cheaper or more expensive, or useful or useless goods. Note that rationality is a behavioral characteristic of making choices. We can analyze consumer choices to see why they were made. There is a logic to it all.

Measurement, as you probably have already guessed, simply means that economists work with numbers. How good are those numbers and what do they tell us? What is it that they can't tell us? How many numbers and what kind do we need? Because markets in which goods and services are bought are places where records are kept, where there are numbers such as prices, incomes, quantities bought and sold, times and places at which sales or purchases took place, qualities of goods, kinds of sellers, and kinds of buyers, the measurement task is to assemble these numbers, to sort them out, and to make them tell what they can about consumer behavior.

If we can show that consumers make choices in ways that can be explained, if we can assemble numbers which describe in some detail what consumers bought and where, when, and how they bought it, and if we can make these numbers into economic models, then we can predict consumer behavior. Indeed, what we need for prediction is simply evidence of a consistency, a tendency for people to do the same kinds of things whenever circumstances are essentially similar.

Time-Series Demand Model

In Chap. 2 you have already seen that it is possible to take the chronological ordering of statistical information called "a time series" and build a time-series model. That model was used to analyze a business cycle. Let us now examine the uses of time-series modeling for demand analysis. Suppose that we had the following information about apple sales in Durham, North Carolina. Table 3.1 is a time series showing apple sales in thousands of bushels per year for each of seven years. We also have the average June price of apples per bushel in Durham for these seven years. By the way, the data are not the result of intensive marketing research but were put together from general observations.

The first thing an analyst does with a time series is check the effect of time by deriving a trend equation that relates changes in the time series with changes in time periods to see what kind of pattern shows up. In this case, there is a clear pattern. Figure 3.1 is a trend plot of the apple price–quantity time series. Apple purchases are plotted against time. The trend equation[1] is

$$Q = 24.46T + 16.43 \qquad R^2 = .9216 \quad \text{(See Chap. 4 for } R^2 \text{ term)[2]}$$

What the trend equation tells us is that apple purchases in Durham over the seven years between 1971 and 1977 tended to increase by 24,460 bushels a year. What is more, there was relatively little variation around this trend so that the trend line explained about 92 percent of the purchase observations. In short, whatever else is true about apple buyers in Durham, their buying behavior seems to have been consistent when examined from the standpoint of time. So we have a time-series model for apple purchases in Durham with a good fit to the available data. And, if consumers don't change their habits, we can use this model to predict how Durham apple buyers will behave in the future.

---

[1]While you did get a taste of algebra and of linear equations in Chap. 2, and while some readers with scientific programmable calculators can readily derive trend and regression equations, Chap. 4 contains the logic of this kind of economic model building.

[2]R^2, as you will see in Chap. 4, is a measure of how well an equation or model fits the data. In Fig. 3.1, the fit was close: R^2 was high. R^2 ranges from 0 to 1.

Table 3.1 Apple price–quantity time series for Durham, N.C.
June 1971 to June 1977

Period	Quantity purchased, thousands of bushels	Average price per bushel, $
June 1971	50	0.90
June 1972	75	0.80
June 1973	65	1.50
June 1974	110	1.00
June 1975	150	0.70
June 1976	150	1.40
June 1977	200	0.90

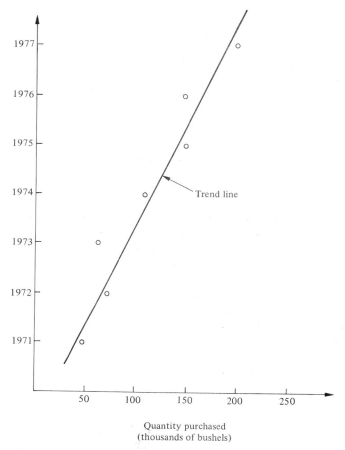

Figure 3.1. Apple demand in Durham, N.C., 1971–1977.

The problem is, though, that while we have measurement and we have a basis for prediction, we really don't have an explanation of why apple buyers in Durham behave as they do. In Chap. 2, our black-eyed-peas model was based on consumer reactions to price changes. And so was our onion cobweb model. As it turns out, there are some price data along with the timed apple-purchase data. Let us see what they can tell us.

The next step in the analysis, then, is to plot the apple prices against the apple purchases and see what kind of pattern emerges (Fig. 3.2). We know what we are looking for. As prices fall, we would expect apple purchases in Durham to increase. But both the plot and the derived equation don't have much to say. The quantity-price equation is

$$Q = -27.71P + 142.78 \qquad R^2 = .0230$$

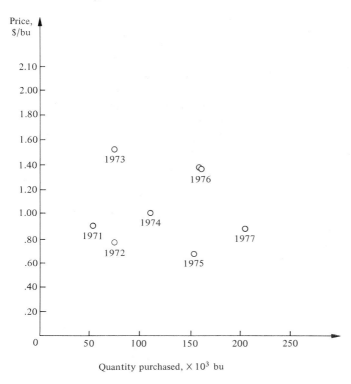

Figure 3.2. Apple demand in Durham; little obvious relationship between price and quantities.

This equation, as you probably have noted already, has the correct sign on the slope. As it stands, it says that for every 10-cent increase in the price of apples, there will be a decrease in apple purchases of about 2771 bushels. But whatever this equation is, it is not a demand model; at least not in its present form.

What is more, the model explains only 2.3 percent of these observations, meaning that a lot more is going on in apple purchases than this model was able to pick up. Our analyst, though, is a resourceful person. A demand model has to work and to work, it must show, at the very least, that rising prices are accompanied by falling purchases. The analyst has a way out of the dilemma.

Why not plot price against purchase deviations? Go back to the trend plot and observe that instead of being right on the trend line, each year's apple purchases were to the right or to the left of the trend line. Table 3.2 shows the deviations for each period. The deviation is derived by subtracting the trend-line purchase amount from the actual purchase amount. The difference is the plus or minus deviation from the trend line. Putting the trend-line purchase deviations and the price together, we plot Fig. 3.3 on the following rule. Negative deviations will be plotted in the left, or negative, quadrant and the positive deviations in the right quadrant. We seem to have struck pay dirt.

Table 3.2 Deviations of apple purchases from trend

Period	Actual sales	Trend sales	Deviation, thousands of bushels
June 1971	50	40.89	9.11
June 1972	75	65.36	9.64
June 1973	65	89.82	−24.82
June 1974	110	114.29	−4.29
June 1975	150	138.75	11.25
June 1976	150	163.21	−13.21
June 1977	200	187.68	12.32

The data scatter ranges from the upper left to the lower right, so that higher prices are associated with negative deviations (those greater than the trend values) and lower prices are associated with positive deviations (those less than the trend values). The equation of this relationship is

$$Q' = -45.36P + 46.65 \qquad R^2 = .9025$$

We have the correct negative sign on the slope. And we have a relationship that explains more than 90 percent of the observations. For every 10-cent increase in price, there was, in general, a decrease in apple purchases of about 4536 bushels in Durham over this seven-year period. Because we have a

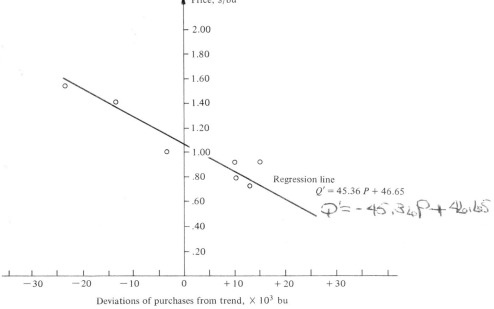

Figure 3.3. Demand for apples in Durham; price variations and purchase deviations.

demand model that is behaving as it should, we could yield to the temptation to give up while we are ahead.

But there is at least one problem remaining.

Surely, over a seven-year period, something more than price changes is affecting apple purchases in Durham. What about changes in consumer tastes or consumer incomes? In fact, let's go back to Table 3.1. Notice that apple purchases increased from June 1972 through June 1973, despite a rise in apple prices. Also, purchases didn't change at all between June 1975 and June 1976 when prices doubled. This and evidence like it suggest that we don't have just one demand model, but perhaps a set of models. Perhaps we have at least one model each for each relevant combination of years.

Let us see then if we can find such combinations of years. And here is how we do it. Begin with the trend deviations in Table 3.2. They are collected in column (2) of Table 3.3. Then, record the regression line values of apple purchases in Durham for the equation

$$Q' = -45.36P + 46.65$$

These values—compared with the actual deviations used to get the data scatter plot—are those along the regression line corresponding to each quoted price. In column (3) of Table 3.3, we have those values. Next, subtract column (3) from column (2). The resultant column (4) gives full effect to the analysis of the trend and of the regression. Finally, subtract column (4) from the trend line purchases in Table 3.2. That gives column (5), which we can call the "adjusted purchases." These adjusted purchases reflect the effects of both the trends over the seven years and the price variations.

The next step is admittedly quite arbitrary. We observe that 1971 and 1972 comprise a set of years in which the price of apples per bushel in Durham fell from 90 cents to 80 cents while purchases rose. This kind of behavior fits a demand model. So does the behavior from 1973 through 1975, when the price fell from $1.50 through $1 to $.70. Meanwhile purchases of apples rose from about 93,500 bushels to 142,000 bushels. By the same token, the behavior between 1976 and 1977 is such as to fit a demand model. Our arbitrariness

Table 3.3 Deviations of regression value from trend line adjusted purchases

Period	(1) Apple prices, $ per bushel	(2) Trend deviations, $q_t(= q')$	(3) Regression values, $q'_t(=q'')$	(4) Deviations from regression, $q' - q''$	(5) Adjusted purchases, actual purchases $[q' + (q' + q'')]$
June 1971	.90	9.11	5.83	3.28	37.61
June 1972	.80	9.64	10.37	−.73	66.09
June 1973	1.50	−24.82	−21.38	−3.45	93.27
June 1974	1.00	−4.29	1.30	−5.59	119.88
June 1975	.70	11.25	14.90	−3.65	142.40
June 1976	1.40	−13.21	−16.85	3.64	159.57
June 1977	.90	12.32	5.83	6.49	181.19

consisted of ignoring the inconvenient fact that when prices rose from 1972 to 1973, purchases also rose, or when prices rose even more sharply from 1975 to 1976, there was still an increase in purchases.

At this stage in our analysis, we are not quite ready to explain what happened between 1972 and 1973 and between 1975 and 1976. It could have been a major shift in consumer tastes, a significant increase in consumer incomes, or maybe a demographic shift in family composition, such as flight to the suburbs. The point, however, is that economists, given the nature of the available data, frequently have to make the data tell the story they think is hidden there somewhere.

Table 3.4 contains the adjusted-purchases data corresponding to the prices of apples per bushel in Durham in each of the seven years surveyed. Table 3.4 is also arranged in combinations of years which look like possible demand models. The next step, of course, is that of plotting these combinations to see what they look like (see Fig. 3.4). It turns out that the three demand models do not look alike. The 1971 to 1972 model, for example, is relatively flat. The other two models are much more steep. What flatness and steepness mean for a demand model, we need to examine further. And we will.

Now, however, let us recapitulate the results of our analysis of a survey of seven years of apple prices and apple purchases in Durham, North Carolina. We have been able to derive at least three price demand models. We have discovered that it may be necessary to "massage" the data to make them yield economic models that work and that can be used. And we have discovered that data that come in a time-series form are not likely—at least in their initial and rough form—to tell us very much about demand. At any rate, we have not gleaned much from data in the way we have learned to construct demand models so far.

What we have done with the Durham apple-purchases data is that we have

Table 3.4   Derivation of three demand curves
Three statistical demand schedules

Period	Price, $ per bushel	Adjusted sales, thousands of bushels
	A	
June 71	0.90	37.61
June 72	.80	66.09
	B	
June 73	1.50	93.27
June 74	1.00	119.88
June 75	0.70	142.40
	C	
June 76	1.40	159.57
June 77	0.90	181.19

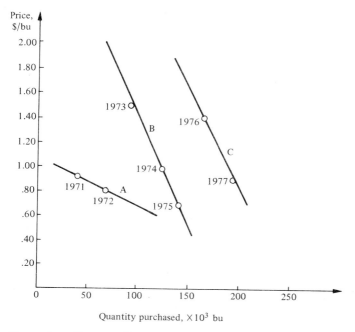

Figure 3.4. Three apple demand curves derived from a time series in Durham, N.C.

derived what can technically be called an "own-price" demand model. That is, the model is designed to tell what happens to the purchases of apples as the price of apples (the own-price) changes. Of equal interest might have been what would have happened to the purchases of apples as the price of oranges changed.

Demand Function for Oranges in Grand Rapids, Michigan

In the early 1960s, a group of agricultural economists made a thorough study of the competition between California and Florida fresh oranges in a typical Midwestern city, Grand Rapids.[3] First, let's take a look at the own-price demand schedule for size 200 Florida interior oranges which the economists worked out for Grand Rapids. Table 3.5 contains a well-behaved demand schedule that differs from the time-series–derived demand models in two interesting ways. On the one hand, this size 200 Florida orange demand schedule is based on market observations taken within a matter of days and often on the same day in different supermarkets. Thus the variations in demand that might be affected by the passage of time are largely eliminated. On the other hand, by limiting the observations to a typical marketplace, Grand

---

[3]M. R. Goodwin, W. F. Chapman, Jr., and W. T. Manley, *Competition between Florida and Valencia Oranges*, Bulletin 7, Economic Research Service, U.S. Department of Agriculture, Washington, D.C., December 1965.

Table 3.5 Own-price demand schedule for size 200 Florida interior oranges

Price, cents per dozen	Quantity, dozens
33	307
37	305
41	281
45	271
49	222
53	219
57	204
61	177
65	164

Rapids, the analysts could and did pick up the effect of other prices on the demand for size 200 Florida oranges.

This demand schedule for size 200 oranges is readily converted into a demand function presented either as an equation or as a line or curve on a graph. The equation is

$$Q = -4.84P + 476.1 \qquad R^2 = .9801$$

So the demand model has the right sign on the slope and appears to explain about 98 percent of the reported observations on orange purchases in Grand Rapids. The graph in Fig. 3.5 shows a relatively close fit between the demand regression line and the data scatter.

The demand regression line reflects the relation between the own-price of size 200 oranges and the quantity sold or purchased in Grand Rapids at the time and under the conditions of the survey. In effect, by using this demand regression line, we can describe—assuming nothing changes—how at higher prices fewer oranges would have been sold, and with some degree of accuracy how many fewer. By the same token, we can describe how many more oranges would have been sold or purchased had the price been lower. So we have a range of quantities demanded as the prices change shown as a demand schedule, a demand regression line (or curve), and an algebraic function. And they all say the same thing.

A change in demand would mean an entirely different demand function. And in that entirely different demand function, more might be purchased or sold at any given price than was true in the function just derived for size 200 oranges in Grand Rapids. Changes in demand functions are shown by movements or shifts in the demand line or curve. An increase in demand means a shift to the right and upward. A decrease in demand means a shift to the left and downward. Our analysis of the apple market in Durham showed us what such a change in demand might mean. Figure 3.4 reflects demand changes in that marketplace.

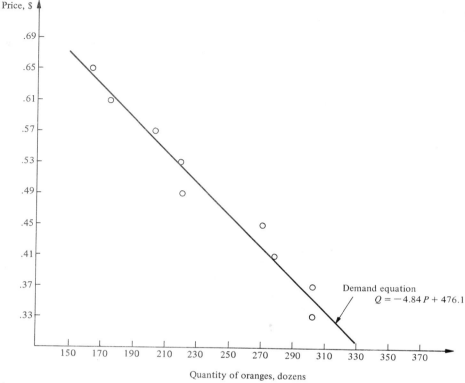

Figure 3.5. Demand curve for size 200 Florida interior oranges in Grand Rapids.

Own-Price Elasticity

In the analysis of the Durham apple market, we referred to the flatness or the steepness of the various demand curves derived from the available information. Now it is time to give more attention to what the flatness or the steepness of a demand curve tells us. What it tells us is called the "elasticity" of the demand relationship.

Own-price elasticity measures the relationship between a percentage change in the own-price of oranges or apples, and the percentage change in the quantity demanded. Own-price elasticity is measured along the demand curve and tells us how sensitive a demand function is to price changes. The following is an arc formula for own-price elasticity:

$$\frac{(q_1 - q_2)/q_1}{(p_1 - p_2)/p_1} = -e_p$$

While there is a variety of possible elasticity formulas, an arc elasticity formula has the advantage of being simple and useful in the analysis of most data such as those in the orange demand schedule in Table 3.5. However, it is better not to regard the arc elasticity obtained from this formula as *the* own-price elasticity of a demand function. This formula may give many elasticity values, depending on which pairs of prices and quantities in a demand schedule are used.

In Table 3.6 are the calculations of the various arc own-price elasticities for size 200 Florida oranges in Grand Rapids. The elasticities range from −.05 between 33 and 37 cents to −2.03 between 45 and 49 cents. The average of these various arc own-price elasticities is −.92. This average arc elasticity may be taken as an estimate of the own-price elasticity of the orange demand function. The value of −.92 for the own-price elasticity of the demand function means that every 10 percent increase in the price of size 200 Florida oranges was accompanied on the average by a 9.2 percent decrease in the purchase and sale of oranges.

An elasticity measure is a first cousin of the slope. But there is an important difference, despite the fact that they belong to the same family. A slope tells us how a given change in prices affects a change in the quantity demanded. An own-price elasticity tells us how a given percentage change in prices affects a change in quantity demanded. If the demand function were plotted in percentage terms (as it would be if double logarithmic graph paper were used), then the slope of the demand function in percentage (or logarithmic) terms would be its elasticity. In the size 200 orange case, the logarithmic slope of the demand function—its own-price elasticity—would be found to be

Table 3.6 Own-price arc elasticities of Grand Rapids orange demand function

Price, cents per dozen	Quantity, dozens	$Q_1 - Q_2$	$P_1 - P_2$	$\dfrac{Q_1 - Q_2}{Q_1}$	$\dfrac{P_1 - P_2}{P_1}$	e_p	Revenue $(P \times Q)$, \$
33	307						101.31
37	305	2	−.04	$\dfrac{2}{307}$	$\dfrac{-.04}{.33}$	−.05	112.85
41	281	24	−.04	$\dfrac{24}{305}$	$\dfrac{-.04}{.37}$	−.73	115.21
45	271	10	−.04	$\dfrac{10}{281}$	$\dfrac{-.04}{.41}$	−.36	121.95
49	222	49	−.04	$\dfrac{49}{271}$	$\dfrac{-.04}{.45}$	−2.03	108.78
53	219	3	−.04	$\dfrac{3}{222}$	$\dfrac{-.04}{.49}$	−.17	116.07
57	204	15	−.04	$\dfrac{15}{219}$	$\dfrac{-.04}{.53}$	−.91	116.28
61	177	27	−.04	$\dfrac{27}{204}$	$\dfrac{-.04}{.57}$	−1.89	107.97
65	164	13	−.04	$\dfrac{13}{177}$	$\dfrac{-.04}{.61}$	−1.19	106.60
					Average =	−.92	
					Log/log e_p =	−.97	

−.97. So the arc elasticity method came fairly close to giving an accurate measure of the own-price elasticity.

You must have noticed that there was a minus sign on the own-price elasticity. The reason for this is the negative monotonic character of the demand function itself. Demand functions relate increases in price with decreases in quantity demanded. And since quantity demanded and price move in opposite directions, the sign on e_p is negative.

Practical Applications of Elasticity

Own-price elasticity can be used to predict changes in sales revenue. For example, if the own-price elasticity is in the range from −.99 to, say, −.001, then any increase in price will be accompanied by an increase in sales revenue. What happens is that despite the decrease in the quantity demanded between one price and a higher price, the drop in quantity demanded is not enough to offset the effect of the higher price on revenue. Note therefore that in the orange demand schedule in Table 3.6, the increase in price from 33 to 37 cents led to an increase in sales revenue (or total consumer outlay) from $101.31 to $112.85. Sales revenue or consumer outlay, of course, is obtained by multiplying price times quantity for each price-quantity–demanded combination. Thus, sales revenue increased as the price of oranges rose from 37 to 41 cents and from 41 to 45 cents. In every one of those cases, the arc elasticity was in the range from −.99 to −.001. Arc elasticities in that range are called "inelastic." Changes in quantity demanded are so insensitive to changes in price that while quantity demanded is lower at the higher price, the revenue at the higher price is greater to the seller than at the lower price.

Let's go back to the three apple-demand functions in Fig. 3.4 derived for the Durham market. Two of them have own-price elasticities in the range from −.99 to −.001. The demand function for the period 1973–1975 has an own-price elasticity of −.56, which means not only that a 10 percent increase in apple prices is accompanied by 5.6 percent decrease in apple purchases but that apple sellers will get more gross revenue from higher than from lower prices. The demand function for the 1976 to 1977 period has an own-price elasticity of −.29, which means that a 10 percent increase in prices was accompanied by a 2.9 percent decrease in apple purchases. That demand model was even more inelastic and thus less responsive to price changes than the earlier one. But observe that the demand model for the 1971 to 1972 period had an own-price elasticity of −2.0, which meant that there was a high purchase responsiveness to price changes.

Own-price elasticities in the range from −1.01 to −3 and beyond are said to be elastic. You will observe that when the price for oranges in Table 3.6 rises from 45 to 49 cents, total consumer outlay (and sales revenue) falls from $121.95 to $108.78. When the demand model is elastic (or, in this case, in the elastic range for the demand model under observation), a change in price is accompanied by a change in revenue in the opposite direction. An elastic response to price changes means that whatever the percentage change in price, the percentage change in quantity demanded will be large and, because it is negative, will more than offset the effect of the price change. Under elastic demand, a falling price will accompany rising sales revenue (and consumer outlays). A rising price will accompany falling sales revenue (and consumer outlays).

There's one more range of elasticity values that needs analysis. It is the range in the vicinity of -1. An own-price elasticity of -1 means that whatever the percentage change in price, the percentage change in quantity demanded will be equal to it but opposite in sign. Thus there will be no change in sales revenue (and consumer outlays) as price varies. This information about own-price elasticities is summarized in Table 3.7.

Empirical Estimates

It turns out that, since own-price elasticity is a first cousin of a slope (and is, in fact, a slope in logarithmic space), all we need to know to use it is an estimate of its value and one set of observations of a price and a quantity. If we can assume that the price-quantity combination or set is part of a demand function, we can predict the values of that function and the possible sales revenues (and consumer outlays) at a wide range of prices.

The basic empirical question is: Do we have dependable estimates that is, estimates that can be applied to a variety of situations, of own-price elasticities?

Table 3.7 Summary of effect of price changes on sales revenue (or consumer outlays) at various possible values of own-price elasticity

Range of own-price elasticity values	Change in price	Change in quantity demanded	Change in sales revenue (or consumer outlays)
From $-.99+$ to $-.001$ "inelastic"	Down Up	Up Down	Down Up
From -1.01 to -3.00 and above "elastic"	Down Up	Up Down	Up Down
Around -1.0 "unit elastic"	Down Up	Up Down	Unchanged Unchanged
Around 0 "absolutely inelastic"	Down Up	No change No change	Wide range of possible values
Approaching a very large value "perfectly elastic"	Small change down Small change up	Large change up Large change down	Wide range of possible values

Answering this obvious and direct question is simply not easy. Taylor in 1975 published a survey of the results of a number of studies of the own-price elasticity of electricity. These studies, conducted in the United States, derived own-price elasticities for residential electricity usage. Table 3.8 is a summary of these results. For residential electricity demand, the values range from an own-price elasticity of -1.02 to -2.0. Needless to say, this is a wide range. Yet, it is clear that nearly every study found electricity demand to be elastic and thus quite responsive to price changes. As energy production costs rose as they did in the 1970s, it could be expected that resultant higher electricity utility rates would reduce the amount each customer purchased by percentages greater than the price increases. Moreover, this would adversely affect the revenues of the electricity utilities.

Taylor concludes that much of the difference in estimates of elasticities is due to the differences in the method of analysis of demand functions. It would be better, Taylor feels, if researchers could begin with the entire demand schedule for residential electricity. In that way, an average elasticity would be derived in a manner analogous to that shown in Table 3.6. But this was not possible. In general, we have to say that, in many demand studies for essentially the same good or kind of good, a relatively wide range of price elasticities has been found.

In Table 3.9 we have Weisskoff's results for underdeveloped countries. He found a wide range of variation in price elasticities for such commodity groups as food, rent, services, clothing, transport, and durable goods. Weisskoff also found that he could not explain these variations by analyses of differences in

Table 3.8   Own-price elasticity of electricity

Type	Research study	Elasticity
Residential	Fisher and Kaysen	0
	Houthakker and Taylor	-1.89
	Wilson	-2.00
	Mount, Chapman, and Tyrell	-1.20
	Anderson	-1.12
	Lyman	-0.90
	Houthakker, Verlegger, and Sheehan	-1.02

Sources: L. D. Taylor, "The Demand for Electricity: A Survey," *Bell Journal of Economics,* Spring 1975; F. M. Fisher, and C. Kaysen, *A Study in Econometrics: The Demand for Electricity in the United States,* Amsterdam, North-Holland Publishing Co., 1962; H. S. Houthakker, and L. D. Taylor, *Consumer Demand in the United States,* 2d ed., Cambridge, Mass., Harvard, 1970; R. A. Lyman, "Price Elasticities in the Electric Power Industry," Department of Economics, University of Arizona, October 1973; K. P. Anderson, "Residential Energy Use: An Econometric Analysis," Rand Corporation, (R-1297-NSF), October 1973; H. S. Houthakker, P. K. Verlegger, and D. D. Sheehan, "Dynamic Demand Analysis for Gasoline and Residential Electricity," Lexington, Mass., Data Resources, Inc., 1973; T. D. Mount, L. D. Chapman, and T. J. Tyrell, "Electricity Demand in the United States: An Econometric Analysis," Oak Ridge National Laboratory (ORNL-NSF-49), Oak Ridge, Tenn., June 1973.

Table 3.9 Price elasticities of various countries in 1955

Country	Food	Rent	Services	Clothing	Transport	Durables
Rhodesia	−0.1279	−0.9104	−1.4700	0.0221	−1.6167	−3.5763
Jamaica	−1.2277	−1.7766	−1.3035	−3.9917	−1.9928	−1.4819
Puerto Rico	−0.2488	−0.3848	−0.7758	−1.6139	0.1852	−0.9667
Peru	−1.0117	−0.5782	−1.0648	−3.5277	−0.9305	−0.8174
Ceylon	−2.3840	−5.7324	−2.2737	0.2597	−2.4805	−4.9572
Korea	−0.1625	−0.3565	−0.3399	−0.2165	−0.2168	−0.2882
Taiwan	−0.0367	−0.1442	0.2024	0.1413	−0.5850	−0.3505
Israel	−1.0662	0.0521	−0.8333	6.3348	−1.0258	−0.0248

Source: Richard Weisskoff, "Demand Elasticities for a Developing Economy: An International Comparison of Consumption Patterns," in H. B. Chenery (ed.), *Studies in Development Planning*, Cambridge, Mass., Harvard, 1971.

life-styles or by homogeneity groupings. There was, he concluded, no basis on which to speak of "the price elasticity" of demand for food, for example.

Are There Meaningful Differences in Own-Price Elasticities?

Sometimes it is said that the more inelastic the demand for any good, the more likely that good is to be a necessity. So we should expect the own-price elasticity for many food items to be in the range from −.99 to −.001. So far, we have seen that the demand models for apples in Durham and oranges in Grand Rapids had own-price elasticities in that range. It has also been held that, the smaller the proportion of the consumer budget for any item, the more likely is its own-price elasticity to be inelastic. Others have suggested that the durability of a commodity affected the own-price elasticity of its demand function. The more durable, the more elastic the demand. What is more, there is the argument that if there are many substitutes for any given good or service, that good or service demand function will be elastic. But a number of cases have been found in which goods having a large number of substitutes were shown to have inelastic demands. The best that can be said is that we should treat with some caution any assertion that the demand for this or that kind of good is elastic or inelastic.

Cross Elasticity

The purpose of the survey of oranges in the fresh fruit market in Grand Rapids was to see whether there was any competition between California and Florida fresh oranges. Two kinds of Florida oranges—Indian River, size 200, and interior, size 200—and one kind of California orange, size 138, were studied to see what their comparative sales at different prices in nine different stores could tell researchers about consumer choices. The measure used to assess the amount of competition among different kinds of oranges is called the "cross elasticity." Cross-price elasticity is the ratio between the percentage change in quantity demanded of one kind of orange and the percentage change in the price of another kind of orange. In order for cross elasticity to have meaning, we have to assume that the quantity demanded of one kind of orange depends not only on its own-price but also on the price of another kind of orange.

The arc elasticity formula for cross-price elasticity is

$$ e_{p_a \, q_b} = \frac{(q_{b1} - q_{b2})/q_{b1}}{(p_{a1} - p_{a2})/p_{a1}} \qquad e \, BP_2 $$

where

p_a = price of good a

q_b = quantity demanded of good b

The number subscripts indicate different amounts of q_b and different prices for a.

In Grand Rapids, researchers found the cross-price elasticities for the various kinds of oranges to be as shown in Table 3.10.

Cross-price elasticities can be both negative and positive. Negative cross-price elasticity means that a rise in the price of one kind of orange caused a decline in the quantity demanded of another kind of orange. When the cross-price elasticity is negative, it indicates that the goods being compared are complements. Complementary goods respond in the same way to a single-price stimulus. Positive cross elasticity indicates that the oranges are substitutes. In the Grand Rapids study, notice that a 1 percent increase in the price of Florida Indian River oranges led to a 1.56 percent increase in the sales of Florida interior oranges. By contrast, a 1 percent increase in the price of Florida Indian River oranges produced only one-tenth of 1 percent change in the quantity demanded of California oranges. The evidence here suggests that Florida oranges are good substitutes for each other but that California oranges are not competitive with Florida oranges.

Another way of interpreting the cross-price elasticity concept is to conceive of it as measuring a *shift* in the demand function of one commodity induced by a change in the price of another commodity. In these terms, a zero cross-price elasticity means no shift in the demand function. Positive cross-price elasticity means an upward shift, while negative cross-price elasticity means a downward shift.

Table 3.10   Results in percentage changes in the sales of oranges

1% change in the price of oranges	Florida Indian River	Florida interior	California
Florida Indian River	. . .	+1.56	+0.01
Florida interior	+1.16	. . .	+0.14
California	+0.16	+0.09	

Total Revenue, Average Revenue, and Marginal Revenue

It is by now clear that there is a relationship between own-price elasticity and revenue. Revenue, of course, is the result of multiplying the price in a demand schedule by the corresponding quantity demanded. While, as we have also noted, we could call this result either a sales revenue or a consumer outlay, most of the time we will be concerned with the use of the demand models and demand schedules as a way of interpreting the effect on sellers. To call $p \times q$ "revenue" would be more useful in these contexts.

Now, here are some definitional distinctions that will be helpful later. Total revenue is said to be the result of multiplying the relevant price times its corresponding quantity demanded of the good in question. Average revenue is obtained by dividing total revenue by the quantity demanded. Therefore, average revenue is the same as price. Marginal revenue is the increase or decrease in total revenue divided by the increase in quantity demanded, as we move up or down the demand schedule.

Suppose that the following demand schedule were the one derived from an economic research effort:

Quantity demanded, units	Price (average revenue), $	Total revenue, $	Marginal revenue	e_p
1.5	12	18		
3	10	30	8	−6
4.5	8	36	4	−2.50
5.25	7	36.75	1	−1.33
6	6	36	−1	−1
7.5	4	30	−4	−0.76
9	2	18	−8	−0.40

Figure 3.6 is a demand function (or line) derived from the demand schedule. Also in Fig. 3.6 is the marginal revenue function (or line). From the schedule and from Fig. 3.6, you can see that as marginal revenue approaches zero, total revenue approaches its maximum value. Marginal revenue is positive when the demand function is elastic. It is negative when the demand function is inelastic. And when marginal revenue is 0, the elasticity is −1.

Geometrically, the marginal revenue function can be derived easily. You will notice that each point on the marginal revenue line is a midpoint on any line drawn parallel to the quantity axis. And, of course, marginal revenue is 0 precisely where the quantity axis between 0 and 10.5 is bisected. You will also notice that the rectangle with sides $p = 7$ and $q = 5.25$ is the largest rectangle that can be drawn under the triangle ODD'. Up to that rectangle, as price decreases from 14 toward 7, the rectangles subtended by the triangle formed by the demand line are growing larger. As the price continues to decrease from 7 toward 0, the rectangles grow smaller. The rectangles represent total revenue (TR).

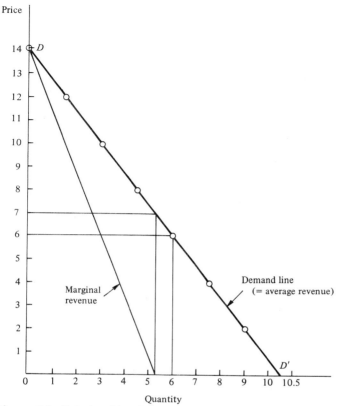

Figure 3.6. Relationship of demand (average revenue) to marginal revenue.

The marginal revenue line tells us how the rectangles are increasing or decreasing. Simply put, to find any point on a marginal revenue curve or line when you know the average revenue curve or line, draw a line parallel to the quantity axis. Bisect that line and the point of bisection, or midpoint, will be a point on the marginal revenue curve or line.

It is useful to know that there is an exact relationship between average revenue (AR) and marginal revenue (MR) which involves own-price elasticity.

$$MR = AR\left(1 + \frac{1}{e_p}\right)$$

e_p is own-price elasticity.

This makes economic sense. In order to increase sales by one unit, a seller must lower the price by some amount. Thus MR, the change in TR, is equal to the receipts from the last unit sold, AR, *less* a loss in revenue.

Consumer Surplus

Consumer surplus is a measure of the benefit consumers receive from a demand situation. "Demand situation" can mean the demand function, a demand schedule, or just a comparison between one quantity demanded at a given price and another quantity demanded at another price within the same demand function. Ilse Mintz,[4] in a study of the effect of import quotas on sugar prices, used the consumer surplus to measure the impact of the quota system on consumers.

She started with the information that the own-price elasticity for sugar is generally estimated to be low, about −.1. In 1970, the "free market," or world, sugar price outside the United States was 5.5 cents a pound. Ms. Mintz estimated that, at 5.5 cents, American consumers would have bought 23.2 billion pounds in 1970. However, the actual price in the United States was 8.07 cents per pound in 1970 and American consumers at that price bought 22.4 billion pounds of sugar.

	Price per pound, cents	Quantity demanded, billions of pounds	Consumer outlay, billions of dollars
	5.5	23.2	1.2760
	8.07	22.4	1.8077
Difference	2.57		.5962 Estimate of consumer surplus lost

Thus Ms. Mintz had two points on a demand function, which she had derived from knowledge about the own-price elasticity and the actual sugar consumption at current prices. If American consumers had been able to buy sugar at 5.5 cents a pound, they would have spent about $1.3 billion. In fact, at the higher price of 8.07 cents, they spent $1.8 billion. Consumer surplus is the difference between what consumers actually spent at a given price and what they would have spent if they had been forced to pay a succession of higher prices on the demand function (or demand schedule). As shown in Fig. 3.7, paying this extra amount would be equivalent to paying an amount more or less equal to the area of the triangle, under the demand curve, above the consumer outlay (or total revenue) rectangle. Because consumers normally pay only one price for a given amount, they obtain a consumer surplus which measures the benefit from their purchases. It is a benefit in the sense that a clever price policy could have been devised to take away every bit of that surplus, a policy which would have made the consumers pay for each additional pound of sugar the additional benefit that sugar gave them.

Ms. Mintz multiplied the difference between the world and the United

[4]Ilse Mintz, *U.S. Import Quotas: Costs and Consequences*, American Enterprise Institute for Public Policy Research, Washington, D.C., February 1973.

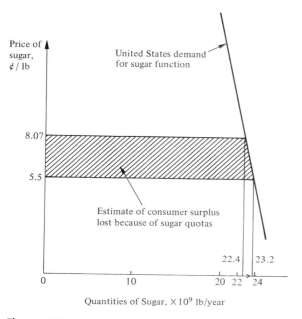

Figure 3.7. American demand for sugar function. Estimate of consumer surplus lost because of sugar quotas.

States price—about 2.57 cents—times the 23.2 billion pounds consumers would have bought at the lower price. This gave the loss in consumer surplus, or an estimate of the shaded area in Fig. 3.7. That loss came to $596.2 million in 1970.

Admittedly, there has been a lot of controversy over the use of this measure of consumer benefits. None the less, the triangular area under the demand curve and above the consumer outlay (or total revenue) rectangle is a very good estimate of consumer surplus. And the consumer surplus is widely used as a market measure of consumer benefits. Willig[5] recently put all the arguments about the consumer surplus together and proved to the satisfaction of most economists that consumer surplus can be calculated from available demand data and that, in most applications, the errors of approximation are quite small.

Income-Expenditure Demand Model: Survey of Consumer Expenditures

There is a wealth of demand data in a variety of forms. One of the richest sources in the United States is the every-decade Survey of Consumer

[5]R. D. Willig, "Consumer's Surplus Without Apology," *American Economic Review*, September 1976.

Expenditures. In the 1960 to 1961 SCE, for example, there is a detail of expenditures and income for the urban United States which can be used to work out, say, a demand model for housing. The following data are taken from Table 29E in Bureau of Labor Statistics Report 237-38 (dated July 1964) and refer to urban three-person—more or less—families. There were 7.3 million such families in the United States in the early 1960s and they had an average size of 3.1 persons. That was 18 percent of the total number of urban families and about the same percentage of the total urban population. What we want to know from this table is whether we can describe and predict consumer spending behavior in the housing market.

All the data we are going to use in our relatively simple model are in Table 3.11. Look carefully at Table 3.11 and what you will see is that about 78 percent of families are in the spending range from about $3950 a year to about $7600 a year. In that range, housing spending varied about 29 percent of total consumer spending for current consumption in the early 1960s. What is more, if you leave out the lower 8.7 percent of the families, for the remaining 91 percent or so, the proportion spent on housing is even closer to 29 percent. That, you will observe, is the average for the entire population group of three-person families. Thus, over a fairly wide range of consumer spending, the share represented by housing remained fairly constant.

To turn this information into a form useful for prediction, let us apply what is called an "income-elasticity formula" to the data. Income elasticity is the relationship between the percentage change in spending for any commodity or service and the percentage change in all spending (taken as a proxy for consumer incomes). Table 3.12 shows how to calculate such elasticity. On this evidence, you could conclude that the income elasticity for housing is in the vicinity of 1. That would mean that for every 10 percent increase in income across the spectrum of three-person family incomes, housing spending in-

Table 3.11   Housing spending and income for 3-person families
United States, 1960 to 1961

Expenditures for current consumption, $	Percent of all 3-person families, %	Total housing spending, $	Percent housing spending of all spending, %
6,207.37	100	1,809.10	29.5
1,044.31	.1	443.01	42.5
1,997.56	3.1	718.61	36.0
2,842.25	5.5	967.24	34.0
3,948.02	10.0	1,211.98	30.7
4,731.17	14.7	1,422.82	30.1
5,411.15	15.2	1,574.66	29.1
6,364.00	19.5	1,884.59	29.6
7,602.80	18.8	2,127.34	28.0
9,834.16	10.2	2,713.84	27.6
13,998.43	2.8	4,158.83	29.7

Table 3.12 Calculation of income elasticity for housing demand of 3-person families
Urban United States, 1960 to 1961

(a) Link relative and change in current spending, %	(b) Link relative and change in housing spending, %	(c) Percent of families in class, %	(d) Unweighted income elasticity b/a	(e) Weighted elasticity $c \times d$
191.3	162.1	3.2	.85	.02720
142.2	134.6	5.5	.95	.05225
138.9	125.3	10.0	.90	.09000
119.8	117.4	14.7	.98	.14404
113.7	110.7	15.2	.97	.14744
117.6	119.7	19.5	1.02	.19890
119.5	112.9	18.8	.94	.17672
129.4	127.6	10.2	.99	.10098
142.3	153.2	2.8	1.08	.03024
Average elasticity			.96	.96777

creased about 10 percent. That would also mean, as we have seen, that housing spending would remain a more or less constant share of total income and spending over this range.

Using different data from the 1960 census, Frank de Leeuw[6] of the Urban Institute in 1971 found the income-elasticity results shown in Table 3.13. Adjusting his data to take account of probable bias, de Leeuw reduced the homeownership income elasticities to an average of about 1.1. His range for the rental family group was 0.8 to 1.0. And his conclusion was that the "preponderance of evidence supports an income elasticity for homeowners moderately above 1.0, or slightly higher than the elasticity for renters."[7]

Frank de Leeuw, of course, isn't the only economist to derive housing

[6]Frank de Leeuw, "The Demand for Housing: A Review of Cross-Section Evidence," *The Review of Economics and Statistics*, February, 1971.
[7]Ibid.

Table 3.13 Income elasticities for urban families by occupancy and family size

Household category	Homeownership income elasticity	Rental housing income elasticity
Two persons	.89	.77
Three or four persons	1.40	.81
Five persons	1.51	.98
Six and more persons	2.01	.72
Weighted average Two and more persons	1.35	.80
All households (unweighted)	1.34	.81

income-elasticity results in the same range. Reid and Muth indicate similar findings.[8]

Housing Demand and the Property Tax

By the way, if the income elasticity for housing is about one, then there are interesting conclusions to be drawn about some controversial matters. One of these is that housing spending is about the same proportion of income in Winnetka or Greenwich as in Chicago or New York. Moreover, as we range over communities classified in rank order of average family incomes, we should expect to find that, as incomes increased, housing spending should match income increases. Thus poor communities and poor neighborhoods should not have significantly different housing spending as a percentage of family income and spending than do middle-class and upper-income towns, neighborhoods, or suburbs. Thus if we add the local property tax as one more housing expenditure—and it is included in the Survey of Consumer Expenditures—we should expect to find that it, too, remains at about the same percentage of income as we move over a cross section of family incomes in different places. Recent studies have at least questioned the assertion that a property tax is regressive, that is, that a property tax becomes a lower percentage of family income and spending as we move from the poor family through the middle-class family to the upper-income family. Some have shown that it is more likely that a property tax is progressive,[9] that is, the share of income paid for that tax increases perceptibly as we move up the income range. Needless to say, not all economists accept this evidence or interpret the available evidence in this way. But you can see how an innocent observation on the numerical value of income elasticity may have fairly far-reaching implications for consumer behavior, for tax policy, and even for the demand for new houses, to say nothing of derivative issues, such as how to finance public education.

Arc Elasticity Formula for Income Elasticity

A simple arc formula for income elasticity is the following:

$$e_y = \frac{(Q_1 - Q_2)/Q_1}{(Y_1 - Y_2)/Y_1}$$

[8]Margaret G. Reid, *Housing and Income*, University of Chicago Press, 1962. Reid finds housing income elasticity to be between 1.5 and 2.0 on the basis of studies of many metropolitan housing markets from 1918 through 1960. R. F. Muth, "Urban Residential Land and Housing Markets," *Issues in Urban Economics*, in H. S. Perloff and W. Wingo, Jr. (eds.), Baltimore, Johns Hopkins Press, 1968.

[9]See Henry Aaron, "A New View of Property Tax Incidence," and Richard A. Musgrave, "Is a Property Tax on Housing Regressive?" as well as comments by Brazer, Netzer, Friedlaender, Rolph, and Peterson in *American Economic Review*, May 1974.

where

Q = amount spent on a given commodity
Y = measure of income or spending

You will have noticed that, in the calculation of housing income elasticities, the proxy for income is some measure of actual total spending. In this way, the analyst gets around the problem of saving out of income. What is being compared is spending on one commodity or service as contrasted with total spending of average income. For this reason, some economists prefer to call income elasticity an "expenditure elasticity."

Income Demand Model for Food

Robert D. Stevens, an economist with the U.S. Department of Agriculture's Economic Research Service, developed a general demand model for food spending based on about sixty-five consumer expenditure surveys in thirty-five countries at two periods in the 1950s and 1960s. These data, like those used for the housing models, are aggregative; that is, instead of referring to a single person or family, they refer to millions of people in a variety of places, under a variety of conditions, and at a wide range of incomes. However, the purpose of aggregation is to derive a model of typical behavior which could be applied to a single typical family. Unlike a single family's experiences, those of many families surveyed fill in all the missing points. But, while aggregative models look like macroeconomic models, they really aren't. They are in the tradition of Alfred Marshall who showed generations of economists how to develop models of typical economic behavior.

Stevens synthesized the food spending and total spending data, converting all monetary units to dollars (at 1953 price levels); his results are shown in Table 3.14.

Table 3.14 Data for an estimated food-expenditure demand model

Food spending per capita, $	Total consumer spending, $	Double logarithmic expenditure elasticity	Arc expenditure elasticity
30	50	.73	
50	100	.73	.66
84	200	.73	.68
164	500	.73	.63
272	1000	.73	.66
366	1500	.73	.70

Source: R. D. Stevens, *Elasticity of Food Consumption*, FAER no. 23, Washington, D.C., Economic Research Service, U.S. Department of Agriculture, March 1965.

The advantage of a double logarithmic demand model is that its slope is its elasticity, in this case, the expenditure or income elasticity.

Figure 3.8 shows Stevens's double logarithmic food-expenditure demand function. Both the total-consumption per capita axis (horizontal axis) and the food-expenditures per capita axis (vertical axis) are calibrated in logarithms. Thus what is being measured on both axes is the percentage change in spending as we move from low figures to high in Table 3.14.

Engel's Demand Model for Food

This food-expenditure model can readily be converted into an Engel model in which what is being measured is the relationship between the percentage change in the share food spending represents of total consumer spending and total consumption itself. Look, for example, at an arc elasticity formula for an Engel food-expenditure model.

$$e_e = \frac{[(Q_{F1}/Q_{TC1}) - (Q_{F2}/Q_{TC2})]/(Q_{F1}/Q_{TC1})}{(Q_{TC1} - Q_{TC2})/Q_{TC1}}$$

where

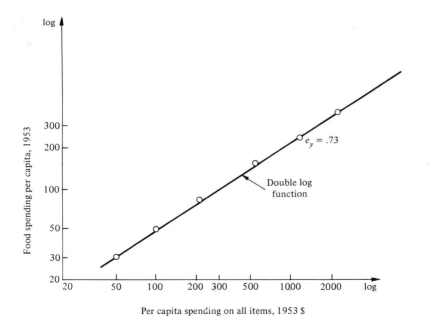

Figure 3.8. Food-expenditure demand model. (Data from R. D. Stevens, *Elasticity of Food Consumption*, USDA Economic Research Service, FAER no. 23, March 1965.)

Q_{F1} = food spending per capita in period 1
Q_{F2} = food spending per capita in period 2
Q_{TC1} = total consumer spending per capita in period 1
Q_{TC2} = total consumer spending per capita in period 2

Figure 3.9 presents an Engel demand model in which the vertical axis is the logarithm of (or percentage change in) the ratio of food spending per capita to total consumer spending (Table 3.15). You will notice that while the expenditure model had a positive slope such that increases in total spending were accompanied by increases in food spending, in this presentation, the Engel demand model has a negative slope. That is, as food spending per capita increased, it became a smaller and smaller share of total spending. You will also notice that

$$e_e = e_y - 1$$

so that $-.27 = .73 - 1 = e_e$.

Thus Engel elasticity is the negative complement of expenditure elasticity. You can use either form of income elasticity and readily convert from one to the other. The economic sense of this relationship is clear. If food-expenditure elasticity is less than one, then each increase in total spending is accompanied by an increase in food spending which is not as large as—in percentage terms—the increase in total spending. Therefore food spending is becoming a smaller and smaller share of total consumer spending. Interestingly, Stevens's results for his summary of sixty-five observations in thirty-five countries at two

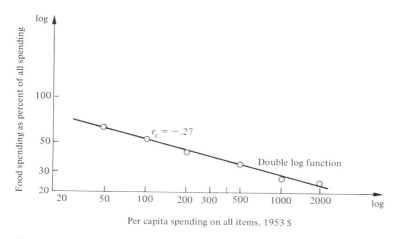

Figure 3.9. Ratio of per capita food spending to per capita spending on all items. (Data from R. D. Stevens, *Elasticity of Food Consumption*, USDA Economic Research Service, FAER no. 23, March 1965.)

Table 3.15   Data for an estimated Engel food demand model

Total consumer spending per capita, $	Ratio of food spending to total consumer spending, %	Engel elasticity, double log	Arc elasticity for Engel model
50	60.8	−.27	
100	50.5	−.27	−.34
200	41.9	−.27	−.17
500	32.8	−.27	−.15
1000	27.2	−.27	−.17
1500	24.4	−.27	−.20

Source: R. D. Stevens, *Elasticity of Food Consumption*, FAER no. 23, Washington, D.C., Economic Research Service, U.S. Department of Agriculture, March 1965.

periods of time more or less correspond to those obtained by others, as you can see in Table 3.16.

The Engel logarithmic demand model Stevens used is

$$\log (Q_{food}/Q_{total\ spending} \times 100) = -.2683 \log \text{total spending} + 2.2399$$

The slope or the elasticity of this demand model is about −.27. From the Engel model, Stevens derives the expenditure model

$$\log Q_{food} = (-.2683 + 1)/\log Q_{total\ spending} + 2.2399 - \log 100$$
$$= .7317 \log Q_{total\ spending} + 2.2399 - \log 100$$

In his expenditure demand model, the slope or elasticity is .73.

Table 3.16   Income elasticities for food

Source	e_y	e_e
Stevens (1965)	.7317	−.2683
Houthakker (1965)	.7440	−.2560
Weisskoff (1971)	.6413	−.3587
ECLA (1958)	.6000	−.4000
Houthakker and Taylor (1966)	.6882	−.3118

Source: R. D. Stevens, *Elasticity of Food Consumption*, FAER no. 23, Washington, D. C., Economic Research Service, U. S. Department of Agriculture, March 1965.

H. S. Houthakker, New Evidence on Demand Elasticities, *Econometrica*, vol. 33, no. 2, 1965.

Richard Weisskoff, Demand Elasticities for a Developing Economy: An International Comparison of Consumption Patterns, in H. B. Chenery, ed. *Studies in Development Planning*, Cambridge, Harvard, 1971.

United Nations, *Economic Development of Columbia*, Mexico City, Economic Commission for Latin America, 1958.

H. S. Houthakker and L. D. Taylor, *Consumer Demand in the United States*, 1929-1970, Cambridge, Harvard, 1966.

Chart of Income-Elasticity Relationships

Table 3.17 is a chart of income-elasticity relationships. The major advantages of demand models using expenditures data revolve around the ready availability of the data and the fact that elasticity coefficients tend to be basically similar whether the data represent the United States or countries overseas, whether the data are in time-series form or are derived from cross-section evidence, or whether the data reflect small samples or large surveys. But expenditures, unlike prices, really represent composite economic information. An expenditure after all is the quantity of the good purchased as measured in physical units such as pounds times the price per physical unit. In effect, then, when we use expenditure data in a demand model, we are asking two interesting questions. One of these concerns price effect: What differences, if any, do changes in price make on the expenditure data? More precisely, what do price elasticities look like?

The other question, which is perhaps more important, is: Are people better off or worse at one expenditure level than another? To be sure, we can infer that, if people buy less food out of additional income (as they apparently do if

Table 3.17 Income elasticity relationships

Elasticity-values expenditure	Engel	Quality of elasticity	Impact on spending	Impact on income shares
1 to .999 .ƏƏ|	−.999 to −.01	Inelastic	Change in spending on good or service less than change in total consumer spending	Spending on good becomes smaller and smaller share of total consumer spending
1	0	Unit elastic	Change in spending on good equals change in total consumer spending	Spending on good remains a constant share of total consumer spending
1.01 up	.01 up	Elastic	Change in spending on good is larger than change in total consumer spending	Spending on good becomes larger and larger share of total consumer spending

the evidence from the food-expenditure demand model is to be accepted), then they are better off. That is, since food is an essential commodity in everyone's consumption budget, if in times of rising incomes less of the budget goes to such an essential, then nonessentials (whatever that term means) are getting a larger share of consumption budgets at those higher incomes. Can such a larger share for nonessentials mean a rising standard of living?

Put these matters into a somewhat different context. Any good which has an Engel elasticity which is inelastic, that is, less than 0, is presumably an essential good. We can use it as an index of "better-off-ness," as the U.S. Department of Labor does in constructing the equivalent income scales for consumer budgets.

Equivalent Income

The ratio of incomes for families of different types is derived from the following formula:

$$Q_{\text{food}_i} = k_i(y_i)^e$$

where

Q_{food_i} = average expenditure for food by family type i

y_i = average net income (or total expenditure) for family type i

e = expenditure elasticity for food

In a 1960 study, a four-person family, with husband, age ranging from 35 to 55, wife, and two older children, aged 6 to 16, was taken as the basic family. In Table 3.18 their income and spending patterns are taken as 100.

The idea of a search for equivalent income appears in various other guises such as the use of consumer price indexes to work out an income to compensate for inflation. In such a case, there is an amount of basic comparative expenditure which we can call a "market basket." Other market baskets are compared with a standard market basket to see whether there has been an improvement or worsening of inflation. An understanding of the market-basket concept can be gained from Fig. 3.10 In Fig. 3.10, the vertical axis measures variations in family size as well as the inverse of the age of the family head. The horizontal axis is the size of the market basket (or, essentially the same thing, the comparative index of equivalent incomes). The meaning of equivalent incomes is that along any line such as EI_1, there is a range of different market baskets, depending on family size, which yield to each family essentially the same level of equivalent income. Larger families need more. Smaller families need less. By the same token, if we take any market basket (or equivalency index) of size 80, then for that market-basket size, there are variations in market-basket composition to account for age difference, such as

Table 3.18 Scale of equivalent income for city families of different sizes, ages, and composition
Typical family = 100

Size and type of family	Age of family head			
	Under 35	35–55	55–65	65 and over
One person	42	50	46	37
Two persons (husband and wife)	63	66	67	63
Three persons (husband, wife, child under 6)	73	80		
Four persons (husband, wife, two children, older child over 18)		116	119	111
Five persons (one parent, four children)	116	123		
Six or more persons (husband, wife, four or more children, oldest 18 and over)		150	153	134

Source: "Estimating Equivalent Incomes," *Monthly Labor Review*, November 1960.

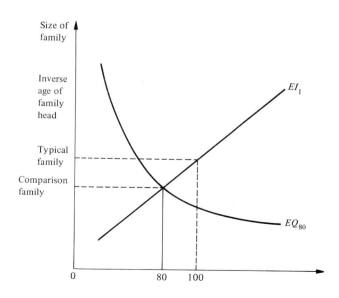

Figure 3.10. Equivalent income.

those on curve EQ_{80}. These variations are designed to retain the same level of equivalent income.

By the way, with this kind of reasoning, the Department of Labor works out budgets for welfare, social security, and similar economic programs. These same kinds of budgets are used to compare Hartford with Scranton or San Francisco as well as San Antonio and Anchorage. With a little thought, it is clear what is meant by a statement that one city has a higher cost of living than another.

All this leads naturally to a basic empirical question: How much do we need to know to establish demand relationships? Paul Samuelson and others developed what is called a "revealed preference model" to try to answer this kind of question. Let us see what revealed preference is all about.

Revealed Preference

Suppose that a consumer market basket at a given point in time was composed of two commodities, tea and eggs. Whatever their tastes, incomes, family sizes, or age composition, as well as the prices of tea and eggs, in consumer situation 1, we find that typical consumer families are buying a certain combination of tea and eggs which we can call "market basket MB_1." Later, another survey reveals that the typical consumer family is buying market basket MB_2. And we are curious. Why did this typical consumer family change from MB_1 to MB_2?

Let us carefully review what we know about consumer behavior. For example, we find that in situation 2, the typical consumer family had a possible choice between MB_1 and MB_2. But they chose MB_2. So not only was there a change from MB_1 to MB_2, but MB_2 was preferred to MB_1. Further research shows that, in fact, in situation 1, MB_2 was not available as a possible choice. So we have a measure of consistency in the consumption behavior of the typical consumer family. The family chose MB_1 when it was the only possible option. When MB_2 became an option, it was selected in preference to MB_1. That must mean something.

Our survey researchers are hard workers and, in the course of their continuing research into consumer behavior, they find another interesting fact. A much later survey turns up situation 3, in which MB_3 is selected. In situation 3, all three market baskets are available as options, but MB_3 is chosen. So now we know that if the options are limited to MB_1, MB_1 is selected. Trivial, perhaps, but important. When the options include MB_1, MB_2, and MB_3, MB_3 is chosen. But here's a question that puzzles us. Is it possible that if only MB_1 and MB_3 were options, MB_3 would be chosen? Fortunately for the course of scientific research, a test market study shows that even in that case MB_3 is chosen.

What we have now is behavior that is not only consistent but also transitive. We can move from one survey of a consumer situation to another survey of a different consumer situation with some assurance that consumers will "always" prefer MB_3 to MB_2, and MB_2 to MB_1, and that this is a rank order of their preferences in "all" cases. They will "never" change that order of preference.

N○D

Inferences from Revealed Preference

In Fig. 3.11, we put together the information that we have collected so far. On the vertical axis is the amount of tea (in pounds) and on the horizontal axis is the amount of eggs (in dozens). MB_1, then, is composed of t_1 pounds of tea and e_1 dozens of eggs. Let us infer from MB_1 the income of consumers in situation 1, as follows: There must be a budget line T_1E_1 which contains MB_1 and indeed other possible market baskets which were spending options at whatever the consumer income level was in situation 1. T_1 is that number of pounds of tea which the typical consumer family would have bought in the unlikely case that they spent all their money on tea. And E_1 is the somewhat more likely number of dozens of eggs that this typical family would have bought if all its money went to proteins. Now for a leap of logic. The slope of the budget line T_1E_1 is the trade-off or price ratio between tea and eggs. This follows from the fact that the consumer family would choose how much to spend on eggs based on the

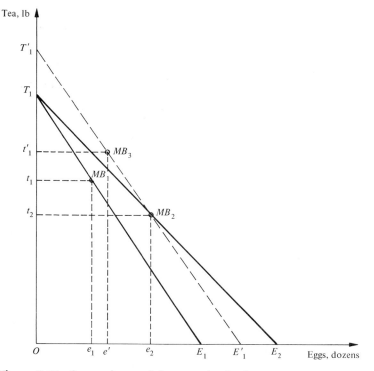

Figure 3.11. Comparisons of three market baskets: MB_1 = situation 1; MB_2 = situation 2; MB_3 = situation 3.

price of eggs per dozen. How much to spend on tea would be based on the tea price. But remember that we don't know these prices. We are inferring them from what we think is typical behavior of typical consumers who are rational and consistent and who behave as if their preferences were transitive.

From these inferences it is not too hard to suppose that MB_2 is also on a budget line. But what kind of budget line? Let us try two possibilities. First, $T_1 E_2$ is drawn on the guess that the price of tea has remained constant between consumer situation 1 and situation 2. But the price of eggs per dozen has gone down. Thus if the typical family so desired, they could buy more dozens of eggs now than before if all their money was spent on eggs. That fits the observations regarding MB_2 which is on the supposed budget line $T_1 E_2$. After all, the difference between MB_2 and MB_1 is that consumers in situation 2 bought more eggs, e_2 greater than e_1, and less tea, t_2 less than t_1. Our guess therefore is that they did this because the price of eggs fell while the price of tea remained unchanged. We already know falling price increases the quantity demanded. And, if the price of tea did not change, nonetheless, the relative price of tea was higher than before; so, with a higher relative price of tea, we would expect less tea to be bought. Our demand logic fits the explanations we have worked out, but we are still only inferring.

Yet we have a clue as to why MB_2 was preferred to MB_1. There were more eggs and lower prices for eggs in MB_2. So, whatever the income level was in situation 1, that same level of money income goes further in situation 2. The same income with a lower price of eggs means a gain in purchasing power.

The second possibility for MB_2 is that it is on budget line $T_1' E_1'$. Such a budget line would have to mean that the family was getting more money since with prices unchanged—the slope of $T_1' E_1'$ is the same as the slope of $T_1 E_1$—more eggs were bought. It is true that less tea was bought. Using that evidence, we have an ambiguous situation. It is not clear that MB_2 is better than MB_1.

Now take the next step. MB_3 by inference is on budget line $T_1' E_1'$. Prices in situation 3 are the same as in situation 1. The logical explanation of the difference between situations 1 and 3 is that the money income of our typical consumer family must have increased. You will notice that, with this higher income, the typical family bought more eggs, e' greater than e_1, and more tea, t' greater than t_1. To put it a little differently, MB_3 is unambiguously larger than MB_1. There are more of both tea and eggs in MB_3 than in MB_1.

Of course, we drew up the budget line $T_1' E_1'$ to include as MB_2 an option at that higher-income level. So now we have an explanation of why MB_3 was preferred to MB_2. MB_3 required no giving up of tea compared with MB_1. More important, while we reached MB_2 from MB_1 by the route of a reduction in the price of eggs, the route from MB_2 to MB_3 involved an increase in money income, whether or not the price of eggs was reduced.

Now a review. Call the triangle $T_1 OE_1$ the whole range of market-basket options out of which MB_1 was chosen. In that triangle, MB_2 and MB_3 just weren't available. By the same token, in triangle $T_1 OE_2$, MB_2 lies farther out, meaning more, while MB_1 lies within triangle $T_1 OE_2$, meaning that a consumer family which chose MB_1 when MB_2 was available wasn't being rational. Why should that family prefer less to more?

Then notice that if triangle T_1OE_2 describes all the possible options in situation 2, MB_3 lies outside the realm of possibility; it is not attainable. To get to MB_3 must have meant an improvement. MB_3 lying farther out on the edge of triangle $T_1'OE_1'$ is better than MB_2 and MB_1.

Let's summarize. Rational and consistent consumers will buy more eggs if prices fall. They will buy less tea if the price of tea rises, actually or relatively. They will buy more of both at unchanged prices if they have more income. So we have by inference a fairly good explanation of what our researchers found.

Price Effects, Income Effects, and Substitution Effects

Earlier we said that it would be interesting to know the price effect of an income change. Since revealed preference has taken us fairly far and has helped us to go from the kind of information we obtain from expenditure surveys to price demand models (at least by inference), why not go the next mile? Every adjustment that a consumer family makes when it shifts from one market basket to another involves either a response to a price change—direct or relative—or a response to an income change. We can separate these responses into three elements:

1. A price effect
2. An income effect
3. A substitution effect

So back we go to tea and eggs. But let us change the order of things a little. Like Fig. 3.11, in Fig. 3.12 we are still dealing with three market baskets, but with a difference. MB_0, which is composed of t_0 of tea and e_0 of eggs was chosen in period O. At a later period, period 1, MB_1 was chosen by our typical consumer family. And in period 2 MB_2 was chosen. So now we are considering a time series of market baskets and the order of these markets is different from that in Fig. 3.11.

As before though there is a budget line in period O. This time around, we become explicit about price so that we designate the period O budget line as Pt_0Pe_0. In the triangle Pt_0OPe_0 are all the available baskets in period O, when the price of eggs was Pe_0 and the price of tea was Pt_0. The consumer family income level in period O is indicated by the height of the budget line. Our revealed preference logic has shown us why MB_0 was a logical choice in the sense that it could easily be shown to be best.

What is more, in period O, one of the choices available to the consumer family was MB_1. Since MB_1 was obviously smaller than MB_0, there was no reason why it should have been chosen. On the other hand, MB_2 was not an available option. To buy it would have required at the very least an increase in income.

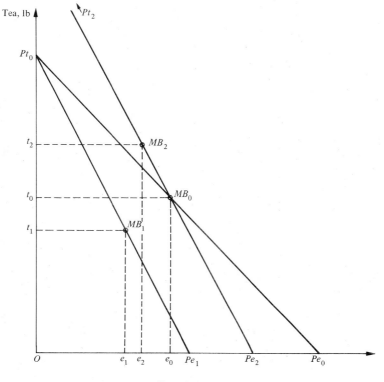

3.12. Price and income effects of an increase in price of eggs.

Situation O
  MB_0 = market basket (t_o, e_o)
  P_o = relative prices of tea and eggs (slope of Pt_oPe_o)

Situation 1 (price of eggs increases)
  MB_1 = market basket (t_1, e_1)
  P_1 = relative prices of tea and eggs (slope of Pt_oPe_1)
Egg-price increase forces a cut in MB.

Situation 2 (income rises to compensate for egg-price increase)
  MB_2 = market basket (t_2, e_2)
  $P_2 = P_1$

	Eggs	Tea
Income effects	(e_1e_2)	(t_1t_2)
Substitution effects	(e_2e_o)	(t_2t_o)

Just as occurred between period 1 and period O, the price of eggs rose from Pe_0 to Pe_1. But the price of tea remained unchanged. As a consequence, the budget line in period 1 became Pt_0Pe_1. So the family faced by a higher egg price cuts egg purchases from the period O level of e_0 to the period 1 level of e_1. Clearly, the decrease in egg consumption (measured by the line segment e_1e_0) is the result of the egg-price change. So we will call it the egg-price effect.

But you will observe that while the price of tea did not change, nonetheless the amount of tea bought also decreased by the line segment t_1t_0. So there was a tea-price effect as well. MB_1 is smaller than MB_0 because of the price effects of an increase in egg prices. The next step is to separate the income and the substitution effects from the price effects. The way we do this is to attempt to restore the consumer family to where it was in period O.

In period 2, the consumer family income is increased by an amount thought to be sufficient to compensate it for the higher price of eggs. That higher income is shown by budget line Pt_2Pe_2 which passes through MB_0. Yet the prices of tea and of eggs are the same in period 2 as in period O. So all that has changed is that the budget line had been shifted farther out, parallel to the budget line Pt_0Pe_0. Of course, budget opportunity triangle Pt_2OPe_2 is not significantly larger than triangle Pt_0OPe_0. But the consumer family can again buy MB_0 if it wants to.

Something interesting has happened. The consumer family, though it has been restored by a compensating increase in income to the possibility of buying MB_0, chooses instead to buy MB_2. Egg consumption, which had been e_1 in period 1, is now e_2. That is a larger egg consumption than in period 1 but not at all as large as in period O.

Let us analyze this development with some care. There was a price effect e_1e_0 and an income effect e_1e_2. The difference must have been the result of an own-price substitution. That difference, e_2e_0, we will call the "own-price substitution effect." What we now know is that this consumer family, as it adjusts to higher incomes, is influenced as well by price changes which change the proportion of eggs in their budget; therefore even if an attempt is made to compensate them for price changes, they do not go back to the same old budget pattern.

The same kind of reasoning helps explain what happened to tea consumption. There was a price effect t_1t_0 and an income effect t_1t_2. But there also was what we can call a "cross-substitution effect" which was the result of the impact of egg-price changes on tea. That cross-substitution effect for tea was t_2t_0. Table 3.19 summarizes this information about tea and eggs.

Table 3.19

Commodity affected	Price effect		Own-price substitution effect	Cross-substitution effect		Income effect
Eggs	e_1e_0	—	e_2e_0		=	e_1e_2
Tea	t_1t_0	+		t_2t_0	=	t_1t_2

In both cases, the income effect was positive. That is, the effect of the income increase was to cause the consumption of both tea and eggs to increase. For tea, the cross-price result (i.e., the result of the effect on tea consumption of an increase in egg prices) was to reduce tea consumption from t_0 to t_1. But the income effect is the sum of the cross-substitution effect and the price effect. By the way, the behavior of tea as a result of egg prices suggests that tea is a substitute for eggs.

It is rare indeed for income effects to be negative for any commodity. However, own-price substitution effects are usually negative. As for cross-substitution effects, all that can be said is that they are added to the price effect to get an income effect if the comparison commodity is a substitute. They are subtracted from the price effect to get an income effect if the comparison commodity is complementary.

Index Numbers

To talk about market baskets and changes in the price of market-basket components from one period of time to another is to talk the language of index numbers. Price index numbers are what economists use to try to determine if consumers are better off or worse as a result of a change in the price of a market basket. Economists also use price indexes to trace the effects of inflation or deflation.

The most common price index number in use is the Laspeyres price index, which is defined as

$$LQ = \frac{\Sigma P_1 Q_0}{\Sigma P_0 Q_0} \times 100$$

where

Σ = sum of
P_0 = the prices in the base (or comparative) period
P_1 = prices in the current period
Q_0 = quantity bought in the base period
$P_1 Q_0$ = base period quantities bought at current prices; it is thus yesterday's market basket priced at today's prices
$P_0 Q_0$ = base period (or yesterday's) quantities bought at the base-period or yesterday's prices; it is thus yesterday's market basket at yesterday's prices

The Laspeyres price index formula is used for the consumer price index (*CPI*) in the United States. As the formula indicates, the *CPI* compares expenditures made in the latest survey period on a fixed market basket with those made on that same market basket in a base period. Dividing the two expenditures gives a decimal value that, when multiplied by 100, yields the index value.

In Fig. 3.13, a change in prices is shown by a change in the slope of the budget lines from Pt_0Pe_0 to Pt_1Pe_1. Following the same shorthand, P_0 is the slope of the budget line Pt_0Pe_0 (and of $P't_0P'e_0$), while P_1 is the slope of budget line Pt_1Pe_1 (and of $P't_1P'e_1$). Our problem is to determine whether MB_0 (yesterday's market basket) at P_1 (today's prices) is better or worse than MB_0 (yesterday's market basket) at P_0 (yesterday's prices). By revealed preference logic, we can demonstrate unambiguously that

$$MB_0 > MB_1 \quad \text{so that} \quad \Sigma P_0 Q_0 > \Sigma P_1 Q_1$$

After all, we know that at P_0 consumers bought $MB_0 (= \Sigma P_0 Q_0)$ and that at P_1 consumers bought a different market basket, $MB_1 (= \Sigma P_1 Q_1)$.

Now since $P_1 > P_0$, if

$$\frac{\Sigma P_1 Q_1}{\Sigma P_0 Q_0} > \frac{\Sigma P_1 Q_0}{\Sigma P_0 Q_0}$$

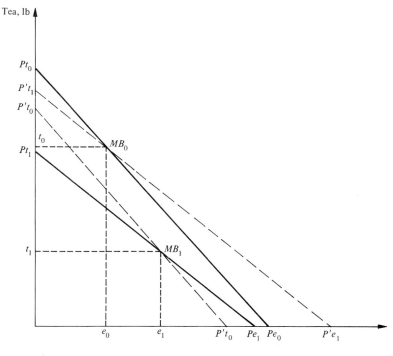

Figure 3.13. Laspeyres price index. Measuring price changes.

Laspeyres price index formula:

$$LI_p = \frac{MB_0 \ (t_o, e_o) \ \text{at} \ P_1 \ (\text{slope of} \ Pt_1Pe_1)}{MB_0 \ (t_o, e_o) \ \text{at} \ P_0 \ (\text{slope of} \ Pt_0Pe_0)} > 1$$

then $LQ_p > 1$, so that

$$\frac{MB_1 \text{ at } P_1 \text{ (slope of } Pt_1Pe_1)}{MB_0 \text{ at } P_0 \text{ (slope of } Pt_0Pe_0)} > \frac{MB_0 \text{ at } P_1}{MB_0 \text{ at } P_0}$$

This formula means that if the ratio of the value of the market baskets at their own prices is less than the ratio of yesterday's market basket at today's prices to yesterday's market basket at yesterday's prices, then the Laspeyres price index will be greater than unity. And the consumers will be worse off in situation 1 than in situation 0.

Index Numbers in Use

The *CPI* is based on the Survey of Consumer Expenditures. From this relatively rich sampling of American consumer spending patterns in a wide variety of places and over almost every possible kind of demographic characteristic, a typical market-basket is constructed. The technique involves, however, not only a sampling of goods and services but also a sampling of retail outlets, a sampling of places, and a sampling of income groups.

The construction of the *CPI* may be illustrated by

$$CPI_{my78} = \frac{\Sigma P_{my78} \%77}{\Sigma P_{77} \%77} \times 100$$

where, for any given commodity such as dress shirts, we multiply the current price, that is, the average of prices found in the sample of retail outlets in May 1978 (designated here as $_{my78}$), times the percentage weight that dress shirts had in the 1970 decade Survey of Consumer Expenditures (designated as %77). Then we divide the results by the dress-shirt price in the survey (designated as P_{77}), itself multiplied by the survey weight for dress shirts (designated as %77). The result of this division is a component of the total *CPI*, called the "price relative," for dress shirts. In a similar manner, the price relatives for each of the component commodities and services in the *CPI* are determined for May 1978.

The index is calculated as a weighted mean or average of price ratio using fixed weights. The formula, which expresses the procedure in symbols, is

$$R_n = \frac{(P_n/P_{n-1}) \, P_{n-1}Q_0}{P_0Q_0} \times 100 = \frac{P_nQ_0}{P_0Q_0}$$

This formula is applicable each time the index is computed. The subscripts n and $n-1$ refer to successive periods (in this case, successive months of the year) for which the index is calculated. The quantities in the market basket, as shown by the use of the zero subscript in Q_0, relate to the same year as that

Table 3.20 Example of calculation of *CPI* elements' index for men's clothing

Commodity	Price relative, May 1978	Base-period price, Jan. 1977	Weighted cost, May 1978
Work trousers	1.032	$10.03	$10.35
Dress trousers	1.016	4.28	4.35
Workshirts	1.13	6.61	7.47
Total		$20.92	$22.17

The index for men's clothing for May 1978 is $22.17/$20.92 = 106.0.

chosen for the base of the index. It is important to note that the quantities in the market basket might have been established in any year (see Table 3.20).

Market Demand

Market demand is a kind of aggregate demand which adds up all the quantities demanded at any price over the range of all consumers (buyers). Typically, either we have a set of demand curves of individuals for a given commodity or a set of demand curves as seen by firms selling the commodity. A market demand curve can either be a summing of all individual demand curves or a summing of all firm demand curves. Some authors prefer to call the latter an industry demand curve.

In either case, the geometry (and algebra) is the same. In Fig. 3.14, we have an individual (or firm) demand curve *dd*. We have also a market (or industry) demand curve *DD*. *DD* is the result of summing all *dd*'s horizontally, that is, over quantities and not over prices. Note that *DD* has a much flatter slope than any given *dd*. What this tells us is that, for any decrease in price, the quantity increase will be much greater along *DD* than along *dd*. Since the summing is over quantities rather than over prices, there is no necessary relationship between the elasticity of the individual or firm demand curve and that of the market (or industry) demand curve. In general, though, the market demand curve will be less elastic than any given individual or firm demand curve. It cannot be more elastic.

Product-as-a-Variable Demand Model

A product-as-a-variable demand model begins with the assumption that the product itself is a variable in addition to prices, tastes, incomes, and other demand elements. Each product is treated as a bundle of attributes. As these attributes change or are changed, changes in the quantity of the product demanded are observed. What consumers want is not a product but a set of attributes. Men don't buy shoes as such. They buy foot comfort and foot protection suited to their foot size, their incomes, the season of the year, their

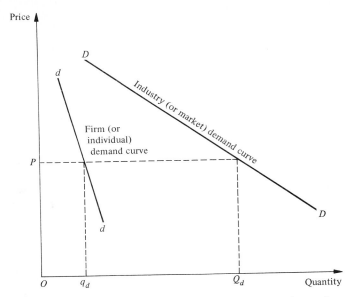

Figure 3.14. Difference between firm and industry demand curves.

color preferences, styles, and tastes. Women don't buy dresses. They buy appearance, attractiveness, personality, and sex appeal. A house is not a house but part of a bundle of housing services including neighbors, schools, trash collection, tax rates, freedom from crime, commuting advantages, prestige, social distance, and other elements of satisfaction. What is more, many goods require inputs from the consumer such as time (including time to enjoy) and effort. In this context, products are bought only as they fit into patterns of satisfaction and convenience. So, along with price, income, and the familiar demand variables come variations in the attributes and even in the nature of the product.

Hans Brems,[10] in analyzing new car registrations for the period 1932–1950, found that the ratio between Ford and Chevrolet was explained not only by the price differential (the ratio between Ford and Chevrolet prices) but also by horsepower which served as an index of attributes of quality. Brems found that

$$v_F/v_C = .782 \, (p_F/p_C)^{-1.79} \, (h_F/h_C)^{1.51}$$

where

v = new car registrations (C = Chevrolet, F = Ford)

p = car prices

h = horsepower

[10]Cf. Hans Brems, *Product Equilibrium and Monopolistic Competition*, Cambridge, Mass., Harvard, 1951. See also P. J. Verdoorn. "Marketing from the Producers' Point of View," *Journal of Marketing*, January 1956, and R. Ferber and D. J. Verdoorn, *Research Methods in Economics and Business*, New York, Macmillan, especially pp. 366 ff.

This function indicates that a 1 percent reduction in Ford prices with Chevrolet prices unchanged was accompanied by a 1.79 percent improvement in Ford's share of the market. A 1 percent increase in Ford's quality, Chevrolet quality unchanged, led to a 1.51 percent increase in Ford's market share.

One possible way of working out a product variation demand model is shown in Fig. 3.15. Suppose that attribute or quality variations are shown by a triangle, a circle, a square, and an X. Each of these is a different form of the product or a different way in which the product may be packaged, financed, or sold. While you might consider just the X's or the squares, look at the kind of pattern that all these attributes together form. There is, first of all, a familiar demand relationship such that higher prices mean less sold regardless of the kind of product variation. In effect, this kind of model combines four different product demand curves and treats them as one because, in fact, there is just one product with different forms.

Chapter Summary

Demand analysis is both theory and practice. In this chapter, we have emphasized the practice of demand analysis. But we have backed up demand analysis with a good dosage of theory since the two really cannot be separated. After all, it is theory that tells us what to look for. From a time-series apple demand model in Durham through orange demand in Grand Rapids to a

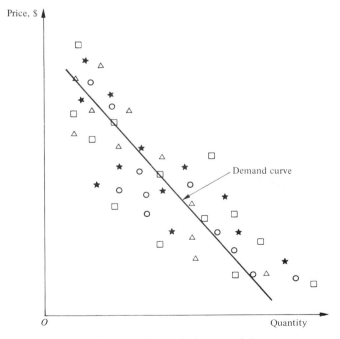

Figure 3.15. Product quality variations model.

three-person-family housing demand model and on to a world food demand model to say nothing of equivalent incomes and the *CPI*, in all of this we were on the trail of what managerial economists actually do. But we tried to reach an operational view of demand analysis without getting too deeply into mathematics and statistics. The resort to revealed preference about halfway through the chapter was made necessary by the kinds of questions that are bound to arise from any use of income demand models. One of the questions surely is what we were trying to hide. Since the answer is nothing, revealed preference does the job of tying together two compatible approaches to demand analysis.

Having seen what demand analysis is when it is being practiced, it is perhaps only natural that we should inquire about some of the problems and techniques involved in finding the kinds of models with which we worked in this chapter. Problems and techniques in model building are the thrust of Chap. 4.

Selected Readings

Hicks, J. R.: *A Revision of Demand Theory*, New York, Oxford University Press, 1959.

Hirschleifer, J.: *Price Theory and Applications*, Englewood Cliffs, N.J., Prentice-Hall, 1976.

Houthakker, H., and L. Taylor: *Consumer Demand in the United States, 1920–1970*, Cambridge, Mass., Harvard, 1966.

Norris, Ruby: *The Theory of Consumers' Demand*, New Haven, Conn., Yale, 1952.

Schultz, Henry: *Theory and Measurement of Demand*, University of Chicago Press, 1964.

Wold, Herman, and L. Jureen: *Demand Analysis: A Study in Econometrics*, New York, Wiley, 1953.

Questions, Problems, and Projects

1. Amtrak measures its ridership by revenue passenger miles (*RPM*). In a review of its operations in 1976, Amtrak tried to determine how to increase *RPM* by adjusting the fare structure. For example, 6.57 billion *RPM* were recorded in 1976 at 6.8 cents per revenue mile. The following are revenue forecasts, *RPM* forecasts, and accompanying adjusted average fares:

National rail passenger corporation (Amtrak)

RPM, billions	Average fare per mile, $	Projected passenger revenues, millions of $
4.61	.085	392
5.61	.073	410
6.57	.068	447
7.53	.060	452
8.63	.056	483

Is the *RPM* demand facing Amtrak elastic or inelastic? Depending on your answer, what kind of price policy would you recommend for Amtrak?

2. MARTA (Metropolitan Atlanta Rapid Transit Authority) decided to test a low-fare policy on bus lines serving the central business district (*CBD*). Whereas the average fare had been 35 cents, it was lowered during the test period to 15 cents. Proponents admitted that MARTA revenues would be decreased but they argued that increased movement into the *CBD*, increased retail sales, increased accessibility for low-income families and individuals, and other indicators of consumer benefit would more than offset any such losses. Moreover, through increased tax revenue on sales and property values, the entire loss might be recovered with a net gain to Atlanta. How would you evaluate this argument? What are some of the economic tools you would have to use to assess the effect of this *CBD* low-fare policy?

3. The corn–hog price cycle is often commented on in agricultural circles. The corn–hog price ratio moves inversely to the change in sows farrowing, so that the higher the corn–hog price ratio, the lower the change in pork supplied. What economic tools can be used to explain why the ratio between corn and hog prices affects the pig crop?

4. The Dow Jones stock price index, as you know, is published daily (and even more often during the business day). What kind of price index is it? What does it try to show? How, in such an index, would you account for stock splits and other changes in stock form? What does any given unit change in the Dow Jones index mean? How would you improve the Dow Jones index?

5. Some of the critics of the Consumer Price Index (*CPI*) say that it ought not be used as a cost-of-living index. They point out that it may not measure product-quality changes adequately, that it might overstate the degree of inflation, and that small changes are probably not statistically reliable. What methodological defense could you give for the *CPI* in its present form?

6. In what sense is a demand function a forecast? What are the data requirements for a good demand forecast, say, for soybeans? Or for automobiles? Or for houses in Maricopa County, Arizona? What do people do with demand forecasts?

7. Contrast and compare (*a*) income and price as demand indicators, (*b*) income effect and price effect in demand analysis, (*c*) measurement of consumer surplus and index numbers.

Case 3.1 Boston & Maine Railroad[1]

The Mass Transportation Commission of Massachusetts contracted with the Boston & Maine Railroad in 1963 to set up a demonstration project to determine the effect of lowering fares and increasing both peak and off-peak service upon commuter revenue and costs. The Boston & Maine Railroad was asked to defer filing petitions for the total discontinuance of railroad commuter passenger service into Boston until after the experiment. The railroad then participated in the experiment, which covered three phases: the first phase lasted for seven months (January to July 1963); the second for five months (August to December 1963); and the third for three months (January to March 1964).

In 1962, the B&M carried some 5.3 million passengers annually into and from the city of Boston on a route structure that fans out from the city's North Station in a northerly and westerly direction. To the northeast, the B&M Eastern Route serves Lynn, Salem, and Beverly (18 miles). The route then splits, with a line to Rockport (35 miles from North Station) and a line to Newburyport (37 miles) that extends to Portsmouth, New Hampshire.

To the north, the B&M Reading Line (12 miles) serves six suburban stations in three towns. Also to the north, the Western Route, which diverges from the New Hampshire Route at Wilmington (15 miles), serves Lawrence (25 miles) and Haverhill (33 miles) and extends to New Hampshire and Maine. The New Hampshire (Lowell) Route serves Lowell (25 miles) and also extends to points in New Hampshire. The Woburn Line diverges from the New Hampshire Route at Winchester (8 miles), continuing to Woburn (10 miles).

The Fitchburg Division serves the western segment of the B&M route structure. Passenger service operates on the Fitchburg line to the industrial center of Fitchburg (50 miles), and the line extends for freight service only to the Connecticut River Line and to points in New York State. Passenger service is also provided on two branches of the Fitchburg Division to Bedford and Hudson.

During the first phase, overall service on the B&M (weekdays and weekends) was increased by 77 percent. Weekday service was expanded by 92 percent, with peak-hour service increasing by 82 percent and off-peak service by 96 percent (see Table 1). This expansion required 386 trains per day, an increase of 182 per day over the 1962 level of service.

Four lines—Eastern, Reading, Lowell, and Fitchburg—had at least a 90 percent increase in total service. Service on two lines—Bedford and Hudson—remained unchanged, so that the effect of the commuter-fare reduction could be more accurately measured.

The fare changes were equally dramatic. Both one-way and twenty-ride commutation tickets were reduced by varying amounts, from as little as 12

[1]Adapted from Mass Transportation in Massachusetts, Transportation Commission, Boston, Mass., 1964, pp. 27–35.

Table 1   Service increases (percentages)

Line	Total service	Weekday service		
		Total	Peak	Off-peak
Eastern	96	120	81	143
Reading	92	111	117	109
Western	35	46	58	44
Lowell	107	118	113	119
Woburn	53	63	86	58
Fitchburg	90	95	68	112
Bedford*				
Hudson*				
Suburban total	77	92	82	96

*No change in schedule.

Table 2   Fare reductions (percentages)

Line	Ticket type	
	20-ride*	One-way†
Eastern	29	36
Reading	22	27
Western	32	37
Lowell	31	30
Woburn	21	30
Fitchburg	30	39
Bedford	24	42
Hudson	30	24

*30-day limit on 20-ride ticket book.
†One-year limit on one-way ticket.

percent for a one-way ticket between Melrose Highlands and Boston to as much as 72 percent for the same kind of ticket between Boston and Fitchburg. The fare reductions, which averaged 28 percent overall (as shown in Table 2), are the average reductions at the major stations on each line, weighted by the number of passengers using each of these stations.

Weekday revenue increased during the first phase on the Eastern Line (by 6.1 percent), the Lowell Line (by 10.4 percent), the Woburn Line (by 2.4 percent), and the Fitchburg Line (by 10.6 percent). There was a decrease in revenue on the Reading and Western lines and on the Bedford and Hudson branches. Weekend revenue increased on all lines except the Western. There

Table 3 Revenue earned

Line	Thousands of dollars		
	1963	1962	% change
Weekdays			
Eastern	522.4	492.3	+ 6.1
Reading	401.8	403.0	− .3
Western	234.4	285.5	−17.9
Lowell	205.7	186.4	+10.4
Woburn	161.1	157.3	+ 2.4
Fitchburg	212.2	191.8	+10.6
Subtotal	1737.6	1716.3	+ 1.2
Bedford and Hudson	39.3	49.3	−20.3
Total*	1776.9	1765.6	+ 0.6
Weekends			
Eastern	68.8	60.8	+13.2
Reading	26.1	24.9	+ 4.8
Western	44.5	54.3	−18.0
Lowell	32.2	29.6	+ 8.8
Woburn	15.0	14.3	+ 4.9
Fitchburg	31.1	23.9	+30.1
Subtotal	217.7	207.8	+ 4.8
Bedford and Hudson†			
Total‡	217.7	207.8	+ 4.8
Grand total	1994.6	1973.4	+ 1.1

*Based on 148 days in 1963 and 147 days in 1962.
†No scheduled service.
‡Based on 59 days in 1963 and 60 days in 1962.

was no weekend service on the Bedford and Hudson branches. Overall, revenue increased slightly during weekdays and by more than 1 percent on weekends (see Table 3).

DISCUSSION QUESTIONS 3.1

1. Do you have enough information to determine whether the demand for commuter rail service in the B&M service area was elastic?
2. How do you account for the differences in elasticity among the various lines? What reason do you assign for the results on the Bedford and Hudson branches?
3. Present detailed calculations for each line and branch.
4. The B&M decided to continue with its petition to end commuter service after these experiments were finished. Why do you think the railroad management made this decision?

Case 3.2 Harris Pine Mills Company[1]

Harris Pine Mills Company is the nation's largest manufacturer of softwood furniture. National distribution is achieved through a network of fifteen branch assembly plants scattered throughout the United States. Approximately 80 percent of the company's sales go to five customers: Montgomery Ward, Gambles, J. C. Penney, Macy's, and Gimbels.

Although the company has some competition, management feels it has had no effect upon sales or pricing decisions. The company's management also feels it can continue to dominate the softwood market so long as it keeps its prices at a minimum.

Because of the relatively small size of the company, management has never invested in formal demand analysis. It has relied upon simple extrapolation to estimate demand.

In 1966, management felt it necessary to work out a new price policy for drawer chests. Though Harris Pine Mills made twenty-six different models of drawer chests, one model, a five-drawer chest, can be considered as typical of the line. This model came in two styles, knotty pine and clear, identified by the numbers 305 and 8205, respectively.

Table 1 contains unit sales and price information for the No. 305 chest by quarters from 1962 to 1966.

[1]Adapted from R. Charles Nagele, *Demand and Sales Forecasting: Five-Drawer Chests,* unpublished study, Berrien Springs, Mich., Andrews University, 1967.

Table 1   Historical sales data: Five-drawer chest unit sales and prices*
1962 to 1966, by quarter

	Unit quarterly sales	Price, $		Unit quarterly sales	Price, $		Unit quarterly sales	Price, $
	1962			1963			1964	
I	9,802	11.95	I	22,605	11.95	I	30,678	12.45
II	12,812	11.95	II	18,195	11.95	II	16,268	12.45
III	22,057	11.95	III	26,986	11.95	III	22,933	12.45
IV	19,744	11.95	IV	21,093	11.95	IV	20,396	12.45
	1965			1966				
I	22,948	12.95	I	23,943	12.95			
II	14,442	12.95	II	19,066	12.95			
III	20,842	12.95	III	20,845	12.95			
IV	23,502	12.95	IV	22,027	12.95			

*Manufacturer's list price, taken as an average of the FOB branch plant prices.

The No. 305 chest has been manufactured for the past thirty years. It has five identical drawers stacked to a height of 44 inches and is typical of the lower end of the company's price and quality range.

The company economist worked out a demand curve for the 305 chest for a five-year period from 1962 to 1966. He adjusted the data to remove changing conditions. The three influences taken into account were price changes, population changes, and seasonal fluctuations. The latter was removed by a moving average centered upon each quarter (see Table 2). Population changes over the five-year period were removed by the use of per capita figures. Sales figures were adjusted for both price and population changes by expressing price as a fraction of per capita disposable personal income.

The company economist found that there were actually two separate patterns of price-quantity relationships: one for the period extending from the

Table 2   No. 305 chest seasonal adjustments
1962 to 1966, by quarter

	Centered quarterly moving average
	1962
III	17,705
IV	19,978
	1963
I	21,267
II	22,051
III	23,229
IV	23,997
	1964
I	23,250
II	22,656
III	21,603
IV	20,408
	1965
I	19,918
II	20,045
III	20,558
IV	21,260
	1966
I	21,839
II	21,655

Table 3 **No. 305 chest population and price adjustment**
1962 to 1966, by quarter

	U.S. civilian population millions*	Disposable personal income, billions of $†	Disposable income per capita, $‡	Sales per capita in units ($\times 10^{-3}$)	Price of chest/disposable personal income per capita ($\times 10^{-2}$), $
			1962		
III	184.097	386.5	2099	96	569
IV	184.954	391.4	2116	108	565
			1963		
I	185.623	395.1	2129	115	561
II	186.222	399.1	2143	118	558
III	186.926	404.4	2163	124	552
IV	187.701	411.2	2191	128	545
			1964		
I	188.328	412.4	2190	123	568
II	188.925	423.3	2241	120	556
III	189.615	429.6	2265	114	550
IV	190.350	435.4	2287	107	544
			1965		
I	190.941	453.2	2374	104	545
II	191.485	461.0	2407	105	538
III	192.075	476.2	2479	107	522
IV	192.635	486.1	2524	110	513
			1966		
I	193.068	495.1	2564	113	505
II	193.451	499.9	2584	112	501

*U.S. Bureau of the Census, *Current Population Reports*, January 1, 1950 to February 1, 1967, Washington, D.C., 1967.

†Council of Economic Advisers, *Economic Indicators, 1962–1967*, Washington, D.C., 1967, p. 1.

‡Expressed in annual rates.

fourth quarter of 1962 to the third quarter of 1964, and another extending from the fourth quarter of 1964 to the second quarter of 1966 (see Table 3). He was puzzled by the downward shift in demand and a drastic change in price elasticity.

DISCUSSION QUESTIONS 3.2

1. Assuming that the company economist was correct, what does the existence of two separate patterns of price-quantity relationships imply about the demand for No. 305 drawer chests?
2. How do you account for the change in price elasticity?
3. Comment upon the method used to obtain the demand curve (*a*) in terms of technique and (*b*) in terms of the measuring and the results.
4. What purpose would the demand curve for No. 305 chests have in developing a sales forecast?

4

STATISTICAL AND ECONOMETRIC ANALYSIS OF DEMAND

Key Concepts

bias
coefficient of determination
dynamic model
econometrics
endogenous
error term
estimation
exogenous
heteroscedasticity
homoscedasticity
hypothesis
identification

least squares
level of significance
linear regression
model testing
multicollinearity
multiple regression
parameters
standard error
statistics
stochastic
variance

What Is Ahead in This Chapter

For economics to be useful and applicable, economists have to develop models of human behavior. This much we have learned so far and we have seen what kinds of models can be developed as well as how they can be used. But in this chapter we are going to spend some time looking at three of the basic ingredients of economic models. These three ingredients are (1) a hypothesis, a combination of insight, logic, guesses, perception, imagination, and intuition; (2) statistical facts as well as statistical methods for analyzing those facts; and (3) econometrics, a special brand of mathematics and statistics developed to help economists test and verify hypotheses. All of this will be focused on demand analysis.

The purpose of empirical economic research on demand and thus of econometrics is to explain as fully as possible how the quantity demanded behaves as one or more variables change in any moment of time, over time, or over a cross section of observations. But there must be a research strategy in such analyses. That research strategy is determined by practical considerations. These involve, for example, the kind and quality of data available, the selection of estimation techniques, and the probable mathematical form of the demand model.

This chapter will not attempt to say all that can be said. There isn't enough room for that. The focus is upon what managerial economists can use and, perhaps just as important, upon the state of the art in demand analysis.

What Is a Hypothesis?

An economic hypothesis is a statement about a relationship between certain economic variables. It is a proposition designed to draw out the logical and empirical consequences of this relationship. It is presented in a form in which the relationship can be tested to see how it works with known relationships and facts or whether it fits and explains facts and relationships that can be determined. There are three kinds of questions to be asked about any economic hypothesis. First, is it in testable form? Second, is it valid? Third, is it accurate? These are tough questions, perhaps too tough to answer in all cases. Indeed, there will be some hypotheses that will go on being used and assumed to be true even if, in fact, they cannot be tested, cannot be proved valid, or cannot be proved accurate. But they are useful, widely accepted, and supported.

A hypothesis is a vital ingredient of any economic model. It is the problem around which the model is developed. Of course, some models may have not one but several hypotheses, several problems to work with. If a model is composed of at least one hypothesis, then what is theory? Well, an economic theory is a working hypothesis or set of hypotheses which have been supported by experimental evidence or by factual or inductive analysis. However, an economic theory becomes an economic law only when it is conclusively proved and accepted. Since conclusive proof in a social science is a rare commodity, we often have to work with hypotheses and theories. The question is, How do we work with hypotheses?

What Is a Statistical Anlysis?

Boot and Cox define statistics as the "body of theory and methodology employed in analyzing and using numerical evidence to choose one among several alternative decisions or actions when not all relevant facts are known."[1] In demand analysis, we seldom know enough about the demand function to be able to state with absolute certainty that it will behave in all places, under all conditions, and at all times in a specified manner. Our data and the state of the statistical art provide us with more modest results. Yet, you should notice three things about statistical methods. First, they use numerical, that is, measurable evidence. Anything that can be quantified, even if only indirectly as with light or human intelligence or simply by assigning a rank order, is usable for statistical purposes. Such evidence can also include opinions, attitudes, fears, hopes, and so-called irrational behavior. All that we require is that it is possible to convert these elements into numbers.

Second, statistics is a way of guiding decision makers through uncertainty. It is a science designed to work when there are major gaps in our knowledge. When the statistician's job is done well, all the available evidence will have been presented in a decision-shaping form. But the statistician doesn't make the decision.

Third, while it is possible to use the word "statistics" as if it meant complete, presumably past knowledge about a city or baseball team or an ant's behavior, that's not quite what is meant by a statistical analysis of demand. In this context, statistics is technique, not knowledge.

A statistical analysis of a demand function, then, is an attempt, using all applicable statistical techniques, to derive from available incomplete and possibly biased observations a relatively simple statement or equation of demand behavior.

What Is Econometric Analysis?

Three of the best-known economists and econometricians have defined econometrics as "the quantitative analysis of economic phenomena based on the concurrent development of theory and observation, related by appropriate methods of inference. . . . Econometrics is a branch of economics."[2] Econometrics uses statistical techniques in the context of economic theory. The purpose of theory is to define both the problem and the nature of the demand

---

[1] J. C. G. Boot and E. B. Cox, *Statistics for Managerial Decisions*, 2d ed., New York, McGraw-Hill, 1974, p. 3.

[2] P. Samuelson, T. C. Koopmans, and J. R. N. Stone, "Report of the Evaluative Committee for *Econometrica*," *Econometrica*, *22*(2):141–146, April 1954.

function that is most likely to be useful. Econometrics can either explain the behavior of demand based on evidence that we have already seen or forecast behavior that we have not seen.[3]

Econometric demand models should be relevant to a significant or interesting problem. They should be simple enough for their meaning to be understood and for them to be used with some degree of facility. They should be plausible and consistent with established theory. They should use available data effectively and have relatively high explanatory value. The coefficients of the models should be as accurate as possible and, in general, the models should be capable of forecasting the future.

Regression Model of Demand

In developing the Grand Rapids orange demand model in Chap. 3 we used linear regression. Here are the basic concepts underlying a linear regression model.

1. There is a dependent variable, in this case, the quantity demanded of size 200 Florida interior oranges in Grand Rapids in 1965 in certain supermarkets. This dependent variable is analyzed to determine its response to one or more other variables.
2. The independent variables such as price of size 200 oranges as well as prices of Florida Indian River and California oranges are used to determine the relationship. It is their behavior which explains the behavior of the dependent variable.
3. The "explanation" which an independent variable provides of the behavior of a dependent variable is obtained by examining the tendency of the dependent variable to respond to the movements of the independent variable(s). For a regression model to have meaning, this tendency to vary must be consistent and systematic. However, the exact and precise form of the tendency is what has to be determined by analysis.
4. A regression model does not need to have a perfect statistical relationship. Some variations between the observed (or sample) data and the derived statistical model are normal. A key question, of course, is, How much variation? Also, what are the reasons for the variations?

Using these basic concepts or characteristics of linear regression modeling, the Florida interior size 200 orange demand model was developed on the following assumptions:

1. Each pair of price–quantity-demanded observations was a sample from a presumably much larger array of possible price-quantity pairs.
2. The linear regression model will apply not only to the sample pairs but to the

[3]C. F. Christ, *Econometric Models and Methods*, New York, Wiley, 1966, pp. 4, 5.

entire population of possible pairs in Grand Rapids at the time the survey was undertaken. The model may also apply to orange demand generally.

3. For each sampled price, there are several possible quantities demanded. By the same token, for each price or independent variable, there is a probability distribution covering the relative likelihood that each price, different values of quantities demanded, or different ranges of quantities demanded might occur.

4. The average or mean of each such probability distribution of quantities demanded or dependent variables fluctuates in a determinable and systematic way as price varies.

What these words mean is illustrated by the linear regression model in Fig. 4.1. The humplike normal curves for each price express the probability distribution of the variation of quantity demanded at that price. At the highest point on the hump of that normal-distribution curve, the average or mean of the distribution of quantities demanded is found. The regression line, as you will observe, is drawn over the range of these means.

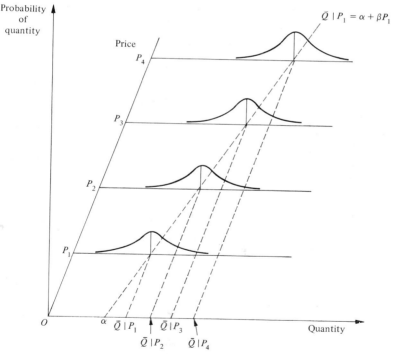

Figure 4.1. Linear regression model.

where
$\bar{Q}$ = mean or average Q
$\bar{Q} \mid P_1$ = probable mean of Q given P_1
α = intercept
β = slope

Statement of the Linear Regression Model

The simplest way to state a linear regression model is by means of an identity such as

$$Q_i = a + bP_i + e$$

where

Q_i = ith observation of the quantity of apples demanded
P_i = corresponding observation of the price of apples
a, b = parameters or constants (one of which, a, is the intercept, while b is the slope of the function)
e = random error term

It is the presence of the random error term which makes this statement of the model different from the linear demand model which we derived,

$$Q = 476.05 - 4.84P$$

The linear demand model was derived by least squares, a technique which uses the concept of deviation. Deviation is the distance of any observation pair or observation point from the regression line obtained. The purpose of the least-squares technique is to find that line or regression relationship which analytically minimizes the sum of the squared deviations of the actual or observed pairs or points from the "best-fit" line or curve. The least-squares technique minimizes

$$\sum_{i}^{n}(Q_i - Q)^2$$

where

Q_i = any observed value of quantity demanded
Q = value of Q on the regression line

and where $Q = a + bP$ is the best-fit demand equation. That least-squares technique permitted us to derive a linear estimate of the demand model. And, by that technique, we also derived parameters such as the slope and the intercept.

An error term may reflect the fact that the demand model is a simplification of reality or that there are difficulties associated with collection and measurement of data. Adding the error term makes the model stochastic, which means that for every value of Q, there is a probability distribution of e as well as a probability distribution of P.

Now we can state the specifications of a variable linear regression model. They consist of the following:

1. The relationship between Q and P is linear.
2. The P_i's are nonstochastic variables with fixed values.
3. The error term has a zero expected value and a constant variance for all observations.
4. To the extent that there is more than one random error, these random errors are uncorrelated, that is, errors corresponding to different observations have a zero correlation.
5. The error term is normally distributed.

What Is a Variance?

Variance is a measure of the dispersion of the estimates of a variable. For example, a normal curve is a distribution or dispersion of estimates of a variable under the assumption that a large number of observations have been taken of a variable in a random fashion that avoids favoring, or biasing, the results toward a certain value. The symbol σ is used to indicate the dispersion or distribution. For a normal curve the mean (or the average) of the distribution plus or minus ($\pm\sigma$) equals about two-thirds of the area under the curve. The area under the normal curve between $+\sigma$ and $-\sigma$ is a measure which indicates that chances are better than two out of every three that an accurate estimate of P will lie within that "distance" or in that area. So σ is a "distance" which is an estimate of the difference between the observed (or sample) value of the variable P and the expected (or true) value of P. Variance is defined as

$$\text{Var}(P) = \sigma P^2$$

So by squaring the "distance" σ, we have variance σ^2 as a number which will always be positive.

Model Estimation

Getting from a statement of a linear regression model to the point where we can assign values to the parameters or constants requires some careful strategic moves. As it stands in its simplest form, a linear regression model is an identity, a tautology. And a tautology is true because you took great care to define it as true. Important as the ability to state a truth is, in the form of an identity it is a hypothesis. What we want to know are the values of the parameters so that we can test the model. Note, too, that as an identity the model is valid in the most vapid meaning of that term. What we want is not validity in any logical sense but accuracy, which means that we have tested and found the model to be "meaningful."

The assumption that error term e has a zero expected value, that is, that we are not making an estimate of its likelihood, is a matter of computational convenience. The assumption of a constant variance means that the error term is "homoscedastic," or that the variance of the error term is the same regardless of the size of the sampling population. Contrast homoscedasticity with heteroscedasticity which might arise in the case where the variance of the error term grew larger as we moved from small markets to larger. To put it another way, whatever the error term was for the Grand Rapids estimate of the orange demand function, the model would be heteroscedastic if choosing Chicago made the variance of the error term larger and choosing Benton Harbor made it smaller.

The assumption that error term e is normally distributed means we can also assume that the dependent variable is normally distributed. From this point, let us go on to the problem of selecting estimated parameters for the stochastic linear regression model.

Selecting Parameters

In the linear regression model for orange demand, least squares minimized the sum of the squares of the deviations from the regression line. This manipulation was supposed to give us a good estimate of the true relationship between the observed points. Yet, how do we know that this regression line is, in fact, a good estimate? Well, for one thing, we can analyze the various possible estimates of one parameter, for example, slope b. The sample we used to give us a set of Q values based on P observations can be repeated again and again with the same P's. We would obtain new and possibly different observations of Q each time we repeated the sampling procedure. We might also obtain a different value for slope b each time. In due time, we would have a distribution of the estimates of the value of b. In the same way, more or less, a distribution of the values of the estimates of a, the intercept, can be derived. Theoretically, something like this procedure could be used to obtain estimates of e, but don't be bullish on the prospects.

Absence of Bias

We can say that any value of b that we obtain is an unbiased estimate of the expected (or true) value of b if the mean of the estimated b's is equal to the expected or true value of the slope. That is equivalent to saying that the distribution of the estimated b's will take the shape of a normal curve. While absence of bias is a desirable property of a good estimate of a parameter, it is hardly enough.

Efficiency

An estimated parameter is said to be an unbiased and efficient estimator if the variance (σ^2) of the parameter is smaller than the variance of any other unbiased estimate of the same parameter. The greater the degree of efficiency of an estimation process, the stronger the statistical statement that can be made about the estimate. That statement would be tantamount to an assertion about accuracy.

Consistency

In general terms, an estimation procedure may be said to be consistent if, as the sample size grows larger and larger, the probability distribution of the estimated variable, in this case, the slope b, grows narrower, until at the limit, it collapses to a single point. In more analytical terms, any procedure for estimating slope b is consistent if the probability limit of the estimated value of slope b is b itself.

What Is Accuracy?

Before we go on, we ought to answer a question which we have been begging all along: What is accuracy? First, accuracy means that the estimated parameter and the results obtained from the use of the regression model fit the observations very well. The closer the fit, the more accurate the model. In other words, the model is accurate if it explains the observations. That is a first step in defining accuracy. Second, it may be more important to know whether the model is an accurate predictor of other future or as yet unobserved values or behavior. It is quite possible for a model to be accurate in the first sense and useless in the second sense. But more of this later.[4]

Confidence Intervals

Given knowledge of estimated distributions of slope and intercept, it is possible to construct confidence intervals and to test hypotheses about estimated parameters. Confidence intervals provide a range of values within which one is likely to find the *true* regression parameters. To each confidence interval is assigned a level of statistical significance. Given any desired level of statistical significance, a confidence interval can be stated so that the probability that the interval contains the *true* parameter is 1 minus the level of significance.

[4]See Chap. 10, especially the discussion of Accuracy of Forecasts.

Testing a Hypothesis

Next, let us see how we test a hypothesis. First, we state rules for accepting or rejecting a hypothesis. To begin with, suppose we say that we want to test our orange demand model at the 10 percent level of significance, which means that we want to examine the 90 percent confidence interval. What we are testing is whether quantity demanded and price are negatively correlated, that is, quantity demanded increases as price decreases. Testing whether slope b is negative will suffice to answer the question. We set up the null hypothesis[5] that the slope is not negative but 0 at the 10 percent level of significance.

To reject the null hypothesis would require that we obtain a value for b sufficiently greater than 0 to permit us to cast doubt on the hypothesis that $b = 0$. It turns out that in our research we get a value of $b = 0.8$. At the 10 percent level of significance, the 90 percent confidence interval for b is

$$-0.6 \leqq b \leqq -1.2$$

This says that the probability that b lies within the range from $-.6$ to -1.2 is .90. In fact, $b = .8$. Thus, we may reject the null hypothesis that $b = 0$ with at least 90 percent confidence.

t Distribution

The statistical test for rejecting the null hypothesis in linear regression analysis often involves the use of the t distribution. The t statistic shows the significance of each explanatory variable in predicting the dependent variable.[6] Generally, any t statistic greater than $+2.0$ or less than -2.0 is acceptable. Basically, the t statistic is a measure of how unlikely it is that there is no relationship between the dependent variable and an independent variable. Thus, the higher the absolute value of the t statistic, the more likely it is that the null hypothesis would be rejected.

---

[5]Testing the null hypothesis is admittedly an easy way out. To demonstrate that a hypothesis is false, you need only one case, but to prove that a hypothesis is true, you have to test *all* the cases. In effect, what the null hypothesis does is to state the hypothesis in the "beyond all *reasonable* doubt" form.

[6]In general, t can be derived as

$$t = \frac{\text{sample statistic} - \text{parameter of sampled universe}}{\text{standard deviation of sampling distribution}}$$

Typically, if we know or suppose that the distribution of a variable such as price is normal but the variance of price is not known, then the use of t is appropriate. In most cases, however, since the value of t is readily obtainable, it is used as additional evidence in testing a hypothesis.

Variance and Correlation

It is generally true that a good regression equation is one which helps to explain or account for a large proportion of the variance of the dependent variable. The variance σ^2 is a measure of the spread or dispersion of any (random) variable around its mean. The positive square root of the variance $\sqrt{\sigma^2}$ is called the "standard deviation." To explain variance,[7] we may break it into two distinct parts. Thus, the variance of

$$Q = \Sigma(Q_i - \hat{Q})^2$$

may be broken into

$$\Sigma(Q_i - \hat{Q})^2 = \Sigma(Q - Q_i)^2 + \Sigma(Q_i - Q)^2$$

Total variance equals variance of error term (unexplained variance) plus explained variance. Dividing the explained variance by the total variance, we get the coefficient of determination,

$$R^2 \leq \frac{\Sigma(Q - \hat{Q})^2}{\sigma^2}$$

R^2 is the proportion of total variance in Q explained by the regression of Q on P. R^2 describes a good fit of regression function to data. Since a regression model is, to some extent, a statement of causality, a high R^2 is also another test of validity of the model. The fact that a model is valid in this instance means that it is a good and logical statement of a relationship, not that it is an accurate statement. "Good and logical" mean that the model deals with the available information effectively and "explains" what is observed.

United States Auto Sales: An Income Demand Model

Pindyck and Rubinfeld[8] examined the relationship between auto sales in the United States (as a dependent variable) and total private wage payments (as an independent variable). The demand model they developed is an income demand function. The identity form of their model is

$$RAS = a + bW + e$$

---

[7]In more precise terms, this is not an analysis of variance but of variation. It would become an analysis of variance by dividing the variations by the appropriate degrees of freedom.

[8]R. S. Pindyck and D. L. Rubinfeld, *Econometric Models and Econometric Forecasting*, New York, McGraw-Hill, 1976, p. 39.

where

RAS = monthly retail auto sales in the United States from January 1963 to April 1970 (in billions of dollars)

W = total monthly wages paid by United States private employers from January 1963 to April 1970 (in billions of dollars)

a, b, e = parameters to be estimated

The regression function was derived by Pindyck and Rubinfeld as:

$$\widehat{RAS} = 1767.1 + 7.48\,W$$
$$(7.4) \qquad (18.5) \quad R^2 = .80$$

In parentheses below the estimated coefficients are the relevant t statistics. Each is greater than $+2$. The hat over RAS tells us that the equation is being used to estimate values of the dependent variable. The R^2 value of .8 shows that the equation is a reasonably good fit to the data available and that its explanatory power is probably adequate. Using the t statistics, we reject the null hypothesis that the true values of intercept and slope are zero (at the 5 percent level of significance and even at the 1 percent level of significance). The auto sales model is a valid analysis and is accurate within defined limits.

Linear Multiple Regression Models

We can extend the two-variable model by making the dependent variable a linear function of a series of independent variables plus an error term. The assumptions of a multiple regression model are practically the same as those for a two-variable model, except that we should add to the five specifications listed earlier:

6. No exact linear relationship exists among two or more of the independent variables.

If such a relationship does exist, we say that the independent variables are collinear. Collinearity presents no problem if the extent of the relationship is known from research. All one does is remove one of the collinear variables without loss of explanatory power. Multicollinearity is a bit more complex. It arises when two or more variables (or combinations of variables) are highly, though not perfectly, correlated with each other. Since, in effect, multicollinearity concerns the efficiency of individual coefficients rather than whether they are biased, an equation may be marred by multicollinearity and still give an unbiased prediction. There is no conclusive technique for dealing with multicollinearity. It is a fact of statistical life, much as a rainy day on a vacation.

In a multiple regression model, there are as many slope coefficients as there are independent variables. R^2 measures the extent to which the multiple regression equation explains the variations in the dependent variable. But a modified measure $\overline{R}^2$ (R-bar squared), or corrected R^2, which takes into account variance in the error term, is much more frequently used.

Naugatuck Candy Company: Solving a Multiple Regression Problem

Even the simplest multiple regression computation involves a "multitude of simple algebraic manipulations." And that phrase usually means that you ought to start looking for a computer multiple regression routine somewhere. In most schools, at least on shared-terminal access computers, you will readily find such programs. What is complicated about multiple regression is not theory but actual paper-and-pencil work. Today, most of that can be avoided. There are even programmable scientific hand calculators with multiple regression routines. Yet, you ought to go through at least one such calculation to see what it is all about. And that is where the Naugatuck Candy Company comes in.

You will recall that, when we left the Naugatuck Candy Company in Chap. 1, we were concerned with a decision whether to turn from television advertising to newspaper advertising. Now let us take some data from the company's records as well as some evidence about newspaper sales and see if we can develop a multiple regression model. The purpose of the model is to relate the total sales of candy to the effects of television and newspaper advertising. The identity form of the model is

$$Y = a_1 + b_1 X_1 + b_2 X_2$$

where

Y = annual sales of candy (in millions of dollars)

X_1 = television ad expense (in thousands of dollars)

X_2 = newspaper ad expense (in thousands of dollars)

a_1, b_1, b_2 = parameters to be estimated

The data used in this model are the results of four tests. Exhibit 4.1 shows a solution of the model.

Exhibit 4.1 Solving a multiple regression problem for Naugatuck Candy Company

Test (n), thousands of $	Sales of candy, millions of $	TV ad expense, thousands of $	Newspaper ad expense, thousands of $
	(Y)	(X_1)	(X_2)
1	7	4	1
2	12	7	2
3	17	9	5
4	20	12	8
Total (Σ)	56	32	16
Mean ($\overline{X}$)	14	8	4

Test (n)	Y^2	X_1^2	X_2^2	X_1X_2	X_1Y	X_2Y
1	49	16	1	4	28	7
2	144	49	4	14	84	24
3	289	81	25	45	153	85
4	400	144	64	96	240	160
Total (Σ)	882	290	94	159	505	276

Normal equations

$$\Sigma X_1^2 = \quad \Sigma X_2^1 - n(\overline{X_1})^2 = 290 - 4(8)^2 = 34$$
$$\Sigma X_1 X_2 = \Sigma X_1 X_2 - n(\overline{X_1})(\overline{X_2}) = 159 - 4(8)(4) = 31$$
$$\Sigma X_2^2 = \quad \Sigma X_2^2 - n(\overline{X_2})^2 = 94 - 4(4)^2 = 30$$
$$\Sigma X_1 Y = \quad \Sigma X_1 Y - n(\overline{X_1})(\overline{Y}) = 505 - 4(8)(14) = 57$$
$$\Sigma X_2 Y = \quad \Sigma X_2 Y - n(\overline{X_2})(\overline{Y}) = 276 - 4(4)(14) = 52$$

So, since

$$b_1 \Sigma X_1^2 + b_2 \Sigma X_1 X_2 = \Sigma X_1 Y$$
$$b_1 \Sigma X_1 X_2 + b_2 \Sigma X_2^2 = \Sigma X_2 Y$$

Therefore

$$34b + 31b_2 = 57$$
$$31b_1 + 30b_2 = 52$$

Solving

$$b_1 = \frac{98}{59} = 1.66 \qquad\qquad b_2 = \frac{1}{59} = .017$$

$$\begin{aligned} a_1 &= \overline{Y} - b_1\overline{X}_1 - b_2\overline{X}_2 \\ &= 14 - 1.66(8) - .017(4) \\ &= 14 - 13.28 - .068 \\ &= .652 \end{aligned}$$

So $Y = .65 + 1.66X_1 + .068X_2 \qquad R^2 = .9751$

$$[\overline{R}^2 = .9767]$$

Since

$$b_1 = \frac{\text{sales}}{\text{newspaper ad expenses}}$$

$$b_2 = \frac{\text{sales}}{\text{TV ad expenses}}$$

Thus every additional dollar of newspaper advertising yields $1.66 in sales. But every additional dollar of television advertising yields only 7 cents in sales.

Retail Sales, Income, and Unemployment

McLagan[9] worked out a simple multiple regression model to explain the relationship among sales of Econ 500, disposable personal income in the United States, and the national unemployment rate. His regression equation was:

$$\text{Sales} = -2.1 \quad + 14.8 \ YD - 173 \ RU$$
$$\qquad\quad (-.01) \qquad (56.14) \qquad (-4.93)$$
$$R^2 = .9971$$
$$s_p = 112.37$$

where

YD = United States disposable personal income per quarter (in billions of dollars)

RU = national unemployment rate

s_p = standard error of registration regression,

The numbers in parentheses below the estimated parameters are the relevant t statistics.

[9] D. L. McLagan, "A Non-Econometrician's Guide to Econometrics," *Business Economics,* 8(3): 38–45, May 1973.

The standard error of the regression, s_p, measures the closeness of the fitted values to the actual values of the data. It is desirable to have the standard error of the regression as small as possible. To say that a standard error is 112 means that about 67 percent of the fitted values are within ±112 (one standard error) of the actual values, that 95 percent of the fitted values are within ±224 (two standard errors), and that 99 percent of the fitted values are within ±336 (three standard errors) of the actual values.

The t statistics indicate that both disposable income and the unemployment rate contribute significantly to explaining variations in the company's retail sales. The constant intercept is not significant and could be dropped. However, whether to drop a coefficient of estimated parameters depends as much on the specifications of the model, that is, the extent to which a factor is expected to explain changes in the dependent variable, as on the t statistic. The fitted variables provide a good estimate of the actual values. If this problem had been worked out on a computer, the printout would have looked somewhat like Table 4.1.

Table 4.1 Computer printout for sales, disposable income, unemployment rate multiple regression

Ordinary least squares
  Frequency: Annual
  Interval: 1959:1 to 1971:1
  Left-hand variable: Sales

Right-hand variable	Estimated coefficient	Standard error	t statistic
Constant	−2.10487	258.938	−.0081288
YD	14.8191	.263968	56.1398
RU	−173.022	35.0928	−4.93043
$\bar{R}^2$	.9971		

Standard error of regression: 112.367

Date	Actual	Fitted
1959	4036	4054
1960	4134	4226
1961	4268	4241
1962	4603	4744
1963	5116	5018
1964	5740	5598
1965	6390	6231
1966	6805	6827
1967	7330	7428
1968	8198	8140
1969	8863	8793
1970	9262	9355
1971	1006	9996

You would read that computer printout as follows:

1. The constant will be the first estimated term, -2.1.
2. The YD coefficient will be 14.8
3. The RU coefficient will be -173.0.
4. The t statistic in the fourth column will be placed below the appropriate coefficient or parameter.
5. The standard error is really the variance of the error term (which is equal to the variance of sales for a given value of YD and/or RU) squared. It gives the range within which chances are slightly better than 2 in 3 that the estimated coefficient will lie.

The computer would also print out a correlation matrix like that shown in Table 4.2.

Table 4.2   Correlation matrix

	Sales	YD	RU
Sales	1.0000		
YD	.9958	1.0000	
RU	-.4807	-.4124	1.000

This matrix shows the correlation between variables in the model. Notice that even though unemployment rate has a relatively low correlation with sales, it still contributes significantly to the explanatory value of the model. One yellow flag here: correlation coefficients alone cannot be used to test the validity of a regression model.

The term "dependent variable" can be replaced by "left-hand variable." The dependent variable may also be called an "endogenous" variable. Such variables are the output of a model; endogenous variables are explained by the model.

Independent variables are "right-hand variables." They may also be called "exogenous" variables. They are the input of a model. Exogenous variables help explain the behavior of the endogenous variables. The purpose of econometric regression models is to explain the behavior of endogenous variables by examining possible relationships and behavior among the exogenous variables.

Projecting United States Consumer Demand

The most comprehensive analysis and projection of consumer demand in the United States by major expenditure categories was that undertaken in the 1960s by H. S. Houthakker and Lester Taylor at Harvard University. The data base was the expenditure category breakdown of the personal consumption expenditure component of the gross national product (GNP). Price, quantity, income, and other data on 83 commodities were available for each quarter from 1929 through 1961 and thus provided at least 132 observations.

Houthakker and Taylor did not specify the mathematical form of the models to be used in estimating demand for each of the eighty-three commodities. Instead, they chose, for each data time series, that form of multiple regression model which provided the best fit, after testing among various forms. Of the eighty-three models, seventy-two are dynamic models, which means that consumer decisions in one quarter depended on data from a previous quarter. The following are two of the Houthakker-Taylor demand models.

Demand for Radio and Television Receivers, Records, and Musical Instruments

To derive a consumer demand model for radio and television receiver demand, Houthakker and Taylor found that it was necessary to use lagged variables. They resorted to this technique because they found that the value of demand in one quarter was influenced by the value of the right-hand variables in previous quarters. While the use of lagged variables is easy enough to demonstrate, the theory of lags is much too complex to analyze here. So, here is an example of a dynamic least-squares consumer demand model.

The multiple regression demand model which Houthakker and Taylor developed for radio and television receivers was

$$q_t = .6599\,q_{t-1} + .0167\,\Delta x_t + .0060\,x_{t-1} - .0946\,\Delta p_t - .0340\,p_{t-1}$$
$$(.2093) \qquad (.0050) \qquad (.0035) \qquad (.0499) \qquad (.0197)$$
$$R^2 = .983$$

where, using the Houthakker-Taylor notation,

q_t = quantity demanded in quarter t of radio and television receivers (per capita consumption expenditures in 1954 dollars)

q_{t-1} = quantity demanded in quarter $t-1$ (per capita consumption expenditures in 1954 dollars)

$\Delta x_t = x_t - x_{t-1}$ = change in total personal consumption expenditure between quarter t and $t-1$ in 1954 dollars

x_{t-1} = total personal consumption expenditures in quarter $t-1$ in 1954 dollars

Δp_t = price relative for commodity in quarter t (1954 is base year)

p_{t-1} = price relative for commodity in quarter $t-1$ (1954 is base year)

In this model, the numbers in parentheses under the estimated parameters or coefficients are not t statistics. So don't be puzzled by their very low values. These numbers are standard errors of the coefficient and indicate the range of the confidence interval within one standard deviation from the coefficient. That is, chances are about 67 in 100 that the "true" value of the coefficient will lie in the range of the estimated coefficient plus or minus the standard error. So for the lagged price coefficient p_{t-1}, the confidence interval is $-.0340 \pm .0197$. Thus, chances are about 2 out of 3 that somewhere between $-.0143$ and $-.0537$ lies the true value of this coefficient.

Houthakker and Taylor found the own-price elasticity for radio and television receivers to be -1.2725. So, for every 10 percent decrease in price, there was a 12.7 percent increase in the amount consumers spent. This highly elastic demand reflected a relatively high and continuing preference for radio and television receivers, a probable indication that these were luxury goods.

The differences between this Houthakker and Taylor demand model and the simpler models we dealt with in Chap. 3 arise from the fact that

1. Houthakker and Taylor included as many right-hand variables as they were able to find. That meant that they were going to let the regression results dictate the form and the content of the demand model.
2. Houthakker and Taylor found it necessary in this time-series analysis to abandon the direct one-on-one relationship between this quarter's demand and this quarter's price. More interesting results were found by lagging the relationship. This suggests consumers remember the past as they decide about the present. Somewhere behind this observation is a theory of consumer habit formation.
3. Houthakker and Taylor had to decide whether the demand model was a price or income model after the regression was completed. This meant that they had to examine not only the R^2 between q_t and the right-hand variables but that they had to examine each correlation coefficient between q_t and each of the right-hand variables. That helped them to decide what to keep in the model and what to drop.

One of the results of the parameter estimation procedures they used was the surprising conclusion that prices are much less important than income in explaining United States consumption of all items (or total expenditures). Prices are excluded from only three of the eighty-three demand models. On the other hand, price appears as a significant right-hand variable in only forty-five of these models. Moreover, price only borders on significance in many of these.

Houthakker and Taylor Food Demand Model

It will be interesting to compare the Houthakker and Taylor food demand model with the Stevens model in Chap. 3. Like the radio-TV model, this food demand model is a dynamic least-squares function. The regression result is

$$q_t = 29.074 + .6044\,q_{t-1} + .1128\,\Delta x_t + .0528\,x_{t-1}$$
$$ (11.727) \quad (.1556) \quad\quad (.0208) \quad\quad (.0221)$$
$$R^2 = .988$$

where

$q_t =$ quantity demanded in quarter t (per capita consumption expenditure on food in 1954 dollars)

$q_{t-1} =$ quantity demanded in quarter $t - 1$ (per capita consumption expenditure on food in 1954 dollars)

$\Delta x_t = x_t - x_{t-1} =$ change in total personal consumption expenditure between quarters t and $t - 1$ in 1954 dollars

$x_{t-1} =$ total personal consumption expenditure in year $t - 1$ in 1954 dollars

Once again, the numbers in parentheses are standard errors. There is no price statistic in this demand model. Oddly enough, the own-price elasticity for food was found to be positive. Estimating the model by using a semilogarithmic form, Houthakker and Taylor did obtain a negative price elasticity. However this semilogarithmic model was subject to autocorrelation, which means that error terms are not independent of one another. The tests of significance turned dubious. For that and other reasons, the price statistic was dropped from the model.

The expenditure elasticity for food in this model was .6882. While the Houthakker and Taylor data were from a time series in the United States and the Stevens data were collected from many cross-section studies in thirty-five countries over a wide range of stages of development and levels of consumer incomes, the closeness of the expenditure elasticities from the two models does support the conclusion that the true food-expenditure elasticity is about .7.

Conflict with Established Demand Theory

There are three possible conclusions to draw about the validity of the Houthakker and Taylor research on American consumer demand functions. One is that if they are right, then for about half of all commodities and services in the American marketplace, consumer spending is not dependent on variations in price. Another possible conclusion is that the Houthakker and Taylor demand functions are not valid tests of the effects of price variations on sales and purchases. And the third is that if another demand function had been used, perhaps a better test of the role of price might have resulted.

J. W. Elliott has pointed out that the nature of available empirical data tends to make it very difficult to produce estimates of price demand functions. He summarizes these factors as follows:

1. The basic demand and supply functional relationships are too volatile to be significantly explained by analytical functions.
2. There are insufficient statistically viable relationships present among candidate variables to identify a demand function (i.e., a model mathematically identified a priori may become underidentified when the statistical evidence is gathered).
3. There is too much multicollinearity inherent in the variables to allow their separate effects to disentangle.
4. The data seriously violate one or more of the statistical assumptions about the error term.

Price demand functions derived by statistical estimating procedures are, in Elliott's words, more of a "navigational mapping of an ocean channel" than a "pure path to reliable estimates."[10]

Problems with Regression Models

Regression modeling is a powerful tool for investigating demand and other economic relationships. But you ought to know that it takes a good deal of skill to know how to avoid misusing or misinterpreting the model and its results. We have already referred to such disturbing factors as homoscedasticity and heteroscedasticity, multicollinearity, lagged variables, and autocorrelation. But they are not all or even the most important problems involved in using regression models. Let us look quickly at two more problems: "hidden" extrapolation and dummy variables. Then, we will turn to the most complex problem, the matter of identification.

There is always a danger that once a nice well-behaved demand model has been developed from the available data, the model cannot be easily extrapolated beyond the limits of the right-hand variable(s). Suppose, for example, we have the Grand Rapids orange demand model. The right-hand variable is price and we have a set of observations about the prices of size 200 oranges. Dare we go beyond these observations to generalize about orange demand? Or suppose that we have the time-series model for apple demand in Durham. Dare we go beyond 1977 to extrapolate the same kind of demand behavior into 1978 and beyond? These two examples involve obvious extrapolation.

If the model contains more than one right-hand variable, then the danger of hidden extrapolation arises. For one thing, it is no longer clear precisely what the limits of the data really are. In the food demand model, we could examine each of the right-hand variables, discover the maximum and the minimum values of each, and then see whether any new value of any one of these right-hand variables was outside the ranges determined. But the fact is that, almost inevitably, as we examine one variable we go outside the limits of

---

[10]J. Walter Elliott, *Economic Analysis for Management Decisions*, Homewood, Ill., Irwin, 1973, pp. 113, 114.

another variable. That is, in our search for price behavior responses, we may go beyond the limits of income responses or of something else like demographic adjustments. We would be extrapolating or predicting income behavior while attempting to concentrate on price behavior without being alert to the degree of hidden extrapolation.

Dummy Variables

In Chap. 2, we observed that not all variables are easily quantifiable. But we said that a way of quantifying the not-so-obviously quantifiable data could frequently be found. That way was called the "method of dummy variables." Suppose that, in analyzing store sales of oranges in Grand Rapids, we found it made a difference whether we were observing sales days or ordinary days. There appeared, in fact, to be two quite different demand functions, one for sales days and one for ordinary days, suggesting the use of a dummy variable such as

$$X_1 = \begin{cases} 0 & \text{if sales day} \\ 1 & \text{if ordinary day} \end{cases}$$

We can now separate price-quantity observations on the basis of these dummy variables and, lo and behold, we have, as we suspect, two demand curves with different elasticities, different slopes, and different intercepts. The point is that failure to use dummy variables to separate data by characteristics such as day of sale, age of buyer, sex, race, and location of buyer's residence may give us regression models which could be misinterpreted.

Urban Housing Demand in Pittsburgh

Professor John M. Quigley, of Yale's Center for the Study of the City and Its Environment,[11] found that many studies of the demand for urban housing ignore several crucial features of the urban housing market. They measure housing consumption in a single dimension, despite the obvious heterogeneity of the housing stock.

Quigley developed an urban-housing demand model which considers choices among types of residential housing. He found that choices among housing types made by urban households were highly responsive to systematic variations in the relative prices households face for the same types of residential housing.

In Quigley's housing demand model the logarithmic odds of the choice between any two types of residential housing are a linear function of the attributes of different housing types. One example of the model is

[11]John M. Quigley, "Housing Demand in the Short Run: An Analysis of Polytomous Choice," *Explorations in Economic Research*, vol. 3, no. 1, 1976.

$$\log p_i/p_j = b_1(CW_i - CW_j) + b_2(APT_i - APT_j) + b_3(BR_i - BR_j)$$
$$+ b_4(AGE_i - AGE_j) + b_5(P_i - P_j) + b_6(ST_i - ST_j)$$

where

CW_i = dummy variable with value of 1 if i is a common wall unit
APT_i = dummy variable with value of 1 if i is an apartment unit
BR_i = dummy variable with value of 1 if i was built before 1930
P_i = effective monthly cost of consuming house type i
ST_i = number of housing units of type i in the sample

The subscripts i and j refer to a choice between two kinds of housing indicated by the dummy variable on an either/or basis. For each cross classification of income and family size, the logistic gives logarithmic odds of the choice. That chance of a certain choice is a linear function of the attributes of the housing types and their effective relative prices.

In this way, Quigley was able, for example, to predict that a three-person family with an income over $15,000 in the Pittsburgh standard metropolitan statistical area had an 82 percent chance of selecting an apartment over a town or row house (with common walls) or a single detached house (Table 4.3).

Table 4.3 Predicted probabilities of housing-type choice for three-person families across income classes

Kind of unit	Less than $3,000	$3,000–$4,999	$5,000–$6,999	$7,000–$9,999	$10,000–$14,999	$15,000+
Common-wall	.54	.37	.54	.59	.36	.01
Apartments	.24	.38	.23	.23	.32	.82
Single detached	.21	.25	.24	.18	.32	.18
Number of bedrooms						
One	.18	.35	.23	.18	.14	.00
Two	.64	.53	.61	.62	.39	.03
Three	.28	.12	.16	.20	.47	.97

Table 4.4 Predicted probabilities of housing-type choice for otherwise identical households at four worksites
Four-person families with income $5000-$6999

Kind of unit	Workplaces			
	CBD	Inner city	Central city	Suburbs
Common-wall	.51	.54	.50	.42
Apartments	.40	.29	.19	.11
Single detached	.09	.17	.30	.47
Number of bedrooms				
One	.16	.13	.13	.14
Two	.63	.63	.61	.57
Three	.21	.23	.26	.28

Table 4.5 Predicted probabilities of housing-type choice for selected incomes across family sizes
Income $5000–$6999

Kind of unit	Family size				
	1	2	3	4	5
Common-wall	.03	.22	.54	.52	.62
Apartments	.94	.60	.22	.11	.08
Single detached	.02	.17	.24	.37	.40
Number of bedrooms					
One	.95	.66	.23	.10	.03
Two	.05	.28	.61	.61	.33
Three	.00	.06	.16	.29	.64

Moreover, 97 times out of 100 that family would select a three-bedroom apartment. The model didn't explain the reason(s) for that many bedrooms.

By the same token, Quigley was able to say (Tables 4.4 and 4.5) that four-person families with incomes in the $5000 to $6999 range and with the head of the family working downtown (in the central business district, *CBD*) had a 51 percent chance of acquiring a common-wall town or row house and a 63 percent chance of selecting one with just two bedrooms. Moreover, a two-person family in that income range would select an apartment 60 times out of 100; 95 times out of 100 that apartment would have only one bedroom.

Thus, the dummy-variable technique is a powerful tool. It carries the model maker further than factors such as income elasticities or price elasticities, interesting and important as they are. You can imagine that real estate people in Pittsburgh would be much more interested in reading Quigley's results than those of Reid or de Leeuw.

Identification

Any set of observed facts can be explained in a variety of ways. Each such way of explaining the facts is called a "hypothesis." The purpose of econometric regression models is to rule out all but a few meaningful hypotheses. The ideal situation is one in which only one hypothesis remains and this hypothesis is consistent with economic theory. But the real situation is likely to be one in which we are never sure about either the quality of the facts or the model. Thus, a hypothesis which is accepted, if at all, can be accepted only provisionally. The concept of identification helps in determining whether a regression model is sufficiently restrictive so that when it is confronted with its data, only one hypothesis is consistent with both the data and the model.

Suppose that we have a simple model of two equations, both having Q in some form as left-hand variables as well as similar right-hand variables.

Endogenous variables: Q_1, Q_2

Exogenous variables: P_1, P_2

$$Q_1 = a + bP_1 + cQ_2 + E_1$$
$$Q_2 = d + eP_2 + fQ_1 + E_2$$

These equations, like any simultaneous equation system, will yield solutions or estimates of the left-hand variable, depending on the values of the right-hand variables and the values of the coefficients (a, b, c, d, e, f). E_1 and E_2 are error terms. These two functions could be demand functions, but until we know the value (and the sign) of parameters or coefficients b and e, we can't tell. It will be noticed that Q_1 depends on Q_2 in the first equation and that in the second equation Q_2 depends on Q_1. Are these two equations separate and unique models? Or is it possible, for example, that changes in P_1 are highly correlated with changes in P_2? If there were such a correlation, then the equation system would give only a small range of solutions or estimates. Both equations in this system would be "underidentified," meaning that there are at least two possible hypotheses and both are consistent with the data and the model. We can't tell which is best.

What we want is a demand model which can be identified. Figure 4.2a and b shows data scatters. Function Q_1Q_1 is a least-squares linear regression model. If it is the only model and thus the only hypothesis that can be derived from the data, then we have a puzzle.

For one thing, Q_1Q_1 has a positive slope. The law of demand tells us that a demand curve in all but truly extraordinary cases has a negative slope. The linear regression model has a high $\bar{R}^2$ with significant t statistics and standard errors of regression. To fit economic theory let us suppose that we have the locus of a shifting demand curve that traces a positively sloped supply curve, the observed Q_1Q_1. This hypothesis makes the supply curve identifiable. Indeed, it can be read from the graph shown in Fig. 4.2a.

However, economic theory also tells us that it is unlikely that a shift in a demand curve takes place without interaction with the supply curve. In that case, Q_1Q_1 in Fig. 4.2b is a "close" estimate of the locus of the points of interaction (the solutions of successive simultaneous equations) of supply and demand. This is a much less precise identification; it is called "nonunique." Indeed, Q_1Q_1, the second hypothesis, would have to be tested against a series of successive hypotheses about each supply and demand equilibrium.

Let's summarize what can be said about the identification puzzle.

1. If a model is *underidentified*, then it will be impossible to estimate the parameters of at least one of the equations in the model.
2. If the model is *nonunique*, there is a tangle of data and more information is needed to untangle the data.
3. An *overidentified* model is one in which the parameters of each equation can be estimated. But these estimates will not be consistent and some parameters may have more than one possible and logical estimate.
4. A *just-identified* model is one in which all the parameters can be estimated

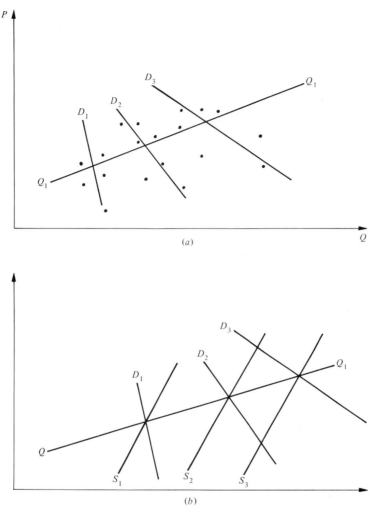

Figure 4.2. The identification problem. What does the data scatter say? (*a*) Hypothesis 1: Rising supply curve, shifting demand functions. (*b*) Hypothesis 2: Both supply and demand curves shift.

by least squares. The method used will probably be indirect in that we may have to move from one set of data to another as we do in Fig. 4.2*a* and *b*.

Keep in mind two key points about identification. First, identification does not really refer to the model itself but rather to the measurability of any single equation within a model. Second, identification is not simply a matter of correctly using statistical tools like linear regression or correctly interpreting data. It is really a relationship between a statistical tool (linear regression) and economic theory. These are the two necessary parts of economic model building. Alert model builders check one against the other as they proceed.

Chapter Summary

Econometrics and statistics can teach us a good deal about models. This chapter couldn't cover it all, but if you now have a feeling for the pitfalls of economic model building, you've gained an insight into why there are more arguments about method than about theory among economists. Managerial economists have the job of selecting models that work, that explain, and that do a presentable job of predicting. You can see that their task is not easy. But, by the same token, you can see what they can do and make up your own mind about the meaning of their results.

We have examined the uses and the methods of linear regression for that is the principal way in which economic models are built. Whether it was simple linear regression or multiple regression, we have tried to see what the methods did to the data so that we could interpret the answers obtained. But the data or the observations themselves pose problems that make identification difficult even after we have tried dummy variables to separate age, sex, and even location, to say nothing of race or day of the week. We can never get very far from the guiding hand of economic theory. Theory tells us what to look for, how to interpret what we have got, and even suggests what kinds of models ought to be used.

This chapter won't make you a statistician, econometrician, or just plain managerial economist, but at least it will tell you what the name tags mean.

Selected Readings

Box, George E. P., and Jenkins, Gwilym: *Time Series Analysis Forecasting and Control,* San Francisco, Holden-Day, 1976.

Christ, Carl F.: *Econometric Models and Methods,* New York, Wiley, 1966.

Elliott, J. W.: *Economic Analysis for Management Decisions,* Homewood, Ill., Irwin, 1973.

Grossack, I. M., and Martin, D. D.: *Managerial Economics,* Boston, Little, Brown, 1973.

Hicks, J. R.: *A Revision of Demand Theory,* New York, Oxford, 1959.

Houthakker, H., and Taylor, L.: *Consumer Demand in the United States, 1929–1970,* Cambridge, Mass., Harvard, 1966.

Johnston, J.: *Econometric Methods,* New York, McGraw-Hill, 1963.

Mills, Richard L.: *Statistics for Applied Economics and Business,* New York, McGraw-Hill, 1977.

Norris, Ruby: *The Theory of Consumers' Demand,* New Haven, Conn., Yale, 1952.

Schultz, Henry: *Theory and Measurement of Demand,* University of Chicago Press, 1964.

Walters, A. A.: *An Introduction to Econometrics,* New York, Norton, 1970.

Wold, Herman, and Jureen, L.: *Demand Analysis: A Study in Econometrics,* New York, Wiley, 1953.

Working, E. J.: "What Do Statistical 'Demand Curves' Show?" in *Readings in Price Theory,* Chicago, Irwin, 1952.

Questions, Problems, and Projects

1. Some years ago, Ruth Mack, of the National Bureau of Economic Research, reported on factors influencing shoe purchases. She found that the "overpowering determinant of what people spend on shoes is what they have to spend." She reported that shoe purchases mirrored "with startling faithfulness" the contours of consumer income. In general, she said, when consumers attain more income, "they seem to spend a certain portion of the increment on shoes—around 1.6 or 1.7 percent." An alternative way of describing the relationship is that a 1 percent change in income was associated with a change of .8 or .9 percent in shoe buying. Though her evidence came from time-series data and "was not as trustworthy as one would wish," the data tentatively indicated that when shoe prices rose out of proportion to other living costs, the physical volume of shoe buying was cut.

By contrast, Houthakker and Taylor, using personal consumption expenditure data from 1929 through 1961, found price to be a significant explanatory variable of the demand for shoes and, additionally, they obtained an own-price elasticity of −.3878. Also included in their demand equation are (negative) changes in automobile registrations as well as consumer expenditures.

What kinds of problems do you see in deriving a shoe demand function? What should be the purpose of this demand function? To what extent are data a problem in deriving such a function? If Houthakker-Taylor found an income elasticity of .47, how do you account for the Mack elasticity?

2. Richard Weisskoff was unhappy with the many consumer demand studies which ignored price elasticity. He wanted to know if it was true that price changes were unimportant in determining patterns of consumption behavior. His results were as follows:

		Expenditure elasticity, B_1	Own-price elasticity, B_2
Food	(1)	.069	−0.68
	(2)	0.69	
Rent	(1)	1.21	−0.71
	(2)	0.90	
Services	(1)	1.23	−1.26
	(2)	1.82	
Clothing	(1)	1.29	−0.64
	(2)	1.31	
Transport	(1)	2.87	
	(2)	1.66	
Durables	(1)	2.33	−1.42
	(2)	2.43	

(1) Unweighted averages, time series.
(2) Unweighted averages, cross-section budget studies.
Source: Weisskoff, R., "Demand Elasticities for a Developing Economy," in H. B. Chenery (ed.), *Studies in Development Planning,* Cambridge, Mass., Harvard, 1971.

He concluded that price elasticities are important and that substitution does take place between all the broad categories of commodities. Thus price increases would reduce excess demand. Any governmental attempt to fix prices for food or transport would lead to an excess demand for food and transport. Would you agree on the basis of his evidence? Why?

3. Pindyck and Rubinfeld worked out the following automobile demand function for the period January 1963 to April 1974:

$$S_t = a + bW_t + cR_{t-1} + d\,CPI_{t-1} - e_t$$

where

S = monthly retail sales of automobiles in current dollars
W = monthly wages paid
R = three-month Treasury bill rate in percentages (interest rate)
CPI = monthly consumer price index for new cars (1957 to 1959 = 100).

The results were

Coefficients	Value	Standard error	t statistic
a	4904.0	1067.0	4.6
b	10.3	1.1	9.6
c	−140.5	57.3	−2.4
d	−35.6	10.6	−3.3

$R^2 = .842$
Standard error of regression = 236.2

What does this demand function say about each of the coefficients? What does the interest rate appear to do in the equation? What does it tell about demand behavior? Evaluate this demand function in standard terms.

4. Just what is the theory of linear regression? What does it say? And how applicable is it to demand analysis? Using it, what are the differences between a theoretical demand function and one derived by linear regression?

5. Contrast and compare (*a*) identification and estimation, (*b*) stochastic and error term, (*c*) standard error and variance, and (*d*) homoscedasticity and multicollinearity.

Case 4.1 Demand for Bus Transit Service in Milwaukee

What should be done about the level of bus transit service in the Milwaukee area? Professor M. A. Abe[1] of Marquette University concluded after a careful study that there was a substantial potential demand for bus service. To provide a basis for transit planning, he developed with an associate a set of demand functions. These functions relate the quality of bus transit service, the level of transit patronage, and the average fare. The basis for Abe's demand functions is a set of time-series observations obtained from the Milwaukee and Suburban Transit Corporation ($MSTC$) for the period 1955–1970.

The following are two of Abe's demand regression equations:

$$\log X_1 = 9.5210 + .8947 \log X_2 - 3.0809 \log X_4 - .2046 \log X_5 \quad (1)$$
$$(8.0084) \qquad (-3.6102) \qquad (-2.8385)$$
$$R^2 = .9948$$

$$\log X_1 = 9.7038 - 2.2141 \log X_2 + 3.0603 \log X_3 - .2367 \log X_5 \quad (2)$$
$$(-2.1971) \qquad (3.1870 \qquad (-3.1870)$$
$$R^2 = .9948$$

where X_1 = number of revenue passengers per year; X_2 = bus miles of route coverage per year; X_3 = bus hours of service per year; X_4 = headway factor (timing between buses on specific routes); X_5 = average fare; R^2 = coefficient of determination. The numbers in parentheses are t statistics.

DISCUSSION QUESTIONS 4.1

1. While the R^2's appear to be high and the t statistics indicate statistical significance, what do you think it means that the sign on the estimated parameter or coefficient for X_2 in Eq. (2) is negative? What reasons would you have for expecting a positive sign? Describe a situation in which the sign might be negative.
2. What is the price elasticity for bus transit in Milwaukee? What kinds of conclusions regarding fare policy can you develop based on your answer? Would you recommend a subsidy for $MSTC$?
3. Look at the other elasticities in Eqs. (1) and (2). What do they imply for the expansion of transit service in Milwaukee? Should fares be increased? Should service be decreased? If not, why not?
4. Abe asserts that "the majority of transit riders [in Milwaukee] are captive riders." Therefore, he recommends that "in order to rescue the deficit-ridden bus transit operation in the city of Milwaukee, massive subsidies or even a government take-over of transit operation" be undertaken, "because it will increase the economic welfare of the community." What do you think of this recommendation?

[1]M. A. Abe, "Pricing and Welfare in Urban Transportation," *Traffic Quarterly*, 27(3): 419–429, July 1973.

Case 4.2   Consumer Food Demand in Ghana[1]

The United States Department of Agriculture sponsors research in demand projection and analysis in many countries. In the early 1960s, H. Wilson Ord and his associates reported on problems they had had in estimating the statistical relationships between demand and household or per capita levels of living in Ghana. The following information is taken from their report.

SCOPE OF ANALYSIS

This is a study of the main determinants of demand for agriculture products imported into Ghana. Since much of the data relating to consumer expenditures cover broad groups of commodities, among which "food, drink," and "tobacco" consistently appear, agricultural products are defined as food, drinks, and tobacco. Included in this definition are purchases of meals and drink away from home and consumption of a few nonagricultural items such as salt, fuel wood, and charcoal for cooking. Our definition covers both domestic output and imports of animal and vegetable products that are classified under "food, beverages, and tobacco." It excludes other commodities that are agricultural in origin, for example, vegetable fibers and textiles, clothing, footwear, soap, and wood products.

The main feature of demand for food is its tendency to increase at a smaller proportionate rate than income. The concept of income elasticity expresses this relationship and provides a valuable tool for prediction of future consumption trends. Income-consumption relationships, or elasticity coefficients, may be derived from either time-series or cross-section studies. The time-series approach would seem the more appropriate for projection studies since it involves an analysis of consumer behavior over time. For Ghana the basic figures of aggregate incomes, population, and consumption by broad commodity groups are not available. A more fundamental problem is the difficulty of isolating the effect on income of changes in consumption attributable to other factors. Unless these can be identified and evaluated and the original data adjusted, the observed income-consumption relationships may provide a misleading guide to future consumption trends.

Demand projections are usually derived under a rigid assumption of constant prices. Neither changes in relative prices nor changes in price elasticities are considered since it is rarely possible to make realistic assumptions about long-term price movements or to have available sufficient data on the many complex relations between prices and consumption. As demand for all food is normally price inelastic, price changes may be expected to influence the composition of food expenditure rather than the total volume purchased.

Any analysis of consumers' expenditures in Ghana must begin with the cross-section data available from family budget surveys, undertaken in various

[1]Adapted from H. Wilson Ord et al., *Ghana: Projected Level of Demand, Supply and Imports of Agricultural Products in 1965, 1970 and 1975*, Economic Research Service, U.S. Department of Agriculture, 1964, pp. 25–40.

parts of Ghana over the period 1953–1962, which provide the only reliable data for measuring the relation between food expenditure and total consumer expenditure.

Total expenditure (including, where possible, consumption of self-produced food) rather than income has been used to classify families and persons for cross-section and regression analyses.

Most of the published data measured purchases in money terms (pq) rather than in quantities (q). This method has a number of practical advantages. First, Ghanaian householders are more able to report the money cost of purchases without necessarily knowing the quantity by weight or volume. Second, changes in quality can be reflected in money terms, thereby explaining why one household spends more on the same quantity of a commodity when, presumably, the same market opportunities are available for all the families in a small sample. Third, specific items can be compared directly with total expenditure and with each other.

We have not been able to derive price effects from Ghanaian family budget data. While implicit unit prices for a wide range of consumer goods may be calculated from published material available for the earlier urban and rural studies, variations in patterns of consumption between different survey locations (and dates) cannot be attributed merely to price differences.

Cross-section analysis showed that Engel's law operated among Ghanaian households, that is, the proportion of income (total expenditure) devoted to food declined as higher levels of family income were attained. For families in the lower-expenditure brackets, it might appear that Engel's law was invalid, that is, the proportion of total expenditure devoted to food did not fall. Part of the explanation may be the underreporting of expenditure on nonfood items or the understatement of income. Many women are traders whose earnings are not likely to be disclosed to other members of the family or to official survey enumerators. The whole concept of the household or family differs markedly from the elementary structure found in developed countries, with the result that microeconomic investigations of consumer behavior are faced with special problems.

A notable characteristic of Ghanaian households was the close association between income and size of family. Opportunities for raising total household income depend largely on the number of potential contributors to total receipts rather than on the capacity of a single breadwinner. However, the number of mouths to be fed will also increase, so that differences in per capita living standards are likely to be much less than differences in household income before taking account of size and composition.

Table 1 summarizes the per capita expenditure elasticities derived from the surveys covering various sectors of the population of Ghana. Regressions obtained by the least-squares method provided linear relationships between income (total expenditure) and consumption of food, drink, and tobacco.

Table 1 indicates that the per capita elasticities derived from the national subsample compare closely with those obtained from earlier cross-section studies for similar income groups or urban-rural strata. In contrast with the earlier urban and rural budget inquiries, this survey took fuller account of

Table 1 Per capita expenditure elasticities (e) and correlation coefficients (R^2) from cross-section studies

Survey locations and dates	Local food		Imported food		Food*		Drink and tobacco	
	e	R^2	e	R^2	e	R^2	e	R^2
Urban								
Accra (1953)	0.81	0.96	0.98	0.90	0.85	0.96	1.67	0.77
Kumasi (1955)	0.52	0.25	1.41	0.93	0.64	0.26	2.25	0.89
Sekondi-Takoradi (1955)	0.45	0.62	1.52	0.75	0.63	0.75	2.96	0.89
National household study†	0.59	0.92	1.11	0.92	0.78	0.98	1.46	0.99
(1961–1962)‡	0.58	0.93	1.17	0.92	0.76	0.98	1.56	0.99
Rural								
Oda-Swedru (1955–1956)	0.50	0.96	1.41	0.93	0.59	0.96	2.39	0.89
Ashanti (1956–1957)	0.31	0.79	1.07	0.92	0.39	0.85	1.51	0.76
National household study†	0.68	0.96	1.11	0.93	0.78	0.98	0.78	0.96
(1961–1962)‡	0.72	0.97	1.32	0.93	0.78	0.98	0.92	0.95
National								
National household study (1961–1962)‡	0.64	0.95	1.30	0.96	0.77	0.97	1.24	0.98

*Total food includes means taken away from home.
†Regression equation excludes "consumption of own produce."
‡Total income and consumption, including "consumption of own produce."

income from and consumption of home produce. The preliminary results of the 1961–1962 survey show that 31 percent of total expenditures among rural households was of income derived from its own produce. In urban areas the proportion was 7 percent. In terms of food consumption, the inclusion or exclusion of a family's produce had no material effect in the urban areas; 52 percent of cash expenditure was devoted to food exclusive of "own produce," 55 percent when own produce was included (in both income and consumption). In Accra the proportions were 50 percent and 51 percent, respectively. In the rural areas the corresponding percentages were 48 and 64. This difference would be large enough to alter both the composition of food consumption and, possibly, the income-consumption relationships. To assess the importance of this factor among both urban and rural consumers, we computed elasticities which exclude "own consumption" from both sides of the equation.

Income-consumption relationships for specific food imports could not be derived from data currently available in Ghanaian budget surveys. The rather narrow definition of imported food adopted in the official inquiries excluded important items of special interest to this study. Another limitation of the cross-section approach was the neglect of demand factors other than income.

Since the analysis dealt almost wholly with food imports destined for final consumer demand, intermediate demands for industrial use or inventory accumulation were assumed to be either a negligible or a constant proportion of total imports. The unit of analysis was "disaggregated" to the level of per capita demand by reference to the population estimates derived under high mortality assumptions.

The next step was to identify and measure changes in the determining variables. The absence of reliable data on personal income or aggregate personal consumption meant that any association using macroeconomic data might be fortuitous and misleading; we therefore selected a component of personal income (personal consumption) that was likely to be both relevant and reliable for time-series analysis of food imports. Accurate records of net cash payments made by the Cocoa Marketing Board to cocoa farmers extending over more than a decade were studied as well as another indicator of cash income movements that consisted of estimates of wages and salaries paid to recorded employees, which was believed to be consistent in coverage for the shorter period from 1954 through 1961. Appraisal of relevant data indicated that consumers receiving these two forms of cash income comprised a major share of the Ghana imported foods market and were representative of other cash-earning households. Net cocoa payments and gross wages in 1961 accounted for approximately 32 percent of personal consumption, or 38 percent, excluding subsistence.

The cash income variable was deflated by the only cost-of-living index available—the Accra Retail Price Index—to obtain real-cash income. The aggregate real-cash income series for the eight-year period of 1954 to 1961 was adjusted to a per capita basis using population estimates.

The time series of per capita consumption of selected imported foods were plotted against per capita real-cash income and price movements for the period 1954–1961. Implicit import prices were used on the assumption that changes in landed cost (CIF prices plus any element attributable to import duty) would be reflected at the final retail stage. The Accra cost-of-living index was then applied to obtain real prices.

The time series were inspected to determine whether changes in the levels of per capita imports were associated with changes in the levels of other specified variables. Of the commodities investigated, namely, rice, wheat flour, sugar, evaporated milk, cattle, canned meat, and salted/dried or canned fish, movements in the levels of imports appeared to relate more closely to changes in per capita cash income than to any other factor, except in the case of cattle, canned meat, and canned fish.

The price of rice showed a downward trend (relative to both the cost of living and the price of wheat flour). This may have been an explanation for the proportionately large increase in per capita imports of rice. There was no overall trend in the price of wheat flour relative to the cost of living, although toward the end of the period the price rose relative to that of rice. This did not appear to have a marked effect on wheat flour imports. The price of sugar (relative to the cost of living) showed no overall trend, and imports appeared to be closely related to the level of cash income. The real price of unsweetened (evaporated) milk showed little variation; but the sharp fall in the price of sweetened (condensed) milk in 1961 to 1962 was probably responsible for part of the decline in unsweetened milk imports. Imports of both cattle and canned meat were at the same per capita level in 1962 as in 1954, and imports of cattle appeared to be quite unresponsive to changes in either price or cash income; imports of canned meat were also unrelated to other variables, with the possible exception of real price. Per capita imports of canned fish were affected by nonspecified factors since the falling trend took place against a decline in price (relative to both the cost of living and the price of imported salted and dried fish). Imports of salted and dried fish did not reflect the relatively large price variations that took place over the period.

Table 2 summarizes the results of our analysis, obtained by applying the various demand models for selected food imports and using time-series data for the years 1954 through 1961. The equations fitted to the consumption and income series were

$$y = a + bx \tag{1}$$
$$y = a + b \cdot \log x \tag{2}$$
$$\log y = a + b \cdot \log x \tag{3}$$
$$dy = a\, dt + b\, dx \tag{4}$$

Table 2   Summary of time-series analysis for some principal food imports

Eq.	R^2	a	b	e (1961)	R^2	a	b	e (1961)
		Wheat flour				Rice		
(1)	0.71	− 6.47	1.86	1.42	0.82	−29.38	2.90	2.95
(2)	0.73	−43.46	23.70	1.19	0.82	−86.52	37.09	2.48
(3)	0.71	− 1.03	1.51	1.51	0.76	−15.64	6.85	6.85
(4)	0.26	0.30	1.35	1.40	0.24	1.03	1.54	0.35
		Refined sugar				Unsweetened milk		
(1)	0.89	−15.89	2.38	1.81	0.83	− 2.17	0.32	1.71
(2)	0.89	−62.54	30.33	1.52	0.82	− 8.43	4.08	1.43
(3)	0.86	− 2.83	2.15	2.15	0.81	− 4.83	2.15	2.15
(4)	0.51	1.11	0.79	0.62	0.13	0.18	0.08	0.15
		Total food imports*				Total food imports†		
(1)	0.91	− 2.49	0.42	1.64	0.96	− 2.73	0.55	1.46
(2)	0.91	−10.82	5.41	1.38	0.96	−13.48	7.00	1.22
(3)	0.89	− 3.79	1.90	1.90	0.96	− 2.74	1.65	1.65
(4)	0.54	0.04	0.40	0.93	0.74	0.11	0.44	0.57

*Ghana total CIF imports of food (S.I.T.C. Section O) deflated by the food component of the import price index (1954 = 100). See *Statistical Yearbook*, 1961.

†Retail value of imported food, including processing margins, deflated by the imported food component of the Accra index of retail prices (June 1954 = 100).

where

y = per capita import quantities

x = per capita real-cash income (cocoa and wage payments)

dy = change in per capita import quantities each year

dx = change in per capita real-cash income each year

a, b = parameters estimated by the least-squares method

Equations (1) through (3) assume a direct relationship between per capita consumption of imports and per capita income. Equation (4) introduces the effect of time on the level of imports, where a is the parameter relating changes in the level of imports to time. As expected, this first difference equation proved to be a poor fit since it introduced a second explanatory variable. Direct comparison between Eq. (4) and the other three is not, therefore, necessarily an indication of the best model. Of Eqs. (1), (2), and (3), in almost every case the linear function fitted the data with the highest correlation coefficient. The semilog and double-log models were almost as good.

We proceeded to estimate future levels of per capita demand on the basis of the parameters derived from Eqs. (1), (2), and (3), giving the best fit and form, Eq. (4). To illustrate the relationship between changes in consumption and income which might be applicable to Ghana at the present time, we have also computed the elasticity coefficient for 1961. This relationship will, of course, reflect changes in tastes as well as in income.

Projected levels of per capita demand for imports have been estimated under the assumption that a linear relationship between per capita cash income and per capita personal consumption applicable to the period 1954–1961 will be maintained. It was necessary to make assumptions about the future behavior of this determining variable since our parameters are related to it and not directly to projections; assumptions about this variable were preferred rather than any alternatives, for example, that per capita cash income will change over the period 1960–1975 at the same rate as total personal consumption, on the grounds that cash income from wage employment, if not from cocoa farming, will continue to grow at a faster rate than total personal disposable income as measured by personal consumption.

DISCUSSION QUESTIONS 4.2

1. Ord and his associates are concerned about isolating the effect on income of change in consumption attributable to other factors. Since most demand research runs the other way, that is, from income change to consumption change, why are they concerned with this issue? What are they looking for? Do they find it?

2. Does this kind of research permit an assessment of the validity of Engel's law? What is the difference between the validity of a theory and the validity of a model? What do you think about the problem of defining a household?

Does this adequately explain those instances in which the validity of Engel's law might be in question?

3. Distinguish demand analysis from demand projection. Does the issue of hidden extrapolation arise in any possible projection of Ghanaian consumer food-spending patterns?

4. Why are many demand projections made under the assumption that prices are unchanging or rigid? Is it safe to assume that the effects of price changes on the distribution of consumer expenditures on broad categories of goods are not important?

Case 4.3 Demand for Network Television Advertising[1]

Gary Bowman developed and tested a relatively simple demand model for network television advertising in the 1960s. He argued that the quantity demanded was the number of people viewing commercials. He worked out the number of minutes households with television sets spent viewing commercials each month. His proxy for demand became the total number of hours watched by all television homes on an average day for any given month.

The identity form of his demand model was

$$\text{Demand} = P = f(Q, I, U, S)$$

where

P = price per home per minute of network commercials in deflated dollars

Q = number of minutes of network commercial messages watched per month by all households

I = real disposable income

U = unemployment rate

S = season of the year

In linear form the demand model was

$$P = a_0 + a_1Q + a_2I + a_3U + a_4D_1 + a_5D_2 + \ldots + a_{15}D_{11} + u_{ad}$$

where $D_1, D_2, \ldots, D_{11}$ are monthly dummy variables and u_{ad} is the normally distributed error term.

Bowman's time variable started with a value of 1 in January 1964 and continued to a value of 72 in December 1969. Bowman obtained the following estimation results for his linear demand model:

[1]G. T. Bowman, "Demand and Supply of Network Television Advertising," *Bell Journal of Economics*, Spring 1976.

Results of estimation of demand parameter

Demand (linear version):

P_t + 32.230 − 0.07434Q_t − 120.22U_t + 0.03200Y_t
(9.948) (0.02542) (81.884) (0.02592)

+ 4.8300 Jan + 4.9955 Feb + 4.3911 Mar + 2.8334 Apr
(1.8959) (1.8193) (1.5832) (0.98267)

− 2.5317 Jun − 4.2924 Jul − 4.5366 Aug + 2.5612 Sep
(0.58597) (0.58697) (0.68083) (0.53090)

+ 8.2292 Oct + 7.7572 Nov + 6.1515 Dec
(0.80353) (1.2611) (1.4441)

$R^2 = 0.943$

The numbers in parentheses are estimated standard errors.

Notes: 71 observations.

Price elasticity of demand $= \dfrac{-1}{\text{slope}}\, \dfrac{\bar{P}}{Q} = .924.$

DISCUSSION QUESTIONS 4.3

1. What does the price-elasticity estimate imply about the effect on network revenues of small decreases in the number of hours of programming?
2. Does the form of Bowman's demand equations bother you? What would you have preferred? What are the basic implications for interpreting results when price is the left-hand variable?
3. Noll, Peck, and McGowan argue that television is a cost-saving innovation. Therefore, they conclude that the demand elasticity for television should be high at higher prices and low at lower prices. Bowman doesn't get this kind of result; even when he uses a logarithmic function, his double log price elasticity is .73.
4. Note and comment on the fact that Bowman's price-elasticity values have a positive sign.

5

ROLE OF COSTS IN MANAGERIAL DECISION MAKING

Key Concepts

average costs
capacity
diminishing average returns
diminishing marginal returns
diminishing returns
economic supply
external economies
fixed costs
input
law of variable proportions
learning curve
least-cost output
long run
long-run costs
marginal cost

opportunity costs
planning context
production process
production run
returns to scale
scale
short run
social costs
statistical cost curves
total costs
total fixed costs
total variable costs
U-shaped cost curve
variable costs

What Is Ahead in This Chapter

The role of costs is crucial in managerial decisions. Yet despite the extraordinary advances in accounting in the past twenty-five years or so, cost measurement is far from simple. What are costs? When and how are they measured? Are long-run costs the same as short-run costs? Does the method of production make any significant difference?

These are the kinds of questions examined in this chapter. The focus is on relevant costs for a manager who has to decide what price to put on a product or service. There is a direct connection between costs, the method of production, and the relation between inputs and outputs. So, this chapter includes more than a set of definitions of the cost elements involved in price decisions. It also answers the question, How can the least-cost combination of inputs for a given output be worked out?

Measurement of Cost

For production purposes cost can be defined in any number of ways. From the accounting viewpoint, costs are outlays—not all of them cash—that arise in the production of goods and services. Accountants analyze cost elements such as direct material, direct labor, and expense. Direct materials are those that become a part of the product. Direct labor is based upon labor time involved in production. Other costs are expense or overhead, sometimes called "burden." Accountants concur that cost measurement should relate directly to the process of production.

Opportunity Costs

Economists agree with accountants generally about cost classifications, but economists stress some cost elements that normal accounting techniques do not pick up. These not-accounted-for costs are included under two general headings: opportunity costs and social costs. By opportunity costs is meant the cost of foregone choices or opportunities. Not only are direct costs to be taken into consideration in a production or pricing decision but so also are those other costs which would have been incurred had another decision been made. Unless the proposed decision is clearly superior to any other possible one or, at least, no worse, there is an opportunity cost. That opportunity cost is the difference between the lower costs in the best decision and the actual cost in the decision made. For example, when there is only so much space in high-sales-density zones in a department store, the use of this space for one sales effort involves the opportunity cost of not having used it for another promotion that could have produced even more profits. The decision of a firm to use retained earnings to finance plant expansion involves the opportunity cost or profit lost by not investing these funds in a better way—if there were a better way. The opportunity cost is thus one measure of the real cost of any production decision. Opportunity-cost thinking forces management to consider all alternatives.

Social Costs

Social costs are costs that are external to the firm but that nevertheless must be borne by society. For example, a paper-making firm in Fitchburg, Massachusetts, that uses a river as its source of water but, through pollution, reduces the quality of the water for drinking, recreational, or industrial usage imposes a loss upon that community. If Fitchburg builds a facility to clean the water somewhere farther downstream, then that loss becomes a measurable social cost. Fitchburg taxpayers have to cover the capital and operating costs of cleaning up the environment, and the municipal government would have to increase taxes on the paper company and other property owners. In the same way, business choices involving air or water pollution, highway utilization, and even unemployment include social costs.

The jewelry industry in and around Providence, Rhode Island, and the apparel industry in Philadelphia, among other industries with relatively low wages and highly seasonal production schedules, necessitate a heavy use of state unemployment compensation funds. Some economists have concluded that, in these cases, the full wage cost is borne in part by the state. The reasoning is that employees and employers alike know in advance the production schedules and adjust employment so as to obtain at least minimum qualifications for unemployment compensation. So that, even though these companies pay a portion of the unemployment cost through state taxes on payrolls, in fact, they are being subsidized by other contributors to the fund and by their employees. The wage cost to the companies is less than the social wage cost in these instances.

In all these cases a private firm or individual does not record as internal cost an outlay that must ultimately be met by someone else, usually the community as a whole.

Costs of Production

Production costs are determined by the amount of inputs used and by the prices of these inputs. Because the questions of how and whether certain inputs are used are important to an understanding of production costs, cost analysis always assumes

1. That there is a known way of combining inputs currently in use or to be used. This way of combining inputs is often called a "production function," to which we will turn in Chap. 6.
2. That the prices of inputs are known or knowable and that there may be a

relationship between prices to be paid for inputs and amount of inputs that will be used.
3. That every decision to use one input or one method of production involves a decision not to use another input or production method, so that a basic measure of cost is the value of what was rejected, directly or implicitly. This is the concept of opportunity cost.
4. That the focus of the analysis is a producing unit, often called a "business firm" (even though, in fact, we may be concentrating on one part of a firm), which makes one product type from inputs.

Cost Definitions

Total costs (TC) are the total money outlays by a firm for the inputs necessary to achieve a given level of output of a specific product (or type of product) in any production run. These total costs may be broken down into total fixed costs (TFC) and total variable costs (TVC). TFC are total money outlays by a firm for the fixed inputs used at a given level of output. Fixed inputs are those factors of production that are bought or hired in lump-sum amounts. Costs of fixed inputs do not vary with different levels of output during any given production run. Examples of fixed costs include rent or initial acquisition cost of land, buildings, machinery, equipment and facilities, interest on borrowed capital funds, property taxes, and security expenses. In short, TFC includes any monetary outlay which does not vary with the level of output for any production run.

TVC represents total money outlays for those inputs which do vary with the level of output in any given production run. TVC includes direct labor, direct materials, assignable heat, light, power, and similar variable costs. It follows that

$$TC = TFC + TVC$$

SB Athletic Products Company

In Table 5.1, we have an illustrative relationship among TC, TFC, and TVC, taken from an analysis in 1971 of production costs for SB Athletic Products Company, a manufacturer of sports equipment.

It should be noted that, when production is at zero, total fixed costs are $156,400, so that at zero production

$$TC = TFC$$

A generalized graph of the relationship among TC, TFC, and TVC is presented in Fig. 5.1.

Average total costs are determined for different production levels by dividing the total costs at that production level by the amount produced. In

Table 5.1   Schedule of total costs of basketballs for SB Athletic Products Company

Output, thousands	TFC thousands of $	+	TVC thousands of $	=	TC thousands of $
64.4	156.4		329.7		486.1
70.4	156.4		350.6		507.0
79.3	156.4		376.7		533.1
83.7	156.4		387.5		543.9
98.4	156.4		421.2		577.6
107.2	156.4		439.5		595.9
113.7	156.4		458.2		614.6
121.7	156.4		486.8		643.2
132.3	156.4		536.1		692.5
143.7	156.4		599.2		755.6

Table 5.2 you can see that, at 79,300 basketballs, the average total cost is $6.72. The average total cost formula is

$$atc = \frac{TC}{q}$$

where q = amount produced.

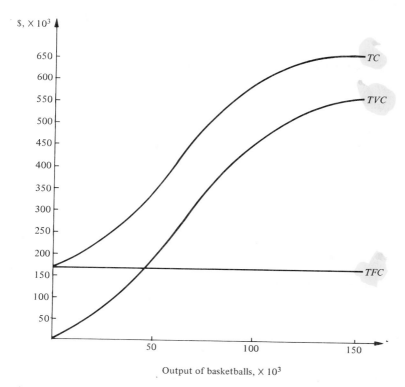

Output of basketballs, $\times 10^3$

Figure 5.1. Relationship between *TC*, *TFC*, *TVC*

Table 5.2 Schedule of average and marginal costs of basketballs for SB Athletic Products Company

Output, thousands	afc $	+	avc $	=	atc $	mc $
64.4	2.43		5.12		7.55	
70.4	2.22		4.98		7.20	3.44
79.3	1.97		4.75		6.72	2.93
83.7	1.87		4.63		6.50	2.45
98.4	1.59		4.28		5.87	2.29
107.2	1.46		4.10		5.56	2.08
113.7	1.38		4.03		5.41	2.88
121.7	1.29		4.00		5.29	3.58
132.3	1.18		4.06		5.24	4.65
143.7	1.09		4.17		5.25	5.53

Average total fixed costs are obtained by dividing TFC by amount produced at any given production level (at 79,300 basketballs, $afc = \$1.97$). The average fixed cost formula is

$$afc = \frac{TFC}{q}$$

Average total variable costs are obtained by dividing TVC by the amount produced at any given production (at 79,300 basketballs, $avc = \$4.75$). The average variable cost formula is

$$avc = \frac{TVC}{q}$$

Of course, if $TC = TFC + TVC$, then $atc = afc + avc$. Figure 5.2 shows a graph of these relationships.

Total Cost Variations

Any conclusion that is valid based on an analysis of total costs is also valid based on average costs. Total costs provide a good starting point for an analysis of the results of a firm's operations. Such costs are not only measures of the burdens which must be reduced to a minimum but they are also indicators of the positive contribution to the profits of the firm. Total costs, then, are measures of the firm's resources when entering income-producing activities. Therefore, they are fundamental to an understanding of the nature of the firm's operations. But these total costs can be divided into those key categories which indicate the pace of utilization of the firm's resources. We may thus have, for example,

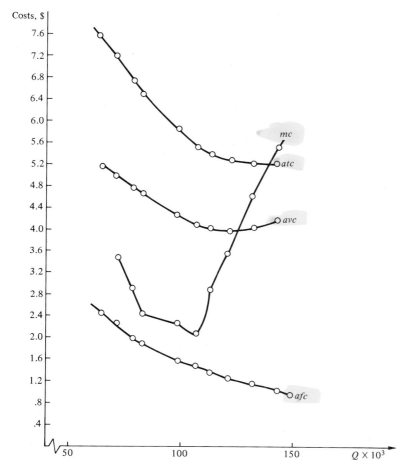

Figure 5.2. SB Athletic Products Company. Basketball production costs: *afc, avc, atc, mc.*

Total labor costs = average or unit labor costs × level of output
Total rental costs = average or unit rental costs × factors such as level of
    output

Not only is the total of all costs a measure of the utilization of the resources to the firm but the composition of or proportion between cost elements is an indication of the nature of decisions the firm must make. For example, if total fixed costs constitute a large proportion of total costs, then it is clear that as that firm varies output the unit fixed costs will dominate the emerging cost picture. This implies that for such a product a firm will have decreasing unit costs up to full capacity utilization.

In contrast, a production run for which the proportion between total variable costs and total costs is very large is one in which the behavior of variable costs will determine the cost patterns of production. In this case, it does not necessarily follow that costs will be increasing over the range of capacity.

Marginal Costs

The last column in Table 5.2, the *mc* column, gives the marginal costs of producing additional basketballs. For example, the increase in total costs from increasing basketball production from 64,400 to 70,400 is $20,660. Divide the $20,660 by the 6000 additional basketballs, and you have the marginal cost per ball, or $3.44. The behavior of total costs over the range of a production run can thus be measured by the changes in marginal cost. The marginal cost curve in Fig. 5.2, then, is a derivative of the total cost curve in Fig. 5.1. You will notice that the marginal cost of basketballs declines through a production level of about 107,000 basketballs. Then the marginal cost begins to climb rapidly, reaching $3.58 in the neighborhood of a production level of 122,000 basketballs.

The simple formula for calculating marginal costs is

$$mc = \frac{\Delta TC}{\Delta q} = \frac{TC_2 - TC_1}{q_2 - q_1}$$

where Δ = "small change in"

TC_1, TC_2 = two different total cost amounts corresponding to two different production levels

q_2, q_1 = two production levels for which TC_1 and TC_2 are determined

The marginal cost of 122,000 basketballs is higher than marginal costs in the neighborhood of 70,000. SB management on this evidence knows that to increase production beyond 107,000 involves significantly rising costs.

Relationship between Marginal and Average Total Costs

Figure 5.3 presents the general functional relationship between average and marginal costs. That relationship may be summarized as follows:

When *atc* = *mc*, *atc* is at a minimum.
When *atc* > *mc*, *atc* is falling.
When *atc* < *mc*, *atc* is rising.

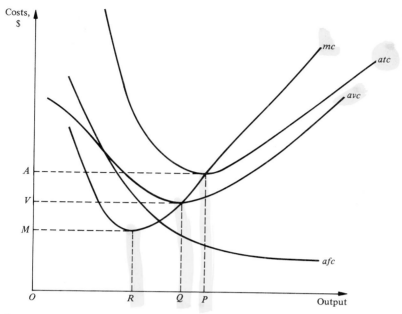

Figure 5.3. Typical cost curves.
Output:
  At *R*, *mc* is at a minimum
  At *Q*, *avc* is at a minimum (and = *mc*)
  At *P*, *atc* is at a minimum (and = *mc*)
The vertical distance between *atc* and *avc* is *afc*

It is also true that

When *avc* = *mc*, *avc* is at a minimum.
When *avc* > *mc*, *avc* is falling.
When *avc* < *mc*, *avc* is rising.

But note that *avc* attains its minimum at a smaller output level than that at which *atc* attains its minimum. The *afc* curve, however, bears no relationship to the *mc* curve and, in fact, is a rectangular hyperbola.

Marginal and Average Cost Relationships at SB Athletic Products Company

Notice that for the SB Athletic Products Company (see Fig. 5.2) the equality between *atc* and *mc* takes place at about a basketball output level of 140,000. At 126,000, *avc* is equal to *mc*. As long as *mc* is less than *atc* or *avc*, *atc* and *avc* continue to fall. They only begin to rise after each in turn becomes larger than *mc*.

Marginal costs are the changes in costs that result from changes in output levels in a production run. Technically speaking, the use of the term "marginal" implies that the production cost relation is continuous and that the space over which the decision is made is very small. In actual practice, such a decision space is frequently quite large, and production is changed from a low to a high level. Accountants often call these "incremental costs" rather than marginal costs.

SB management is now in a position to analyze the impact of production decisions on the behavior of costs. It is clear that average costs vary over the possible production run in a kind of U-shaped curve. This means that the minimum average cost occurs at about 140,000 basketballs. The minimum average variable costs occur in the neighborhood of 126,000 basketballs. But all decisions to increase production beyond 107,000 basketballs will mean increased marginal costs. Marginal costs are decision costs. They are the real decision costs since they tell SB management what the result would be in cost terms of a decision to increase production. So long as the essence of the decision facing SB management is the cost of moving from one production level to another, marginal cost information is going to be very helpful.

Analysis of Production Costs at Unitechnology, Inc.

Unitechnology, Inc., is a small firm producing gundrills. The inputs which the firm purchases are bought at prices reflecting market conditions at the time of purchase. Unitechnology management thinks that gundrill technology can be summarized in terms of five possible input combinations (Table 5.3A).

Now, if capital in the current market costs $5 per machine-hour and labor costs $10, then the costs of these five processes or input combinations are as shown in Table 5.3B.

In Table 5.3, it is clear that the least-cost process is UC. And if management chooses the least costly process the production cost of gundrills for Unitechnology is $45 per 100.

This cost of course is tied to a specific process. If input prices change (e.g., the machine-hour prices fall while labor-hour prices either rise or remain constant), it will likely mean a change not only in cost but also in the production

Table 5.3A

Process	Capital, machine-hours	Labor, worker-hours	Output, number of gundrills
UA	10	1	100
UB	8	1.3	100
UC	5	2	100
UD	3	3.3	100
UE	2	5	100

Table 5.3B

Process	Output costs/100 gundrills $(P_K = \$5,^* \ P_L = \$10\dagger)$, $
UA	60
UB	53
UC	45
UD	48
UE	60

$^* P_K$ = machine-hour costs.
$\dagger P_L$ = labor-hour costs.

process selected. For example, if labor costs fall to $5 and machine-hour costs rise to $10, then UE becomes the least costly process for making gundrills as Table 5.4 shows.

In the choice among these five production processes, which are alike in that each can produce 100 gundrills but unlike in that they have different total output costs, it is the input costs which determine which is the least-cost process. A change in input costs causes management to shift from one process to another in a search for the best, that is, the least, cost. Of course, the least-cost process is also that process which yields the most output per unit of input at input costs.

Another way of showing how to minimize production costs, given input costs and a choice among different processes, is shown in Fig. 5.4. Along a single curve, called an "isoproduct curve" because it shows different ways of producing 100 gundrills, are such processes as UA, UB, UC, UD, and UE. But observe that UA and UE also lie on an "isocost line," along which the costs of production are $60. This $60 line runs from a point on the K axis (where $60 buys at the given input prices twelve machine hours and no labor hours) to a point on the L axis (where $60 buys zero machine hours and six labor hours). Obviously, any isocost line, at those input prices, parallel to but below the $60 isocost line is that isocost line which is just tangent to the 100 gundrill isoproduct curve at UC. Thus, given the $10 per machine-hour price and the $5 per labor-hour price, UC is that process for making 100 gundrills which has the lowest cost. You can infer from this figure that any set of production processes for making, say, 150 gundrills would describe an isoproduct curve lying above

Table 5.4

Process	Output costs/100 gundrills $(P_K = \$10, \ P_L = \$5)$, $
UA	105
UB	86.50
UC	60
UD	46.50
UE	45

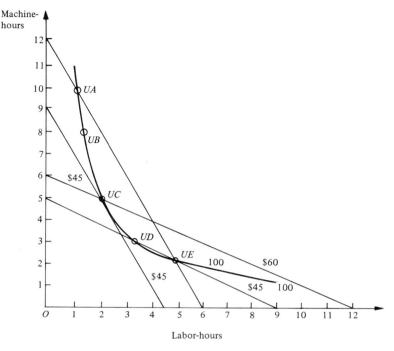

Figure 5.4. Least-cost production.

and to the right of the curve for 100 gundrills. You can also infer that any gundrill isoproduct curve for, say, 60 drills would lie to the left and below the 100-gundrill curve.

Change in Input Prices

In Fig. 5.4 we can also see what happens when the prices of the inputs change. We get a different set of isocost lines, the slopes of which reflect the relative prices of the input.

Marginal Rate of Substitution

The slope of the isocost line is the ratio of the input prices. By the same token, the slope of the isoproduct curve is a measure of the substitution of one input for another as we shift from one process to another. The technical name for this isoproduct curve slope is "marginal rate of substitution" (MRS). MRS is obtained by dividing a small change in machine hours (one input) by a small change in labor hours (another input). In general, then, we can tell Unitechnology that its maximum production efficiency will be obtained when for any one of its gundrill processes the *MRS* of the isoproduct curve is just equal to the ratio of the input prices.

Meaning of Production Process and Scale Changes

A production process, as we have been using the term so far, has meant a single combination of inputs for which there is a single possible output. Thus, we called UA, UB, UC, UD, and UE production processes. To be more general, we need a different definition which allows us to vary the inputs in order to vary the outputs. So, if a production process is all those combinations of inputs which will produce a given kind of product at many levels of output as the inputs vary, we can call the changes in the inputs which yield changes in the output "changes in scale." A choice among different production processes does not involve a change in scale. A choice among different levels of output for the same production process does involve a change in scale. Variations in cost can involve a change in (or a choice among) production processes, a change in scale of a given production process, or both.

Capacity

The production capacity of a firm for a given product is the maximum range of production-process choices. It is determined by fixed cost elements such as plant size, machine capacity, and land available. It may also be affected by limits on the utilization of some of the variable inputs such as a restriction to a forty-hour week. A change in production capacity is a scale change such that there is a shift from one set of fixed cost elements to a new or different set of fixed cost elements.

Planning Context: Meaning of Short Run and Long Run

An analysis of decisions about how much to produce and at what cost is undertaken against a background of at least two possible planning contexts. If we assume that management wishes to know how both total and average costs will vary as output varies within the current capacity of the firm, then the economic term for that planning context is the "short run." The short-run planning context covers all those possible decisions about output which do not involve enlarging the plant or changing the size, scale, or capacity of the operation.

In contrast, if what management wants is to compare costs of production at different sizes, scales, or capacities of production facilities, then this is called a "long-run" analysis. While there is, to be sure, some artificiality in the distinctions between these two planning contexts, it is nonetheless important to keep in mind what economic cost analysis is all about. Given an understanding of relationships among various possible inputs, economic cost analysis seeks to explain how costs vary (1) in the short run, with respect to changes in the level of utilization of the capacity of existing plant facilities; and (2) in the long run, with respect to changes in the capacity of these facilities.

Law of Variable Proportions

Back to Unitechnology again. Suppose all the firm's production processes were alike in that each requires the same level of capital input, 10 machine-hours. These processes, U_a through U_m, are listed in Table 5.5. As the amount of labor-hour input increases over the range of the processes, the output increases. Thus, over this range of processes, capital input is fixed and labor input is varied so that the choice among processes (or, what is the same thing, the choice as to output level) is a short-run choice. Note that, over this range of production processes, not only does the labor input vary but the proportion between the fixed and the variable input changes. What is called the "law of variable proportions" concerns what happens to the total output as at least one input is held constant while one (or more) inputs are varied (with scale or capacity of the operation unchanged).

Diminishing Returns

One interpretation of the law of variable proportions holds that there is likely to be a diminishing average return to the increased labor input. This is the "principle of diminishing returns," as stated by Alfred Marshall, an English economist who contributed much to economics early in this century. In Fig. 5.5

Table 5.5   Unitechnology: Alternate gundrill processes

	Inputs			(Average product) Output/ units of labor	(Marginal product) Change in output/ change in units of labor
Process	Capital, machine-hours	Labor, worker-hours	Output		
U_a	10	1	100	100.0	100
U_b	10	1.5	226	150.7	252
U_c	10	2	290	145.0	128
U_d	10	3	380	126.7	90
U_e	10	4	443	110.8	63
U_f	10	5	490	98.0	47
U_g	10	6	525	87.5	35
U_h	10	7	551	78.7	26
U_i	10	8	569	71.1	18
U_j	10	9	580	64.4	11
U_k	10	10	583	58.3	3
U_l	10	11	580	52.7	−3
U_m	10	12	569	47.4	−11

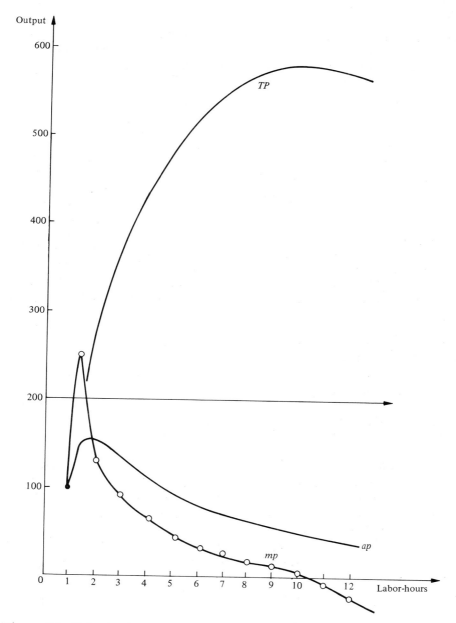

Figure 5.5. Unitechnology, Inc.: How output for production varies as labor input is increased in the short run (capacity unchanged).

TP = total product (output)
ap = average product
mp = marginal product

is a picture of how Unitechnology's output would vary as more labor is used. The average product—output per unit of labor—increases between processes U_a and U_b, where total output rises from 100 to 226 gundrills. However, average product declines from U_c through U_n. Process U_b could be called the "point of diminishing average returns to labor."

Another statement of the law of variable proportions, the principle of diminishing marginal returns, holds that if the quantity of one input is increased by equal increments while the quantity of at least one other input is held constant, then somewhere in the output range output will be increasing at a decreasing rate of increase. Put differently, there will be diminishing marginal returns to the increasing input. In Table 5.5, the marginal product of labor— change in total product brought about by a change in labor-hour input—rises from U_a through U_b, then declines throughout the rest of the range of process

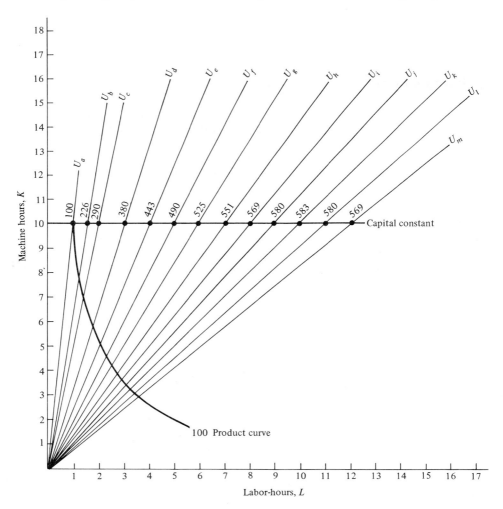

Figure 5.6. Comparison of fixed output with fixed input.

change, as labor inputs increase. Process U_b is the point of diminishing marginal returns. But note that process U_k is the last one for which the marginal product of labor is positive. The choice of either process U_l or U_m would mean that an increase in labor input had decreased total output. In this context, while U_l and U_m are feasible processes, Unitechnology's management is unlikely to choose them.

Figure 5.6 shows the relationship between isoproduct curves and different processes. Each line through the origin is a production process. We can see how much is produced by each process with capital input constant by reading along the capital input–constant line. Process U_a produces 100 gundrills when capital input is 10 machine-hours. Process U_b produces 226 gundrills with the same capital input. And so on along the capital input–constant line. The 100-gundrill isoproduct curve swings down to the right connecting all those points on each successive production-process ray at which the gundrill output is 100. Of course, we could also trace a 226-isoproduct curve or a 380-isoproduct curve as well.

Changes in Scale

The law of variable proportions, as we have noted, deals with a choice among different production processes. It shows that if there is a fixed cost element in the production process, returns to varying inputs will ultimately decline. Scale changes, by contrast, occur when all the inputs are changed, when there is no fixed cost element. Yet, just as there are diminishing returns when scale or capacity remains unchanged, there can also be diminishing returns when scale is changed. "Diminishing returns to scale" means that for any production process, as we increase both inputs, the increase in total output would be decreasing. But, as Table 5.6 illustrates, there can be constant returns to scale as well as increasing returns to scale. Just as the empirical basis for the law of variable proportions is weak, just so is there some question about the meaning

Table 5.6 Unitechnology: How output changes with scale changes

Input changes		Decreasing returns to scale	Constant returns to scale	Increasing returns to scale
Machine-hour	Labor-hour			
2	.2	64	20	48
3	.3	72	30	51
4	.4	79	40	55
5	.5	85	50	60
6	.6	90	60	66
7	.7	94	70	73
8	.8	97	80	81
9	.9	99	90	90
10	1.0	100	100	100

of returns to scale.[1] But we will soon see how these concepts affect cost functions.

Cost Functions

A cost function traces the relationship between production output and its cost. We have noted the existence of total cost functions, average cost functions, and marginal cost functions. And we have discovered some of the relationships among these different cost functions. But what is the relationship among cost functions, variable proportions, and scale factors? What is the typical cost curve (see Fig. 5.7)?

To begin, let us examine a U-shaped average cost curve such as a cost function for SB Athletic Products Company. What this function shows is that while average production costs are high at low production levels, they decline as output increases in any production run. But they also stop declining at some determinable output level and begin to rise again. Keep in mind that this U-shaped average cost curve is a short-run function and that, therefore, there is no scale effect involved in its construction, only a variable input proportion effect.

Bela Gold[2] has pointed out that a U-shaped average total cost function depends on three cost elements:

[1]But see F. T. Moore, "Economies of Scale: Some Statistical Evidence," *Quarterly Journal of Economics, 73*:232–245, May 1959.
[2]Bela Gold, *Explorations in Managerial Economics*, New York, Basic Books, 1971, p. 140 ff.

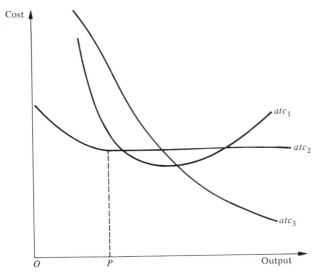

Figure 5.7. Which is the typical average cost curve?
  atc = U-shaped cost curve
  atc_2 = constant average cost after op
  atc_3 = declining average costs

1. Average total fixed costs which are rectangularly hyperbolic, that is, they decline for any production run up to capacity.
2. Average total variable costs which, if not constant, follow a shallow dish-shaped pattern.
3. Fixed cost elements which are substantial compared with variable cost elements.

A distinction may be made between the effect of fixed cost elements in setting the capacity of the production run and the effect of the fixed cost elements in limiting the effectiveness of increasing variable inputs. Spreading the capacity costs over larger and larger production amounts lowers the average fixed cost and reduces its impact on average total costs. But the fact of the capacity limit means that increasing amounts of variable input are subject to diminishing returns. The former leads to the declining phase of the U-shaped cost curve and the latter helps explain its rising phase.

Not all firms, however, would have U-shaped average cost curves for their products. Nor would all products of a firm have U-shaped average cost functions. It is common to find constant cost functions. Under constant costs average total costs are at the same level throughout a production run. This is tantamount to saying that management can determine the average cost of a production run at any level of output.

It is also common to find, for some kinds of products, declining average costs over a production run. The capacity–cost-spreading effect extends to capacity. This is the case when a production process has an overwhelmingly large fixed input component.

Bela Gold's research on empirical cost functions displays a broad range of cost functions, but he found a dominance of rising average total cost functions. However, as he adjusted for real cost changes over time, he found that deflation by appropriate index numbers increased the proportion of cost curves which had a negative slope, that is, exhibited declining costs. Perhaps the most significant outcome of Gold's empirical cost function research was his failure to find a typical average total cost curve.

Many attempts have been made to establish the shape of cost curves by theoretical arguments. For example, the shape of the short-run average cost function is asserted to be deducible from the principles of diminishing returns. But the law of diminishing returns does not necessarily follow even from what is required for most cost functions. Perhaps all that we can deduce is the principle of diminishing average product. The most common alternative to the U-shaped cost function is a constant marginal cost function over wide ranges of output for any production run. It is used by cost accountants and is supported by many investigators of firm cost behavior.

Economic Supply

The concept of economic supply proceeds logically from the concepts of cost curves and cost functions. If marginal costs are the decision costs for firms, then the economic supply for any firm is that amount of production for which market prices cover marginal cost. The basis of the economic supply curve is the assumption that a potential supplier will respond to any price that covers the relevant production costs by making available in the market all units produced up to the last one for which cost is covered. Marginal costs are relevant costs because they measure the cost of increasing production from one production level to another. Obviously, if marginal costs are rising, then the supply curve will also be rising. Suppose, though, that, rather than rising or remaining constant, marginal costs were decreasing so that the supply curve fell through much of its range. Each additional unit of production would then cost less to produce than did the last unit and the average costs of increasing production would fall.

In order to have a falling supply curve, several things must be true. Fixed costs must be significantly large. Observe, for example, that when the initial investment is very large—like railway track and equipment or a multi-KWH generator—the average variable costs of producing a unit of service will contain a larger amount of user cost or depreciation than out-of-the-pocket cost elements. If we assume that these user costs are allocated on the basis of total user costs per units produced, then the average user costs will fall as output increases.

External Economies

Decreasing cost/supply curves frequently involve what economists call "external economies." These are effects that arise from the size of any one firm or the number of firms in an industry. A large railroad might take so large a share of the production of things it needed that it and smaller railways would find the cost of these necessary factors dropping. If a large number of airlines created such a large demand for, say, airline pilots that it paid for them to set up a school for pilots, then the direct as well as the social costs of pilot training would decline.

Of course, all supply curves must ultimately rise somewhere along their length. To assume otherwise would be to overlook the basic scarcity of resources. Whatever the cost function, the concern of the economist is with those cost elements that enter into management decision making. If we assume that these decision costs are used rationally, then we gain some idea of the supply characteristics of production. These supply characteristics trace the response of producers to changes in market prices and give the amount of product likely to be made available in the market at each successive possible price.

Long-Run Costs

The analysis of long-run costs is in a planning context in which all cost elements, including fixed cost elements, are to be considered variable. Whereas, in a short-run cost analysis we had to face the implications of fixed costs, limitations of scale, diminishing returns to any given input with scale limited, and the effects of capacity utilization, in a long-run planning context the focus is on that size or scale of operations which is optimal.

There are at least three kinds of long-run cost approaches. One is to regard the long-run cost problem of a firm as a choice among alternative plant sizes. The most efficient among these plant sizes is that which, given cost and demand information, minimizes cost. Another approach is to examine the effect of expanding a known operation by enlarging plant size, assuming essentially the same techniques. The question is that of determining whether it pays to expand. Finally, there is the much more complex long-run problem of adjusting to changes in techniques, changes in market demand, and changes in markets themselves as well as in costs of inputs.

Long-Run Planning for Unitechnology, Inc.

Suppose that Unitechnology has decided to expand output to a level not attainable within the current capacity of the firm. How does Unitechnology choose the correct amount of capital investment in plant and facilities to minimize total costs at the expanded size? One way to proceed would be for management to draw up short-run average cost curves for each of a number of possible plant sizes. In Fig. 5.8, based on Table 5.7, we have four such average cost curves, including one for the current size or scale of operations. The minimum average cost for Unitechnology's current facilities is $19.80 per gundrill at a production run of 640 gundrills. In effect, the economic capacity of the current facility is 640 since any increase in production beyond that level would be accompanied by faster-rising marginal costs than average costs. Alternative plant size 1 has an economic capacity of 1500 gundrills, of which the average cost is $18.80. Alternative plant size 2 has an economic capacity of 3300 units at an average cost of $16.70, and the economic capacity for alternative plant size 3 is 6600, where average cost would be $16.

Each alternative requires a given amount of capital outlay. The decision as to which size to select will depend not only on the long-run declining average cost of production over the range of available alternative plant sizes but also

Table 5.7   Unitechnology: Output and average costs for different plant sizes

Current size		Size 1		Size 2		Size 3	
Output	Average cost	Output	Average cost	Output	Average cost	Output	Average cost
320	$23.50	640	$22.10	1500	$21.00	2900	$19.00
480	20.90	1000	20.90	2200	18.00	4400	17.00
640	19.80	1500	18.80	3300	16.70	6600	16.00
880	20.80	1800	20.00	4000	19.00	7200	18.00

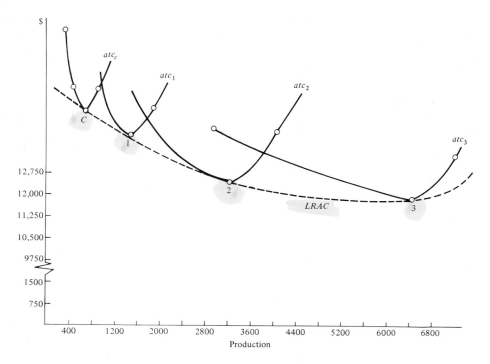

Figure 5.8. Unitechnology, Inc.: Long-run average cost curve with short-run average cost curves for four different capacity levels.

upon the estimated likely demand for output. Indeed, it was an increase in demand for gundrills which had caused Unitechnology to consider whether and how to expand. Looking closely at the cost data for each alternative size, it is apparent that Unitechnology could produce 880 units in its current facilities at a lower average cost than the same production level would cost in plant size 1. However, 1000 units could be produced for less in plant size 1 than in the current facility. Thus plant size 1 and its accompanying required capital outlay would be appropriate only if the demand for gundrills were in excess of about 900 units. In a similar fashion, the output level at which it would be appropriate to choose either of the other two plant sizes can be determined. Clearly, then, the decision as to the cost-minimizing amount of capital will depend on demand.

Long-Run Cost Curves

Long-run costs are total costs associated with different scales or plant sizes. In Table 5.8 are the total costs for each of the four plant sizes of Unitechnology at each of several different output levels. The development of long-run total costs and of a long-run total cost curve would involve moving from, say, 640

Table 5.8   Unitechnology: Total costs at different plant sizes

TC_c		TC_1		TC_2		TC_3	
320	$ 7,520	640	$14,144	1500	$31,500	2900	$ 55,100
480	10,032	1000	20,900	2200	39,600	4400	74,800
640	12,672	1500	28,200	3300	55,110	6600	105,600
880	18,304	1800	36,000	4000	76,000	7200	129,600

gundrills at a total cost of $12,672 for the current plant size, to an output of 1500 gundrills at a total cost of $28,200 for plant size 1. Then plant size 2 would produce 3300 units at a total cost of $55,110 and, finally, plant size 3, 6600 units at a total cost of $105,600. This long total cost curve thus connects the total costs associated with the lower-cost output at each plant size.

The long-run total cost curve (LTC) is constructed to summarize the relationship between the quantity to be produced and the total cost at each possible production level over the range of alternative plant sizes. If returns to scale are constant, then long-run total costs will rise by an amount proportional to the increase in output. If returns to scale are decreasing, then long-run total costs will be increasing at a rate greater than the rate of increase in output. If returns to scale are increasing, long-run costs will be increasing at a slower rate than that of output. In this instance, returns to scale are decreasing so that LTC rises at a rate slower than output.

Once we have LTC, it is not hard to work out the long-run average cost curve ($LRAC$) and the long-run marginal cost curve (LMC). $LRAC$ is an envelope curve in the sense that it envelops all the short-run average cost curves ($SACs$). It does this by connecting the various $SACs$ by a series of tangencies between the $LRAC$ and the $SACs$. Suppose, for example, as in Fig. 5.9, which is a generalized picture of the relationship between $LRAC$, the $SACs$, the short-run marginal costs ($SMCs$), and LMC, that we have five alternative plant sizes. Each such plant size, of course, reflects a feasible production level for which there is assumed to be an adequate demand forecast.

You will note that as we move from SAC_1 through SAC_3, the minimum average costs decline, meaning that there are economies of scale from plant size 1 through plant size 2 to plant size 3. If $LRAC$ is drawn to envelop these three plant sizes, $LRAC$ will be tangent to SAC_1 and SAC_2 to the left of the minimum-cost point for each SAC. However, since plant sizes 4 and 5 involve minimum costs successively higher than that at plant size 3, plant size 3 is the most efficient size in terms of minimum cost. $LRAC$ will thus be tangent to SAC_3 right at the bottom of SAC_3. Then, $LRAC$ will swing around and begin to climb. As it climbs, $LRAC$ will be tangent to SAC_4 and SAC_5 at points to the right of their minimum-cost levels.

Recapitulating, $LRAC$ will fall through the range of plant-size alternatives for which there are economies of scale, and $LRAC$ will rise through those plant-size alternatives for which there are diseconomies of scale. The minimum

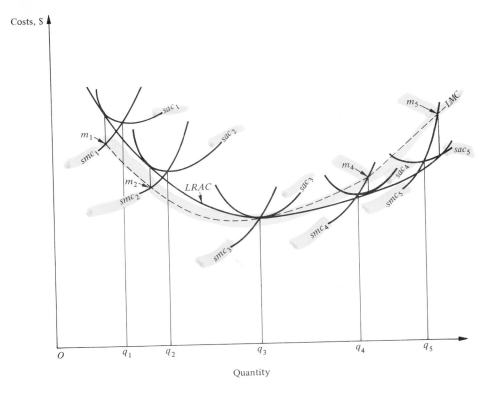

Figure 5.9. *LRAC* and *LMC* in relation to *sac* and *smc*.

point of *LRAC* is where it is just tangent to the most efficient plant size, in this case, *SAC₃*. If there had been constant returns to scale so that there were no economies of scale, then *LRAC* would have been a line parallel to the output axis. That *LRAC* would be tangent to a series of plant sizes, all of which would have the same minimum-cost level. For the Unitechnology case, at least through plant size 3, there are increasing returns to scale, as shown in Fig. 5.8.

To derive the long-run marginal cost curve, *LMC*, here's a geometrical technique that will work. When there are economies of scale, take a point on *SMC* directly below the tangency between *LRAC* and *SRC*. That will be a point on *LMC*. In this way, points M_1 and M_2 are found. At the minimum point on *SRC₃*, *LMC* will cut *LRAC* from below. Then, for *SRC₄* and *SRC₅*, that point on *SMC* directly above the point of tangency between *LRAC* and *SRC* will be a point on *LMC*. This is how points M_4 and M_5 on *LMC* were derived. The long-run marginal costs are, then, the costs of moving from one alternative size to another. You will notice that minimum *LMC* is the same as minimum *LRAC* and indeed the same as the minimum point on the most efficient *SRC*. If we know one of the following—the most efficient *SRC*, the lowest point on *LRAC*, or the point where $LRAC = LMC$—we have defined the best alternative plant size, given the availability of adequate demand.

However, the concept of "bestness" must be treated with some care. Obviously, if demand is greater than could be met efficiently by plant size 3, then the firm should select a larger alternative plant size, even if there were diseconomies of scale. Why? Because to continue to use plant size 3 would involve an SAC for plant size 3 significantly higher than the comparable SAC for plant size 4. Thus there is no reason a priori why a firm should not continue to increase the scale of operations in response to increasing demand even if there are diseconomies of scale. At least, in cost terms and without consideration of the implications of resource allocation, there is no reason for the most efficient plant size to be the most economic size, given the demand. Here is a paradox for which cost reasoning has no answer.

Economists call economies of scale "internal economies." That is, these are economies which accrue to a firm and presumably to its customers. There are external economies as well.

Externalities

The external economies situation is one in which an increase in a firm's production produces benefits—in terms of costs and revenues—that accrue to other firms and individuals. This phenomenon may arise in at least two ways. Take the case of a textile firm that as it expands, creates the need for training textile engineers. Obviously this training of textile workers at all levels of technical and managerial skills makes possible the creation of new textile firms and, indeed, a more efficient industry overall.

But there is more to externalities than that. Textile machinery suppliers, textile wholesalers, textile educators, textile bankers, and textile transport firms will find that they can supply the necessary services to a larger industrial output at reduced unit costs—assuming, of course, economies of scale in these services. This will mean even lower costs to all firms in the industry. The problem, though, at least in part, is that the benefits generated by the first firm accrue increasingly to other firms. Indeed, the first firm may derive little additional benefit from these externalities. That, however, is not likely.

It isn't all peaches and cream, to be sure. There are some detrimental externalities, such as increasing air and water pollution, increasing urbanization as well as an increasing shift of resources from agriculture, fishing, and even the arts and music to textile making. Just as important, there may be detrimental economies of consumption. As we have shown above, there is no a priori reason for any firm to choose the most efficient size, since, as demand increases, demand would cover costs of production and associated costs of scale increases. Yet, consumers might be induced to increase consumption because of a keeping-up-with-the-Joneses approach to demand inducement. One consumer is affecting another consumer and the result is an increase in demand which may—just may, not that it necessarily will—cause an uneconomic use of the nation's resources. In view of the now-obvious limits on energy resources, there may be reason to question whether or not there are detrimental consumer externalities of some importance. The fact that economists speak of internal or external economies does not permit the complete inference that they always know the best level of output.

Measuring Economies of Scale

Using cost information or cost functions to estimate scale effects is one approach by which scale can be determined and its effect separated from the data. In such regulated industries as electricity and natural gas, where the quantity and price of the outputs are determined exogenously (i.e., output quantity and price depend on factors beyond the direct control of the company itself), cost functions are estimated for plants of different sizes. It is inferred that the differences in average costs reflect differences in scale.

An alternative way of estimating the likely or probable scale effects is to work out a relationship between size of plant and profit rate. Sometimes, the same kind of result is sought by correlating plant size with market share of the firm in the industry. It is believed that if larger plants have higher profit rates than smaller plants, then there are scale effects such that they could be regarded as economies of scale. By the same token, if, over time, a plant is able to increase its share of the market, it is inferred that there are economies of scale. However, an alternative explanation of these results might be that they show not the scale economies but market power or the monopoly position of the firms studied.

Still another way of estimating scale economies is to obtain cross-section comparisons of per capita value added in different industries. If in a survey across many nations it is found that per capita value added increases in a given industry in close correlation with increases in indices of market size such as population or per capita gross national product, it is inferred that there are economies of scale. The basic problem with this kind of analysis is one of identification. Given the range of data being used, it is possible that there were other explanations of what was observed. Probably results from analysis of per capita value added should not be used as evidence of economies of scale.

The approach used by engineers is much more promising. Suppose that C_a and C_b are the costs of two machines A and B and Q_a and Q_b are their rated capacities; then

$$C_b = C_a \left(\frac{Q_b}{Q_a} \right)^s$$

This engineering rule says that the additional cost of machine B, $C_b \geqq C_a$, is given by the increase in capacity, $Q_b \geqq Q_a$, raised to the power s. In other words, the increase in capital cost for the new machine is less than the increase in the capacity obtained. This engineer's rule generally uses .6 as the value of s, so that cost varies as capacity varies to roughly the .6 power.

A value of $s = 0.6$ means that there are economies of scale. A value of 1 implies no economies of scale or, what is the same thing, constant returns to scale. If $s > 1$, then there are diseconomies of scale.

Moore generalized this engineering rule as

$$C = aQ^s$$

where

C = capital costs or outlays
Q = capacity measured in output terms
a, s = parameters to be estimated

In logarithmic form, a linear relationship is obtained,

$$\log C = \log a + s \log Q$$

In Table 5.9 are estimates of the value of s in a number of different engineering and economic research analytical studies.

Table 5.9 Estimates of economies of scale (value of s)

Industry, product of process	Chilton	Haldi & Whitcomb	Manne	Moore	OECD	Silber-ston	UN
Aluminum ingots	0.90	0.72–0.87	0.77–0.90	0.92–1.0			
Bread						0.62	
Cement	0.70		0.54–0.68	0.77–0.61		0.77	0.64
Chlorine soda		0.75	0.77				0.76–0.80
Detergents						0.74	
Ethylene						0.62	0.54
Magnesium	0.62						
Gasoline	0.51	0.71–0.83				0.66	
Pulp and paper		0.74–0.98			0.82		
Rubber	0.82	0.78–1.33		1.10			
Styrene	0.53	0.65–0.75		0.90			0.76
Sulfuric acid	0.68–0.91	0.66–0.90		0.80		0.75	0.65–0.80
Vegetable oil		0.70			0.46		0.40

Sources: C. H. Chilton, "Six-tenths Factor Applies to Complete Plant Cost," *Chemical Engineering,* April 1950; J. Haldi and D. Whitcomb, "Economies of Scale in Industrial Plants," *Journal of Political Economy,* August 1967; A. S. Manne (ed.), *Investments for Capacity Expansion,* Cambridge, Mass., M.I.T., 1967; F. T. Moore, "Economies of Scale: Some Statistical Evidence," *Quarterly Journal of Economics,* May 1959; OECD, *Industrial Profiles: Manual of Industrial Project Analysis in Developing Countries,* Paris, 1968; A. Silberston, "Economies of Scale in Theory and Practice," *Economic Journal,* March 1972; United Nations, various sources including: "Pre-investment Data for the Cement Industry," *Studies in the Economics of Industry,* 1963; FAO, *State of Food and Agriculture,* Rome, 1966; "Plant Size and Economies of Scale," *Industrialization and Productivity,* December 1964.

The studies summarized in Table 5.9 do reveal that the engineering rule of 0.6 for the value of s is a good general statement. Nonetheless, there is considerable variation around that value. The higher the value of s, the less the extent of economies of scale. Rubber and aluminum did show evidence of possible diseconomies of scale. It should, of course, be remembered that various methods of estimation and the quality of the data may themselves account for the variations in the value of s. Chilton (see Table 5.9) thinks that, given these factors, the value 0.6 for s stands up pretty well.

Empirical Analysis of Long-Run Costs

Most empirical studies of $LRAC$ have revealed a modified L-shape which means that there are economies of scale up to a determinable plant size or scale of operation. Beyond that scale, returns to scale tend to be constant. George Borts found Southern and Western railways had decreasing $LRAC$s. F. W. Bell and Neil B. Murphy found declining $LRAC$s for commercial banks, while Nerlove found declining $LRAC$s for United States electric utilities. J. Johnston's exhaustive studies found L-shaped $LRAC$s in English electricity production, road passenger transport, food processing, and coal mining.

Statistical Cost Functions

In practice, as Joel Dean[3] and many others have shown, measuring cost functions is not a particularly difficult task. There are adequate accounting data and more than adequate statistical estimating procedures. The problem, though, does not involve technique but interpretation of the statistical results.

Economic theory defines as cost to the firm those payments which have to be made to induce suppliers of the goods and services the firm needs for production purposes to continue to provide these necessary elements. The economic definition of costs involves significant difficulties in application. Take the matter of payments to the suppliers of entrepreneurial talents, a question that is discussed in detail in Chap. 8. Presumably, total costs ought to be calculated, less such payments, but how do you determine what these payments are or, more precisely, what is the proper level of such payments? Many empirical studies have been based on a definition of total costs as total disbursements to outsiders.

There are also accounting problems. One is that the basic accounting period is usually one year, which is longer than most definitions of the short run. Yet it is not so much a question of time as that in a typical year scale decisions have to be made apart from capacity utilization decisions. Another

---

[3]See, for example, J. Dean, "Statistical Cost Functions of a Hosiery Mill," *Journal of Business,* 1941. But for a serious criticism of statistical cost curves, see M. Friedman, *Price Theory,* Chicago, Aldine, 1976, p. 145.

problem is that depreciation is usually calculated by a routine formula which probably does not adequately capture user costs. Then, too, the value of fixed assets is often set at acquisition costs rather than at replacement costs which may understate actual costs. Add to these the fact that inventory evaluation, too, is often routine. Yet, none of these difficulties is insurmountable. Such is the nature of accounting data that allowance can be made for them. Moreover, increasingly, accounting experts have indicated how to solve for true costs.

Rail Cost Functions

George Borts, in his study of rail cost functions,[4] developed a linear cost equation

$$C = aX_1 + bX_2 + u$$

where

C = allocated freight-operating expenditures
X_1 = total loaded and empty freight car-miles
X_2 = total freight carloads/total loaded and empty freight car-miles
a, b = constants
u = random error term

In this equation, the marginal cost of carloads is defined as the change in cost accompanying an incremental change in car-miles and carloads such that

---

[4]G. H. Borts, "The Estimation of Rail Cost Functions," *Econometrica,* 28:1, 108–131, January 1960.

Table 5.10

Region	Size class of railroad in decreasing order of size	Marginal cost	Average cost
East	1	.25	.25
	2	.22	.22
	3	.12	.12
South	1	.05	.17
	2	.14	.18
	3	.15	.26
West	1	.15	.18
	2	.13	.18
	3	.13	.19

the average length of haul remains constant. Thus the marginal cost is the coefficient a in the equation. One of Borts's statistical cost functions was

$$C' - \overline{C}_j' = .9769 \, (X_1' - \overline{X}_{1j}') + .0471 \, (\overline{X}_2' - X_{2j})$$
$$(.0367) \qquad\qquad (.0153)$$
$$\overline{R}^2 = 0.72$$

The figures in parentheses are the standard errors of the regression. $\overline{C}'$, $\overline{X}_1$, and $\overline{X}_2$ are the means of the samples of the data; subscripts refer to regional data.

Borts found average and marginal costs of carloads with respect to size of railroad as shown in Table 5.10. Only in the East were marginal costs observed to intersect and exceed average costs. It is also to be observed that the larger the railroad (and thus the longer haul), the higher the marginal costs in the East. On the other hand, in the South, marginal costs decline with size suggesting economies of scale in that region in contrast with apparent diseconomies of scale in the East. In the West, there were nearly constant returns to scale.

Johnston's Review of Cost Functions

John Johnston, an English economist, concludes that "the various short-run studies more often than not indicate constant marginal cost and declining average costs as the pattern that best seems to describe the data that have been analyzed."[5] His review covered the results of statistical cost analysis from about the middle 1930s through the late 1950s. These included Joel Dean's research in costs, in a furniture factory, in leather belt production, in hosiery mills, and in department stores, which were pioneer efforts to obtain empirical cost curves. Also included are Lester's wage-employment cost study, Nordin's coal-fired electric generating plant study, Yntema's analysis of costs at United States Steel, as well as work in hat production costs, railway operating costs, shoe stores, and farms.

Johnston noted that a relatively hostile reception had been accorded to these cost study results because they seemed to contradict assumptions in theoretical models of cost behavior. His judgment was that most of the conflict was apparent rather than real since firms in actual production are not operating under ideal conditions either with respect to competition or with respect to certainty of information about business conditions.

Walters's Review of Cost Study Results

Table 5.11 shows a summary by Prof. A. Walters of statistical cost function studies done in many industries over a twenty-five-year period through the early 1960s. Walters noted that many of these studies had taken place in public

[5]J. Johnston, *Statistical Cost Analysis*, New York, McGraw-Hill, 1960, p. 168.

Table 5.11A Results of studies of cost curves: General industry studies

Name	Industry	Type	Period	Result
Bain (1956)	Manufacturing	Q	L	Small economies of scale of multiplant firms.
Eiteman and Guthrie (1952)	Manufacturing	Q	S	mc below ac at all outputs below capacity.
Hall and Hitch (1939)	Manufacturing	Q	S	Majority have mc decreasing.
Lester (1946)	Manufacturing	Q	S	Decreasing average variable cost to capacity.
Moore (1959)	Manufacturing	E	L	Economies of scale generally.
T.N.E.C. Mon. 13	Various industries	CS	L	Small- or medium-sized plants usually have lowest costs. Blair (1942) draws different conclusions.

Table 5.11B Results of studies of cost curves: Industry studies

Name	Industry	Type	Period	Result
Alpert (1959)	Metal	E	L	Economies of scale to 80,000 lb/month; then constant returns.
Johnston (1960)	Multiple product	TS	S	Direct cost is linearly related to output. mc is constant.
Dean (1936)	Furniture	TS	S	mc constant. $SRAC$ failed to rise.
Dean (1941)	Leather belts	TS	S	Significantly increasing mc. Rejected by Dean.
Dean (1941)	Hosiery	TS	S	mc constant. $SRAC$ failed to rise.
Dean (1942)	Dept. store	TS	S	mc declining or constant.
Dean and James (1942)	Shoe stores	CS	L	$LRAC$ is U-shaped (interpreted as *not* due to diseconomies of scale).
Holton (1956)	Retailing (Puerto Rico)	E	L	$LRAC$ is L-shaped. But Holton argues that inputs of management may be undervalued at high outputs.
Ezekiel and Wylie (1941)	Steel	TS	S	mc declining but large standard errors.
Yntema (1940)	Steel	TS	S	mc constant.
Ehrke (1933)	Cement	TS	S	Ehrke interprets as constant mc. Apel (1948) argues that mc is increasing.
Nordin (1947)	Light plant	TS	S	mc is increasing.

Symbols: Q = questionnaire data.   S = short-run cost curve.   CS = cross section.
L = long-run cost curve.   E = engineering data.   TS = time series.

Table 5.11C   Results of studies of cost curves: Public utilities

Name	Industry	Type	Result
Lomax (1951)	Gas (United Kingdom)	CS	*LRAC* of production declines (no analysis of distribution).
Gribbin (1953)	Gas (United Kingdom)	CS	*LRAC* of production declines (no analysis of distribution).
Lomax (1952)	Electricity (United Kingdom)	CS	*LRAC* of production declines (no analysis of distribution).
Johnston (1960)	Electricity (United Kingdom)	CS	*LRAC* of production declines (no analysis of distribution).
Johnston (1960)	Electricity (United Kingdom)	TS	*SRAC* falls, then flattens, tending toward constant *mc* up to capacity.
McNulty (1955)	Electricity (United States)	CS	Average costs of administration are constant.
Nerlove (1961)	Electricity (United States)	CS	*LRAC* excluding transmission costs declines, then shows signs of increasing.
Johnston (1960)	Coal (United Kingdom)	CS	Wide dispersion of costs per ton.
Johnston (1960)	Road passenger transport (United Kingdom)	CS	*LRAC* either falling or constant.
Johnston (1960)	Road passenger transport (United Kingdom)	TS	*SRAC* decreases.
Johnston (1960)	Life assurance	CS	*LRAC* declines.

Table 5.11D   Results of studies of cost curves: Railways

Name	Industry	Type	Result
Borts (1952)	United States	CS	*LRAC* either constant or falling.
Borts (1960)	United States	CS	*LRAC* increasing in East, decreasing in South and West.
Broster (1938)	United Kingdom	TS	Operating cost per unit of output falls.
Mansfield and Wein (1958)	United Kingdom	E	*mc* is constant.

Symbols: CS = cross section.   TS = time series.   E = engineering data.
Source: A. A. Walters, "Production and Cost Functions," *Econometrica, 31*(1–2): 1–66, January 1963.

utilities and railways, probably because of the ready availability of data. For those industries, established theory seems to have been confirmed because there one would expect increasing returns to scale or at least decreasing costs.

In general, Walters felt that "for competitive industries, the U-shaped [curve] hypothesis does not inspire great confidence," yet, as he concludes, "there is no large body of data which convincingly refutes the hypothesis . . . and the fruitful results that depend on it."[6]

[6]A. A. Walters, "Production and Cost Functions," *Econometrica, 31*(1-2):1–66, January 1963.

Learning Curve

The learning curve is a tool for "costing" the production of a relatively large number of units of one kind of product. Although it is similar to other cost or productivity relationships, there is an essential difference. The learning curve traces a change in output when there has been no change in input. The same amount of input produces more output as the production run is repeated. Or, put another way, the same output requires progressively less input. Input costs decline because of the "learning" that takes place once production has begun. But to what can learning be attributed? Does the worker on the line gain skill in doing a repetitive job? Does management adopt changes in product and process design? Do indirect costs decline under conditions of unchanging input? Probably learning can be attributed to all of these factors.

The equation for an exponential curve gives the general form of the learning curve as

$$y_i = y_1{}^{i-b}$$

where

y_i = input required to produce the ith unit of an uninterrupted series of products that are all alike

y_1 = first such product

i = cumulative count of units produced (experience in producing the product)

$-b$ = rate at which input effort declines as experience increases

The logarithmic form is often preferred because of the fact that it yields a straight line.

$$\log y = (\log y_1) - b(\log i)$$

The angle of descent, or slope, of this line is a function of the learning rate. The greater the learning, the steeper the slope of the learning curve. Figure 5.10 and Table 5.12 present a learning curve with a slope such that, as output quantity continues to double (1, 2, 4, 8, 16, . . .), there is a uniform 20 percent decrease in the time necessary to produce a unit amount of output. On double logarithmic graph paper, this uniform decline is shown as a descending straight line.

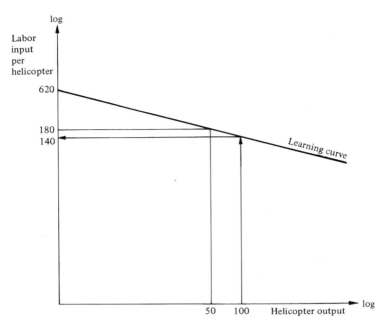

Figure 5.10. Determination of labor input per helicopter at 100th unit.

In the learning curve unit costs drop very rapidly in the early production runs. Because unit costs decrease in a predictable way, we can forecast what costs will be at any production run if we know y_1 and $-b$. The learning curve is thus an accurate tool for predicting costs of a given production run.

**Table 5.12   Housatonic Aircraft:
80% learning curve for helicopter**

Labor input/ helicopter	Helicopter output
620	1
496	2
396.8	4
317.4	8
253.95	16
203.16	32
162.53	64
130.02	128
104.02	256

Application of the Learning Curve to Prices and Costs

To establish contract sales prices and production cost goals, the average-unit–direct-labor-hours built into a unit selling price are usually based upon a learning curve positioned on the graph by estimated standard hours, either at unit 1 or at some subsequent unit on the curve. The ratio of standard hours to anticipated hours at a given unit is expressed as a percentage.

Housatonic Aircraft, Inc., has produced a prototype helicopter with a labor-hour input of 620 hours. The problem is to find what the labor-hour input per helicopter would be for a production run of fifty helicopters. Assume an 80 percent cumulative learning curve. Housatonic engineers have set a standard labor input per helicopter at the 100th unit at 70 hours to meet the requirements of Department of Defense contracts. They expect a 55 percent realization of standard, so that

$$\begin{pmatrix}\text{Projected direct labor-hour input} \\ \text{per helicopter at 100th unit}\end{pmatrix} = \frac{\text{standard labor-hours}}{\text{percent realization}}$$
$$= \frac{70}{55} = 127.3 \text{ hours}$$

To this direct labor input, the engineers add inspection costs which are equal to 10 percent of direct labor so that

$$127.3 + 12.7 = 140 \text{ hours}$$

In Fig. 5.10, you will see that this corresponds to the unit cost of 100 helicopters in labor-hours, on an 80 percent learning curve.

To determine the cost per helicopter if fifty units are produced, read off the labor input along the 80 percent curve at fifty helicopters. That is approximately 180 hours.

In effect, what this technique does is to determine (using a protractor, e.g.) two positions on an estimated learning curve. Then, any intermediate position, as in the example above, is interpolated. Housatonic engineers knew that on an 80 percent cumulative learning curve, at unit 1, labor-hour input would be 100 percent of prototype costs. They worked out a ratio of 77.4 percent, which is the amount by which the prototype costs would be anticipated to have been reduced at unit 100. At unit 50, then, costs or labor input would be, by interpolation, 71.0 percent below prototype costs.

Some Possible Pitfalls in Learning Curve Analysis

The learning curve theory cannot adequately deal, for example, with situations where

1. Changes are made in the usual size of the production run.
2. The concern is rapidly growing in size.

3. New employees are learning faster than older ones.
4. There are varying and substantial differences in rates of production.
5. Improvements in the direct labor functions reduce the direct labor content of the product.

For economists, a learning curve is a useful approximation of a cost concept which arises in many studies. What has to be explained is how production costs vary when there is no change in the input-output relationship. Though the learning curve concept is distinct from the concept of productivity, nevertheless it is likely that a good share of what are called productivity gains is traceable to learning.

Other Applications of Learning Curve

The learning curve can be used for a wide variety of management purposes

1. To forecast labor costs and to set selling prices
2. For "make or buy" decisions
3. For financial planning decisions
4. To set standards and guide production performance
5. To show the effects of design changes
6. To forecast delivery dates
7. For manpower utilization scheduling

Examples of Learning Curves in Use

The Xenia Company is faced with a threatened cutback in sales. Yet Xenia has already contracted with Youngstown Assembly Company for the supply of a key subassembly. Increasingly depressed conditions in the industry are forcing a reconsideration of this contract. With a learning curve, Xenia is able to put things into perspective. Xenia in its own facilities has already produced 165 subassembly units. The labor input for the 165th unit was 445 worker-hours. Along the learning curve, it was estimated that the proposed 372 additional subassemblies would require 111,000 additional worker-hours. By contrast, Youngstown was just getting started in subassembly production. What had appeared to be necessary earlier could now be reevaluated.

Youngstown's learning curve was such that while the 165th-unit subassembly would require a labor input of 402 worker-hours, some 43 worker-hours less than Xenia had used in its 165th-unit production, continuation along the Youngstown learning curve indicated a likely requirement of 164,000 additional worker-hours for the 372 units remaining. That, of course, meant that labor costs to completion would be the equivalent of 53,000 more worker-hours in the

Youngstown subcontract than production of the remaining 372 units at Xenia. It would pay Xenia to cancel the Youngstown contract if depressed conditions are forecast to continue.

Tashua Corporation and Financial Planning

Tashua has been encountering considerable difficulty because suppliers are reporting losses on supply contracts in the initial phase of production of small electrical motors. In one reported case, involving a contract for 300 subassemblies, the Emmons Company found itself losing on the first 90 to 100 units because production costs exceeded selling prices to Tashua. Using learning curves for the subassemblies, the Tashua corporate treasurer explained the situation to Emmons's personnel by the use of Fig. 5.11.

There was no surprise, he pointed out, that there was a financial drain on the first 90 units. However, if Emmons would calculate its learning curve, it would find that there was a significant financial return on the remaining 210 units ordered. But having worked out the problem for Emmons, the treasurer decided that, at least from Tashua's viewpoint, there was an even better way to contract for supplying the subassembly. Why not break the contracts to companies like Emmons into two or more contracts with successively lower

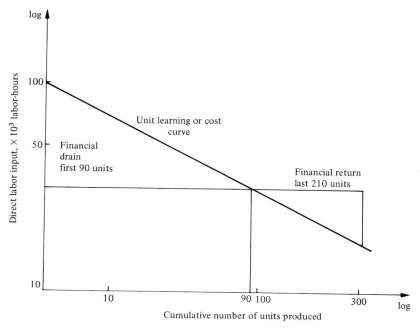

Figure 5.11. Emmons Co.: How Tashua's treasurer analyzed Emmons's problem.

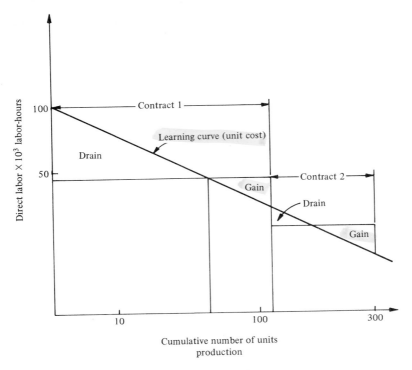

Figure 5.12. Tashua strategy: two contracts.

unit prices based on the successively lower average labor costs? In Fig. 5.12 is the new supply contract strategy for Tashua.

Chapter Summary

Cost analysis in economics is crucial because such analysis provides the basis both for pricing decisions and for evaluating effectiveness of production. What is more, cost analysis pinpoints the essential elements in determining how much to produce and whether to increase or decrease the size of production facilities. The key decision cost is marginal cost, the changing cost resulting from increasing production.

It is, however, one thing to spell out a theory of economic costs and how to measure them. It is quite something else to derive those costs in the "real world." Economic cost analysis, however, does stand up well in statistical studies. Yet, it does appear from such studies that there is rather less reason to support the concept of varying marginal costs than theory itself would suggest.

Economies of scale and, indeed, the concept of scale itself are matters of long-run analysis. The long run like the short run are planning concepts with the difference between them pivoting on whether scale is varied or not. Scale economies ranging from increasing returns through constant returns to decreasing returns are not to be confused with the law of diminishing returns. That law is really part of the law of variable proportions, which deals with changes in input proportions when the scale or capacity of a production unit does not itself change.

Selected Readings

Arrow, K. J.: "The Economic Implications of Learning by Doing," *Review of Economic Studies*, vol. 29, no. 3, 1962.

Bell, F. W., and N. B. Murphy: "Costs in Commercial Banking: A Quantitative Analysis of Bank Behavior and Its Relation to Bank Regulation," *Federal Reserve Bank of Boston, Research Report* 41, Boston, 1968.

Borts, G.: "The Estimation of Rail Cost Function," *Econometrica*, 28, January 1960.

Christ, C. F.: *Measurement in Economics*, Stanford, 1963.

Eisenstadt, K. M.: *Factors Affecting Maintenance and Operating Costs in Private Rental Housing*, New York, Rand Institute, 1972.

Gold, Bela: *Explorations in Managerial Economics*, New York, Basic Books, 1971.

Grossack, I. M., and D. D. Martin: *Managerial Economics*, Boston, Little, Brown, 1973.

Huettner, David: *Plant Size, Technological Change and Investment Requirements: A Dynamic Framework for the Long-Run Average Cost Curve*, New York, Praeger, 1974.

Johnston, John: *Statistical Cost Analysis*, New York, McGraw-Hill, 1960.

Nelson, J. R.: *Marginal Cost Pricing in Practice*, Englewood Cliffs, N.J., Prentice-Hall, 1964.

Olson, Charles E.: *Cost Considerations for Efficient Electricity Supply*, East Lansing, Michigan State Institute of Public Utilities, 1970.

"Social Costs: Should They Be Incorporated in Capital Budgets?", *Management Adviser*, *10*:10, March 1973.

Staehle, Hans: "The Measurement of Statistical Cost Functions: An Appraisal of Some Recent Contributions," *Readings in Price Theory*, Chicago, Irwin, 1952.

Viner, Jacob: "Cost Curves and Supply Curves," *Readings in Price Theory*, Chicago, Irwin, 1952.

Questions, Problems, and Projects

1. De Leeuw and Ekanem noted that the elasticity of the housing supply is a critical unknown in federal housing-policy analysis. By a technique involving cross-section evidence on housing demand, they derived the following results:

Elasticity of housing supply with respect to:	Value of elasticity
Rent per housing unit	From .3 to .7
Price of capital inputs	From −.2 to −.5
Price of operating inputs	From +.1 to −.3
Number of households	About 1.1

They concluded from this evidence that any program which subsidized low-income demand for housing would drive up rents. Would you agree? What other possible conclusions about the operation of the rental housing market would you draw from this evidence?

2. Examine Borts's finding that, because Western railroad marginal costs were essentially similar for the three size categories of railroads, there were constant returns to scale. What kind of evidence do we need to establish different kinds of returns to scale? What is the special case for Eastern railroads? Is there in this evidence an explanation of the problems of Eastern railroads?

3. What is the meaning of the process concept? How is it used in cost analysis?

4. Distinguish between long-run costs and historical cost trends. Do historical cost trends aid in developing long-run cost curves? How? Why?

5. Explain the meaning of learning and compare it with the concept of productivity. How, if at all, does learning affect scale economies?

6. Why do many analysts ignore fixed costs in determining decision costs? What is the effect of fixed costs upon analysis of average and marginal cost behavior?

7. Diminishing returns is a concept difficult to establish empirically. Is it necessary for cost analysis?

Case 5.1   Housing Supply in Springfield, Massachusetts, in October 1972

The following data are taken from an internal memo of the United States General Accounting Office (Tables 1 through 4). They refer to a survey of newspapers and other rental housing listings for October 2 and 3, 1972, in Springfield, Massachusetts. They were developed in an attempt to assess the accuracy of estimates of rents in the city of Springfield and to provide the basis for an evaluation of certain federally financed housing programs.

C* rents (shown in Table 4) are levels set by the Commonwealth of Massachusetts Department of Community Affairs as those which would assure tenants units meeting adequate and decent housing standards.

Table 1 Analysis of housing units available in Springfield, Massachusetts
October 2 and 3, 1972

Rooms	Units available	$20	$40	$60	$80	$100	$120	$140	$160	$180	Not stated
1	32	—	—	—	1	4	11	1	—	—	15
%	3.8	—	—	—	3.1	12.5	34.4	3.1	—	—	46.9
2	68	1	—	4	10	4	5	2	—	—	42
%	8.2	1.5	—	5.9	14.7	5.8	7.4	2.9	—	—	61.8
3	216	—	1	7	21	14	3	20	10	4	136
%	26.0	—	.5	3.2	9.7	6.5	1.4	9.3	4.6	1.8	63.0
4	291	—	—	12	17	16	12	12	10	18	194
%	35.0	—	—	4.1	5.8	5.5	4.1	4.1	3.4	6.2	66.8
5	168	—	—	6	21	6	5	11	8	6	105
%	20.2	—	—	3.6	12.5	3.6	3.0	6.5	4.8	3.6	62.4
6	48	—	—	—	1	2	6	6	6	4	23
%	5.8	—	—	—	2.1	4.2	12.5	12.5	12.5	8.3	47.9
7	3	—	—	—	—	—	—	—	2	—	1
%	.4	—	—	—	—	—	—	—	66.7	—	33.3
8	6	—	—	—	—	—	—	—	3	3	—
%	.6	—	—	—	—	—	—	—	50.0	50.0	—
Total	832	1	1	29	71	46	42	52	39	35	516
%	100.0	.1	.1	3.4	8.5	5.5	5.0	6.3	4.8	4.3	62.0

Source: Springfield newspapers of October 2 and 3, 1972.

187

Table 2 Springfield housing survey: Comparison of 1970 census figures with information from current newspapers

	Rooms								
	1	2	3	4	5	6	7+	Total	Total
Census, 1970	136	61	310	545	510	116	46	1724	
%	7.9	3.0	18.0	31.6	29.6	6.7	2.7	100.0	
Survey, 1972	32	68	216	291	168	48	9	832	
%	3.8	8.2	26.0	35.0	20.2	5.8	1.0	100.0	
	$50	$59	$79	$99	$119	$149	$199		
Census, 1970	136	167	547	547	148	114	42	20	1721
%	7.9	9.7	31.8	31.8	8.6	6.6	2.4	1.6	100.0
Survey, 1972	2	11	18	71	46	65	103	N.A.	316
%	.6	3.5	5.7	22.5	14.6	20.6	32.5		100.0

Median size

Census	4 rooms	(1970)
Survey	4 rooms	(1972)

Modal size

Census	4 rooms	(1970)
Survey	4 rooms	(1972)

Median rent

Census	$80	(1970)
Survey	$120–$139	(1972)

Modal rent

Census	$80–$99	(1970)
Survey	$80–$99	(1972)

N.A. = not available.

Sources: Metropolitan housing characteristics for Springfield, Massachusetts, Bureau of Census, 1970; Springfield newspapers of October 2 and 3, 1972.

Table 3   Rental housing break-even comparison in Springfield, Massachusetts

Rooms	Estimated monthly break-even rent, $	Monthly real estate taxes, $	1970 census: Percent of rental housing units with rents below	
			Break-even	Taxes
1	87	43	68.9	35.2
2	97	48	79.5	12.6
3	107	53	61.5	4.0
4	121	60	71.2	6.5
5	144	71	73.4	9.2
6	167	82	85.2	9.6
7	185	91	94.5	6.2
8	192	95	81.0	7.6

Table 4   Comparison of reported rents with break-even title and taxes

Bed-rooms	Housing resource history	News survey	Relocation service survey	Census gross rent	C*	Break-even point, $
0		90		70	125	97
1	90	100	101	87	140	107
2	100	120	121	97	150	121
3	110	100	111	108	160	144
4	140	140	129	116	180	167
5		160	135	126	200	185

Sources: Housing resource history column is the median rent by bedroom of a list of available units compiled by the Springfield city planning department, June 30, 1972. The news survey column was taken from newspaper ads on October 2 and 3, 1972. The relocation service survey is also a newspaper survey taken sometime in April 1972. The census figures were taken from the 1970 census of housing. C* figures are from the Strategic Plan for Springfield Housing Allowance Research Program.

Table 5 Rental rate comparison for Springfield, Massachusetts

Number bedrooms	Housing resource history	News survey	Relocation service survey	Census gross rents	C* rents
0		$ 90		$ 70	$125
%C*		72.0		56.0	100.0
1	$ 90	$100	$101	$ 87	$140
%C*	64.3	71.4	72.1	62.1	100.0
2	$100	$120	$121	$ 97	$150
%C*	66.7	80.0	80.7	64.7	100.0
3	$110	$100	$111	$108	$160
%C*	68.7	62.5	69.4	67.5	100.0
4	$140	$140	$129	$116	$180
%C*	77.8	77.8	71.7	64.4	100.0
5		$160	$135	$126	$200
%C*		80.0	67.5	63.0	100.0

Sources: Housing resource history column is the median rent by bedroom of a list of available units compiled by the Springfield city planning department, June 30, 1972. The news survey column was derived from newspaper ads on October 2 and 3, 1972. The relocation service survey is also a newspaper survey taken sometime in April 1972. The census figures were taken from the 1970 census of housing. C* rents are estimated at levels necessary to cover all landlord costs, including depreciation, maintenance, property taxes, interest costs, and a standard rate of profit. C* figures are from the Strategic Plan for Springfield Housing Allowance Research Program.

DISCUSSION QUESTIONS 5.1

1. Can you develop a rental housing supply schedule and supply curve from these data? Are there sufficient data to provide a demand schedule?
2. How do you account for the fact that the census gross rents are generally lower than those in newspaper listings?
3. As you compare break-even costs for different-sized units with actual census gross rents reported in 1970, how do you account for the willingness of landlords to rent at below cost?

Case 5.2 Merritt Aircraft Company

The Merritt Aircraft Company has been investigating possible revisions of one of its standard aircraft models, the UA-2. The following is a summary of correspondence between the marketing department and the engineering department concerning the UA-2.

In general, marketing wrote, the proposed design appears to satisfy the requirements, as best we know them. However, both development and production costs are considerably higher than anticipated, and these have resulted in escalation of estimated seat-mile costs. The purpose of this memo is to show the effect of these elements of direct operating costs (*DOC*s) and to request engineering suggestions on ways to reduce them.

*DOC*s are used as a tool because they are understood and recorded by the airlines. ABC Airways, using UA-1s, is now operating at a *DOC* of 7 cents per seat-mile and expects to attain 6 cents this year. If a larger aircraft like the UA-2 is used, some frequency and flexibility is sacrificed in return for a lower *DOC*.

The minimum change, a three-engine UA-2, has a computed *DOC* of 5.6 cents, using as basic data:

60 passenger seats
161 miles per hour cruising speed
2000 hours per year utilization
$1.75 million unit cost, fully equipped
$45 million research and development, test, certification spread over fifty aircraft

Figure 1 shows that 2.86 cents of the 5.6 cents is determined by purely operational costs and the remainder by the initial aircraft cost. Figure 2 shows that a reduction in initial unit cost, without changing research and development (R&D) cost, will lower the *DOC* by about 0.4 cents per $500,000. R&D cost is based on UA-2 experience and, although high in total, amounts to only 0.55 cents for fifty aircraft, as shown in Fig. 1. If fewer aircraft are made, however, R&D cost effect increases rapidly.

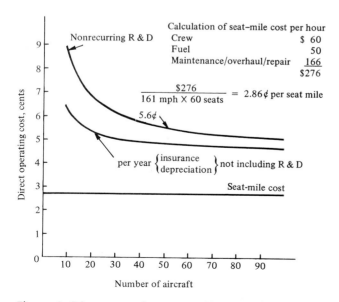

Figure 1. Direct operating costs, 2000 hours per year.

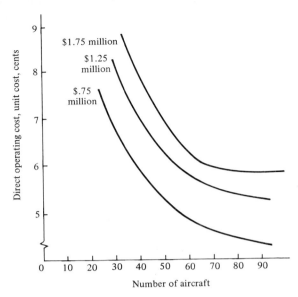

Figure 2. Effect of aircraft cost on direct operating cost, 2000 hours per year.

Additional reductions of *DOC* can be made by increasing speed, utilization, and number of seats. For example, *DOC*s can be reduced 0.5 cents by either increasing cruise speed to 195 miles per hour, increasing seats to 75, or increasing utilization to 2,500 hours per year—all based on 50 aircraft. By assuming 75 seats and 2500-hour utilization *DOC* would be reduced to 4.6 cents. Further reduction might be possible if review of the design could achieve some decrease in initial cost and possibly some increase in cruising speed.

The following information is supplied in reference to the alternatives offered.

1. We feel there is a greater potential market volume for the 60- to 65-passenger, 50-statute-mile, intracity helicopter than for the intercity 200-mile-range aircraft. Even with *DOC* of 5 cents a seat-mile a breakeven fare price for a 200-mile run would have to be 20 cents a mile or $40, which would be too high a premium to draw sufficient volume. On the other hand, a 50- or even 75-mile run might still be salable at the same per mile cost since it would result in a ticket of only $15.

2. We are concerned at the steep drop-off in cruising speed with an increase in gross weight (reducing from 150 knots at 36,000 pounds to 125 knots at 44,000 pounds, which, in percentage, is three-quarters as much as the percentage increase in gross weight). While operators recognize that cruising speed does not affect the number of passengers carried, it does have a

significant effect on per-mile operating cost. Block speeds of current helicopter operations are at least 85 percent of the cruise speed for a 30-mile distance; increasing the cruise speed from 140 knots to 180 knots, a 28 percent increase, would still result in a 23 percent increase (128 to 148 knots) in block speed with a reciprocal reduction in per-mile cost, assuming that hourly costs are constant.

3. Cabin ventilation and air conditioning must be comparable to the comfort level afforded by modern jet aircraft.

The following additional comments or suggestions are offered for future consideration and perhaps joint discussions.

To provide a substantial safety factor, we are aware that consideration of a "V tail" might have certain advantages.

1. In event of tail-blade or tail-rotor damage, it could be jettisoned. The remaining section would provide reasonable remaining control.
2. Twin tail rotors would result in a net saving of up to $180 per unit.
3. The tail gearbox becomes considerably smaller and lighter. Inertia at the rotor is greatly reduced as only a bearing retention and torque shaft are required for each tail rotor.
4. Also, torque and moment loads caused by thrust are eliminated, which reduces tail vibration.
5. Tail-rotor tip speeds should be reduced substantially as this item is the biggest noise offender and a larger rotor, lower tip speed, may provide even more benefits in lower stress vibration and in power consumption.
6. Another real benefit would be the ability of differential trim of the V tail to keep the fuselage level in landing and takeoff or in forward flight.

With 8000 horsepower transmitted through the drive system, engine noise level would be even higher than the present UA-2. Soundproofing is a problem and would have to be very heavy to be effective.

The longer fuselage and the distribution of more passengers farther forward and aft of the main rotor would generally result in increased vibration to be felt by the passengers at the outermost locations.

The tail rotor is a major source of noise, and this effect would be more pronounced as it would be absorbing even greater power.

While the pod concepts of the UA-3 would have definite advantages, our cost estimates do not indicate that this type of aircraft will produce lower seat-mile costs than the currently available UA-1, which costs 6 cents per seat-mile. This is true basically for two reasons:

1. The empty weight of the UA-3 plus the pod is greater than a comparable conventional configuration.
2. Its speed is slower.

However, in favor of the pod concept are the following factors:

1. Because of the detachable nature of pods there can be potentially higher airframe utilization.
2. Pods can provide substantial isolation from noise and vibration which could be further improved with an isolator-type mounting.
3. The pod, being a separate package, also provides good noise reduction that can be improved even further by soundproofing. The pod provides an ideal structure to soundproof.
4. The pod can be varied in design for many seating arrangements and baggage-handling arrangements. (Doors in rear would allow four-rows inboard-outboard-facing seating arrangements and carry-on–stow baggage arrangement. This will result in a shorter and lighter structure.)
5. The aircraft is also useful for carrying more than one type of pod for passenger and/or cargo.
6. A good safety feature is that no fuel would be carried in the passenger structure. Also, fuel would be well isolated from the ground and thereby protected from minor landing accidents.
7. All services to the pod, like air conditioning, heat, electricity, and hydraulics, would be umbilically connected between the aircraft and pod. This would provide a safety factor in survivable accidents. There would be no equipment to damage in the passenger pod, thus less passenger hazard.
8. The floor is "one step height to ground," eliminating need of air stairs. This would speed up loading and unloading.

These comments are set forth here in the event that engineering disagrees with this conclusion and might therefore wish to continue consideration of a UA-3 concept as our next-generation commercial airliner.

The pricing objective is a *DOC* of 4 cents per mile.

DISCUSSION QUESTIONS 5.2

1. Merritt Aircraft uses potential sales prices as indicators of the benefit of a production decision. Would DOCs give a different answer than price?
2. Would you on the basis of the information presented advise the abandonment of the production of UA-2?
3. Should R&D costs be included in the investment-choice criteria?
4. Do we know enough about UA-2 to evaluate the costs and benefits of further work on the aircraft? What would you require for a decision on this aircraft?

6

PRODUCTION

Key Concepts

closed-path evaluation
Cobb-Douglas production function
contribution margin
degree of homogeneity
dynamic programming
elasticity of substitution
empirical profit function
feasibility box
flowchart methods
implicit values
interindustry inputs and outputs

Lagrange multiplier
Leontieff production function
linear programming
marginal rate of substitution
northwest corner rule
open path evaluation
production frontier graph
production function
simplex
transportation method

What Is Ahead in This Chapter

This is a chapter about production. Production means the conversion of inputs such as labor, materials, land, and capital into an output, a product. Where to put this chapter in a book on managerial economics is a puzzle. Should we have looked into production before we discussed costs? Or having discussed costs and the pitfalls of cost analysis, should we then have turned to production to see what the underlying technical problems were? But the fact is that economists know a good deal more about costs than they do about production. Indeed, much that is known about production is deduced from cost information. That is what we saw in our analysis of economies of scale. We think that this is the place to put this piece about production into the economic jigsaw puzzle. But you will find that even if you had read this chapter before the one on costs, nothing much would be out of order.

Production can be examined in at least four ways. In this chapter, the first of these ways is with the help of an engineering concept, the production function, which details how inputs become outputs. We economists take as given the fact that engineers can define with facility what a particular production function is. That definition, of course, involves complex matters like technology, the state of the art, innovation, and efficiency. We will use the production function to try to understand management production decisions.

The second way to look at production is to develop and test actual or empirical production functions. Certainly since Professors Cobb and Douglas at Amherst College in the early 1930s did their seminal research, we have learned a good deal about empirical production functions. What this research means and whether it means what it appears to say are questions that occupy more than a little space in this chapter.

A third way to examine production, from empirical production functions to linear programming, is a move back toward theory again. But the move is not too far since linear programming is a tool which permits a fruitful and practical analysis of the accounting and engineering data many firms are likely to have. Linear programming was invented during World War II as a decision algorithm. Simple as it is, it turns out to be powerful in application.

Linear programming is but one in a family of optimizing tools that can be used in production analysis. To round out this chapter with a fourth way to evaluate production, we put linear programming into context and compare it with other possible production decision-making tools.

One point of warning before we begin our analysis of production: A production function in its engineering form implies that the technical maximization or optimization problems have already been solved. To put the matter a little differently, a production function is not a statement of how to get from here to there but draws on the assumption that we have already gone from here to there and need to know the path we have trod. Not every economist thinks he knows where the path leads. Some even doubt that the path exists. In other words, production functions and production theory in general, while tools of convenience for engineers, economists, and management, are kettles of worms for economists. One of these worms is the meaning of technological change or progress. But let's get on with production analysis.

Characteristics of Production Functions

There are at least five important characteristics of engineering production functions that are worth examining as we begin our analysis of production:

1. The production function as an explanation of how inputs get turned into outputs is a statement about the technology in use.
2. The production function permits an evaluation of how efficient a technology is. Efficiency, of course, will be a measure of how the inputs are used to get a particular output.
3. The production function describes the intensity with which any particular technology employs capital or labor or land. Capital intensity is a question of how large a share of the inputs capital, for example, represents and, therefore, how large a part capital plays in the output.
4. The production function defines and describes economies of scale.
5. The production function describes how one input such as labor is substituted by capital or land as well as the other way around. Indeed, substitution of one input for another is at the heart of the production function concept.

A Production Process

We have already attempted to define a production process. In the Unitechnology example in Chap. 5, a process was a specific combination of capital and labor inputs. In reality, the mechanical, chemical, and electronic processes used by manufacturing firms are incredibly complex. Any attempt to speak of processes and technology available to a firm must of necessity be a summary of many facts. Nonetheless, the economic concept of process can be defined relatively simply. A production process can be regarded as a "schedule of the inputs associated with each level of output." As we have seen, process UA was a way of combining 10 machine-hours and 1 labor-hour to get 100 gundrills. Suppose that as the scale of process UA was expanded the output of gundrills increased in some proportion to the increase in input.

Production process UA

Capital input	Labor input	Number of gundrills produced
10	1	100
20	2	175
30	3	245
40	4	310
50	5	370

Clearly, process UA gives evidence of decreasing returns to scale. In Fig. 6.1, we have traced process UA as a process ray. The vertical axis is the amount of capital input (in machine-hours) and the horizontal axis is the amount of labor input (in labor-hours). But since, as the scale changes, output also changes, it will be convenient to indicate in parentheses the amount of gundrill output at each point on the production or process ray. Indeed, if we knew the price per unit of output or the unit contribution to profit, we could multiply that value times the amount of output and indicate again in parentheses the value of the output.

By the way, there is no reason a priori to assume that any particular process ray will have constant decreasing or increasing returns to scale. The output number gives evidence of the returns to scale. And if those output numbers had been put in parentheses along the process ray, we would see that we have decreasing returns. Note the fact that the process ray is a straight line

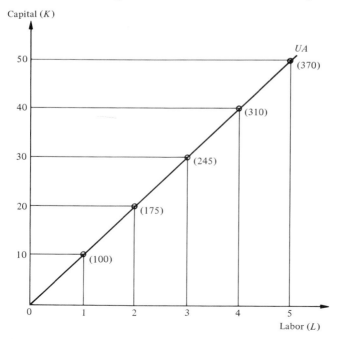

Figure 6.1. Process ray *UA*. Output in parentheses.

does not imply constant returns to scale. You have to determine the value of the output at each level of input combinations.

A Production Function Map

The next step is to take not just one process ray but a "pencil" of many such rays. A pencil of rays is simply all those rays passing through a single point, in this case the origin. Figure 6.2 shows such a pencil of rays, each ray being a different combination of capital and labor. Along each such ray are measured inputs, outputs, and even values of outputs.

Next, connect all those points on each ray which represent the same output level. That would give us an isoproduct curve such as IP_{100}, which connects all 100 gundrill points on the pencil of process rays. And if there were an IP_{100}, there is also an IP_{175}, and so on, up or down the range of possible outputs. The resulting mapping of process rays and isoproduct curves gives us a production map, which illustrates the complexities of a single production function. To put it simply, the production map is the production function.

We can now observe that economies of scale are measured along the process rays or as we move from one isoproduct curve to another. To determine the extent and kind of return to scale or scale economies, we can compare changes in inputs with changes in outputs. By contrast, if we hold one

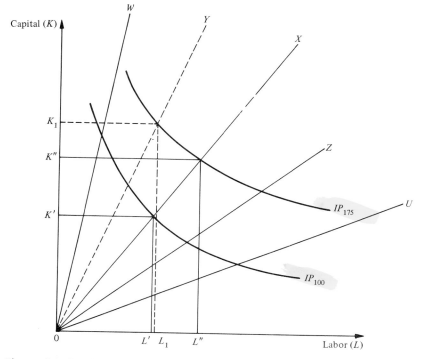

Figure 6.2. Production function map. A "pencil" of process ray.

input constant and vary another input, the output changes will reflect the law of variable proportions.

While we are repeating what we stated in Chap. 5 about the law of variable proportions, let's keep in mind that, regardless of whether returns to scale are constant, increasing, or decreasing, if one or more inputs are held constant then the scale factor is held constant. For example, if that scale factor is plant capacity, a concept which can be measured in terms of maximum or optimal number of machine-hours available (or something similar), then with a fixed capacity changes in variable inputs will probably give evidence of diminishing returns. Testing for the presence of diminishing returns is not the same as saying that all production functions necessarily have diminishing-return characteristics.

Selection of an Efficient Process

A plant manager selects a production process with a ratio of three units of labor input to one unit of capital input not because he has any preference for the labor-capital mix, but because his evidence indicates that this is the most efficient way to produce. He reached that decision by comparing various cost alternatives among different processes. The most efficient process is the one with least cost. All this we saw in Chap. 5.

Differences in efficiency among different processes can be shown by comparing the amount of any given input necessary to reach any given isoproduct curve or level. The process OX, for example, requires less of K to reach isoproduct curve IP_{175} than does process OY.

Frequently, average and marginal products are used to measure efficiency, but they must be used with care. In effect, for each production function there is a different marginal productivity function. Thus, for each production function we can work out the marginal productivity function for labor or for capital or for land. Remember that the concepts of average productivity and marginal productivity apply to the short run, that planning period during which no decisions are being made about changes in scale. Short-run average and marginal productivities assume the law of variable proportions is valid and that there are diminishing returns.

By contrast long-run average and marginal productivities would be measures of economies of scale since the output increase was the result not just of one or more inputs varying while capacity remained unchanged, but of all inputs changing.

The way to obtain average and marginal productivities from a production function is, of course, to assume a fixed scale and to determine how the increase in output is related to the level of one input as well as the changes in the level of that one input. The marginal productivity of labor or capital or any other input is, it turns out, a good proxy for the price of that input. The marginal product of labor becomes the wage. The marginal product of capital becomes the price of capital. The reasoning behind this relationship is that labor, for example, is bought and used as an input because of what it will add to the output. What one more unit of labor adds to the product or output is the measure of the value of labor to the firm. An alert producer would surely pay no more for the labor input than its value in production, its marginal productivity.

Profit Maximization

One of the assumptions we have to make about a firm and its production function is that the goal of production is to maximize the difference between costs of inputs and the price of the product. We already know that production costs vary with output. That, however, is not quite the same as saying that those cost variations which we examined in Chap. 5 are entirely caused by variations in the employment of all or specific inputs. The matter is more complex than that. It turns out that, if managers pay for the inputs a price no more than their marginal products for any level of production and if managers select the best level, presumably the lowest cost level of output, based on what they know about demand and prices and possible revenues, they will get maximum profits. Just how they do this and what it really means is reserved for Chap. 7. But we need the concept of profit maximization here for one basic reason. There is no point to production function analysis unless we can assume that managers are actually looking for and have found the best, that is, the most profitable, way of combining the inputs to make a given level of output. That is what the production function supposedly tells management.

The Marginal Rate of Substitution

The marginal rate of substitution (often called the "marginal technical rate of substitution" of one input for another) is the slope of the isoproduct curve. What it measures is the amount of one input that must be substituted for another input in order to retain the same level of output. For example, in Fig. 6.2, the move from process OY to process OX along isoproduct curve IP_{175} means that less of K ($OK_1 - OK''$) is used while more of L is used ($OL'' - OL_1$). L_1L'' is substituted for $K''K_1$ while the level of output along the isoproduct curve IP_{175} remains unchanged. Thus

$$MRS = \frac{\Delta K}{\Delta L}$$

along any isoproduct curve.

What this means is that, along the isoproduct curve as we move from process to process, labor is being substituted for capital. Unless there are constant returns to scale, the marginal rate of substitution also means that labor is becoming a better and better substitute for capital as we move down to the right along the isoproduct curve. This is the "law of diminishing marginal rate of substitution." This law describes the way in which the marginal products of labor and capital behave along any given isoproduct curve. The marginal rate of substitution of labor for capital is equal to the ratio of the marginal product of capital to the marginal product of labor, so that

$$MRS = \frac{\Delta K}{\Delta L} = \frac{MP_L}{MP_K}$$

Thus it is that as we increase the amount of labor moving from process to process along any isoproduct curve, the ratio of the marginal productivity of capital to that of labor decreases.

What is the marginal rate of substitution all about? Just this: Management must pay in efficiency for choosing among different processes. All processes in a production function are not equivalent. As a consequence, given the prices (and by inference the marginal productivities) of the inputs, some firms will choose capital-intensive processes. Other firms, perhaps in different parts of the nation or the world, may choose labor-intensive processes for the same product. Certainly as you run over the range of processes by which the whole array of products is listed in the Standard Industrial Classification code used for the Census of Manufacturers, one explanation for differences in capital intensity would be the marginal rate of substitution.

Be careful, though, for this does not say that capital-intensive processes are always more efficient than labor-intensive processes. It says only that given the prices (which reflect the market supply and demand as well as marginal productivities) of inputs in a given period in time, capital-intensive processes were more efficient. One result of energy shortages in recent years is that we have been moving rapidly away from those kinds of capital-intensive processes which are also fossil-fuel–intensive. That is further evidence, if you needed it, that the marginal rate of substitution is a useful concept.

Empirical Implications of the Production Function

The main concern of production theory is to show how firms choose from among many alternative processes open to them those which contain optimal combinations of input (optimal in the sense that the cost of production will be minimized). The production function as a physical or engineering relationship between inputs and outputs may be expressed in a simple linear equation

$$X = a \cdot i_1 + b \cdot i_2 + c \cdot i_3 + \cdots + m \cdot i_m + n \cdot i_n$$

where a, b, c, through n, are parameters indicating the productivity of the inputs. The larger these parameters or coefficients, the more productive is the function or process and the more productive is each input. These coefficients also measure the marginal products of each input (changes in output owing to a unit change in input). A linear production function implies that the inputs have constant marginal products. A "constant marginal product" means a change in the amount of an input in use does not affect its marginal product.

The same amount of output can also be produced, in a linear production function, by alternative combinations of inputs. For example, if there are two inputs L and K and

$$X_0 = aL_0 + bK_0 + n$$

then

$$
\begin{aligned}
X_0 &= a(L_0 + \Delta L) + b(K_0 - a\,\Delta L/b) + n \\
&= aL_0 + a\,\Delta L + bK_0 - a\,\Delta L + n \\
&= aL_0 + bK_0 + n
\end{aligned}
$$

If output in a linear production function does not vary as one input is substituted for another (ΔL for $a\,\Delta L/b$ units of capital), the price of $L(p_L)$ and the price of $K(p_K)$ must be such that the ratios of the coefficients of (marginal) productivity must be equal to the ratios of the prices. Since

$$p_L\,\Delta L = p_K\,a\,\Delta L/b$$

then

$$p_L/p_K = a\,\Delta L/b\,\Delta L = a/b$$

So long as the ratio of market prices for inputs (those external to the firm) is equal to a/b, it won't make any difference to the firm whether L or K is used in the production process. The contribution of one dollar's worth of L to output is the same as one dollar's worth of K. Thus L and K can be combined in any proportion.

Yet, if the market-price ratio is different from a/b so that, for example, the one dollar's worth of L produces less output than one dollar's worth of K, then only K will be used in the production process.

Homogeneous Production Functions

A homogeneous production function is one in which there is a discernible proportionality between changes in inputs and changes in outputs. A familiar case is that of constant returns to scale. Here is an equation of a constant return to scale production function,

$$X = f(XK^a L^b)$$

where $a + b = 1$.

Mathematicians say that this production function is homogeneous of degree $(a + b = 1)$. Turn this function into a logarithmic function,

$$\log X = a \log K + b \log L$$

The sum of the exponents or the coefficients (in the log form) is 1. Given the input proportions indicated by the values of a and b, doubling input will double output.

Increasing returns to scale would mean that $a + b > 1$ and the function would be of a degree greater than 1. By the same token, if $a + b < 1$, then the returns to scale are decreasing. Put a little differently, homegeneity is a question of proportionality between inputs and outputs. The degree of homogeneity indicates the nature of the returns to scale.

There are some rather interesting properties of homogeneous production functions.

1. Along any process ray in a production function map, the marginal rate of substitution between inputs is the same regardless of the level of output.
2. Along any process ray, the slope of all the isoproduct curves is the same.
3. Returns to scale are the same along any process ray as along any other process ray.
4. We need know only the process selected, not the level of output along that process, to know the marginal rate of substitution.

The Cobb-Douglas Production Function

The Cobb-Douglas production function is and has been a very popular statistical form. In its best-known form it is

$$X = bL^\alpha K^\beta \qquad \begin{matrix} X \geqq 0 & \alpha \geqq 0 \\ K \geqq 0 & \beta \geqq 0 \\ L \geqq 0 & b \geqq 0 \end{matrix}$$

where

X = a varying level of industry or national output which depends on L and K

L = units of labor input

K = units of capital input

b = constant which represents the state of technology or the productivity of the system

α, β = exponents reflecting both the degree of homogeneity and the proportionality between inputs. Obviously, if $\alpha + \beta = 1$, then returns to scale are constant

The properties of the Cobb-Douglas production function are

1. Exponents α and β are the elasticities of production with respect to labor and capital.
2. The marginal physical productivity of labor decreases if $\alpha \leqq 1$ as increasing amounts of labor are added.
3. The marginal rate of substitution is $\alpha K/\beta L$ so the elasticity of substitution is 1.

Converted to logarithms, we have

$$\log X = \log b + (\alpha \log L + \beta \log K)$$

If the prices of the output are known along with the prices of the inputs themselves, it is possible to derive a cost function from the Cobb-Douglas production function,

$$\text{Cost} = i \left(\frac{\alpha + \beta}{\beta} \right) \left[\left(\frac{\beta w}{\alpha i} \right)^{\alpha} \cdot \frac{x}{b} \right]^{1/(\alpha + \beta)}$$

This cost function assumes a competitive market and is linear in the logarithms of wage rate w, price of capital i, and amount of production x. If $\alpha + \beta = 1$, the costs are proportional to output, and the supply curve (marginal cost curve) is parallel to the horizontal axis. This means that supply has a very high, probably infinite, elasticity. We have already seen in Chap. 5 that this assumption fits the results of many statistical cost studies. Of course, with more complicated algebra, it would be possible to derive cost curves and functions under assumptions of monopoly.

In the Cobb-Douglas function the marginal product of labor (L) decreases as the amount of labor input increases and it increases as the amount of capital (K) increases. By the same token, the marginal product of capital (K) decreases as the amount of capital input increases and increases as the amount of labor input increases. In the Cobb-Douglas production function (and generally as well), if substitution among inputs is possible, then the minimum cost output will be obtained when the price ratio of the inputs is equal to the ratio of the marginal products.

Cobb and Douglas found that the best-fitted statistical equation for the United States private, nongovernmental production function gave values of $\alpha = a = .75$ so that $\beta = 1 - a = .25$. These values mean that to produce a unit of X, .75 units of L and .25 units of K are needed. It follows that an increase in X by any proportion would be accomplished by increasing L and K in the same proportion while, of course, preserving the input ratios. It also means that for any given amount of United States national product, 75 percent of that product is attributable to labor's input and 25 percent to capital input. Moreover, as would be expected, this would be the proportional distribution of output between laborers and capitalists.

Constant Elasticity of Substitution
Production Function

The Cobb-Douglas production function does well both as a method of testing actual production functions empirically and as a statement of production theory. But it does have some shortcomings. One of these is the extent to which it permits the substitution of one production factor for another. For example, the marginal rate of substitution of labor for capital is in terms of units of capital divided by units of labor. The value of the marginal rate of substitution thus depends on the units in which the inputs are measured. It is more useful to have a concept such as the elasticity of substitution which may be defined as

$$b = \frac{\text{percentage change in } K/L}{\left(\begin{array}{c}\text{percentage change in} \\ \text{marginal rate} \\ \text{of substitution}\end{array}\right)} = \frac{\text{percentage change in } K/L}{\left(\begin{array}{c}\text{percentage change} \\ \text{in relative} \\ \text{prices of } K \text{ and } L\end{array}\right)}$$

The value of the elasticity of substitution of the Cobb-Douglas production function is 1.

Suppose, however, that the facts of a particular production situation don't fit the unitary elasticity-of-substitution case. There are at least two possibilities. One is the fixed-proportions case which we will take up shortly when we discuss the Leontieff production function.

The other is to have a production function with a constant elasticity of substitution, where b may take any admissible value. Consider production function

$$X = v \left[\delta K^{(p-1)/p} + (1 - \delta) L^{(p-1)/p}\right]^{(p/p-1)}$$

where

X = output
L = labor inputs
K = capital inputs
v = a parameter which varies between zero and 1
p = elasticity of substitution
δ = a distribution parameter which works together with the substitution parameter to determine how the product is to be distributed among the inputs. The distribution parameter must never exceed $+1$

A constant-elasticity-of-substitution (CES) production function need not always have constant returns to scale as does the Cobb-Douglas function, though it is common to make this assumption. CES functions may have increasing or decreasing returns to scale, depending on specifications of the data.

The Leontieff Production Function

The Leontieff production function is a fixed-proportions production function. This function allows no substitution among the inputs. In this function, the physical input-output relationship is

$$X = \alpha \text{ (minimum } L/a \text{ or } K/b)$$

where

α = a coefficient indicating the productivity of the process

a, b = constants indicating the unchangeable way in which *L* and *K* are to be combined

The amount of *X* produced is determined by multiplying *X* times *L/a* or *K/b*, whichever is smaller. There is thus only one efficient way of producing *X*, and that is in the proportion of *a* to *b*. Constant returns to scale in the Leontieff production function are the result of the technical nonsubstitutability and the fixed input proportions. Constant returns to scale are not the result of any optimizing procedure in the Leontieff production function. The cost of a product unit is the same at all levels of production. In the Leontieff production function, all variations are variations in scale. This production function is more restrictive than the Cobb-Douglas production function in that the Leontieff function is simply additive in an accounting sense. The production process for any industry is described as consisting of the sum of the inputs.

Empirical Cobb-Douglas Production Functions

Going from statistical and accounting facts to a meaningful production function is hardly easy. First, as Walters observes,[1] there is the gap between theory and fact. There are simply too many facts to be accounted for by theory alone. Second, there is the problem of which statistical techniques to use. And, third, there is the problem of what it all means when we derive a statistical production function.

A production function is a model of a production process in a business firm. The key assumption is that during a period of observation or over a range of observations at any one point in time, conditions do not change very much. One of the conditions that clearly had better not change is technology. But what is technology if it is not a way of combining labor and capital?

If we start with labor, a variable about which we are sure to have more accounting and statistical information than any other, we can begin to see what the measurement problem is. It is not enough to count wages paid or persons employed. We have to reduce labor to a standard such as worker-hours. But

---

[1] A. A. Walters, *An Introduction to Econometrics*, chap. 10, New York, Norton, 1970.

then there's the problem of different kinds and qualities of labor. What is frequently done is to classify labor into categories of age, wage level, stage in process, sex, and educational and skill levels. But at least we have something to start with.

Capital, however, is a much more complex matter. Obviously, to count the number of machines in use would never do. What we want is a "flow of services" from machines, something like machine-hours. But the machines themselves are arrayed over different stages in their economic lives. And capital has to include inventories and buildings, as well as a variety of equipment items. The money value of a flow of services is a way of adding apples and oranges, but often researchers resort to index numbers. What is done is to get times-series or cross-section observations of net capital, capital less depreciation. In this way, the addition to the capital goods in use is offset by the actual using up of capital to obtain a kind of perpetual inventory of capital.

The problem of statistical estimation for a Cobb-Douglas production function is one of finding values of coefficients for labor, for capital, and for other inputs. Table 6.1 is a summary of several studies. In each case, the logarithmic form of the Cobb-Douglas function was used. The coefficient for each input is the proportion in the production function of that input used. The sum of the coefficients, of course, indicates the nature of the returns to scale. Most of the studies indicate constant returns to scale with the sum of input coefficients in the neighborhood of 1.

The coefficients derived in this way have another possible meaning. They may also indicate the share of income generated by an industry which goes to the input in question. In the United States examples, the labor share runs about 80 percent of income. One should be careful about drawing too many conclusions from this fact. It is quite possible that the reason why the labor coefficient and the labor share have been found in most studies to be almost equal may simply reflect the use of accounting rules which ensure that all income is allocated to one input or another.

The marginal product of the input can also be determined by use of the Cobb-Douglas production function. While, in fact, the input coefficient is a marginal product, Liu and Hildebrand[2] worked out a marginal physical product in terms of value added per dollar of wage cost. Yotopoulos[3] computed his marginal productivities by multiplying the input coefficient times the relevant output-input ratio (expressed in monetary units per worker-day, per land unit, or per monetary value of capital). Table 6.2 shows 1957 marginal productivities for 15 two-digit industries in the United States. These marginal productivities were developed by Liu and Hildebrand in their production studies based on the Census of Manufacturers for 1957.

Marginal productivity of capital is relatively high in the machinery, electrical machinery, transportation equipment, and instrument industries.

[2]G. H. Hildebrand and T. C. Liu, *Manufacturing Production Functions in the United States, 1957*, Ithaca, Cornell University Press, 1965.
[3]P. A. Yotopoulos, "On the Efficiency of Resource Utilization in Subsistence Agriculture," *Food Research Institute Studies*, vol. 8, no. 2, 1968.

Table 6.1 Cobb-Douglas coefficients

Study	Log labor			Log capital	Log other inputs	Sum of coefficients
	Total	Production	Nonproduction			
Greek farms, 1968	.441			.093	.478	1.012
United States industries, 1919	.76			.25		1.01
Canadian industries, 1937	.43			.58		1.01
United States food products, 1957	.536			.618		1.154
United States apparel products, 1957		.591	.258	.144		.993
United States lumber, 1957	.792			.183		.975
United States paper and products, 1957		.547	.270	.159		.976
United States chemicals, 1957		.348	.570	.156		1.074
United States petroleum, 1957		.274	.500	.136		.910
United States rubber, 1957	.851			.140		.991
United States leather and products, 1957	.849			.041		.890
United States stone, clay, and glass, 1957		.671	.299	.077		1.047
United States primary metals, 1957	.958			.099		1.057
United States fabricated metals, 1957		.529	.337	.086		.952
United States machinery except electrical, 1957		.467	.272	.190		.929
United States electrical machinery, 1957	.584			.337		.921
United States transportation equipment, 1957	.887			.252		1.139
United States instruments, 1957	.666			.362		1.028

Source: G. H. Hildebrand and T. C. Liu, *Manufacturing Production Functions in the US, 1957*, Ithaca, New York State School of Industrial and Labor Relations, Cornell University, 1965.

Only in the lumber industry did nonproduction labor have a lower marginal product than production labor. Interestingly, production-labor marginal products varied less over the range of 15 two-digit industries than did either the marginal products of capital or nonproduction labor. Liu and Hildebrand also found that variations in marginal products of production labor between different states in the United States were not wide in most cases.

Whether these aggregative production functions can be taken to represent typical firms in the chemical, transportation equipment, or other industry is a matter of interpretation. The intent of the research done by Liu and Hildebrand as well as others is to obtain a microeconomic production function. The difficulty lies in the availability and nature of the data. Liu and Hildebrand could disaggregate to the level of a given two-digit industry in a particular state. For New York State, the number of firms observed for any given production

Table 6.2   Marginal productivity of inputs of manufacturing industries in the United States, 1957

Marginal physical product in value added per dollar of wage costs

Industry	Production labor, $	Nonproduction labor, $	Capital, $
Food	1.11	2.03	1.34
Apparel	1.14	2.12	.93
Lumber	1.19	.97	.63
Paper	1.46	1.98	.49
Chemicals	1.58	3.83	.68
Petroleum	1.09	3.87	.30
Rubber	1.48		.86
Leather	1.32		.97
Stone, clay, glass	1.69	2.32	
Primary metals	1.69		.51
Fabricated metals	1.26	1.92	.96
Machinery	1.16	1.35	1.42
Electrical machinery	1.13	1.22	1.76
Transportation equipment	.88	1.58	3.00
Instruments	1.06	.68	1.86

Source: G. H. Hildebrand and T. C. Liu, *Manufacturing Production Functions in the US, 1957*, chap. 4, Ithaca, Cornell University Press, 1965.

function ranged from about 15 to 150 with most examples toward the lower end of this range. Provided that data were handled correctly, that the least-squares procedures used involved no more than an acceptable amount of bias, and that demand and supply elasticities were reasonably correctly estimated, these data may be taken to be representative and possibly able to provide a meaningful basis for microeconomic conclusions.

Technological Change

The available technology is a list of all available production processes. To be sure, such a list is so long that almost nobody will be familiar with everything on it. Moreover, the list is always changing. Some processes are being dropped; others are being added. Technological change typically means addition of a new process. A process can be new in a variety of ways.

1. It uses the same inputs as at least one older process, but one or more of these inputs is used in a different, more efficient way. That different or more efficient way could involve less of one or more inputs with no change in the other inputs. Or it could involve less of some inputs and more of others. These you will recognize as simply changes in input proportions.
2. It uses inputs that either have not been available before or have not been used in this way to produce a familiar product at lower cost.

3. It produces a new product, one that was not produced before from existing inputs and that requires at least one new imput.

A further distinction between a neutral and a nonneutral technological change can be made. A neutral technological change is one which does not affect the marginal rate of substitution for labor. Thus, it neither saves nor increases the use of labor. A nonneutral technological change alters the production function, making it either labor saving (therefore capital using) or capital saving. What is at issue in this definition of technological change is the intensity of use of capital (or labor).

Changes in technical efficiency or in demand cause changes in the list of technologies. Technical efficiency simply means the relative productivity of inputs with respect to an output. Technically inefficient and therefore less productive technologies will be dropped. Demand operates through changes in tastes to be satisfied by entirely new products.

Linear Programming

Efficient production is a matter of selecting the most efficient process. In linear programming (LP), there is a set of mathematical techniques for selecting such processes. The process in linear programming is a specifically defined production function. The linear programming production function is "homothetic," which is a way of saying that it is linear, homogeneous, and of degree 1. Thus it has the characteristic of constant returns to scale and full proportionality. This proportionality greatly simplifies the description and the algebra of the process.

Linear programming is more than a way of describing production. It is a way of solving production problems. It was developed in response to real problems and not surprisingly it is widely used. The production problem for which linear programming is best suited is one in which a firm with known resources or inputs, known processes or techniques, and known prices of inputs and outputs wants to find the production program that will either make the profits of the firm as great as possible or reduce the costs of production as much as possible. Note the elements: inputs, outputs, and processes.

Suppose that Unitechnology could produce four gear types by using the processes shown in Table 6.3

Table 6.3

Gear type	Output	Hobbing machine input in machine-hours	Automatic screw machine input in machine-hours
A	2000	16	16
B	1333	20	12
C	1000	12	15
D	2000	10	20

And assume that Unitechnology faces the technical and economic constraints indicated in Table 6.4.

In algebraic terms, the problem is to maximize the contribution margin

$$100x_A + 150x_B + 200x_C + 100x_D$$

subject to

$$16x_A + 12x_B + 15x_C + 20x_D \leq 63$$
$$16x_A + 20x_B + 12x_C + 10x_D \leq 84$$

All quantities must be positive, that is, $x_A, x_B, x_C, x_D \geq 0$.

In Fig. 6.3, we have four production processes, one each for gear types A, B, C, and D. Each process is identified by two points, the origin and the input coordinates corresponding to a particular level of output. These production processes differ in that they have different slopes though they use the same inputs. The production constraints are shown as a "feasibility box." All feasible production levels for gear types lie within the limits imposed by 63 machine-hours of the automatic screw machine (ASM) and 84 machine-hours of the hobbing machine (HM). Full utilization of this capacity would require using a process which, in effect, went from the origin to the corner where the two production frontiers meet. However, none of the production processes available would use up that capacity.

Efficiency in this context is simply making the most money with the least input. To find out which process is most efficient, solve for the maximum contribution margin. This maximum contribution margin, of course, is limited by what is feasible for each process. In effect, this means moving along the process ray to that point at which it reaches the frontiers of the feasibility box. Gear type A, for example, reaches the frontier at 63 ASM machine-hours. At

Table 6.4

Gear type	Contribution margin per 1000 units of gear type, $	Variable cost/1000, $	Price/1000, $
A	100	275	375
B	150	300	450
C	200	325	525
D	100	275	375

Machine capacity available	
Automatic screw machine	63 machine-hours/day
Hobbing machine	84 machine-hours/day

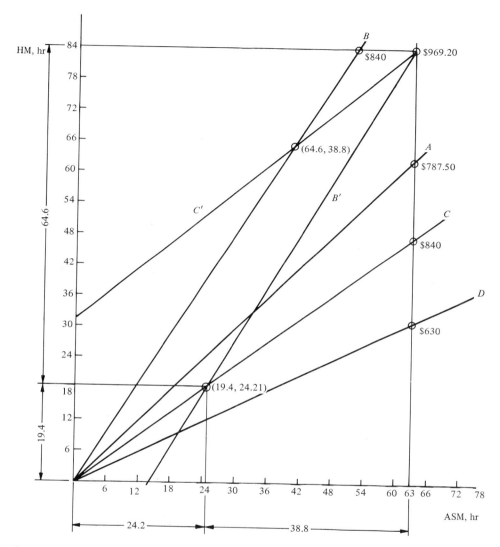

Figure 6.3. Linear programming for Unitechnology, Inc.

Gear	Produce	HM	ASM	Earn
B	4308	64.6	38.8	$646.20
C	1615	19.4	24.2	323.00
		84	63	969.20

that point, the maximum output of gear type A is 7875 units. Since the contribution margin per 1000 units of gear type A is $100, then multiplying 7.875 times $100 gives a contribution margin of $787.50 at maximum feasible output of gear type A.

Table 6.5 Comparisons of gear-type production efficiency

Gear type	Maximum output	*HM* input	*ASM* input	Contribu-tion margin, $
A	7875	63	63	787.50
B	5600	84	50.4	840.00
C	4200	50.4	63	840.00
D	6300	31.5	63	630.00

Table 6.5 shows the maximum feasible outputs for each gear type, the comparable machine inputs of *HM* and *ASM* at the frontier as well as the contribution margins for each gear type. It is clear that processes B and C are the most efficient. The other two processes are much less efficient. The general solution rule for linear programming problems is that the number of processes in the optimal solution need never be greater (though it can be less) than the number of effective constraints imposed in the problem. Therefore, there is a possible combination of at least two efficient processes in this case: Processes B and C are the two which will compose an efficient production program.

Any maximally efficient production program must use all the available resources. One geometric way to ensure that a production program containing B and C is maximally efficient is to create the pseudo-production processes B' and C', which do pass through the corner of the feasibility box and thus use up all available resources. Each pseudoprocess is parallel to its corresponding actual production process. Process B left unused 12.6 *ASM* machine-hours. Pseudoprocess B' will use up those 12.6 *ASM* machine-hours. It is drawn from (0, 12.6) to (84, 63). Process C left unused 33.6 *HM* machine-hours. Pseudo-process C' will use up those 33.6 *HM* hours. It is drawn from (33.6, 0) to (84, 63).

The intersection between B' and C allocates 19.4 *HM* hours to the production of C and the remaining 64.6 *HM* hours to the production of B. By the same token, the intersection of C' with B allocates 24.2 *ASM* hours to C and the remaining 38.8 *ASM* hours to the production of B. This means a production level of 4308 units of gear type B and 1615 units of gear type C. The net contribution margin for this combination of B and C gear types is $969.20. This is the most efficient use of the plant resources for Unitechnology. The characteristics of this production program are shown in Table 6.6.

Table 6.6 Unitechnology: Maximum contribution margin linear program

Gear type	Produce	Contribution margin per 1000, $	Total contribution margin	*HM* input	*ASM* input
B	4308	150	$646.20	64.6	38.8
C	1615	200	323.00	19.4	24.2
Total			$969.20	84.0	63.0

Table 6.7

Gear type	HM	ASM	Contribution margin, $
B	96.9	58.2	$969.20\pi^0$
C	58.2	72.7	$969.20\pi^0$

Implicit Values

The implicit or imputed value (or shadow price) of an input is its opportunity cost. Implicit values measure the amount of payoff (in this case the contribution margin) obtained per unit increase of each of the inputs. To calculate the implicit value of *HM*, there is a simple three-step algorithm. First, determine for each gear type the *HM* and *ASM* inputs necessary to obtain $969.20, the maximum contribution margin (Table 6.7).

Points (96.9, 58.2) and (58.2, 72.7) are on an equal line π^0, whose value is $969.20, and which passes through the corner point (84, 63) of the feasibility box (Fig. 6.4).

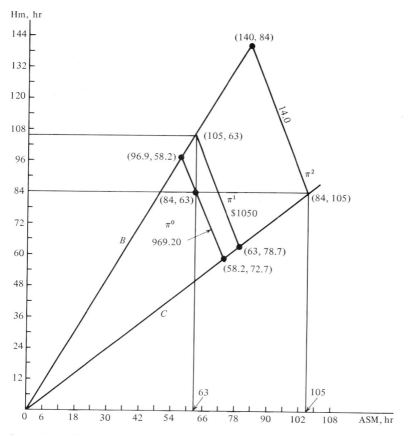

Figure 6.4. Calculation of implicit values of *HM*, *ASM*.

Second, find π^1 an equal revenue line parallel to π^0, the \$969.20 line, such that it uses up all the available ASM. The π^1 equal revenue line will have a value of \$1049.13. Third, divide increase in revenue \$80.80 by increase 21 in HM input. This yields an implicit value of \$3.85 per unit. You will notice that this procedure created a new feasibility box of 105 HM and 63 ASM and that π^1 passes through its corner.

There is also π^2, an equal revenue line such that all available HM is used up. π^2 will have a value of \$1400 and will pass through the corner point (84,105) of the third feasibility box. Again, divide \$430.08, the increase in revenue, by 42.0, the increase in ASM input. This yields an implicit value for ASM of \$10.26.

Implicit values

HM per unit of gear type	\$ 3.85
ASM per unit of gear type	\$10.26

Minimizing Costs

The Jaeckle Machine Company uses three machine setups to manufacture four different automobile parts. Jaeckle management wishes to know how to develop a production program which will minimize production costs. Production, cost, and capacity information is presented in Table 6.8. In studying the table, let's assume

1. Downtime for job setups and minor maintenance has already been deducted from available machine-hours.
2. All job orders compete for the available machine-hours. The sequence in which jobs are assigned to the machine setups does not affect the answer to the problem.
3. There are no variations in actual machine costs.

Table 6.8 Jaeckle Machine Company

Part class type	Costs/machine-hour, \$ Machine Setup			Standard machine-hours required/part class type
	I	II	III	
A	10	15	10	100
B	20	10	15	50
C	30	25	15	300
D	40	22.50	30	50
Standard machine-hours available	50	150	300	500

4. Duplicate tool sets are provided so that it is possible to set up any one job on any machine.

Minimize variable machine costs per part type:

$$10x_{AI} + 15x_{AII} + 10x_{AIII}$$
$$20x_{BI} + 10x_{BII} + 15x_{BIII}$$
$$30x_{CI} + 25x_{CII} + 15x_{CIII}$$
$$40x_{DI} + 22.50x_{DII} + 30x_{DIII}$$

subject to machine-capacity constraints

$$x_{AI} + x_{BI} + x_{CI} + x_{DI} \leq 50$$
$$x_{AII} + x_{BII} + x_{CII} + x_{DII} \leq 150$$
$$x_{AIII} + x_{BIII} + x_{CIII} + x_{DIII} \leq 300$$

and to customer requirements

$$x_{IA} + x_{IIA} + x_{IIIA} = 100$$
$$x_{IB} + x_{IIB} + x_{IIIB} = 50$$
$$x_{IC} + x_{IIC} + x_{IIIC} = 300$$
$$x_{ID} + x_{IID} + x_{IIID} = 50$$

as well as to the requirement that there be no negative values for x.

This is a linear programming problem for which a so-called transportation algorithm can be used. We begin by framing the problem as shown in Fig. 6.5.

Machine group	I	II	III	Standard machine-hours available
Part class type A	10 50	15 50	10	100
B	20	10 50	15	50
C	30	25 50	15 250	300
D	40	22.50 50	30	50
Standard machine-hours available	50	150	300	500

Figure 6.5. Obtaining a linear program by the transportation method. Display for first trial program using northwest corner rule.

Each cell in this matrix corresponds to a machine capacity constraint (down any column) and to the demand for use of machine-hours (across any row). In the upper right-hand corner of each cell is the machine-hour cost for the indicated operation. For example, to produce part type A, using machine setup I will cost $10 per machine-hour.

The essence of the transportation algorithm is that an initial program is proposed and tested; then, by iteration, successive programs are proposed and tested until (in this case) a least-cost program is determined. The opening gambit used here is the "northwest corner rule."

The "rim coefficients" are the machine-hours available (for each column) and the machine-hours required (for each row). There are, thus, seven rim coefficients. More generally, the sum of the number of columns and the number of rows is the number of rim coefficients. A basic feasible solution for this algorithm requires that an optimal program contain no more elements (or cells filled) than the sum of the rim coefficients less 1 ($m + n - 1$).

Using the northwest corner rule, we begin with cell AI. Into that cell, we place 50 machine-hours by using the available machine-hours from machine setup I. However, another 50 machine-hours is required to meet the A output. Those 50 machine-hours we place in cell AII. We next observe that this allocates only 50 of the available 150 machine-hours from machine setup II. We place 50 of these machine-hours in cell BII and thus meet the output requirements for B. The remaining 50 machine-hours we assign to cell CII. For C, though, the output requirement is 300 machine-hours, so that we place 250 machine-hours in cell CIII. This leaves 50 machine-hours from machine setup III which we assign to cell DII. In this way, we have met the requirements and availabilities indicated by the rim coefficients.

The opening program derived by the northwest corner rule is

Produce	50 A at $500, using machine setup I	
	50 A at $750, using machine setup II	
	50 B at $500, using machine setup II	
	50 C at $1250, using machine setup II	
	250 C at $3750, using machine setup III	
	50 D at $1500, using machine setup III	

This opening program has a cost of $8250. You will note that there are six elements to this program. Can a less costly program be developed? If so, how?

One test procedure is the following. Examine the matrix for cells with lower cost coefficients than those currently occupied. Evaluate the net cost of a program change which shifts from a currently occupied cell to a less costly cell. For example, in Fig. 6.6 cell DII has a lower cost than cell CII. Cell CIII has a lower cost than cell DIII. Therefore, $(-1)(25) + (+1)(22.50) + (+1)(15) + (-1)(30) = -17.5$, which means that any move to those lower cost cells will yield a program with lower total costs. You will note, of course, that the rules for developing a program apply to the test, that is, since rim coefficients remain unchanged, any move must be intercompensating. In this case, the test

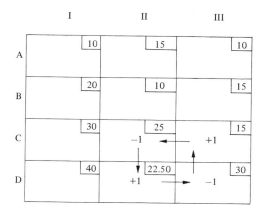

Figure 6.6. Closed path test.

procedure can be called a "closed-path evaluation" since the matching of plus and minus moves, given the rim coefficients, produces a circlelike pattern of moves. This is said to be closed path since we begin with an empty cell and test occupied cells until the starting point is reached again. If we cannot trace such a closed path because four empty cells are available to be evaluated, we follow an open path.

The second program is

Produce 50 A at $500, using machine setup I
50 A at $750, using machine setup II
50 B at $500, using machine setup II
50 D at $1125, using machine setup II
300 C at $4500, using machine setup III
Program cost = $7375.

You can test to see whether there is any less costly program than the second program. Note that this program has only five elements. This means that the second program exhibits degeneracy. That is, the cells occupied by this second program are less than $m + n - 1$ (or 6). Thus it is no longer possible to use the closed path evaluation. Every path available to be tried is open.

To resolve this problem, make use of Δ, an artificial quantity, which, when placed in a cell, can be taken to indicate that a very small but positive number occupies the cell. This number is so small that it is not affected by the rim coefficients, nor will it have any value if it appears in a final program. Then proceed with a closed path evaluation test.

Solving Linear Programming Problems

Linear programming offers an extremely useful analytical decision model for both describing and solving resource allocation problems in terms of the kind of information contained in a production function. Both accounting and technological information can be handled with facility in the typical linear programming model which consists of

1. An objective function to be maximized or minimized. This objective function is the weighed linear sum of all the decision variables in the stated problem. The weight is the contribution margin of each product.
2. A set of constraints describing resource availability, limitations (or scarcities), and their relationships to products.
3. A requirement that all problem values be positive.

We have used two methods thus far to solve linear programs. One is graphic, though it is not the only graphic method in use. We have chosen graphing of the production process since it relates most directly to the production function concept with its constant returns to scale. Many analysts prefer a production frontier graphic solution method which follows on page 223.

The other solution method we have used is the transportation algorithm. But the general method for solving linear programming problems is the simplex. The term "simplex" implies a multidimensional analog of a triangle. The computational procedure for the simple method consists of six steps:

1. State the problem in terms of its relevant variables and constraints, expressing the relationships among all variables and constraints in the form of equations.
2. Develop an initial feasible program, one which does not violate any constraint.
3. Evaluate alternative variables that might be brought into the initial feasible program, selecting those alternative variables which are favorable in that they either reduce or increase the value of the objective function (depending on whether the problem is to maximize or minimize). At the same time, certain variables in use in the first program are found to be unfavorable and are rejected.
4. Develop a revised program using revised equations which express the new relationships among variables and constraints.
5. Repeat steps 3 and 4 until there are no further favorable alternatives and, thus, no better programs.
6. Interpret the optimal program for implementation.

The specific mathematical and computational content of these rules can be found in any good book on linear programming. Moreover, students and others have ready access to LP computer routines which will permit quick solutions to most linear programming problems. Indeed, for most purposes, the real difficulties in linear programming lie not in solutions of problems but in problem setups and very often in interpretations of the program.

Other Production Optimization Techniques[4]

Production optimization problems are not always by nature linear programming problems. Consider the following problem:[5]

> A company makes two kinds of leather belts. Belt A is a high-quality belt, and belt B is of lower quality. The respective profits are $0.40 and $0.30 per belt. Each belt of type A requires twice as much time as a belt of type B, and, if all belts were of type B, the company could make 1,000 per day. The supply of leather is sufficient for only 800 belts per day (both A and B combined). Belt A requires a fancy buckle, and only 400 per day are available. There are only 700 buckles a day available for belt B.

Assuming that all the A belts and B belts the factory can make can be sold, how should the manager schedule production to gain the most profit?

The problem is stated as

Z = profit

X_1 = number of A belts produced

X_2 = number of B belts produced

X_3 = remaining A buckles

X_4 = remaining B buckles

X_5 = remaining units of leather

X_6 = remaining time units

The objective function is now specified as

$$Z = 0.40X_1 + 0.30X_2$$

and the constraint equations as

$X_1 \leq 400$

$X_2 \leq 700$

$X_1 + X_2 \leq 800$

$2X_1 + X_2 \leq 1000$

What is your first reaction? An engineer might say, "That's a Lagrange multiplier problem." Of course he is right. Change the inequalities to equalities

$$X_1 = 400$$
$$2X_1 + X_2 = 1000$$
$$X_1 + X_2 + X_5 = 800$$
$$X_2 + X_4 = 700$$

[4]Based on J. E. Mulligan, "Basic Optimization Techniques: A Brief Survey," *Journal of Industrial Engineering,* 16:3, May–June 1965.

[5]M. Sasieni, A. Vaspan, and L. Friedman, *Operations Research: Methods and Problems,* New York, Wiley, 1959, p. 236.

and create the lagrangian expression

$$L = 0.40X_1 + 0.30X_2 + \lambda_1(X_1 - 400)$$
$$+ \lambda_2(X_2 + X_4 - 700)$$
$$+ \lambda_3(X_1 + X_5 - 800)$$
$$+ \lambda_4(2X_1 + X_2 - 1000)$$

Differentiating with respect to each of the eight variables, setting the resulting expressions equal to 0, and solving the simultaneous equations would yield

X_1 = A belts produced = 400
X_2 = B belts produced = 200
X_4 = B buckles remaining = 500
X_5 = leather units remaining = 200
λ_1 = +0.20
λ_2 = 0
λ_3 = 0
λ_4 = +0.30

Our engineer would then point out that the optimum had not yet been found. "The +0.20 value for λ_1 means that $0.20 can be made by eliminating an A buckle (and hence an A belt)." He might then proceed to revise his constraint equations so that

$$X_1 + X_3 - 400 = 0$$
$$X_2 + X_4 - 700 = 0$$
$$X_1 + X_2 - 800 = 0$$
$$2X_1 + X_2 - 1000 = 0$$

From this there would result a new lagrangian expression, new simultaneous equations, and a new result,

X_1 = 200
X_2 = 600
X_3 = 200
X_4 = 100
λ_1 = 0
λ_2 = 0
λ_3 = -0.20
λ_4 = -0.10

The engineer might claim this was the optimum solution. "Two hundred A belts and 600 B belts. The negative λ's mean that money would be lost if one

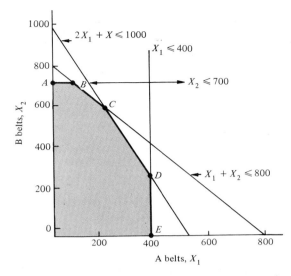

Figure 6.7. Production frontier linear programming solution.

less A belt or one less B belt was produced. Let's see, the profit would be $260."

But this is also a linear programming problem. In Figs. 6.7 and 6.8 the equal cost curve through extreme point C is farthest from the origin and yields $260 profit. The engineer notes that if the profit or constraint equations turn out to be nonlinear, linear programming is in trouble. On the other hand, Lagrange multipliers could still be used. The linear programmer replies, "There's still

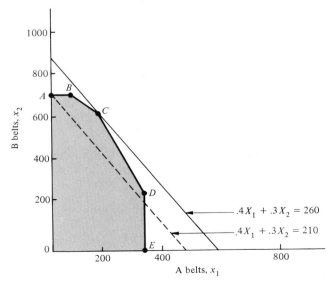

Figure 6.8. Production frontier linear programming solution.

nonlinear programming. Seriously, I can see you taking months to come up with some multivariable, nonlinear representation of this problem, spending hours of computer time inverting a huge matrix, and finally concluding that this factory should make 199.51 A belts and 599.49 B belts for a profit of $259.999. How would you tell a computer to go from the first pass you made to the second pass?"

A pacifier rises and says, "Linear or nonlinear, dynamic programming gives you the general method of solution. Further, when this business expands, we're ready to handle new products." He then proceeds to draw up Tables 6.9 and 6.10. "You can see $260 is the right answer as the problem is stated and, furthermore, we're ready to take on a new belt."

At this point another person might well rise and say, "Although the solutions you've suggested may be elegant, you're all off on the wrong track. Your objective of trying to fit mathematical functions to real-world problems is impractical. The only way to research real-world problems is simulation. Logically structure the problem—identify the blocks or modules—then prepare flowcharts. This way you are not trying to avoid nonlinearities or invert them." He then proceeds to draw up Fig. 6.9 and, after noting that an event-type model would be more efficient than a time-step model, he draws Figs. 6.10 and 6.11.

"And if you can fit your logic on a computer, I suppose you are going to recommend a Monte Carlo solution," sneers the linear programmer. "Then you'll run case after case and never know whether you've really found the optimum. You're just as bad, if not worse, than the engineer and his nth degree polynomials. You'll replace every term in his equations with a subroutine."

The dynamic programmer starts to point out that his method of solution will cover this structure as well as any other. But the engineer—finally recovering his poise—advances to the board.

"You don't have to code a modified simplex algorithm, or fill in all those boxes in the dynamic programming tables, or draw numbers out of a hat. There is a perfectly logical way to find optimums in all cases—derivatives will point the way to the top. And just like dynamic programming, this method applies to either structure, but it will save a lot of computation. I was using derivatives in the lagrange multiplier solution. Let's use the gradient method to find the summit of the profit mountain structured by these flowcharts. Let's start with a base point of 200 B belts."

Pointing out that the gradient (Δ) shows that more B belts should be produced, he moves on to a base point of 500 and, eventually, after cutting step size, comes up with Table 6.11 and Fig. 6.12.

He admits that there could be greater saving. He would not have had to evaluate so many derivatives had he taken time to "sample the profit space" before using the gradient method. Several samples are suggested and numerous points are added to Fig. 6.12. All this and more can result from such a discussion among experts. One thing, though, needs to be kept in mind: In practice, optimizing or maximizing is a search procedure. There is no one right way to determine maximum or optimum production under all conditions. It is worth the candle to look for more.

Table 6.9 Dynamic programming solution: Profit possibilities for X_1 and X_2

		X_1 made										
		Tenths of days producing X_1										
		0	1	2	3	4	5	6	7	8	9	10
		0	50	100	150	200	250	300	350	400	450	500
X_2 made												
0	0	0	20	40	60	80	100	120	140	160		
1	100	30*	50	70	90	110	130	150	170	190		
2	200	60*	80	100	120	140	160	180	200	220		
3	300	90*	110	130	150	170	190	210	230			
4	400	120*	140	160	180	200	220	240				
5	500	150*	170	190	210	230	250					
6	600	180*	200	220	240	260*						
7	700	210*	230*	250*								
8	800											
9	900											
10	1000											

Tenths of days producing X_2

$X_1 = 400$

$X_1 + X_2 = 800$

$X_2 = 700$

$X_1 + X_2 = 700$

$X_1 + X_2 = 800$

Table 6.10 Dynamic programming solution: Profit possibilities for X_1, X_2, and X_{new}

X_1 and X_2 made	Tenths of days producing X_1 and X_2										
	0	1	2	3	4	5	6	7	8	9	10
X_{new} made	0	100	200	300	400	500	600	700	750	800	800
	0	30	60	90	120	150	180	210	230	250	260
Tenths of days producing X_{new}											
0											
1	—	—	—	—	—	—	—	—	—	—	
2	—	—	—	—	—	—	—	—	—		
3	—	—	—	—	—	—	—	—			
4	—	—	—	—	—	—	—				
5	—	—	—	—	—	—					
6	—	—	—	—	—						
7	—	—	—	—							
8	—	—	—								
9	—	—									
10	—										

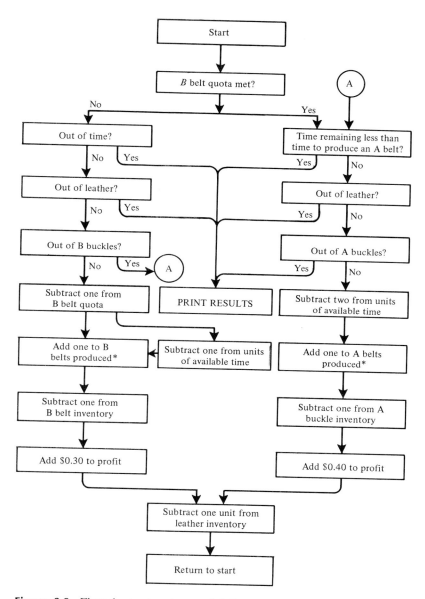

Figure 6.9. Flowchart, stepping model. Boxes marked with asterisks are what makes this a "stepping" model. Belts are produced one at a time.

Chapter Summary

Production analysis for economists is a matter of input and output. A production function relates the inputs to the outputs in a way that permits a variety of interesting conclusions about productivity to be drawn. But the

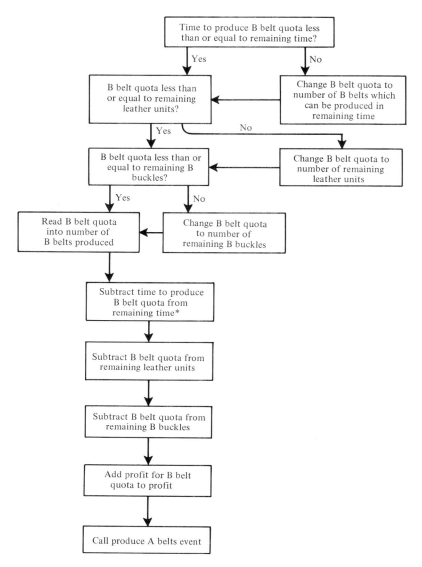

Figure 6.10. Flowchart, event-type model, B belts. * All B belts to be produced are produced at one time.

theory of the production function can only carry us so far. Sooner or later, someone is going to want to see how a production for the XYZ industry is really derived. And, then, he will want to see what it means. So this chapter has gone from theory to the statistical derivation of production functions.

But production function thinking leads quite readily into linear programming, another concept which is really more engineering than it is economics. Ways to solve and to use linear programming as well as other ways to obtain and to measure production optimums or maximums close out the chapter.

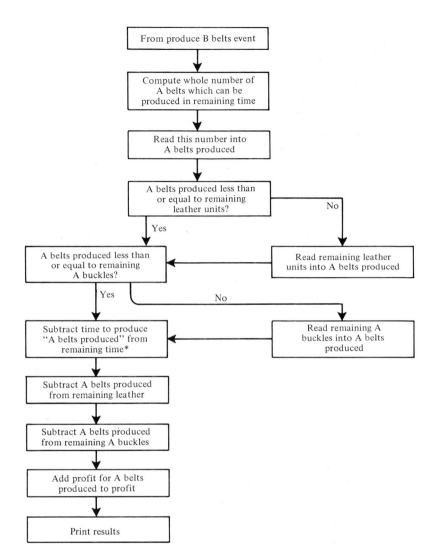

Figure 6.11. Flowchart, event-type model, A belts. ∗ All belts to be produced are produced at one time.

Table 6.11 Gradient method

Condition	Resulting A belts	Resulting profit, $	Δ
B, 100 belts	400	190	−30
A, 200 belts	400	220	−30
C, 300 belts	350	230	+10

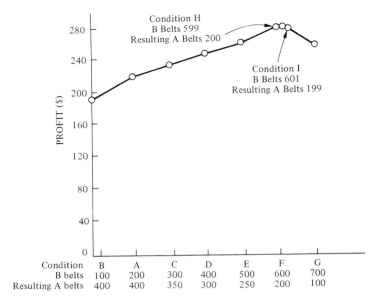

Figure 6.12. Empirical profit function.

Selected Readings

Arrow, K. J.: "The Economic Implications of Learning by Doing," *Review of Economic Studies*, *29*(3):155–173, 1962.

Brown, M.: *On the Theory and Measurement of Technological Change*, London, Cambridge, 1966.

Gamson, R. H.: "Linear Programming in Capital Budgeting," *Management Accounting*, *52*(10):43–46, April 1971.

Griliches, Z., and V. Ringstad: *Economics of Scale and the Form of the Production Function: An Econometric Study of Norwegian Manufacturing Establishment Data*, Amsterdam, North-Holland, 1971.

Hague, D. C.: *Managerial Economics*, New York, Wiley, 1969.

Johnston, J.: *Statistical Cost Analysis*, New York, McGraw-Hill, 1960.

Smith, Caleb: "The Cost-Output Relation for the US Steel Corporation," *Review of Economic Studies*, *24*(4):166–178, November 1942.

Walters, A. A.: "Production and Cost Functions: An Econometric Survey," *Econometrica*, *31*(1, 2):1–66, January–April 1963.

Questions, Problems, and Projects

1. Sir John Hicks argues that the concept of the production function does not belong in any explanation of the growth of industries. What is there about the problem of measuring technological progress that weakens the concept of a production function?

2. The Wilton Corporation makes autoscopes and flexibars. Each autoscope yields $40 in profit, each flexibar $50. Wilton management wants to know the best combination of product to make efficient use of the plant facilities. It also wishes to know whether there is adequate testing capacity, as well as whether the product mix can be changed without reducing profits. The three main operations in the plant are machining, assembling, and testing.

	Machining, hr	Assembling, hr	Testing, hr
Each autoscope requires	1	5	3
Each flexibar requires	2	4	1
Total production time available	720	1800	900

Spell out a profit-maximizing linear program for Wilton which will help company management to answer its questions.

3. Chowchilla sewing machines have for years been made in a New England location. Chowchilla is now planning to phase out its New England subassembly operations and shift them to a Texas location. The subassemblies needed for final assembly at the Texas location as well as in New England are the following:

	Thousands of subassemblies required	
Quarter	New England	Texas
I 1976	25	15
II 1976	50	20
III 1976	50	35

The New England plant has the capacity to produce 50,000 subassemblies a quarter. The Texas facility will be built up gradually from 20,000 capacity in I1976 to 40,000 in II1976 and to 60,000 in III1976. The cost per subassembly unit averages $25 in New England but only $15 in Texas. Shipping costs from New England to Texas average $5 per unit. From Texas to New England, shipping costs are higher, averaging $7 per unit assembly. Inventory holding costs per quarter per assembly unit have been estimated at $2.75. If Chowchilla's objective is to minimize production costs, how much should be produced in each location per quarter? How much should be shipped each way per quarter? How much production should be put into inventory? When, if at all, should the New England plant be shut down?

4. What can linear programming tell us about prices? Examine the meaning of implicit values.

5. Wittstanley-Pequonnock-Ansonia is a manufacturer of kitchen utensils. One of WPA's plants in Indiana can produce four different products, using processes requiring the same inputs. The following is a table of processes and products:

| Product | Daily inputs, in thousands | | Output, in thousands |
	Machine-hours	Labor-hours	
Roasters	4	8	6
Toasters	2	2	1.5
Griddles	6	4	7
Warmers	3	1	4

The Indiana plant on a daily basis can effectively use no more than 18,000 labor-hours and 15,000 machine-hours. The cost of labor for each labor-hour is estimated at $4. A machine-hour's cost has been estimated at $3.

WPA's prices on the kitchen-utensil items are as follows:

Roasters $12.50
Toasters $15.00
Griddles $ 6.00
Warmers $ 6.00

Describe the best production program for WPA's Indiana plant. How many of each utensil should be produced? What is the maximum possible profit per day at the Indiana plant?

6. Contrast and compare (*a*) Cobb-Douglas and *CES* production functions, (*b*), homogeneity and substitution in a production function, and (*c*) economies of scale in the Cobb-Douglas and the Leontieff production functions.

7. "Engineers look at things somewhat differently from economists ... The production function short-circuits certain aspects of production analysis that the engineer cannot afford to neglect ... Linear programming talks the engineer's language." Comment.

8. What kind of information would be needed to derive a production function from statistical data?

Case 6.1   Economies of Scale and Organizational Efficiency in Banking

Donald J. Mullineaux[1] of the Federal Reserve Bank of Philadelphia concluded, on the basis of his research, that

1. The production function of banks located in states which permit either limited or statewide branches is characterized by constant returns to scale.
2. The production function for banks located in unit-banking states is characterized by increasing returns to scale. Doubling all inputs would increase

[1]Donald J. Mullineaux, "Economies of Scale and Organizational Efficiency in Banking: A Profit-Function Approach," *Research Papers*, Philadelphia Federal Reserve Bank, October 1975.

output by about 122 percent. These advantages of scale, however, cannot be currently realized because of legal restrictions.

3. Banks in multibank holding companies are more profitable than their non-holding-company counterparts.
4. One-bank holding-company banks are more profitable than their non-holding-company counterparts.
5. The banking industry is characterized by imperfect competition.
6. The hypothesis of an underlying Cobb-Douglas production function was not rejected by the data.

Though these conclusions were still tentative in 1975 because of problems with the samples used, they were sufficiently different from other results to be worthy of notice.

As one of the elements of his research Mullineaux used a profit function which expressed the *maximized profit* for a bank in a competitive situation as a function of *prices* of output and variable-input factors and quantities of the fixed factors of production. The profit function is nonnegative, convex, increasing in output prices, decreasing in input prices, and increasing in the quantities of fixed factors of production. The profit function is homogeneous of degree 1 in input and output prices. The assumptions in formulating a profit function are (1) banks are profit maximizing, (2) banks are price takers in both output and variable-input markets, and (3) the production function is concave in the variable inputs. The derivative of the profit function with respect to an input price yields the factor demand equation for that input. The output supply function can also be derived from the profit function.

Differences in relative economic efficiency across banks of different size and organization can be hypothesized and tested within this framework. Efficiency is divided into technical efficiency and price efficiency. A bank is said to be technically efficient if it consistently produces more output from the same quantities of inputs than another bank. Price efficiency is implied by profit maximization.

The profit function has a number of desirable properties in studying bank efficiency. First, there is a one-to-one correspondence between the set of concave production functions and the set of convex profit functions. Hence, the characteristics of the bank production function can be identified from the parameters of the profit function. Second, the level of output is not a variable in the profit function. Third, bank cost studies relate solely to technical efficiency, while the profit function, since it considers prices, entails a more complete concept of efficiency.

Mullineaux defined profits as the total revenue minus the cost of the variable factors of production. The profit identity therefore is:

$$\pi = R'Y - P'X$$

where R' is a $(1 \times m)$ vector of exogenous prices and interest rates for bank services and loans. P' is a $(1 \times n)$ vector of given input prices and interest rates. Both flows and stocks appear in the profit identity. Because of the

Table 1   Variables in the bank-profit function

Output prices:
GARLRE   Real estate loan rate
GARLI   Consumer installment loan rate
GARLCA   Commercial and agricultural loan rate
SDB   Safe-deposit rental fee

Input prices:
ATW   Average total wages
AWO   Officers' wage rate
AWE   Employees' wage rate
RDD   Demand-deposit rate
RTD   Savings- and time-deposit rate
RCD   Certificate-of-deposit rate

Quantities of fixed factors:
FSB   Full-service branches
LSB   Limited-service branches
PRS   Paying and receiving stations
IBMON   On-premise computers

Organizational status:
MBHC   Multiple-bank holding company
OBHC   One-bank holding company

Market-structure variable:
RNE   Relative numbers equivalent

balance sheet constraint, banks cannot freely choose every element in the balance sheet.

The profit function is derived by solving first-order conditions for the optimal quantities of the variable factors, then substituting the profit identity. Profit is expressed as a function of output and input prices, and the quantities

Table 2   Definitions of deposit rates used in estimating bank-deposit function

$$RTD = \frac{\text{annual interest on time and savings deposits}}{\text{average time and savings deposits*}}$$

$$RCD = \frac{\text{annual interest on certificates of deposit}}{\text{average volume of certificates of deposit*}}$$

$$RDD = \frac{\text{cost of servicing demand deposits less demand-deposit service charge revenue}}{\text{average volume of demand deposits*}}$$

*Monthly average for the year.

Table 3 OLS Estimates of Eq. (3) for 1971 and 1972

Variables	1971	1972
Intercept	1.308	4.15
	(3.42)	(19.69)
ln ATW	−2.284	−1.446
	(−7.70)	(−4.62)
$(\ln AWO)^2$	−0.342	−0.057
	(−0.65)	(−0.23)
$(\ln AWE)^2$	−0.422	−0.200
	(−0.64)	(−0.62)
(ln AWO) (ln AWE)	1.246	0.438
	(1.06)	(0.79)
ln RDD	−0.183	−0.047
	(−4.16)	(−1.08)
ln SDB	0.200	0.295
	(2.43)	(3.57)
ln FSB	0.790	0.720
	(14.92)	(13.70)
ln LSB	0.072	0.071
	(3.12)	(2.98)
ln PRS	0.090	0.110
	(3.41)	(3.98)
ln IBMON	0.290	0.319
	(11.25)	(12.05)
MBHC	0.048	0.089
	(1.32)	(2.25)
OBHC	0.151	0.136
	(5.61)	(4.79)
ln RNE	−0.333	−0.482
	(−4.72)	(−6.79)
DUM 1	−0.228	−0.206
	(−6.66)	(−6.14)
DUM 2	−0.212	−0.165
	(−7.70)	(−5.97)
$\bar{R}^2$	.6816	.6317
SE	.3019	.3131
F	135.42	105.28

of the fixed factors, all of which are presumed to be exogenous. Estimation of the profit function thus allows consistent identification of the technology parameters of interest (through duality) for price-taking banks. It is well known that the ordinary least-squares estimation of the production function does not yield a consistent estimate of these parameters because of the simultaneity problem. A hybrid profit function that is a special case is employed to test the hypothesis that commercial bank production functions are of a Cobb-Douglas type in labor inputs.

The data base for this Mullineaux study is the Functional Cost Analysis Program of the Federal Reserve System. There were about 892 banks in the 1971 sample and 859 in the 1972 sample drawn from all 12 Federal Reserve districts. The data coincide with the income and expense reports of commercial banks.

The following equation was estimated separately for 1971 and 1972 by ordinary least squares using the functional cost data. (See Tables 1 and 2 for codes for variables.)

$$
\begin{aligned}
\text{PROF} = \ln a_0 &+ b_1 \ln \text{ATW} + b_2(\ln \text{AWO})^2 \\
&+ b_3(\ln \text{AWE})^2 + b_4(\ln \text{AWO})(\ln \text{AWE}) \\
&+ b_5 \ln \text{RDD} + b_6 \ln \text{RTD} \\
&+ b_7 \ln \text{RCD} + b_8 \ln \text{GARLE} \\
&+ b_9 \ln \text{GARLI} + b_{10} \ln \text{GARLCA} \\
&+ b_{11} \ln \text{SDB} + b_{12} \ln \text{FSB} \\
&+ b_{13} \ln \text{LSB} + b_{14} \ln \text{PRS} \\
&+ b_{15} \ln \text{IBMON} + b_{16} \ln \text{MBHC} \\
&+ b_{17} \ln \text{OBHC} + b_{18} \text{DUM1} \\
&+ b_{18} \text{DUM2} + e
\end{aligned}
$$

where
$$\text{DUM1} = D_1 x \ln \text{FSB}$$
$$\text{DUM2} = D_2 x \ln \text{FSB}$$
$$\ln = \log \text{ natural (base } e = 2.71828+)$$

so that $D_1 = 1$ if the bank is located in a statewide branching state, 0 if located elsewhere; $D_2 = 1$ if the bank is located in a limited branching state, 0 if located elsewhere; e is a random error term which reflects the divergences of expected prices from realized prices, imperfect knowledge of efficiency parameters, and differences in technical efficiency across banks of the same organizational form.

DISCUSSION QUESTIONS 6.1

1. Outline the essential differences between a profit function and a production function. How can a profit function have a Cobb-Douglas form?
2. Explain the meaning of constant returns to scale in this profit function context. The meaning of increasing returns to scale?
3. Why is it important to know the relative efficiency of banks in different types of organizations and in different kinds of state regimes of branching permission? Does it make any difference if we use technical or economic efficiency in these comparisons? Why or why not?
4. Examine the policy implications of Mullineaux's findings for a restructuring of the commercial banking system.

Case 6.2   Forecasting Agricultural Supply Response in France[1]

The Department for Study and Synthesis of the French Ministry of Agriculture financed research which led to a linear programming model developed by L. Desport. For many years, the French economy had been studied to determine what could be forecast and, based on these forecasts, what could be controlled effectively to achieve balanced growth.

Description of the Model

GEOGRAPHICAL BREAKDOWN

The geographical breakdown of the model conforms to the twenty-one program regions set up by the plan commissariat. In these twenty-one regions are about 100 subregions or groups with an average size of 340,000 hectares.

VARIABLES

The principal variables measure cultivated areas according to production systems. These production systems are characterized by the volumes of products sold commercially, the various necessary inputs (fertilizer, cost of capital, insurance, rent of the farm, amount of worker-power employed), and the farmers' average skill. The production systems correspond to each of the various ranges of size of farms. For any given type of farm k with output d, the productive system is characterized by a yield A^{kd} of the commercially sold product d, the paid worker-power d^{ks}, family worker-power d^{kf}, intermediate consumption C^k, and amortization of capital R^k.

   Secondary variables I^d represent for product d the possible imports (used to prevent large rises in domestic prices). Secondary variables E^d represent supplementary exports (used to prevent too great a drop in domestic prices). The function of these supplementary variables is to ensure that market prices and equilibrium prices (which should reflect actual real costs of production) are relatively close to each other. For worker-power, the secondary variable is D^f for family worker-power (which might be in shortage). These variables are manipulated to assure that wages do not vary out of line with normal supply and demand situations.

CONSTRAINTS

The total supply of each product must equal anticipated or forecast demand. The forecast demand can lie between an upper bound P^d and a lower bound P^{*d}. The relevant relationships, taking into account exports and imports, are

[1] L. Desport, "Forecasting the Supply Response of French Agriculture with a Linear Programming Model," *European Economic Review*, *1*(2):212–256, Winter 1969.

$$\sum_k A^{kd} X^k - E^d \le P^d$$
$$-\sum_k A^{kd} X^k - I^d \le -P^{*d}$$

where X^k is the output of d on k farms.

The agricultural labor force is made up of paid and family workers. One constraint, M^s, for the paid labor force, is the maximum number of such laborers. A second constraint, M^f, is the minimum number of family workers. The relevant relationships are

$$\sum_k d^{ks} X^k - D^s \le M^s$$
$$\sum_k d^{ks} X^k - D^f \le -M^f$$

Cultivable area S is limited. No production system can extend beyond this resource. The constraint is

$$\sum_k X^k \le S$$

The behavior of farmers will also lead to constraints on production systems. This behavior may arise from rigidity of the land market, special-equipment requirements, or other unusual characteristics of a production system. The exact value and significance of these constraints will have to be specified in each case.

The weight of the past and of tradition will be such that the production of some crops will remain close to certain volume levels. In cases of this type the constraint is of the type

$$\sum_k \epsilon_I X^k \le S^y$$

where I is the group of indices k, corresponding to the system on which the constraints bear.

CHOICE CRITERIA

A farmer has a choice among the various possibilities. His decision is guided by the search for maximum income. Maximum income can be expressed as value added, net income from the farm operation, or by profit.

The Rapid Average-Term Operation (RATO)

GOALS

Launched at the end of 1965 and completed at the end of 1967, RATO pursued several goals. The model described above was perfected only for a single-program region, that of Poitou-Charente, for which data were available even though they were deficient.

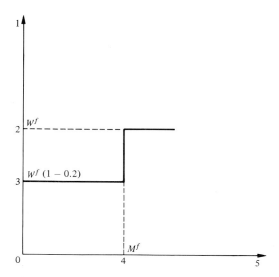

Figure 1. Supply curve for family agricultural labor. (1) Remuneration for family labor, W^f. (2) 1970 base remuneration. (3) 1970 base remuneration less 20 percent. (4) INSEE forecast. (5) Family labor M^f, employed in the agriculture of the region.

INITIAL HYPOTHESES

1. The production systems were characterized qualitatively (grazing systems, cereal systems) and quantitatively (yield, fertilizer). The first hypothesis consists of considering that the 1970 production systems can be, on the average, qualitatively close to those observed in 1962. The quantitative characteristics of the various systems selected for 1970 are taken as equal to those of systems constituting a point group in the accounting of the management centers.
2. The areas in each category are deduced from inquiries concerning the years 1955 and 1962 to 1963 or are determined according to experts. The useful area of the agricultural subregions in 1970 is not very different, except for special cases, from that noted for 1963.
3. The hypotheses relative to the active population relate directly to the amount of worker-power deducted from the work by INSEE (National Institute for Statistics and Economic Studies) relative to 1970, to which are added supplementary hypotheses distinguishing between paid and family labor.

   The link between income and worker-power is derived from wages in 1964, ascertained by the management centers and duly corrected in relation to the objectives selected in the Fifth French Plan, and also from the following hypotheses. A 20 percent drop in income expected for 1970 implies a possibility of decrease in family worker-power employed. A 20 percent increase in the base wage expected for 1970 makes available an amount of paid worker-power greater than that expected by INSEE. Figures 1 and 2 depict these two hypotheses. The relationship of the model is

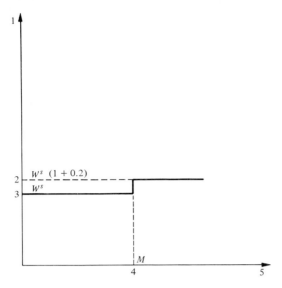

Figure 2. Supply curve for paid agricultural labor. (1) Wage. W^s. (2) 1970 base wage plus 20 percent. (3) Base wage. (4) INSEE forecast. (5) Paid labor M employed in the agriculture of the region.

$$\sum_k d^{kf}X^k - D^f \le -M^f$$

4. The hypotheses concerning the demand for products are simple and mainly relate to setting maximum and minimum prices. Figure 3 schematizes the method selected for describing the demand curves that are centered on the plan forecasts. The relationships are

$$\sum_k A^{kd}X^k - E^d \le P^d$$

and

$$-\sum_k A^{kd}X^k - I^d \le P^{*d}$$

In fact, the relationships used effectively introduce a demand curve approximated by a step curve (Fig. 4). The relationships are

$$\sum_k A^{kd}X^d_k + I^d_1 + I^d_2 + I^d_3 - E^d_1 - E^d_2 - E^d_3 = P^d_0$$

$$I^d_1 \le l^d_1$$
$$I^d_2 \le l^d_2$$
$$E^d_1 \le L^d_1$$
$$E^d_2 \le L^d_2$$

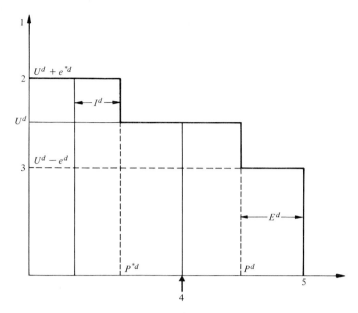

Figure 3. Simplified demand curve. (1) Price. (2) Maximum price. (3) Minimum price. (4) Plan forecast. (5) Quantity.

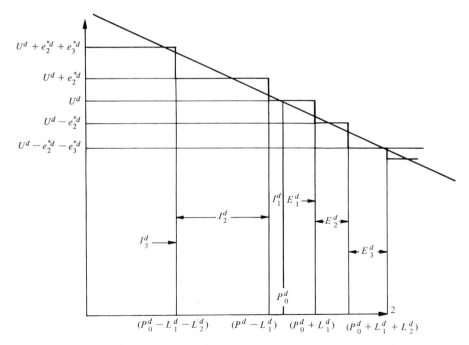

Figure 4. Utilized demand curve. (1) Approximated demand curve. (2) Quantity.

The economic function then includes the terms

$$-e_2^{*d}I_2^d - (e_2^{*d} + e_3^{*d})I_3^d - e_2^{*d}E_2^d - (e_2^{*d} + e_3^{*d})E_3^d$$

Checking Initial Hypotheses

Checking is performed in several phases and relates to different hypotheses.

1. An initial check of reliability concerns characteristics of the production systems, which are evaluated by taking account of various statistical sources and by comparing them with each other.
2. Use of the model as a method of aggregating data pertaining to a region opens the possibility of estimating to what extent there is coherence between the prospects selected in the Fifth Plan and the hypothesis made that the 1970 average is identical to the yield of point operations in 1962.
3. The perfecting and resolving of three interregional models grouping six or seven program regions provides the occasion for a supplementary check. This mainly relates to the coherence of information between regions. In fact, lack of coherence in developing the regions' production systems will be revealed by solutions displaying exaggerated production shifts. For example, it thus has proved necessary to modify the intermediate levels of consumption of the production systems for an entire region.

First Results of the RATO Operation

PRICES

The coefficients are calculated using a hypothesis on prices. The latter, which are not necessarily coherent with the production and use hypotheses, are initial prices. Resolution of the model defines dual prices that are coherent with the group of hypotheses. These prices are called "equilibrium prices."

The initial prices retained were to the advantage of cereal and sugar beet growers (agreements made within the framework of the European Common Market) and of beef producers but were noticeably lower for other surplus products (milk, fruit, hogs, and poultry).

The model, considered to represent market mechanisms, has caused equilibrium prices to appear with a slight but general drop in relation to the initial prices for all products extensively produced, because, it seems, of the hypothesis made of a considerable extension of large farms, oriented in general toward crops requiring but little worker-power. The price drops were retained for the case of milk, because of increase in productivity and in the orienting of some of the farms toward the production of milk rather than meat.

Table 1 Initial and equilibrium prices
Indices calculated in 1964 constant francs

Products	1970 initial price / 1964 price	1970 equilibrium price / 1964 price	1970 equilibrium price / 1970 initial price
Wheat	102.5	100.9	98.4
Corn	106.0*	98.5*	92.9*
Secondary cereals	108.5	105.1	97.0
Potatoes	117.6	112.6	95.9
Sugar beets	109.8	107.3	97.7
Industrial and specialized crops	100.0	100.0	100.0
Vegetables	100.0	100.1	100.1
Apples	75.0	75.3	100.4
All fruits	81.1	81.3	100.2
Wine (current consumption)	105.0	107.0	101.9
All wine	105.5	105.5	100.0
Milk	99.2	95.1	95.9
Beef	106.1	111.0	104.6
Veal	104.4	110.1	105.4
Pork	94.9	96.0	101.1
Mutton	99.5	99.5	100.0
Various animal receipts (mainly eggs and poultry)	92.0	92.0	100.0

*The price of corn was exceptionally high in 1964, a year of low production. Consequently, the index of 106 is certainly too high. This explains the importance of the drop recorded in the programming.

The great demand for meat makes the anticipated rise in prices insufficient, no matter how marked already.

The results are summarized in Table 1.

QUANTITIES

The results relative to quantities confirm those given by analysis of prices, namely, greater production than anticipated of cereals and sugar beets and a relative drop in animal products. In particular, the production of sugar beets exceeded the first quota provided by the regulations of the European economic community, a quota associated with a slight drop in price, but did not attain the level starting from which the much lower world rates come into play. Table 2 compares the results of resolution of the model for all of France with various other forecasts.

Table 3 gives the distribution in various units of measurement for the results of three interregional models for the north, west, and east.

Table 2   Comparison of products obtained by the model with forecasts coming from other sources for all of France

In millions of quintals

Product	Forecasts, RATO	Forecasts, D_1	Forecasts, D_2	Forecasts, ONIC
Wheat	124.0	109.9	114.0	122.8
Corn	32.0	30.0	25.0	30.0
Other secondary cereals	58.7	53.8	46.5	54.1
Sugar beets	179.3	157.0	174.0	
Milk	231.8	248.0		
Beef	14.2	15.4	14.5	
Veal	4.1	4.8	4.5	
Pork	13.2	13.5		

D_1 = based on forecast labor requirement
D_2 = adjusted for regions
ONIC = national office of research

Table 3   Distribution in various units of measurement for three interregional models

Expressed in percent

Product	%	1963			RATO		
		North	West	East	North	West	East
New wheat	Quintals	63.0	28.0	9.0	64.2	27.6	8.2
Dry cereals	Quintals	86.7	9.4	3.9	82.9	11.6	5.5
Corn	Quintals	32.0	59.0	9.0	33.2	59.1	7.7
Sugar beets	Quintals	96.6	2.1	1.3	97.4	0.8	1.8
All fruits	Francs	15.4	29.7	54.9	13.0	36.0	51.0
All wine	Francs	17.4	29.7	52.9	16.1	32.7	51.2
Milk	Quintals	36.1	43.3	20.6	34.9	44.9	20.2
Beef	Quintals	36.4	46.0	17.6	37.6	44.9	17.5
Veal	Quintals	23.2	47.9	28.9	22.7	46.2	31.1
Pork	Quintals	30.7	47.0	22.3	29.7	51.2	19.1
Gross added value	Francs	34.2	40.2	25.6	35.2	39.9	24.9
UAS (useful agricultural area)	Hectares				35.6	39.3	25.1
UHL (unit of human labor)	Labor units				25.4	47.8	26.8

Marginal Studies

MODIFICATION OF A DEMAND CURVE

The approximation of a demand curve by a step curve makes it possible to modify readily the characteristics of the demand curve. Modification of a demand curve for a product causes a variation in production of this product

Table 4   Elasticities in the supply of several products in relation to the price of meat for three zones and for all of France
In millions of quintals

Product	North	West	East	France
Wheat	−1.0	−1.0	1.5	−0.6
Corn	0.1	−0.6	3.8	0
Other secondary cereals	−0.8	−0.6	−2.0	−0.8
Sugar beets	−0.2	0	0	−0.2
Milk	0.5	−0.8	0.3	−0.1
Beef	1.9	1.3	0.5	1.4
Veal	−0.6	1.5	3.1	1.4
Pork	−0.6	0.1	1.1	0

and possibly of other products. For that very reason it causes a variation in the equilibrium prices. Depending on whether production of two products is complementary or competitive, the equilibrium prices of the products vary in the same or opposite directions.

It should be noted that the connection between the two products can depend on the zones of variation considered and be either of the two types considered. The same is true for the effect of the price of beef on that of milk. This was studied for experimental purposes at the level of a single program region, that of Rhone-Alps (Fig. 4).

Table 4 gives an indication of average elasticities in the supply of various products in relation to variations in the price of beef. These average elasticities, calculated for a rise of 1.78 percent in the price of beef, differ noticeably enough depending on the region.

These already valuable results can be completed by analysis of elasticities at the level of characteristics of the operations. As an example, Table 5 presents elasticities in the production of beef and milk, in relation to a rise in the price of beef for four categories of operations classified according to their income. Competition between beef and milk increases with income, that is, with adaptation of the farm to the market mechanisms.

Table 5   Elasticity in the supply of several products in relation to the price of meat
By classes of income

Classes	I	II	III	IV	France
Indices of income	$R \le 55$	$55 < R \le 85$	$85 < R \le 115$	$R \ge 15$	100
% useful agricultural area	11	24	24	41	100
% total units of human labor	18	27	23	32	100
Elasticity in the production of beef	0.5	−0.05	0.2	3.0	1.4
Elasticity in the production of milk	0.5	0.05	−0.08	−0.5	−0.1

Table 6 Elasticity in the supply of several products in relation to structural evolution*

Product	North	West	East	France
Wheat	0.6	0.3	1.4	0.6
Corn	−1.2	0.8	−0.2	0
Other secondary cereals	−0.1	0.6	4.0†	0.2
Sugar beets	1.8	−4.0†	2.2†	1.9
All fruits	−0.5	−0.5	1.4	0.6
All wine	−0.5	−0.7	−0.2	−0.4
Milk	0.6	−1.0	0	−0.1
Beef	−1.0	1.0	0	0
Veal	−0.6	0.4	0.4	0
Pork	0.4	−0.2	−0.1	0
Net revenue of exploitation/units of family worker-power	0.8	0.5	0.6	0.7

*Elasticity in supply of product equals percentage increase in supply of this product per percent total useful agricultural area transferred from one structure to another.
†Relates to negligible amounts.

The supply curves depend on the production systems and on various constraints, especially those determining structural deformations. To explore the possibility of using the model for measuring the effects of a structures policy, a trial was carried out in considering that 1.75 percent of the useful agricultural area had been transferred from small farms to large ones. The results obtained (see Table 6) conform qualitatively to those expected. The values of the elasticity coefficients are low, but it is not possible in the present state of studies to draw conclusions from this.

DISCUSSION QUESTIONS 6.2

1. Admittedly, in a complex case like this one from France, it is difficult to redo the mathematics and statistics, but what do you make of a linear programming model that permits you to derive demand and supply curves? How is this possible in the logic of linear programming? Is there a basic production function relationship that helps the analyst? What is that relationship?
2. In what sense is this linear programming model a "stage" model? What, if any, are the stages? Of what use is this staging technique?
3. What levels of accuracy would you require from such a model as a basis for policy decisions? Does the fact that there is precision about linear programming methods assure accuracy?
4. Can you conceive of this model as a "transportation" or "assignment" model? Try to outline in conceptual terms how such a model could be set up.

Case 6.3   Canadian Plywood Manufacturing[1]

D. B. Kotak of a British Columbia firm, Canadian Forest Products, Inc., developed a linear programming model in 1967 to determine an optimum balance between the available wood mix and projected sales requirements with production constraints known.

Introduction to Plywood Manufacturing Process

Generally, plywood manufacture involves the following basic steps:

Peeling   Converting logs or round wood into thin sheets of veneer by peeling at the lathe.

Veneer Preparation   Drying the green veneer and then preparing the dry veneer plywood layup by patching small defects, such as knotholes, clipping out large defects such as splits or bark, and edge-gluing narrow pieces into sheets. This is where the opportunity exists for improving the veneer grade.

Panel Layup and Pressing   Preparing plywood panels of various grades and thicknesses by gluing together three, five, or seven layers of veneer of different grades, thicknesses, and species, and then pressing these layers in a hot press.

Sizing and Finishing   This step involves processing rough plywood into the finished product by first sawing it to an exact size and then sanding and patching the surface to obtain a smooth finish.

There are seven grades and species of peelable logs available from five major sources, which can be peeled into four veneer thicknesses (140 possible combinations). Peeling results in veneer of four thicknesses, two species, and twelve grades (96 possible combinations). Plywood may be laid up from veneer into ten thicknesses, twelve grades, three widths, and five lengths, and may be sold in two separate markets (3600 possible combinations). Also to be considered is that logs can be peeled to veneer on four different lathes, dried in one of the seven different dryers, and pressed into plywood on five different presses.

What seems to be a simple problem shapes up into a complex process presenting a multitude of choices. When wrong choices are made they represent serious problems, but, conversely, correct choices represent experience, gut feel, and intuition. This had been successful because the gap between the prices and the costs was large enough to absorb the cost of wrong decisions. However, the costs were going up, and somehow the prices did not keep pace. It was realized by management that linear programming might help in identifying areas of opportunities—by making a few more right choices. A decision to implement linear programming was made in 1966.

The LP model optimizes the contribution margin, defined as sales incomes

---

[1]D. B. Kotak, "Application of Linear Programming to Plywood Manufacture," *Interfaces*, 7(1, pt. 2):56–68, November 1976.

minus the variable or wood costs. Labor, maintenance, and administration were considered to be fixed once the basic assumptions were made regarding, for example, how many shifts to operate. Machine centers, that is, the four lathes, seven dryers, and five presses, will be considered in aggregate. It was realized that by doing this the gains to be made by changing the utilization of one press versus another press for a particular product would not be realized; but, on the other hand, by doing this the problem became less complex and hence the solution more practical to implement. Capacity of the plant will be limited by the volume of plywood pressed (measured in $^1/_{16}$ to 1 inch square foot) rather than by maximum utilization of pressing time. This was a major assumption but it was justified because the press cycle times and downtimes were difficult to record and it was almost impossible to maintain the reliability of these records because of constant plant modifications. Also, volume measurement is a physical measurement which is easy to identify and visualize.

Finally, it was decided to pursue the choices related to balancing the available raw material against the product mix desired by the sales division, because the sales income and wood costs were truly variable with volume; wood costs accounted for almost 55 percent of the total costs; and the labor costs, which were relatively fixed, did not offer significant potential savings owing to their nature.

In summary, the LP model was designed to balance the raw material (wood) mix as close as possible to the desired sales mix within the constraints imposed by those in charge of raw material supply, production, and sales, with an objective to maximize the difference between sales income and the variable costs defined as the contribution margin. Table 1 shows the basic structure of this model.

Impact

Tables 2 through 5 present the information developed to give management the necessary data on which to base planning and decisions.

Physical Impact This is measured in terms of the achievement to target as shown in Table 2. By being able to achieve this it is possible to provide good customer service, a very important part of this highly competitive business.

Raw Material and Product Mix Table 3 shows the impact of the LP model on raw material and product mix on a yearly basis since its inception in 1969, with 1969 as the base year. The dollars shown are on the basis of 1976 prices. This has been achieved by being conscious of the raw material and product mix and of the balance between the two.

Evaluation of New Products Whenever a new product is being developed, the LP analysis is used to study the physical impact of this product on raw material and product mix balance. In addition to this it also provides guidance as to the price/volume relationship for the proposed product. This information provides an important basis for both sales and production plans for development and introduction of the new products into the market.

Table 1   Structure of the LP model

Rows	Logs consumed	Logs peeled by grade	Veneer purchases	Veneer upgrading/downgrading transfer	Products pressed	Products sold by market	RHS
Logs available	1						$\leq$ Limits forecast by raw materials division
Peelable logs	x_1	-1					$=$ 0
Veneer generated		x_2	x_3	-1			$=$ 0
Limits on purchased veneer			1				$\leq$ Limits set by RM coordinator
Veneer available for use				-1 $+1$	$-x_4$		$=$ 0
Products generated					x_5	-1	$=$ 0
Mill constraints					x_6		$\leq$ Limits set by production division
Sales limits						1	$\leq$ Limits forecast by sales division
Objective function	$-$ Log costs	$-$ Log processing costs	$-$ Purchasing veneer costs	$-$ Veneer processing costs	$-$ Production costs	$+$ Sales income	$=$ Maximize contribution margin

Evaluation of Raw Material Alternatives   From time to time opportunities arise to supplement the available raw material mix by purchasing veneer rather than logs. One major decision was made in 1970 to supplement the logs by buying as much as 35 percent raw material in veneer form. This was based upon extensive LP analyses and over the years it has played a significant role in maintaining the profitability of the division.

Intangible Impact   Last but not least is the impact of this program on people themselves. The planning procedure itself has resulted in a better dialog between raw material, production, and sales personnel, which has resulted in more cooperative teamwork and a more coordinated effort in achieving the plans. This in itself is a valuable benefit.

Table 2 Plywood press performance (May 24–June 4, 1976)

Line no.	Name	Summary					
		Biweekly schedule			Year to date		
		Schedule	Actual	Percent	Target	Actual	Percent
600.0	A items:						
610.0	$1/4''$ G1S	20000	22011	110	216375	265556	123
615.0	$1/2''$ G1S	15000	14819	99	182940	164859	90
620.0	$3/4''$ G1S	25000	23562	94	281244	277160	99
680.0							
690.0	M 16"S to target	17920	17270	96	204304	197398	97
695.0							
700.0	B items:						
710.0	$5/16''$ etchwood	1000	2028	203	12788	17059	133
715.0	$3/8''$ specialty	10000	9453	95	87517	127824	146
720.0	$5/8''$ roughsawn	0	0	0	83953	84809	101
725.0	$3/8''$ G1S	12000	14001	117	140622	158667	113
730.0	$5/16''$ select	7000	8383	120	131104	85612	65
735.0	$5/8''$ select	14500	15199	105	168639	140519	83
780.0							
790.0	M 16"S to target	10528	10423	99	152155	135878	89
795.0							
800.0	C items:						
810.0	$5/8''$ G1S	5000	5748	115	60476	54378	90
815.0	$11/16''$ formply	2000	2764	138	45101	30563	68
820.0	$3/8''$ select	0	0	0	12983	0	0
825.0	$1/2''$ select	7000	6592	94	60378	70400	117
830.0	$3/4''$ select	7000	6908	99	60573	68510	113
835.0	$5/16''$ standard	2000	2303	115	11812	15037	127
840.0	$3/8''$ standard	3000	3390	113	31678	35092	111
845.0	$1/2''$ standard	2000	1991	100	27285	43169	158
850.0	$5/8''$ standard	2000	1887	94	25332	10287	41
855.0	$3/4''$ standard	1000	720	72	11373	9019	79
880.0							
890.0	M 16"S to target	9440	9154	97	107246	91306	85
895.0							
900.0	D items:						
910.0	$1/2''$ roughsawn	900	930	103	0	9631	0
915.0	$1/4''$ G2S	1000	1226	123	0	10658	0
920.0	$3/8''$ G2S	0	0	0	0	4009	0
925.0	$1/2''$ G2S	1500	1592	106	0	18275	0
930.0	$5/8''$ G2S	0	0	0	0	4704	0
935.0	$3/4''$ G2S	3000	3074	102	0	41200	0
980.0							
990.0	M 16"S to target	2070	2070	100	0	0	0
995.0							
996.0	Grand total						
997.0	M 16"S to target	37888	36847	97	463705	424582	92
998.0	M 16"S—actual	39958	41078	103	463705	485167	105

Table 3   Wood supply and plywood product mix
Statistics for 1969–1975

Wood supply, 1000 CCF								Estimated budget
	1969	1970	1971	1972	1973	1974	1975	1976
Fir logs	90	75	60	62	63	45	47	59
Balsam logs	24	25	21	22	23	14	14	13
Total logs	114	100	81	84	86	59	61	72
Purchased veneer, log equiv	25	37	36	41	48	41	36	52
Total wood	139	137	117	125	134	100	97	124
Wood mix, % of total wood								
Fir logs	65	54	51	50	47	45	48	48
Balsam logs	17	18	18	17	17	14	14	10
Purchased veneer, log equiv	18	28	31	33	35	41	38	42
Product mix, % of production								
Specialties	5	5	7	8	9	12	11	10
Sanded	46	46	51	57	58	59	65	59
Unsanded fir	47	43	37	33	32	28	23	31
WSP & others	2	6	5	2	1	1	1	

Gain or loss in $1000 due to mix, in 1975 dollars, compared to 1969								Total since 1969
Wood mix	0	337	370	424	548	455	374	479	2987
Product mix	0	−94	282	630	842	1056	945	977	4638
Total mix	0	243	652	1054	1390	1511	1319	1456	7625

In addition, the information required for linear programming has resulted in a much better data base being kept for the operation, leading to a better understanding of divisional operations by all concerned.

These two benefits have made a significant contribution to the ability of the team to plan and achieve more and more ambitious goals with or without the use of LP as a tool. The key factor in the success of LP and its supporting systems has been their use as tools to help people in making decisions.

Table 4 details major sensitivity points and Table 5 contains operating plan variances. These elements helped management determine opportunity costs.

Table 4 Major sensitivity points

	For every 1% change	
	$ per day	$ per year
Product mix:		
Change in average price of products due to mix: no change in volume or prices	1132	269,000
Wood recovery: With total wood cost	551	131,000
Production volume: Wood and resin costs are associated with the volume. Hence it is less than the change due to mix	518	123,000
Grade mix of logs only: Change in the average price due to log mix	337	80,000
Falldown grades @ 14.4%: For 1% decrease in falldown grades from 14.4% to 12.4%	252	60,000
Total	$2790	$663,000

DISCUSSION QUESTIONS 6.3

1. Test this plywood model to see how it works. Spell out your method for testing it. And give your results.
2. Tie the results of this model into the planning function of the management of Canadian Forest Products. What outcomes from linear programming does management need for market and production planning?
3. This is an example of linear programming in use. What does such a model tell you about the production function in plywood production?
4. Examine the constraints in the linear programming model. What role do they play in the results? Are they valid constraints?

Table 5 Variances to the operating plan

	Plywood							
	Month				Year to date			
	Products	Wood	Contribution margin	Cont. index	Products	Wood	Contribution margin	Cont. index
Budget	1,924	872	1,052	1.21	19,901	9,395	10,506	1.12
Price	+ 72	+ 24	+ 48	+ 0.02	+ 1,307	+ 442	+ 865	+ 0.04
Expected budget	1,996	896	1,100	1.23	21,208	9,827	11,371	1.16
Mix	− 8	+ 22	− 30	− 0.06	+ 377	− 82	+ 459	+ 0.05
Volume	− 155	Production volume − 70 Recovery + 21 Source mix − 15	− 91	− 0.02	− 864	Production volume − 362 Recovery + 216 Source mix − 29	− 689	− 0.05
Actual	1,833	854	979	1.15	20,721	9,580	11,141	1.16

	Month	Year to date
Performance index	93.4%	100.6%
Recovery	97.5%	97.7%
3-ply	94.7%	101.5%

253

Case 6.4   Acme Plastics

Mortimer McCarthy has just inherited 100 percent of the stock of Acme Plastics Company. Acme produces a number of specialized machines for extruding and finishing small plastic items and manufactures them for other companies that in turn market them under their own brand names.

At present, Acme has contracts to make the following four products per week:

Product	Number produced per week	Unit price
Toothbrushes	20,000	$ .08
Toothbrush cases	10,000	.06
Lipstick cases	10,000	.13
Pocket flashlights	10,000	.155

Their selling prices have been fixed for the most part by the purchasing companies. All of their buyers would take additional quantities if they were available. Unfortunately, the finishing machine is now working at full capacity, and therefore no additional business has been sought. It has been a policy of Acme Plastics not to work overtime.

McCarthy feels that there is an opportunity to increase the total profits of the business but is not sure where to begin. He has spent the first few weeks letting operations continue at the normal level. On that experience he allocates direct cost as follows:

Product	Materials	Labor	Equipment	Total
Toothbrushes	$.025	$.02	$.02	$.065
Toothbrush cases	.025	.01	.015	.05
Lipstick cases	.04	.03	.04	.11
Flashlights	.04	.04	.05	.13

In determining these direct costs, McCarthy finds that each of the four products goes through a similar process, except the toothbrush cases, which are not painted. To mix a batch of plastic that will make 1000 pieces takes 3 hours for each of the four items. The number of pieces processed per hour for each item is as follows:

	Toothbrushes	Toothbrush cases	Lipstick cases	Flashlights
Extruding	500	333	200	250
Finishing	333	1000	1000	250
Painting	1000		500	1000
Packaging	1000	1000	1000	500

McCarthy is stumped at this point, however. His finishing machine is his bottleneck, but if he tries to upgrade profits by moving production from toothbrushes to flashlights, his most profitable item, he still will not have enough finishing time. If he runs overtime costs will go up.

Assimilating all the information given, the following table has been devised:

	Hours per 1000 units				Machine-hours available
	Tooth-brushes	Toothbrush cases	Lipstick cases	Flashlights	
Mixing	3	3	3	3	180
Extruding	2	3	5	4	240
Finishing	3	1	1	4	120
Painting	1		2	1	160
Packaging	1	1	1	2	80
Contribution per 1000 units	$15	$10	$20	$25	

DISCUSSION QUESTIONS 6.4

1. Work out a program that will permit McCarthy to maximize profits.
2. Is this the same program which would permit him to minimize his costs for any predetermined production level?
3. What advantages does linear programming offer over other possible methods of solving the problem faced by McCarthy?

7

MANAGERIAL PRICE DECISIONS

Key Concepts

average revenue
bilateral monopoly
break-even model
contribution margin
cost-plus pricing
dominant firm demand curve
kinked demand curve
long-run price decision
marginal cost pricing
market
$MC = MR$
monopoly
monopoly pricing rule
monopoly profits
oligopoly
oligopoly pricing rule

output determination
price dimensions
price discrimination
price lining
pricing objectives
product differentiation
profit maximization
pure competition
shadow prices
short-run price decision
shut-down price
target pricing
third-degree price discrimination
time pattern of prices
transfer prices

What Is Ahead in This Chapter

The focus in this chapter is on prices. The key questions are How is a price set?, Who sets the price?, and What kind of reasoning guides the price setter? The answers to these questions require basic understanding of the structure of the marketplaces in which business operates. Even if government is left out of the picture, it just isn't true that most firms can charge whatever they wish. Or that if they could they would.

Competition and monopoly, supply and demand, and revenue and cost are at least some of the elements of price decisions that this chapter deals with. Underlying the discussion about pricing are the following assumptions. Business firms exist. These business firms have managements that are assumed to be rational. Management knows costs, knows what happens when a price is set, and is intelligent enough to select a price that is best for the firm. Its only limits will be those imposed by competition. That's a good beginning and we will see how far such relatively unrealistic reasoning can take us. It turns out to be far indeed.

The gap between how firms function and how they could function is a matter of considerable interest to economists and to businessmen themselves. A study of real businesses helps supply many facts about the gap. But there are also some interesting explanations of business behavior that reduce the size of the gap. It may just be that firms can't do all that some theories assume they can. This idea leads to more than a battle of theories. Instead, it helps us to assess the real behavior of General Motors, General Tire, General Electric, and General Time.

The pricing rules spelled out in this chapter are designed to help management make intelligent price decisions. But they are also designed to help students of business management understand how and why price decisions are made. While demand theory explains how the quantity demanded is related to price and cost theory explains how the costs which underlie prices are determined, neither theory is enough. The pricing rules take elements from demand and cost theory and give both a setting and a rationale for price decisions.

This, then, is a chapter about prices, about firms and their managements, which make price decisions, and about the impact of these price decisions on the firms themselves and upon society.

The Key Elements of the Pricing Decision

When management makes a price decision what are the key elements of that decision? There are two elements which we have already considered in some detail. The cost of a product at a variety of different production levels and even at various possible plant sizes is one of these. The other is the reaction of consumers to any one price or to a range of prices. That, in part at least, is what demand is about. But cost analysis and demand projection are not all there is to price decision making. At least three more elements of the price decision process require being put into place:

1. The objectives of the firm itself
2. The competitive structure of the market in which the product is or will be sold
3. The present and future business environment in which a firm expects to sell its product or services

But before we analyze each of these price decision elements, we really need to look at the dimensions and importance of a price as such.

The Dimensions of a Price

First, as you probably know from looking at price stickers on automobiles, there is sometimes a considerable difference between a quoted price and the price actually paid by the consumer. What is more, there is often a difference between the price paid by the consumer and the average revenue per unit sold received by the seller or producer. Yet interesting as these observations are, their importance revolves around determining which is the price that matters. Which is the price about which management decisions are made? Which is the price which motivates consumers to buy or not to buy, as well as how much to buy? Which price affects profit? We can ignore these kinds of problems, if we wish. But they persist.

The answers are not easy or obvious. Indeed, there is no one answer. But there appears to be a relationship such that the closer the pricing decision is to the final consumer, the more frequent the sales, the more competitive the sales atmosphere, the more elastic the demand, the smaller the relative unit size of the product as well as the shorter the life of the product in use, the more likely it is the price on the tag is the same for all buyers and for the seller and that this price is also the average revenue. By inference, the further the product is from the final consumer market, the less frequent the number of times it is purchased, the more durable the product, the more likely it is that some form of credit or extended terms will be used in its purchase, the larger the unit size of the product, and the less competitive the market; the more complex the product, the less likely it is that the price on the tag—if indeed there is a price on a tag—will reflect reality. There will be some bargaining. There will be differences in price depending on extras, options, and terms. There may be trade-ins, salvage value, and product life to consider. The more complicated the pricing process, the less likely it is that a given price decision means as much at wholesale as at a retail grocery market. Or that the average revenue—the total revenue divided by the number of units sold—will be the same as the price on the tag.

Some prices change frequently. Stock and bond prices vary greatly over a given business day. Other prices such as transit fares remain the same for protracted periods of time. Some prices vary from Louisville to Indianapolis to Chicago and back through Peoria, Springfield, St. Louis, and Paducah. Other prices are the same everywhere. Some prices depend on quality differences in the product. Others depend on how much we buy and even when we buy. There are even differences in price that depend on who we are and what kinds of business we are in. Telephone service is priced this way. There are prices that are penalties or rewards such as a fee system for public goods.

Prices are affected by sales taxes and tariffs directly and by property taxes, income taxes, and corporate profits taxes indirectly. Prices reflect qualitative perceptions, for example, high prices at Neiman-Marcus in Dallas or at Chicago's Blum's Vogue or at Gump's in San Francisco are marks of at least some snob appeal. Or prices on Maxwell Street in Chicago or Seventh Street in Washington are low because of so-called borax quality. Low prices at Filene's basement in Boston, though, are regarded as bargains.

A general and too-fast-upward movement in prices of all or at least key commodities and services is called "inflation." And that is bad, leading to one set of buyer and producer behavior patterns. Falling prices generally are regarded as "deflation" and possibly "depression." That is bad, too. Every price is part of a system such that prices are compared with each other for the same good, for comparable goods, for complementary goods, or for substitution goods. Then, too, even wages, interest rates, rents, and exchange rates are prices.

The dimensional context of a pricing decision is not a simple one. To analyze such a decision, as you can guess, does at times require some heroic assumptions. But if we focus on a particular firm in an attempt to understand how such decisions are made, there are three basic dimensions:

1. The frequency of price change during any period of time
2. The amount of a price change compared with a previous price
3. The direction of a price change, whether up or down

Each of these dimensions can be interpreted in terms of the specific circumstances a firm faces, the size of a firm relative to other firms in that industry, the overall state of the market at the time of a price decision, the adequacy of cost and demand information available to a firm's management, and the expected reactions of government, customers, and competitors.

How Important Is the Price?

Udell[1] found, in a survey of 200 producers of industrial and consumer goods, that half of the firms surveyed did not regard pricing as one of five key policy

[1] J. G. Udell, "How Important Is Pricing in Competitive Strategy?", *Journal of Marketing*, 28:44, January 1964.

reasons for their marketing success. These firms regarded as more important product research and development, sales research, management and training of sales personnel, advertising and sales promotion, and product (and customer) service.

Houthakker and Taylor, as we noted in Chap. 4, found that price and price variation were not adequate explanatory variables in their analysis of the demand behavior of more than half the commodity categories in the United States from 1929 through the early 1960s. Perhaps too much emphasis on a pricing decision alone obscures the rich tapestry of business decision making as firms adjust to market changes.

Objectives in Pricing

A number of economists have tried to determine by case studies just how firms *really* price. Kaplan, Dirlam, and Lanzilotti[2] concluded, after a case study of many large businesses ranging from primary metals firms (such as Republic Steel) through major finished-goods producers (including General Motors) to leading retailers (Safeway, e.g.), that in most firms the following pricing practices are widely used:

1. Pricing to obtain a specified return on an investment, so-called target pricing
2. Pricing to stabilize market prices and to maintain that profit margin that is set as a goal
3. Pricing to maintain or improve share of the market
4. Pricing to meet competition
5. Pricing to maintain distribution among product lines

Kaplan, Dirlam, and Lanzilotti also found that pricing was seldom undertaken as a separate management function. It was instead closely related to a wide range of company objectives and the executives involved included accountants and sales managers, finance, engineering, and public relations division heads, and product development and line production chiefs. It was difficult for these economists to find direct evidence that profit maximization played a consistent role in the setting of prices, though the efficiency of different departments and the sales effectiveness of particular product lines were clearly measured in terms of profit. Thus, though there was a connection between pricing and profit, the tie was often not direct.

Looking at pricing objectives in terms of the kinds of companies following each, they found that General Motors, International Harvester, Alcoa, Union Carbide, and Standard Oil of New Jersey, among others, did set target returns of profit rates as companywide and divisional objectives. There was evidence, however, that the companies surveyed had difficulty both in reaching their

[2]A. D. H. Kaplan, J. B. Dirlam, and R. B. Lanzilotti, *Pricing in Big Business: A Case Approach*, Washington, D.C., Brookings, 1958.

targeted profit margins and in separating this objective from other company-wide policies.

Not surprisingly, such companies as United States Steel and Kennecott Copper Company, which have potentially unstable markets, tend to stress price stability and the maintenance of a specific profit margin as major pricing objectives. Once again, though, if we look at the pricing practices of the companies involved against the background of their presumed objectives, we can find discrepancies that suggest rather less success in achieving these objectives than they might have hoped.

Retail enterprises, like A & P, and those that were retail-oriented, like Exxon, tended to regard volume and market share as primary objectives and seemed almost to disregard the necessary price consequences. A study of A & P's pricing policies indicated that the essential elasticity of the grocery market almost dictated low prices aimed at sales volume. In the case of those firms that had announced goals of maintaining or increasing their market shares, there was considerable evidence that these goals were being attained, although pricing at retail does permit a clearer view as well as a better measure of the effectiveness of any pricing policy than pricing at other levels.

Meeting or following competition was the announced goal of some tire companies, Gulf Oil, and a major food retailer, Kroger, among others. The companies surveyed by Kaplan and his associates typically were industry leaders, either in production capacity or in sales. Such firms can either choose to set prices that keep unused capacity at a minimum or, at the very least, to avoid competitive price wars that promise no real advantage for any of the parties.

Product differentiation policies like those followed by General Foods and General Electric emphasized the quality differential between one line and product and another. The pricing policies in this category were designed to give the customer a way of recognizing the difference. Advertising was used to stress brand name and quality and generally to differentiate the product.

Competitive Structure of the Market

What a firm can do about the prices of its products and therefore the kind and nature of its price decisions depends not only on its pricing objectives but upon the "competition." Competition is a tricky word in economics. In some places, competition means "the other guys" and what they may or will do if your firm changes its prices. In other places, competition means the structure of the market. The structural approach to competition analysis, though, is broad enough to cover most of the ways in which the word competition is used to describe business situations.

Table 7.1 is a schematic outline of the elements of competition and how these elements relate to two broad categories of competitive structure. An industry or market is competitive if there are many firms selling the product which identifies the industry and its market. An industry is monopolized and

Table 7.1 Competitive structure

	Competition		Monopoly	
	Pure competition	Imperfect competition	Oligopoly	Pure monopoly
Number of firms selling product	Many	Many	Few	One
Product characteristics	Homogeneous	Differentiated	Differentiated or homogeneous	Unique; without good substitute
Market price behavior	Volatile, flexible, up and down	Frequent though not volatile change	Infrequent change	Infrequent change
Character of price decision	Firm accepts market price. Firm cannot set its own price	Firm has some but not much latitude in price setting	Firms set their own price but with careful consideration of competitive reaction	Firm has complete price-making latitude, subject to demand
Ease of entry	No limits on entry	Minor limits on entry	Major limits on entry	Industry closed; no new firms
Ease of exit	No limits on exit	No limits on exit	Substantial capital investment inhibits exit	Unless there is a public franchise, exit easy
Market information	Excellent to all sellers and buyers	Adequate, favoring seller	Poor to adequate, favoring sellers	Control by firm
Advertising	Little value	Widespread use	Widespread use	Infrequent use
Production economies of scale	None	Rare	Common	Frequent
Typical industries	Stock market, commodity exchange, wheat, corn	Toothpaste, retail grocery, soap, dress making	Automobile, sugar, steel, rubber, milk	Telephone service, electricity, gas

thus not very competitive if there are only a few firms. But numbers are only part of the competitive structure, important as the number of firms is to an understanding of competitive behavior. The kind and nature of the product set the whole context within which competition can be analyzed.

For example, if the product is wheat or soybeans or common stocks, homogeneity is a basic characteristic. No meaningful distinction for pricing purposes can be made between what "we" make and sell and what "they" make and sell. However, sugar, too, is homogeneous but it is produced under conditions of economies of scale so that, unlike wheat, the sugar market is characterized by oligopoly. If the product can be made to have significant differences depending on who makes it, then there can be different prices set by different sellers. This product differentiation is going to be related to advertising, to market information in the hands of buyers and sellers, and to that vague but important category called "consumer tastes."

Given the competitive elements, there are but two options or different kinds of price decisions that a firm can make:

1. The firm can take the market price as given and try to sell as much as possible, or
2. The firm can attempt to set its own price for the product.

Under pure competition, only option (1) is available. Under pure monopoly, only option (2) is available. In oligopoly, there may be firms that are price leaders and others which are price followers. Most oligopolistic firms use option (2), though some of the smaller firms appear to use option (1). In imperfect or monopolistic competition, option (1) is seldom available and most firms are forced into option (2).

The fact of the matter, though, is that many managements for many products tend to avoid changing prices for as long as possible. There is a general feeling that consumers will react negatively to any upward price change and this makes management reluctant to act until most other revenue-generating options have been tried.

The Business Environment

The business environment in which a firm makes decisions is presented in schematic form in Table 7.2. This table examines some of the possible impacts of changes in business environment. The purpose is to give you an idea, if not all the details, of the complexity of the business environment. Everything from technological changes which lower production costs to sales taxes which raise prices (and reduce product demand) and on to air pollution controls which affect costs and prices. The point is that the business environment–price decision interface is circular. Business environmental changes impinge on price decisions and sometimes force price changes. Price changes even at the firm level are bound to have an effect on the business environment.

Table 7.2 Possible impact of changes in business environment

	Technology	Law	Taxes	Business cycle
Product	New technology lowers production cost	Air pollution controls increase cost	Income and property taxes increase cost	Recession changes family tastes
Price	Economies of scale reduce prices on larger sales volume	Requirement of unit pricing	Sales taxes increase prices	Inflation affects all prices
Competition	New products redefine industry	Antitrust action changes competitive structure	Investment credits favor larger firms	Recession and inflation kill smaller firms

When Must Pricing Decisions Be Made?

There is a variety of situations in which a price decision has to be made, regardless of the preference of management for the status quo. Such situations occur

1. When the firm introduces a new product
2. When the firm enters a new market which is distant from the current markets it serves
3. When competition changes the price
4. When underlying production costs change significantly
5. When new production facilities are necessary to meet increasing demand

   Given the product demand and cost situations, the firm's pricing objectives, the competitive structure of the market, and the business environment present and future, are there any rules for making a pricing decision? The answer, of course, is "yes." And what follows is a catalog of those rules with suggestions on how to apply them.

Pricing Rules

There are five sets of economic rules for pricing which can be classified according to their effect:

1. Profit maximizing pricing rules
2. Gross revenue maximizing rules
3. Firm investment value maximizing rules
4. Satisficing rules
5. Firm survival rules

Profit Maximizing Rules for Price Decisions

The most effective profit maximizing rule for price decisions is: Along the demand function for the product the firm is selling, select that price at which the falling marginal revenue from increases in sales is just equal to the rising marginal cost of producing the output to be sold.

Figure 7.1 shows how to use this $MR = MC$ rule. Notice that the effective range for possible price decisions is between p_1 and p_2. At price p_1, average revenue which had been higher than average total costs at lower output (and sales) levels just covered costs. At p_1, with output at OB_1 then, there is a break-even point. At output (and sales) levels from OB_1 to OB_2, average revenue is above-average total cost. OB_2 is the second break-even point. The question is Which among these prices ranging from p_1 down to p_2 is the one

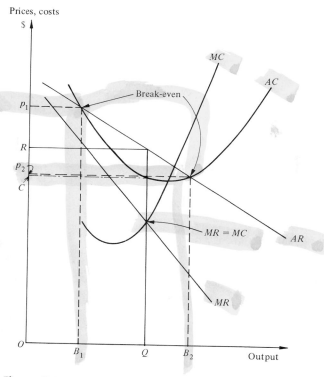

Figure 7.1. $MR = MC$ pricing rule, short run.

$p_1 p_2$ is range of prices over which profit ≥ 0
OR is best price where profit (CR) is maximized
OQ is best output
$B_1 B_2$ is feasible operating range

$CR \times OQ$ = total profit
$OR \times OQ$ = total revenue
$OC \times OQ$ = total cost

which will yield not only a revenue over costs but the most profit, the most net revenue? In terms of Fig. 7.1, we are looking for that output and that price at which the vertical gap between AC and AR is the largest. The geometric solution is to find the intersection between MR and MC. The gap between average revenue and average total cost will be RC. The price will be OR and the best output (and sales) level will be OQ.

This rule will work just as well if the best possible situation is a minimized loss. $MR = MC$ will indicate at what price and at what output (and sales) level losses will be minimized. In addition, the rule works as well for firms in perfect competition as in pure monopolies. It works for oligopolies and for imperfect or monopolistic competition. However, since demand conditions and competitor reactions differ depending on the competitive structure, it will be helpful to see, in diagrammatic form, how the $MR = MC$ rule is applied in pure competition. And how it is applied, later in this chapter, in oligopoly.

Imperfect Competition and Monopoly

Figure 7.1 will serve well for imperfect competition and monopoly. You see, this figure implies that there is a price decision to make. But it implies something else of equal importance. For there to be an MC curve and an MR curve, this situation would have to be one in which short-run planning considerations are paramount. In a short-run planning context the price decision (and the accompanying production and sales decision) involves no change in the scale of the firm. Fixed costs do not enter the picture. By the way, the firm is assumed to have a U-shaped cost curve.

The $MR = MC$ Pricing Rule in Pure Competition

In Fig. 7.2 the demand curve, the marginal revenue curve, and the average revenue curve are all one because, in pure competition, the firm has available only pricing option (1). It must take the market price as given and react to it. From the firm's viewpoint, demand is highly elastic. The firm can sell all that it cares to produce at the market price. It won't do that, of course. It still makes sense to move along the marginal revenue curve to where it equals marginal cost and set sales (and production) levels there.

In Fig. 7.2, because the AC curve falls below the demand curve, there is a range of sales (and output) from OB_1 to OB_2 for which, at the market price, revenue exceeds cost. In that range, the best output is OQ where the unit revenue cost gap PC is the greatest. The maximum possible net revenue or profit is $OQ \times PC$. This, too, is the short run. It is supposed that in a long-run planning context, because of the likelihood that a firm somewhere in the market has the most efficient cost curve, this firm will find itself forced to match the lowest possible price. Taking advantage of all possible efficiencies will probably mean that the demand curve will drop to a tangency with the AC curve. Thus, in the long run, this firm will have no profit. It will just cover its costs. But

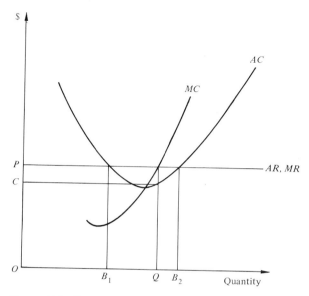

Figure 7.2. Pure competition, short-run price decision. At P, a price set by competition in marketplace, set $P = MC$ to determine best output Q. CP is profit.

$CP \times OQ$ = total profit
$OC \times OQ$ = total cost
$OP \times OQ$ = total revenue

the pricing rule, set $MR = MC$, will still give it the best output (and sales) position. It can't do any better.

Obviously, in pure competition, $MR = MC$ is not really a pricing rule. There is no pricing decision to make other than to accept what is. It is, in this pure competition context, only a production and revenue maximizing rule.

Oligopoly Pricing

Oligopoly is a different story. Two models of oligopoly pricing policies can be used to describe how those few firms in an oligopolistic industry use the $MR = MC$ rule. One is the kinked demand curve analysis that seeks to explain the fact that prices in an oligopolistic industry are relatively unchanging or rigid. This appears to be the case in such industries as automobile manufacture, tobacco and tobacco products, and tires and tubes. If any oligopolist firm were to try to cut prices, then rival firms with essentially similar production processes available to them and with relatively complete knowledge of the demand would quickly match any price cut. Yet, it probably would not match a price increase. By the same token, so long as any one oligopolistic firm did not change its prices, it is unlikely that rivals would "rock the boat."

In Fig. 7.3, the demand curve for an oligopolist's output has two segments.

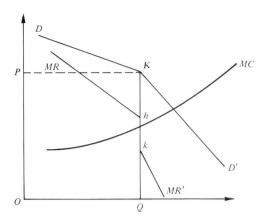

Figure 7.3. Oligopoly kinked demand curve.

DK is the more elastic for price increases and *KD'* is less elastic for price decreases. The whole demand curve is *DKD'*. *Op* is the current market price and *K* is the point at the "kink" in the demand curve. There are two *MR*'s: *MRh*, for demand curve section *DK* and *KMR'* for demand curve section *KD'*

Because of these two *MR*'s, interpreting the *MR* = *MC* rule in oligopoly is more difficult. For example, *MC* at no point actually crosses either *MR* curve. There is no *MR* = *MC* point.

However, between *h* and *k* on the vertical line *KQ*, there is a segment which could be said to be part of a continuous *MR* function. It is clear that any output less than *OQ* or greater than *OQ* would be less profitable than *OQ*. So long as *MR* (between the values *h* and *k* on line *KQ*) is equal to *MC*, the *MR* = *MC* rule holds, meaning, of course, that over a fairly wide range of industry marginal costs (between *h* and *k*) the price and output would remain the same.

Dominant Firm Approach to Oligopoly

Another oligopoly pricing model, developed by K. J. Cohen and R. M. Cyert, operates on the assumption that there is a dominant firm or at least a price leader in an oligopolistic industry and that there are smaller firms that will adjust their product prices to follow the leader. This dominant firm sets the price and allows the other firms to sell all they can sell at this price. Given the market structure, the dominant firm has a share sufficiently large to assure it of a satisfactory sales level and profit.

In Fig. 7.4, at any high price such as *Om*, market demand curve *DD'* intersects supply curve *Sm*. The share of the dominant firm will be 0 and *Sm*, the supply curve of the smaller firms, will also be the supply curve of the industry. But at any price *Oc* (lower than *Om*), the amount supplied by the smaller firms is *OQc* (= *cd*), read off the small firms' supply curve *Sm*. But the market demand is *OQf* (= *df*). Moreover, at any price *Or* (lower than *Oc*),

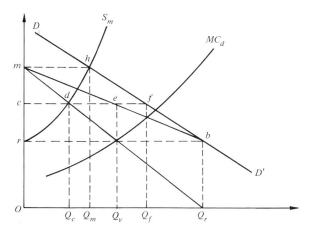

Figure 7.4. Dominant firm in oligopoly.

the smaller firms' share of the market demand dwindles to 0 and the entire demand OQr (= rb) is supplied by the dominant firm.

With this information, we can now trace the dominant firm's demand curve. It contains points m, e, b, and D' and is the kinked line $mebD'$. Thus, too, MR of the dominant firm is mQr. So, if the dominant firm chooses to act as a monopolist and maximizes profit it will set its price at Oc where $MR = MC$ and produce OQv. Out of total industry output OQf, OQc will be the smaller firms' share and the rest goes to the dominant firm.

Cartel and Oligopolistic Pricing Agreements

Simply, a cartel is an agreement among business firms to cooperate to their mutual advantage. A frequently found form of cartels is a price-setting agreement designed to permit profits to be maximized jointly. Admittedly, cartel agreements, especially when the industry members have diverse and even conflicting interests, are hard to administer. The key issue in analyzing a cartel is how the members arrive at mutually satisfactory prices for the products they sell. Electric switchgear pricing procedures in an illegal cartel may illustrate the problem. Court testimony revealed that each seller in the cartel after much negotiation was assigned a share of the sealed-bid government contract business. For example, General Electric's share was set at 40.3 percent in 1958. Allis-Chalmers' share was 8.8 percent. The cartel members, then, coordinated bids so that each was a low bidder in just enough cases to gain the agreed-upon share of the market.

The cartel was a success if measured by higher prices and profits. But there is always a temptation to cheat. And, as one General Electric executive admitted ruefully, "on every job, someone would cut our throat . . ." Thus there are two basic problems with price-setting cartels. One is that mutually agreed-on prices, market shares, and profit levels are very hard to reach. The second is that, once an agreement is reached, there is a strong temptation to cheat, since all participants know the advantages of undercutting the agreement.

Needless to say, cartels are generally illegal in the United States, with the milk industry an important exception. Yet cartels or restrictive agreements can take many forms. Such agreements are likely to be effective only when the main customers are public agencies or regulated companies such as public utilities.

A Summary Comment on the $MR = MC$ Pricing Rule

The major criticism of the $MR = MC$ rule is that it requires a kind of information management may not have. After all, marginal revenue calculations require management to know how market demand will react to alternative prices. If, as we have observed in our review of the state of demand analysis, there are problems for experts in estimating and even in identifying demand relationships, it is reasonable to assume that some managements may not be able to use demand information effectively, even if, indeed, it is available in usable form.

By the same token, marginal cost calculations require a good understanding of the short-run production level alternatives. What is more, if, as Bela Gold, J. Johnston, and others suspect and as a good many empirical cost studies have apparently shown, marginal costs are constant over much of the range of short-run production for many firms in a wide variety of industries, they may not even be necessary. Average costs will serve as well.

The temptation is to reduce the $MR = MC$ rule to a simple setting of price equal to average cost plus some arbitrary margin for profit. Cost-plus pricing involving the use of a learning curve can be a very efficient way to keep defense procurement prices under control as Department of Defense contract procedures will show.

However, the kind of reasoning that goes into the $MR = MC$ rule is still valid, even if there are some practical problems in application. The $MR = MC$ rule amounts to a statement that if, in setting prices, management observes the resultant sales are such that the increase in total revenue is greater than the increase in total cost, then there is more profit to be made. A lower price would be even more profitable than the one set.

Or if management finds that a given price induces an increase in revenue which is less than the increase in costs, this is evidence that a higher price would have brought higher profits. Some economists have pointed out that it is this rough, marginal kind of reasoning that shows evidence of rational price decisions. It is not necessary, they have argued, that each firm know its MR and MC, every time, with precision.

One more point must be made about the $MR = MC$ rule. There are obviously some problems in applying the rule when short-run costs are decreasing. In that case, often called "natural monopoly," the firm with the lowest costs at capacity should be the single seller to assure society of the most for the least. The seller may find that if the demand for the product is elastic, it will pay to keep lowering the price since costs decrease per unit with volume increases.

Gross Revenue Maximizing Pricing Rule

A number of years ago, Professor Baumol of Princeton suggested that many sellers really try to maximize gross revenues or total sales rather than profits. He argued that there was a good deal of rationality in such behavior and proposed a pricing rule to fit this pricing decision. There are two elements of the sales revenue maximizing pricing rule. One is a management profit goal. The other is the price that will permit the attainment of this goal.

How the rule is to be applied is spelled out in Fig. 7.5. Along the vertical axis in Fig. 7.5 are measured dollars of profit, revenue, and costs. Along the horizontal axis are measured units of output. In Fig. 7.5, price lines pass through the origin. The slope of a price line is total revenue divided by output and is thus the average revenue. Obviously, the steeper the slope the higher the price (and the average revenue).

Price OP_q is a price which meets the $MR = MC$ rule and will maximize profits. At price OP_q, the sales will be OQ_q. And, at that sales level OQ_q, the surplus of total revenue over total cost will be at a maximum. This is indicated by the topping out of the profit curve (profit $= \pi_q$).

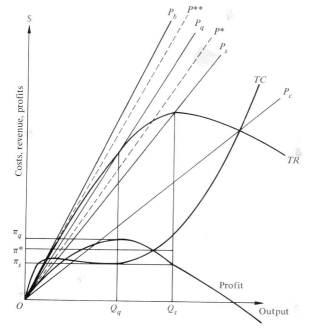

Figure 7.5. Maximizing gross revenue versus maximizing net revenue.

The price OP_s will maximize total revenue. It will also permit a profit of π_s to be earned. Price OP_c will be one that just permits total revenue to cover total cost. Profit will be zero at that price. Profits will also be zero at price OP_b.

If the management profit goal is π^*, then price OP^* will meet that objective; and so will any price between OP^* and OP^{**}. The sales revenue maximizing price policy, then, involves selecting any price in the range that permits achievement of a given profit goal or constraint.

Observe that a strategy of lowering the price from OP_b to OP_q would have the effect of increasing both sales and profits. In that price range, then, the $MR = MC$ rule and the revenue maximizing rule would give the same answer, that is, lower the price. Lowering the price below OP_q would run counter to the $MR = MC$ rule; nonetheless, the lower price would still yield an increase in total revenue as well as a good profit.

There are three advantages to management application of the sales revenue maximizing price rules:

1. It is easier for management to trace the relationship between prices and sales.
2. For a significant range of prices, the rule will also maximize profits.
3. Use of the rule will almost never incur losses.

Nevertheless, the truth is that the sales revenue maximizing price rule is a second-best rule. A firm using this rule will sell (and produce) more than it would if it were following a profit maximizing policy. It will also charge lower prices and, of course, make lower profits.

A Pricing Rule for Maximizing the Value of the Investment in a Firm

Price decisions not only affect the sales of the products of a firm. Since they affect the level of profit that a firm can earn, price decisions also affect the value of the firm itself. The value of a firm is, in the simplest possible terms, the price of its common stock. The price or value of common stock can be determined by

$$V = \frac{E}{k}$$

where

E = earnings (or profits) of a firm for any given accounting period
k = interest rate which discounts or capitalizes earnings (thus turning earnings into a price)

So, if the earnings of the Putney Corporation in 1977 were reported at

$1,750,000, if the expected rate of return on common stocks in 1977 were 4.7 percent, and if Putney had a million common shares outstanding, then

$$V = \frac{\$1,750,000}{.047} = \$37,234,043$$

V per share = $37.23.

But E is directly affected by the price at which Putney's products sell. Here's a way to determine E, keeping in mind that what we are looking for are the net earnings available to common stockholders of Putney,

$$E_t = p_t Q_t - \Sigma\, b_t X_t - r_t D_t$$

where

E = earnings available to pay dividends to common stockholders
p = price of the product Putney sells

Q = quantity sold of the product
b = cost of product inputs
X = level of output of products
r = contract rate of interest on Putney's debt
D = dollar value of Putney's debt
t = accounting period

Thus, the firm's earnings depend on a price decision, the effect of that decision on sales, the costs of production, and the amount owed to lenders of money capital to the firm.

We could have added corporate taxes, so that $E(1 - T)$, where T is the tax rate on corporate earnings. In any case, the key variable in this equation is the product price. Other things being equal, the higher the price the higher the earnings, depending, of course, on demand elasticity of product sales and also on the firm's cost curve. So there is at least one certain price which will maximize the firm's earnings. That price will also maximize the firm's value and thus raise the price of the firm's common stock.

No such relationship is simple. But the point is that Putney's management has to be concerned with the cost of the money capital it needs. The value of the firm's common stock depends directly on profits or earnings. And those earnings depend on price and sales volume. The higher (and more secure) the flow of the firm's earnings, the higher the price of its common stock on Wall Street. And the lower will be the cost of the money capital Putney can obtain by selling more stocks or by borrowing from banks.

In general, the $MR = MC$ rule will also maximize the investment value of the firm. However, since investors are more interested in tomorrow than in today, it is not the short-run price decision that matters but the long-run impact of that decision and the pattern of short-run price decisions as they affect profits. Investors take whatever evidence they have of the performance of a firm's management or a likely change in the firm's market. The E they are concerned with is the future flow of Es. Of course, the past behavior of E is not overlooked by any means.

Satisficing Rules and Price Decisions

The $MR = MC$ rule and profit maximization assume that management, with knowledge of current and future costs, current and future markets, and current and future assets, will set prices that maximize profits. The emphasis in profit maximization theory is on performance. Profit measures permit comparison of effectiveness of one policy, one action, or one decision against another. A profit maximizing firm is one in which management is responding to objective signals in the most effective way.

However, the longer the period over which price and other decisions have to be made, the less precise management can be about which acts will maximize profits. When corporate managements have to make long-range decisions that involve

1. Long design and implementation periods
2. Consequences that will unavoidably be felt over long periods
3. Irreversibility, that is, extreme difficulty in modifying or correcting decisions once made, even if subsequent experience indicates shortcomings

they cannot always be sure about the objective criteria implicit in the profit maximizing theory of behavior.

Herbert Simon[3], one of the most perceptive critics of the profit maximizing theory of firm behavior, feels that the firm cannot choose effectively from any set of alternatives on a continuous basis without knowing exactly what the results of these choices will be. The future is uncertain. Competitive structure, economic conditions, innovations, and many other factors can cause such uncertainty that businessmen cannot know the best alternatives. Therefore, they cannot maximize. What businessmen search for, according to Simon, are those behavior patterns which produce satisfactory results with some degree of assurance. Being unable to maximize in a world of limited knowledge, business firms "satisfice."

Satisficing could mean selecting those courses of action which achieve performance criteria at least equal to reference projections. A reference projection is based upon the assumption that a company will continue to react in the future in the way it has reacted in the past. For Syco, one of the nation's largest manufacturers of electronic products, a reference projection takes account of adjustments for inflation, expected costs, and most likely produc-

[3]H. A. Simon, *Models of Man*, New York, Wiley, 1957; also *Administrative Behavior*, 2d ed., New York, Free Press, 1957.

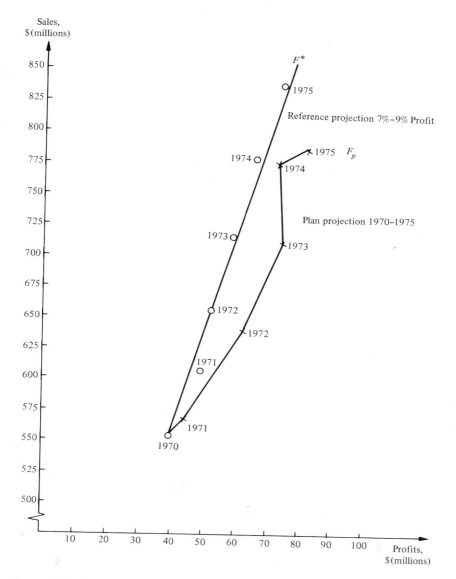

Figure 7.6. Syco, 1970–1975 plan, BPT divisions. Satisficing is achieved whenever forecast lies to the right of reference projection.

tion levels (see Fig. 7.6 and Table 7.3). If Syco's management concludes that a proposed course of action will not meet the minimum requirements of a reference projection, then it will know that it ought not to take that course of action.

Syco's price decisions are designed to achieve a satisfactory level of profit, a level that will not lower Syco's common stock prices and at the same time will generate enough funds for continuing growth. While it is possible that

Table 7.3 Comparison of plan with actual performance
BPT divisions, Syco, 1970–1975

	Year	Forecasts,* F_p		Reference projections,† F	
		Sales $\times\ 10^6$	Profits $\times\ 10^6$ (%)	Sales $\times\ 10^6$	Profits $\times\ 10^6$ (%)
Actual	1970	$554.8	$39.0 (7.0)	$554.8	$39.0 (7.0)
	1971	567.3	44.7 (7.9)	609.0	48.9 (8.0)
	1972	636.4	61.2 (9.6)	654.1	52.0 (7.9)
	1973	709.8	73.8 (10.4)	712.2	58.7 (8.2)
	1974	771.2	71.9 (9.3)	777.4	65.5 (8.4)
	1975	785.2	80.3 (10.2)	835.8	73.6 (8.8)

*A projection in current dollars based on management's best estimates.
†Takes into account inflation offsets and necessary divisional profit contributions.

Syco's satisficing price policies might also occasionally maximize profits, this would be a pleasant accident. In this instance forecasted profits exceed reference projections—a good satisfice!

Firm Survival Pricing

There is nothing in economic theory that says a business firm has to survive. On the other hand, it is not hard to understand that management is much concerned about the problem of business survival. A number of years ago, Kenneth Boulding[4] pointed out that a firm is composed of sets of assets. A firm can survive, he argued, only if management policies maintain those assets in a form and in amounts sufficient to meet changing conditions in the marketplace.

Survival pricing, then, involves price levels set

1. To preserve a firm's existing assets
2. To permit a buildup of necessary future assets for growth and adaptation to market changes
3. To permit a transformation of existing assets to preserve their value

Survival is attained and assured when there is an effective coordination between price policy and asset management and when there is viable equilibrium among all elements, an equilibrium that can be maintained.

So far so good, but what Boulding doesn't say is exactly how to set prices for firm survival. Here, then, are some elements of survival pricing. First, there is the matter of a shut-down price. A shut-down price is one which just covers out-of-pocket or average variable costs. A shut-down price does not allow for coverage of fixed or asset costs. Clearly, that is the minimum survival price. Clearly, too, such a survival price will work only in the short run. Yet, there are

[4]K. E. Boulding, *A Reconstruction of Economics*, New York, Wiley, 1950.

many businesses such as public utilities, steel production, railroads, and chemicals where the relative size of the investment is so large that coverage of variable costs can sustain a firm and keep it viable for fairly long periods of time.

Depreciation generated by capital invested in facilities can provide a considerable cash flow. Failure to replace or to maintain assets in such industries, even if possible for the short run, entails substantial risks of severe service curtailment if prices remain at or near the shut-down point.

The concept of contribution margin is used to define that amount of fixed cost coverage any particular price may offer. In effect, the contribution margin is the difference between the shut-down price and the price that would cover all costs. Sometimes, of course, the concept is used to refer to a situation where a firm has a specific cost-plus objective. In that instance, the contribution margin is the difference between the shut-down price and the total cost plus a fixed profit percentage.

The larger a contribution margin is, the better the asset management and preservation. The point of the contribution margin concept is that full-cost pricing is not always possible. Contribution margin calculations permit determination of the degree of cost coverage a particular price involves and, thus, the degree of implicit survival.

Putney Corporation: Using Break-Even Analysis to Set Prices

Putney Corporation is a small vacuum-tube manufacturer in the Northeast. To get a special order for 75,000 vacuum tubes, the sales and marketing manager reported that it might be necessary to quote $1.50 per tube. The production manager felt that Putney should stay out of the market unless it could get at least $2. He added that, even at $2, a production run of at least 60,000 tubes would be necessary to make it worthwhile. The corporate treasurer wanted $2.50 a tube. Company records, he pointed out, showed that, on average orders of about 30,000 tubes, it had been difficult to make a profit. The treasurer prepared a best-estimate of costs at successive output levels for the executive committee. Table 7.4 shows the figures the treasurer prepared, along with an estimate worked out by the executive committee of the profit or loss from each of the proposed price options. Figure 7.7 presents the break-even chart worked out by the treasury staff.

The production manager opened the meeting of the executive committee with a presentation showing that, with current vacuum-tube production facilities, the treasurer's total fixed costs estimates were more or less correct. He observed that the normal operating range for these vacuum-tube facilities did not exceed a production run of 78,000 tubes and seldom fell below 10,000 tubes. The direct labor input for this production range ran from 1000 to 9000 production hours.

The treasurer's presentation stressed the profit curves in Fig. 7.7. The break-even production level for the $2 price option was 50,000 tubes. The break-even point for the $2.50 price option was about 33,000 tubes. There was

Table 7.4 Putney Corporation: Vacuum-tube production outputs and profits

					Revenue at three price options, × 10^3			Profit (loss) at each price option		
					A	B	C			
Direct					$2	$1.50	$2.50			
labor-hours, × 10^3	Output, × 10^3	*TVC*, $ × 10^3	*TFC*, $ × 10^3	*TC*, $ × 10^3	TR_2 $	$TR_{1.5}$ $	$TR_{2.50}$ $	A $	B $	C $
0	0	0	30	30	0	0	0	(30)	(30)	(30)
1	10	30	30	60	20	15	25	(40)	(45)	(35)
2	18	38	30	68	36	27	45	(32)	(41)	(23)
3	26	46	30	76	52	39	65	(24)	(37)	(11)
4	34	54	30	84	68	51	85	(16)	(33)	1
5	42	62	30	92	84	63	105	(8)	(29)	13
6	50	70	30	100	100	75	125	0	(25)	25
7	58	78	30	108	116	87	145	8	(21)	37
8	68	88	30	118	136	102	170	18	(16)	52
9	78	98	30	128	156	117	195	28	(11)	67
10	88	128	30	158	176	132	220	18	(26)	62

no break-even level for the $1.50 price option. He added that it would take a price of $1.64 for Putney to break even on tube production at 78,000, the top of the normal operating range. There would, he noted, be no contribution margin below a price of $1.26 a tube. At the $1.50 price, a contribution margin would appear at about the 37,000 output level. There would be a contribution margin at the $2 price beyond the 20,000 output level, and, for the $2.50 price, there would be a contribution margin beyond an output of 13,000 tubes. In the light of this analysis, the treasurer insisted that the best and safest price policy would be to bid at no lower than $2.50.

But the marketing manager argued that Putney would not get the special order at $2.50 per tube. He said that this one order was needed to round out a good year. The fixed costs would be there whether or not this order was obtained. He had surveyed the competition and was sure that, to be the lowest bidder and the winner of the contract, Putney's bid had to be below $2.00. "To ice this order, I strongly urge $1.50," he concluded.

At about this point, the recording tape broke. Nobody knows quite how the price decision was made, but Putney didn't get the special order. However, we can see the advantages of break-even analysis even if Putney did make the wrong price decision. The shut-down price was $1.26 per tube. Any price above that would not have threatened the firm's short-run viability. What is more, just how close to that shut-down price the actual price should have been depended on management's assessment of the competition.

Notice, too, that, beyond the normal operating range, that is, beyond the capacity of Putney's tube operation, total costs climbed at a faster pace and profits for each of the options declined. The capacity level of about 78,000 tubes was a least-average-cost operating level. It was also the level at which

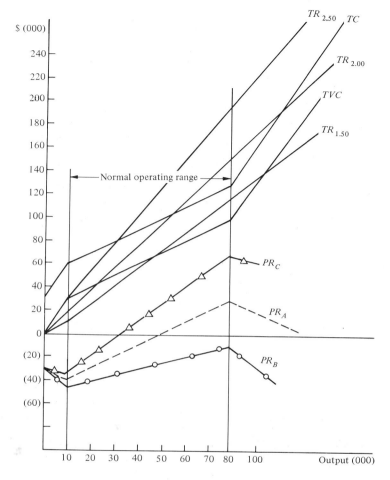

Figure 7.7. Putney Corporation: prices and break-even analysis.

profits were maximized. In fact, even though nobody around the table mentioned marginal revenue or marginal cost, much less the $MR = MC$ pricing rule, implicitly that was the pricing rule that was used. In this break-even analysis, since the slope of the total revenue line is really the average revenue and also the marginal revenue and since the slope of the total cost curves is the average cost and also the marginal cost, it was at capacity that

$$AR = MR = MC = AC$$

Therefore at capacity profits were maximized or losses were minimized for each profit option. Figure 7.8 spells out the break-even story in terms of the average and marginal curves. But what needs to be stressed is that Putney, like any other firm using break-even analysis, was playing the $MR = MC$ game even if they did not know the name of the game.

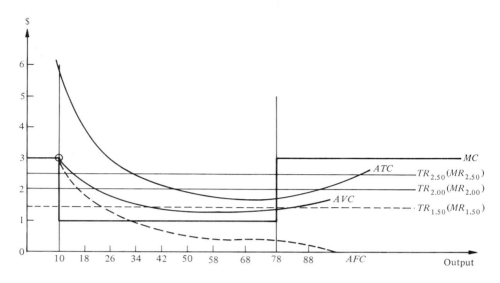

Figure 7.8. Putney Corporation: $MR = MC$ at 78,000 units for all price options.

Nonlinear Break-Even Analysis

The break-even chart used by the Putney Corporation executives goes back to the work of Columbia University's Prof. Walter Rautenstrauch in the early part of this century. It is neither complicated nor novel, and it is very helpful since it focuses on three elements of short-run price setting:

1. The meaning of capacity and its effect on cost behavior
2. The effect on profit of various price options facing a firm
3. The effect on profit of different elements of a firm's cost structure, given a price

There isn't any reason, though, to suppose that break-even analysis has to be linear. Figure 7.9 shows a total cost curve which rises sharply from a zero output total fixed cost level of $15,000. Total costs then level off in the vicinity of an output of 3000 units before beginning to rise again. This total cost reflects the effects of diminishing average and marginal productivity. Average cost is obtained by dividing the total cost at any output level by the output indicated. Obviously, if we know total fixed costs, we also know total variable costs and can obtain average variable costs.

In this case suppose there are three total revenue lines: TR_1, corresponding to a market price of $7.50, TR_2 for a market price of $9, and TR_3 for a market price of $10. At an output of 8000 units, $TC = TR_2$, so that, with a price of $9, TR is $72,000 = TC$. At 8000 units, $AR = AC = \$9$. But, since $TFC = \$15,000$, $TVC = \$57,000$ and $AVC = \$7.13$. At that same output of 8000 units, TR at $10 is $80,000. While a price of $9 just covers total cost, a price of $10 yields a unit profit of $1 and a total profit of $8,000. Table 7.5a and b spells out these relationships.

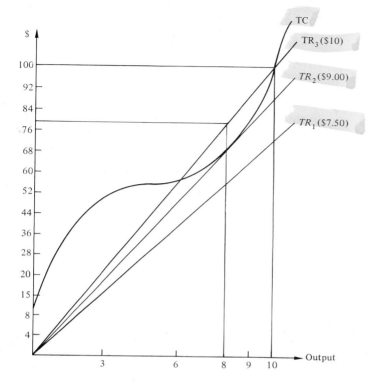

Figure 7.9. Nonlinear break-even analysis.

A price of $7.50 yields a profit at no one of the output levels, but at 8000 units, the loss $(TC - TR_1)$ is $12,000. Thus, the revenue at a price of $7.50 from the sale of 8000 units is enough to cover the total variable cost ($57,000) and

Table 7.5a

Out-put, $\times 10^3$	Total costs Fixed $\$ \times 10^3$	Total costs Variable $\$ \times 10^3$	Total costs $\$ \times 10^3$	TR_1, $\$ \times 10^3$	TR_2, $\$ \times 10^3$	TR_3, $\$ \times 10^3$	Profit$_1$, $\$ \times 10^3$	Profit$_2$, $\$ \times 10^3$	Profit$_3$, $\$ \times 10^3$
6	15	45	60	45	54	60	−15	−6	0
8	15	57	72	60	72	80	−12	0	8
10	15	85	100	75	90	100	−25	−10	0

Table 7.5b

Output, $\times 10^3$	AFC, $	AVC, $	ATC, $	P_1, $	P_2, $	P_3, $
6	2.50	7.50	10.00	7.50	9.00	10.00
8	1.88	7.13	9.00	7.50	9.00	10.00
10	1.50	8.50	10.00	7.50	9.00	10.00

leave a contribution margin of $3000. What is more, at 6000 units, TR_1 = $45,000 = TC.

In Table 7.5b the shut-down price is $7.13, the minimum AVC. At a $10 price, the break-even levels of output are 6000 and 10,000. A break-even level occurs at the $9 price at an output of 8000. A $7.50 price covers out-of-pocket costs from an output of 6000 to a little less than 9000 units. These outputs, at the $7.50 price, give the minimum feasibility range at the lowest market price.

The nonlinear break-even model, of course, is a succinct statement of the $MR = MC$ rule. If a firm knows its total cost curve, its fixed costs, and its price options, the rule for price setting is: Select that price from the range of available options for which, at an output level within a feasible range, profit (loss) is maximized (minimized). The minimum possible price is that which just covers out-of-pocket or variable costs.

Monopoly Prices and Price Discrimination

A monopoly firm with the same cost conditions as a firm in pure competition faces a qualitatively different pricing decision. Unlike the purely competitive firm, the monopoly management is aware that not only does it have a range of prices which it can charge but also that there will be a different quantity demanded at each such price. Therefore, it is looking for that price which will permit it to produce at a cost as far below price as possible, that is, to maximize profit.

So $P \geqq MC$ at any level of production or output at which a monopoly firm is likely to operate. While distinctions can be made for the short-run price-output decision (especially when the monopoly firm is in the unusual position in which the only price decisions available would fail to yield enough revenue to cover all costs but would cover variable costs) and in the long run, there is little practical reason to make such distinctions. To be sure, the case of regulated monopoly is a different matter, for there the monopoly firm is not free to set any price it wishes.

A monopoly firm does not have a supply curve in the sense that how much it should supply to the market can be calculated from knowledge about its costs. In an attempt to find the best market position (equals the most profit position), a monopoly firm adjusts either its price or its production and sales level to the demand situation. In that context, a monopolist may find it possible to charge different groups different prices either because of their location or because of their reactions to prices. This is price discrimination.

We can distinguish between first-, second-, and third-degree price discrimination. First-degree discrimination frequently is found in public utility pricing. For example, if the demand curve of any customer is known, the public utility can divide that demand curve into small segments so that, in effect, it becomes many customers. For each segment, from the highest portion of the demand curve to the lowest, the utility can charge a different price, one which reflects the willingness of the customer to buy a given amount of, say, electricity at that price.

As Fig. 7.10 illustrates, effective first-degree discrimination means that the utility captures all of the customer's consumer surplus. Actually, first-degree discrimination is too difficult to administer and thus most utilities prefer second-degree discrimination where customers are divided into different user groups, such as residential, industrial, commercial, high volume, and low volume. Each group is charged a different set of rates; though this pricing technique does not capture all the available consumer surplus, it is much more practical to administer. By the way, in this example of price discrimination as in others, there is nothing necessarily illegal or immoral about the practice. Indeed, the paradox of first- and second-degree price discrimination is that any policy attempting to ensure that public utilities (which generally have declining average and marginal cost curves) price along their marginal cost curves must also permit price discrimination. The reason is that marginal cost pricing for decreasing cost industries means losses and discriminatory pricing makes up for these losses.

Third-degree discrimination is that situation where in each of several

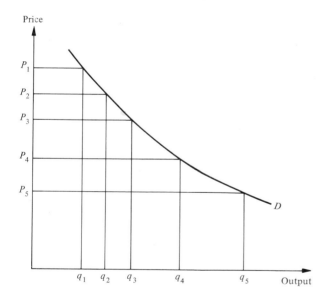

Figure 7.10. First- and second-degree price discrimination. If consumer's total outlay for q_5 is

$$P_1 \times q_1 + P_2 \times q_2 + P_3 \times q_2 q_3 + P_4 \times q_3 q_4 + P_5 \times q_4 q_5$$

then he has paid a good share of his consumer surplus.

If monopolist could price to take all the consumer surplus, this would be *first-degree discrimination*.

But if, as in this figure, monopolist misses some because of a step price schedule, this is *second-degree discrimination*.

markets there is a separate demand function. Suppose, for example, that in Fig. 7.11 DD_1 is the demand function in market 1 and MR_1 is the marginal revenue function for that market. Then, DD_2 and MR_2 are the demand and marginal revenue functions in market 2. The discriminating monopolist firm will, first, add the demand functions horizontally to obtain a total demand curve for all markets in which it sells. And in the same manner, the monopoly firm will obtain a total marginal revenue curve. Next, the monopolist finds that output level at which the total marginal revenue function just equals the marginal cost of the total output. This is the output level for which monopoly profits are maximized. Then, the monopolist will allocate the output so determined among the two markets so that the marginal revenue obtained in each market from the output allocated there is the same in each market. In effect, then, this means setting a price in each market such that $MR_1 = MR_2 = MC_t$. The price in each market, of course, will depend on that market's demand function.

It turns out that if the own-price elasticity of demand is higher (i.e., more elastic) in one market than in another, the discriminatory price will be lower in the market with the higher own-price elasticity. Furthermore, if the own-price elasticities are the same in both markets, there can be no price discrimination.

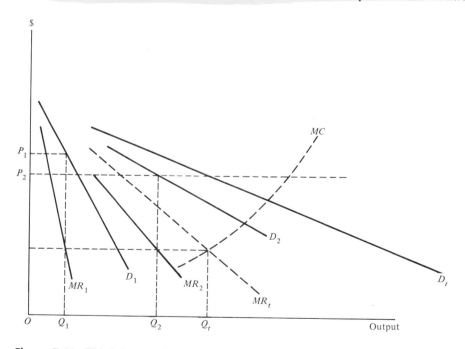

Figure 7.11. Third-degree discrimination: charging what traffic will bear.

Market	Price	Output
1	P_1	Q_1
2	P_2	Q_2

Thus, effective price discrimination depends on a difference in the (logarithmic) slope of the different demand functions among different markets.

Empirical research into price discrimination indicates a far more varied range of price behavior than this simple model implies. In fact, it is just as likely that a firm with a buyer's monopoly may discriminate among markets and pay different prices for the same commodity in each market, depending in this case on the relative strength of its position in each market (i.e., on the elasticity of supply of each potential supplier).

Comparison Between Competitive and Monopoly Pricing

It is difficult to make a meaningful comparison between the performance of a monopoly firm and a firm in pure competition. In pure competition, there are many firms in an industry (even if we concentrate on the behavior of only one); in monopoly, there is only one firm. The essential differences in performance arise in three areas: the level of output, the level of profit, and the relationship between price and marginal cost.

In most cases, monopoly output is less than would be produced if the monopoly firm set its price equal to marginal cost. But, if we were to ask "What would happen to the level of total output if a purely competitive industry were to be monopolized?", the answer is not so apparent.

The answer is not apparent partly because the question is not specific enough. We must inquire whether the monopolist firm would continue to operate all the individual plants which it would be taking over. If all plants were to be continued in operation, then, very likely, total industry output would fall as the monopoly firm took over. But it is also likely that the reason for the monopoly take-over is that there are economies of scale. In that case, the monopoly firm would consolidate operations, reduce the number of plants, and increase the sizes of the remaining plants. Moreover, the monopolist would probably increase research and development spending, introduce product differentiation, begin advertising, and change distribution procedures. If all these actions lead to greater efficiency, then it is possible that output will be larger in the monopoly situation than in the competitive one. Both socialists and hard-nosed capitalists can use this same argument for monopoly; socialists, of course, prefer state monopolies. It needs to be added that observation of the current world suggests that monopolies are found in industries which are different from those which are competitive. There are differences in technology, scale, markets, and type of products.

The difference in level of profit is a complex problem. While, in the long run, a purely competitive firm would just break even, there is nothing in monopoly theory to ensure that a monopoly would always make a profit. In the short run, both monopolistic and competitive firms could be making profits but little of value can be said about the relative size of such profits. They also could be suffering losses. The point is that economic theory does not answer the question whether monopoly profits would be higher than competitive profits in an industry which moved from competition to a monopoly structure, except perhaps in the special case of constant returns to scale. There is, moreover, no convincing evidence that in practice monopolies are always profitable. Nation-wide railroad and local transit situations would be quite different if there were an assurance of profit.

As to the relationship between price and marginal cost, the difference is that a competitive firm will always operate at an output level where price equals marginal cost. A monopoly firm will always operate at a level of output where price exceeds marginal cost. The essence of this difference, though, lies in resource allocation, not in the specific relationship between price and marginal cost. If a purely competitive industry is monopolized, the presence of monopoly can mean a less efficient utilization of productive resources than would exist in the long run in pure competition. But this is more a hypothesis than an easily provable assertion.

Shadow Prices

Sometimes market prices are inadequate indicators of true costs. For example, in a major engineering proposal such as a highway, a bridge, or a rapid transit system, labor and materials costs may be based on local or unusual conditions. These conditions may exaggerate the true value of the labor or undervalue the true cost of materials. If the true or economic cost of the project is to be determined where market prices are out of line, it may be necessary to adjust prevailing prices by estimating the extent to which they fail to match actual costs of capacity utilization or to which they deviate from normal or equilibrium prices. The adjusted prices are known as "shadow prices" (and sometimes as "accounting prices"). Shadow prices may be substituted for prevailing prices and thus permit a more correct comparison among alternative projects. Shadow prices, thus, allow for the determination of opportunity costs. However, because the determination of shadow prices is surrounded with considerable uncertainty, it is not always easy to obtain reliable shadow prices to substitute for market prices.

Higgins[5] distinguishes between those market prices which are inadequate because they reflect excessive monopoly control, government price and wage controls, or discontinuities, and those market prices which are inadequate because they do not assign a correct value to education, health and environmental factors, transportation utilization, or other considerations of a social nature.

Linear programming can be used to estimate fairly accurately those shadow prices which reflect the extent to which a firm uses its resources optimally. The key to understanding and computing shadow prices is to realize that the sum of the contribution margins in linear programming for each product is equal to the sum of the total values imputed to each product in each

---

[5] B. Higgins, *Economic Development*, rev. ed., New York, Norton, 1959, pp. 370–372. See also A. Waterson, *Development Planning*, Baltimore, Johns Hopkins, 1965, p. 322.

operation or process. Shadow prices reflect sacrifices of profit (or social benefit) if resources are not used (and paid for) optimally.

Shadow prices can also be used to determine whether to add to a firm's capacity. A shadow price is the contribution margin arising from the use of more of a given process. Then, if an additional unit of capacity in this process can be acquired for less than the shadow price, capacity should be expanded.

Transfer Prices

In any large multiproduct, multidepartmental firm, goods and services are often exchanged between divisions. What prices should be assigned to those exchanges or transfers? This is a troublesome question which must be answered by comparing one division (treated as a separate firm or profit center) with another division. For many purposes in markets where there is competition, market prices are desirable transfer prices because they reflect actual market price-cost decisions. But, as with shadow prices, there are reasons why, on occasion, market prices are not good guides to optimal decisions.

The pitfalls in using market prices are that few markets are perfectly competitive and that in some cases no comparative market for the good or service actually exists. A general rule for transfer pricing may be stated as follows: A transfer price should reflect the variable costs (or the additional out-of-pocket costs incurred to the point of transfer) plus opportunity costs for a firm as a whole.

Many firms have different practices with respect to transfer pricing. Some firms deliberately set low prices on goods moving into states that levy taxes on inventories to reduce tax liabilities. Other companies use their transfer price system as a management control device. Transfer prices between foreign and domestic operations are sometimes used to permit repatriation of dollars from foreign operations when such repatriation through payment of dividends may be blocked by exchange controls.

Taking into account opportunity costs or alternative uses for capacity is a complicated process.[6] In practice, simple rules tend to be used such as full cost, standard cost plus markup, simulated interdivisional negotiation, or variable cost plus lump sum.

Price Lining

Price lining takes place when, as in many retail markets, there are distinctions among different grades or lines of goods. For example, shirts may, in large department stores, sell at popular prices in a giant basement store. In the main floor men's department, shirts will sell at somewhat higher prices. And in the

---

[6]For an authoritative discussion of transfer pricing, see chap. 22 of C. T. Horngren, *Cost Accounting: A Managerial Emphasis*, 3d ed., Englewood Cliffs, N.J., Prentice-Hall, 1972.

specialty men's shop, shirts may sell at substantially higher prices. To be sure, there are differences in the quality of the shirts sold in each department, but quality differences would not normally account for the price differences. There is, also, a difference in markup over cost, depending largely on the volume of sales (the number of times inventory has to be replenished in a sales year). But this too won't fully account for the price differences. Perhaps, as many observers insist, this is a more sophisticated and common form of price discrimination. Actually, retailers are trying to maximize gross margin dollar returns rather than net revenue on any one item in any one department.

When the Price System Does Not Work

In the neat and orderly world in which economists like to work, every price is a market-clearing price. Consumers buy all they want, depending on their incomes, their tastes, and their expectations. There are no waiting lines, no problems with shortages, and nothing under the counter. Sellers sell all they want and there are no effective surpluses. But this is not what really happens.

Consider the following four situations as partial illustrations of the nonworking of the price system. First, there is the market for jobs, where there is an obvious problem with persistent unemployment (job seekers exceed the job supply at the going wage). Then, there is the case of the not-for-profit enterprise like a hospital or a university where the price charged probably does not reflect cost and where, what is more, the price is not expected to make demand equal supply. Third, there is the case of zoning where property owners are restricted in the uses they can make of their land, regardless of price. Finally, there is the question of public goods, which, like television, pose knotty problems for regulators.

We will not go into a complex review of how labor markets operate but will give a short description of the problem. If there were a perfect labor market system with adequate information, then, at a given market wage, the supply of worker-hours offered by job seekers would just equal the demand for worker-hours of labor. And the market would clear. But, in reality, not only is it likely that at times more worker-hours will be offered than the market can use but, just as important, lowering the wage would not decrease the supply of worker-hours very much. This labor surplus is a problem that price and pricing policies alone cannot solve.

A not-for-profit enterprise may not know its costs. Even if it does, it may not expect to recover these costs from the prices charged. Should a hospital charge very low prices to avoid burdening those who cannot afford higher prices but who can benefit from its services? If so, then how does it recover its costs? By a drive for funds? By charging the rich more than the poor? By seeking direct grants from government agencies to make up for the difference between revenue and cost? In short, should the price reflect the costs, the benefits, or the hospital's need for meeting its own survival requirements?

In a free market, every property owner could sell holdings to any buyer for any use at the best possible price. But how does that fit into an attempt to preserve the so-called quality of a neighborhood? How, under such a policy, do you protect the ecological environment? If a free market is not allowed to operate, can society be sure that results are better under a zoning law which imparts the basic decision making to planners? Are they wiser than the market would be?

Should a public good like television be controlled by the marketplace so that whatever anyone is willing to pay determines programming? What about controls on excessive violence, sex, or political propaganda?

If there are more questions than answers in this section, that's the way things are. There are cases where prices are not good enough arbiters to determine who gets what. Economics has something to say, but other disciplines also have roles to play.

Chapter Summary

This chapter has set forth a series of pricing rules. The key to these pricing rules is the comparison between marginal revenue and marginal cost. A business firm is assumed to be alert enough to know how both revenue and cost behave as different short-run price alternatives are tried. It turns out, though, that it doesn't matter whether a firm can determine exact marginal cost or exact marginal revenue. The essence of the $MR = MC$ pricing rule is not precision but rationality. A business decision that is in the direction of maximizing the difference between total revenue and total cost meets the $MR = MC$ test of rationality.

Pricing decisions also reflect other considerations, such as the desire of a firm's management to survive under all possible conditions, or the desire to meet certain investment target rates of return, or the intention to operate according to long-range plans. These decisions, too, can be rational by the $MR = MC$ test. Indeed, unless a price decision is made with complete lack of concern for its impact on a firm's well-being (an unlikely situation), it is not too hard to establish useful tests of rational behavior.

The point, of course, is that a chapter dealing with the ways firms set prices is an important contribution to a theory of how firms operate. Price decisions are revenue decisions. Price decisions are also production decisions. But, even more important, price decisions are measures of management. Prices lead to profits and profits determine whether a firm will survive or not. Even in pure competition, where management has few if any pricing decisions to make, management's reactions to market prices involve production decisions which affect the firm's survival.

Selected Readings

Adelman, Morris A.: *A & P: A Study in Price-Cost Behavior and Public Policy,* Cambridge, Harvard, 1959.

Baumol, W. J.: *Business Behavior, Value and Growth,* rev. ed., New York, Harcourt Brace Jovanovich, 1967.

Chamberlin, N. W.: *The Firm in Time and Place*, New York, McGraw-Hill, 1968.

Friedman, Milton: *Price Theory*, Chicago, Aldine, 1976.

Haynes, W. W.: "Pricing Practices in Small Firms," *Southern Economic Journal*, 30(4):315–324, April 1964.

Kamerschen, D. R.: "The Return of Target Pricing," *Journal of Business*, 48(2):242–252, April 1975.

Kaplan, A. D. H., J. B. Dirlam, and R. F. Lanzilotti: *Pricing in Big Business*, Washington, Brookings, 1958.

Marris, R.: *The Economic Theory of "Managerial" Capitalism*, New York, Free Press, 1964.

Palda, K. S.: *Economic Analysis for Marketing Decisions*, Englewood Cliffs, N. J., Prentice-Hall, 1969.

Thompson, A. A., Jr.: *Economics of the Firm, Theory and Practice*, 2d ed., Englewood Cliffs, N. J., Prentice-Hall, 1973.

Waite, W. C., and H. C. Trelogan: *Agricultural Market Prices*, New York, Wiley, 1948.

Weston, J. F.: "Pricing Behavior of Large Firms," *Western Economic Journal*, 10:1–18, March 1972.

Questions, Problems, and Projects

1. United Nuclear Corporation, a major supplier of uranium ore, found the commercial spot price of the ore rising sharply throughout 1975. From 1950 through 1965, the Atomic Energy Commission had been the sole buyer of uranium ore. A commercial market for domestic requirements began in 1965 and, by 1972, AEC purchases ceased. The domestic ore price, which had been as high as $14 per pound in 1959, had been drifting downward and had actually fallen to about $6 when a commercial spot market price was established in 1968. In 1973, new projections about the production capability of known reserves indicated that reserves would be rising from about 30 million pounds in 1973 to about 60 million pounds in 1978 or 1979. Thereafter, through 1985, known reserves would be falling toward 40 million pounds. Domestic requirements that were at about 15 million pounds in 1970 would be reaching 85 million pounds by 1985. How does all this explain the behavior of the commercial spot price per pound of uranium ore in 1975?

2. In the middle 1970s there was a price war in the metropolitan Chicago area among national and local supermarket chains. Supermarket officials blamed the high prices of food, the recent recession, and the lower per capita consumption of food—the lowest, in fact, in seven years—for the price war. They also pointed out that there were too many stores in the Chicago area. "What is happening in Chicago is irrational," said one non-Chicago chain executive. Is a price war "irrational"? What does it mean for a marketplace to be "overstored"? Is there a limit to price wars?

3. Regulation Q sets limits to the interest rates paid by commercial and savings banks as well as savings and loan associations on savings deposits. It also, in 1976, maintained .25 percent differential in favor of the savings institutions for small savings accounts. Mrs. Carol Greenwald, Massachusetts Banking Commissioner, proposed that ceiling interest rates be raised .50

percent every six months "until Reg Q has zero effect." How can rising ceiling prices ultimately have zero effect? How does such a ceiling price system affect competition among banks?

4. Contrast and compare (*a*) target price and pricing to maintain steady profit margins, (*b*) discrimination and exploitation, and (*c*) transfer price and shadow price.

5. Is there ever a defense for price control? Under what conditions? With what results?

6. Examine the meaning of "shut-down point" and its effect on competitive pricing.

Case 7.1   The Government Accounting Office (GAO) Assesses Impact of Deregulating the Price of Natural Gas

ECONOMICS OF NATURAL GAS PRODUCTION

There are costs associated with the production of reserves and pipeline shipments for all three phases of natural gas production. However, some phases of production are more susceptible to cost and price changes than other phases. Extraction costs are closely related to the current level of output. As the pressure from a reservoir drops, output slows down and extraction costs increase. A well will usually be "shut-in" (closed down) for economic reasons when the wellhead price of natural gas falls below current extraction costs. Thus, a higher wellhead price for natural gas is likely to postpone shutting in wells and to bring some shut-in wells back into operation. The exploration phase is further removed from such economic incentives as higher prices. However, higher prices for natural gas should marginally increase the intensity of exploration for new fields.

Development costs are likely to be the most sensitive to short-term economic incentives and therefore the most responsive to increases in wellhead prices. Development, exploration, and extraction expenditures each account for about one-third of total production expenditures.

In general, higher prices for natural gas at the wellhead could be expected to have their largest impact on the development phase because producers would more actively extend and revise their existing fields. Onshore, this extension would be primarily in deeper drilling; offshore, it would mean deeper drilling over larger areas. All these activities are costly in terms of time and money. Any great increase in extraction would probably require a lead time of at least five years. The crucial factor is the discovery of new reserves.

ECONOMIC REGULATION OF THE INDUSTRY

Before 1954 the Federal Power Commission (FPC) regulated pipeline prices only. The public utility nature of pipeline companies provided the underlying rationale for that regulation. During that time the wellhead prices were unregulated. After the 1954 Supreme Court decision in the Phillips case[1], the

---

[1] *Phillips Petroleum Co.* v. *Wisconsin*, 347 U.S. 674 (1954).

FPC was instructed to regulate the wellhead price. It has been argued that the volume of new reserves has not kept up with increased demand because the regulated price has not increased rapidly enough to reflect increased costs of exploration, development, and extraction.

Buyers of reserves at the wellhead are natural gas pipeline companies seeking to deliver gas under long-term contracts to industrial consumers and retail public utility companies. Their scheduled annual deliveries to utilities and industry determine their demand for reserves to be dedicated at the wellhead.

Prices paid by a distributor to a pipeline (wholesale or "city-gate" prices) depend on field prices and delivery charges for transportation of gas from the wellhead to the distributor.

Markup prices for interstate pipelines are determined by the historical average costs of transportation and by the transportation profit margins allowed under FPC regulation. The regulation of wholesale prices creates a considerable lag between changes in field prices and changes in consumer prices. FPC policy has been to allow wholesale prices to equal historical average field prices paid for gas at the wellhead plus markup. The average wellhead price, or "rolled-in price," changes slowly as prices rise because new contracts in any year provide only 5 to 15 percent of all gas under contract. This lag softens the impact of large increases in new contract prices in field markets. Distributors deliver gas to the final consumer, and for delivery they also charge a markup over their wholesale purchase price. Distributors are normally regulated by state public utility commissions.

DEREGULATION PROS AND CONS

Proponents of continued regulation contend that

1. FPC prices have not been too low but have provided adequate incentives for exploration and development and have provided for recovering costs plus a reasonable rate of return.
2. The natural gas market is not competitive. Evidence cited to back up this claim includes the fact that 85 percent of the natural gas produced is controlled by about twenty-five major companies.
3. Pipeline companies which purchase gas have no incentive to obtain low prices since they pass these costs along to consumers who have no choice of supplier.
4. The current gas shortage is the result of industry strategy to gain deregulation of prices. While comprehensive information about withheld reserves is unavailable, many investigations have concluded industry reserve reports are understated.
5. Regulation should be extended to the intrastate market to end the inequities of uneven distribution.
6. Deregulation would not guarantee added natural gas production but would certainly lead to increased prices and windfall profits.
7. Continued regulation is necessary to equitably distribute natural gas and to ensure that critical users obtain a supply.
8. Gas prices are low only in relation to oil prices established by a cartel, the

Organization of Petroleum Exporting Countries (OPEC), not by cost of production nor by free market standards, and deregulation would result in economic disruption for consumers.

Proponents of deregulation contend that

1. Low natural gas prices as set by the FPC have caused the present gas shortage.
2. Price regulation based on costs provides inadequate industry incentive; exploration costs vary widely as do costs among competitive companies.
3. Price regulation has resulted in prices below those of alternative fuels, thereby encouraging excessive use of natural gas.
4. Effective market competition is reflected in frequent changes in market shares among producers, and the market positions of the major companies change materially within short periods of time.
5. There are 30,000 producers; the four largest control 24 percent of the market, and the eight largest control 42 percent which is low when compared with other industries.
6. The amounts added to reserves each year are far below the amounts needed to sustain current production levels.
7. Economic imperatives and legal obligations prohibit producers from holding back their supplies.
8. Inequitable distribution of natural gas supplies between the intrastate and interstate markets has been caused by regulation. Restriction of the interstate gas prices has caused the price differences between these markets.
9. After deregulation, consumer prices would certainly increase, but not excessively, because the wellhead price constitutes only a small portion of consumers' final prices.
10. Without deregulation natural gas production will probably continue to decline, thus increasing dependence on foreign oil.

THE PROCESS OF DEREGULATION: OBJECTIVES

A deregulatory action should attempt to balance the following factors:

1. The need for more exploration and development
2. The impact of increases on retail prices
3. The effect on the overall national economy
4. Excessive growth in industry profit levels

Balancing the above factors involves considerations of timing (phasing) and coverage of deregulation in terms of the extent to which natural gas supplies will be deregulated. For example, immediate termination of price regulation on the total supply would provide

1. The greatest economic incentives
2. The harshest end-user impact
3. The harshest national economic impact
4. The maximum windfall profits

The deregulation approach would satisfy only one of the four objectives, that is, it would provide the greatest economic incentives; but, by moderating timing and coverage, impact on the consumer and windfall profits can be moderated. The coordination of timing and coverage is the key.

TIMING

Timing of deregulation can be either immediate or phased. Immediate means that, on a specified date, a major portion of, or perhaps the total, gas supply price is decontrolled and the price is determined by market forces from that time forward. Phased means that the price of gas is deregulated gradually, for example, over a three- to five-year period.

The immediate approach has the advantage of being the simplest to execute and would tend to maximize capital investment response in the short term. However, it could also result in a period of high prices until supply and demand stabilized under the new price scheme.

Under the phased approach, fewer investment incentives would be present for a few years until the price was fully deregulated, but it would also avoid the impact of sudden large price increases.

Phasing is generally approached in two ways:

1. Pro rata, which is a succession of price increases gradually moving toward an assumed market price for unregulated gas and competing fuels over a period of time.
2. Price ceiling, which is an immediate movement to a price which is near the market price but is still controlled. The regulator adjusts the price periodically on the basis of the prevailing market price for natural gas and competing fuels until the end of the phasing period, at which time price controls are dropped.

The phased approaches are intended to reduce the shock of extreme price movements, pending additional supplies. The pro rata method eliminates the shock best but still is unrelated to the market price. The price-ceiling approach provides more shock but is related to the market price while still maintaining the element of control. It could restrict upward movements in the market price, depending on the volumes involved and the policy of the regulator in adjusting prices in response to the prevailing market price. The price-ceiling method also has the advantage of rising more quickly to a point near the market price for natural gas and competing fuels. This method would help the interstate market compete more effectively with the intrastate market for new gas supplies.

Figure 1 illustrates the approaches to immediate and phased deregulation.

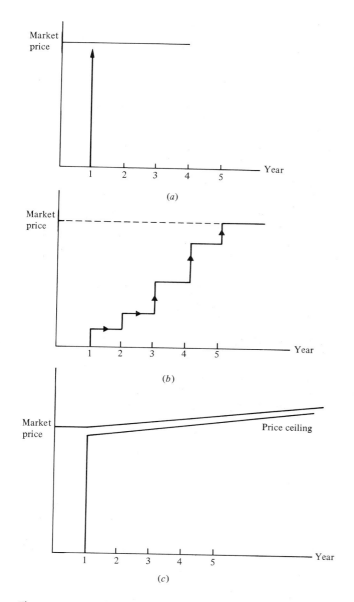

Figure 1. Deregulating timing methods. (*a*) Immediate termination. (*b*) Pro rata phased termination. (*c*) Price ceiling phased termination.

PROCESS OF DEREGULATION: FINDINGS AND CONCLUSIONS

Energy implications

1. Natural gas production in 1975 is expected to be about 21 trillion cubic feet (21 tcf). The major impact of deregulation on future natural gas supplies

between now and 1985 would be on production from the lower forty-eight states. It would have little or no positive impact on natural gas from Alaska, liquefied natural gas imports, or Canadian imports. It could have a negative impact on synthetic pipeline quality gas. Under continued regulation at or near current prices, natural gas supplies in 1985 would be about 17 tcf, or 20 percent below 1975 supplies. With deregulation natural gas supplies would fall about 13 percent below 1975 supplies to 19 tcf. Only under highly optimistic, unlikely circumstances could natural gas supplies in 1985 remain at or near 1975 levels.

This conclusion is based primarily on an analysis of the level of reserve additions that will be required to attain a given amount of production within the next ten years. The level and composition of reserve additions over the last thirty years indicates the probable limits of future levels of reserve additions. The fact is that over the last several years the United States has been producing and consuming natural gas at a faster rate than additional reserve finds, and any significant increase in reserve additions requires an unprecedented rate of new finds. The probable major impact of high prices on production in the lower forty-eight states would be to slow down, but not to reverse, the trend of production.

2. The additional production that deregulation might generate could reduce requirements for imported oil by about 750,000 barrels per day if it displaced imported oil on a one-for-one basis. At current prices this would improve the annual balance-of-payments position, which would increase to an annual figure of $3 billion by 1985.

Environmental implications

If deregulation of natural gas prices should increase the supply of natural gas, the most severe impacts would be accidents such as blowouts or explosions, especially if the gas were produced in association with oil. The maximum damage in such a case would occur in the offshore area. If increased natural gas supplies substitute for imported oil, the environmental advantages and disadvantages in the production and transportation stages would be about equal. However, with the clear advantages of natural gas over other fuels in the consumption state, deregulation of natural gas would seem to have an overall beneficial impact on our environment.

Economic and social implications

1. Continued regulation and deregulation cases indicate no real difference in macroeconomic activity. The economic indicators used in our study, growth of gross national product (GNP), rate of inflation, and rate of unemployment, are substantially the same under regulation or deregulation. This is as expected since the market value of gas is only about $20 billion (1973) in an economy with a GNP of $1300 billion.

2. Deregulation will smooth the distribution of supplies between the intra- and interstate markets. Under continued regulation virtually the entire shortfall in future production would occur in the interstate market (31 percent below

1971 levels). With deregulation the interstate market will be able to compete for supplies on an even basis, and future production is expected to be spread accordingly (about 13 percent below 1975 levels in each market).

3. In the aggregate, additional fuel costs for industry resulting from either deregulation or the need to use alternatives should not be large. Total industry expenditures in 1974 represented less than 1 percent of the monetary value of industrial output. However, some industries will be severely affected. These can generally be classified as industries (1) for which natural gas costs represent a large portion of their selling price (such as the cement industry) or (2) which depend upon natural gas for its unique material value rather than for its energy value and for which there is no practical substitute (such as fertilizer, plastics, and certain textile and baking industries).

4. Since FPC regulations give priority to residential customers in times of shortages, most interstate residential customers would continue to receive supplies under continued regulation; but deregulation would increase residential consumer costs by 40 percent in 1980 and 10 percent in 1985 over the level expected with regulation. This increase amounts to $94 and $30, respectively, over the level of the average residential bill with continued regulation.

5. Deregulation would increase producers' gross revenues from an estimated $9 billion in 1975 to $31 billion in 1980 versus $18 billion with continued regulation. But net earnings would not be increased proportionately. The cost of future natural gas production from the offshore continental shelf (OCS) and deeper onshore reserves is expected to be high. The added revenues would provide added incentives to develop these expensive resources.

DISCUSSION QUESTIONS 7.1

1. While higher prices would increase supplies of natural gas, what is the likely elasticity of the natural gas supply?
2. Can natural gas prices be prevented from rising? With what effect? Upon whom?
3. What would be the result of a free market in natural gas?
4. How do you balance profits to the natural gas suppliers with consumer well-being?

Case 7.2 Memorial Hospital: Reimbursement of In-Patient Laboratory Service

Memorial Hospital has been experiencing a rapid growth in the utilization of its laboratory services. The chief pathologist has been endeavoring to automate as many laboratory tests as possible. As a result, while the average unit cost has been steadily reduced, the average margin per unit has increased, so the average charge per unit has remained the same (Exhibit 1).

Exhibit 1   Comparative analysis of 1969 laboratory gross charges, total cost, allowance, and potential cash for 3 months

	Units of service	Gross charges	Total cost	Contractual allowance	Potential cash
Self-pay	91,513	$ 13,167	$ 9,218	None	$ 13,167
Blue Cross	780,556	110,627	76,816	$33,811	76,816
Commercial insurance	298,893	42,074	29,292	None	42,074
Compensation	14,380	2,046	1,434	612	1,434
Medicaid	78,185	11,369	7,989	3,380	7,989
Medicare	791,461	115,423	80,091	35,332	80,091
Total	2,054,987	$294,705	$204,841	$73,135	$221,571

Medicare, Blue Cross, and Workmen's Compensation allow only cost reimbursement. Any amount over the cost is written off as a contractual allowance. This amount is not recoverable from the patient.

Self-pay and commercial insurance patients reimburse the hospital at published charges. Exhibit 2 presents a summary of the laboratory's charges, costs, allowances, and potential cash.

The controller has developed the following terms and ratios to assist the hospital administration in its evaluation of operational performance (Exhibit 3):

1. Net cash represents the potential cash the hospital can expect to receive if all patients pay their total proportionate amount. No provision has been made for bad debts.
2. Gross charges represent the total published charge to patients for services received.
3. Total cost represents the combined direct and indirect costs of the department.
4. Allowances represent the difference between gross charges and net cash.
5. Net cash: gross charges represents a ratio. Whenever this ratio is greater than 100.0, gross charges are less than net cash, that is, charges for services are less than costs of services.
6. Net cash: total cost represents the relationship between potential cash to be received and cost of service. This ratio must be maintained at least at the

Exhibit 2   Comparative analysis of 1968 actual and 1969 estimated laboratory activity

	1968 actual	1969 estimated
Total units of in-patient service	7,197,084	10,219,948
Margin between charge and cost	4.6¢	4.3¢
% of third-party cost reimbursement	78.6%	81.2%
Units reimbursed at cost	5,657,694	8,298,598
Estimated contractual allowance	$260,254	$292,540

Exhibit 3 Ratio comparisons, fiscal 1968 and 1969 (3 mo.)

	Fiscal 1968	1969, 3 mo.
Net cash/gross charges	74.1%	75.2%
Net cash/total cost	110.5%	108.2%
Total cost/gross charges	67.1	69.5
Gross charges	$1,024,989	$294,705
Total cost	$ 687,351	$204,841
Net cash	$ 759,218	$221,571
Contractual allowance	$ 250,680	$ 69,259

100.0 level or greater. A ratio less than 100.0 would indicate that cash to be received from patients is less than the cost of service.

7. Total cost: gross charges represents a ratio that must be maintained below the 100.0 level. If the ratio is above the 100.0 level, the gross charges are less than cost. However, if the ratio is substantially below 100.0, the margin between costs and charges may be too great. It would appear that a maximum of 80.0 would be reasonable, since Blue Cross and Medicare are making their interim payments at 80 percent of gross charges.

The controller recommended that the hospital administration seek the following three goals:

1. Strive to have the department carry its own total costs
2. Maintain a direct relationship between unit cost and unit charge
3. Adjust rates to reduce contractual allowances while preserving current cash flow

There also appeared to be three alternatives the hospital administration could consider in reviewing the laboratory rate structure, funding, and reimbursement:

1. Reduce rates, knowing that the current cash flow will be less but that there will be a smaller year-end liability to Blue Cross and Medicare
2. Accept the theory of a wide margin between costs and charges and adequately fund the margin in investment for income to help meet the pending liability
3. Maintain the present charge structure and increase the percentage of "hold-back" (20 percent) from Blue Cross and Medicare.

The liability to Blue Cross and Medicare is the difference between total costs and total interim payments. If gross charges are in excess of cost, the interim payment would be larger than total costs. Medicare and Blue Cross reimburse the hospital at 80 percent of gross charges (hold-back equals 20 percent). After a year-end cost study, an adjustment is made to the hospital or to the paying agents to match total reimbursement with total costs.

DISCUSSION QUESTIONS 7.2

1. What is the pricing philosophy at Memorial Hospital?
2. Assess the impact of a marginal cost pricing policy at Memorial Hospital.
3. Work out a break-even analysis, showing price, cost, and volume relationships.
4. In what sense is Memorial Hospital's pricing policy cost-plus?

8

PROFITS, MANAGERIAL EFFECTIVENESS, AND ENTERPRISE

Key Concepts

accumulation
business product
cash flow
compensation theory
costs
deficit
earnings per share
equity, stockholders'
exploitation theory
innovation
innovation profits
loss
monopoly theory of profits

program evaluation
risk premium
romantic theory of profits
Joseph A. Schumpeter
socially necessary labor
statement of changes in financial
    position
surplus value
survival
systems analysis
venture
working capital

What Is Ahead in This Chapter

Corporate profits play a fundamental role in the economy of the United States. They govern the allocation of corporate resources and they encourage the production of goods and services. The profit motive appears to stimulate corporate investment and economic growth and to create new jobs for a growing labor force. Indeed, so essential are profits that it is hard to imagine how our system could operate without them. Samuel Gompers, a founding leader of the early American Federation of Labor once said, "The worst crime a corporation can commit against the working man is to fail to make a profit."

In this chapter, we examine the roles of profit. One of its principal roles is surely that of measuring the effectiveness of corporate management. Another role is that of allocating the flow of investable funds among competing uses. Still another role for profit is that of determining whether a particular corporation or business should be permitted to continue to operate.

But to understand profit and its role in the economy, we must first agree on how to define profits. Then we have to determine the actual and potential level of profits. We must also assess the degree to which profits are really necessary to the survival of the corporate economy.

There is a difference between the way economists and accountants measure profits. That difference will be explained and its significance assessed so that there is a minimum of confusion. Try as hard as they can to avoid it, most economists, in practice, use accounting definitions.

A large and growing share of the gross national product of the United States is produced by enterprises which supposedly don't operate to make a profit. Some of these enterprises are government agencies like the power and light department of the City of Seattle or the Massachusetts Bay Transportation Authority or the Tennessee Valley Authority. Many are hospitals, colleges and universities, research organizations or charitable corporations. But these not-for-profit concerns generally do operate as if they were businesses. Should we measure profits for them? If we do, do we measure profits in the same way as for profit-making corporations? And in the case of these not-for-profit enterprises shouldn't we try to see whether management and other resources are being employed efficiently? So, if not a standard of accounting or economic profit, then what should we use to measure the success of these organizations?

Questions about Profits

Profits are controversial. We have already questioned how to define and measure profits. For accountants, the focus of that question is on When does a corporation, a partnership, or an individual proprietorship actually have a profit? Everyone knows that the Internal Revenue Service has one point of view on this subject, while many accountants have other equally valid but different points of view.

Then, there is a question about profits that is of more significance to economists. What social and economic purposes do profits serve? If a firm maximizes profits, as economists assume, what is the firm maximizing? What is the result of this maximizing behavior? Is society better off, worse off, or unaffected by this behavior?

Another question, assuming that accountants agree on a definition and economists agree on a role, is Are profits too high? Are they too low?

The Facts about Profits

Facts about profits are plentiful. The United States Department of Commerce, *Business Week*, the *Wall Street Journal*, and Citibank in New York City along with thousands of corporations publish detailed information about profits, profitability, trends, and comparisons. Facts, though, require definitions. As you read through the facts we present in the next several pages, keep in mind that they are based on definitions and measures of profits which not all accountants and certainly not all economists accept. Many critics of currently used profits measures feel that profits are actually substantially smaller than the published figures. They would want a better assessment of real costs as well as the full influence of inflation to be taken into consideration.

Of course, there are critics on the left who feel that profits are understated in the United States. However, here are the facts as they come from United States government agencies, based on definitions the federal government uses in its national income accounts (Table 8.1).

How High Are Profits?

Corporate profits before taxes in 1974 came to $132.1 billion. That represented about 13 percent of the business product, that portion of the gross national product which is contributed by corporate production and sales. That is, while the costs of sales and production came to 87 cents out of every corporate dollar, profits were 13 cents in 1974. But, in 1965, for example, profits were 14.4 cents of every corporate dollar. And, in 1970, they were as low as 9.9 cents on every corporate dollar of sales and production. Certainly, during the ten years from 1964 through 1974, there is no clear trend upward in profits.

Total corporate profits before taxes at the end of World War II were $24.6 billion (in 1946). And, by 1974, they had reached $132.1 billion. Exclude corporate profit taxes, thus removing the share that the government takes of this income flow, and the change was from $15.5 billion in 1946 to $79.5 billion in 1974. In 1949, 1952, 1954, 1957, 1958, 1967, and 1969, profits on

Table 8.1 Corporate profits in the United States, 1964–1974

	% of business product*		% of stockholder's equity†		% of sales†	
Year	Before taxes	After taxes	Before taxes	After taxes	Before taxes	After taxes
1964	13.5	7.7	19.8	11.6	8.9	5.2
1965	14.4	8.5	21.9	13.0	9.5	5.6
1966	14.2	8.3	22.5	13.5	9.3	5.6
1967	12.9	7.5	19.3	11.7	8.1	5.0
1968	13.1	7.1	20.6	12.1	8.8	5.1
1969	11.9	6.3	20.1	11.5	8.4	4.8
1970	9.9	5.1	15.7	9.3	6.8	4.0
1971	10.6	5.7	16.5	9.7	7.1	4.2
1972	11.2	6.4	18.4	10.6	7.5	4.3
1973	12.3	7.3	20.3	13.1	8.3	5.0
1974	13.0	7.8	23.4	14.9	8.7	5.5

Survey of Current Business, January 1976.
†*Quarterly Financial Report for Manufacturing, Mining and Trade Corporations*, Washington, D.C., Federal Trade Commission.

both a before- and after-tax basis were lower in each of these years than the year before.

Just as significant, whereas profits were 16.2 percent of the business product in 1946, they were, as we see in Table 8.1, only 13 percent in 1974. In after-tax terms, the fall was from 10.2 percent in 1946 to 7.8 percent in 1974. In 1950, corporate profits as a percent of the gross business product of the nation represented nearly 20 percent or 11.5 percent after taxes. But, in 1970, on this same measure, before-tax profits came to only 10 percent of the business product. After tax, they were 5.1 percent. There's hardly a trend in those measures to indicate any significant growth in profitability of corporate business in the past twenty-five years.

Many observers regard the 1960s as a period of unusually high and steady prosperity. Yet, in that decade, profits as a percentage of the business product were on the average lower than in the 1940s and 1950s, whether on a before- or after-tax basis. The 1975 profit performance of major United States corporations is shown in Table 8.2.

Some surveyors of American public opinion have found that many Americans think that profits are quite high. Frequently, such surveys have reported that the man on the street believes after-tax profits to be over 30 percent on sales or net investment. What people think is not always the same as fact, of course, but it is obvious that correct comparisons are necessary to give an adequate basis for understanding; especially if the actual before-tax 1975 margin, for example, was 5.0 percent. (Table 8.2)

One thing seems clear. Given the actual size and trend of United States corporate profits, you couldn't substitute a 100 percent corporate profits tax for a personal income tax and collect anywhere near as much tax revenue as the personal income tax collects. It also should be pointed out again that profit

Table 8.2 Profit performance of major United States corporations, 1975

Company	Sales 1975, × 10³	Profits 1975, × 10³	% Margin*	% return on common equity	P/E*	EPS*
American Can	$ 2,870.2	$ 77.3	2.7	10.3	8	$ 4.17
American Express	2,490.2	165.0	5.8	16.3	16	2.29
American Machine & Foundry	1,004.7	32.1	2.8	11.0	12	1.71
American Tel. & Tel.	28,614.1	3,143.7	10.7	10.1	11	5.15
Anderson, Clayton	803.9	32.4	4.1	12.0	8	5.11
Anheuser-Busch	1,645.0	84.7	5.3	15.3	18	1.88
BankAmerica	4,742.7	301.7	6.6	17.4	11	4.37
Bucyrus-Erie	353.1	29.9	8.4	16.8	17	1.53
Columbia Broadcasting System	1,938.9	122.9	6.2	20.9	13	4.30
Cessna	482.3	18.8	4.9	12.9	10	2.45
Chesebrough-Pond's	647.6	47.9	5.3	18.4	19	3.01
Chrysler	11,598.4	−207.2	1.1	−8.0		−3.46
Cincinnati Milacron	450.2	9.9	1.3	6.5	10	2.69
Delta	1,415.0	37.4	4.9	7.9	22	1.88
Duke Power	954.2	128.3	16.1	9.6	10	1.84
Du Pont	7,221.5	271.8	7.2	7.4	28	5.43
Eastern Airlines	1,624.0	−49.7		−16.1		−2.65
Eastman Kodak	4,958.5	613.7	13.1	17.5	28	3.80
Exxon	44,748.0	2,500.0	5.4	15.7	8	11.18
Federated Department Stores	3,534.8	139.3	3.8	14.4	18	3.14
First Union (No. Car.)	173.7	7.6	2.1	7.0	9	1.24
Foremost-McKesson	2,500.0	33.3	1.3	15.9	7	2.54
General Dynamics	2,160.0	81.1	4.2	17.1	6	7.62
General Electric	13,399.1	580.8	5.9	16.0	17	3.17
Harcourt Brace Jovanovich	241.3	14.9	4.3	16.1	7	3.60
Hewlett-Packard	981.2	83.6	7.6	16.4	36	3.02
Holiday Inns	917.0	41.4	1.1	9.5	13	1.36
International Business Machines	14,436.5	1,989.9	14.5	19.1	19	13.35
Kaiser Industries	1,031.9	76.7	3.2	12.6	4	2.72
Laclede Gas	206.6	11.5	5.6	11.8	8	2.50
Liggett & Myers	813.0	35.9	2.5	9.6	8	4.22
McDermott (J. Ray)	1,065.7	136.4	14.8	33.1	5	8.74
McGraw-Hill	536.5	33.1	7.3	14.5	11	1.35
McLean Trucking	331.4	12.6	3.6	19.4	11	4.51
Merrill Lynch	953.2	95.7	9.7	18.9	11	2.69
Miles Laboratories	413.8	13.1	2.4	9.4	10	2.45
Nashua	304.9	1.4	1.0	1.7	47	0.31
Portland General Electric	179.9	46.0	22.3	14.2	7	2.52
Republic of Texas	357.1	44.0	10.8	16.0	7	4.01

Table 8.2 Profit performance of major United States corporations, 1975 (continued)

Company	Sales 1975, × 10³	Profits 1975, × 10³	% Margin*	% return on common equity	P/E*	EPS*
Safeway Stores	9,716.9	148.7	1.6	29.3	8	5.74
Sante Fe Industries	1,432.2	109.2	8.7	7.3	8	4.23
Sears, Roebuck	13,291.1	404.0	3.5	7.6	28	2.56
Simmons	434.3	10.3	2.8	6.6	15	1.51
Levi Strauss	1,015.2	64.7	6.0	29.2	8	5.90
Texas Industries	128.8	3.8	2.3	7.5	11	1.25
United States Steel	8,380.3	559.6	5.7	12.5	8	10.33
United Technologies	3,877.8	117.5	2.2	14.2	7	7.80
Babcock & Wilcox	1,656.0	42.3	3.5	12.2	8	3.49
Winn-Dixie Stores	3,138.0	56.9	1.7	20.3	15	2.74
Crown Zellerback	1,758.1	74.5	6.0	10.1	16	3.01
All industry composite	334,380.1	59,912.2	5.0	11.8	12	2.89

*Margin = profits/sales; P/E = price-earnings ratio; EPS = earnings per share.
Source: Survey of Corporate Performance, Fourth Quarter, 1975, *Business Week*, March 22, 1976.

facts are determined as accountants, not economists, would measure them. And not all accountants would accept them either.

Measurement of Profits

From the point of view of managerial economics, the key profit measurement issue is whether relevant costs have actually been covered. Assuming that the profit measure is correct in the sense that all relevant economic costs are

---

Exhibit 8.1 Calculation of corporate profits

Gross corporate income less costs incurred in producing and selling the output that provides the corporate income = corporate profit, adjusted where possible for

1. Inflation
2. Real costs of money
3. Real costs of inventory
4. Real costs of resources employed
5. Changes in market value of replaceable fixed capital resources

---

Exhibit 8.2 Distribution of corporate profit

Payments to governments	Federal and state, corporate profits, taxes, franchise taxes
Payments to stockholders	Dividends
Increases in corporate net worth	Used to acquire additional productive assets, to provide reserves against possible losses, to increase stockholders' equity, to increase corporate working capital

---

subtracted from income and assuming that income is properly recorded, the role of profit in a managerial context needs stressing. Profits are used to rate the success or degree of success of a venture or a firm's annual or periodic performance. Profitable activities are likely to be approved and continued. Those which incur losses are likely to be terminated and those resources to be transferred elsewhere. Moreover, if activities are ranked in order of profitability, some of the just barely profitable lines or divisions may be cut back or discontinued. Every manager soon comes to be aware that what counts is a good level of profit. His or her ability to meet this kind of goal will be the measure of eligibility for better and better positions in management. What is more, these are accounting profits, not economic profits.

Profit is residual. It is what is left over after all costs, however calculated, have been covered. The key issues are whether, in fact, all relevant costs have been covered and, then, whether what has been recorded as profit is a surplus. The accounting task is to determine what these costs are, to estimate them with reasonable accuracy, to assign them to the proper activity and time period, and to determine therefore the extent of the profit or surplus.

Profit[1] is also an indication of productivity. The more profit after cost, the more productive the enterprise has been. And, no matter who shared in this productivity, the profit flow is a source of income that did not exist before.

The Purpose of Economic Theories of Profit

The essential purpose of an economic theory of profit is to define the social role of profits. Just as there is a theory of wages which explains the social role of wage payments to labor and a theory of interest as well as a theory of rent, there is need for a theory of profits. However, while economists generally agree that wages, interest, and rents would, in certain ideal conditions, be equivalent

---

[1] For a thorough analysis of how to measure profits, see R. R. Sterling, *Theory of the Measurement of Enterprise Income*, Lawrence, Kans., University of Kansas Press, 1970. Also R. J. Chambers, *Accounting, Evaluation and Economic Behavior*, Englewood Cliffs, N.J., Prentice-Hall, 1966.

Exhibit 8.3   Things corporate profits are not used for

---

1. High management salaries
2. Contributions to charities
3. Personal expenses of owners, stockholders, management

---

to the marginal product of labor, capital, and land, there is no such general agreement about a theory of profits.

There are two basic problems about a theory of profits. One is the definition of the social resource being employed. And the other is whether this social resource is actually necessary to achieve the production results society requires.

In the five economic theories of profit which follow, we assume that we can identify a resource called "management," or the entrepreneurial ability of the capitalist. These, you should be warned, are not exact equivalents. One cannot readily be substituted for another in the different theories. We also assume that it is rational for a business firm to seek to obtain the maximum amount of profits consistent with the demand and supply situation faced. In short, there is no argument, in these theories at least, about how businessmen behave. The argument is about what happens to the economy when they behave this way and whether society couldn't get as good or perhaps even better results if they didn't conduct business along certain lines or if, in fact, another type of organization were substituted for them.

Marginal Productivity and Profit

Economics teaches that the demand for any resource is determined by the marginal product of that resource. The business firm faces two markets, one in which it is selling its products and the other in which it is buying its input. One of these inputs is management ability or entrepreneurial ability. The best quantity and quality of management ability to demand or buy (hire or employ) varies, of course, with the costs and returns on the employment of that resource in production. Whether a firm is a monopolist or a competitor in the product marketplace, its demand for inputs such as management will depend on the demand for the product sold and the prices at which it sells as well as the price (or marginal product) and productivity of the input itself.

The concept of marginal revenue product is used to measure demand for inputs. Marginal revenue product is the marginal product of any productive input, including management, multiplied by the unit price of the output for which that input was used. This is the economically proper method of evaluating the contribution of the input. The marginal revenue product of an input times the amount of the input used (or employed) in production, of course, becomes the total cost of the input (See Fig. 8.1).

So, for example, if MRP_L = marginal revenue product of labor, MRP_K =

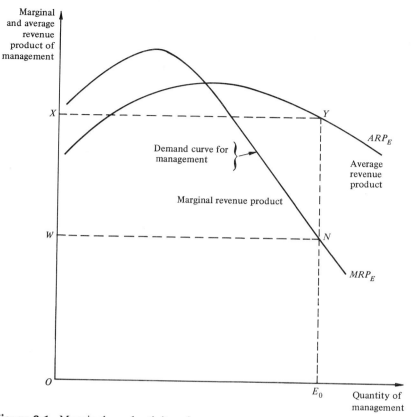

Figure 8.1. Marginal productivity of management.

$$OW \times OE_0 = \text{total cost of management } (= \text{profit})$$
$$WX \times OE_0 = \text{amount available to cover all other input costs (or profit from management).}$$

marginal revenue product of capital, MRP_T = marginal revenue product of land, MRP_E = marginal revenue product of management, then

Labor cost	Capital cost	Land cost	Management cost

$$(MRP_L \times L_0) + (MRP_K \times K_0) + (MRP_T \times T_0) + (MRP_E \times E_0) = TRP$$

Thus, the total revenue product of a firm consists of the sum of the marginal revenue product (or input price) of each input times the amount of that input employed. Or, put differently, the total revenue product will equal the total input costs.

It follows that, if we regard only labor, land, and capital as inputs and if we treat management as a different kind of input, then whatever (positive) difference there is between TRP and the sum of the input costs will be a surplus or profit. So, a profit-maximizing firm will operate under a condition such that

$$MRP_L \times L_0 + MRP_K \times K_0 + MRP_T \times T_0 \leq TRP$$

The right-hand side of this inequality is the revenue and the left-hand side is the cost. Obviously revenue minus cost is profit, which can exist only if revenue exceeds cost. A firm would regard a situation in which revenue only just covered the costs of the inputs (not including management) as a break-even or perhaps as a shut-down point. Thus, profit is residual. But we have not really constructed a theory of profit since all that we have done is explain that there is a difference sometimes between firm revenue and firm costs. There is a theory of firm behavior that says that, for reasons not fully explained, firms attempt to maximize profits, the residual difference between revenue and cost.

Uncertainty

In what follows, we examine various theories of profit, some of which, like the compensation or the monopoly theories, are based on the marginal productivity theory. The Schumpeter and risk theories attempt to explain the role of profit in an uncertain world. Only in such a world does it make sense to discuss profits as the earnings of a successful innovator or as the earnings of a risk taker. Uncertainty, of course, arises when decision makers don't have the necessary information to allow them to remove uncertainties. Though we don't spell it out here, uncertainty could be described in terms of the subjective probabilities associated with events and hence outcomes of decisions. Whenever management makes decisions under uncertain conditions two elements of managerial preference are relevant. One is the preference with respect to the reward, its amount and its utility. The other is the preference with respect to risk. By assigning measurable utility numbers to preferences, management behavior that is consistent with those preferences will seek to maximize expected utility. That is, management will choose the probability distribution of profits or rewards (or payoffs) that has the highest value in terms of expected utility.

What Is a Productive Resource?

The exploitation theory of profits is at base an argument about productivity. What is at issue is whether any input factor other than labor can really add to the social surplus over social costs. If, as Marxists and other economists assert, labor is the only resource that can give value to produced goods and is, therefore, the only resource that yields a surplus over cost, the calculation is

$$MRP_L \times L_0 \leq TRP$$

There are only two problems remaining. One is to remind ourselves that labor can take various forms, including stored-up or transformed labor, which looks like what we call capital. And the other is to note that, if the left side of the equation is smaller than the right side, then the surplus arises because of market imperfections in a rigged social system. The surplus has no economic justification since it is a payment for nothing, the marginal product of a nonproductive resource, the exploited difference between revenue and true social cost.

The Compensation Theory of Profits

The compensation theory says that management or entrepreneurial ability is a scarce resource. The demand for that resource tends to exceed its supply so that the price of management or entrepreneurial ability is high. Management is a quality which encourages corporations to produce new products, enter new markets, create new jobs, and innovate cost-saving, more productive activities. In effect, the compensation theory is really about how to measure profits. What it says is that whatever is paid for management or entrepreneurial ability is a cost. If profit is that cost, then profit, at least insofar as it goes to management or entrepreneurial ability, is not a surplus left over after all costs have been covered.

The compensation theory does not say, however, that there will be no surplus above costs or that corporations and other kinds of business never earn surpluses above the cost of management.

The Monopoly Theory of Profits

Monopoly profits are those surpluses above costs which persist in the long run. They persist because there are monopolistic barriers to entry into the industry. Firms which might desire to enter the monopolized industry cannot do so because the required investment is too high, because the monopoly firm has a substantial scale advantage and decreasing costs, because there is patent protection, or because of other effective barriers. If these barriers can be maintained and if the demand for the monopoly firm's production is sustained, monopoly profits may persist indefinitely.

You see, if there were pure competition and no natural monopoly, then the effects of competition, such as homogeneous product, adequate information, freedom of entry, and large numbers of buyers and sellers, would be to drive costs and prices down to the level of those firms that are efficient. Profits would disappear. If profits persist in the American economy, it is because monopolies exist and the effects of a competitive market are not allowed to have sway.

Notice that there is nothing in the monopoly theory which denies the validity of the compensation theory. The monopoly theory is not about profit measurement but about the effects of the lack of pure competition. It follows, of course, that an empirical test of the monopoly theory would require economists to take reported corporate profits and convert them to economic profits. A reported profit which persisted into the long-run expansion of an industry must be an economic profit to be evidence of a monopoly.

In the long run in a monopolized industry there is no tendency for price to be equal to marginal cost. But it must be pointed out that this condition does not assure profits. It only assures that the monopolistic firm, in seeking its best level of production, will not take average total costs into consideration. Monopoly losses are as likely to occur under this criterion as monopoly profits. It is clear that a monopolistic firm's market strength must really come from the demand and not from the cost side of the equation.

Monopoly profits are the results of market imperfections. Some of these imperfections result from natural monopoly where, given a production function that has a high proportion of capital and other fixed elements, average costs decline both as the installed capacity is more fully utilized and as the scale of operation increases. Natural monopoly is the case where only one very large supplier or producer in an industry is necessary to achieve fully scale and production economies. But if natural monopolies are controlled through government regulation then people benefit from low price and adequate production even without pure competition.

Contrived monopolies that result from research and development (R&D) expenditures, invention, advertising, location, barriers to entry, lack of information to potential competitors, or size of initial investment and franchises can also be controlled. The contrived monopolies can be broken up, with an increase in the number of competitors and other changes in market conditions. At the very least, the degree of monopoly can be ameliorated with more competition.

The basic conclusion of the monopoly theory is that monopoly profits serve no useful social purpose. That is, they cover no necessary costs. They are a waste. Society ought to attempt to eliminate that waste by increasing competition.

Schumpeter's Theory of Monopoly Profits

Joseph A. Schumpeter, a seminal economist of the first half of the twentieth century, attempted to understand how the capitalist process actually worked. His theory of monopoly profits is an interesting and useful combination of the compensation theory and the monopoly theory. It differs from the monopoly theory by putting the monopoly firm into a different and perhaps more relevant historical context. Suppose, Schumpeter said, a national economy had reached equilibrium. There would be full employment not only of labor but of land, capital, and all other resources. Because there was a long-run equilibrium, growth, of course, would have ceased. There would be no tendency for incomes to increase, for GNP to rise, or for productivity to improve. Obviously, all profits would have disappeared.

Into such a state of affairs, a monopolist innovator enters with a proposed new way of producing goods at a lower cost. To introduce the innovation in a static society, this entrepreneur would need capital, labor, and land, all of which are fully employed at the best available return. Suppose a banker with some daring, attracted by the possibility of profit, lends money to the monopolist-entrepreneur-innovator. The banker is taking a chance that at least enough additional production over current levels could be achieved to permit the entrepreneur to pay back the loan and obtain a profit, too. Then, with this money, the entrepreneur goes into the marketplace to acquire production equipment, land for plants, and workers. The entrepreneur would have to pay more for these factors of production than their current price, just to induce their sellers either to increase their supply or to transfer some of these resources from their current employment.

If the entrepreneur obtained these factors at higher prices, two things would happen. First, prices in the economy would go up—inflation—and production would decline as resources were diverted to the innovative product. Higher prices and lower production would mean what is now called "stagflation," but not for long.

Next, suppose that the innovation is a success. The production efforts of the entrepreneur recover costs (even at the higher prices for the inputs) and earn a profit too, all this after having paid for the borrowed money (at the interest rate the banker charged). The innovation, whether it is a new and more productive way to make a familiar good, a new good meeting existing wants, or even a new good meeting tastes that were cultivated by the advertising which introduced it, by any means, would have the effect of increasing the total production of the economy, permitting not only the recovery of the production lost during the gestation period for the innovation but an increase beyond the previous equilibrium. All this plus monopoly profit.

Now, note that in the Schumpeter theory of monopoly profit the profit earned is the cost of the entrepreneurial ability used. This compensation induces a key resource to be supplied. This resource, management or entrepreneurial ability, is the source of the growth in GNP, in productivity, in income, and, of course, in profit. In this kind of analysis, there is a beneficial social role for profits, even if they come from monopoly. The Schumpeter theory of monopoly profits is very much like theories of wages, rents, and interest. Profits result from a productive resource, management, under conditions of monopoly.

As Schumpeter saw the matter from his analysis of long-term changes in the United States and other capitalist economies, monopoly profits are short-lived. As it becomes apparent that innovations can succeed and that there is adequate compensation for managerial or entrepreneurial ability, its supply will continue to increase. Many new innovations will be introduced, but the rate of return on management or entrepreneurial ability will obviously decline as its supply increases. Monopoly profits drop across the board.

What is more, one of the effects of the increase in the supply of management or entrepreneurial ability is the growth of competition. Schumpeter, you see, didn't believe that effective entry barriers can exist for long if monopoly profits are high. Instead, he saw a succession of stages in an industry created through innovation as it moved from monopoly to competition and perhaps to oligopoly. Each stage will depend on the amount and the quality of management or entrepreneurial ability employed.

Another effect of the capitalist process Schumpeter analyzed was that, because management or entrepreneurial ability as well as other resources were withdrawn from firms, industries, and activities which were unprofitable or which became less profitable in the face of innovations, these weaker firms would fail. Thus, the very process that was creating new jobs, growth, increased productivity, and other good things was also killing off the unproductive sectors. That, in fact, is how Schumpeter thought capitalist growth took place. For him, monopoly profits were both an engine of creation of the new order and of destruction of the old order.

The Exploitation Theory of Profits

Karl Marx, in his powerful critique of the capitalist process, conceded that capitalism was decidedly superior to any previous form of national economic organization such as mercantilism or feudalism. Moreover, Marx found that capitalism had performed a useful social role in destroying older economic orders. One of the key questions he sought to answer was whether, in any new or better society, it would be necessary to have capitalists. His conclusion was that capitalists did not perform a function so important that they could not be replaced by the workers in a socialist society.

Marx came to these points of view largely because of the theory of value which he used. The labor theory of value holds that all productive and therefore sales value in any good or commodity comes only from the amount of labor used to produce it. In one sense or another, according to this theory of value, every resource, whether we regard it as capital or land or parts or raw materials or management, has value only because of labor. The purpose of a theory of value is to determine the productive resources. Therefore, if only labor is the source of value in any item for sale, then no other resource is productive. It follows that capital is not productive. And if capital is not productive, then the owners and suppliers of capital, the capitalists, are not productive either.

But labor is sold in a capitalist market which is rigged institutionally to favor capitalists. Because, in a capitalist society, the supply of labor always exceeds demand and because there is, as a consequence, an industrial reserve army of unemployed, capitalists buy labor at a price or wage well below its intrinsic value.

The difference between the market price of a good and what labor receives for producing it is a surplus value. This surplus value, exploited from workers in the marketplace, is the source of all payments in a capitalist society such as rent for the landlord, interest for the sellers of money capital, and even profits for the capitalists. The reason for the surplus value is thus exploitation in capitalist society. The superior market power of capitalist employers is what creates surplus value.

In a socialist society, the workers would be organized so that they could manage their own enterprises or, perhaps, they would organize the state or government in a way so that it could manage business enterprises without capitalists. More important, in that way, surplus value would all go to labor.

While Marx was careful to distinguish between capitalism and socialism as stages in a historically inexorable upward movement, many Marxian critics of capitalism conclude that even now capitalists can readily be replaced. They say that the existence of profits is unjust since what is paid as profits is not only exploited from workers but, perhaps even more significantly, provides no additional resource that society could not possess without its payment.

Profits and Profitability in the Soviet Union

It is useful and interesting to compare industrial profits in the largest socialist country with those in the largest capitalist country. Obviously, of course, socialist profits accrue to state-managed and -run enterprises, while in the United States, as in other capitalist economies, corporate profits are earned by the private corporation, though a significant share is paid to the state as a corporate profits tax (Table 8.3).

Contrast this overall profitability of 33 percent for the industrial production sector of the Soviet Union with an after-tax rate of 5.1 percent in the United States in 1970.

In Soviet management practice, wages paid include the direct labor cost plus social insurance and imputed income from such items as free lunches at the factory. In Soviet industry in 1970, the total wage bill, not including social insurance and imputed incomes, was 31 percent of total expenses of 48.8 billion rubles. Adding social insurance and imputed incomes, wages exceed profits by only 2.6 billion rubles, suggesting that the state exacts an even larger rate of exploitation from the total value of production in this socialist nation than does private industry in the United States.

Table 8.3   Profits by industry, USSR, 1970

Industry	Profits, billions of rubles	Profits as % of social product
Electric power	3.2	44.3
Petroleum products	4.0	42.8
Coal	0.8	15.8
Nonferrous metals	2.5	51.7
Chemicals	3.4	42.2
Machine building and metal working	12.9	31.7
Ferrous metals	3.7	45.1
Forest products	2.0	27.8
Pulp and paper	0.5	29.6
Construction materials	1.5	22.0
Light industry	6.4	24.8
Processed foods	6.8	26.1
Other industry	4.2	64.2
All industry	52.0	33.1

Source: USSR, GNP accounts 1970, Research Aid.
CIA, November (A)(ER), 75–76.

The Risk Theory of Profit

The risk theory of profit pinpoints an intuitively obvious factor in the analysis of business investment practices. There is no assurance of gain or profit from any investment for an investor in a capitalist economy. Since the investor does not know what the precise likelihood is that there will be a return on funds invested and since past experience provides many examples of failure, it is prudent to insist upon a "risk premium." This risk premium is a payment which compensates for past losses or which takes account of any possible future losses. It is the cost of inducing investors to risk their funds.

The risk theory takes two forms. One is the venture approach, a kind of "when-your-ship-comes-in" analysis. The analysis assumes that the investor approaches each investment as a venture. Money capital is supplied now for a fixed period or for a known time-limited venture. With the end of the venture, if it is successful, the gains are divided in such a way that all costs are covered. One of those costs is the risk premium. Only after it is paid is there any true surplus.

More typical of the day-to-day investment market is a second form of the risk theory. If the behavior of investors is observed, you will see that higher and higher returns must be promised to suppliers of funds as financial risks increase. There is an evident risk aversion among such suppliers of capital funds, so there must be a trade-off between promised returns on investments and the variabilities of expected returns. For any given degree of risk and cost of management, there is a premium for risk aversion which must be added to the risk-free interest rate. While this may be considered a profit upon settlement of accounts, it is a payment necessary to induce an increase in the supply of investment funds.

The difference between the risk theory in its various forms and the compensation theory is the identification of the factor being paid for. The compensation theory identifies that factor as management. The risk theory identifies the factor as risk. In point of fact, both theories may well be correct with respect to what they identify. Both the entrepreneurial manager and the risk-taker may be necessary to provide for success in business.

The Romantic Theory of Profits

The romantic theory of profits holds that profits are a payment to a class of people whose value systems are "wrong." St. Thomas Aquinas taught that the "just society" was one in which people devoted their highest efforts to God, the Church, society in general, and the needy everywhere. Work was to be rewarded but the rewards for selling, for producing goods, for banking, and for providing one's daily bread were not to be out of line with their true relative value. Man was not to live by bread alone. The danger of profit is that its pursuit to the exclusion of good endeavors can only pervert men and women and lead to their ultimate destruction.

A theological basis for profits can be found, of course, in the parable of the

Table 8.4 Comparisons of economic theories of profit

Theory	Profit is a necessary cost	Profit is an incentive in-creasing the supply of a necessary factor	Profit is a waste-not necessary to pay to increase production	Profits are a maldistribution of society's in-come. Takes from one group to give to another
Compensation	X	X		
Monopoly			X	
Schumpeter	X	X		
Exploitation			X	X
Risk		X		
Romantic				X

talents where it is observed that the evil servant who did not invest his talent was consigned to damnation. The dilemma of the romanticist is that of ensuring the obvious benefits, including far less poverty, from a productive society based on profits while directing society to higher, more noble goals.

Much of the disenchantment with profits prevalent in our society today arises from this dilemma rather than from the Marxist position. Romanticism is a critique of profits, based on a search for a better society, one with its priorities set straight. In Table 8.4 is a comparison of the romantic with other theories of profit.

Frigitronics: A Case Study in Profit Analysis

Table 8.5 shows the 1975 consolidated statement of earnings for Frigitronics, Inc., a manufacturer of optical and medical supply specialties.

Notice the elements of this statement. Included among Frigitronics' sources of income is a flow of royalty payments received from Warner-Lambert. From 1973 through 1990, Warner-Lambert will be manufacturing and selling soft contact lenses under license from Frigitronics. The provisions of the agreement call for Warner-Lambert to pay Frigitronics a percentage of net sales.

Research and development costs for Frigitronics are substantial. The rules of the Financial Accounting Standards Board require that practically all R&D costs, including those acquired by business mergers, be charged to operations as they are incurred. The rule was put into effect in 1975 and caused Frigitronics to change significantly its reported 1973 and 1974 earnings.

In 1974, Frigitronics acquired the ITD Corporation, which had an exclusive license for application in North America of new technology in cancer detection and therapy. The purchase of ITD also entitled Frigitronics to a transfer of Bulgarian technology as well. In compliance with Financial Accounting Standards Board rulings, in 1975 the company transferred its ITD acquisition costs from assets to costs.

Table 8.5 Frigitronics, Inc., and subsidiaries: Consolidated statement of earnings

	Year ended May 31	
	1975	1974
Revenues:		
Net sales	$40,681,546	$37,968,556
Royalty	283,442	253,741
Other	158,862	54,252
	41,123,850	38,276,549
Costs and expenses:		
Cost of products sold	24,121,351	22,150,537
Selling, general and administrative	13,480,597	12,062,614
Research and development costs, including $396,297 and $169,379, respectively, for cancer research program	656,743	367,027
Interest	215,636	200,660
	38,474,327	34,780,838
Earnings before income taxes and extraordinary item	2,649,523	3,495,711
Income taxes	1,380,000	1,698,000
Earnings before extraordinary item	1,269,523	1,797,711
Extraordinary item: Income tax benefit from operating loss carryovers	140,000	121,000
Net earnings	$ 1,409,523	$ 1,918,711
Earnings per common and common equivalent share		
Earnings before extraordinary item	$.43	$.61
Extraordinary item	.05	.04
Net earnings	$.48	$.65
Average common and common equivalent shares outstanding	2,951,479	2,933,388

Though the Frigitronics statement of earnings may reflect current accounting practice, it does not reflect economic profit. In Table 8.6 is such a statement of economic profit for fiscal year 1975. It includes adjustments necessary to record actual costs of production of goods and services sold in 1975. Obviously, other adjustments would be necessary if an audit of accounts showed further elements of cost, elements of income not recorded, or situations where internal accounting procedures have not permitted normal market valuations to influence costs and revenues. The rate of economic profit is about 4.5 percent compared with 6.4 percent reported before taxes. Income taxes are not subtracted from economic profits since such taxes are a distribution of profits

Table 8.6 Frigitronics, Inc.: Statement of economic profit
Fiscal year 1975

Revenues as stated	$41,123,850
Less royalties*	283,442
Economic revenues	$40,840,408
Costs and expenses as stated	$38,474,327
Less research and development costs†	656,743
	$37,817,584
Plus additional interest on retained earnings, opportunity cost at 12%‡	1,200,000
Economic costs and expenses	$39,017,584
Economic profit	$ 1,822,824

*Royalties are income on products not produced or sold by Frigitronics in this fiscal year.
†Research and development costs are not production costs for products sold in 1975.
‡Retained earnings represent a borrowing from the stockholders. If this sum had been borrowed at prime rates plus adjustment for risk premium at 12 percent, $1.2 million would have been added to interest costs.

rather than a cost of doing business. It could, of course, be argued that governments, federal, state, and local, provide services for which taxes are a price.

Changes in Financial Position

In the statement of changes in financial position (Table 8.7), we can see the effect of after-tax earnings, depreciation, and amortization as well as extraordinary income on the flow of funds through the company. We can also see how the company financed its operations by the use of long-term debt and sales of land and buildings, as well as merger activity. Just as important, we can see how funds provided by cash flow (profit plus depreciation) and extraordinary and external sources were used to build up productive facilities and to increase working capital. Notice that no dividends were paid to stockholders so that the entire profit flow was retained and used to build company assets.

What Is a Loss?

Losses are negative profits. Losses occur when, during any accounting period, costs of operation exceed revenue from the normal operations of the business. Losses are a reduction in capital or net worth accounts.

A railroad or electric utility with large amounts invested in fixed capital and with a low percentage of direct or variable costs to total costs can sustain persistent losses. A grocery store with an active and perishable inventory and a

Table 8.7 Frigitronics, Inc., and subsidiaries: Consolidated statement of changes in financial position

	Year ended May 31	
	1975	1974
Source of funds:		
Operations:		
Earnings before extraordinary item	$1,269,523	$1,797,711
Depreciation and amortization	575,609	554,769
Gain on sale of land and building	(106,946)	
	1,738,186	2,352,480
Extraordinary item:		
Tax benefit from		
net operating loss carryovers	140,000	121,000
	1,878,186	2,473,480
Proceeds from common stock issued in connection with acquisition of ITD Corporation	177,600	
Proceeds from sale of land and building	171,069	
Proceeds from exercise of options and warrants		545,360
Proceeds from issuance of long-term debt		325,774
Other	77,186	5,000
Total source of funds	2,304,041	3,349,614
Application of funds:		
Additions to property, plant and equipment	542,931	871,495
Payments and maturities of long-term debt	106,959	105,421
Additions to goodwill	1,475	202,205
Other		37,168
Total application of funds	651,365	1,216,289
Increase in working capital	$1,652,676	$2,133,325
Changes in components of working capital:		
Increases (decreases) in current assets:		
Cash	$ 168,765	($ 268,851)
Accounts receivable	310,311	930,245
Inventories	577,421	2,367,949
Prepaid expenses	38,580	2,850
Total	1,095,077	3,032,193
Increases (decreases) in current liabilities:		
Notes payable to bank	100,000	100,000
Accounts payable	(120,604)	562,565
Income taxes	(86,924)	(39,853)
Other current liabilities	(450,386)	439,315
Current portion of long-term debt	315	(163,159)
Total	(557,599)	898,868
Net increase in working capital	$1,652,676	$2,133,325

high percentage relation between direct and total costs cannot sustain long-term persistent losses. What causes the difference?

For one thing, the cash flow of a company with high fixed assets and low direct-cost ratios has a larger component of depreciation than of profit. The available cash in such companies is not reduced greatly by a loss in any one year. The cash flow of a grocery store, on the other hand, is used to help finance inventory turnover, and it consists largely of profit. A loss reduces the viability of the store significantly. Unless there are capital reserves or bank loans to replace the cash, the store may not survive.

In an unchanging world, the minimum requirement for survival is the preservation of the net asset value of a company. But in a dynamic world, it is not enough just to preserve the net asset value. The minimum level of net asset value would be determined by the growth requirements that would allow a firm to maintain the same relative position in a certain industry. The effect of a weak profit addition in the dynamic case might be equivalent to a loss in the static industry case.

Wiltek, Inc.: A Case Study in Loss Management

The statement of loss and deficit for Wiltek for fiscal years 1974 and 1975 shows that while the company had net sales of $10.4 million in 1974 and $14.4 million in 1975, costs and expenses were even larger. The company, therefore, had to report a loss (after adjustment) of $7.2 million in 1974 and, for 1975, a loss of about $2 million. (See Table 8.8.) The deficit—the accumulated losses over recent years—came to $8.4 million. Moreover, the actual value of stockholders' equity in 1975 was minus $6.6 million.

Table 8.9 is the statement of changes in financial position which permits an analysis of how Wiltek survived. The company borrowed an additional $1.3 million, sold $306,000 in assets, and received advance payment from customers of $389,000. These items (including smaller sources) plus a reduction in working capital of $409,000 and depreciation of $353,000 gave Wiltek about $3 million in 1975.

Wiltek used the $3 million to finance its loss, acquire additional productive facilities and equipment, and meet current debt payments. But Wiltek can't go on this way forever. It offers its investors (stockholders and lenders) the prospect that some day soon the risks they have taken will be compensated. The very fact that Wiltek survived through 1975 indicated that these investors thought the products and service innovative enough for there to be a likely (profitable) market for them. In 1977, however, Wiltek filed for bankruptcy. Losses overcame the viability of the firm.

Table 8.8 Wiltek, Inc.: Consolidated statement of loss and retained earnings, deficit

Year ended October 31	1975	1974
Net sales:		
Equipment	$12,773,900	$ 9,335,600
Service	1,666,300	1,019,700
	14,440,200	10,355,300
Gain on disposal of assets	169,900	
Costs and expenses:		
Cost of goods sold	7,450,200	7,462,600
Service expense	3,378,000	3,124,700
Selling, general and administrative expenses	2,988,700	2,858,300
Product research, development and engineering	1,158,500	1,090,700
Interest expense, net	1,614,800	1,481,400
	16,590,200	16,017,700
Loss before cumulative effect of accounting change	(1,980,100)	(5,662,400)
Cumulative effect on prior years (to October 31, 1973) of accounting change		(1,542,900)
Net loss for the year	$(1,980,100)	$(7,205,300)
Per common share:		
Loss before cumulative effect of accounting change	$ (1.43)	$ (4.13)
Cumulative effect of accounting change		(1.13)
Net loss	$ (1.43)	$ (5.26)
Retained earnings (deficit) at beginning of year	$(6,386,400)	$ 818,900
Net loss for the year	(1,980,100)	(7,205,300)
Deficit at end of year	$(8,366,500)	(6,386,400)

The Anomalous Position of Some Nonprofit Organizations

Frequently, hospitals, schools, colleges, and similar concerns do not earn enough from regular revenue sources—fees, room charges, tuition—to cover total costs. Yet they somehow go on surviving and indeed growing. They suffer budget deficits but their net asset values are not reduced because they regularly turn to nonrevenue sources for support. They conduct fund drives, seek foundation assistance, and solicit their alumni and the general public. Evidently, these sources provide enough not only to cover operating costs but to construct buildings, improve facilities, and expand services. Their budget deficits, then, are the measure of the amounts by which regular revenue sources do not provide enough to cover all costs. But the deficits are covered by nonrevenue sources.

In Table 8.10 is a schematic statement of revenue for a moderate-sized private Eastern university. The figures, of course, are not precise, but they do

Table 8.9   Wiltek, Inc.: Consolidated statement of changes in financial position

Year ended October 31	1975	1974
Financial resources were used for:		
Loss before cumulative effect of accounting change	$ 1,980,100	$ 5,662,400
Add (deduct) items not affecting working capital:		
Depreciation and amortization	(352,500)	(270,300)
Gain on disposal of assets	169,900	
Working capital used in operations	1,797,500	5,392,100
Cumulative effect of accounting change		1,542,900
Acquisition of property, plant, and equipment, net of normal retirements	762,000	404,500
Current maturities of long-term debt	115,100	3,594,500
Increase in other assets		27,200
	2,674,600	10,961,200
Financial resources were provided by:		
Decrease in other assets	19,100	
Proceeds received on disposal of assets	306,000	
Increase in long-term portion of notes payable to banks	1,300,000	2,500,000
Deferred payments from customers	389,000	
Proceeds from sale of 9% convertible subordinated notes		3,000,000
Proceeds from exercise of stock options		107,700
Other changes	170,300	92,000
	2,184,400	5,699,700
Increase (decrease) in working capital	$ (490,200)	$(5,261,500)
Analysis of changes in working capital		
Increase (decrease) in current assets:		
Cash	$ 160,900	$ (104,900)
Refundable federal income tax	(498,300)	498,300
Accounts receivable	(126,200)	(6,517,900)
Inventories	(4,064,800)	2,752,200
Other	(44,600)	39,300
	(4,573,000)	(3,333,000)
Increase (decrease) in current liabilities:		
Current portion of long-term debt	(3,479,400)	3,594,500
Accounts payable	37,600	(2,225,800)
Accrued expenses	(33,100)	(338,700)
Federal and state income taxes		(289,400)
Deferred income and advance payments from customers	(607,900)	1,187,900
	(4,082,800)	1,928,500
Increase (decrease) in working capital	$ (490,200)	$(5,261,500)

Table 8-10 Schematic statement of revenue for a private university
Academic year, 1974 through 1975

Revenue	
Tuition	$12,000,000
Fees	1,500,000
Dormitory rents	6,800,000
Service fees and charges	3,000,000
Gross revenues	$23,300,000
Costs	
Instruction (inc. library)	$10,800,000
Maintenance & repairs	2,700,000
Dormitory expense	6,900,000
Heat, light	1,300,000
Materials	1,100,000
Depreciation	1,200,000
	$24,000,000
Loss	$ 700,000
Loss financed by	
Yield on endowment funds	$ 1,500,000
Gifts & grants from alumni,	
foundations, individuals	$ 400,000
Government grants & subsidies	$ 300,000
Change in net worth,	
loss less nonrevenue	$ 1,500,000

help explain the financial management problems of private higher education. The statement shows a loss for the 1974 to 1975 academic year of $700,000, the amount by which tuition and dormitory charges failed to cover the actual operating costs (including depreciation) of the institution. However, this loss was not carried into the net worth of the university since there were other sources of funds. For example, endowment funds yield $1.5 million while alumni, private foundations, and individuals during the 1974 to 1975 academic year gave unrestricted amounts of $400,000. Government grants and subsidies, including scholarship funds and other unrestricted amounts which could be applied to operating costs, came to $300,000. So it was that in 1975 the actual change in the net worth of the university was an increase of $1.5 million. To be sure, this did not take into account a substantial but restricted gift of $2 million to be used for a chapel complex.

Do Governments Lose Money? Why?

Government accounting cannot serve the same purposes as corporate accounting. The emphasis in government accounting is upon the budget process. A budget is not just an estimate of revenues and expenses for the budget year. It is a legal statement and authorization of what the government intends to spend based on what it expects to obtain in revenue. A budget deficit, then, is an estimate of the extent to which revenues will fail during the budget year to cover expenses.

Deficits in most cases do not threaten the survival of the government. They can be financed by borrowing from the general public, by using surpluses, if any, from previous years, and by transferring (or borrowing) funds from other government activities.

Because there is seldom an accounting of the assets and liabilities of governments, there is no way to determine the effect of these deficits and surpluses on the financial position or net worth of the government in question. However, Arthur Andersen & Co., one of the nation's largest accounting firms, in 1975 prepared an illustrative consolidated balance sheet for fiscal years 1973 and 1974 (see Exhibit 8.4a and b). That balance sheet showed gross assets for the United States federal government of about $329 billion in 1974. The effect

Exhibit 8.4a   United States government: Illustrative consolidated balance sheet

June 30, 1974 and 1973

Assets		
	Millions	
	1974	1973
Cash and cash equivalents	$ 18,127	$ 22,797
Gold, at official rate	11,567	10,410
Receivables, net of allowances:		
Accounts	5,490	4,859
Taxes	14,960	12,844
Loans	65,836	62,985
	86,286	80,688
Inventories, at cost		
Military and strategic system supplies	28,019	25,173
Stockpiled materials and commodities	11,526	12,693
Other materials and supplies	11,026	12,012
	50,571	49,878
Property and equipment, at cost:		
Land	6,686	6,415
Buildings, structures, and facilities	88,649	86,129
Strategic and tactical military assets	119,913	117,670
Nonmilitary equipment	39,708	37,377
Construction in progress	19,400	17,169
Other	2,118	1,848
	276,474	266,608
Less accumulated depreciation	129,000	122,000
	147,474	144,608
Deferred charges and other assets	15,297	15,369
	$329,322	$323,750

Source: Sound Financial Reporting in the Public Sector, Arthur Andersen & Co., Chicago, 1976.

Exhibit 8.4*b* United States government: Illustrative consolidated balance sheet
June 30, 1974 and 1973

	Liabilities and deficit				
			Millions		
			1974		1973
Federal debt:					
Gross debt outstanding			$ 486,247		$ 468,426
Less intragovernmental holdings					
Trust funds			(129,745)		(114,852)
Federal Reserve			(80,649)		(75,182)
Other			(10,449)		(10,529)
Debt outstanding with the public			265,404		267,863
Less unamortized discount			2,506		2,243
			262,898		265,620
Federal reserve liabilities:					
Federal Reserve Notes outstanding			64,263		58,754
Deposits of member banks			26,760		25,506
Other			2,286		1,725
			93,309		85,985
Accounts payable and accrued liabilities:					
Accounts payable			32,491		30,757
Accrued interest, annual leave and other			11,187		11,819
Deferred revenue			6,734		6,565
			50,412		49,141
Other liabilities			18,991		19,836
Retirement and disability benefits:					
Civil service			108,000		97,000
Military			80,380		70,950
Veterans			110,980		110,850
			299,360		278,800
Accrued social security			416,020		340,930
Contingencies					
Total liabilities			1,140,990		1,040,312
Less accumulated deficit			811,668		716,562
			$ 329,322		$ 323,750

Source: Sound Financial Reporting in the Public Sector, Arthur Andersen & Co., Chicago, 1976.

of contingent liabilities in the Social Security trust fund and other military and civilian retirement and disability payments owing was to increase gross liabilities from $425,610 million to $1,140,990 million.

It is interesting that the debt of the United States to the public is $263 million (after adjustment for amounts held by government agencies and funds), only a relatively small portion of gross liabilities. The accumulated deficit came to $812 billion in 1974. However, the statement of revenues, expenses, and transfer payments prepared by Arthur Andersen for the 1974 fiscal year gives a somewhat more revealing picture of the nature of the financing problem the federal government faces (see Exhibit 8.5).

In fiscal 1974, after covering operating expenses, the United States federal government had $157 billion left out of revenues received. Of this amount, $139 billion went to states, local governments, and individuals in the forms of grants, pensions, assistance, and unemployment compensation and benefits. Another $17 billion paid (net of interest income) interest on the national debt. Even so, the federal government had a small cash surplus of $544 million for fiscal year 1974. At least that's the way the Arthur Andersen & Co. accountants figured out the matter. A deficit arose because there was a necessary provision for benefits payable under the various retirement and disability programs of the United States. While these amounts are not payable any time soon in cash, they are nonetheless liabilities which were incurred in 1974.

Analyses like these seldom clarify the mysteries of government finance completely, but they do help explain why corporate accounting rules can't and won't apply. From the data just presented, you could say (*a*) Uncle Sam made a profit in 1974, (*b*) Uncle Sam went badly into the hole in 1974, or (*c*) much more study is necessary before meaningful conclusions about the operations of the federal government can be compared to those of other sectors of the national economy.

The Allocative Role of Profit in the United States

In the highly competitive market for capital funds, those companies that do not earn a profit equal to the going rate of return always run the risk of having the capital invested in them withdrawn and channeled toward more profitable uses. In a very laissez-faire economy, earned profit would be the only criterion for determining whether or not a business should survive. Governments may protect some companies from loss by taxing the products of their overseas competitors, by limiting the number of firms in some kinds of businesses, by direct subsidies and grants, and by making capital available at low cost.

While some interference is presumably justified by general economic welfare considerations, there is always a risk of misallocation of the nation's capital funds. The fact that one protective device or subsidy worked toward the general good does not ensure that the next one will be equally beneficial.

Governments are not the only agencies that may interfere with the free flow of capital to its most productive use. Banks and other financial agencies may have traditional and hidebound investment policies. Labor unions may

Exhibit 8.5   United States government: Illustrative consolidated statement of revenues, expenses, and transfer payments
For the year ending June 30, 1974 (in millions)

Revenues		
Individual income taxes		$118,952
Social Security, unemployment		
Taxes and retirement contributions		76,780
Corporate income taxes		40,736
Excise taxes		16,844
Estate and gift taxes		5,035
Rents and royalties		6,748
Other		6,539
		$271,634
Less operating expenses		
National defense	$72,479	
Other departments	41,982	114,461
Available for transfer payments		$157,173
Grants to states and local governments		41,500
Income security payments to individuals		69,381
Health care for individuals		11,300
Veterans benefits		10,400
Other grants to individuals		6,900
		$139,481
Interest charges, net of interest income		17,148
Remaining to cover noncash provisions		
for contingent retirement and disability payments		$544
Noncash provisions for retirement and		
disability payments		
Social Security		$ 75,090
Other		20,560
		$ 95,650
Excess of noncash provisions for retirement		
and disability payments over available funds,		
deficit		$ 95,106

Source: Sound Financial Reporting in the Public Sector, Arthur Andersen & Co., Chicago, 1976.

seek protection against losses of jobs and privileges that endanger the viability of the economy. Inflation may distort the price structure so that funds flow toward secure investments in real estate rather than toward more productive areas of economic growth.

The existence of profits in any sector is the measure of the growth potential of that sector. Assuming free flow of capital, these profitable sectors will always attract capital. A nation with profitable sectors will attract capital from every possible source, including those overseas.

Undesirable Social Outcomes from the Profit System

There are probably at least three situations in which a profit-seeking company may produce a socially undesirable outcome. One of these occurs when the business in which the firm is operating lacks the full stimulation of competition. Another occurs when the social costs of adequate product information are high. And still another occurs when the business does not bear its proper share of the full costs of production.

The man on the street tends to overestimate the profitability of large companies in relatively uncompetitive industries—companies like IBM, Exxon, Xerox, and Pacific Gas and Electric—because bigness is often confused with monopoly. Also, when the public learns that a big company is under scrutiny for, say, antitrust violations, its bigness makes the story sound more incriminating. Then, too, many observers really are thinking of the manufacturing industries when they are talking about profits. Actually, two-thirds of the national output is produced in other sectors, many of which are highly competitive. What is more, the manufacturing sector is continuing to decrease in relative importance.

We discuss the whole question of industry structure later, but the man on the street who can't be expected to know all there is to know about economics often underrates the effect of economic forces which tend to reduce noncompetitive behavior. Indeed, profit itself tends to induce competition. In addition, there are technological changes in transport and communication, the impact of overseas producers on the domestic market, changes in the locational pattern of Americans as they move to the suburbs, all of which weaken what might appear casually to be monopoly advantages.

There have been times when firms, by failing to provide correct or sufficient information about their products, have induced consumers to buy in the belief that the products were better than they really were. This, of course, is cheating. And if a supplier, in this manner, charged more than a product was worth, that excess profit was unjustified. But cheaters get found out; even if they don't, such is the process of competition that other cheaters will appear to share the excess profits so that the profits from cheating will be driven down to zero. Deception is a burden—there is no condoning it. More regulation may be part of an answer, but there is little evidence that product deception is widespread or that the problem is a serious social one. More important, excess profits from such cheating are probably extremely rare.

Many have noted that the pollution problem is associated with profit-seeking firms. Paper mills along the streams of Massachusetts, New Hampshire, and Maine, for example, have been accused of fouling the air and water that they use. And if there is no way of compensating the public for the pollution of the environment, then the mill costs recorded in their reports to stockholders and investors clearly understate actual social costs. By the same token, if there are profits, they are excessive in the social sense. But the situation is undesirable not because of excess profits or even of a lack of competition, but because there is too much pollution. The way to handle a situation like this is to find a way of assessing the social costs and fining the polluters. That would reduce paper mill profits, probably cause paper prices to go up, and possibly even reduce paper mill employment, but the price mechanism would have operated effectively to eliminate a situation in which the profits were excessive because cost calculations were wrong.

Put simply, such is the normal operation of the profit system that it would appear better on balance to correct the defects in the system when and where they take place. Such adjustments are preferable to discarding the profit system entirely.

Chapter Summary

In this chapter on corporate profits, we have outlined five basic theories of profits:

1. Compensation theory
2. Monopoly theory
3. Schumpeter's theory of monopoly profits
4. Exploitation theory
5. Romantic theory

The purpose of this outline of theories was to set the stage for an understanding of how actual corporate profits work, why they work that way, and how much they are. The outline also enabled us to understand criticisms of corporate profits.

Analyses of actual reported profits in the Soviet Union, in a major research and development corporation and in a corporation in trouble, were presented to help you see profit measurement and profit utilization in context. Profit and loss were compared as sources and uses of funds in a corporation.

A short examination of the possible meaning of profits of not-for-profit enterprises as well as a summary examination of the implications of federal government deficits and losses were presented to distinguish between corporate profits and their social uses and similar concepts used for other kinds of businesses and concerns.

The chapter closes with a frank analysis of possible undesirable social outcomes of the profit system. Since the basic thrust of the chapter is that corporate profits are generally misunderstood and their amounts and rates often overestimated, this last section considers how justified are some of the criticisms of profits.

Selected Readings

Chambers, Raymond J.: *Accounting, Evaluation and Economic Behavior*, Englewood Cliffs, N.J., Prentice-Hall, 1966.
Edwards, E. O., and P. W. Bell: *The Theory and Measurement of Business Income*, Berkeley, Cal., University of California Press, 1961.

Fellner, William: *Probability and Profit*, Homewood, Ill., Irwin, 1965.

Gross, Malvern J., Jr.: *Financial and Accounting Guide for Nonprofit Organizations*, New York, Ronald, 1972.

Haynes, W. W., and W. R. Henry: *Managerial Economics*, 3d ed., Dallas, Business Publications, 1974.

Lamberton, D. M.: *The Theory of Profit*, New York, Kelley, 1971.

Little, I. M. D., and J. A. Mirrlees: *Project Appraisal and Planning for Developing Countries*, New York, Basic Books, 1974.

Marris, Robin, and Adrian Wood (eds.): *The Corporate Economy*, Cambridge, Mass., Harvard, 1971.

Page, Alfred N.: *Utility Theory: A Book of Readings*, New York, Wiley, 1968.

Seater, John J.: "Profit in a Free Economy," *Business Review*, Philadelphia Federal Reserve Bank, May–June 1976.

Spulber, Nicholas, and Ira Horowitz: *Quantitative Economic Policy and Planning*, New York, Norton, 1976.

Sterling, Robert R.: *Theory of the Measurement of Enterprise Income*, Lawrence, Kans., University of Kansas Press, 1970.

Sterling, Robert R. (ed.): *Asset Valuation and Income Determination*, Lawrence, Kans., Scholars Book, 1971.

Summers, Edward L.: *An Introduction to Accounting for Decision Making and Control*, Homewood, Ill., Irwin, 1974.

Questions, Problems, and Projects

1. "In 1974, the construction of some 235 electric power plants was postponed or cancelled. In part, these deferrals were the result of revised demand projections, but for many utilities they reflected an inability to generate funds internally or raise outside capital at an acceptable price. Almost all of the utilities' common stocks were selling in 1974 below book value. The marked deterioration was largely explained by the decline in the return on equity relative to yields on alternative investments, such as AAA industrial bonds." Explain these remarks by an economist of the Federal Reserve Bank of Boston in 1975. In what sense do they adequately explain why New England utility rates were high and likely to remain high?

2. A Yugoslavian economist, Stevan Kupoleca, has reported the following deficiencies of a command economy, based on his research in Yugoslavia: (*a*) Failures in selecting products to be manufactured, (*b*) lack of worker interest in increasing productivity, (*c*) unsatisfactory allocation of resources and funds for increased production, (*d*) slow turnover of capital, (*e*) lack of interest in innovation, and (*f*) difficulties in organizing scientific research and development. Would a profit system operate differently? How?

3. William G. Shepherd examined whether monopoly power regularly yields higher profits. He found no easy answer. The profitability of a company embraces at least two dimensions, he noted, the raw rate of return on investment and the degree of risk in these profit rates. So a low-risk 6 percent profit rate might represent greater genuine profitability than a high-risk 12 percent. How do you explain his findings?

4. Is the marginal productivity measure of profit relevant? What are the implications and limitations of such a measure of profit? In what sense is profit a price? And, if it is a price, how does it affect the distribution of the gross national product?

5. Hard as they are to obtain, try to get a copy of your or another college's balance sheet and a statement of gifts, grants, and value of the endowment. Determine the profitability of the college. Now assess the meaning of profit in terms of the price system used in determining tuition. Do these profits measure the full social benefits resulting from educating students?

6. Deficits and losses are frequently confused. What is the difference between the two? In what sense does a government lose? What is the relationship between the net worth of an organization and its deficits? Its losses?

7. Thomas G. Moore, in an analysis of the over-the-road trucking industry, observed that the total assets of class I and class II common carriers were $2.42 billion in 1968. Since net operating revenue was $499 million and since, given a market rate of interest of 10 percent, total equity financing would require less than $499 million, what were the monopoly profits in the trucking industry? What would be the effect on freight rates of deregulating the trucking industry? On the national economy? On the Teamsters' Union?

Case 8.1   United Nuclear Corporation

In 1975 the United Nuclear Corporation reported that, in the fiscal year ending March 31, 1975, the company had returned to profitability, although earnings were marginal and included a significant profit from a venture with the Tennessee Valley Authority (TVA). Earnings of $423,000 (8 cents a share) compared with the 1974 net loss from continuing operations of $1,495,000 (29 cents a share) and net loss of $4,667,000 (90 cents a share) after provisions for losses of discontinued operations.

Previous years were difficult for the company. They have been characterized by problems and circumstances which have adversely affected profitability. The absence of a functioning economic uranium market precluded realistic prices for one of the company's most significant products, and uranium deliveries had been made under old contracts at relatively low prices. The commercial nuclear fuel fabrication business did not develop as anticipated and so was divested along with certain other related activities. Despite absence of a viable uranium market and a consequent lack of profits during this period, the company had to sustain its mining capabilities and protect and extend its sources of uranium through continued exploration and development.

1975 saw a number of significant events. Steps were taken to realign and strengthen the company's management organization. Uranium sales contracts were negotiated that totaled $84 million plus escalation, with $24.6 million in advance payments, providing for delivery of 5.8 million pounds of uranium in the period 1976 through 1979.

Table 1   United Nuclear Corporation: Operations highlights
Year Ending March 31

	1975	1974
Operating results:		
Revenues	$83,261,000	$67,543,000
Income from continuing operations, loss	423,000	(1,495,000)
Loss from discontinued operations		(3,172,000)
Net earnings, loss	423,000	(4,667,000)
Depreciation, depletion, and amortization	4,599,000	5,254,000
Per share		
Income from continuing operations, loss	.08	(.29)
Loss from discontinued operations		(.61)
Net earnings, loss	$.08	$(.90)
Average number of shares outstanding	5,085,157	5,172,709
Financial position:		
Working capital	$ 9,028,000	$ 8,264,000*
Property, plant, and equipment		
Capital expenditures during the year	19,570,000	9,981,000
Balance, net of depreciation, depletion, and amortization	69,531,000	57,480,000
Long-term debt, net of current portion	48,623,000	44,058,000
Shareholders' equity	46,594,000	47,808,000
Equity per outstanding share	9.45	9.24
Price range of common shares		
High	14$^{1}/_{8}$	20$^{1}/_{2}$
Low	6	6
Price range of debentures		
High	67	80
Low	43	54$^{1}/_{4}$
Number of registered shareholders	18,319	18,271
Number of debenture holders	1,392	1,349
Operating highlights:		
Approximate number of employees	3,300	2,900
Uranium reserves in pounds		
$15 reserves 1975; $8 reserves 1974*	79,800,000	63,800,000
Uranium delivery commitments in pounds,		
including customer options	38,386,000	33,859,000
Uranium production in pounds	1,550,000	1,446,000
Exploration drilling on company properties in feet	1,093,000	1,135,000
Tons of coal produced	354,000	294,000

*The 1974 amount has been reclassified to conform to 1975 presentation.
†Reserves were recomputed effective April 1, 1975.

Notwithstanding the progress made, much remained to be achieved. It was necessary to rebuild production capacity in uranium from the low rate sustained in the past three years and to correct the disproportionate mix of lower-price uranium contracts calling for deliveries this year. The company's priorities would have to be directed to increasing uranium production capacity, more specifically,

1. Continued development of Church Rock mine consistent with a balance of current production to meet commitments
2. Successful completion and operation of the first Uranium Recovery Corporation plant to extract uranium from Florida phosphates
3. Planning and development of Morton Ranch and other mining properties

Improving price and delivery terms of certain existing uranium supply contracts was under study, but the degree of success was as yet conjectural.

These priorities constituted a formidable program and required substantial capital expenditures. Capital requirements in 1976 would exceed the internally generated cash flow. The net additional requirement would be obtained from outside resources, probably from "front-end payments" under further uranium supply contracts. The company's capacity to meet the capital requirements of its present business from internal cash flow was expected to improve after 1976.

Opportunities and prospects in the supply of energy products and services were promising. The company's uranium reserves, both before and after existing commitments, caused the company to be a significant factor in its industry and represented material values. As is typical for natural resource companies, the accounts of the company reflected only the investment in but not the prospective value of such reserves. An exploration program under way in 1976 should help to evaluate the extent and the significance of the Western coal reserves held by the company. This program was expected to confirm that coal reserves were another potential source of material profitability.

Notwithstanding the continuing dialog with the nuclear opposition, each passing day further seemed to prove the critical need for and the value of both the actual contribution in 1976 and the potential future contributions of nuclear power in the generation of electricity. There appeared to be no feasible alternative to the rapid development of nuclear power generation to meet the nation's growing requirements for electricity.

SUMMARY OF SIGNIFICANT ACCOUNTING POLICIES: LONG-TERM CONTRACTS IN PROCESS

The percentage-of-completion method of accounting is used to record sales values of performance under long-term government contracts (predominantly fixed-price and fixed-price incentive contracts). Sales values, including a portion of the profit expected, are recorded as costs are incurred. Profits expected are based on estimates of total sales values and costs at completion.

These estimates are reviewed periodically and adjustments to estimated profits resulting from such review are recorded when appropriate. Profits under certain contracts may be increased or decreased in accordance with cost-incentive provisions which measure actual costs against established targets. Losses on contracts, if any, are recorded in full as they are identified.

INVENTORIES

Valuation of inventories is at the lower of cost or market. Cost of uranium ore is determined by the first-in–first-out method. The costs of all other inventories are determined by averaging methods.

EXPLORATION

The costs of exploring and examining prospects in which property interests are not acquired and general administrative costs relating to overall exploration are charged to earnings as incurred. Acquisition costs and exploration costs relating to properties acquired for specific exploration projects within limited geological areas are capitalized. Such capitalized costs are amortized against production or written off immediately when it is determined that a project is unsuccessful.

DEPRECIATION, DEPLETION, AND AMORTIZATION

Producing mining properties, including capitalized exploration and development costs, are amortized by the unit-of-production method, based on estimated ore reserves. In arriving at rates under the unit-of-production method, commercially recoverable reserves are estimated by the company's geologists and engineers. Such estimates are revised as data becomes available to warrant revision. Mill site, plant, and equipment are depreciated over their estimated economic lives, determined in relationship with associated ore reserves to be processed. Other facilities and equipment are depreciated over their estimated useful lives by use of the straight-line method, except for recently expanded facilities in the naval products division which are being depreciated by the sum-of-the-years' digits method.

Maintenance, repairs, and minor renewals and "betterments" are charged to earnings when incurred. Major renewals and betterments are capitalized and subsequently depreciated. Upon sale or other disposition, costs of asset and accumulated depreciation, depletion, and amortization are eliminated from account and any resulting gain or loss is reflected in earnings.

DISCUSSION QUESTIONS 8.1

1. Would you and, if you would, how would you adjust the reported profits of United Nuclear for 1974 and 1975?
2. What do you think of the market situation facing United Nuclear? What difference does it make that it is not easy to determine prices of products when profits are being calculated?
3. As you examine the statement of accounting policies, do you see reasons why economic profit might vary significantly from accounting profits for United Nuclear?

4. Does the fact that United Nuclear is in an industry which is sometimes accused of being environmentally damaging have any effect on your previous answers? How would you account for any possible environmental damage in estimating profits in this case?

Case 8.2 Connecticut Natural Gas Corporation

The following is the letter of an exasperated utility executive to a state public utility commissioner:

Mr. Albert J. Kleban, Chairman
Public Utilities Control Authority
State Office Building
Hartford, Connecticut 06115
Dear Commissioner Kleban:

As you know, the Federal Power Commission in its Opinion 770, issued on July 27, 1976, authorized major increases in the wellhead price of natural gas committed to production, starting on January 1, 1973.

Current FPC rate filings by our pipeline suppliers indicate that the effect of this opinion on CNG's wholesale gas costs will be very substantial and far more than previously estimated by the FPC. For this reason, I believe it is important for me to provide you with the best review possible at this point of the potential effect on our gas costs.

Opinion 770 permits a wellhead price of $1.01 per 1000 cubic feet for new gas committed to production between January 1 of 1973 and December 31 of 1974 and a rate of $1.42 for gas committed to production after that date, compared with the 52 cents previously allowed for new gas. An escalation clause permits further increases of 1 cent every three months for gas produced after January 1, 1975.

Various intervenors protested the price increase and other aspects of the order to the FPC and later appealed to the courts. The court stipulated that the new prices must be subject to refund and the FPC agreed to a rehearing of the matter. However, the FPC also announced that it would permit the new prices to go into effect subject to refund, pending announcement of its findings following the rehearing, in connection with which it heard oral arguments in September.

The FPC opinion also included a provision permitting pipelines to utilize their Purchased Gas Adjustment Clauses as the vehicle to pass along the full amount of the wellhead price increases to customers effective October 27, subject to refund. This use of the PGA mechanism results in the increases becoming effective 30 days after filing rather than being suspended for five months and then permitted to go into effect subject to refund.

Our pipeline suppliers, Algonquin Gas Transmission Company and Tennessee Gas Pipeline Company, have now filed new rate schedules to recover the costs established in Opinion 770 and have notified us that these will go into effect on October 27, 1976.

We have computed the impact of these increases at approximately $8 million annually, nearly a 28 percent increase in our cost of gas. While CNG recognizes that an increase in the price of *new* gas is necessary to accelerate exploration and production, we also believe there are many unanswered questions in regard to these pipeline rate increases and do not endorse the FPC philosophy of allowing increases in the price of previously committed gas as opposed to placing the incentive on the price of *new* gas.

I am chairman of a group of New England gas companies known as the Algonquin Customer Group because all are customers of Algonquin Gas Transmission Company. The steering committee of this group has voted unanimously to file petitions to intervene, protests, and requests for stay in the filing of Algonquin Gas and in the underlying filings of Texas Eastern Transmission Corporation and United Gas Pipeline Company, through which Algonquin receives gas. These documents will be filed by October 15.

We also plan to participate in a similar intervention against the Tennessee Gas increase, and are demanding full disclosure of data on which applications of all suppliers concerned are based.

The wellhead price of gas included in deliveries to us will obviously now vary widely. It could be as low as 29 cents per thousand cubic feet under old contracts, and at special prices granted small producers. It will be 52 cents for gas sold to pipelines under new contracts but not committed for sale prior to January 1 of 1973, $1.01 for gas committed in 1973 and 1974, $1.42 for new gas committed in early 1975, and up to $1.50 for gas committed at the end of this calendar year.

This is a confusing situation. We have no proof regarding when gas being sold to us was committed to production and of the percentage of gas which should be charged for at each of the varying rates. In addition, there are many aspects of Opinion 770 which will probably be subject to legal determinations for years to come. For example, what price will ultimately be allowed for new wells drilled into existing reservoirs after January 1, 1975? The Algonquin filing rests solely on the Texas Eastern and United Gas filings, which we do not see since we are not a customer of either. Being a direct customer of Tennessee, we have been able to determine that their total gas supply vintage is made up of 53 percent prior to 1973–74, 26 percent 1973–74, and 21 percent since 1975. The price effect on each is not yet known.

I can assure you that CNG people are doing everything within their power to find answers and to explore every possible avenue of appropriate action for protecting our customers.

As I am sure you recognize, increases the size of those scheduled for October 27 will have extremely broad long-range ramifications. For example, they will affect the competitive relationship of seasonal and interruptible gas sales to large industrial and commercial users as related to oil. This could adversely affect our load factor, total sales volume, and rate structure within a relatively short period.

Meanwhile, the FPC recently announced figures on gas production for the first quarter of 1976, showing that sales to interstate pipelines dropped to the lowest quarterly level in eight years and a considerable deepening of pipeline gas curtailments on a national basis is anticipated during the coming winter.

As you know, we are fighting hard for our fair share of gas due us under contractual commitments. In mid-September, for example, I wrote Frank G. Zarb, administrator of the Federal Energy Administration, in sharp protest of an FEA practice of changing our data to treat our synthetic natural gas purchases as additional volumes of natural gas rather than as a replacement for natural gas curtailed.

In other words, the effect of such a procedure would be to withhold from Connecticut consumers additional contracted amounts of pipeline gas costing about $1 per thousand cubic feet and forcing us into increased reliance on synthetic gas at over $5 per thousand cubic feet. Obviously, this would have an adverse economic effect on our customers and be patently unfair, but it is typical of the supply and price problems we are facing every day.

CNG continues to believe that decontrol of *new* gas discoveries remains the only real or lasting solution to the complex problems of the type outlined in this letter, but the FPC action on higher ceiling prices will possibly cause such adverse public reaction as to set back the decontrol movement for some time. However, the FPC's actions in Opinion 770 were forced upon it by Congressional failure to decontrol the price of new gas discoveries. If the FPC had done nothing, exploration and development of new gas for interstate commerce would certainly continue to degenerate toward total national disaster.

The chances are that the new wellhead prices permitted by the FPC will result in more gas than would otherwise be available. However, costs of drilling vary greatly. An onshore well may be relatively inexpensive, while the cost of offshore drilling in deep water is tremendous. Imposing equal prices for dissimilar sources cannot be productive. Similarly, free market prices would encourage use of methods to develop additional gas from depleted fields or tight formations.

Meanwhile, we face the totally ridiculous situation in which Connecticut gas users are being harmed by the constantly rising pipeline prices inherent in a shortage situation plus the resulting need for synthetic gas at $5 per thousand cubic feet and up . . . obviously far above the new FPC wellhead prices or any conceivable price for natural gas under decontrol.

Another incredible facet of today's entire situation is that most of the money the producers are receiving under the FPC price schedule will not even be retained by them. The FPC opinion recognizes that 55 percent of the increase must be paid out in income taxes . . . making the Federal Government the chief beneficiary, a situation that probably will void much of the impact of the new prices in improving the pace of exploration.

To put this another way, the bulk of the substantial increase which Opinion 770 threatens in terms of Connecticut gas bills will in substance represent additional tax payments passed along to producers by Connecticut gas users for the benefit of the Federal Government. Producers need over twice the extra money they are presumed by the FPC to require for drilling, since the lion's share goes to Washington. This is a strange and weird situation in a time of energy crisis.

Our lack of a national energy policy is an even worse villain than inflation in squeezing gas customers. Mr. Ford has strongly endorsed decontrol and Mr.

Carter has stated that it should at least be given a try. The Senate, of course, has also approved it. Adequate decontrol legislation, embodied in the Murphy-Kreuger-Brown bill, is now before the House, but is stagnating there.

The passage of such legislation can, in our opinion, halt the deteriorating and threatening natural gas supply and price crisis now facing our country and Connecticut consumers, but achievement of a supply-demand balance may be hastened by the FPC higher prices.

Meanwhile, we will do our best to keep you informed of the difficult situation created by the pipeline rate increases due to go into effect on October 27 and of our efforts to obtain adequate underlying data and fair treatment for CNG customers under the circumstances.

I will be happy to provide you with any additional information you may desire on this matter or to meet with you or any other representatives of the Public Utilities Control Authority to outline the problem created by FPC Opinion 770 in more detail, along with the steps we are taking to meet it. Sincerely,

Connecticut Natural Gas Corporation
R. H. Willis
Chairman and President

DISCUSSION QUESTIONS 8.2

1. Although you don't have the Connecticut Natural Gas balance sheets and statements of income, what kinds of adjustments do you think would have to be made to account for the situation of which Mr. Willis complains?
2. Remembering that, to a great extent, prices are determined at least with the guidelines set by such agencies as the Federal Power Commission and the Connecticut Public Utilities Control Authority, what elements enter the calculation of Connecticut Natural Gas profits that make those profits difficult to compare with other corporate profits?
3. How would you calculate economic profits in the light of the obvious conflict over purpose and policy in Opinion 770? Why should CNG be permitted to earn any economic profit?
4. Find a role for management in the CNG case such that there could be a defense for profits. Is there a risk issue here? How would a Marxist analyze this situation? To what extent are there real and potential areas of exploitation?

9

MARKET STRUCTURE, MARKET POWER, AND ANTITRUST

Key Concepts

Alcoa case
Antitrust division of Department
   of Justice
case law
classical merger
Clayton Act
common law
competitive structure
concentration
concentration ratio
conglomerate
control of market power
determinants of market
   structure
discrimination
divestiture
du Pont case
du Pont–General Motors case
economic size
enforcement
entry
excessive profits
fair competition
Federal Trade Commission
Fortune 500
freedom of exit
homogeneity of product
horizontal mergers

industry
information
market behavior
market performance
market power
minimum optimum scale
monopoly capitalism
Morton Salt case
pecuniary cost advantages
per se violations
potential competition
price discrimination
pure competition and market
   dimensions
relevant market
Robinson-Patman Act
Schumpeter on monopoly and
   economic structure
Sherman Act
SIC code
social power
Standard Oil case
substitutability
technical cost advantages
trust busting
trusts
two-digit industry
vertical mergers

What Is Ahead in This Chapter

This chapter considers how markets are organized and the effect of market organization on public welfare. Market organization is a matter of structure; the elements of the structure are the dimensions of competition. The dimensions of competition—number of firms, kind of product sold, amount of market information available, ease of entry and exit in an industry—permit a classification of markets ranging from pure competition to monopoly. Competition, though, is more than a way to describe market organization. It is also a theory about how firms and their managements behave. Therefore, it is a theory about the exercise of market power.

Market power arises from the ability of firms to set prices, to determine how much they are going to produce and sell, and to decide how much profit they are going to derive from their business activities. The more competitive the structure, the less market power any firm has. And the less competitive and more monopolized the structure, the more market power management has.

The control of market power is what antitrust laws are about. The commitment of the United States to a system of free—that is, competitive—markets is expressed in these antitrust or antimonopoly laws. How and whether these laws accomplish their social purposes are matters we carefully consider in the later portions of this chapter.

Readers who seek an assessment of the social and political power of giant corporations may find the discussion somewhat technical and unsatisfactory in those contexts. Social forces and political power, while possibly resulting from use or abuse of market power, are not the same. In political science, it is the absolute bigness of the corporation and its ability to use the resultant social and political power to further its own interests in society that are at issue. In economics, the focus is not upon the corporation but upon a market where a certain division of a corporation is regarded as a firm manufacturing and selling a product. Market power refers only to a strictly defined product market.

Perhaps it is because definitions of market and of corporation are not quite the same that antitrust enforcement is never quite what popular literature depicts. In short, in economics, market power is seldom an exciting concept, and whether it actually makes much difference in the operation of the national economy is a question that we will examine in detail in this chapter.

The paradox is that the more we understand the competitive structure of American markets and how firms behave in those markets, the less substance there is to the prevalent negative image of corporate management. It isn't that monopoly doesn't matter, but just how much does it matter? Let's consider the facts.

State of the Argument

Some years ago J. S. Bain[1] divided the subject matter of competitive market structure into three parts: (1) structure, (2) behavior, and (3) performance. Structure determines the extent to which an industry is competitive. It is largely a question of taxonomy, of classifying all the variations in degree of competitive structure. Behavior is a matter of observing what firms do and of developing hypotheses about patterns of action and reaction. And performance is an attempt to measure the effect of structure and behavior on a firm, an industry, and the national economy.

In recent years, market structure has been increasingly studied in terms of concentration, the extent to which one firm or a small group of firms dominates an industry. Such studies generally assume that, in the absence of unnatural or contrived elements in the structure of an industry or in the behavior of firms, the natural structure and behavior of most markets would be competitive.

Competition

"Pure competition" is a market concept in which there are large numbers of both buyers and sellers and in which there is no effective market power available to or possessed by any single participant. Market benefits—prices, profits, and satisfaction—are distributed in a manner as nearly free from discrimination as possible.

Note that competition includes several economic dimensions. The first such dimension is the number of participants. The more participants, the more competitive the market. The fewer participants, the more monopolized the market. In this dimension, competition is not a matter of what the participants do or how they behave, but what it is possible for them to do. Thus, the more competitive the market, the less can any one participant set a price, change the quality of merchandise, advertise, increase profits, improve satisfaction, stabilize market variations, or otherwise effect a gain accruing solely to that participant. Where pure competition is present, no firm has any economic power.

The next key economic dimension is price. The "ruling price" concept is a hallmark of competition but to the extent that persistent price differences appear that reflect advantages in the market location of the seller or the buyer, special production cost variations, and induced consumer preferences for one firm's product over another, there is less competition and more monopoly.

Another dimension is product homogeneity, which is partly a question of nature and/or technology. Monopoly power is unavoidable when a product by

---

[1] J. S. Bain, *Industrial Organization*, rev. ed., New York, Wiley, 1967.

one firm is unique. Uniqueness may arise from a patent granted to and possessed by a firm or it may arise from the fact that technology or state of the art limits the manufacturers and sellers to a given place or number.

But homogeneity is also a question of consumer perception. If consumers, because they intuitively believe there is a difference or because they have been induced through advertising to perceive a unique quality in the output of one firm compared with that of another, choose to pay a higher price for a specific product, then the fact that there may be no chemical or physical difference is not relevant.

The degree of homogeneity or substitutability is not dependent on physical similarities or qualitative comparisons. All that is necessary is that consumers behave as if the purchase of one good is affected by the price and/or availability of another good or service.

Still another economic dimension is information. In the nineteenth century poor communications and lack of market information made markets which could have been competitive behave as if they were monopolized. Indeed, it was because of their control of market information that the Rockefellers and the Goulds converted competitive markets into trusts and monopolies.

Another dimension of competition is the "relevant market," a market which contains all those sellers (and buyers) who actually participate regardless of the geographic location of their place of production. To define relevant markets it is necessary to define industry. An industry consists of all those firms which produce and/or sell a given product. Note that the definition of industry turns on the product. By implication, each industry is so separate from any other industry that there can be no confusion. However, it is not enough to define an industry by its product; one must also define the geographic range. Thus, we have not only the steel industry, but the United States steel industry. We have not only the department store business but the metropolitan Dallas department store business. In these terms, then, a relevant market is competitive to the extent that it contains a large number of participants, that its product is homogeneous, that information about product, price, and competitive behavior more or less affects all participants, and that the ruling price is a basis for production decisions.

One more dimension to competition is worthy of note, that of entry. So long as there are limits on the number of participants in a relevant market, those limits can be conducive to monopoly power. The limitation may be legal eligibility as defined in a license, permission, or charter. Those who have the necessary charter can participate. Those who do not, cannot. And if a charter is relatively difficult to obtain, then there are possibly fewer market participants than there could or even should be. The limitation may also be financial; the technology, say, of steel making, requires so large an initial investment that few can be expected to obtain such funding. Whatever the barrier to entry, its presence is a potential or real monopoly power element.

Other forms of discrimination may also limit entry. Race, sex, or age discrimination may prevent potential sellers of labor from participating in the marketplace. Discrimination may also exist in such areas as tariffs, public health laws, zoning codes, building restrictions, pollution control, language, culture, and social class structure.

Freedom of entry implies freedom of exit. Odd forms of monopoly power arise because market participants who wish to terminate their businesses in particular areas or in particular lines are not permitted to do so for public convenience. The position of the urban transit service in New Orleans and the dominance by Allegheny Airlines of Midwest air routes arose in this fashion.

A point to be stressed is that any act which reduces a dimensional element of a competitive market is a monopolizing act. Monopoly power in a market increases as that market becomes less competitive.

Concentration

Concentration is a measure of the competitiveness of an industry or a relevant market. The appropriate index of concentration is not intuitively obvious. The most common index is the percentage of economic activity (assets, sales, value of shipments, value added, and employment) in an industry held by one, two, four, or more firms.

To calculate a concentration ratio, three basic elements must be determined: (1) industry, (2) firm, and (3) a firm's share of an industry's activity. The Bureau of the Census uses a standard industrial classification (SIC) code which, by number of digits, describes the detailed product structure of an industry (Table 9.1). For most purposes, four-digit industries are used in the calculation of concentration ratios.

For census purposes, a firm may simply be part of a corporation, a part engaged in making the particular product upon which the SIC code is focused. What the concentration ratio measures is not the market power of the Ford Motor Company, for example, but the market share of the motor vehicle manufacturing operations of the Ford Motor Company in the motor vehicle manufacturing industry.

SIC industries may not be true economic industries. For one thing, SIC industries are national in scope and may not reflect local or regional concentration. Obviously, they do not reflect international concentration. Yet SIC codes are probably reasonably accurate in defining manufacturing, mining, and

Table 9.1 Example of SIC code breakdown of two-digit industry

SIC code	Name of industry
36	Electrical equipment and supplies
361	Electrical and distributing equipment
3611	Electrical measuring instruments
36111	Electrical integrating instruments

transportation markets. They are used less effectively to measure concentration in retailing, wholesaling, services, and construction.

Changes in Concentration in the United States

Is concentration increasing or decreasing in the United States? SIC code concentration ratios provide part of the answer, but evidence from the 1972 economic census does not establish a clear trend (Tables 9.2 and 9.3). Of the 180 more or less comparable four-digit industries for which value-of-shipments concentration ratio series are available from 1947 through 1972, 97 industries showed an increase in their concentration ratios, 6 showed no change between the beginning and the end of the period, and 77 showed a decrease in concentration. These 180 four-digit industries represent less than half of the four-digit industries in the nation. Between 1967 and 1972, 39 four-digit industries showed no change, 176 showed an increase in concentration, and 158 showed a decrease. Of these 373 industries for which data are comparable for the two censuses of manufacture, 47 percent, then, recorded increasing concentration.

Table 9.2 Number of four-digit industries reporting change in four-firm concentration ratios
Value of industry shipments, 1972

SIC industry	No change, 1947–1972	Decrease, 1947–1972	Increase, 1947–1972
20	1	7	16
21	0	2	2
22	0	4	8
23	0	4	14
24	0	4	3
25	0	2	1
26	0	1	1
27	0	4	5
28	0	5	3
29	0	3	1
30	0	2	0
31	1	1	2
32	2	3	8
33	1	3	3
34	0	10	3
35	1	5	5
36	0	9	4
37	0	2	5
38	0	2	3
39	0	4	10
	6	77	97

Table 9.3 Number of four-digit industries reporting change in four-firm concentration ratios

Value of industry shipments, 1972

SIC in- dustry	1967–1972			SIC in- dustry	1967–1972		
	No change	De- crease	In- crease		No change	De- crease	In- crease
20	7	15	21	30	2	1	1
21	0	1	3	31	0	3	6
22	3	10	13	32	3	11	12
23	2	6	25	33	1	11	8
24	0	0	6	34	5	15	7
25	1	8	2	35	4	19	15
26	2	5	8	36	2	18	11
27	3	4	8	37	0	5	7
28	2	12	6	38	0	4	7
29	0	3	2	39	2	7	8
				Totals	39	158	176

Economic Size

Economic size is the relative position of a firm in an industry. It is not the absolute financial, asset, or sales size of the firm. A firm has significant economic size if it controls a large share of the business of an industry. Few will doubt that General Motors is large in this sense since it controls somewhere between 40 and 50 percent of the sales of American-made automobiles in the United States, but a ten-seat barber shop in a small community in which there are only five barber shops, all the rest having no more than two seats, is also economically large. By the same token, American Motors, a multibillion-dollar corporation, is economically small.

The Fortune 500

The Fortune 500 is an annual listing by *Fortune* magazine of the 500 largest corporations in the United States. But the Fortune 500 listing is not based on the concept of market size, or of monopoly power, or of concentration. To count, for example, the share of the total sales of all United States corporations held by one or all of the Fortune 500 firms does not address the issue involved in the construction of a concentration ratio. In the Fortune 500, the economic power that is being measured is the assumed financial position of the giant corporation vis-à-vis the economy. Economic analysis deals with control in individual markets over prices, profits, costs, and wages.

Determinants of Market Structure

Shepherd[2] outlines four possible general determinants of the presence of monopoly elements in a market. The first is the stage of growth of an industry. For example, industry may begin as a monopoly and gradually progress toward a more competitive structure. But a mature industry is likely to be characterized by tight and collusive oligopolies. The automobile industry began as a monopoly, rapidly became competitive, then turned oligopolistic. The state of growth is not, however, a helpful determinant, he says.

A second determinant is the combination of technical and demand conditions in an industry. Such conditions may involve patents, financial and technological barriers to entry as well as barriers to exit, lack of homogeneity of product, and actual and potential size of the market itself.

The third determinant concerns the quality of information. The more specialized knowledge and inside information about prices, sales, costs, market trends, and market positions of individual participants compared with relative lack of knowledge outside the industry, the greater advantage to insiders in gaining and maintaining market power. Information may reduce uncertainty for the favored firms, reducing their risks and increasing the profitability of their activities.

Finally, there is the role of government policies. Governments may set up procurement procedures which favor one firm over others. They may institute subsidies and price and production controls, provide research support, administer taxes, and otherwise encourage development of monopoly power.

Evidence on Concentration, Size, and Profitability

Unfortunately, there is no undisputed evidence among firms in an industry about the effect of economic size on profits. J. S. Bain[3] examined twelve multiplant industries; of these, he found six in which there appeared to be no economies of scale. In four of the remaining six, economies were small or slight and in only two of these industries did Bain find convincing evidence of scale.

Willard F. Mueller, William H. Kelly, and Russell G. Parker,[4] in a 1969 report to the Federal Trade Commission (FTC) argued that "our conclusions clearly substantiate the theory that market structure has a significant influence on market performance," but James A. Dalton and David W. Penn[5] in a 1971 report to the FTC said that their "analysis demonstrates that reliance on data

[2]William G. Shepherd, *Market Power and Economic Welfare*, chap. 3, New York, Random House, 1970.

[3]J. S. Bain, "Economies of Scale, Concentration and the Condition of Entry in Twenty Manufacturing Industries," *American Economic Review*, 44(1):15–39, March 1954.

[4]W. F. Mueller, W. H. Kelly, and R. G. Parker, *On the Influence of Market Structure on the Profit Performance of Food Manufacturing Companies*, Economic Report to the Federal Trade Commission, Washington, D.C., September 1969.

[5]J. A. Dalton and D. W. Penn, *The Quality of Data as a Factor in Analyses of Structural Performance Relationships*, A Report to the Federal Trade Commission, Washington, D.C., July 1971.

from public sources is likely to underestimate the explanatory power of structural variables on firm profitability. . . . More importantly, it is not possible with public data to measure the impact of a firm's market share on profitability."

Collins and Preston[6] found that, over the range of four-digit manufacturing industries in 1963, for every 10 percent increase in the four-firm concentration ratio, industrywide average rates of return appeared to increase from 0.8 to 1.0 percentage points. Eatwell,[7] in summarizing major empirical research on relationships among profitability, growth, and size of business firms, found no simple linear explanation of the effect of firm size on profitability. Instead, Eatwell reported that larger firms tended to have more certainty of profits. He suggested that they traded this certainty for somewhat lower-than-expected rates of return.

Market Power and Market Performance

There is a subtle difference between measuring market performance in a microeconomic context and in a macroeconomic context. Microeconomics is concerned with the individual firm and how it performs in terms of profits, prices, sales, production, and efficient use of inputs. In reviewing the performance of an industry, it is by summing the performances of individual firms in that product market that conclusions about industry performances are drawn. Macroeconomics looks at national goals such as full employment, stability in prices or avoidance of inflation, adequate growth of the national economy, technological progress, fairness in distribution of benefits of growth and technology, and relative economic position of our nation compared with other nations.

How does the presence of market power in one, several, or many industries affect the ability of the national economy to achieve such goals? Would the level of employment be higher and the level of unemployment lower with a more competitive structure in the American economy?

Arnold Harberger[8] attempted to estimate, in dollar terms, actual losses caused by monopolistic resource misallocation in American industry. His judgment was that eliminating monopolistic resource misallocation in the period 1924–1928 would have increased consumer welfare by slightly less than 0.1 percent of the gross national product. David Schwartzman[9] reached

---

[6]Norman R. Collins and Lee E. Preston, *Concentration and Price-Cost Margins in Manufacturing Industries*, Berkeley, University of California Press, 1968.

[7]John L. Eatwell, "Growth, Profitability and Size: The Empirical Evidence," in Robin Marris and Adrian Wood (eds.), *The Corporate Economy*, Cambridge, Harvard University Press, 1971, Appendix A.

[8]Arnold Harberger, "Monopoly and Resource Allocation," *American Economic Review*, 44(2):77–92, May 1954.

[9]David Schwartzman, "The Burden of Monopoly," *Journal of Political Economy*, 68:627–630, December 1960. See also his "The Effect of Monopoly on Price," *Journal of Political Economy*, 67:352–362, August 1959.

essentially similar results. Even if we conclude that perhaps as much as 6 percent of the gross national product (GNP) is monopoly waste, an admitted exaggeration, how does that waste compare with a loss of potential GNP traceable to inadequate tax or monetary policies? More important, how do we translate what is effectively a loss of consumer surplus into a measurement of loss of employment? In other words, if we reduce monopoly power effectively, can we have better national economic performance?

The review by H. Demsetz[10] of evidence on market performance is informative. Demsetz found no broad statistical support for a tie between market concentration and inflation and, for price inflexibility, he found no link.

Minimum Optimal Scale

F. M. Scherer[11] and his associates found that the number of minimum optimal scale plants compatible with domestic consumption in the United States varied from 523 in the case of shoes down to a little over 7 in the case of refrigerators. Where the minimum optimal scale is relatively small, the number of plants operated by the leading firms in an industry tends to be large, over thirty in the textile weaving industry, for example.

Multiplant operations reduce transport costs where these are important (as with breweries). They permit product specialization and coordination of investments over time and space. But, for other markets, where buyers prefer to deal with broadline suppliers, there are economies of scale in marketing and promotion. Moreover, lenders charge lower interest rates to multiplant operators because such operations spread the risk.

Scherer concluded that in many instances the market share held by the top three firms was larger than it needed to be to take advantage of all significant multiplant scale economies. Yet, because many of the multiplant industries are regionally distributed, any attempt at divestiture would mean a reduction in the national concentration ratio, with but little if any change in the regional indexes of concentration. But see discussion in the section on the limits of antitrust at the end of this chapter.

Monopoly Capitalism

The Marxist critique holds that the giant business corporation—defined in terms of its total assets or size or employment—is a focus of superior and

---

[10]Harold Demsetz, *The Market Concentration Doctrine*, Washington, D.C., American Enterprise Institute for Public Policy Research, August 1973. See Louis Philips, *Effects of Industrial Concentration*, Amsterdam, North-Holland, 1971, in which, after a study of common market nations, Philips concludes essentially (as does Demsetz) that statistical evidence for any relationship between price behavior, inflation, and profitability on the one hand and indexes of concentration on the other is weak and unreliable.

[11]F. M. Scherer et al., *The Economics of Multiplant Operation*, Cambridge, Harvard University Press, 1975.

overweening economic power. Marxists point up the allegedly self-perpetuating and self-serving character of the giant firm which, with other giant firms, interacts to provide complete or near complete control of the economy. Bigness is bad, however, less because of monopoly per se—since socialism would replace the private big firm with a state-owned big firm with presumably disinterested management—than because of a confirmed tendency of the capitalist class to deny the working class a fair share of the benefits from operation of the economic system.

By extension, the position of the United States in the world economy is that of a monopolist, a wielder of economic power solely for the good of the ruling classes in the United States. What is at issue is the distribution of the social surplus, the difference between the wages received by laborers and the gross product at market prices. Monopoly power, in the Marxist critique, means the power to induce a massive maldistribution of income and wealth.

Whether one accepts this critique or not, it is at least useful to be aware of what it implies. Basically, such analyses tend to become detailed statements of the deeds of alleged corporate malefactors, statistical derivations of the amount of social surplus exploited by big business, and identifications of certain individuals and families as archetypes of capitalist misbehavior.

Antitrust Policy

There are three basic elements to antitrust policy. One is the control of market power. Another is the preservation or promotion of fair competition. And the third is the restriction of mergers, combinations, and collusive behavior. Antitrust principles are a mixture of economics and law. The underlying economic doctrines are those of pure competition, efficiency in production, and equity in distribution. Antitrust law, deriving in part from English and American common law, is a statement of the desire of Americans to prevent the marketplace from becoming dominated by the few, the rich, the powerful, urban centers, Wall Street, and giant corporations. If we can assume that there is a thread of consistency to the economic doctrines, we cannot be so charitable about the law. The best we can say is that, as antitrust law now stands, it is the result of a complex and tortuous process of social response to a set of monopoly problems about whose specific aspects there seldom was general agreement.

Attitudes toward Antitrust

Antitrust policy can be understood by examining the laws and court decisions that relate to the prohibition of combinations in restraint of trade,[12] the prohibition of price fixing and interlocking directorates, and the control of

---

[12]Robert H. Bork, "The Goals of Antitrust Policy," *American Economic Review*, 57:242–253, May 1967.

discriminatory practices that might lessen competition. Before we analyze this policy more carefully, it may be useful to examine five widespread attitudes toward antitrust policy.[13]

Some observers have said that antitrust legislation is both actually and potentially beneficial to the business and national economics of the United States. This group essentially argues that the very existence of the free private enterprise system depends upon such laws. As it stands, this viewpoint is rather more an expression of faith than an easily demonstrable fact.[14]

Another group contends that antitrust legislation could be beneficial if existing legislation were better enforced. This second set of attitudes does not lead to conclusions distinctly different from the first. Observers in this category, however, tend to point to actions that might have been taken in defense of free private enterprise if there had been adequate enforcement. They think they see either a design or a suspicious set of circumstances that over the years has denied enforcement agencies the necessary funds for the prosecution of their assigned duties. They argue that an inadequate number of personnel have been given the task of enforcement and suggest that government has tended to favor, both by indirection and by specific action, the development of monopolistic and oligopolistic enterprises.[15]

The third group of critics has asked for substantial changes in the laws themselves in order to increase the effectiveness of antitrust action. Obviously, this set of opinions turns not so much on enforcement as on enforceability of legislation. For many, the basic cure is an automatic law that depends for results not so much upon the punishment it inflicts as upon the degree of respect it inspires in the prospective violator when contemplating a potential violation. By far, the greater portion of the commentators belong in this group.[16]

A fourth, admittedly smaller, and less representative group, which includes many distinguished European scholars, holds that antitrust laws are most applicable to the United States alone. Actions taken in competitive markets in the United States have paradoxical monopolistic and even imperialistic impact overseas, especially in the underdeveloped primary producer countries. The retail price of bananas is surely determined in a competitive way, but the effects in Guatemala, Honduras, Costa Rica, and Ecuador are the same as if the price was set by an international banana cartel. On the other hand, the economic well-being of the Netherlands and Switzerland clearly depends upon the success of domestic and international monopolies and cartels such as those represented by Shell, Phillips, and Nestlé.

The last school of experts questions whether there is a relationship

---

[13]T. J. Kreps, *An Evaluation of Antitrust Policy: Its Relation to Economic Growth, Full Employment and Prices*, Study Paper 22, Washington, D.C., U.S. Congress Joint Economic Committee, January 30, 1960.

[14]R. W. Miller, *Can Capitalism Compete? A Campaign for Free Enterprise*, New York, Ronald, 1959.

[15]G. J. Stigler, "The Case Against Big Business," *Fortune*, May 1952.

[16]See *American Economic Review*, vol. 39, June 1949, for a symposium on the effectiveness of the antitrust laws.

between antitrust policy and economic growth, employment, and price and wage levels. Although John P. Miller has insisted that "Antitrust policies have played an important role in promoting high standards of living and growth in the American economy,"[17] Corwin Edwards has pointed out the difficulty of obtaining any measure of the results.[18] Donald Dewey finds that the achievements of antitrust policy have been slight indeed.[19]

It would be useful, suggest members of this last school, to study the performance of the economy before and after antitrust action or to compare an economy that had antitrust with one that did not. But such comparisons would be difficult. We know of the recent outstanding performance of Japan, where the degree of monopoly is high, and of Brazil, where it has been low. We also know that the United States growth rate in the last quarter of the nineteenth century was, in fact, greater than that in America after World War II. But was this because of or despite the trusts?

How Big Should a Firm Be?

The issue of economic size involves a concern with freedom and economic justice. One of the first major pieces of legislation designed to preserve competition and perhaps even to promote it was the Sherman Antitrust Act of 1890. Americans had come to feel that the general issue of monopoly versus competition was one of control over their economic destinies. Monopoly, it appeared to them, threatened to concentrate economic power in the hands of a very few. It seemed to be destroying the small farmer, the small businessman, or the local economy in favor of giant enterprises centralized in large cities, especially New York City. Monopolists allegedly used tactics and market strategies that were widely condemned.

The Sherman Act expresses its objectives in two short sections:

Section 1. Every contract, combination in the form of trust or otherwise or conspiracy, in restraint of trade or commerce among the several states, or with foreign nations, is hereby declared to be illegal.

Section 2. Every person who shall monopolize, or attempt to monopolize or combine or conspire with any other person or persons, to monopolize any part of the trade or commerce among the several states, or with foreign nations, shall be deemed guilty of a misdemeanor.

The first section, then, gives the legal definition of monopoly. Quite clearly, every act designed to combine or conspire to restrain trade or

---

[17]John P. Miller, Testimony before U.S. Congress, Joint Economic Committee, September 23, 1959.

[18]Corwin Edwards, "Public Policy and Business Size," *Journal of Business*, 24:280–292, October 1951.

[19]Donald Dewey, *Monopoly in Economics and Law*, Chicago, Rand McNally, 1959. See also M. Alexis and C. Z. Wilson, *Organizational Decision Making*, Englewood Cliffs, N.J., Prentice-Hall, 1966.

commerce is interdicted. The courts have interpreted monopoly and restraint of commerce to mean essentially the same thing. The second section turns its attention to the conduct of persons and/or firms in the marketplace. It says that monopolizing is a misdemeanor, no matter how it is attempted, by whom, or where, within the jurisdiction of federal courts.

The Sherman Act was not really concerned with market structure or ideal market behavior patterns but with prohibiting detrimental behavior that was thought to be taking place in the American marketplace.

Structural Changes

The nineteenth century saw significant structural change. By the 1840s New York City had become the industrial and financial center of a fast-growing nation. The focus of investments had shifted from domestic commerce and foreign trade to industry. Monetary, banking, transport, exchange, and inter-governmental systems had emerged that had combined the original thirteen colonies with the rich Midwest and South into a nation. An economic culture with laws, institutions, sanctions, and, most of all, increased viability had grown up. And at the very heart of this economic culture were the corporations and the free market, the elements of viable and aggressive capitalism.

Capitalism was dynamic in that it led to new techniques of production, marketing, financing, and even organization and control. It developed a means of transferring liquid capital from one type of investment to another so that, as one industry grew obsolescent, it was possible to salvage the liquid investment and channel funds toward other productive uses. This process involved a constant comparison of profitability among industries and possible investments already in existence and put a premium upon the search for new, more productive, less costly, and more labor-saving investment. Stimulated by a continental market in which volume rather than price provided tremendous profits, capitalism drove prices down, destroyed weak firms, took power from older, established classes in the society, and provided for continual dynamic change.

The most striking discovery of the last thirty years of the nineteenth century was that costs could be lowered by combining plants into trusts. The scale of enterprise became a key to profitability. Scale gave control over supply markets—farm produce, mining output, even labor—and it also gave control over demand markets. The same classes that in general had favored the North in the Civil War—farmers and urban workers—found themselves in direct and vigorous opposition to these large trusts. They objected to the tendency of trusts to lower farm prices and factory wages. To these groups, the falling prices of the goods they bought were not adequate compensation. Small businessmen, manufacturers, and merchants saw their businesses threatened by the mass production of stoves, shoes, kerosene lamps, clothing, and furniture that replaced small shop output. Trusts, too, were changing the character of marketing, and farmers, urban workers, and small businessmen were determined to fight them. For these classes, monopolizing—the economic behavior forbidden by the Sherman Act—was weakening and destroying the basis of their economic existence.

Effect of Antitrust Laws

Antitrust policies did not prevent many big companies from becoming bigger.[20] In every respect but one, firms and industries are bigger in the 1970s than they were when the Sherman Act was passed. But that one respect is vital. Relative to their markets, there are fewer firms occupying the positions of dominance held by the trusts at the turn of the century. Although firms are now much bigger than they were, markets themselves have far outdistanced them in growth. United States Steel, for example, is much bigger than it was but it is smaller relative to the steel market.

Changes in Economic Theory

As public concern shifted from monopoly to oligopoly, from monopolizing to concentration ratios, studies by economists reflected the changing character of industrial and market structure by a shift in emphasis. A theory of imperfect or monopolistic competition[21] was worked out to amend and even to replace classical and neoclassical analyses of perfect competition. It was now possible to analyze in detail a wide range of competitive behavior, including product changes, advertising, model changes, and price policy. The means of competition were shown to be far more varied than had been previously recognized.

Key Antitrust Cases

In 1911, the Supreme Court held that two very large trusts, Standard Oil and American Tobacco, had restrained trade unreasonably. About 91 percent of the refining capacity of the country was controlled by Standard Oil, and 90 percent of the market for tobacco products (except cigars) was in the hands of the so-called tobacco trust. These firms also had the reputation of using doubtful tactics to force smaller, rival firms out of the market or to sell to the trusts under conditions favorable to the larger companies. The Supreme Court held that monopolizing behavior had been interdicted by the Sherman Act. This

[20]M. A. Adelman, "Concentration in Manufacturing," in Edwin Mansfield (ed.), *Monopoly, Power and Economic Performance*, New York, Norton, 1964; Solomon Fabricant, "Is Monopoly Increasing?", *Journal of Economic History*, *13*:89–94, Winter 1953; and C. W. Nutter, *The Extent of Enterprise Monopoly in the United States, 1899–1939*, University of Chicago Press, 1951.

[21]E. H. Chamberlin, *The Theory of Monopolistic Competition*, Cambridge, Harvard University Press, 1933; and Joan Robinson, *The Economics of Imperfect Competition*, New York, Macmillan, 1934. For the opposite point of view, see Harold Demsetz, "The Welfare and Empirical Implications of Monopolistic Competition," *Economic Journal*, *74*:623–641, September 1964; and Donald J. Dewey, "Changing Standards of Economic Performance," *American Economic Review* *50*:1–12, May 1960.

same judgment was later extended to mean that, if a trust had gained monopoly power without monopolizing, it was beyond the enforcement powers of the act. In the United States Steel case of 1920, for example, the Supreme Court did not find the company in violation of the Sherman Act because it could not find that United States Steel mistreated its competitors or had conspired to fix prices. Furthermore, "the law," the court said, "does not make mere size an offense or the existence of unexerted power an offense."

By 1945, the federal courts had shifted their emphasis. In the Alcoa case, Justice Learned Hand held that the company had violated the second section of the Sherman Act by monopolizing the manufacture of newly refined aluminum. By defining Alcoa's market so that it included about 90 percent of the virgin aluminum produced in the United States, Justice Hand was able to establish the existence of a monopoly. But the mere presence of a monopoly had not hitherto been regarded as violating the Sherman Act. In Justice Hand's view, the fact that Alcoa had systematically expanded with the market was sufficient to show that it had intended to keep its monopoly. Monopolizing was thus shown to have existed to the court's satisfaction. But the decision suggested that possession of a monopoly power, that is, power to bar entry and to control prices, was in itself evidence of intent to achieve it.

The key to the new doctrine was the definition of market structure. The factual underpinning required by this new doctrine was illustrated in the du Pont case in 1947. A suit was brought against E. I. du Pont de Nemours & Co. for monopolizing the manufacture and sale of cellophane. Finally settled in 1956, the case revolved around one question: Which market is relevant for the definition of monopoly? Instead of taking the market for cellophane as relevant, the federal district court in Delaware considered the whole field of flexible packaging materials. Because there were many competing products in this area, it rather easily followed that du Pont, despite its position in the manufacture and sale of cellophane, faced substantial and continuing competition. Hence, it was not guilty of violating the Sherman Act. In addition, the district court was undoubtedly influenced by the fact that du Pont was aggressive in research and development, had consistently lowered its prices, and had expanded output.

Though the power and intent to monopolize are, in fact, in violation of the Sherman Act, decisions on Section 2 have necessarily been made pragmatically. The courts have had to balance intent to monopolize against definition of the market. This has left a degree of flexibility in federal antitrust policies that is disconcerting to business but tempting to management and the Department of Justice alike.

Per Se Violations

Some types of antitrust offenses, of course, do not require an interpretation by a federal court. By their very nature, "per se," they violate the law. In 1961, the assistant attorney general in charge of the antitrust section defined six practices as per se (intrinsically) unreasonable restraints under Section 1 of the Sherman Act. They were as follows:

1. Agreements not to compete when not ancillary to an otherwise legitimate contract
2. Collusive price fixing
3. Agreements to divide markets
4. Group boycotts
5. Certain tie-in agreements
6. Agreements among competitors to pool profits and losses

The Clayton Act

The Clayton Antitrust Act was enacted in 1914 specifically to prohibit various procedures and market control devices that were believed to contribute to lessening of competition and to promoting of tendencies toward monopoly. The greatest complexities arise under Section 2, which deals with price discrimination by buyers and/or sellers in market situations in which there is a substantial question whether competition has, in fact, been lessened. The issue is whether price discrimination tends to create a monopoly in any line of commerce "or to injure, destroy, or prevent competition with any person who either grants or knowingly receives the benefit of such discrimination, or with customers of either of them." Later Congress changed the Clayton Act through a 1936 amendment called the Robinson-Patman Act, which was designed to aid the small businessman, especially the small retailer.

Section 3 of the Clayton Act prohibits tying agreements and exclusive contracts that would substantially lessen competition. Because Congress intended to remove the barriers to entry into an industry and to prevent already large and well-established firms in an industry from engaging in practices that would make it difficult for smaller businesses to grow or to continue in a particular line, the courts have been liberal in interpreting Section 3. They have tended to hold that certain borderline practices are monopolizing simply because they were undertaken by firms holding a reasonably large share of the relevant market. In fact, the courts have sometimes held that even small firms were guilty of an antitrust violation when they used a specific market arrangement that other firms in the industry were using for the purpose of monopolizing.

Section 7 of the Clayton Act refers to mergers. The reasons for and varieties of mergers are without practical limit. In some cases, they help salvage an unsuccessful firm with a good reputation and asset structure. On the other hand, both firms may be in good financial condition but see an advantage to combining operations. For the purposes of Section 7, however, the essential question is whether the merger had or was intended to have an anticompetitive effect.

A landmark case is the du Pont–General Motors case. Between 1917 and 1919, du Pont acquired about 23 percent of General Motors stock as a by-product of a successful attempt to reorganize General Motors, a company with a previous record of rather poor management. Over succeeding years, du Pont became a major supplier of automotive paints, finishes, and fabrics to

General Motors. The propriety of being both a major supplier and a major stockholder was challenged in 1949 when the federal government instituted proceedings to force du Pont to divest itself of its holdings.

The heart of the case was whether du Pont's dominant position as a General Motors supplier had developed because its products were superior or because it held stock in the company but the case, from a legal point of view, turned on the definition of a relevant market. The Supreme Court chose to limit the definition of the market for finishes and fabrics to the automotive industry, and du Pont's position was thus found to be well within the defined limits of monopoly. The suit resulted in the eventual distribution of du Pont's holdings of General Motors stock to its own stockholders over a ten-year period. The court, surprisingly enough, did not require the government to establish "intent to monopolize." It was apparently enough to show a "reasonable probability" that the stock holdings would or could result in the market restraints condemned by Section 7.

In more general terms, the courts and the Federal Trade Commission have tended to reject mergers that give the combined firms control of more than 15 percent of their relevant markets. In addition, they have looked at evidence that would indicate whether a merger or other forces operating in the relevant market were tending toward a high degree of concentration. In recent bank merger cases, for example, even though the merged firms might not reach the 15 percent guideline, the courts have not permitted merging because it would reduce the competitiveness of the banking market in a particular city. Section 7 has also served to block the formation of vertical mergers, for example, the case of a manufacturer who sought to acquire a chain of retail outlets. Note that the enforcement of Section 7 had an essentially different effect from that of Section 2, which apparently tries both to protect a market from loss of competition and to shield small businesses from the effects of competition. Whether such goals are antithetical should at least be questioned.

Problems in Antitrust Enforcement

Antitrust laws are often self-enforcing and, in this respect, they have been regarded as similar to traffic laws. Although these laws have public support, few people regard antitrust violations, or speeding, as serious offenses unless carried to extremes. These laws thus keep speeding and antitrust violations down to a level society can tolerate. But it is also true that the amount of actual speeding or antitrust violation depends to a considerable extent upon the kind of enforcement effort the community attempts. Nevertheless, the prospect of becoming embroiled with the Department of Justice and/or the Federal Trade Commission is an important consideration in business planning. For this reason, large firms have a legal staff whose responsibilities include antitrust considerations. Smaller companies often retain legal firms for the same purpose.

The agency charged with enforcement of the Sherman Act is the antitrust division of the Department of Justice. Enforcement of the Clayton Act has been assigned to the Federal Trade Commission, but the Justice Department can and does enter the enforcement picture if there is any chance that the Sherman Act is also involved in a Clayton Act proceeding. Whereas the FTC is an independent executive agency, the antitrust division is an arm of a cabinet-level office. Hence, overall administration of antitrust matters is in the purview of the Attorney General. Yet, although the Attorney General is a member of the President's Cabinet, it is not normally true that antitrust enforcement reflects presidential attitudes or administration policies.

The pace of antitrust enforcement has varied considerably from period to period and has, in general, been correlated with appropriations made available by Congress. Another measure of antitrust activity is caseload. Yet, even with a large budget, the antitrust division is hardly in a position to keep watch over the whole possible range of antitrust violations. In addition, individual cases tend to be extremely difficult and costly to prosecute. The antitrust division has estimated that the average case taken to litigation requires about five and one-half years and hundreds of thousands of pages of testimony and exhibits.

Price Discrimination

Legal definitions of price discrimination differ significantly from the economic concept. The Robinson-Patman Act, for example, assumes that if the price of a seller is not equal to his average cost of production plus a fair markup, there is price discrimination. But a rational producer will seek to equate the marginal cost of what he sells with the marginal revenue by setting a price which permits him to sell, in every market in which he participates, enough of his output for this to be true. The seller's average cost of supplying customers' demand is not relevant. It is unfair competition, as defined by law and by the courts, which is the essence of legal price discrimination. Since, by and large, the question of unfair competition arises in the retail-wholesale sector, it is there that most cases have been adjudicated.

Morris Adelman argues that the Robinson-Patman Act had but one purpose, namely, to enforce discrimination against a lower-cost buyer or a lower-cost method of distribution.[22] Its main provision forbids a seller "to discriminate in price between different purchasers of commodities of like grade and quality" under certain specified conditions. The seller may not discriminate, the act further provides, when the result "may be substantially to lessen competition or tend to create a monopoly in any line of commerce." This last provision changed the preexisting Clayton Act very little. But the amendment adds that discrimination is interdicted when the effect "is to injure, destroy, or prevent competition with any person who either grants or knowingly receives the benefits of such discrimination." In economic terms, it would appear that to the extent that it requires price uniformity in the face of cost differences, the amendment actually requires discrimination.

Caves points out that to designate as illegal a discrimination that harms

---

[22]M. A. Adelman, "The Consistency of the Robinson-Patman Act," *Stanford Law Review*, December 1953.

competitors as well as competition involves the Robinson-Patman Act in a contradiction.[23] If there are more competitors, there is not only more competition but also more possible harm to the competitors themselves. The competitors would be happy, indeed, to have less competition. By the same token, to preserve competition may call for action to increase entry, cut costs, introduce innovations (e.g., the chain store), and provide for much more flexibility in prices. The latter, of course, was what the shooting was all about; for flexible prices, illustrated by bargains, one-cent sales, or closeouts obviously upset a market area.

It is not surprising that one judge said of the law, "I doubt if any judge would assert that he knows exactly what does or what does not amount to violation of the Robinson-Patman Act in any and all instances."[24] The breadth and complexity of the act created a tremendous enforcement problem both for the Federal Trade Commission and for the courts. In practice, of course, not all sections of the act have been invoked with equal vigor.

The application of that portion of the law dealing with quantity discounts is uncertain largely because court decisions have been in conflict. In the Bruce's Juices case, the Supreme Court said: "It would be a far-reaching decision to outlaw all quantity discounts. Courts should not rush in where Congress feared to tread." But the Morton Salt case raised new doubts. Morton had argued that granting quantity discounts on sales of table salt to wholesalers, jobbers, and large retailers had no effect on competition because less than 1 percent of its sales were in less-than-carload lots. Morton also argued that table salt was a very small part of retail and wholesale grocery trade. The court found the commission's evidence that the discount structure was not based on actual cost differences convincing. It held that the Robinson-Patman Act "does not require that the discriminations must in fact have harmed competition, but only that there is a reasonable possibility that they 'may' have such an effect."

The FTC does not and probably cannot know the costs of the sellers it polices. If there is a complaint about a seller's price, the FTC seeks to find out whether harm has been caused by a practice forbidden by the Clayton Act. Usually, given the nature of the complaint and the complainant, this information is not hard to establish. In their defense, sellers can argue that the buyers allegedly injured were not actually in the same product market. Or they may say that the discount that is the cause of the complaint was offered to meet the low price of a competitor. Of course, the best defense would be to insist that the discount structure did reflect cost savings to large buyers. Yet few sellers have presented this argument largely because, at least until recently, the FTC has judged that cost savings can occur in sales and delivery but not in manufacturing.

The effect of Robinson-Patman upon the retail-wholesale area is highly problematical. It would be difficult, indeed, to show that it has affected the nature of competition, the pace of changes in price levels, or even the practices

---

[23]Richard Caves, *American Industry: Structure, Conduct and Performance*, Englewood Cliffs, N.J., Prentice-Hall, 1964.
[24]See *FTC* v. *Ruberoid Co.*, 343 U.S. 470, 1952.

of businessmen. Yet it probably has caused wholesalers and retailers to look carefully into the relation between their costs and their discount structures. To establish a definite cause-and-effect relation between Robinson-Patman and the way in which the retail-wholesale sector has developed would require demonstrating that the act was responsible for the vast changes going on decade by decade and for the ways in which market changes have been channeled into certain paths or prevented from continuing along other paths. A careful look at local markets suggests that income changes, urban sprawl, use of the automobile and other means of transport, and, in fact, all the factors that have changed the economic landscape have had a far more important impact on development of the retail-wholesale sector in recent years than the Robinson-Patman Act.

We are left, then, with the rather odd conclusion that significant effort has been devoted to the prevention of discrimination and monopoly in the one sector of the national economy least likely to be affected.

Conglomerate Mergers

A "conglomerate" is a corporation combining productive activities in a variety of unrelated and independent markets. It may be large in absolute size, but it can be small in each market in which it participates. Whether the conglomerate device was intended to do so is not clear, but it is a way by which a corporation may acquire the substance of social power without the accompanying market power. Conglomerate movement even more than vertical mergers would likely have little or no effect on concentration indexes in individual markets.

Conglomerate mergers have been a tempting target for the antitrust division.[25] But, except for the Hartford Fire Insurance case, little real success has been attained. Part of the reason resides in the apparent lack of corporate desire to increase market control. Some have observed that perhaps there are fewer scale economies left to take advantage of, and consequently, the case against conglomerate mergers has to be based on broader economic and social issues than market power. Indeed, the "portfolio corporation"—as one observer has entitled the conglomerate—seems to have only size maximization as a goal. Moreover, available evidence[26] suggests that conglomerates are not as profitable nor do they exhibit as much stability in growth as do traditional horizontal or vertical mergers.

Charles Berry[27] found that for the period 1960–1965 increasing diversification was related to the growth of large firms. But he did not find that diversification was a cause of growth. He found that conglomerate mergers had led to reduction in the relative size of the leading firm in those industries

---

[25]W. G. Shepherd, "Conglomerate Mergers in Perspective," *Antitrust Law and Economics Review*, Fall 1968. See also J. F. Weston and S. K. Mansinghka, "Tests of the Efficiency Performance of Conglomerate Firms," in J. F. Weston and S. I. Ornstein (eds.), op. cit. *The Impact of Large Scale Firms on the U.S. Economy*, Lexington, Mass., Heath, 1973.

[26]S. R. Reid, "The Conglomerate Merger: A Special Case," *Antitrust Law and Economics Review*, 2(1):15–32, Fall 1968.

[27]C. H. Berry, *Corporate Growth and Diversification*, Princeton University Press, 1975.

affected. Either one competitor was replaced by another as the conglomerate expanded by acquisition into independent markets or the conglomerate was big enough to make an effective entry and thus induce a substantial reduction in concentration.

Potential Competition

The most telling argument against merger and acquisition, whether by traditional or conglomerate mergers, is that of potential competition. To permit the merger or acquisition of one firm in a given industry by another in a different industry where there is a likelihood that such a merger or entry prevents a potential competitor from entry constitutes a primary danger to public antitrust policy.The issue is whether a reduction in concentration could have been accomplished by a firm already in the industry or a de novo entry by a nonconglomerate firm.

Limits of Antitrust

If the purpose of antitrust enforcement is to restructure the economy, then how far should restructuring go? Monopoly power can be reduced by breaking up or divestiture of firms with too large a share of given markets. It can also be reduced by preventing growth of existing large firms, by inducing growth of other potentially competitive firms, by encouraging new entry, and by restricting use of market power. To the extent that some form of restructuring does not take place of itself over time, then what remains is an option among policies to induce it.

Trust busting or divestiture is the most complex and time consuming of the restructuring policies and legal remedies. It is not clear that there is either a bloodless or a painless way of trust busting. If a firm has monopoly power which it used to its advantage, this power must have been capitalized in the value of the securities of the corporation. The noninsider holders of these securities would suffer loss from trust busting, which would reduce the value of the securities. The loss might be substantial and without adequate recompense. Employees whose wages were above average because of the strength of their unions vis-à-vis a corporation with strong market power would surely lose if their wages fell to competitive levels. Since the evidence is doubtful that monopoly has led to too high prices, little benefit can be foreseen for the consumer which would provide a broad social offset to the losses sustained by corporate stockholders and employees. Courts, by and large, have been very careful to structure divestitures so as to minimize losses to all parties with the result that what little social benefit might have been presumed to be available from such action was probably lost.

All other restructuring options probably need no new laws or administrative procedures. But there is a haunting doubt whether a marketplace as dramatically changeful as it is might not have achieved an even more beneficial structure had there been less governmental interference. Government's role in transport, communication, energy, land use, banking, and other areas of regulation may have been so anticompetitive as to offset all antitrust activities.

Chapter Summary

You have been led through a detailed analysis of how to define and classify varieties of market organization. You have seen how to measure concentration, relevant markets, potential competition, and the likely impact of market power. You have also seen that it is not easy to establish the alleged negative effects of market size, market power, or excess profits. At least from the point of view of economics and economic research, there is not a lot of evidence on which to build a strong case against monopoly. Indeed, there is not even sufficient and convincing evidence that there is very much monopoly or monopoly power in the American economy. Certainly, the thesis that the economy has been growing more and more monopolized is a doubtful proposition. None of this, of course, says that monopoly is a good thing. It just says that if it is a bad thing, what we have of it in the United States hasn't been bothersome.

Is this relatively toothless monopoly situation the result of effective antitrust laws and their enforcement? It would be comforting to be able to answer "yes." The only problem is that the same kinds of statistical tests that cast doubt on the arguments about how monopoly power is hurting the national economy provide little substantive evidence of the impact of antitrust enforcement. It could be inferred that, without the panoply of antitrust law, the nation would now be controlled by one small set of interlocking directorates. But that inference would have to be based on romanticism, not on economic fact. The most that we can say is that we don't know. And, because we don't know, there are doubters who suggest that there might have been more rather than less competition had there been less law and less interference by federal and state regulatory authorities in the operations of the marketplace.

Selected Readings

Ansoff, Igor H., et al.: *Acquisition Behavior of U.S. Manufacturing Firms, 1946–1965*, Nashville, Vanderbilt University Press, 1971.
Bain, J. S.: *International Differences in Industrial Structure*, New Haven, Yale University Press, 1966.
Berry, Charles H.: *Corporate Growth and Diversification*, Princeton University Press, 1975.
Demsetz, Harold: *The Market Concentration Doctrine: An Examination of Evidence and a Discussion of Policy*, AEI-Hoover Policy Study 7, Washington, D.C., American Enterprise Institute for Public Policy Research, August 1973.
Dewey, Donald: *Monopoly in Economics and Law*, Chicago, Rand McNally, 1959.
Eichner, Alfred S.: *The Megacorp and Oligopoly*, New York, Cambridge University Press, 1976.

Koch, James V.: *Industrial Organization and Prices*, Englewood Cliffs, N.J., Prentice-Hall, 1974.

McGee, J. S.: *In Defense of Industrial Concentration*, New York, Praeger, 1971.

Moroney, J. R.: *The Structure of Production in American Manufacturing*, Chapel Hill, N.C., University of North Carolina Press, 1972.

Philips, Louis: *Effects of Industrial Concentration: A Cross-Section Analysis for the Common Market*, Amsterdam, North-Holland, 1971.

Phillips, Almarin: *Promoting Competition in Regulated Markets*, Washington, D.C., The Brookings Institute, 1975.

Posner, R. A.: *Economic Analysis of Law*, Boston, Little, Brown, 1973.

Weston, J. Fred, and S.I. Ornstein: *The Impact of Large Firms on the U.S. Economy*, Lexington, Mass., Heath, 1973.

Questions, Problems, and Projects

1. Table 1 shows data taken from the June 30, 1975, Federal Deposit Insurance Corporation (FDIC) *Summary of Accounts and Deposits*. Included are concentration ratios for commercial banks in eleven New England and Northwest cities having both commercial and mutual savings banks. In the light of the Phillipsburg doctrine that savings banks and commercial banks operate in separate relevant markets, how would you assess the relative degree of concentration in each city? Suppose that as the powers of the two financial institutions become essentially alike, the Phillipsburg doctrine no longer held; what would this do to your analysis of degree of concentration? What is the relative size of these banking markets, with or without combining the two types of banking institutions? In your opinion, what is the best way to assess the relative competitiveness of banking markets?

Table 1   Size and concentration, banks in 11 SMSAs* having both commercial and mutual savings banks

SMSA	% of CB deposits in banks ranked by size					Total CB deposits, millions of $	Total MSB deposits, millions of $	No. of CBs (offices)	No. of MSBs (offices)
	A	B	C	D	E				
Seattle	41.0	19.4	11.0	8.1	4.2	4499.0	415.4	35 (314)	5 (48)
Hartford	47.5	36.1	3.6	1.6	1.5	2515.8	2092.1	23 (133)	22 (84)
Providence	42.5	23.7	20.9	3.2	3.1	3150.0	372.7	20 (217)	10 (68)
Portland	33.7	32.4	5.5	5.4	4.9	2988.5	49.2	23 (188)	2 (5)
Bridgeport	31.2	30.9	12.8	7.5	4.8	764.1	1469.9	17 (84)	6 (35)
New Haven	30.5	23.4	17.0	11.6	4.8	761.2	1206.6	14 (79)	8 (36)
Springfield	31.3	30.5	15.4	4.3	3.6	793.4	585.1	14 (102)	18 (65)
Worcester	47.4	25.0	17.4	5.4	3.6	634.7	379.0	8 (59)	13 (42)
Spokane	36.3	28.9	17.5	5.5	3.0	796.0	89.4	10 (62)	2 (10)
Tacoma	34.7	31.0	10.7	9.7	3.9	814.4	58.0	11 (80)	4 (15)
Anchorage	36.9	35.4	11.4	7.9	4.4	666.1	17.3	6 (30)	1 (2)

*Standard Metropolitan Statistical Areas.

2. The legal guideline for regulation of "natural monopolies," based on *Federal Power Commission* v. *Hope Natural Gas Co.*, 1944, requires that regulatory policies provide a return to the equity holder "commensurate with returns on investments with corresponding risks." However, economic theory has not provided a definitive concept of fair return under conditions of risk and this lack of clarity has led to costly hearings and litigation. Can you be of any help to the attorneys in this area?

3. In his study of the effect of deregulation of air fares and entry in the domestic airlines industry, George C. Eads concludes that the industry "suffers from excessive attention to service rivalry—termed by some 'competition.'" He suggests that the experience of California where there was much less regulation indicates that "deregulation would lead only to lower fares, more efficient operations, and a quality of air service more in line with consumer tastes and would not cause safety standards to deteriorate." If Eads is correct, what would you do about the likely failure of some airline companies if deregulation were to take place? Build an argument defending regulation. And then one opposing it. Be careful to use your economic tools wisely and avoid circular arguments.

4. R. A. Posner says that there are two theories of government intervention or regulation in the marketplace. One is the "public interest" theory, which holds that government has to act to correct inefficient or inequitable market practices. The other is the "capture" theory, which holds that regulation takes place because interest groups are struggling among themselves to maximize their own or their members' incomes. From the point of view of managerial economics, which is the more defensible? Expound on this matter.

5. In examining a long list of reasons why big corporations are not loved, one author concludes that largely it is because educated people just do not understand how the market system operates or the role of profits. He adds that many people like to believe in the potential danger from a sinister giant corporation. But if corporations are generally efficient and if they are no more guilty and probably less guilty than small firms of such crimes as pollution, advertising waste and exploitation of consumers, what other reasons than these can you find for the bad press, resulting in political and legal action against big business? What is the economics of the matter?

6. In 1960, T. J. Kreps told the Joint Economic Committee of Congress that "giant enterprise . . . has grown irrevocably beyond the point of no return [and is now] vital to modern economic, political and military survival." He concluded that "the problems of monopoly power . . . will require other remedies than those available under the antitrust laws." Assuming that Kreps is as right now as then, where do you suggest we go from here?

7. Earl Kintner, once Chairman of the Federal Trade Commission, noted that economics is legally neutral. Moreover, he observed, antitrust laws deal with acts and their effects, not merely the results. For example, antitrust laws proscribe the act of conspiring to fix prices. It makes no difference whether the fixed price is high or low, reasonable or unreasonable, or benefits or hurts consumers. Is there in these remarks the seed of the problem for economists in analyzing antitrust performance?

8. Concepts derived from theories of monopoly, monopolistic competition, measurements of concentration, definitions of relevant markets, assessments of economic power, all are involved in many descriptions of the operation of retail food marketing enterprise. Also involved are the prescriptions and proscriptions of the Robinson-Patman Act, the Federal Trade Commission Act, the Celler-Kefauver Act, and other legal provisions. Compare the facts of market operation in a typical metropolitan market with theory. What meaning has concentration or competition in such a market? How can you determine the effect of antitrust enforcement?

Case 9.1 Chartering, Branching, and the Concentration Problem

These remarks by Donald I. Baker, Director of Policy Planning, Antitrust Division, United States Department of Justice, Ross M. Robertson, Professor of Business Economics, Indiana University, and Leonard Lapidus, Vice President, Federal Reserve Bank of New York, reflect the tone of a conference held in Nantucket, Massachusetts, in June 1972 to consider policies for a more competitive financial system.

THE CONCENTRATION QUESTION AND MERGER POLICY GENERALLY

Donald I. Baker

The Hunt Commission did not seem to put great weight on "concentration" in its deliberations. This is perhaps just as well, since the concept of "concentration" is often subject to a great deal of loose usage—especially among us noneconomists— in discussing bank structure questions. The concept is used at at least three levels—local market concentration, statewide concentration, and national concentration. At the price of parading my ignorance, let me give you my views on each of these concepts.

"Local concentration" in banking seems to me to be the most important. It is the economist's classic sort of market concentration: It is a means of measuring market position of competitors in the local service market in which they all operate. In banking, local concentration is generally quite high.

"Statewide concentration" will in most instances represent an aggregation of local competitive retail market positions. The results of such statewide aggregation vary greatly: In a few states, such as Oregon and Rhode Island, we can see that two banks dominate the state entirely, while in some other states a reasonable degree of diversity and choice exists even among the larger banking organizations.[1] In addition, statewide concentration may be an appropriate

[1]See "Recent Changes in the Structure of Commercial Banking," *Fed. Res. Bull.*, 56:195–210, 1970.

market measure of certain wholesale type services offered on a statewide basis (such as correspondent banking or perhaps factoring).

"National concentration" is almost pure aggregation of local market positions. Of course, on a national scale, banking is a quite "unconcentrated" industry, with over 13,000 banks. Taking total bank deposits as a universe, one finds that the largest institutions in the country—although very large indeed—do not dominate the country. This, by my calculations based on December 1971 figures on domestic deposits. In addition, there are a few national wholesale markets for large commercial borrowers and customers in which national concentration figures would be appropriate.[2]

. . . Merger policy in general, and antitrust merger policy in particular, have been primarily concerned with competition and concentration at the local level. Banking is always a local business, and for larger banks it may often be a regional or national business. The antitrust laws and enforcement have stressed local markets because convenience is a vital factor to retain customers and local business; and effective choices are the most limited at the local level. Economic performance in local markets has often been quite poor, with the "quiet life" the order of the day. Thus, the district judge in the Phillipsburg case summarized the situation in a passage noted by the Supreme Court:

> . . . Most of the small banks in the area have not been interested in building up banking services except to the extent that aggressive competitors led the way. An ultraconservative policy of banking seems to have been prevailing with reluctant change occurring only when profits and future growth were threatened by virulent competitors. There is an attitude of complacency on the part of many banks. They are content to continue outmoded banking practices [rather than] . . . extend services over a greater area to a larger segment of the population.[3]

Ever since the Philadelphia National Bank decision in 1963[4], antitrust enforcement in banking has stressed concentration in local markets. Section 7 of the Clayton Act represents a strong congressional mandate that increases in market concentration which are created by merger are generally not to be tolerated. The Department of Justice and the Supreme Court have vigorously applied this policy of preventing local concentration. This policy applies in smaller markets which are usually more concentrated than large metropolitan ones. The Supreme Court was very clear on the point in its 1970 *Phillipsburg* decision: "Mergers of directly competing small commercial banks in small communities are subject to scrutiny under these (antitrust) standards. Indeed, competitive commercial banks, with their cluster of products and services, play a particularly significant role in a small community unable to support a large variety of financial institutions."[5] The alternative, said the Court, "would be

[2] See *United States* v. *Manufacturers Hanover Trust Company*, 240 F. Supp. 867, 901–922 (S.D.N.Y. 1965).
[3] 306 F. Supp. 645, 661 (D.N.J. 1969).
[4] 374 U.S. 321 (1963).
[5] *United States* v. *Phillipsburg National Bank*, 399 U.S. at 358 (1970).

likely to deny customers of small banks—and thus residents of many small towns—the antitrust protection to which they are no less entitled than customers of large city banks. Indeed, the need for that protection may be greater in a small town . . . " where the alternative institutions are more limited.[6]

Concentration—or more accurately dominance—at the statewide level is something that has been a matter of growing concern to the Department of Justice. Here, however, we are not talking about concentration in a real market sense so much as the elimination of potential competition into local banking markets within a state. The state boundaries are of course significant to competitive analysis in banking, because they delineate the widest area from which potential competitors can be drawn. I am therefore concerned when I see a trend in a state in which the leading banking organizations move on to a position of statewide dominance by acquiring the leaders in local banking markets throughout the state. In most of the states where the Department has brought suit, there were only a handful of banks or holding companies which could enter a market de novo or by a small toehold acquisition, and from the outset be a competitive source to be reckoned with in that market. Any time one of these few significant potential entrants enters a concentrated local market through acquisition with the local market leader, then that loss of potential competition is likely to occur. Therefore, the government argues that a Section 7 violation can be found in a bank merger case if the government proves that (1) the acquiring defendant is one of but a fairly small number of capable potential entrants legally eligible to enter a market; (2) the acquired bank is a leader in a concentrated local market; and (3) the acquiring defendant has an alternative means of entry (e.g., either the market is growing fast enough to support additional banking facilities de novo now or in the future or a small competitor is present in the market as an entry vehicle).

National market figures have not really played any significant role in antitrust enforcement. Defendants in antitrust cases—including the Philadelphia and Houston cases—have frequently asserted that they needed to engage in horizontal local mergers in order to effectively compete on a national or international basis. The courts and the Department have generally rejected this plea on two grounds. The national wholesale market is generally better served and has more competitors than local retail markets, and therefore this does not provide a basis for upholding anticompetitive local mergers. Moreover, in the Philadelphia case, the Supreme Court stressed that alleged procompetitive effects in one market were not a justification for allowing anticompetitive effects in another.[7] Quite apart from the question of law, this seems sound as a matter of policy so long as an adequate level of competition exists in the first market, for surely it is the need of the banking public for service and not the desire of particular banks to participate in the market which should be the controlling issue of policy.

---

[6]399 U.S. at 361–2 (1970).

[7]*United States* v. *Philadelphia National Bank*, 374 U.S. 321, 371 (1963).

REGULATION BY ANTITRUST?

Ross M. Robertson

I must say a word or two in conclusion about the very last part of Don Baker's paper. This is where the punch comes. You can skip over all that smooth talk you get in the first twenty pages, and when you come up right to the end it is clear that Mr. Baker feels that the saving grace in this whole question of regulation is the Antitrust Division of the Justice Department. Now, I am going to say something that is going to start a row, but I am comforted by the reflection that the function of speakers at a conference is to start the talk going. The Justice Department really has no business interfering in the regulation of banking in this country. Here I wish that I were an attorney and could comprehend a little better the obscure wording of decisions in such cases as Philadelphia National Bank and Houston. I could then understand a little better how it is that, in its efforts to prevent mergers, the Justice Department can proceed under Section 7 of the Clayton Act and just forget all about the intent of Congress as expressed in the Bank Merger acts of 1960 and 1966. I insist that if Congress had wanted to bring banks under Section 7 of the Clayton Act, it would have done so in the Celler-Kefauver amendments to the Clayton Act, which carefully omitted banks from their application. It is my belief that Congress intended, particularly in the Bank Merger Act of 1966, to allow the Justice Department to intrude only in flagrant cases of merger approvals by federal banking agencies. Of course, Don can respond that all of the Comptroller's approvals have been flagrant—but it seems to me that twenty-odd objections is a little much. So I close in concurrence with at least one point that Don made and that is that we should have deregulation, a lot of deregulation, and the first step should be to get the Antitrust Division of the Justice Department out of it.

CONCENTRATION RATIOS

Leonard Lapidus

Just a final short word on concentration ratios. The kinds of concentration ratios one can easily calculate from published figures should be used very carefully. They can't be given fixed meanings. The larger the geographical area covered, the less certain they have any meaning. Concentration ratios for carefully defined markets are useful. Local areas come closest to being true banking markets and concentration ratios may be useful. However, state and national figures are treacherous. Don indicates that statewide figures have three uses. They can suggest whether a reasonable degree of choice exists within a state's borders; they are an appropriate market measure of certain wholesale type services offered on a statewide basis; and finally the share of state market may be a measure of the strength of a potential competitor. None of these propositions holds up very well. First, where customers search for, or find, banking alternatives is not usually related to state lines. Also, markets are not apt to follow state lines even for services offered on a statewide basis; out-of-state banks may offer services over state lines. Finally, share-of-market figures are so affected by the structure laws in a state that their use as indexes of potential competitive strength is not recommended.

The treachery of state figures is evidenced by the case of New Jersey prior to the 1969 change in that state's structure laws. The state ranked among the half-dozen least concentrated states in the nation, largely because branching and merging were limited to county lines. County concentration ratios were very high. The low statewide ratios for the leading banks did not mean that New Jerseyans had wide choices. Also, because of the happenstance of the county of location, a bank's share of state deposits might be a poor indication of how aggressive a competitor it might have been if merging and branching opportunities had been available.

DISCUSSION QUESTIONS 9.1

1. How does local concentration differ from national concentration? Why does it make a difference to limit the geographic area to which a concentration measure is applied?
2. What is a procompetitive effect compared with potential competition?
3. Does antitrust enforcement really constitute industry regulation rather than legal action?
4. In an industry with an oligopolistic structure, what does competition mean?

Case 9.2   Economic Concentration—Some Further Observations[1]

CONCENTRATION RATIOS

Between 1947 and 1967, the share of value added by manufacturing accounted for by the nation's 200 largest manufacturing corporations rose from less than one-third to more than two-fifths. As impressive as these aggregate data may be in pointing toward the growth of large enterprise in our economy, they do not shed much light on the extent of economic concentration within particular industries or product classes; here, one can make use of concentration ratios. These ratios typically refer to the share of output accounted for by the four largest firms in an industry and are customarily expressed in terms of the value of shipments. The economic significance of these measures lies in the fact that established theory clearly suggests that where a relatively few firms may possess a sufficiently large share of the market, none can or will remain indifferent to the actions of the others and their response to changes in market demand conditions will be quite different than if there were more numerous competitors. This behavior was amply documented in the Temporary National Economic Committee (TNEC) hearings.

TRENDS IN CONCENTRATION

Data on concentration trends are shown in Table 1 for various industry groups during the post-World War II period through 1967, the last year for which published Census of Manufactures' data are available. The table is based on

[1]By Sheldon W. Stahl and C. Edward Harshbarger in *Monthly Review*, Federal Reserve Bank of Kansas City, January 1974.

Table 1   Concentration in industry groups for selected years (percent)

	1947	1954	1958	1963	1967
Food and kindred products					
Increasing					
Prepared feeds for animals and fowls	19	21	22	22	23
Bread, cake, and related products	16	20	22	23	26
Confectionary products	17	19	18	15	25
Malt liquors	21	27	28	34	40
Bottled and canned soft drinks	10	10	11	12	13
Flavorings, extracts, and syrups	50	53	55	62	67
Soybean oil mills	44	41	40	50	55
Decreasing					
Meat-packing plants	41	39	34	31	26
Ice cream and frozen desserts	40	36	38	37	33
Distilled liquor	75	64	60	58	54
Textiles; apparel					
Increasing					
Weaving mills, cotton	n.a.	18	25	30	30
Weaving mills, synthetic	31	30	34	39	46
Knit outerwear mills	8	6	7	11	15
Men's and boys' suits and coats	9	11	11	14	17
Men's dress shirts and nightwear	19	17	16	22	23
Men's and boys' separate trousers	12	12	9	16	20
Women's and misses' suits and coats	n.a.	3	3	8	12
Women's and children's underwear	6	8	8	11	15
Decreasing					
Knit fabric mills	27	17	18	18	15
Lumber, stone, clay, and glass					
Increasing					
Logging camps and logging contractors	n.a.	8	13	11	14
Decreasing					
Glass containers	63	63	58	55	60
Primary metals					
Increasing					
Gray-iron foundries	16	26	24	28	27
Iron and steel forgings	24	27	31	30	30
Decreasing					
Blast furnaces and steel mills	50	55	53	48	48

analysis of a number of industries with a value of shipments of more than $1 billion and with concentration ratios that changed three or more percentage points during the period 1947–1967. The Food and Kindred Products group clearly was an area of increasing concentration; seven of the ten large industries showed increases. The decline of the small independent brewer is clearly evident in the sharp increase in concentration in the malt liquor industry. Also, given the growing importance of soybean products as a source of protein, the sharp reversal of a declining trend in concentration since 1958 in soybean oil mills is of particular interest. At the same time, the advent of the

Table 1 (continued)

	1947	1954	1958	1963	1967
Transportation equipment					
Increasing					
Motor vehicles and parts*	56	75	75	79	78
Decreasing					
Aircraft engines and parts	72	62	56	57	64
Railroad and street cars	56	64	58	53	53
Instruments; miscellaneous products					
Increasing					
Photographic equipment and supplies	61	n.a.	65	63	69
Games and toys	20	18	13	15	25
Chemicals and allied products					
Decreasing					
Industrial organic chemicals	n.a.	59	55	51	45
Plastics materials and resins	44	47	40	35	27
Pharmaceutical preparations	28	25	27	22	24
Increasing					
Toilet preparations	24	25	29	38	38
Tobacco; Petroleum products					
Decreasing					
Cigarettes	90	82	79	80	81
Tobacco stemming and redrying	88	79	73	70	63
Petroleum refining	37	33	32	34	33
Printing and publishing					
Decreasing					
Newspapers	21	18	17	15	16
Periodicals	34	29	31	29	24
Fabricated metals; nonelectrical machinery					
Decreasing					
Metal cans	78	80	80	74	73
Sheet metalwork	21	19	15	11	10
Screw machine products	17	11	9	5	6
Miscellaneous fabricated wire products	20	18	13	13	11
Valves and fittings	24	17	17	13	14
Ball and roller bearings	62	60	57	57	54

*The 1967 concentration ratio for motor vehicles and parts, as published by the Census Bureau, is 76%. However, it excludes automotive stamping plants operated by automobile producing companies, which had formerly been included in the motor vehicle and parts industry. For the year 1963 the bureau has compiled ratios both including and excluding these stamping plants; the figures were 79% and 77%, respectively. Therefore, to retain comparability, the published ratio for 1967 has been increased 2 percentage points to 78%.

n.a. Not available.

Source: Bureau of the Census, Department of Commerce, *Concentration Ratios in Manufacturing, 1967*, Special Reports, 1970, Pt. 1, Table 5.

large commercial feedlot and the changing technology of the meat-packing industry involving a proliferation of smaller, more specialized plants are evidenced by the decreasing concentration ratios for that industry throughout the postwar period. The Textile and Apparel groups were marked by generally increasing concentrations, with eight of nine industries showing gains compared with a decline for only a single industry.

In the Primary Metals group, two industries showed an increase in concentration for the period, although the changes have been rather moderate since 1958. For the largest industry in this group, blast furnaces and steel mills, the ratio fell after a sharp rise in concentration between 1947 and 1954. Nonetheless, as of 1967, the four largest firms in that industry still accounted for nearly half the output, a degree of concentration which remained unchanged between the 1963 and 1976 census dates. The Transportation Equipment group is dominated by the motor vehicles and parts industry which accounts for more than one-half the group's output. Within this industry, the disappearance of a number of automobile manufacturers may be clearly seen in the very sharp rise in concentration between 1947 and 1954. As of 1967, the four largest firms continued to account for nearly four-fifths of total output. Even in those two industries in the group where there was a decline in concentration relative to 1947, the trend was somewhat irregular and the concentration ratios as of 1967 still reflect substantial market power by the four largest firms.

The growing market dominance of the large firm is apparent in the photographic equipment and supplies industry. On the other hand, the Chemicals and Allied Products group was one in which decreases outnumbered increases in concentration among three of its four large industries. The general tendency for declining concentration is also apparent in the six large industries in the Fabricated Metals and Nonelectrical Machinery groups, as well as in the Printing and Publishing group, a development which reveals nothing about the extent of regional concentration. The Tobacco and Petroleum Products groups are both dominated by single large industries, cigarettes and petroleum refining. In both these industries, the decline in concentration occurred between 1947 and 1954. Since that time, no change in the dominant industries has been evident.

The data in Table 1 reflect concentration trends among a relatively limited number of large industries. Table 2 provides data which illustrate the trend of concentration among smaller and medium-sized as well as large industries and includes a much larger sample than Table 1. There are more than 400 industries for which 1963 and 1967 census concentration ratios are available. However, because of SIC revisions dating from 1963, only 191 industries remained comparable throughout the entire 1947 to 1967 period. In addition, 18 other industries that remained comparable beginning in 1954 have been included, for a total of 209 industries constituting more than one-half of the value added by all manufacturing industries.

The 1971 *Economic Report of the President* expressed the view that there was little objective evidence that economic power had increased in recent times. Yet, Table 2 shows that, with the introduction of 1967 census data,

Table 2   Distribution of changes in concentration ratios

Size of industry, value of shipments in millions of $	Number of industries	
	1947 (or 1954) to 1963	1947 (or 1954) to 1967
Increases:		
$2500 or over	4	9
$1000–$2500	13	14
$500–$1000	14	18
Under $500	54	54
Total	85	95
Less than 3 percentage points	43	39
Decreases:		
Under $500	44	30
$500–$1000	17	21
$1000–$2500	13	15
$2500 or over	7	9
Total	81	75
Total	209	209

industry concentration has risen. Those industries in which concentration ratios changed by less than three percentage points are shown separately so that attention might be focused on those industries with more significant changes. In the period 1947– (or 1954–) 1963, there were 85 increases, 43 cases of relative stability, and 81 decreases in concentration ratios. Thus, increases had been roughly offset by decreases. The inclusion of 1967 data clearly changes that picture. Industries with an increase in concentration ratios number 95—a gain of 10 over 1963; there is relative stability in 39 cases; and decreases number 75—a net loss of 6 from 1963. It is interesting to note that of the 10 increases in concentration between 1963 and 1967, one-half took place in the very large industries with shipments of $2.5 billion or more. At the same time, the number of small industries with declining concentration in the period of 1947– (or 1954–) 1963 fell off sharply—from 44 to 30—in the 1963 to 1967 period. Thus, the data do show that concentration among the large industries has risen.

ANOTHER ASPECT OF CONCENTRATION

It has been recognized for some time that substantial economic power can impede the market's effective operation. Competition among the few will produce quite different results than under the assumptions of classical competition among the many. The early TNEC hearings illustrated this, but the implications for public policy were not grasped for a variety of reasons set forth earlier. However, the behavior of prices among concentrated industries during the recession of 1969 to 1970 provides anew evidence of the difficulties besetting the traditional stabilization tools of monetary and fiscal policy in slowing inflation in our current economic environment. The policy implications of these difficulties might again be ignored in the face of evidence showing that concentration is diminishing, but with clear evidence to the contrary the 1969 to 1970 experience presents a strong reason to reassess economic policy assumptions and actions.

Beginning late in 1968 and continuing through most of 1969, a combination of monetary and fiscal restraint was applied to the American economy in an attempt to reduce the rate of inflation. In part as a consequence, a reduction in aggregate demand did occur—aggravated by a major strike in the auto industry late in 1970—culminating in the recession of 1969 to 1970. At the same time, prices not only continued to rise, but their rate of increase accelerated. In this connection, the price behavior of certain concentrated industries is quite instructive. Table 3 compares price changes for 347 product classes with census concentration ratios for the industry groups within which those products are found. These products comprise more than one-half the value of all manufacturing output. The price changes are shown for the period between December 1969 and December 1970, these dates having been officially designated by the National Bureau of Economic Research as the beginning and the trough of the 1969 to 1970 recession.

During this recession, classical competitive behavior was evident in only 52 product classes where prices clearly fell. These declines ranged from 2 percent to more than 5 percent. Among the other product classes, 65 remained relatively stable—with price changes of from +2 percent to −2 percent. However, for the remaining 230 product classes—or nearly two-thirds of the total sample—prices rose. In fact, more than one-half of these price increases were at a rate of 5 percent or more. Thus, it appears clear that a good deal of perverse price behavior occurred during this recession, behavior which does not comport with the kind of competitive performance suggested by classical economic theory.

A closer look at the data confirms that the extent of such perverse behavior is clearly related to the degree of economic concentration which pertains. For example, the preponderant share of price decreases—about four-fifths—was associated with concentration ratios under 25 percent or from 25 to 49 percent. On the other hand, only one-sixth of the price declines occurred where concentration ratios were 50 percent or more. At the same time, price increases were dominant in the moderate to highly concentrated product classes and conspicuously less so where concentration ratios were under 25 percent.

Table 3   Concentration ratio and percentage price change of 347 product classes
December 1969 to December 1970

Industry grouping	Total	Increases 5.0% and over	Increases 2.0% to 4.9%	Changes of less than +2.0% or −2.0%	Decreases −2.0% to −4.9%	Decreases −5.0% and over
Farm, food, and tobacco						
50% and over	21	12	5	3	1	—
25% to 49%	32	12	7	3	3	7
Under 25%*	29	12	2	1	1	13
Total	82	36	14	7	5	20
Textiles, apparel, and leather						
50% and over	9	1	2	3	—	3
25% to 49%	14	1	1	7	3	2
Under 25%	11	1	6	3	1	—
Total	34	3	9	13	4	5
Lumber, furniture, and paper						
50% and over	6	3	3	—	—	—
25% to 49%	15	3	3	6	1	2
Under 25%	13	—	5	3	4	1
Total	34	6	11	9	5	3
Chemicals and petroleum						
50% and over	12	—	2	8	2	—
25% to 49%	15	8	5	2	—	—
Under 25%‡	1	—	1	—	—	—
Total	28	8	8	10	2	0
Stone, clay, and glass						
50% and over	10	4	3	3	—	—
25% to 49%	5	2	3	—	—	—
Under 25%	3	3	—	—	—	—
Total	18	9	6	3	0	0
Primary metals						
50% and over	26	12	5	6	2	1
25% to 49%	12	6	4	0	—	2
Under 25%‡	2	1	—	—	1	—
Total	40	19	9	6	3	3
Machinery and fabricated metal products						
50% and over	21	10	9	2	—	—
25% to 49%	27	14	11	2	—	—
Under 25%	8	5	2	1	—	—
Total	56	29	22	5	0	0

Table 3 (continued)

Industry grouping	Total	Increases 5.0% and over	Increases 2.0% to 4.9%	Changes of less than +2.0% or −2.0%	Decreases −2.0% to −4.9%	Decreases −5.0% and over
Electrical machinery						
50% and over	19	6	8	5	—	—
25% to 49%	14	9	2	1	1	1
Under 25%	2	1	1	—	—	—
Total	35	16	11	6	1	1
Transportation equipment						
50% and over	3	3	—	—	—	—
25% to 49%	1	—	—	1	—	—
Under 25%	—	—	—	—	—	—
Total	4	3	0	1	0	0
Miscellaneous						
50% and over	7	2	1	4	—	—
25% to 49%	5	—	4	1	—	—
Under 25%	4	1	3	—	—	—
Total	16	3	8	5	0	0
All product classes						
50% and over	134	53	38	34	5	4
25% to 49%	140	55	40	23	8	14
Under 25%	73	24	20	8	7	14
Total	347	132	98	65	20	32

*Includes 19 farm product classes.
†Includes 1 product class, wastepaper.
‡Includes 2 product classes of scrap metal.
Source: Prices: Bureau of Labor Statistics, Department of Labor, Wholesale Price Index. Concentration ratios: *Concentration Ratios in Manufacturing Industry, 1963,* 1966, Pt. 1, Table 4.

DISCUSSION QUESTIONS 9.2

1. Define "administered price." What does the concept of administered pricing have to say about the contradictory phenomenon of inflation during a recession?
2. What does the evidence say about changes in concentration? Relate concentration to economic performance.
3. Are competition and free enterprise "models which do not exist, which never have existed and which Americans do not permit to exist, yet which assuage our frontieristic, democratic spirit"?

4. Is there a danger that control over markets may be lost because "public policy may not perceive the ultimate impact of forces in motion until it is too late"?

Case 9.3   Forced Divestiture in Oil?[1]

Morgan Guaranty Trust Company of New York publishes the *Morgan Guaranty Survey*, from which this worried article is taken. It is one point of view on antitrust action against the oil industry:

A feeling has persisted among many people that the earlier shortages and the present high prices of gasoline somehow have been due to oil company "conspiracies." Frustrated by inflation at the gas pump (which aggravates the problem of generalized inflation), and upset at the inability of the United States government to counter the Organization of Petroleum Exporting Countries (OPEC), public sentiment has taken on a decidedly antioil bias.

LASHING OUT

The tendency to lash out at "big oil" is evident in the halls of Congress. In the past year, nearly forty bills which would importantly affect oil industry operations have been popped into the legislative hopper. In mid-June 1976 the Senate Judiciary Committee approved and sent to the Senate floor the most far-reaching of those bills. Called the "Petroleum Industry Competition Act," it would force the top eighteen oil companies to divest themselves of either their exploration and production functions or their refining-marketing functions as well as, in either case, all their transportation operations (mostly pipelines). In addition, refining companies would not be permitted to extend their marketing operations through owned service stations beyond the number of such outlets they owned at the beginning of this year. Thus, integrated operations—from drilling rig to the refinery and then to the gas pump—would be banned.

A companion measure in Congress would require "horizontal divestiture," which would prohibit oil companies from operating in other types of energy such as coal, nuclear power, or geothermal steam.

LITTLE ONES OUT OF BIG ONES

Vertical or horizontal divestiture (or the two combined) would bring about major restructuring of a giant industry with an impact far greater than the historic 1911 breakup of Standard Oil. That action sixty-five years ago resulted in merely a geographic dismemberment in which individual companies confined their operations to specific regions. Many of the companies continued as integrated operations.

The worldwide assets of the companies affected by currently proposed divestiture legislation are estimated at $149 billion at the end of 1975. Those companies employed 693,000 workers. Their aggregate long-term debt amounted to nearly $23 billion and their off-balance-sheet debt exceeded $10 billion.

[1] *Morgan Guaranty Survey*, June 1976.

Stock in the companies, valued at $72 billion, is held by several million investors directly—and, indirectly, by several million more through pension and mutual funds.

The bill to break up the oil companies declares: "It is the purpose of the Congress in this act to facilitate the creation and maintenance of competition in the petroleum industry, and to require the most expeditious and equitable separation and divestment of assets and interests of vertically integrated major petroleum companies."

Companies producing 100,000 barrels of oil a day or more in the United States could not engage in refining, transportation, or marketing of oil. Companies refining or marketing 300,000 barrels a day or more in the United States could not produce or transport oil. And companies of any size that transport oil through domestic pipelines could not produce, refine, or market oil.

The bill's timetable calls for vertical disintegration of the oil companies within five years.[2] Table 1 lists the eighteen companies that would be affected by divestiture.

[2]Horizontal divestiture, which is contained in a separate bill not acted upon as yet, would have to be completed within three years. Alarm within the industry is greater over proposed vertical disintegration, although oil companies are very much concerned with forced divestiture horizontally. The oil industry, which has engaged in research and development for alternate energy sources for many years, feels that it has much to contribute. And quite aside from technological know-how and expertise, segmented coal or nuclear power companies would not have the capital base needed for massive development programs.

Table 1   Major producers, refiners, and marketers

| | Barrels per day | | |
U.S. operations only in 1974	Crude production	Refinery throughout	Marketing
Exxon	890,000	1,123,000	1,782,000
Texaco	807,000	945,000	1,338,000
Shell	586,000	1,005,000	1,060,000
Standard Oil of Indiana	539,000	936,000	1,012,000
Gulf	476,300	813,000	860,600
Mobil	420,000	823,000	928,000
Standard Oil of California	413,080	867,000	1,006,000
Atlantic-Richfield	383,100	653,500	697,600
Getty	300,300	214,500	254,000
Union	268,400	439,100	441,200
Sun	265,588	489,988	570,546
Phillips	244,700	523,000	541,000
Continental	218,000	322,000	364,000
Cities Service	212,300	231,800	348,400
Marathon	174,039	264,415	280,106
BP-Sohio	29,646	323,336	332,996
Amerada Hess	98,816	530,000	591,000
Ashland	23,071	329,789	457,007

Source: National Petroleum News Factbook, mid-May 1975.

Significantly, the oil companies are not charged with violating any laws. Instead, a breakup of the oil industry is called necessary to foster competition. Proponents of the bill argue that legislation is needed because antitrust laws have been "too slow and inadequate."

Traditionally, when looking for indications of possible anticompetitive conduct in an industry, analysts consider three criteria: concentration ratios, profitability, and ease of entry into the field.

Concentration Ratios Such ratios show the proportion of industry production or sales accounted for by a small number of firms—usually the top firm, the top four companies, and the top eight companies. The evidence is clear that oil concentration ratios are lower than for United States businesses generally. Data from the Census of Manufactures and other sources (Table 2) show that the four-firm concentration ratio approximates 27 percent for crude oil production, 34 percent for refining capacity, and 30 percent for gasoline sales. These numbers are appreciably lower than the weighted average four-firm concentration ratio for United States manufacturing, which works out at about 40 percent.[3]

Indeed, many other United States industries are decidedly more concentrated than is oil. For example, the four top companies in the copper industry account for 75 percent of production; the auto industry has one producer which accounts for half the market for American cars; more than 90 percent of aluminum output is accounted for by four producers. In a list of twenty-seven major industries, oil-industry concentration ranks lowest of all.

Charges of monopolistic behavior raised by proponents of divestiture seem strange in an industry where there are 50 integrated oil companies; 10,000

[3]Share of the market accounted for by top four firms in various industries, with the shares for a particular industry weighted by value added.

Table 2 U.S. oil industry concentration ratios

	Percent of U.S. industry output accounted for by		
	Top firm	Top 4 firms	Top 8 firms
Crude oil production, 1970	8.5	27.1	49.1
Refining capacity Gasoline, 1970	9.2	34.0	59.8
Product sales Gasoline, 1973	8.0	10.0	52.4

Sources: Crude oil production from "Concentration Levels and Trends in the Energy Sector of the U.S. Economy," by Joseph P. Mulholland and Douglas W. Webbink, Staff Report to the Federal Trade Commission, Washington, D.C., March 1974, pp. 63–65. Gasoline refining capacity from U.S. Federal Trade Commission, "Preliminary Federal Trade Commission Staff Report on Its Investigation of the Petroleum Industry," Washington, D.C., 1973, Table 11–3. Gasoline product sales from Harold Wilson, "Exxon and Shell Score Gasoline Gains," *Oil and Gas Journal,* June 3, 1974. Reproduced from page 2231 of hearings of Senate Subcommittee on Antitrust and Monopoly, Part Three.

producers of oil and natural gas; 100 interstate pipeline companies; 130 refining companies; 18,000 marketers of fuel oil; and 300,000 retailers of gasoline—95 percent of them independent businessmen who compete for motorists' business.

Proponents of divestiture concede that concentration ratios in oil are low, but they insist such ratios should not be conventionally interpreted. The reason they cite: The oil industry is prone to joint ventures, swap agreements, and joint services affecting pipelines, refineries, international production and distribution, domestic oil exploration and development, and bidding for federal oil leases. Such arrangements are said to create a "community of interest" which tends to bring about a "unity of attitude and action."

Unquestionably, the oil industry enters frequently into joint ventures. An obvious reason for this is the cost—and enormous risks—involved in oil exploration and development. Joint bidding on offshore oil tracts can be procompetitive rather than anticompetitive since more companies can participate than would be the case if joint bidding were not allowed. (Actually, under a recent government ruling the seven largest oil companies can no longer bid jointly; they must bid singly or as partners with smaller companies.) Moreover, exchange and processing agreements among oil companies provide for economical use of resources. Oil is rarely found near a company's own refinery but can be exchanged with other companies for a supply which can be more efficiently used—and which is of the specific type and quality needed for each refinery. As for monopolistic control by owners of pipelines, the Interstate Commerce Commission tightly regulates pipeline transportation to be sure that nonowners get access to the lines.

Profitability　Relatively large profits for an industry over a long period of time traditionally are considered an indication that the industry possesses monopolistic power. That kind of profitability is not the case in the oil industry. In 1974, it is true, oil profits hit record highs. But that was due to inventory profits made possible by the quadrupling of the world price of oil by OPEC and by overseas sales at the higher prices. After that one-shot effect, profits dropped back to normal levels. For the years 1960 through 1975, the oil industry's rate of return on shareholders' equity—what the company earns on the money the stockholders have invested—averaged just over 12 percent, only a bit higher than the 11.4 percent average return on all American manufacturing. Many other industries did better than oil companies—including soft drinks, drugs, medicines, soap, cosmetics, office equipment, and tobacco.

Entry by Competitors　The third test of uncompetitive conditions is the existence of barriers to entry into the field.

The record indicates freedom of entry for individuals and groups into all phases of the oil business. For example, independent oil companies have shared in four of every five winning bids on tracts for offshore lease sales. And independents selling nonbrand gasoline have increased their share of the market from 23 percent of the total in 1967 to roughly 32 percent in 1975.

VERTICALLY UNCOMPETITIVE?

On the three standard tests, it is not at all clear why anyone should think that the oil industry needs to be dismembered. Perhaps recognizing this, those who are pushing a breakup have been emphasizing a different argument: Because the oil industry is vertically integrated, its market structure lends itself to uncompetitive action. Here again, a look at the record makes the claims for divestiture appear unconvincing.

In the first place, an industry should not be presumed to be anticompetitive just because it is integrated. Economists who have written on the subject generally argue that vertical integration does not have an adverse impact on competition. Second, vertical integration is not peculiar to the oil industry; it is used by all sorts of businesses, large and small.

Such integration is commonplace in business. Some auto companies make their own steel and glass and some operate auto dealerships. Steel companies are integrated "backward" through ownership of coal and ore mines and "forward" into production of finished products. Some newspapers own timber to assure supplies of newsprint. The industry list of integrated firms is almost endless. The key point is that there must be very strong advantages to be derived from vertical integration in order to make it so universal a method of organization.

Moreover, as a study of Prof. M. A. Adelman of Massachusetts Institute of Technology has shown, the oil industry ranks far down the list in its degree of vertical integration among United States manufacturing industries.[4] As Prof. Edward J. Mitchell of the University of Michigan put it in testimony before the Senate Antitrust and Monopoly Subcommittee in January: "The average U.S. manufacturing firm would have to divest itself of from 30 to 60 percent of its assets and employees just to get down to the low level of integration that exists in the petroleum industry."

ADVERSE CONSEQUENCES

Against a background of competitiveness in oil, an industry which is less integrated than most others, and one which has served consumers well over the years, why the proposals for a breakup?

Would such action bring important benefits for consumers? Would a splintered oil industry be more capable of the major task of developing domestic energy resources? And would a larger group of smaller United States companies have more muscle and be better able to stand up to the OPEC cartel?

The answer to each of those questions must be "no." Dismemberment in all probability would lead to higher costs and a narrowing capital base, resulting in more expensive fuel for consumers and impeding hopes for developing an effective energy program. Such an impact on the energy program, monumentally jarring as it would be initially, would continue to be felt for years to come.

---

[4]See "Concept and Statistical Measurement of Vertical Integration," in *Business Concentration and Public Policy*, Washington, D.C., National Bureau of Economic Research.

The reason: Divestiture standards are based on the size of production and refining-marketing operations; as today's smaller oil companies got larger and reached those artificial limits, they automatically would have to break their operations into pieces. A government sword, thus, would be hanging over their heads. Where, then, would be the incentive for such companies to expand and grow? Obviously, there would be strong disincentives—just the opposite of what's needed if this country ever is to achieve its goal of energy independence.

Divestiture could also result in reduced effectiveness in dealing with OPEC since the larger number of buyers would still be faced with the same concentration of supplier power. Moreover, a dismantled United States oil industry, with a multitude of smaller companies, would be at a distinct disadvantage trying to compete with the foreign giants for scarce supplies of foreign oil.

The proposed divestiture legislation is glaringly lacking in specificity as to how it would apply abroad. Still the broad intent of the bill is clear: United States companies would be required to break into segments their overseas as well as their domestic companies. For example, Exxon's production activities in the United States and overseas could be retained, but the company would have to divest its refining, marketing, and distribution operations in this country and abroad. Moreover, as experts in corporate law warned the Senate Antitrust Subcommittee, any long-term contracts entered into between the prohibited United States overseas subsidiaries and foreign companies or foreign governments would have to be terminated.

The international legal snarls that would be created by such action clearly would be immense. Foreign courts almost surely would support the contentions of foreigners that contractual obligations of American overseas oil companies could not unilaterally be abrogated by the United States. Foreign debts of American overseas oil companies might be accelerated by foreign creditors concerned about the impact of dismemberment. Foreign courts might very well uphold claims for damages for breach of contract against splintered United States overseas companies. In short, a breakup of the United States oil companies would bring severe headaches abroad as well as at home.

A case of need for divestiture has not been made; appeals have been largely emotional—and proponents of a breakup have been vague about the resulting benefits. What is not at all fuzzy, however, are the tremendous risks that would be run if dismemberment is pursued.

Chief among these are the enormous procedural problems which would arise if Congress were to enact divestiture. Tearing apart a major industry is easier said than done. It would be a long, drawn-out affair dealing with immensely complicated issues. Legal experts at the hearings on the divestiture bill estimated that such a move by the government might well take ten to twenty years to complete.

Those involved in the case would include federal agencies, federal courts, oil companies, investment bankers and other financial institutions, and squadrons of lawyers. All would be caught up in a costly and arduous exercise in revising a maze of contractual arrangements on which the oil industry's financial and organizational structure now rests.

In the meantime, what would happen to this country's energy industry? How could the industry function during a period of extended litigation which would breed extreme uncertainty?

In one word, as witnesses testified, the condition of the oil industry would be chaotic. Until a divestiture plan was agreed upon, until the inevitable litigation that would follow was settled in the courts, and until dismemberment was actually carried out, no one would have any idea of what the postdivestiture oil industry would be like. Stockholders would not know what they owned—or what had been "spun off" by divestiture. How would the debts of the present companies be apportioned to each of the fragments? What kind of capital structure would the new, smaller units have? How to judge their earnings potential? And would the smaller units be able to make it on their own in a tough, competitive industry? No one, quite literally, can know in advance the answers to those critical questions.

The financial market implications of divestiture, quite obviously, would be sizable. Investment analysts warned the lawmakers at the hearings that a breakup of the majors—making seventy-two companies instead of the present eighteen companies—would effectively close off a major portion of the oil industry from the capital markets for an indefinite period of time. With reduced investment, the inevitable result would be growing weakness for the oil industry in this country—and enlarged dependence on foreign suppliers of energy.

SHEER-SIZE SYNDROME

Fundamentally, the dismemberment drive grows out of the deep-rooted antipathy toward bigness that keeps surfacing in American political dialog. Fortunately, from the standpoint of the nation's economic development, the legal framework within which business operates has not heretofore reflected a preoccupation with sheer size. Size, indeed, is irrelevant in judging anticompetitive conduct; the law requires evidence of collusion or other anticompetitive behavior as the only grounds for government antitrust action.

The pervasive yearning for smaller economic units simply overlooks reality in today's world of high-cost energy. It takes unprecedented amounts of capital to find and deliver energy to consumers. The trans-Alaska pipeline, coming into operation next year, will cost something over $7 billion when completed. A single drilling platform in the North Sea, together with its associated wells and production facilities, is currently estimated to cost upward of $750 million. An economically competitive oil refinery can cost well over $500 million these days. Such projects require companies of a size capable of raising massive amounts of capital. Smaller units in a postdivestiture market environment, if able to raise money at all, surely would have to pay much more for it, adding to operating costs. Moreover, smaller companies would either have to build smaller, less efficient units or operate on the basis of cumbersome joint ventures; one or the other alternative, however, would further add to production costs—and to the bill the consumer would have to pay. Splintering the oil companies, thus, might yield short-term political gains but, over the longer run, prove to be an economic disaster.

Radical legislative surgery, as is called for in the divestiture bill, would make sense only if it were clear that the oil industry is badly malfunctioning—and if the surgery could cure the problem without devastating after effects. By reasonably objective tests, the oil industry is performing well.

DISCUSSION QUESTIONS 9.3

1. If divestiture is "the bottom line" in antitrust policy, how would you evaluate its impact in the oil industry? Who would benefit?
2. What concept of bigness is relevant to an analysis of the national (or worldwide) oil market? Relate bigness to economic power and then to social well-being. Is there a question of national security at issue here? If so, in what sense?
3. What does the doctrine of conspiracy mean as applied to antitrust enforcement? Is conspiracy avoidable in an oligopolistic market?
4. What is the other side of the Morgan Guaranty argument?

10

FORECASTING: MAKING THE FUTURE PART OF TODAY'S DECISIONS

Key Concepts

accuracy
composite index of leading
   indicators (CLI)
diffusion indexes
economic causality
economic time series
endogenous variables
exogenous variables
extrapolation
fine tuning
input-output forecast models
judgment
large-scale econometric models
leading indicators
logical flow of a model
macroeconomic forecasting
matrix
mean absolute error

microeconomic forecasting
micrometrics
naive forecast
neo-Keynesian models
observable constancies
purposive intervention
quantity theory
reference trough
sensitivity
symptomatic forecasts
systems dynamics
technical coefficients
technological forecasting
Thiel coefficient
turning points
verification

What Is Ahead in This Chapter

This is a chapter about business forecasting. Business forecasting involves predicting the environment in which the management of business firms must make decisions. While the future business environment is affected by changes in laws, shifts in the competitive structure of the industry, tax increases, and the changing phases of the business cycle, among many other things, most forecasting involves the business cycle.

Forecasting the business environment is situation forecasting. The purpose of situation forecasting is to give the management of a firm the economic setting—national income, consumer attitudes, price changes, and unemployment. While situation forecasting focuses on macroeconomic variables, the use of forecasting results is basically microeconomic. The underlying assumption of most managements is that the firm's activities—sales, production, employment, prices, profits—are going to be affected by the so-called big picture.

What kind of situation forecasts are available? What are the methods used by forecasters? In what sense are forecasts accurate? What are the new developments in forecasting? Do all forecasters derive the same results? If they don't, who does the best job at forecasting? Why? These and related questions are answered in this chapter. Given the rapid pace of improvement in forecasting methodology, this chapter handles economic forecasting in a state-of-the-art context.

Studying one chapter doesn't make you a forecaster, but it can help you understand what forecasters do and can give you the reasons why so many firms depend heavily on economic forecasting. In effect, the most obvious and continuing use large and small firms alike make of managerial economics is economic forecasting. That, too, is why so many firms hire economists and spend substantial sums on the development of economic research capability. Successful forecasting reduces business risks and thereby increases the profitability of firms. In a word, economic forecasting pays. So long as marginal revenue from better knowledge about the future in which a firm will have to operate equals or exceeds the marginal cost of operating in the dark, more and more economic forecasting will be used.

Relationship Between Microeconomic and Macroeconomic Forecasting

Business firms can readily hire the services of economic consultants. They can also buy the forecast output of major forecasting firms. In addition, a company can hire its own economic staff. Whatever the method, management is looking for a way to correlate future operations of the firm with the probable pattern of behavior of national variables.

Suppose the following elements constitute what the management of one major firm wants to know from its economic staff about the business environment:[1]

1. Growth patterns of products and product lines—based on sales, production, inventory, and other data.
2. Performance benchmarks—derived both from large-scale models and from growth patterns and used to provide management with a comparison between actual and potential sales and production.
3. Market penetration—a comparison of a firm's sales and production with that of its industry to determine whether the firm is gaining, losing, or maintaining market share.
4. Product and product-line profitability—a continuing indication of the relationship between cost and revenue, before and after taxes for each product and product line, set in a context of corporate profit performance (and expectations), as well as of industry performance.
5. Customer analysis—a plot of the changing purchases of customers, together with a forecast of their likely purchases.
6. Competition analysis—an estimate of sales and other data for each of the five or ten largest competitors. Though these data may not be precise, salesmen will probably have a good idea of what is happening.
7. Distribution analysis—a continuing breakdown of the major channels of distribution, such as factories, internal use, wholesalers, distributors, retailers, governments, export and direct sale, to assess changes in relationships, as well as the extent of dependence on any one channel.
8. End-use analysis—to what kind of customers do the products go? In what form are they finally used? How much is used in industrial as opposed to consumer products?

Each of these elements requires both internal and external information. Company records, sales and marketing staff, and type of data picked up from industry associations will supply part of the desired information. Outside research will supply more. But the resultant corporate microeconomic forecasting model would be limited in scope and effectiveness. While the micro-forecasting model would be detailed and broken down into terms of individual products, divisions, impact areas, and profits centers, it would lack outside trends and developments. No matter how good the micromodel, it would have to tie into a parent national situation model.

The point is this. No matter how complete the inside information, its validity depends on outside relationships. It is for that reason that even very large companies with extraordinarily good inside information capabilities turn to outside macroeconomic models. Imagine, for example, a product sales forecast, a basic premise in managerial decision making. How will it be tested

[1]R. L. McLaughlin, "The Corporate Economist in the Microeconomy," *Business Economics,* 8(3):7–14, May 1973.

for its reasonableness, its accuracy? Obviously dependent on that sales forecast is the corporate financial situation next year and the next. That includes the projected income statement, the balance sheet, and the financial plan (borrowing, stock issue, debt reduction). Also dependent on the sales forecast are new product plans, price policies, market penetration, promotion moves, and other types of decisions. But the sales forecast hinges on the national forecast.

Approaches to Economic Forecasting

In essence, all economic forecasting involves one or more of the following basic approaches:

1. A careful analysis of past and currently available data regarding business and general market situation will produce a model that can be used to produce answers about the future, provided the right data are used.
2. There are broad general and usually cyclical movements in the basic economic indicators that trace an undulating path for national, regional, and local economies. The relation between these broad general economic movements and those of the firm or product is forecast by a model of the cycle.
3. There were difficulties, recessions, crises, or mistakes in the past from which lessons can be learned. It is necessary to find both a way of recognizing the symptoms of trouble and a knowledge of the applicable remedies.
4. There are at any moment important structural changes taking place in the local, regional, national, and international economies that will produce economic reactions quite different from those known in the past. Nevertheless, it is possible to base a prediction of future events on a study of such changes.

Each approach to forecasting involves a strategy. For each possible strategy, there is one basic rule: Never use more data input than you need to get the result. Each approach can be used with detail and sophistication. There is no reason to call upon a computer to do simple sums. The hunches, instincts, and psychological reactions of a trained observer should not be overlooked. The human mind is the most complex of calculating machines, and there is no question that it can deal with some forms of data input that no other device can be expected to handle.

Forecasting with Large-Scale Econometric Models

An econometric model used for forecasting is a set of mathematical and statistical relationships that is designed both to describe and to project economic behavior. The models are based on economic theory but are derived from data available in a form which may or may not meet the specifications of theory. Relationships in the model are estimated from these data and the results are tested against actual performance. Most such models are quite large, ranging from 40 to more than 400 equations and/or relationships. These macromodels are intended to predict the gross national product (and its components), price levels (at the consumer, wholesale, and sometimes export/import levels), employment and unemployment rates, interest rates, money supply and rates of exchange, and changes in inventories, investment, and government finances (deficits, surpluses).

The variables in the models are either endogenous (internal) or exogenous (external). Endogenous variables are determined within the model and to a large extent influence each other. For example, the GNP is directly related to national income and in turn to disposable personal income. Disposable personal income affects consumer expenditures on goods and services as well as consumer saving. However, these endogenous variables, in turn, are affected by or depend on other exogenous variables such as government spending, taxes, exports, and Federal Reserve bank policy in respect of money supply and interest rates. Some of these endogenous variables, of course, may not be purely economic in nature. The external variables are called "exogenous" because they are not explicitly determined by the model. In using such a model a forecaster supplies estimates of these exogenous variables.

Whether a variable is endogenous or exogenous to a model is determined by the model-builder. Some model-builders, for example, consider government expenditures to be exogenous because they feel that such spending depends primarily on economic activity. All models will distinguish between endogenous and exogenous variables, though they may differ as to which is what. The reason is that unless a model has some givens, some exogenous variables, it posits an everything-depends-on-everything-else situation, which is very difficult to handle mathematically.

A Simple Econometric Forecasting Model

Liebenberg, Hirsch, and Popkin[2] some years ago developed a simple econometric model of the United States

$$C_t = a_0 + a_1 Y_t + a_2 C_{t-1} \tag{1}$$
$$I_t = b_0 + b_1 P_t + b_2 K_{t-1} \tag{2}$$
$$W_t = c_0 + c_1 Y_1 + c_2 t \tag{3}$$
$$Y_t = C_t + I_t + G_t \tag{4}$$
$$P_t = Y_t - W_t \tag{5}$$
$$K_t = K_{t-1} + I_t \tag{6}$$

where

[2]M. Liebenberg, A. Hirsch, and J. Popkin, "A Quarterly Econometric Model of the United States: A Progress Report," *Survey of Current Business*, 5:13–39, May 1966.

C = consumption spending
Y = national income
W = wage income
P = property and other nonwage income (industry profits)
I = investment (net after capital consumption allowances)
K = capital (productive investment in place) at end of relevant accounting period
G = spending by governments on goods and services
t = time marked off in accounting periods

These six equations and eight variables spell out certain hypothesized relationships derived from economic theory. The relationships are of two kinds: One is a behavioral equation that describes an empirically testable hypothesis about how a certain endogenous variable is determined. The other is an identity, a form of accounting or economic definition. In this model, there are three behavioral equations: One is about consumption, one about investment, and a third about wages. And there are three identities: One is that national income is the sum of consumption spending, investment spending, and government spending; another identity holds that property or nonwage income is that part of national income not derived from wages; and the third identity states that capital stock of the economy at the end of the current accounting period is the sum of the capital stock available at the end of the previous period plus the additions to it from net investment which took place in the current accounting period. Thus, there are six endogenous variables, each explained by an equation, and two exogenous variables, time and government spending.

The logical flow in this model can be illustrated by the following flowchart shown in Fig. 10.1. Thus a rise in government spending leads first to an increase in national income, Eq. (4). Rising national income induces higher consump-

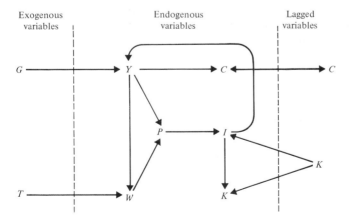

Figure 10.1. Logical flow in a simple macroeconometric model. (From "Econometric Models: The Monetarist and Non-Monetarist Views Compared," *Monthly Review*, Federal Reserve Bank of Richmond, February 1973.)

tion, Eq. (1); increased property income (and profits), Eq. (5); and increased wages, Eq. (3). Consumption, then, feeds back into national income, Eq. (4), and after a lag of one period induces a further increase in consumption. Rising property income and profits lead to higher investment outlays, Eq. (2), resulting in a further increase in national income, Eq. (4). Increased investment outlays also increase the capital stock of the nation, Eq. (6). Changes in wage and nonwage payments (including profits) are offsetting as income is distributed between them, Eq. (5).

Whys and Wherefores of Econometric Forecasting

Econometrics is used in developing forecasting models to make them more explicit and quantitatively precise. If there are regularities, they are to be stated as explicitly as possible, making them subject to systematic tests. If, for example, it appears that whenever the sales tax goes up 10 percent, the consumer price index rises by about 17 percent, there's a testable regularity. The test might show that there is a 1 in 3 chance that the consumer price index (CPI) will go up by more than 19 percent or less than 15 percent. And there are 2 chances in 3 that it will increase between 15 and 19 percent.

Far from selecting estimating and testing techniques at random from the toolbox, econometricians, as they build their forecasts, preselect certain properties they consider desirable and then choose methods that combine these properties in a satisfactory way. The two properties most frequently looked for are (1) the expected value of the estimates and (2) the sensitivity of the estimates to any given sample of data chosen. Since the mass of available data is very large, econometricians have devised techniques that yield estimates with desirable properties even when a sufficiently large number of estimates may not be obtainable. For forecasting purposes, the usefulness of a forecast is considerably increased if the user knows its standard error of estimate (SEE). The standard error is a measure of the extent to which predictions deviated from their actual values in a sample of data. A low SEE means that the estimated values were near their expected values.

Econometric forecasting is objective, meaning that it is explicit about the nature of the reasoning in the forecast model and that the model is quantitative. An econometric model cannot always be accurate. It cannot even eliminate controversy.

Three basic model-building problems face an econometrician who wants to develop good forecasting techniques. The first problem is the form of the model. Should it deal with correlations between, say, prices and car sales, or between percentage changes in car prices and percentage changes in car sales, or perhaps even better between a percentage change yesterday in prices with a percentage change today in car sales? Should every available market contour be modeled by a separate equation? Or will a small number of equations do the trick?

If too few equations and variables are used, then a second problem arises, whether too much was omitted. Econometricians can never be sure that they have considered all the relevant variables—even if all were available. But they will try, nonetheless.

The last problem involves the use of predetermined variables. An econometrician is limited to indicators that are known at the time the forecast is being made. But suppose that the model turns up unsuspected regularities? If there are surprises of this kind, the econometrician may want to develop structural estimates that will try to probe the economic system for further underlying relationships. Or, if an econometrician is not willing to dig deeply into the structure, he may choose reduced-form models that spell net relationships. The more structural the model, the more room for error. On the other hand, the reduced form may overlook key variables.

In any case, econometrics points out the problems in trying to understand a complex social reality like next year's level of gross national product. And econometricians are getting better all the time at helping us understand and even predict.

A Choice Among Models: Keynes v. Friedman

Without a thorough analysis of the theoretical merits of a Keynesian versus a Friedman econometric model, it is nonetheless useful to distinguish between the two in terms of their structure, their relative predictive accuracy, and their data requirements. The Federal Reserve Bank of St. Louis has generally been known as a proponent of the Friedman or quantity theory approach. A typical quantity equation[3] (based on observations from IV1958 to IV1966) is

$$\Delta Y_t = 5.61 + 3.94 \, (\Delta M)_{t-3}$$
$$(.67)$$
$$R^2 = .553$$

where

ΔY_t = change in GNP in period t
ΔM = change in the money supply

This quantity theory single-equation system says that in each quarter the GNP will rise by $5.61 billion (at annual rates) plus $3.9 billion for every $1 billion increase in the money supply M three quarters previously. The number in parentheses is the standard error of the estimate. It will be noted that this standard error is about one-sixth of the value of the coefficient, indicating a relatively high degree of statistical significance. The R^2 value indicates that about 55 percent of the variation in ΔY can be explained by the changes in $(\Delta M)_{t-3}$.

[3]"Economic Theory and Forecasting," *Review*, Federal Reserve Bank of St. Louis, March 1967.

A Keynesian or income-expenditure single-equation model also derived by the Federal Reserve Bank of St. Louis for the same period is

$$Y_t = 4.94 + 1.08 \, (\Delta A)_{t-1}$$
$$(.24)$$
$$R^2 = .400$$

where A = autonomous spending.

This result says that for each quarter the GNP will increase $4.9 billion (annual rate) for every $1 billion increase in A, autonomous spending, in the previous quarter. The coefficient is statistically significant and 40 percent of the change in ΔY can be explained by changes in $(\Delta A)_{t-1}$.

An analysis of the time path of these two equations shows that they generally share the same upper turning points, but the quantity equation leads the income-expenditure equation on the lower turning point by two to three quarters. It is this latter feature of the quantity model which has made it attractive to forecasters. What is more, the relationship indicates that even relatively small variations in money supply lead to variations in GNP.

As the St. Louis bank points out, it is possible to combine these two approaches as

$$\Delta Y_t = 4.00 + 2.52 \, (\Delta M)_{t-3} + .670 \, (\Delta M)_{t-1}$$
$$(.80) \qquad\qquad (.241)$$
$$R^2 = .658$$

This result says that quarterly changes in GNP will equal $4 billion (at annual rates) plus $2.52 billion for every $1 billion rise in the money supply three quarters earlier plus $670 million for every $1 billion increase in autonomous spending one quarter earlier. The values of the coefficients for ΔM and ΔA are statistically significant and the model explains 66 percent of the variation in ΔY.

Autonomous spending consists largely of business investment and government spending. The money supply concept used is money stock. The Federal Reserve Bank of St. Louis[4] economics staff argue that because their small model is not designed for quarter-to-quarter forecasting and because many factors are known to influence short-run variations in economic activity, the best performance test for the St. Louis model extends over a six-quarter period.[5] In whatever form the St. Louis model has been used, it has had a strong impact on forecasting, model building, and economic policy making and assessment.

[4]The forecasting discussion is based on "Economic Theory and Forecasting," *Review*, Federal Reserve Bank of St. Louis, March 1967. See also K. M. Carlson, "Projecting with the St. Louis Model: A Progress Report," *Review*, *ibid.*, February 1972, for a much more detailed statement of the model. Frequent analyses of the model and its performance have appeared in the *Review* through 1976.

[5]See, however, K. M. Carlson, "The St. Louis Equation and Monthly Data," *Review*, Federal Reserve Bank of St. Louis, January 1975.

Timing in Econometric Models

On their own, without adjustment, large-scale econometric models cannot be used for good turning-point forecasts. Some critics have asked why large-scale models should be used at all. One answer is that, even in their present form, they can be used as an explicit and well-organized framework for the application of a forecaster's judgment. Another answer is that, as adjustments are made based on new and "unavailable" information, these data can be fed into the model in ways consonant with the forecaster's concepts of economic structure. Even more important, the model-user is provided with a range of policy options. A forecast can never take the place of managerial decision making.

On the whole, however, there is little doubt that the cyclical tracking capability of large-scale econometric models leaves room for improvement. Those[6] close to the Wharton econometric model have outlined two general ways to "hone the tracking and predictive abilities" of such models. The first method is to adjust numerically current model predictions to correct for past misses. The second method is to refine and improve the model itself.

The first method involves the use of past error patterns—the differences between actual and forecast variables. If, for example, a model typically understates GNP growth during a recovery period and overstates GNP growth during the downturn, the model-builder (and the user, too) can adjust predicted growth upward or downward by a probabilistic estimate of actual growth rates. This is called "fine tuning."

The second method of adjustment involves trying to incorporate additional predictive information such as anticipations data. Adams and Duggal[7] have shown that the forecasting performance of the Wharton Mark III model could be improved by incorporating plant and equipment investment anticipations, thus reducing forecast errors of business fixed investment. Some have used frequent reestimating techniques by adding new observations and by recalculating the prediction equations. The smaller the model, that is, the fewer the equations, the less expensive and time-consuming are the adjustments. Yet, there is evidence that not even frequent reestimating is enough; further error patterns and possibly incorrect forecasters' judgments must always be considered.

Accuracy in Forecasting

Economic forecasting has advanced to a point where most large corporations and many small ones depend on the output of one of about six major econometric models. The federal government, of course, has its own economic

---

[6]N. Behravesh, "Forecasting the Economy with Mathematical Models: Is It Worth the Effort?" *Business Review*, Federal Reserve Bank of Philadelphia, July/August 1975.

[7]F. G. Adams and V. G. Duggal, "Anticipations Variables in an Econometric Model: Performance of the Anticipations Versions of Wharton Mark III," *International Economic Review*, *15*:267–283, 1974.

forecasting staffs, but it also buys forecasts from the forecasting firms. Such is the general dependence on econometric models that questions regarding their accuracy are of considerable importance. A number of evaluations of forecasts have been made in recent years, using a variety of coefficients of accuracy.

Stephen McNees[8] of the Federal Reserve Bank of Boston used two summary forecast error measures in an evaluation of the commonly used forecast models. One is the mean absolute error (MAE), which is

$$\text{MAE} = \frac{1}{m} \sum_{t=1}^{m} \left| e_{t+n} \right|$$

where

> e = forecast error (by how much did actual exceed or fall behind forecast?)
>
> m = number of forecasts of horizon n
>
> n = forecast horizon (date for which forecast is made)
>
> t = period in which forecast is made

The MAE has the same units of measurement as the forecast errors themselves. These units of measurement may be dollar differences between actual and forecast data or they may be differences between forecast and actual growth rates.

The other summary error measure was developed by Henri Thiel. The Thiel coefficient is, the square root of the ratio of the sum of squared forecast errors to the sum of squared actual changes,

$$u = \sqrt{\frac{\displaystyle\sum_{t=1}^{m} (e_{t+n})^2}{\displaystyle\sum_{t=1}^{m} (A_{t+n} - A_t)^2}}$$

where

> e = forecast error
>
> A = actual value of variable
>
> m = number of forecasts of horizon n
>
> n = forecast horizon
>
> t = period in which forecast is made

The Thiel coefficient has the following significant characteristics. First, it is

[8]S. K. McNees, "An Evaluation of Economic Forecasts," *New England Economic Review*, pp. 3–39, Federal Reserve Bank of Boston, November/December 1975.

based on squared errors, not simple errors. Large errors are penalized out of proportion to their size. Second, the Thiel coefficient is a relative measure. It is the ratio of the squared errors to the squared actual changes. Thus, the Thiel coefficient is 0 only when all forecast elements are on target and is 1 only when the forecasts are as accurate as a simple no-change extrapolation. Third, using a simple no-change extrapolation as the standard of comparison, the Thiel coefficient permits a comparison of forecasting accuracy between different forecast models across the forecast variables. Finally, the Thiel coefficient can be decomposed to show the importance of various sources of forecast error such as bias.

Table 10.1 shows the use of MAEs to assess the relative accuracy of six large-scale econometric models and a judgment survey over the span from the third quarter of 1970 to the second quarter of 1974. Evaluated in this table are forecast outputs by a combination of members by the American Statistical Association and the regular survey panel of the National Bureau of Economic Research, the Bureau of Economic Analysis of the United States Department of Commerce, Chase Econometrics, Inc., Data Resources Inc., Princeton professor Roy C. Fair's short-run forecasting model of the United States,

Table 10.1 Mean absolute errors in forecasts of inflation
Percent of annual rate

Horizon: Econometric model	Period of forecast, quarters				
	1	2	3	4	Average
Span: III1970 to II1974					
ASA/NBER	1.7	1.7	1.7	1.7	1.7
BEA	1.4	1.5	1.7	1.7	1.6
Chase	1.4	1.8	1.8	1.6	1.7
DRI	1.8	1.8	1.7	1.7	1.7
Fair	2.0	2.1	2.1	2.1	2.1
GE	1.1*	1.4*	1.4*	1.4*	1.3*
Wharton	1.1*	1.6	1.8	1.8	1.5
Quarterly changes: III1970 to II1974					
ASA/NBER	1.7	2.1	2.6	2.6	2.2
BEA	1.4	1.9	2.6	2.6	2.1
Chase	1.4	2.5	2.3	2.3*	2.1
DRI	1.8	2.4	2.5	2.8	2.3
Fair	2.0	2.6	2.8	3.1	2.6
GE	1.1*	1.7*	2.2*	2.3*	1.8*
Wharton	1.1*	2.1	2.8	2.7	2.1

*Best.

Source: S. K. McNees, "How Accurate Are Economic Forecasts?" *New England Economic Review*, November/December, 1974.

General Electric's economic staff, and the Wharton School's Economic Fore-casting Unit. The Fair forecast model is designed to operate without the interference of the model-builder's judgment. It is a modified "naive forecast" which "rides the trend." The ASA/NBER forecasts are judgment based, yet there is likely to be some influence on the panelists by the output of some of the large-scale models. The GE model involves an interplay of econometrics and economic judgment. The GE economics staff uses an iterative process in which initial values are obtained from smaller econometric models but the final results are derived from a strong interplay among the experiences, instincts, and intuition of economists specialized in all the important sectors of the national economy. The GE, Chase, DRI, and Wharton models produce outputs which are sold as a service to an increasingly large number of business and government clients.

The GE model, in this comparison, had the least MAE both on a span and on a quarterly change basis. The Fair naive forecast had the largest MAE in both cases. But, before the score is counted, it will be useful to look at the Thiel coefficients for the same array of forecasts for the same time span. Table 10.2 shows the Thiel coefficients, using the Fair forecast as a standard of compari-son. Recalling that the closer the Thiel coefficient is to 0, the more accurate is the forecast, it is apparent that the GE forecast with the five lowest values among the ten forecast variables is the best. But note that, in the inventory investment forecast, it was the worst and that in the unemployment rate forecast, its performance was worse than that of the Fair naive forecast. The average performance of the commercial forecasts (GE, Chase, DRI, and Wharton) was consistently better than the Fair naive forecast on nine of the forecast variables but on the unemployment rate was significantly worse.

Table 10.2 Thiel coefficients, using Fair forecast as comparison standard
III1970 to II1974

Forecast variable	Fair	BEA	Chase	DRI	GE	Wharton	ASA/NBER	Commercial
Growth rates								
Nominal GNP	.1914	.1467	.1211	.1539	.1134*	.1576	.1561	.1365
Real GNP	.4815	.3777	.3315	.3307	.3005	.2770*	.3468	.3099
Inflation	.5311	.4173	.3927	.4301	.3496*	.4146	.4255	.3967
Dollar values								
Residential construction	.8734	.6400	.7252	.5963	.6461	.4493*		.6042
Business fixed investment	.3967	.2912	.1937*	.3678	.3866	.2478		.2983
Consumption								
Total	.1840	.1901	.1908	.1582	.1327*	.1428		.1561
Durables	.5611	.5943	.5299	.4896	.4608*	.5738	.5347	.5134
Nondurables	.1919	.1653	.2117	.1964	.1414*	.1691		.1794
Inventories	.9962	.9483	.9093	.8826	1.1080	.8394	.8348*	.9348
Unemployment Rate	.6833	.5420*	.5868	.5785	.6048	1.0420	.6483	.7030

*Best.

Moreover, the commercial forecasts did better on four of the six variables on which the combined panels of ASA and NBER were polled. Wharton appears to be the next best of the commercial forecasts after GE. In no case was the Fair naive forecast superior to either the large-scale econometric models or to the judgmental forecast. However, the judgment forecast was superior in respect to inventory investment forecasts. By the way, McNees[9] found in a test of the St. Louis model from IV1969 to II1972 that it had higher MAEs than did the Fair model.

It is not entirely fair to judge a forecast output on one such set of comparisons. More important, these measures leave out the turning point. The Federal Reserve Bank of Boston ended its survey at the second quarter of 1974. It is now well known that a serious economic crisis, the worst since the end of the depression of the 1930s, was developing then. But not one of these forecasting services picked up the turning point. Thus, forecast accuracy was vitiated by the failure to predict what to management would have been much more important than the actual value of any forecast variable or the rate of change. To have known that a serious recession was to begin by the third quarter of 1974 would have been vital information.

Input-Output Forecasting

A Leontieff input-output econometric model (I/O) has at least two advantages over other large-scale econometric models. The linear equation system in the Leontieff model can absorb a vaster array of data than other models. As such, it is much more detailed and probably more realistic. Moreover, input-output models yield a more accurate picture of interindustry dependencies. The major disadvantage of I/O is that because of the complexities and costs of data collection, tables of technical coefficients are late in being developed; the most recent table available is 1972.

As early as the 1950s, Western Electric was obtaining reasonably good forecasting results with I/O. Later the A. D. Little Co., Clopper Almon at the University of Maryland, the Batelle Institute, General Electric, IBM, and North American Rockwell developed and used ambitious and comprehensive applications of I/O in forecasting. At A. D. Little, Inc., a management consulting firm, an I/O model is used annually to provide forecasts for more than forty corporate clients. These forecasts cover between 215 and 230 series for the year ahead, in current and constant dollars.

In I/O forecasting there are two basic tasks. One is to update the data input and the second is to change the technical coefficient matrix. A. D. Little provides not only a forecast in as much detail as its clients desire but also interpretations of I/O output. Realistic forecasts by I/O methods require forecasts of the likely structural shifts in the economy that will take place over time. In effect, this requires estimates of the changing size and position of given

[9]S. K. McNees, "A Comparison of the GNP Forecasting Accuracy of the Fair and the St. Louis Econometric Models," *New England Economic Review*, pp. 29–34, Federal Reserve Bank of Boston, September/October 1973.

industries. There are also quarterly I/O forecasts available. Yost and Stowell[10] have shown how such forecasts can be used to evaluate corporate profit center performance by adjusting actual performance to reflect changes in the business environment.

Input-Output Structure

There are two kinds of linear equations in I/O. The first is a demand or output equation

$$X_1 = [x_{11} + x_{12} + x_{13} + \ldots x_{1n}] + [x_{1C} + x_{1I} + x_{1G}]$$

where

X_1 = output of industry 1

x_{ij} = output of industry i as supplied to industry j

$\left.\begin{array}{l} x_{1C} \\ x_{1I} \\ x_{1G} \end{array}\right\}$ = output of industry 1 as supplied to final-use sectors, such as consumption, investment and government

The first set of brackets in the equation includes the interindustry allocation of industry 1's output and the second set of brackets includes the final-use allocation. The equation is an accounting identity and requires, as it turns out, intensive statistical analysis to break down the x_{ij}'s by SIC industries.

In an I/O matrix, the demand equations are read as rows and there are as many demand equations as there are industries (and value-added sectors). The vertical sum of the first set of brackets of these demand equations constitutes the interindustry demand, that is, the demand of each and every industry for the output of each and every industry. The vertical sum of the second set of brackets is the GNP, decomposed by industry.

Then there are supply or production functions, such as

$$X_1 = [x_{11} + x_{21} + x_{31} \ldots x_{m1}] + [x_{v1} + x_{y1} + \cdots x_{z1}]$$

where

X_1 = total output of industry 1

x_{ji} = amounts purchased from the jth industry by the ith industry

$\left.\begin{array}{l} x_{v1} \\ x_{y1} \\ x_{z1} \end{array}\right\}$ = inputs of labor, capital, and other nonproduced inputs (or value-added inputs)

These equations are columns in the Leontieff I/O matrix. The horizontal sum of the first set of brackets of these equations is the set of input requirements of each and every industry for the output of each and every industry and sector.

[10]S. W. Yost and C. E. Stowell, *Using Input/Output Analysis for Evaluating Profit Center Performance*, Paper for the Institute for Management Sciences, London Conference, July 1970.

Table 10.3 Hypothetical input/output table

Output → Input Industry	Intermediate sector 1	2	3	4	Final demand sector	Total output
1	20	25	15	80	60	200
2	0	25	0	120	105	250
3	0	25	45	40	40	150
4	0	0	0	80	320	400
V	180	175	90	80		
X	200	250	150	400		

The horizontal sum of the second set of brackets of these equations constitutes the industrial value-added components of the economy.

The relationship between the dependence of industry 1 on the output of any other industry j is given by dividing input requirement x_{1j} by the output of industry 1, X_1,

$$\frac{x_{1j}}{X_1} = a_{1j}$$

The resultant is a technical input/output coefficient. It is called "technical" because the industry requirements' column in the I/O matrix clearly reveals the technology of production. The entire submatrix x_{ij} may be replaced by the submatrix a_{ij}. It follows, of course, that

$$x_{1j} = a_{ij}X_1$$

The a_{ij} or technical coefficient submatrix is the heart of the I/O system. Each a_{ij} is dependent on the actual values of x_{ij} and X_1. Updating the a_{ij} submatrix requires continuous new information about these values, but they are only obtained on a massive basis once every five years from the economic censuses. Yet, as Almon and others have shown, there are ways of updating the a_{ij} matrix with a reasonable degree of accuracy. One thing is certain: Leontieff's original assertion that the a_{ij} matrix did not change (very much) over time is not realistic.

The a_{ij} matrix is changed in three ways. One is by the addition of new industries requiring new sets of input requirements and new production functions as well as adjustments in demand equations. Another is by the change in the actual and usually therefore the relative values of the inputs and outputs. The last is by splitting up industries to reflect more detailed and more realistic definitions of industries.

Further, account must be taken of ripple effects in the I/O matrix. A useful distinction can be made between direct technical coefficients which are derived by successively adjusting across each row and down each column for any given unit change in the value of X_1. Obviously, for example, a $1 billion increase in

Table 10.4 Technical coefficient matrix, a_{ij}

Output → Input ↓		1	2	3	4
	1	0.1	0.1	0.1	0.2
	2	0	0.1	0	0.3
	3	0	0.1	0.3	0.1
	4	0	0	0	0.2
	V	0.9	0.7	0.6	0.3

aircraft output means initially a change of a_{1j} times X_1 (where the aircraft industry is industry 1). But an increase in the demand for industry j's output means that industry j will have to expand its output. That will require industry j to buy more of industry 1 and many other industries. And so on through the system. The total technical coefficient has taken account of these ripple effects.

The solution techniques for I/O involve treating some of the variables as exogenous—usually some or all of the GNP or final demand components—and others as endogenous.For example, suppose that Table 10.3 is the hypothetical I/O array for the United States in a recent year. There are four industries. In the second quadrant, the interindustry matrix shows as rows the output distribution of each industry so that industry 1 supplies $20 billion of its output to itself, $25 billion to industry 2, $15 billion to industry 3, and $80 billion to industry 4. The remaining $60 billion is supplied to consumers, to government, and to business for investment and inventory buildup, and some is exported. The sum of the intermediate (or interindustry) sector and the final-demand (or demands of GNP) sector is the total output of industry 1. Likewise, the rows are the demands of the individual industries and the final-demand sector for each of the other industries. The V (or value-added) row is the sum of the demands of the individual industries for labor, capital, and other nonproduced inputs.

Table 10.4, the technical coefficient matrix, was derived by dividing the cell component in each column by the sum of the column. With the technical coefficient matrix, we can state the demand equations for each industry as

$$X_1 = (0.1X_1 + 0.1X_2 + 0.1X_3 + 0.2X_4) + 60$$
$$X_2 = (\qquad 0.1X_2 \qquad + 0.3X_4) + 105$$
$$X_3 = (\qquad 0.1X_2 + 0.3X_3 = 0.1X_4) + 40$$
$$X_4 = (\qquad\qquad 0.2X_4) + 320$$

Table 10.5 Assume changes in final-demand sector

Industry	% change	Forecast final demand for 1980
1	+20	72
2	−15	89.25
3	+30	52
4	+10	352
Net	7.6	565.25

Table 10.6 Solving an I/O problem by iteration

	x_1 60	x_2 105	x_3 40	x_4 320
First iteration				
Second iteration	$+0.1x_1$ 6.0 $+0.1x_2$ 10.5 $+0.1x_3$ 4.0 $+0.2x_4$ 64.0 84.5 Δx_1 144.5	$+0.1x_2$ 10.5 $+0.3x_4$ 96.0 106.5 Δx_2 211.5	$+0.1x_2$ 10.5 $+0.3x_3$ 12.0 $+0.3x_4$ 32.0 54.5 Δx_3 94.5	$+0.2x_4$ 64.0 Δx_4 384.0
Third iteration	$+0.1x_1$ 8.45 $+0.1x_2$ 10.65 $+0.1x_3$ 5.45 $+0.2x_4$ 12.80 37.35 Δx_1 181.85	$+0.1x_2$ 10.65 $+0.3x_4$ 19.20 29.85 Δx_2 241.35	$+0.1x_2$ 10.65 $+0.3x_3$ 16.35 $+0.1x_4$ 6.40 34.40 Δx_3 127.98	$+0.2x_4$ 12.8 Δx_4 396.8
Fourth iteration	$+0.1x_1$ 3.74 $+0.1x_2$ 2.99 $+0.1x_3$ 3.44 $+0.2x_4$ 2.56 12.73 Δx_1 194.58	$+0.1x_2$ 2.99 $+0.3x_4$ 3.84 6.83 Δx_2 248.18	$+0.1x_2$ 2.99 $+0.3x_3$ 10.32 $+0.1x_4$ 1.28 14.59 Δx_3 142.49	$+0.2x_4$ 2.56 Δx_4 399.36
Fifth iteration	$+1.0x_1$ 1.27 $+0.1x_2$ 0.68 $+0.1x_3$ 1.46 $+0.2x_4$ 0.51 3.92 Δx_1 198.50	$+0.1x_2$ 0.68 $+0.3x_4$ 6.77 1.45 Δx_2 249.63	$+0.1x_2$ 0.68 $+0.3x_3$ 4.35 $+0.1x_4$ .26 5.29 Δx_3 147.78	$+0.2x_4$ 0.51 Δx_4 399.87
Final answer	200.00	250.00	150.00	400.00

Table 10.7   Forecast of industry output

Industry	1980 forecast/output, billions	Percent change
1	$ 224	12
2	$ 246	−1.6
3	$ 171.5	14.3
4	$ 440	10
Total	$1081.5	8.2

Table 10.5 shows a forecast of changes in the final-demand sectors as follows: This forecast amounted to a predicted increase of 7.6 percent in GNP for the forecast period. The problem is to determine the impact of this forecast increase on each industry's output. In essence this solution is relatively easy and is presented as an illustration of the development of an I/O forecast. Obviously, computer programs are readily available, but the basic mathematical solution is by matrix inversion.

The method used in Table 10.6 is an iterative algorithm for simultaneous equations. In the demand equations, we replace the original final-demand components by the forecast components and begin the solution process by taking these forecast components as the values of the industry output which is to be forecast. That gives a first estimate. The results of this first estimate, each multiplied by the appropriate a_{ij} and added horizontally, yield an increment in the industry output. This increment, added to the initial or opening estimate, yields a second estimate of industry output. Then, in each successive iteration, the indicated increments times the appropriate a_{ij} will, when added horizontally, yield a further increment. As is apparent, these increments decline in size and the industry output estimates begin to emerge.

Table 10.7 contains the forecast of industry output. An average 7.6 percent increase in final demand for industry output will yield an average 8.2 percent increase in total industry output. Note particularly that while the final demand for the output of industry 2 is forecast to decrease by 15 percent, output in that industry will decrease by only 1.6 percent. Though it is a major part of the GNP, it is an even more important part of the inputs of the intermediate (or interindustry) sector.

Comparison of I/O with Econometric Forecasting

I/O provides complete, compared with partial, forecasts obtained with other econometric models. The other models estimate their functions by stochastic variables or error terms and use time-series or cross-sectional data. I/O begins with total information and to the extent that the linear general equilibrium assumptions implicit in the I/O models are reasonable, the forecast results will be consistent and accurate.

More important, the kind of detail possible from I/O forecasting gets very close to microeconomic forecasting. It is more likely to be of use to corporate management than a pure situation forecast. Theoretically, it is quite possible to get down to six-, seven-, eight-, or nine-digit SIC industries. The theory fails only because of the complexity of obtaining data. When data are available as they sometimes are for individual corporations, they can develop I/O models of their own operations. But preparing the data for use at the national level has thus far proved too costly and too time consuming.

Testing with Sensitivity in I/O

It is possible to use I/O to answer "what if" questions. What if the pace of growth of the economy slows down? What if the structure of the economy changes in a certain way? What happens if industry X introduces a new product next year? I/O can provide the basis for spelling out a variety of possible scenarios.

For example, we can focus on residential construction[11] which, during most of the 1970s, was a relatively weak sector and inquire what would have happened if housing demand had increased by, say, 10 percent. Further, we can ask what difference it would have made if this 10 percent demand-for-housing increase were met by high-rise apartment construction, or mobile homes, or walk-up apartments, or two-to-four-unit structures, all in contrast with single-family houses.

Table 10.8 shows the direct requirements per dwelling unit from the 1963 national I/O table. They show that in terms of materials and services as well as value added, single-family house units have a greater effect on the demand for

[11]A. H. Young and C. M. Ball, "Industrial Impacts of Residential Construction and Mobile Home Production," *Survey of Current Business, 10*:14–17, October 1970.

Table 10.8   Direct requirements per dwelling unit in 1963 dollars

Single-family house			
A. Materials	6,044	B. Services	3,359
Millwork	544	Wholesale trade	981
Ready mixed concrete	509	Retail trade	676
Sawmills & planing mills	485	Miscellaneous professional	
Prefabricated wood structures	317	services	462
Veneer & plywood	304	Real estate	298
Metal doors, sash & trim	268	Railroads & related services	259
Blast furnaces & basic steel		All other	683
products	221	C. Value added	5,685
Concrete products, n.e.c.	209	D. Total (A+B+C)	15,088
Forest, greenhouse & nursery			
products	185		
Heating equipment, except			
electrical	178		
All other	2,824		

Table 10.8 Direct requirements per dwelling unit in 1963 dollars (continued)

Two- to four-unit structure		Walk-up apartment	
A. Materials	3,800	A. Materials	4,107
Sawmills & planing mills	483	Ready mixed concrete	260
Ready mixed concrete	318	Metal doors, sash & trim	255
Veneer & plywood	203	Sawmills & planing mills	193
Metal doors, sash & trim	181	Sheet metal work	183
Millwork	165	Millwork	181
Blast furnaces & basic steel		Blast furnaces & basic steel	
products	150	products	174
Wood household furniture	135	Forest, greenhouse & nursery	
Heating equipment, except		products	152
electrical	121	Architectural metal work	136
Concrete block & brick	99	Gypsum products	132
Forest, greenhouse & nursery		Heating equipment, except	
products	97	electrical	131
All other	1,848	All other	2,310
B. Services	2,327	B. Services	1,992
Wholesale trade	740	Wholesale trade	482
Retail trade	511	Retail trade	463
Miscellaneous professional		Miscellaneous professional	
services	382	services	390
Railroads & related services	208	Railroads & related services	139
Motor freight transportation		Motor freight transportation	130
& warehousing	140	All other	389
All other	346	C. Value added	3,898
C. Value added	3,871	D. Total (A+B+C)	9,998
D. Total (A+B+C)	9,998		

High-rise apartment		Mobile home	
A. Materials	4,885	A. Materials	2,272
Ready mixed concrete	550	Veneer & plywood	268
Metal doors, sash & trim	498	Millwork	206
Sheet metal work	293	Motor vehicles & parts	202
Miscellaneous metal work	264	Aluminum rolling and drawing	194
Blast furnaces & basic steel		Heating equipment, except	
products	176	electrical	144
Architectural metal work	153	Metal doors, sash & trim	141
Wiring devices	152	Sawmills & planing mills	112
Gypsum products	149	Blast furnaces & basic steel	
Elevators & moving stairways	145	products	107
Pipe, valves & pipe fittings	120	Electric housewares, fans	91
All other	2,385	Coated fabrics not rubberized	78
B. Services	2,141	All other	729
Miscellaneous professional		B. Services	1,148
services	471	Retail trade	567
Wholesale trade	452	Wholesale trade	315
Retail trade	449	Railroads & related services	56
Motor freight transportation		Motor freight transportation	51
& warehousing	157	Business travel entertainment	
Railroads & related services	116	& gifts	49
All other	496	All other	110
C. Value added	4,615	C. Value added	1,123
D. Total (A+B+C)	11,641	D. Total (A+B+C)	4,543

Table 10.9 Sales of two selected industries to their customers per dwelling unit in 1963, dollars

A. Sales of the plastics materials and resins industry to other industries

Type of unit	Total	New construction	Mobile homes	Coated fabrics not rubberized	Veneer and plywood	Paints and allied products	Miscellaneous plastic products	Asbestos products	All other industries
Single-family house	96	0	0	1	4	13	43	9	26
Two- to four-unit structure	64	0	0	1	2	8	29	7	17
Walk-up apartment	60	0	0	1	1	8	22	7	21
High-rise apartment	69	0	0	1	1	9	30	4	24
Mobile home	50	0	0	8	3	5	21	(*)	13

B. Sales of the railroads and related services industry to other industries

Type of unit	Total	New construction	Mobile homes	Sawmills and planing mills	Industrial inorganic, organic chemicals	Ready-mixed concrete	Blast furnaces and basic steel products	Primary aluminum	All other industries
Single-family house	479	259	0	13	3	18	20	2	164
Two- to four-unit structure	344	208	0	10	2	11	13	2	98
Walk-up apartment	274	139	0	4	2	10	18	2	99
High-rise apartment	284	116	0	2	3	19	26	4	114
Mobile home	128	0	56	3	1	(*)	10	4	54

*Less than $0.50.

interindustry output. You will notice also that, whereas the largest suppliers for single-family construction are wood product industries, ready-mixed concrete, metal product industries, and greenhouse and nursery products, there is no wood product industry among the top ten suppliers of materials for high-rise apartments. Moreover, the top ten suppliers to the mobile home industry include four industries that are not among the top ten for any of the other types of new housing construction. But just as surprising is that the two largest direct suppliers to mobile home construction are wood product industries. It would make a good deal of difference to particular industries how the 10 percent housing-demand increase were met.

Table 10.9 concentrates on the plastics materials and resins industries and the railroad and related industries. Table 10.9 gives the sales in dollars for each additional dwelling unit by type of construction. It is apparent that single-family construction would represent for the plastics industry twice as much additional demand as mobile home construction. But, for the railroads, single-family construction would mean more than three times more demand than that for mobile homes.

Other Uses of I/O

I/O can also be used for flow and structural analysis as well as sorting and screening. For example, during the energy crisis of the early 1970s, when it became evident that there might be a possible lack of petrochemical feedstock, A. D. Little[12] used I/O to determine what direct petrochemical inputs the chemical industries required and what industrial and employment repercussions would occur if these inputs turned out to be in short supply. A. D. Little has also sorted all industries, on the basis of their energy-intensiveness or usage, and can array about 40,000 markets by perhaps as many as 20 different key configurations. This sorting and screening process makes it possible to forecast direct market impacts of particular corporate decisions, especially if these are the decisions of large-market suppliers.

Indicator Approach to Forecasting

Each month, *Business Conditions Digest*, a publication of the Statistical Indicators Division of the United States Department of Commerce, presents the key economic indicators. Table 10.10 shows a recent cross-classification of these indicators by economic process and cyclical timing.

The underlying model of economic activity in which the concept of economic indicators has relevance is that of the business cycle, a set of alternating periods of expansion and contraction in aggregate economic

---

[12]A. A. Gols, "The Use of Input-Output in Industrial Planning," *Business Economics,* *10*(3):19–27, May 1975.

Table 10.10 Cross-classification of cyclical indicators by economic process and cyclical timing

Economic process: Cyclical timing	I. Employment and unemployment (13 series)	II. Production, income, consumption and trade (9 series)	III. Fixed capital investment (14 series)	IV. Inventories and inventory investment (9 series)	V. Prices, costs, and profits (14 series)	VI. Money and credit (20 series)
Leading indicators (40 series)	Marginal employment adjustments (5 series)		Formation of business enterprises (2 series) New investment commitments (8 series)	Inventory investment and purchasing (7 series)	Sensitive commodity prices (1 series) Stock prices (1 series) Profits and profit margins (5 series) Cash flows (2 series)	Flows of money and credit (7 series) Credit difficulties (2 series)
Roughly coincident indicators (26 series)	Job vacancies (1 series) Comprehensive employment (3 series) Comprehensive unemployment (3 series)	Comprehensive production (3 series) Comprehensive income (2 series) Comprehensive consumption and trade (4 series)	Backlog of investment commitments (2 series)		Comprehensive wholesale prices (2 series)	Bank reserves (1 series) Interest rates (5 series)
Lagging indicators (13 series)	Long-duration unemployment (1 series)		Investment expenditures (2 series)	Inventories (2 series)	Unit labor costs (3 series)	Outstanding debt (2 series) Interest rates (3 series)

Source: Business Conditions Digest, p. 2, May 1976.

activity. The indicators are used to forecast turning points. As a result of the work of the National Bureau of Economic Research, there is general agreement about how these turning-point indicators trace out the cyclical movements of the economy.

Indicators use economic time series. Some of these time series are leading in the sense that they normally tend to anticipate the turning points in the cycle. Others are coincident with the turning points. Still others are lagging with respect to the turning points.

Composite Indicator Series

A composite indicator series provides a simple summary measure of the average behavior of selected groups of indicators. Each component of such a series or index is weighted according to its value in forecasting or identifying short-term movements in aggregate economic activity. The components are standardized mathematically so that, apart from their relative weights, each has an equal opportunity to influence the composite index.

The Composite Index of Leading Indicators (CLI) is widely used because it tends to forecast turning points with reliability.

Included in the CLI in 1976 were average work week of production workers in manufacturing, index of net business formation, index of stock prices of 500 common stocks, index of new building permits for private housing units, layoff rate (inverted) in manufacturing, new orders in 1967 dollars for consumer goods and materials, contracts and orders in 1967 dollars for plant and equipment, net change in 1967 dollars (smoothed) of inventories on hand and on order, percentage change in sensitive prices in the wholesale price index of crude materials excluding foodstuffs and feed (smoothed), vendor performance as percentage of companies reporting slower deliveries, money balance (M_1) in 1967 dollars, and percentage change in total liquid assets (smoothed).

The rationale behind the weighting structure of the CLI reflects the general opinion among economists that in most circumstances a combination of forecasts is more accurate than any single model taken by itself. The weights used for combining these elements are based upon relative forecast errors or other objective method which stresses desirable statistical attributes.

In Table 10.11 is a scorecard that Boschan and Zarnowitz[13] developed on the record of the CLI in forecasting turning points from 1948 through 1975.

If the lead time is only a few months, the CLI is not very helpful since there is a one-month reporting lag. This is especially true with an unusually long lead time, because the peak may be rather difficult to adjust for if there is a danger of serious inflation. By and large, available evidence suggests that the CLI is a reasonably good forecast tool for discerning turning points.

[13]C. Boschan and V. Zarnowitz, "Cyclical Indicators: An Evaluation and New Leading Indicators," *Business Conditions Digest*, May 1975. See also I. Broder and H. O. Stekler, "Forecasting with a Deflated Index of Leading Series," *New England Economic Review*, September/October 1975.

Table 10.11   Official leads and lags of the composite leading index at cyclical turning points, 1948–1975

Peak	Lead(−) or lag(+) in months	Trough	Lead(−) or lag(+) in months
November 1948	*	October 1949	−4
July 1953	−4	May 1954	−6
August 1957	−23	April 1958	−2
April 1960	−12	February 1961	−2
December 1969	−11	November 1970	−1
November 1973	−5	March 1975	0

*Not available.

Using the CLI as a Forecast Model

Harris and Jamroz[14] of the Federal Reserve Bank of New York evaluated the CLI as a general forecasting model. For the periods I-1953 through II-1970 and III-1970 through I-1976, they developed the following forecast equations.

I-1953 through II-1970:

$$\% \Delta \text{ Real GNP}_t = \underset{(7.32)}{2.89} + \underset{(6.30)}{.21} \ (\% \Delta \text{ CLI})_{t-1} \qquad \begin{array}{l} R^2 = .37 \\ SEE = 3.24 \end{array}$$

III-1970 through I-1976:

$$\% \Delta \text{ Real GNP}_t = \underset{(2.98)}{1.67} + \underset{(4.59)}{.48} \ (\% \Delta \text{ CLI})_{t-1} \qquad \begin{array}{l} R^2 = .24 \\ SEE = 3.56 \end{array}$$

Numbers in parentheses are t statistics; SEE = standard error of estimate of forecast coefficient.

For the earlier period, percentage changes in the CLI in one quarter explained 37 percent of the variation in real GNP in the following quarter, and, for the later period, about 24 percent of the variations in real GNP were explained. Normally, in equations measuring percentage rather than absolute or level changes, R^2's are lower. These equations were designed to forecast with a lag of one quarter but when models using two quarter lags were tried, their results were substantially worse. As a forecasting model, the CLI has a very short lead time.

When compared to large-scale econometric models, Harris and Jamroz found, the CLI model had lower MAEs than the Fair model, but somewhat higher MAEs than those of DRI, Chase, Wharton, or GE. McNees reported a composite MAE of 1.9 percent for his forecast sample through II-1974, while for the same period the MAE for CLI was 2.9 percent. Harris and Jamroz recommended that because large econometric models are costly and results

[14]M. N. Harris and D. Jamroz, "Evaluating the Leading Indicators," *Monthly Review of the Federal Reserve Bank of New York*, 6:165–171, June 1976.

often reflect adjustment of the pure model with information not included in the model, forecasters should at least use the CLI in combination. The CLI performed well enough to make it a good substitute for the DRI, Chase, or Wharton models.

Indicators will remain useful so long as models use economic information and data directly rather than reactions to these data. Many of the indicators give economic information beyond the boundaries of most models. For example, indicators are available monthly, while the data used by the large-scale models are seldom available more often than quarterly. Some are available weekly and even daily. Hence, these data can be used for correcting the large-scale models, updating them, and providing for turning-point adjustments.

Technological Forecasting

Technological forecasting is that forecasting technique in which the focus is upon when and with what effect the products of a new technology will be introduced. In terms of the industrial structure, seen, for example, as an I/O matrix, the problem is one of adding—and, indeed, the timing of the adding—of one more industry. That one more industry will appear both as a row and a column and it will clearly affect the a_{ij} matrix as well as the final-demand and the value-added sectors. Moreover, the rate of growth of this new industry can be measured in terms of its income elasticity of demand which, if greater than unity, means that it will be becoming an ever larger share of the national economy and will be using an ever larger share of the nation's inputs, though it may affect the nation's imports as well. More than likely, there will be other industries for which income elasticities are very low and which are falling rapidly in their share of the nation's output.

We know that if, for example, a new technology introduces a product for which the income elasticity is, say, 1.3, then its Engel or share elasticity will be positive. For each 10 percent increase in total spending, the share going to this new product would increase by 3 percent. But the effect would not stop there. After all, the production function for the new product involves labor, land, capital, and the rest of the inputs. As demand for the new product grows, so will the demand for the inputs. If you read these inputs in the way a Leontieff production function would, you would be able to judge the impact of the new industry on each of the older industries as well. It would be possible by examining input utilization elasticities for each input (the effect of a 10 percent increase in total spending on the demand for inputs for this new industry or by I/O sensitivity analysis) to determine how it would affect the pattern of demand (and even the location of industries), this year and in the years to come.

Technological change is a structural change, a redistribution in the use, allocation, employment, and even location of inputs, as well as a change in the industrial complex. Technological forecasting will explain the rise of new cities and the decline of older ones. It will forecast, for example, effects on the balance of payments and changes in the structure of employment.

Raymond S. Isenson[15] developed a technological forecast equation,

$$K(T) = \int O^T I(t)\, dt$$

where

$K(T)$ = state of knowledge at time T

$I(t)$ = number of information units added during an increment of time. This expression is also a function of time

He points out that, in the most general case, where the forecaster is simply trying to measure advancing technology in the broadest sense,

$$I(t) = n(t) \times p(t) \times Q$$

where

$n(t)$ = number of scientists actively engaged in research at time t

$p(t)$ = probability that a scientist will make a contribution during a given year

Q = productivity factor

Floyd,[16] Fisher and Pry,[17] Blackman,[18] as well as Sharif and Kabir,[19] have worked out more specific models for forecasting technological substitution. The mathematical formulations for these models are

Blackman: $\quad \ln \dfrac{f}{F} = C_1 + C_2 t$

Fisher and Pry: $\quad \dfrac{f}{1-f} = \exp 2\,\alpha\,(t-t_0)$

Floyd: $\quad \ln \dfrac{f}{F-f} + \dfrac{F}{F-f} = C_1 + C_2 t$

Sharif and Kabir: $\quad \ln \dfrac{f}{1-f} + \sigma\, \dfrac{1}{1-f} = C_1 + C_2 t$

where

f = market share of product at time t

F = upper limit of market share

[15]R. S. Isenson, "Technological Forecasting in Perspective," *Management Science,* 2:B70–B83, October 1966.

[16]A. Floyd, "Trend Forecasting: A Methodology for Figure of Merit," in *Proceedings of the First Annual Technology and Management Conference,* J. Bright (ed.), Englewood Cliffs, N.J., Prentice-Hall, 1968.

[17]J. C. Fisher and R. Pry, "A Simple Substitution Model of Technological Change," *Technology, Forecasting and Social Change,* 3:75–88, 1971.

[18]A. W. Blackman, "The Market Dynamics of Technological Substitutions," *Technology, Forecasting and Social Change,* 6:41–63, 1974.

[19]M. N. Sharif and C. Kabir, "A Generalized Model for Forecasting Technological Substitution," *Technology, Forecasting and Social Change,* 8:353–364, 1976.

t = time measured in standard units
t_0 = time at which technological substitution is half-complete
2α = slope of the regression lines
$\left.\begin{array}{c} C_1 \\ C_2 \end{array}\right\}$ = constants
σ = dimensionless factor, positive but less than unity

These equations specify the shape of S-shaped growth curves, such as those in Fig. 10.2. In effect, the higher the value of σ, the flatter the growth curve; the closer to zero the value of σ, the more S-like the growth curve.

In a more general sense, it can be shown that the changing slopes of the S-shaped growth curve reflect changing income elasticities and that the point of inflection in these curves is when the Engel share elasticity shifts from positive to negative values. The problem remains, with this and similar analyses, that while it is useful in predicting structural changes in the economy once the nature and time of introduction of the technology are known, we need to know more to be able to predict what will be introduced and when.

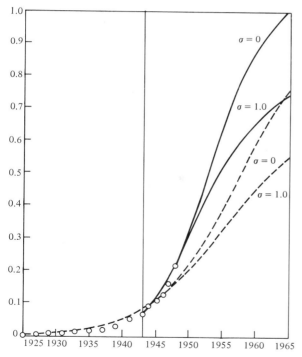

Figure 10.2. Substitution of diesel and electric locomotives for steam locomotives in American railroads. o, historical data; (dashed line, model predictions at $f = 0.2$ with available data from $f = 0.006$ (upper curve for $\sigma = 0$ and lower curve for $\sigma = 1.0$); solid line, model predictions at $f = 0.2$ with available data from $f = 0.08$ (upper curve for $\sigma = 0$ and lower curve for $\sigma = 1.0$). M. N. Sharif and C. Kabir, "A Generalized Model for Forecasting Technological Substitution," *Technology, Forecasting and Social Change*, 8:357, 1976.)

Delphi Forecasts

Delphi is one of several methods designed to answer this kind of question. Essentially it is a successive-panel method by which first the contours of possible change are obtained from a set of experts; then, iteratively, the likelihood, nature, and timing of appearance are determined. Like the Isenson method, Delphi is likely to project the development of what is already known but not yet in production.

The German electrical manufacturer Siemens has used the Delphi method in technological forecasting for many years. Siemens found that selection of experts is of overriding importance in the success of a Delphi study. The experts' answers must be analyzed with care. Siemens discovered that general agreement among the experts was not too valuable. More important was the direction answers took in the successive rounds of questions. The interaction between management and the experts provided a basis for effective use of forecasts. Siemens found the Delphi method expensive since the time of experts required high compensation. Indeed, the more valuable the answers derived from the Delphi study, the more costly was the study itself.

Long-Wave Forecasting

Nikolai Dmitriyevich Kondratyev, whose major work appeared in the 1920s, theorized the existence of a long wave of capitalist economic development extending over a period from forty to sixty years, averaging about fifty-five years. And though there has been some reluctance to accept long wave as a basis for short-range forecasting and its underlying assumption, there has recently been a resurgence of interest in long-wave analysis. Even the *Wall Street Journal* (October 14, 1974) noted that

> The Kondratyev wave idea can be applied to the United States economic record, going back at least into the late 18th century. Prices—and prosperity—increased markedly from the 1780s until just after the War of 1812, when an abrupt price drop occurred. This period constituted, under Kondratyev theory, a "primary" recession within the super-cycle. Then, until about 1819, a "plateau" period persisted in which prices declined only moderately and economic activity seemed to recover somewhat. But after that a deep "secondary" slump set in. Prices and economic activity declined sharply for a prolonged period of joblessness and business failures. The bottom did not come until the mid-1840s. Then a super-cycle expansion phase ensued, reaching a super-cycle peak around the end of the Civil War, half a century after the War of 1812.
>
> Kondratyev theory argues that after the Civil War peak a super-cycle pattern developed remarkably similar to the pattern after the War of 1812—a brief primary recession, a plateau until 1874, a prolonged secondary slump until 1896 and finally a period of renewed prosperity and rising prices until 1920.
>
> The price collapse and 18-month recession that began in July 1921, according to Kondratyev theory, marked still another primary recession within the super-cycle. The balance of the decade witnessed a plateau period. The Great Depres-

sion, until the late 1930s, marked a secondary-slump stage. A renewed expansion phase has been in progress since then, Kondratyev disciples contend, and it is due to end about now.

If such a view should prove correct, a relatively short-lived recession, in which prices will drop sharply, would appear to be in prospect now. Beyond that, until perhaps the early 1980s, a somewhat sluggish plateau stage would seem likely, to be followed by a deep secondary slump.

Jay W. Forrester of the MIT Sloan School of Management has developed a systems dynamic model incorporating the Kondratyev wave. In that model the Kondratyev long wave forecasts structural changes to take place in the economy. Pervasive nonlinear relationships such as the impacts of infrequent but periodic introductions of new energy sources (water power, steam, electricity, internal combustion engines) become the vehicles for innovation shocks. These innovation shocks generate broad changes in the pace of economic development and lead to long waves. They also change the social and especially the leadership structure of the nation. As they do so they rearrange the locational characteristics of industry, economic power, and urban development.

Forrester's model is a serious attempt to model the Kondratyev long wave. The Forrester model is capable of absorbing technological forecasts and using them to predict structural change. In early 1976, Forrester published preliminary findings from his research.[20]

1. Several and perhaps many simultaneous periodicities of economic fluctuation can exist in the economy at the same time.
2. Capital investment may have less to do with contributing to short-term business cycle movements than it has in generating longer-wave cycles such as that observed by Kondratyev.
3. The severity of the recession that took place from 1974 through 1976 may have been an indication that it was the top of a Kondratyev long wave of capital expansion.

Microanalytic Simulation

The newest approach to the construction of models of socioeconomic systems is the microanalytic approach developed by Guy Orcutt.[21] While of the same general statistical type as other models of national economies, microanalytic models are, nevertheless, general in terms of their statistical structure in that

[20]J. W. Forrester, "Business Structures, Economic Cycles and National Policy," *Business Economics*, *11*(1):13–24, January 1976. See also N. J. Mass, *Economic Cycles: An Analysis of Underlying Causes*, Cambridge, Wright-Allen Press, 1975.

[21]Guy Orcutt et al., *Policy Exploration Through Microanalytic Simulation*, Washington D.C., the Urban Institute, 1976. See also, G. H. Orcutt, H. W. Watts, and J. B. Edwards, "Data Aggregation and Information Loss," *The American Economic Review*, *53*:775–787, September 1968, and J. B. Edwards and G. H. Orcutt, "Should Aggregation Prior to Estimation be the Rule?" *The Review of Economics and Statistics*, *51*:409–420, November 1969.

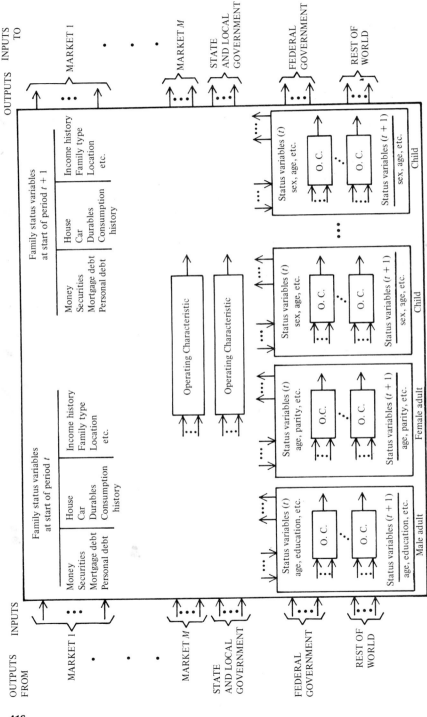

Figure 10.3. Incomplete flow diagram of a model of a nuclear family. (Guy H. Orcutt et al., *Microanalytic Simulation of American Family Behavior: A Tool for Policy Analysis*, Working Paper no. 509-5, Urban Institute, Washington D.C., August 1973.)

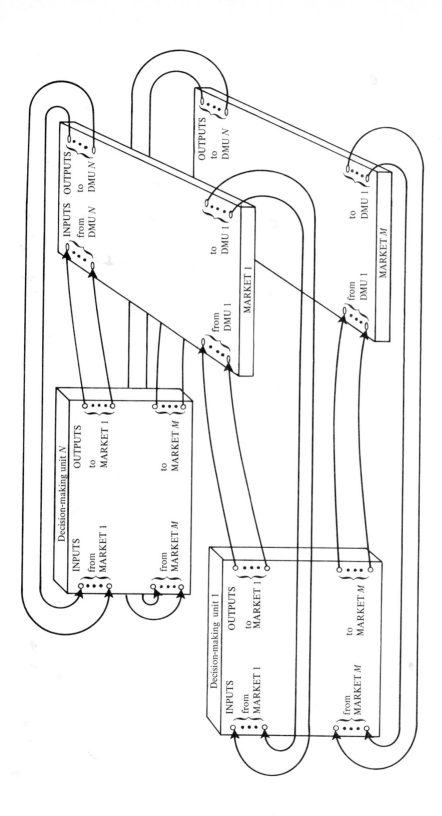

Figure 10.4. Incomplete flow diagram of a model of an economic system. (Guy H. Orcutt et al., *Microanalytic Simulation of American Family Behavior: A Tool for Policy Analysis*, Working Paper no. 509-5, Urban Institute, Washington D.C., August, 1973.)

they contain one or more populations of microunits such as individuals, families, and firms. Both the Leontieff type and the aggregate type of national income models contain but a single case of each kind of unit.

The key element of microanalytic modeling strategy is concern for modeling the behavior of persons, families, firms, and other microunits. The objective behind a microanalytic model is to represent an entire economy or social system as the interaction of the component populations of microunits. The concern for the behavior of individuals, as opposed to masses or aggregates, returns to a traditional economic perspective.

In microanalytic models of an economy the components represent recognizable entities met in everyday experience. The type of component occupying center stage is called a decision unit. Decision units include individuals, nuclear families, households, manufacturing firms, retailers, banks, insurance companies, labor unions, and local, state, and federal government units. Individuals are embedded within more extensive family or household units. Firms are embedded within industry units.

The decision units in microanalytic models interact with each other either directly or indirectly through a second major type of component called a market. The markets in a model represent markets in the economy, and it is through them that the third type of component flows from decision unit to decision unit.

Figure 10-3 illustrates how decision units such as persons are embedded in a more extensive decision unit, the family. Figure 10-4 shows how the outputs of an entire set of N decision units are transmitted and distributed by the M markets. The outputs of the decision units become inputs into the markets. After being summarized and distributed, they appear as outputs of the markets. These market outputs then become inputs into the decision units again.

Arguments Favoring a Microanalytic Strategy

Economists have gradually become aware of a variety of estimation and testing problems associated with the analysis of highly aggregative time-series data. Among these are problems associated with simultaneous equations, multicollinearity among explanatory variables, and autocorrelated error terms. Somewhat forgotten are problems associated with errors of observation. The presence of these problems seriously reduces the information available in aggregate time-series data for testing and estimation. No method of analysis is a substitute for evidence that has not been generated or that has been lost in aggregation. Even in the absence of statistical problems associated with use of national accounts data, the ratio of potential observations to parameters to be estimated is woefully small.

Anyone who recommends primary reliance upon estimation and testing based solely on the use of national accounts data is surely one of the world's greatest optimists. Highly aggregative time series simply do not contain enough degrees of freedom to permit extensive testing and estimation.

Microanalytic models were devised to improve estimation and testing possibilities. One central reason why they do this is that although many components are introduced, these components are replications of one or another of a small number of types.

In the analytic approach an attempt is made to deduce a relationship for each endogenous or output variable of the model. The set of such relationships is the general solution of the model. Specific solutions of a model are obtained by evaluating these functions for specific sets of endogenous variables for specific time periods, and for given values of initial conditions and exogenous variables.

MASS—A Microanalytic Simulation System

MASS (MicroAnalytic Simulation System) is a set of computer modules designed to implement microanalytic models. MASS modules are of several types. Model modules specify operating characteristics and identities, and the operating characteristic agenda (the order in which operating characteristics are applied). Other modules in MASS are service modules, which execute input, output, and statistical arithmetic. Control modules control the execution order of the program. A principal design goal of MASS is execution efficiency. The updating of variables by operating characteristics is performed in core. MASS is unadorned, almost to the point of being primitive. MASS is a collection of microsimulation modules. The modules are relatively independent of each other, so that modules can be added, deleted, or modified with ease.

The advantages of modular programming are efficiency and flexibility, program development and overlaying. One disadvantage: modular programming does entail overhead costs.

Applications of Microanalytic Forecasting

Fairly significant progress has been made in developing reasonably good forecasting in such fields as demographic analysis, including forecasts of geographic mobility, educational levels of segments of the population, family formation and dissolution. In labor force analysis where labor force participation rates, wage-rate impact, unemployment, transfer income (including welfare and unemployment-compensation payments), property income, income taxes, savings, and wealth behavior have been simulated with considerable success, microanalytic techniques have provided insights not possible otherwise. A recent intriguing use of microanalysis involved a study of the dependence of probability of death (by cause of death) on environment.[22]

Although applications are being developed constantly, it is still true that microanalysis despite its obvious advantages will be developing rather slowly as a substitute for other forms of econometric forecasting. Yet disenchantment

---

[22]Guy Orcutt, S. D. Franklin, R. Mendelsohn, and J. D. Smith, "Does Your Probability of Death Depend on Your Environment?" *American Economic Review*, February 1977.

with imprecision in such forecasts may step up the substitution of microanalysis for macroanalytic models.

Annual Review of Forecasts

For a number of years, the Federal Reserve Bank of Richmond has been publishing an annual review of forecasts. This booklet contains excerpts from econometric and judgmental forecasts from a wide variety of forecast producers. This review serves as a reference file of representative opinions. The advantage of the Richmond bank review is that forecast output can be compared. Many managements and most managerial economists use this report to check the accuracy of the report they have bought or produced against other forecast products. Particularly useful, too, is the detailed prose analysis of forecast logic underlying the work of many forecast producers.

Chapter Summary

Forecasting of the business environment in which vital managerial decisions must be made is a relatively rapidly expanding field of knowledge. Large-scale econometric models employing time-series analysis, linear regression analysis, judgmental inputs, computers, and complex algebra are in widespread use. In recent years major forecasting firms have expanded to supply forecasts to a large and growing list of corporate and governmental clients. While the typical situation forecast is macroeconomic in form and spells out the likely level and behavior of a series of macroeconomic variables such as GNP, employment, consumer price index, interest rates, consumer spending, and balance of payments, this macro forecast is used in microeconomic decision making. Frequently firms will supplement the macro forecast with a micro forecast based on internal relationships and data. The fact that forecasting is itself a successful industry indicates the need corporate managements feel for such inputs into their decision-making processes.

Given the demand for forecasts, a key question is their accuracy. At base, the accuracy question involves a trade-off between expensive forecast models with high costs and lower-cost models. Management will be willing to pay for the higher-cost model only if that expenditure consistently yields a significant increase in accuracy. The marginal revenue from forecast accuracy is set off against the marginal cost of attaining the required level of accuracy.

Input-output forecasting, despite its enormous appetite for data, promises to be the most accurate and relevant forecast model for corporate decision making. Technological forecasting is being incorporated more and more into corporate planning since it focuses on basic structural changes. And, in recent years, there has been a revival of interest in long-wave forecasting because of apparently increasing evidence that basic innovative shocks have changed the nature of the operation of the economic system.

Yet, whichever way management turns, the essence of the forecast problem is not whether to forecast; forecasting is unavoidable in a world of uncertainty. The essential question is how best to forecast. We are learning a good deal more in this area, now that management has given a high priority to its need for accurate forecasts.

Selected Readings

Behravesh, Nariman: "Forecasting Inflation: Does the Method Make a Difference?", *Business Review*, Federal Reserve Bank of Philadelphia, September/October 1976.

Blom, Hans, and Karl Steinbuch: *Technological Forecasting in Practice*, Lexington, Mass., Saxon House, 1973.

Brigham, E. F., and J. L. Pappas: *Managerial Economics*, 2d ed., Hinsdale, Ill., Dryden, 1976.

Butler, William F., and Robert A. Karesh (eds.): *How Business Economists Forecast*, Englewood Cliffs, N. J., Prentice-Hall, 1966.

Graham, D. A.: "A Geometrical Exposition of the Input-Output Analysis," *American Economic Review*, March 1975.

Klein, Lawrence R.: *An Essay on the Theory of Economic Prediction*, Chicago, Markham Publishing Co., 1971.

McNees, Stephen K.: "An Evaluation of Economic Forecasts," *New England Economic Review*, November/December 1975.

McNees, Stephen K.: "An Evaluation of Economic Forecasts: Extension and Update," *New England Economic Review*, September/October 1976.

Mincer, Jacob: *Economic Forecasts and Expectations*, New York, National Bureau of Economic Research, 1969.

Pindyck, R. S., and D. L. Rubinfeld: *Econometric Models and Economic Forecasts*, New York, McGraw-Hill, 1976.

Stekler, Herman O.: *Economic Forecasting*, New York, Praeger, 1970.

U.S. Department of Labor, Bureau of Labor Statistics: "The Structure of the U.S. Economy in 1980 and 1985," *Bulletin 18*:31, Washington, D.C., 1975.

Questions, Problems, and Projects

1. Robert Platt, senior economist with the Wall Street firm of Andersen and Co., argues that the forecasting task of the Wall Street economist differs from that of other business economists. "Over the last year," he said in 1974, "our portfolio strategy group has been developing a methodology which attempts to bridge the gap between traditional economic forecasts and forecasts of factors essential to investment decision making." One of the particularly serious problems Platt and his group faced was that of finding the appropriate trade-off between the degree of disaggregation needed to develop reasonably homogeneous industry definitions and the need to keep industry groupings large enough to find statistically stable macrorelationships. Comment on and suggest outlines for a trade-off as well as a method for solving Andersen and Co.'s forecasting and investment-analysis problems.

2. The following is an outline of the investment-decision process at the Security Pacific National Bank in Los Angeles. In what way is the forecast integrated into the investment decision? What other kinds of economic analysis are required for these decisions?

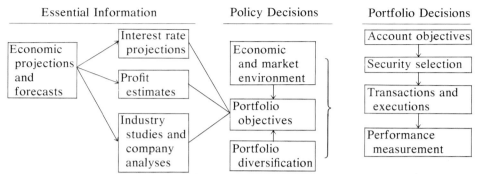

In this context, how does one evaluate the accuracy of a forecast in contrast with the correctness of an investment decision?

3. Data Resources, Inc., offers its clients an inflation monitoring service. In 1976 the main features of this service included:

(*a*) Forecasts of over 120 prices and wages out 10 quarters and 15 years, with alternative economic assumptions.

(*b*) Monthly analysis of price and market developments.

(*c*) On-line access to econometric models so that clients can incorporate their own information and generate different forecasts as well as test thoroughly and simulate DRI and their own models historically.

Suppose that an automobile company used this service and was faced with the problem of whether to switch from zinc die castings to plastic injections for decorative trim. What kinds of price information would the company need? What kinds of price forecasts and what kinds of industry reaction (by the zinc and the plastics industries, among others) would the car-maker want to use? In what sense is this kind of data a measure of inflation?

4. If you were going to build an econometric forecast model, your first question might be: What economic variables should I describe? You might also ask what economic theory had to say about the behavior of these variables. Or what do the data show about the past behavior of the variables? Take the relationship between disposable income and personal consumption expenditures and see what you can do.

5. Combustion Engineering has an input/output forecast model consisting of two basic parts:

(*a*) Technological coefficients supplied by Arthur D. Little and the United States Department of Commerce.

(*b*) Final demand (GNP) obtained from Arthur D. Little and L. D. Edie.

How would final demand be used to get industry or even large-company forecasts? How could I/O be used to take account of technological change? Do techniques such as I/O provide an actual forecast or just the likely ranges of such forecasts?

6. Why is there an affinity between the concept of structural change in a national economy and that of technological forecasting? Between technological forecasting and the concept of long waves? Does Forrester's systems dynamic approach provide a final breakthrough for effective technological forecasting?

Case 10.1   Charleroi County Savings Bank

There is no Charleroi County Savings Bank anywhere in the United States, but there are many savings banks not unlike it. This case was prepared for use by savings bank executives to train them to use effectively knowledge or forecasts about the future. Put yourself in a bank executive's position as you work your way through this case.

CHARLEROI COUNTY SAVINGS BANK (CCSB)

Late in 1974, CCSB management was startled to see a slowdown in its rate of growth relative to that of Harrison City Savings Bank (HCSB) and of Hawthorne Savings Bank. Explaining this was not difficult: HCSB had opened two new branches (in Hope Village and in Jenkinstown) and in early November Hawthorne had raised its rates to the maximums allowed just after its quarterly crediting date. The latter move appeared to be part of a general reorientation of Hawthorne's financial objectives.

No local institution had yet raised its rate to the nominal 7.75 percent recently allowed on six- to seven-year accounts. Henry Arnold, CCSB's president, thought that soon a move to this rate was likely, although he found himself a little queasy concerning his bank's being the first locally to go to that rate: "Big Charlie has always led the local parade to higher rates; for once, maybe some other bank should lead the way." His holding back from recommending to the board that CCSB go to this new rate was partly a result of his caution concerning 1975 conditions. Although Arnold had long (and accurately) been regarded as a chronic optimist, in late 1974 he found himself wary of the general health of the national economy: There were many unpredictables to take into account in evaluating possible conditions in 1975. Although the economic health of the county and of the city was much like that of the nation, he concluded that the country could be near a sort of turning point in its economic health, but which economic scenario—recession, depression, recovery, boom—he expected was not clear, even to him.

To help crystallize his thinking and to involve his officers in as meaningful a way as possible, he convened an informal meeting as soon as the year-end financial statements were available. Although he prided himself on having perceived that there were major differences in the points of view they took, he was not prepared for the wide variety of opinions and expectations they stated.

Present at the January 17 meeting were Dan Fair (executive vice president and trustee), T. M. Wright (comptroller), D. N. Smith (mortgage officer), Paul Keith (vice president—operations), and Stan Olander (assistant to the president and secretary to the board). Although Olander was not a senior officer, he was senior in point of service and in age. This was to be his last attendance at a meeting of this type, for, on April 1, he would become manager of the branch opening that day in Heritage City, a large retirement community 23 miles south of Harrison.

Arnold decided that he should take notes during the day-long meeting, not as formal minutes but as a guide to his memory. What follows is a portion of these notes. In some places, the officer making the statement is identified; in other places, the name of the speaker is lost.

Assets Smith: "I don't care what happens to the economy, or to our growth. I want a fair share of our assets to put into residential mortgages in 1975. I remember several years ago that we offered education loans and payroll savings, too, in order to build long-term relationships with potential mortgage borrowers. I've been greatly embarrassed in recent years at having to turn them down, good applications, too, because we ran out of mortgage money."

Olander: "I agree with Smith. And if that branch is to be a success, we'll have to allocate a large amount for condominium financing, too. These older folks need financing just as much as others do."

Fair: "I disagree with you. If I'm to do the job expected of me, I must be allowed to build the bank's liquidity up to an appropriate level. And don't ask me what 'appropriate' means unless you can first tell me how long this recession will last, and how soon rates on bonds will fall."

Wright: "Take it easy, Dan. My studies show that we've been rather insulated from open-market competition ever since we began offering high-rate accounts. Except for that large block falling due in late June, I see nothing to fear. Amount maturing then? $6.3 million."

Fair: "I anticipate a runoff of no more than 10 percent of that amount if rates go the way I think. And if rates do go down that way, we can safely hold back on any major movement into mortgages. Think along these lines: The new money we put into long corporate bonds will give us a nice gain as yields soften. But mortgage rates will stay high. So then I sell the bonds and release money to you for mortgage acquisitions. Mortgage rates will still be high at that time."

Smith: "Isn't this contradictory? Add to liquidity, you say, but also add to long bonds? How do you explain this?"

Fair: "Take another look, a close one, at the balance sheet."

Services Arnold: "The bank is committed to publish again this year the supplement to the Harrison City *Sunday Examiner* on Sunday, January 26. You know that we always get a great local reaction to that "Big Charlie Reports to You" theme. We planned to stress our 1974 community involvement and to announce a new financial counseling program. Do you agree that this combination is OK?"

Keith: "It's not enough. How about announcing a new rate, 7.75 percent?"

Fair: "We can't afford it. If we go to that rate and roll over the June maturities and shift over a large portion of our regular accounts, we'll be in earnings trouble by year-end."

Smith: "If you can't carry the ball on this, give it to me. My people can be ready to put the money out, at twice or more our recent gross rate, in thirty to sixty days."

Unidentified officer: "We've got no time to wait on this supplement. A decision by Monday is a must. If we go to a higher rate, we can stress it; if we don't, maybe we'll be forced into it when some other bank goes to it."

Arnold: "My information is that Hawthorne expects to have completed soon (if not already) a 'management audit' of its marketing area. The question becomes: What should we anticipate from this competitor?"

Current assets   Fair: "Maybe you're right that we've got to think ahead here and lead the parade again. If so, I've got to be allowed to make many more changes than I usually do in our portfolio, both long-term and short-term."

Smith: "What asset changes worth mentioning here have you made recently?"

Fair: "First in early December I reduced our federal funds by $3 million and bought three bonds:

Firestone Tire $8^{1/2}$'s, 1983, Aa, NC 81, at par;

Columbia Gas $9^{5/8}$, 1989, A, MR 79, at par;

General Electric Credit, 8.60, 1985, NC 83, at par;

and four common stocks:

Schlumberger, at 100;

Federal National Mortgage Association, at 16;

Sears, Roebuck, at 44;

IBM, at 170.

"The rest of the money was used to help you meet your mortgage commitments."

Smith: "If I were allotted all the money I think I can use, what types of securities would you sell?"

Fair: "I'd be very distressed to reduce long bonds, corporates now—so I'd sell each of the commons that we have a profit in now. And likewise, as to preferreds. If even more were needed, I'd cut Treasuries back, first long, then short. I'd hate to do this, of course, but would if I had to. And then? Taking into account what I would like to see in our surplus account—and how it would be affected by losses we might have to take—I'd use those warehousing arrangements that we've had so long but never used. Then rather than sell any more, I'd go for selling debentures . . ."

Unidentified officer: "Even at a rate above 7.75 percent?"

Fair: "Yes, in order to keep those long corporates at high coupons. They'll sit on the balance sheet indefinitely, and earn much more than we'd have to pay on the debentures we might then sell."

Keith: "Noah, what rates do you expect locally on mortgages?"

Smith: "Rates, terms, and other factors: the same locally as nationally. My feeling is that the best guide to the future is the past—and in the past, our mortgage experience has pretty well matched the national picture."

Arnold: "It's coming through to me very clearly now—we need an overall

1975 strategy now, before any major decision is made. And before we come to grips with asset mix, changes in holdings, and so on, we've got to decide on the likely economic scenario."

DISCUSSION QUESTIONS 10.1

1. Take a forecast for 1975, any forecast, including one you might make up. Include in it the level of economic activity, changes in monetary and fiscal policy, prices, employment, personal income, savings, and interest rate. With that forecast in mind, assess the problems that will probably be faced by Charleroi County Savings Bank.
2. Select a strategy for Charleroi County Savings Bank—a greater emphasis on long or short assets, more or less emphasis on high-quality assets, more or fewer treasuries, agencies, Federal Housing Administration–Veterans Administration mortgages, or state and local (municipal) securities. What about 7.75 percent accounts for savers?
3. Examine the asset structure of a typical savings bank, and determine probable areas of bank weakness in your forecast.
4. If you take Dan Fair's recommendations seriously, what is your reaction to the changes he had recently made—one asset reduction, seven purchases— as they affect CCSB's asset mix? In the light of your forecast, would you improve on his policies? How?

Case 10.2   The 1976 RCA Forecast

Radio Corporation of America (RCA) has a large and well-staffed business research department. In 1975, Robert J. Eggert was its staff vice president and chief economist. RCA developed and used its own econometric models as well as those of national economic consulting firms. In addition, the staff kept a running count of all key economic variables.

The following are pages taken from a January 1976 management presentation entitled "The Economic Outlook for 1976—Boom or Gloom?"

A BETTER ECONOMY AHEAD

Two years of severe marketplace turbulence are now behind us. The downdraft of real consumer incomes, the severe upward pressure on prices paid by consumers, and the prolonged high level of unemployment resulted in a new low for the past quarter of a century in public economic confidence.

The good news is that the United States economy has clearly turned the corner (as President Ford emphasized in his recent State of the Union message) in spite of the many doubts that were so prevalent six months ago. Between the first half of 1975 and the second half, real gross national product (seasonally adjusted) advanced at an 8 percent annual rate and expanded consumer spending accounted for over one-half the increase. Also, inflation as measured by the GNP deflator settled down to a 6 percent annual rate during the last six months of the year.

This improvement in both real incomes and in the lowered rate of inflation

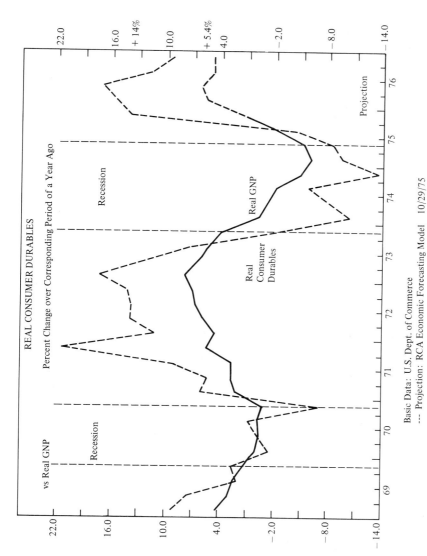

Figure 1. This chart shows the strong cyclical relationship between real GNP and real consumer durables. Highly postponable items, durables, adjusted for the effects of inflation, are expected to rise 14 percent in 1976, reversing 1975's poor showing.

Table 1 Both real growth and prices now continue to forecast in the 5–6% range for 1976

	Percent change in 1976 from 1975					
	Con- stant GNP	(Price) GNP deflator	Current consumer durables	Pretax corporate profits	Current $ GNP, (billions)	1976 unem- ployment rate, %
Conference Board (Jan 5)	6.9H	6.1	18	28	1677H	8.0
Chase Econometrics (Jan)	6.7	5.5	18	33H	1663	7.7
Manufacturers Hanover Trust (Nov)	6.6	5.5	13	19	1659	7.4L
W. R. Grace (Nov 26)	6.5	6.5H	17	23	1674	7.7
Union Carbide (Jan 13)	6.4	5.0	18	29	1651	7.8
B. F. Goodrich (Jan 7)	6.3	5.4	18	21	1654	7.4L
Data Resources (Dec 31)	6.2	6.2	17	28	1666	7.5
Harris Trust (Oct 27)	6.2	5.5	17	26	1652	7.8
Equitable Life (Nov 26)	6.0	6.2	17	25	1660	7.7
Schroder, Naess & Thomas (Oct 27)	5.9	5.4	16	23	1647	7.9
ASA/NBER Survey (Dec)	5.9	6.0	15	23[1]	1657	7.8
Security Pacific Nat. Bank (Dec 30)	5.7	5.7	16	23	1650	7.7
Irving Trust (Dec 8)	5.7	6.0	19H	26	1654	7.3
American Express (Dec 16)	5.7	6.1	15	27	1657	7.6
Bankers Trust (Dec 22)	5.7	6.1	15	24	1655	7.8
UCLA Business Forecast (Dec 4)	5.6	5.2	NA	15	1640	8.1
Wells Fargo Bank (Nov 13)	5.6	5.5	17	32	1641	7.8
Mellon Bank (Dec 1)	5.6	5.8	16	24[2]	1645	7.7
Wharton EFU (Dec 11)	5.6	6.1	NA	31	1655	7.9
E. I. du Pont de Nemours (Oct 29)	5.5	6.3	19H	33H	1655	7.4L
Prudential Insurance (Nov 30)	5.5	6.5H	14	25	1658	7.8
RCA (Oct 29)	5.4	5.3	18	24	1635	8.0
General Electric (Dec 31)	5.4	6.5H	12	25	1659	8.0
C J Lawrence (Nov 20)	5.3	4.5	12	20	1624	7.7
A G Becker (Dec 4)	5.3	5.4	8L	22	1641	8.3
Lionel D Edie (Nov 28)	5.2	5.0	14	15	1630	7.7
U.S. Trust (Dec 4)	5.1	4.9	13	17	1627	8.4
First National City Bank (Nov 21)	4.4	4.4L	12	13	1608	8.4
Dean Witter (Nov 15)	3.1L	5.5	8L	10L	1600L	8.5H
Table mean	5.7	5.7	15	24	1648	7.8
Table mean last month	5.6	5.7	15	23	647	7.8

NA: Not available.   H: highest forecast in column.   L: lowest forecast in column.

[1]After tax, not included in table mean.

[2]Federal Reserve Board, 170 large manufacturing companies, after tax, not included in table mean.

Of the 24 forecasts tabulated last time which are included this month, 2 revised real growth down, 4 up, the rest unchanged; 4 revised price inflation down, 1 up, the rest unchanged.

Source: Published forecasts and personal communication from the economics departments of the firms listed. RCA Forecast: RCA Economic Forecasting Model, 10/29/75.

is expected to continue in 1976. Specifically, real growth this year is forecast to be about 5¹/₂ percent above 1975 levels. Inflation is also expected to be in the 5 to 6 percent range, about one-half the rate of increase that prevailed during the latter part of 1974.

Also encouraging is the expectation that there will be about 4 million more jobs by the end of 1976 than at the low point of the business cycle last spring. But unemployment is still expected to hover in the over 7¹/₂ percent area, owing largely to continuing increases in the labor force (individuals looking for work).

In brief, the economy during our Bicentennial Year will be better but no boom! (Table 1.)

HOW CAN WE BE REASONABLY SURE THAT CONSUMERS WILL SPEND MORE IN 1976?

The following factors (many overlapping) will contribute to an upturn in consumer expenditures throughout 1976:
1. Personal tax cuts extended—election years tend to be expansionary.
2. Expanded money supply and improved velocity will provide support to spending programs.
3. Real spendable pay of wage-earners has advanced during recent months.
4. Renewed expansion in the use of consumer credit—improved income and use of credit go hand in hand.
5. Better food and feed grain crops last year and improved productivity should help curb inflation this year.
6. Expected reduction in the rate of inflation should further improve consumer confidence.

Table 2 RCA's track record in economic forecasting
Real gross national product—Forecast in January for year ahead vs. actual

| Year | Change from previous year | | |
	RCA forecast, in Jan. for year ahead	Actual, 1 yr. later	Percentage point, Actual ± forecast
1970	0.8	−0.4	−1.2
1971	2.4	3.3	+0.9
1972	5.6	6.2	+0.6
1973	5.9	5.9	0.0
1974	1.6	−2.1	−3.7
1975	−3.0	−2.0	+1.0
		Average error	1.2

Source: Forecast based on RCA's economic forecasting model. Projections were those made at the end of the first month of the year (January) for the full year ahead. Actual through 1974 from the U.S. Department of Commerce.

7. Backlog of consumer demand for durables after two years of slow growth.
8. Consumer buying plans for most durables up over depressed levels of a year ago.
9. Auto sales are expected to jump 17 percent from depressed 1975 levels—to a total of 10.2 million.

In my judgment all of these short-term factors will provide support to the expected plus 5 percent improvement in real consumer expenditures during 1976. Put this against our track record. (Table 2.)

DISCUSSION QUESTIONS 10.2

1. Assess the accuracy of the RCA forecasts.
2. How does the RCA forecast fit into the decision process at RCA? While you can't be expected to know this answer in detail, try to work out what you think the role of this forecast might be.
3. Despite the use of econometric models, why does Dr. Eggert stress judgment? What does "judgment" mean in a forecast context?
4. What one element of a forecast is likely to be of more importance to management than any other?

11

CAPITAL BUDGETING

Key Concepts

absorbing chain
acceptance rules
capital budget
capital budgeting
capital rationing
capital theory
cash flow
contingent dependencies
cost of capital
cost of money
demand-for-capital schedule
depreciation
discounted cash flow
discounted payback
economic life
equity funds
financial evaluation

internal rate of return
investment priorities
marginal cost of capital
Markov chain
mutually exclusive
net present worth
NPW profile
payback
projected dependence and independence
random walk
reinvestment rate
relative costs
sequential decision theory
supply-of-funds schedule
yield

What Is Ahead in This Chapter

This chapter will show that capital budgeting encompasses all those techniques and criteria that a firm would use for key long-range investment projects for a given accounting period. A capital budget indicates all the possible alternative uses for available capital funds as of that accounting period. The problem, though, is how to select from that capital budget those investment projects which will maximize long-run profit. It is to make such investment decisions that choice criteria have been worked out.

This chapter presents and analyzes four investment criteria: cutoff rates, net present worth, internal rate of return, and payback. Among these, net present worth is shown to be the correct choice criterion. The importance of using the correct choice criterion is highlighted by the fact that most investment decisions once made cannot be reversed without great cost.

Thus, capital budgeting often affects not only the profitability of a firm at any moment in time but the very existence of the firm in the future. Capital budgeting decisions involve investments in assets, machinery, facilities, land, buildings, product research, attainment of a market penetration position, marketing and distribution systems, and major personnel decisions. The capital budgeting process helps determine not only what to invest in but how much and when to invest and even the order of investment over time. This chapter outlines and assesses many, though hardly all, of the methods available to management to arrive at the best investment decision.

Capital budgeting is a part of capital theory which discusses such fundamental issues as the nature and function of interest rates, optimal investment programs for firms, effects of time on the programming of investment, increasing returns, external economies, and measurements of the productivity of capital.

Capital budgeting is about as practical an exercise in managerial economics as can be imagined. It makes use of every possible talent and bit of economic knowledge. And, even more important, it is a humbling activity: The chances of being wrong are not low.

Interstate Acromatics, Inc.

We owe much of the current interest in capital budgeting to the work of Joel Dean,[1] who stressed the viewpoint of the business firm. He recommended that a firm, facing a choice among alternative investments, compute for each alternative investment its expected profitability and then list the projects in

[1]Joel Dean, *Capital Budgeting*, New York, Columbia University Press, 1951.

Table 11.1 Interstate Acromatics, Inc.: Capital budget for 1980

Project	Amount required, $	Expected profitability, %*
A	2,660,000	10
B	1,845,000	18
C	1,225,000	41
D	4,125,000	32
E	2,750,000	25
F	510,000	20
G	5,235,000	31
H	275,000	47
I	525,000	45
J	4,145,000	21
K	1,175,000	38

*Expected profitability is an estimate of the annual rate of return on the capital to be invested.

decreasing order of profitability. To illustrate this approach to capital budgeting, take the Interstate Acromatics capital budget for 1980 shown in Table 11.1

This capital budget was prepared from the submissions of each of the departments of Interstate Acromatics. In this form, the capital budget is a shopping list. In Table 11.2 the budget is rearranged on a cumulative basis to become a schedule of demand for capital funds that relates the amounts presented by the various departments for inclusion in the capital budget to the estimated profitability of the individual projects. This schedule is a summary statement of Interstate's capital investment opportunities in 1980.

In Fig. 11.1 the schedule becomes a demand curve. The decline in the curve shows that the marginal efficiency of additional capital for the current planning period decreases over the range of the proposed projects. But, as it stands, the capital funds demand curve does not reveal anything about the costs of employing capital. Where is the money coming from?

Table 11.2 Interstate Acromatics, Inc.: Schedule of demand for capital funds, 1980

Expected profitability, %	Cumulative amount required, $	Add project
47	275,000	H
45	800,000	I
41	2,025,000	C
38	3,200,000	K
32	7,325,000	D
31	12,560,000	G
25	15,310,000	E
21	19,455,000	J
20	19,964,000	F
18	21,810,000	B
10	24,470,000	A

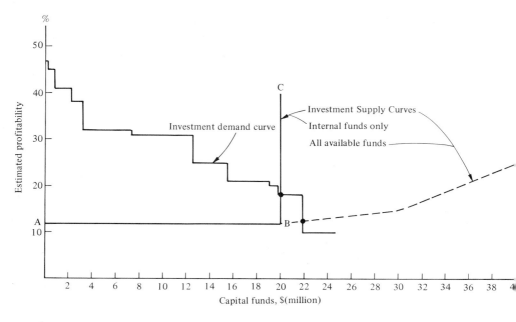

Figure 11.1. Interstate Acromatics, Inc.

Interstate Acromatics expects to finance its capital budget from a pool of capital funds that consists partly of internal funds, partly of new equity funds, and partly of new debt. Its internal funds are generated by accumulating depreciation and by retained earnings. They tend to comprise about half of Interstate's capital budget funding. The rest is normally supplied either by new equity or by borrowing.

Interstate's comptroller has estimated that, for 1980, about $20 million will be available from internal sources. The comptroller has determined that were he to try to invest these funds at the going interest rate, he could expect to earn an average of 12 percent on such funds in the money market. That 12 percent rate would represent the opportunity cost of the internal funds. The comptroller pointed out that despite the fact that the internal funds had no apparent cost, nonetheless the real cost of such funds was what they could earn in the best alternative investment.

If only internal funds are available, then the supply-of-capital-funds curve in Fig. 11.1 is ABC. The ABC supply curve shows that any amount up to $20 million is available at 12 percent, but no more than $20 million will be available no matter what the rate. ABC intersects the demand function at slightly above 18 percent. Thus, with $20 million available, only those projects earning more than 18 percent will be eligible for consideration.

This 18 percent rate is a cutoff rate. Projects with expected profitability estimates at 18 percent or lower will be rejected. The projects to be considered for inclusion in the 1980 Interstate Acromatics capital budget will be H, I, C, K, D, G, E, J, and F. Each of these proposed investments has an expected profitability greater than 18 percent. Projects A and B are rejected.

The project acceptance rule for Interstate Acromatics can be stated as follows:

Accept any project with an expected profitability equal to or greater than the cutoff rate.

The key question in applying this project acceptance rule is: What is the correct cut-off rate? The use of both internal and external sources changes the cutoff rate for Interstate Acromatics' 1980 capital budget. Local banks have indicated a willingness to lend $10 million at a rate of interest which, with the requirement of compensating balances, comes to 15 percent. The comptroller has found that to issue new common stock to obtain an additional $10 million would require a cost that, with the required dividend taken into consideration, would be 25 percent. Table 11.3 shows a supply of capital funds schedule.

From this supply-of-capital-funds' schedule, the total capital funds supply curve ABS is derived. The intersection of total supply of capital funds curve ABS with the demand-for-capital-funds curve is at about 12.5 percent. This lower cutoff rate would appear to be a more realistic and, indeed, a more correct rate than 18 percent. The 12.5 percent rate is based on all funds available, internal as well as external.

At the 12.5 percent cutoff rate, project B, for which there are not enough funds at the 18 percent, or better, cutoff rate, now becomes an attractive choice. It will be added to the Interstate Acromatics 1980 capital budget. However, Project A remains, as before, on the rejected list. The correctness of the 12.5 percent cutoff rate lies in the fact that at that rate all capital projects for which there are funds available can be accepted. However, at the 18 percent, or better, rate, an arbitrary limitation on the supply of capital funds had the effect of reducing the Interstate Acromatics capital budget for 1980. This reduction or this omission of Project B would have meant that the capital budget would not have permitted Interstate Acromatics to maximize its long-run profits.

The limitation of capital funds availability to internally generated funds alone is an example of capital rationing. Capital rationing, in this instance, takes place because an arbitrary higher price for capital funds is used rather than the price which would have derived from a full use of all market sources of funds. Capital rationing, obviously, has the effect of denying the Interstate Acromatics management an opportunity to maximize investment opportunities. A capital budget selected under rules which induce capital rationing is not an optimal selection of available capital projects.

In the Interstate Acromatics case, we have the following elements of capital budgeting:

Table 11.3 Interstate Acromatics, Inc.: Supply of capital funds schedule, 1980

Amount, millions		Sources	Cost, %
Individual	Cumulative		
$20	$20	Internal, profits plus depreciation	12
$10	$30	Bank loan	15
$10	$40	Common stock issue	25

1. A method for selecting projects to be included in the capital budget. This method uses an acceptance or rejection rule to determine which projects to include.
2. A relationship between internal measures of project acceptability and the cost of capital funds (money) determined in the marketplace.
3. A statement of the purpose of capital budgeting. This purpose is to find those capital projects to include in a capital budget which will permit a long-run maximization of the firm's profits.

Long-Run Costs and Capital Budgeting

In Chap. 5, the discussion on long-run cost curves involved a comparison between a number of short-run cost curves. Each such short-run cost curve represented the short-run capacity of a firm. The firm's short-run capacity was, of course, limited by the amount of investment in fixed facilities. A larger capacity required a larger investment in fixed facilities. A long-run average cost curve showed that, as fixed investment was increased (or what is the same thing, as a firm moved from one short-run cost curve to another), there were constant, increasing, or decreasing returns to scale. But there was an element missing in that analysis.

The missing element was an explanation of why a firm would want to increase the scale of its operations. Obviously, such an explanation turns on questions of demand and profitability. Only if the demand for a product or service increases sufficiently would there be enough revenue to cover costs at the larger size or scale of production. In effect, long-run cost curve analysis was a first stage in the analysis of capital budgets. The different-size facilities represented by different short-run cost curves can be regarded as alternative capital projects. The profitability of each such scale of operations would depend on the intersection of short-run marginal revenue and marginal cost curves in each case. In the case of constant returns to scale, there would be no difference in profitability from one size or scale to another, so that, other things being equal, any increase in a firm's capacity and thus any choice among different investment levels would be determined only by the need to meet increased demand and not by improved profitability.

Under certain conditions, both increasing returns and decreasing returns might lead to increased profitability with increasing size. Most of the empirical evidence suggests that economies of scale in industries with elastic product demands lead to significant increased profitability with larger sizes of operations. The case of decreasing returns is less clear, but assuming inelastic demand for product or service, increasing size would lead to increasing profitability.

Capital budgeting as a management tool does not take such concepts as long-run planning directly and explicitly into consideration. Nonetheless, the use of capital budgeting by a firm is an act seeking to establish a long-run production equilibrium. The ultimate test of benefits from a particular capital budget is whether, in fact, long-run profits are maximized.

Cash-Flow Analysis and Capital Budgeting

While, in the Interstate Acromatics case, we looked at each investment project as a proposed amount of outlay in 1980 and we ranked each project by its expected profitability, that analysis assumed that how we estimated profitability was understood. For most analytical purposes, it is better to regard each investment proposal as a set of cash flows over the economic life of that investment. Using these cash-flow estimates, then, we can evaluate each project by using a variety of choice criteria. The choice criteria will be derived from the cash flow. Capital budgeting spells out a series of methods for evaluating projects as cash flows in the light of available investment funds and their costs. The point is that, in capital budgeting, it is not the technical character of a project that is being compared with other projects but the cash-flow–based profitability criteria.

Each investment project, as we can see, generates a flow of funds during its economic life. This flow of funds, in any accounting period, consists of a net after-tax profit contribution for that period plus the depreciation recognized and recorded for that period. The net profit contribution can be positive or negative but the depreciation amount is always at least 0 and usually positive. It is a frequently employed practice to treat the initial outlay to acquire the investment as a negative cash flow for the period in which it takes place. Negative cash flows may also take place during the first several periods as the investment is being put into place. There may be negative cash flows toward the end of the economic life of the asset when there are often removal or salvage costs.

In Fig. 11.2 the cash-flow pattern from an investment is visualized. The economic life of the asset lasts to period n. In period 0, the first major outlay

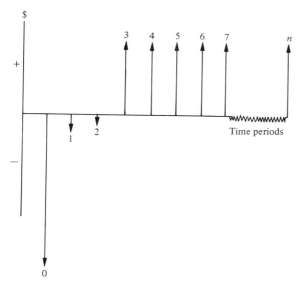

Figure 11.2. Cash flow diagram.

occurs. In periods 1 and 2, the asset is still being brought on-line and installation outlays are required. Finally, in period 3, there is a positive cash flow and these positive cash flows last to period n.

To illustrate the computation of cash flows, consider a proposed investment in a new machine that will cost $18,000 installed and will save $7600 in production costs in each of five years. At the end of five years, it will be removed at zero net cost (salvage value equals removal cost). Preventive and expected maintenance costs are $1800 in the first year of operation, increasing $200 per year thereafter. The corporate income tax rate is 50 percent, depreciation is straight-line, and no investment tax credit is allowed. The cash-flow calculations are shown in Table 11.4, where all revenues and expenditures are assumed to occur at year's end. In the table cash flow is the net profit contribution (after taxes plus depreciation).

Depreciation

Depreciation is an accounting cost as well as a tax cost; it is the periodic recovery of the acquisition cost (net of salvage value) of an asset. Accounting procedures and tax laws do not normally permit the acquisition outlay to be deducted totally from income earned in the period in which the purchase or investment was made. Instead, depreciation is allocated by formulas intended to make each period bear a partial cost which recognizes the source of the income.

In Table 11.4, the $18,000 investment outlay, the cost of acquisition, is allocated over five earning or accounting periods at $3600 per period. Yet, in none of these periods will $3600 actually be paid in cash. Instead, the $3600, plus profit, will be available cash, the increment in the cash flow. Obviously, the method used to allocate depreciation, straight-line (as in this instance), sum-of-the-years' digits, or other methods, can make quite a difference in the determination of cash flow.

Table 11.4   Calculation of cash flow

Year: Period:	1976 0	1977 1	1978 2	1979 3	1980 4	1981 5
Gross profit contribution from new machine	−$18,000	$7600	$7600	$7600	$7600	$7600
Less maintenance cost	0	1800	2000	2200	2400	2600
Less depreciation	0	3600	3600	3600	3600	3600
Equals increase in profit before taxes	−$18,000	2200	2000	1800	1600	1400
Less corp. income taxes	0	1100	1000	900	800	700
Equals increase in after-tax profit	−$18,000	1100	1000	900	800	700
Plus depreciation	0	3600	3600	3600	3600	3600
Equals cash flow	−$18,000	$4700	$4600	$4500	$4400	$4300

Discounted Cash Flow

In Chap. 2, in both the determination of the profitability of the Boylston Street restaurant and the Pierpaoli decision whether to buy a Pacific Heights condominium, we used discounted cash flow. Now let us analyze the concept in more detail. Elements of a discounted cash flow are (1) cash-flow pattern, (2) discount factor, and (3) net present worth.

The cash-flow pattern is the array of cash-flow estimates, period by period, over the economic life of the proposed investment project. Each investment will have a different cash flow and possibly even a different cash-flow pattern. Some cash-flow patterns will be composed of one large negative outlay amount in period 0 and a steady, even amount of positive cash flow over the life of the asset. Other cash-flow patterns will be much more irregular. But these cash-flow patterns can all be reduced to a basis of comparison. The net present worth of a cash flow is such a basis of comparison.

The technique required is a method to adjust for futurity to permit determination of worth of each cash-flow pattern (and thus each investment), as of now. This "now" worth of the various cash-flow patterns or streams is called the "net present worth." The "net" in net present worth refers to the fact that the present worth calculations include both negative and positive cash flows.

To derive the net present worth (NPW) in each cash-flow pattern, we will multiply the individual cash flow by the discount factor. Discount factor d is defined as

$$d = \frac{1}{1 + r}$$

where r is the interest rate.

Using the cash-flow stream calculated in Table 11.4, we can now illustrate discounted cash-flow (DCF) computations at three constant interest rates: 0, 7, and 10 percent.

For $r = 0$ $d = 1$

For $r = 0.7$ $d = \dfrac{1}{1.07} = 0.9345794$

For $r = 1.10$ $d = \dfrac{1}{1.10} = 0.9090909$

Table 11.5 shows the discount for each value of r to the end of 1981.

Computer programs significantly relieve the burden of such calculations. However, with electronic calculators, manual computation is not difficult.

Several points need stressing. First, the algebraic sum of the nondiscounted cash flows, $4500, is always greater than the net present worth of the discounted cash flows. And the difference between the nondiscounted cash flow and the discounted cash flow grows as the interest rate increases.

Second, the discounted cash flow grows smaller the longer the time over

Table 11.5 Net present worth computations

Year end	n	$r = 0\%$ CF_n	$r = 7\%$ d	$d \cdot CF_n$	$r = 10\%$ d	$d \cdot CF_n$
1976	0	$ −18,000	1.0000000	$ −18,000	1.0000000	$ −18,000
1977	1	4,700	0.9345794	4,392.52	0.9090909	4,272.72
1978	2	4,600	0.8734386	4,017.82	0.8264462	3,801.65
1979	3	4,500	0.8162977	3,673.34	0.7513147	3,380.92
1980	4	4,400	0.7628949	3,356.74	0.6830133	3,005.26
1981	5	4,300	0.7129858	3,065.84	0.6209211	2,669.97
		NPW (0%)=$4,500		NPW (7%)=$506.26		NPW (10%)=$ −869.48

which discounting takes place. Beyond ten years, the amount added to any cash flow by additional discounting is small, and it is that much smaller the higher the rate of interest used as a discount factor.

Third, net present worth can be positive, negative, or zero. For simple even-amount cash-flow patterns, the net worth is a decreasing monotonic function of the interest rate. But not all cash-flow time patterns are of this nature.

Financial Evaluation of Projects

The Conference Board[2] has pointed out that financial evaluation of investment projects involves two steps. One is the setting of a realistic company standard or market goal against which all projects can be judged. The second is to develop mathematical formulas that can be used to evaluate correctly the relative profitability of each project and thus to rank projects in comparison with company-set goals. The fact of the matter, though, is that, while the concept of financial evaluation is not difficult, there are many problems in applying financial criteria in specific situations. The following is a review of a number of project-choice criteria.

Payback

Payback is the number of accounting periods over which income earned or amounts saved on an investment project will accumulate sufficiently to cover the proposed investment outlay. Payback is attained when 100 percent of a proposed investment outlay is recovered; its calculation is a NPW problem where you are solving for the period when NPW = 0.

Payback calculations can be made either by accumulating the undis-

[2] Conference Board, *Managing Capital Expenditures*, New York, 1963, p. 39.

Table 11.6   Payback calculations for Project A*

Year	Initial investment outlay	Incremental cash flow, $	Cumulative cash flow, $	Present value of $1 discounted at 20%	Present value of cumulative cash flow, $	% recovery of investment
1980	$80,000					
1981		20,000	20,000	.8333	16,666	20.8
1982		20,000	40,000	.6944	30,554	38.2
1983		20,000	60,000	.5787	42,128	52.7
1984		20,000	80,000	.4823	51,774	69.7
1985		20,000	100,000	.4019	59,812	74.8
1986		20,000	120,000	.3349	66,510	83.1
1987		20,000	140,000	.2791	72,092	90.1
1988		20,000	160,000	.2326	76,744	95.9
1989		20,000	180,000	.1938	80,620	100.8
1990		20,000	200,000	.1615	83,850	104.8

*Cost: $80,000; expected project life: 10 years; incremental cash flow: $20,000; discount rate: 20%.

counted cash-flow amounts or by accumulating a discounted cash-flow amount. Payback has been reached when the accumulated cash flow (undiscounted or discounted) is equal to the proposed initial investment outlay. Having determined the payback, we have a financial criterion to be measured against a company goal. Suppose that management has set a payback horizon of five years; then any project with a payback of five years or less is acceptable.

Table 11.6 shows the payback calculations for project A. On an undiscounted basis project A will have a payback of four years. Over its ten-year expected life, A will return $200,000, 250 percent of the initial investment outlay. On a discounted basis, at 20 percent, the payback will be eight years, ten months, and the discounted percentage of recovery of initial investment will be 104.8 percent at the end of the ten-year project life.

Table 11.6 is accompanied by Fig. 11.3, which illustrates the relationship between management payback horizon, undiscounted payback, and discounted payback.

Payback Project Acceptance Rule

Accept any project for which the payback is equal to or less than management horizon. Or accept any project for which percentage of recovery of initial investment at management horizon is equal to or greater than 100.

Percentage of recovery of proposed initial investment outlay at end of project life is also an indication of gross profitability. The higher the percentage of recovery, the more profitable the project would be.

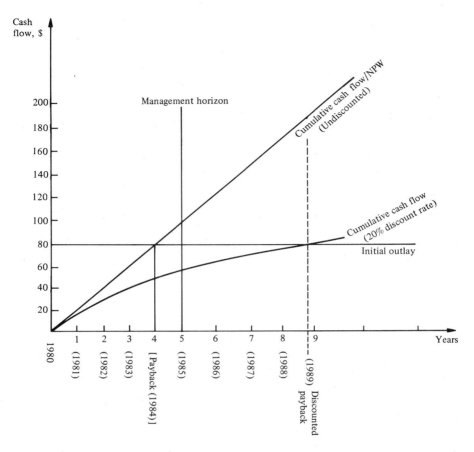

Figure 11.3. Payback calculation.

NPW(PW − outlay) @ 0% = 0 at 4 years
NPW(PW − outlay) @ 20% = 0 at 8 years 10 months

Criticisms of Payback

Payback is a widely used financial evaluation criterion. Its failings, however, need stressing. Payback does not take explicit consideration of any portion of the cash flow to be received after payback. Undiscounted payback does not take into account the time value of money. However, as Weingartner[3] has pointed out, payback is a kind of break-even analysis that indicates to management how rapidly confirmation can be expected that a good investment

[3]See Martin Weingartner, "Some New Views on the Payback Period and Capital Budgeting Decisions," R.F. Byrne, et al., (eds.), *Budgeting Interrelated Activities—2:* Studies in Budgeting. Studies in Mathematical and Managerial Economics, vol 2. New York, American Elsevier, 1971, pp. 138–57.

choice has been made. Moreover, given the uncertainty in which capital budgeting decisions are made, payback yields information on the rate at which the uncertainty about a project can be resolved. While payback is not the best solution to both these problems, it is not a bad solution.

Project Dependence and Independence

Before proceeding to an explanation of how the net present worth criterion can be used, let us set the stage. How and when to use that and other criteria (including, though not necessarily, payback) depend on whether proposed investment projects are independent of each other, whether they are mutually exclusive, or whether there is a contingent dependence among them. Independent[4] projects are those whose acceptance or rejection neither affects nor is affected by any other project under consideration. Mutually exclusive projects are units in a set of projects from which only one can be accepted. For example, a proposed increase in production capacity could be achieved by expanding existing capacity, by acquiring a going manufacturing concern, or by building an additional plant. Any one of these would provide the extra capacity required, but only one can be chosen. They are mutually exclusive. There is the possibility that none will be chosen, that is, that the proposed expansion will not be accepted at all. Sometimes, mutually exclusive projects are mistakenly said to be independent. In fact, there exists no greater degree of dependence than mutual exclusivity.

Contingent dependence exists when one project requires the acceptance of another project. For example, suppose project A is the building of a new plant and outfitting it with conventional but modern machinery and equipment; project B is the addition to this new plant of a numerically controlled machine tool. Clearly, B can be accepted for inclusion in a capital budget only if project A is accepted. The converse is not true, of course.

Extending the concept of contingent dependence, C may be contingently dependent on B, which in turn is dependent on A. In addition, D may be contingently dependent on B, and E on both C and D.

In making capital budgeting decisions, only two project relationships need be considered: independence and mutual exclusivity. Contingent dependencies can be replaced with a mutually exclusive and collectively exhaustive set of equivalent composite projects.[5] In terms of five contingently dependent projects A–E, this set is

1. Project A—A alone
2. Project AB—A and B
3. Project ABC—A and B and C
4. Project ABD—A and B and D, since contingence on B implies contingence on A

---

[4]These definitions imply riskless investments and sufficient capital.

[5]"Collectively exhaustive" means that all feasible combinations are included.

5. Project ABCD—A and B and C and D, since C and D are not mutually exclusive
6. Project ABCED—A and B and C and D and E.

NPW as an Investment-Choice Criterion

The NPW of an investment project, as we have observed, is the "now" value of the cash-flow pattern generated by that investment over its expected economic life. To calculate the NPW of a project, we need to establish the discount factor to use. The discount factor choice is a choice among interest rates to find that interest rate which will yield a discount factor that reduces the NPW of the investment project cash pattern to zero. Call that interest rate the "reference rate." Clearly, any investment project whose NPW is not equal to or greater than zero is not acceptable. Zero net worth is an intuitive standard. Positive net worth is better than standard. How is the reference rate determined?

Go back to Table 11.5. Of the three interest rates used in Table 11.5, 0 percent yielded an NPW of $4500, 7 percent yielded an NPW of $506, and 10 percent yielded an NPW of −$869. Clearly the reference rate must lie somewhere between 7 and 10 percent. As we shall show later in considerable detail when we examine the internal rate of return, the reference rate is 8.06 percent. If you are impatient to find out how this reference rate is calculated, turn at once to Table 11.11. For the remainder of this analysis of NPW as an investment-choice criterion, however, we don't need to know the reference rate. We need only to know that such a rate exists. In short, we need to know what NPW = 0 means.

Use of the Net Present Worth Criterion

Given an interest rate which yields a net present worth at least equal to zero, the project acceptance rules are

1. For independent projects—accept all projects whose NPW are positive.
2. For mutually exclusive projects—consider that project (perhaps composite) from the mutually exclusive set whose NPW is largest. If this NPW is positive, accept the project. If this NPW is zero or negative, do not accept any project from this mutually exclusive set.

To illustrate the application of these acceptance rules, consider the ten candidate projects shown in Table 11.7. A, D, F, and J are independent projects. B, C, and E form one mutually exclusive set; G, H, and I form another. The net present worths of each project are shown for three discount rates.

At 10 percent, all independent projects would be accepted. For set 1, C would be accepted; B and E would be rejected. For set 2, either H or I, but not both, would be accepted.

Table 11.7   Net present worth of capital budgeting projects

Project	Mut. excl. set no.	NPW, thousands, at discount rate		
		10%	15%	20%
A	. . .	$100	$ 80	$ 40
B	1	30	20	− 10
C	1	50	30	− 20
D	. . .	70	− 10	− 20
E	1	20	0	− 15
F	. . .	80	60	30
G	2	10	5	− 5
H	2	40	30	20
I	2	40	10	5
J	. . .	15	10	0

At 15 percent, all independent projects except D would be accepted. C and H would be accepted for sets 1 and 2, respectively.

Finally, at 20 percent, only A and F (among the independents) and H (for set 2) would be accepted. As the most positive NPW in set 1 is negative, no project from this set would be acceptable.

Marginal Cost of Capital

Three interest rates are included in this illustration. In the application of the net present worth criterion only one rate would be used. That rate is the highest interest rate at which the investment funds could otherwise be lent, that is, a firm's marginal cost of capital.[6]

All a firm's funds can be thought of as external or borrowed funds. Debt, of course, is borrowed capital. Equity, stocks or shares, owned by a firm's shareholders (to the extent that they are not used to reduce debt or returned to the shareholders by repurchase of shares or by payment of dividends) is also borrowed capital in the sense that shareholders expect a return.

There are three possible relationships between the rate of interest at which a lender or shareholder might wish to lend to a firm and a firm's marginal cost of capital. The lending rate could be higher than the cost of capital. But market arbitrage would soon eliminate the difference. Or the two rates could be equal. Or the marginal cost of capital could be higher than the lending rate. If that were true, then a firm would not borrow. Thus, ignoring risk, a firm's marginal cost of capital is the rate at which lenders will lend.

Of course, there could be and there frequently is an interest rate imposed by management that is higher than the marginal cost of capital. Since this target rate is higher, it obviously increases a firm's cost of capital.

---

[6]Under the assumed conditions, it would be more accurate to say: *risk-free* marginal cost of capital. The actual cost of capital includes a market-generated premium for risk.

There is no reason, to be sure, to expect that the marginal cost of capital will remain constant as the demand for capital increases. In the Interstate Acromatics case, the marginal cost of capital was constant only over the range of internal funds. As larger and larger external funds are required to meet the capital demand, the marginal-cost-of-funds curve will rise. Determination of the marginal cost of capital or what we have called the cutoff rate requires the solution of a simultaneous demand and supply equation.

NPW as a Choice Criterion: A Supply-Demand Example

To illustrate the use of the NPW criterion in a case analogous to Interstate Acromatics, suppose capital funds are available as shown in Table 11.8. At each rate, the NPW criterion is applied to the projects in the capital budget and the initial outlays required by the accepted projects are totaled (see Table 11.9). A blank entry indicates nonacceptance of the project at the given rate.

Finally, the funds available and the funds required are compared in the supply-demand schedule (see Table 11.10). This table shows that 20 percent is the marginal cost of capital, that is, it is the rate at which sufficient funds are

Table 11.8 Supply of funds

Source	Amount available	Cost, %
Internal	$150,000	10
Bank 1 loan	75,000	12
Bank 2 loan	50,000	15
Insurance company loan	60,000	18
Bond issue	250,000	20
Common stock issue	300,000	25

Table 11.9 Funds required

Project	Mutually exclusive set no.	Initial outlay	10%	12%	15%	18%	20%	25%
A	. . .	$150,000	$150	$150	$150	$150	$150	$150
B	1	70,000						
C	1	100,000	100	100	100			
D	. . .	120,000	120	120				
E	1	50,000						
F	. . .	130,000	130	130	130	130	130	130
G	2	25,000						
H	2	90,000	90	90	90	90	90	
I	2	105,000						
J	. . .	25,000	25	25	25			
			$615	$615	$495	$370	$370	$280

Table 11.10 Supply-demand schedule

Cumulative funds available	Marginal cost, %	Funds required
$150,000	10	$615,000
225,000	12	615,000
275,000	15	495,000
335,000	18	370,000
585,000	20	370,000
885,000	25	280,000

available to meet the required initial outlays. It is, therefore, the rate at supply equals demand.

The marginal cost of the entire funding package is the 20 percent of the last funding increment needed. In contrast, the average cost of these funds is 13.3 percent.

Internal Rate of Return

Like NPW and payback, the internal rate of return (IRR) is a choice criterion for investment analysis. IRR is also called the "yield." But, as it turns out, it is also the reference rate used to define the meaning of NPW = 0. Indeed, IRR is that rate of interest for which the discount factor applied to the cash-flow pattern will give an NPW of zero.

IRR is internal in the sense that it can be calculated independently of the marginal cost (and the supply function of capital). The estimated profitability rates in the Interstate Acromatics case were IRRs. An IRR is a gross rate so that working it out does not require any knowledge of target rates or marginal costs of capital or cutoff rates. To illustrate the general principles though not the precise method of calculating the IRR, the data in Table 11.5 are repeated in Table 11.11. We know from Table 11.5 that the reference rate—the rate at

Table 11.11 Calculation of internal rate of return (IRR)

Year end	CF_N	$r = 7\%$ d''	$d''CF_N$	$r = 8.06\%$ d''	$d''CF_N$	$r = 10\%$ d''	$d''CF_N$
1976	−$18,000	1.0000	−$18,000	1.0000	−$18,000	1.0000	−$18,000
1977	4,700	0.9346	4,393	0.9254	4,349	0.9091	4,273
1978	4,600	0.8734	4,018	0.8562	3,939	0.8264	3,802
1979	4,500	0.8163	3,673	0.7924	3,566	0.7513	3,381
1980	4,400	0.7629	3,357	0.7331	3,226	0.6830	3,005
1981	4,300	0.7130	3,066	0.6791	2,920	0.6209	2,670
NPW	4,500		507		0		−869
IRR = 8.06%							

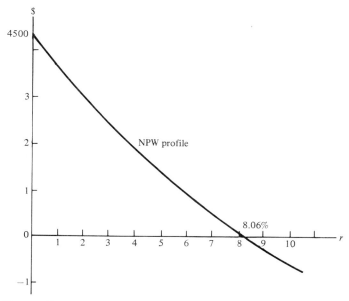

Figure 11.4. NPW profile.

which NPW = 0—must lie somewhere between 7 and 10 percent. In Table 11.11, we find that the reference rate or IRR is 8.06 percent.

Table 11.11 involves a search procedure. And that procedure can be pretty tedious. But the average scientific hand calculator has an IRR program and, in no more than five minutes, you can work out the IRR by inputting the tables. Table 11.11 shows that the successive discount factors at $r = 8.06$ percent, when multiplied by the individual cash flows, do, in fact, give an NPW of zero.

If we took each of these NPWs at their respective interest rates, we could, as in Fig. 11.4, trace out an NPW profile of this investment. The NPW profile begins at 0 percent and an NPW of $4500 and crosses the horizontal axis at $r = 8.06$ percent. Since the vertical axis is the NPW and the horizontal axis is the rate of interest, the fact that the NPW profile crosses the r axis at 8.06 percent indicates the rate at which NPW is zero.

Project Acceptance Rules Using IRR

For independent projects, accept all those projects for which the IRR is equal to or exceeds the cost of money (however calculated), hurdle rate, or target interest rate set by management.

For a set of mutually exclusive projects, accept any project or any combination of projects in that set for which the IRR is equal to or exceeds the cost of money (however calculated), hurdle rate, or the management target interest rate.

Comparison of NPW and IRR

For cash-flow patterns composed of one or more initial outlays followed by cash inflows, NPW and IRR will usually give the same evaluation. Yet there are problems with IRR both in theory and in practice. IRR is derived mathematically by a polynomial equation of degree N with N roots, any one of which could, in principle, be IRR. Which root is *the* IRR? Sometimes there is no positive root to the equation; therefore, there is no IRR. No IRR would mean either that all possible NPWs were positive or that they all were negative. The key point is this: You can always determine the NPW of a cash-flow stream, but there are times when you cannot determine the IRR for some cash-flow streams.

No Positive IRR

Here is an example of a case where there is no positive IRR. Suppose that the cash-flow stream were

Year	Period	CF_N
1976	1	$18,000
1977	2	−20,000
1978	3	6,000

For this cash-flow stream, any positive discount rate will yield a positive NPW. But your hand scientific calculator will give you IRR = −75.43 percent. This will not do: A negative IRR has no meaning. Hence, there is no effective IRR for this admittedly unusual cash flow. You could not make a decision on the acceptability of this investment with the IRR criterion. Using the NPW criterion at a 7 percent marginal cost of capital, you would accept it. At 7 percent, NPW = $4251.

Two or More IRRs

Now suppose that an investment project had the following cash-flow stream:

Year	Period	CF_N
1976	0	$− 8,000
1977	1	17,900
1978	2	− 10,000

This product has two IRRs, 7.87 percent and 15.88 percent.

In Table 11.12, we can see the problem more clearly. If we use the IRR

Table 11.12 Calculation of IRR and NPW when there are two IRRs

Year end	CF_N	$r = 0\%$ discount factor	$d^n CF_N$	$r = 7.87\%$ discount factor	$d^n CF_N$	$r = 10\%$ discount factor	$d^n CF_N$
1976	$- 8,000	1.0000	$- 8,000	1.0000	$- 8,000	1.0000	$- 8,000
1977	17,900	1.000	17,000	0.9270	16,594	0.9091	16,273
1978	- 10,000	1.000	- 10,000	0.8594	- 8,594	0.8264	- 8,264
	$ 100		$- 1,000		$ 0		$ 9

Year end	CF_N	$r = 11.73\%$ discount factor	$d^n CF_N$	$r = 15.88\%$ discount factor	$d^n CF_N$
1976	$- 8,000	1.0000	$- 8,000	1.0000	$- 8,000
1977	17,900	0.8950	16,021	0.8630	15,447
1978	- 10,000	0.8010	- 8,011	0.7447	- 7,447
	$ 100		$ 10		$ 0

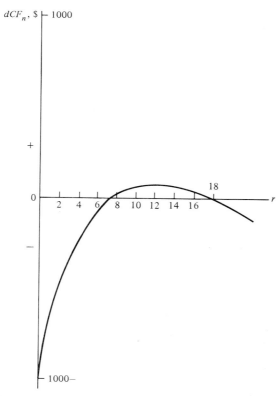

Figure 11.5. NPW profile for Table 11.12.

acceptance criterion for 7.87 percent, then we would accept this project at any cost of money or target rate up to 7.87 percent. But at interest rates below 7.87 percent, the NPW is negative. Thus, the two criteria are in conflict.

Only at a cost of capital between 7.87 percent and 15.88 percent would NPW be zero or positive. At 11.73 percent NPW is at a maximum, but this is above one IRR and below another.

Figure 11.5 shows the NPW profile of this investment. Using the NPW criterion, this product is acceptable at costs of money between 7.87 and 15.88 percent.

Economic Life of Capital Projects

The shorter the economic life of the project, the lower the prospective NPW at any interest rate. Project economic life estimates are based on calculations that are not independent of the use to which the project is to be put or, for that matter, of the possible alternatives to the project at various times in the future.

The economic life of a project is that period during which it can be expected that there will be no superior alternative investment. The economic life of a project will be dependent on anticipated relative obsolescence, expected deterioration, intensity of use in production, comparative operating costs as well as changing costs of money or capital. If forecasts could be made with any certainty about the future value of each possible factor affecting the economic life of a project, it would be possible to work out the total cost of retaining that project in service for any given period of time. In such a calculation, there would be two opposing sets of costs. On the one hand, the longer the facility or project is to be kept in operation, the lower will be the NPW of the service value remaining in the project and, thus, the lower the capital recovery costs. On the other hand, the higher will be the operating costs. In Fig. 11.6 the two costs are plotted as annual averages against expected service life. Summing the capital recovery costs and the operating costs, a total cost is obtained. The lowest point on this total cost curve would mark the effective economic life of the project.

The point to be stressed is that no project has a built-in economic life. Economic life must be estimated in advance to permit a calculation of depreciation and of expected profit contribution (or cost saving) and thus of cash flow. Such estimates ought to be made carefully; otherwise, a cash flow estimated to extend over a longer set of accounting periods than would appear to be warranted on the basis of careful economic life estimates would distort the NPW or IRR calculations.

Here is an example of a way to estimate economic life. Tashua Enterprises is considering a machine tool installation at a cost of $500,000. Management wants a minimum rate of return of 15 percent on the installation and wishes to know its likely economic life. Engineering staff estimates of inherent costs are assembled for each of seven possible service years ahead. In addition to the

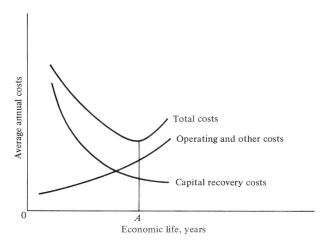

Figure 11.6. Calculation of economic life of an asset.

operating and maintenance costs, there are costs of downtime, declining productivity, and loss of effective capacity. These inherent costs are presented in column 1 of Table 11.13. In column 2 are relative costs which include the differences in cost of operation between the proposed machine tool installation and such newer, more efficient facilities as are likely to be available in the future. Engineering staff estimates show these relative costs becoming larger than inherent costs by the sixth year ahead. Relative costs can also be regarded as opportunity costs, costs incident upon this choice.

In column 3 are the total operating costs. In column 4 are estimates of changes in salvage value of the facility. These are subtracted from the acquisition cost of $500,000 at the beginning of each service year to obtain an estimate of book value of the facility for that year. These book values are in column 5. In column 6 are the expected earnings on the book value at 15 percent.

The estimates of total cost in column 7 are the sum of the total operating costs and the earnings on book value. These two costs (in columns 3 and 6), when combined, provide an estimate both of capital recovery costs and of operating costs. The capital recovery costs decline throughout each of the seven service years for which engineering staff has made estimates. In contrast, the total operating costs increase steadily over the same service years. When the present worth of these annual estimated costs of service are determined at 15 percent (column 8), it is apparent that they decline through the third service year but then begin to climb (column 9). This fact indicates that the expected economic life of this facility is certainly no more than four years.

An economic life calculation depends on the target rate of interest: The higher the rate, the longer the economic life. Indeed, at some high target rate, economic life could become infinite. This calculation also depends on estimates of obsolescence or relative costs: The higher these are, the shorter the economic life. By the same token, with obsolescence and interest rates constant, the larger the investment, the longer its economic life may be expected to be.

Table 11.13 Tashua Enterprises, Inc.: Calculation of economic life of a $500,000 facility

	(1)	(2)	(3)	(4)	(5)	(6)	(7)	(8)	(9)
Year	Inherent costs*	Relative costs*	Total operating costs*	Annual change in salvage value*	Book value at beginning of year*	Earning on book value at 15%*	Total annual cost of service*	Single-payment present worth at 15%	Present worth of cost of service*
1	60	5	65	200	500	75	140	.8696	121.7
2	65	15	80	100	300	45	125	.7561	94.5
3	71	30	101	50	150	22.5	123.5	.6575	81.2
4	78	50	128	30	120	18	146	.5718	83.5
5	86	75	161	20	100	15	176	.4972	87.5
6	95	111	206	15	85	12.8	218.8	.4323	94.5
7	105	150	255	5	80	12	267	.3759	100.4

*In thousands of dollars.

Selection of Priorities

Capital budgeting has three phases: measuring the firm's objectives, determining evaluation criteria, and setting priorities. The difference between evaluation criteria and firm priorities is essentially one of focus. Evaluation criteria, whatever their nature and their theoretical correctness, use techniques that can be applied to all firms regardless of size, position, future, market share, and competitive stance. Priorities, on the other hand, provide the perspective that makes evaluative criteria meaningful for a particular firm. A firm sets its priorities in terms of its short-run and long-run goals or objectives and its specific economic situation.

Although it is not possible to know completely the course of future economic events that may affect the firm, there are tools that allow management to see evaluative criteria against the background of possible and probable changes in the economic environment, such as sequential decision theory, linear programming, and Markov chain analysis.

Sequential Decision Theory

Although an evaluation criterion tells us which investment is best at the moment, it does not tell us the difference between the paths implicit in each investment choice. The choice of one facility over another, for example, may imply that a whole new line of products has also been chosen involving new market decisions, new research and development expenditures, new personnel acquisition problems, advertising campaigns, and different methods of handling cash and working capital needs. And this decision chain will be more profitable to the extent that the entire train of events is successful. At least some of a firm's decisions thus lead not only to some definite outcome in terms of immediately measurable returns or present-value considerations but also to still other decisions. A method that can distinguish the final values of the various decision paths is therefore useful.

Kettletown Appliances has a well-established product line. However, Kettletown is now contemplating an investment in new plant and equipment to produce a new complementary product line. Competition has made the existing product line increasingly less profitable than it has been. Kettletown management wants to regain previous levels of profitability. All the possibilities facing Kettletown are presented in a decision tree in Fig. 11.7. Kettletown could (1) build a new plant at a cost of $5 million and immediately begin making the new product; (2) authorize marketing research at a cost of $100,000 to determine the feasibility of the new product; or (3) acquire Smith and Sons, an old-line manufacturer of the proposed new product, at a cost of $3 million together with whatever problems such an acquisition may mean for the firm. A high demand level for the new product would mean a continuing average annual sales total of $600,000 after its production began. If there were a high initial demand, average annual sales would be $400,000 for the first five years. A high initial, then low, subsequent demand would mean an average annual sales figure of $200,000, and a low demand level would mean $100,000 in annual sales.

At decision 1, what are the values of the possible paths to be taken? Assume that the elapsed time between each decision is one year, so that decisions 3 and 4 take place a year later than decision 1. Decisions 2, 5, and 6 take place two years after decision 1. The expected value of deciding to build a new plant at a cost of $5 million is the present value of the average annual sales times the probability that such sales would be forthcoming. This value would be $600,000 times 0.60, or $360,000.

Kettletown management calculated the expected value of decision 3 at the time of decision 1. At decision 3, the indicated decision is to build the new plant at the cost of $5 million. The NPW of the annual sales would be $545,460, with an 87 percent likelihood that this figure would be achieved. That would give a value of $474,550. By contrast, at decision 4, the best indicated choice would be to build the new plant and obtain a probable present worth of $190,911. The next step would be to multiply $474,550 by 51 percent (the chance of a highly positive research finding) and add the result to $190,911 multiplied by 49 percent (the chance of a weakly favorable research finding), giving a result of $335,567. The cost of marketing research ($100,000) is subtracted from this sum to obtain a net expected value for decision 3 of $235,567. The net expected value of decision 2 at decision 1 is $221,392.

The best apparent path is to do marketing research and then build the new plant. With the horizon pushed back one accounting period, however, the issue is in doubt. Kettletown must take into account the conditional probabilities of high demand after expansion to meet the initial high response to the acquisition of Smith and Sons. Acquisition of the older plant would turn out to be the best decision.

Pushing the decision horizon back beyond today removes the initial advantage of building a new plant and gives preference to a different investment alternative. Kettletown must, of course, still assess its own ability to afford the risk of postponing expansion, its financial resources, and the relative

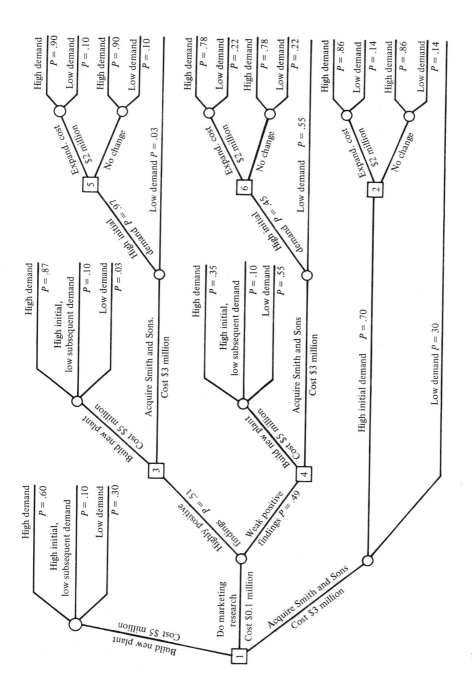

Figure 11.7. Kettletown's decision tree. *P* is probability of event expressed in percentages.

market implications of each path. Setting down the possible paths and their values is not easy, but it forces management to think through the less obvious alternatives that lie ahead and presumably results in more rational decisions.

Linear Programming

Often the determination of a capital budget or a choice among possible courses of action frequently involves more than a decision among an array of potential alternatives and more than the application of project acceptance criteria. Resources and alternative investments may have to be combined in order to accomplish those objectives. Linear programming enables management to work out solutions to investment problems involving such combinations.

Take the case of Sanmarco and Sullivan, a small manufacturer of automobile parts, that until now has been producing only parts for automobiles at an average output of some 50,000 a week. The manager of the marketing division has strongly urged that the firm make truck parts as well. Truck parts would, he has been insisting, complete the line, improve the marketing image of the firm, and, even more important, increase profits. If management decides to produce truck parts, it must decide whether to expand current facilities or to attempt to use the existing facilities for the production of both car and truck parts. Management thus needs to know whether profit could be increased by combining truck with car parts in the current production line. If management discovers that the firm's profit position could be increased within the existing plant capacity, this increase in profit could then be compared with the profit to be obtained from a new, all-truck-part facility.

Sanmarco and Sullivan's current facilities are divided into two shops, an assembly shop and a finishing shop. Each major automobile part requires two worker-days in assembly and three worker-days in finishing. At capacity operation, assembly averages 180,000 worker-days a week; finishing, about 150,000 worker-days a week. Each part contributes $200 to gross profit. Since it is obvious that the finishing shop limits production to 50,000 parts, the maximum obtainable gross profit at capacity is $10 million a week.

Engineering research has shown that, if truck parts are made in existing facilities, each part will require five worker-days in assembly and three worker-days in finishing. The gross profit contribution of each part has been estimated at $300. The limiting factor for truck parts is the assembly shop. Maximum possible production of truck parts would then be 36,000, yielding a weekly gross profit of $10 million. All-truck-part production would thus be more profitable than all-auto-part production. But the marketing manager argues that this turnaround, even if possible, would not solve the problem he has posed, because it would obviously not complete the line for the company's dealers.

The automobile- and the truck-part production functions (or rays) are worked out on the basis of information supplied by the engineering research staff. Capacity is plotted in Fig. 11.8. The maximum obtainable revenue for combined auto- and truck-part production works out to $12 million a week.

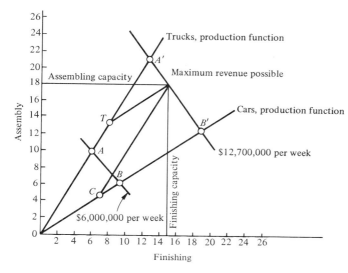

Figure 11.8. Sanmarco and Sullivan, Inc. Capital budgeting for new facilities by linear programming technique.
Note: AB connects points of equal profit on car and truck production functions at $6 million per week. *AB* is parallel to *A'B'*.
Solution: $(OC)(200) + (OT)(300) = \$12.7$ million
$$OC = 23,400 \text{ cars per week}$$
$$OT = 26,700 \text{ trucks per week}$$

Solving for production levels, the recommended production combination is 23,400 car and 26,700 truck parts a week. Thus management learns that by producing both car and truck parts, it can improve its profit position over the all-car or all-truck-part options. It also has learned that unless a new all-truck-part facility can improve this profit position, it ·will not be a worthwhile investment.

Integer Programming

Not all investment problems are this simple, of course. Suppose, instead, that the investment committee of Amiri-Girouard had the problem of spreading a fixed annual budget allocation among a number of competing proposals. This is another example of "capital rationing." The investment proposals are indivisible; that is, the investment committee has to allocate funds for the purchase of a whole machine or no machine, a whole factory addition or none. Half a machine or quarter of a factory is not possible. Nevertheless, for the sake of illustrating the nature of the problem, it may be useful to begin by assuming that fractional elements of each proposal could be obtained with the available funds.

The machine in question, a jig borer, can be purchased in a wide variety of sizes with a linear variation in purchase cost that is equivalent to saying that it is divisible. Similarly, the plant addition can be put up to suit the requirements of the firm in any agreed-upon dimension. Figure 11.9 shows the solution to the investment committee's problem. On the vertical axis is the budget available for the current year. That total budget will be equivalent to length OC_p. Along the horizontal axis, we measure next year's budget, length OC_f. Thus, the frontier $C_pC_tC_f$ represents all the money available for investment this year and next.

Ray OA represents all the various sizes in which jig borers are made. Likewise, OB represents all the optional sizes of the proposed plant addition. With funds C_t available, including this year's and next year's budget allotment, the solution is a fairly simple one. The committee should select the O size of the jig borer and the OP dimension of the plant addition because these decisions would provide the best possible allocation of its funds. But this demonstration, interesting as it is, will be of little use to the committee, because jig borers come in discrete sizes and plant additions just cannot be constructed in a wide variety of dimensions.

Integer programming may help Amiri-Girouard out of this dilemma. To illustrate the use of integer programming technique, we will change the problem slightly. Now the committee has to choose between two different jig borers. The machines will be used to produce 130 parts a day. One type of jig borer can produce fifty parts per day and the other eighty parts a day. The per part cost for the smaller machine is estimated to be 34 cents and for the larger machine 30 cents. As it stands, the problem is not difficult to solve. But suppose that it were a very complex calculation. Call X_1 the number of times the larger machine would have to be used to produce 130 parts and X_2 the number of times the smaller machine must be used to produce the same number. The daily production requirement then would be

$$80X_1 + 50X_2 = 130$$

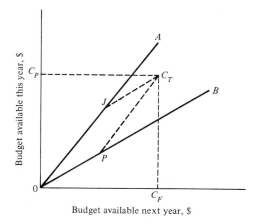

Figure 11.9. Amiri-Girouard. Best allocation of funds under capital rationing: divisible investments.

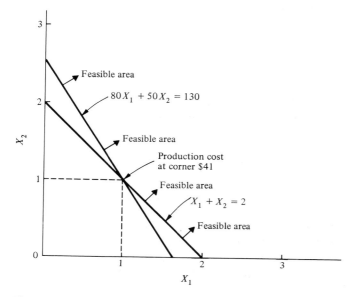

Figure 11.10. Integer programming solution to capital budgeting problem: indivisible investments.

Note: (80) (.30) + (50)(.34) = $41

We draw this line in Fig. 11.10. But there is a further requirement for an integer solution, one that does not involve divisible or variable-size machines.

$$X_1 + X_2 = 2$$

which is another way of saying that the investment committee must purchase, at a minimum, one each of the two machines. Together, these equations or lines define the area of feasibility for production purposes, which is the entire area above these two lines. In other words, these lines form a production frontier downward. The production costs on the larger machine will be $24 and on the smaller $17; the total cost will thus be $41. And, in an integer solution, no lower production cost is possible.

Markov Chain Analysis

Markov chain analysis is a mathematical device that stacks up information available about possible events and uses that information to predict where these events, if they occur in sequence and at some known or determinable probabilities, will lead. We may start by discovering what effect one decision chosen from among alternative decisions has upon other successive and possible decisions. There is a probability of outcome for each decision, given the outcome of a previous decision. The outcomes are called "states" and the probabilities are called "transition probabilities." Now all we need to know is how the process starts in order to deduce the likely direction the chain of events will take.

A particular form of Markov chain, sometimes called the "random walk" or "absorbing chain," is interesting because one or more of the transitions is irreversible and we can thus work out models that will tell us what inputs may be needed to maintain the process at a desired level. A good but quite simple example is that of Bird-Invalido, a car rental firm, in the New York metropolitan area. Bird-Invalido has three car pickup and drop-off points—Kennedy Airport, Grand Central Station, and Pennsylvania Station. In addition, the customers may drop off their cars out of town. This is an "absorbing state" because cars dropped off out of town do not return readily to the city pickup and drop-off points. A further absorbing state is the garage used for repairs. The number of cars that are dropped off out of town or are sent to the garage for repair determines both how quickly the in-town points will run out of cars and what sort of schedule must be worked out for returns from out of town and/or new car acquisitions.

Table 11.14 shows what is known about the movement of cars. The percentages are probabilities that a car starting from Grand Central Station, for example, will return within a day to that starting point. The problem is to determine the number of days that will pass before it will be necessary to replenish the supply of cars at any one pickup point, assuming that all cars leaving it are subject to the same probability.

Table 11.15 arranges the available information in computational (or canonical) form. The solution presented in Table 11.16 is that, for cars that leave Pennsylvania Station and are dropped off at Kennedy Airport, it will be one day before the supply runs out. Similarly, Kennedy Airport will run out of cars with respect to Grand Central Station in half a day.

The car rental case has a general analogy with investment problems in which machinery available for various alternative uses will be used in some

Table 11.14 Pickup and drop-off points for rental cars
Percentages of cars from pickup point

Pickup point	Grand Central Station	Pennsylvania Station	Kennedy Airport	Out of town	Garage
		Drop-off point			
Grand Central Station	0	50	0	50	0
Pennsylvania Station	50	0	50	0	0
Kennedy Airport	0	50	0	0	50
Out of town	0	0	0	100	0
Garage	0	0	0	0	100

Table 11.15   Computational format

	Out of town	Garage	Grand Central Station	Pennsylvania Station	Kennedy Airport
Out of town	1	0	0	0	0
Garage	0	1	0	0	0
Grand Central Station	.5	0	0	.5	0
Pennsylvania Station	0	0	.5	0	.5
Kennedy Airport	0	.5	0	.5	0

Notes: (1) The row probabilities add up to 1.
(2) The absorbing state always has a probability of 1.

Table 11.16   Number of days each pickup point will have cars with respect to any drop-off point

Pickup point	Drop-off point		
	Grand Central Station	Pennsylvania Station	Kennedy Airport
Grand Central Station	1.5	1	0.5
Pennsylvania Station	1.0	2	1.0
Kennedy Airport	0.5	1	1.5

probabilistic order. The absorbing states are those in which capital equipment is used up, depreciated, or "obsoleted." Markov chain analysis yields an investment replacement schedule based upon a dynamic sequence. This kind of solution has wide applications in capital budgeting.

Uncertainty in Capital Budgeting

An example taken from the Allis-Chalmers Company may be helpful in focusing on the issues involved in uncertainty in capital budgeting.[7] The problem is how to plan growth in a proposed lawn mower division. Allis-Chalmers could build a new plant especially designed to handle lawn mower production. It could acquire a lawn mower producer. It could buy the lawn mowers in some stage of production and finish and market them under the Allis-Chalmers name.

A significant part of the decision was the forecast by the marketing division with respect to the growth of demand for lawn mowers over the

---

[7]Victor Chou, "The Use of Gaming Models in Company Planning," *Business Economics,* I(2):62–64, 1965.

planning period. The forecast alternative growth rates with their associated probabilities were

	Annual growth rate, %	Probability, %
Low growth	2	10
Moderate growth	4	20
Rapid growth	7	70

Based upon financial analysis, various rates of return on the proposed alternative investment projects were projected as

	Projected rates of return		
Growth rates	Low, 2%	Moderate, 4%	High, 7%
Alternative investments			
Build plant	1	7	13
Acquire plant	5	10	10
Buy lawn mowers	8	8	8
Probabilities	.10	.20	.70

Now management was in a position to work out a defensible decision. Regarding the growth rates as events, the financial staff obtained the expected values of each investment project by multiplying each project's rate of return by the relevant probability value:

Expected value × project rate of return	Expected rate of return	Decision
$0.01(0.1) + 0.07(0.2) + 0.13(0.7) =$	10.6	Build
$0.05(0.1) + 0.10(0.2) + 0.10(0.7) =$	9.5	Acquire
$0.08(0.1) + 0.08(0.2) + 0.08(0.7) =$	8.0	Buy

On this reckoning, building its own plant appeared to be the best-paying alternative for Allis-Chalmers.

The role of logical deductions under conditions of uncertainty needs to be understood, though, in fact, no really new principles are at issue. Logic reduces uncertainty to a group of "if, then" statements. An outcome or probability matrix informs a decision-maker of the probable outcome of a decision if a certain forecast about the business environment comes true. Since managers may have different attitudes toward risk, this information does not of itself point to the preferred decision. However, it permits decision-makers to reach well-informed choices that are in accordance with their views of the risks involved.

Sensitivity Analysis

Another technique for taking account of the impact of uncertainties on the future outcome of investment proposals is that of sensitivity analysis. Hammersmith Trucking Enterprises is considering the investment attractiveness of a subsidiary operation in leasing. The proposal will require an initial outlay of $100,000 for a fleet of trucks to be leased. Current expectations are that the subsidiary will be successful, but a planning horizon of five years is set after which the decision to operate a leasing business will be reconsidered. The salvage value of the truck fleet at that time is estimated to be $10,000. Estimated lease income per year is $35,000. After taxes the expected cash flow then is $53,000 per year. The net present worth value of this cash flow, assuming a required rate of return of 20 percent, is $55,986. That, of course, is nearly a 56 percent return on the initial investment, which is quite favorable.

Yet the decision is sensitive to certain key parameters. Among these are the revenue estimate, the salvage value of the trucks at the end of five years, the time horizon used, and the required rate of return on investment. A significant variation in any one of these can be important. Table 11.17 shows an outline of management objectives and probable outcomes. Review of each in terms of probabilities included the following: Hammersmith management used a series of sensitivity tests staged in order of highest probability of adverse outcome (shown in Table 11.17) to try each likely adverse combination of outcomes. Management found that at every one of these uncertainty thresholds there was reason to proceed with the proposed investment. Test D, which

Table 11.17 Hammersmith Trucking Enterprises, Inc.

	Chance of outcome		
Outcome	20% higher, %	As predicted, %	20% lower, %
$35,000 annual profit	20	50	30
$10,000 salvage value	30	60	10
Five-year horizon	10	50	40
20% required return	20	70	10

Sensitivity tests	Net present worth, $
A Profits 20% lower	37,567
B Profits 20% lower	
Salvage value 20% higher	29,792
C Profits 20% lower	
Salvage value 20% higher	
Four-year horizon	12,350
D Profits 20% lower	
Salvage value 20% higher	
Four-year horizon	
Required rate 20% higher	2,494

combined all the adverse outcomes thought likely, still yielded a positive net present worth.

Case of Unknown Probabilities

ITADCO, a subsidiary of a major chemical and plastics company in the United States, was set up to develop new manufacturing facilities in various Latin American countries. Management prepared a set of proposed alternative facilities for a relatively wide variety of locations, political conditions, market demand possibilities, and access to transport and raw materials. These alternatives are grouped, as indicated in Table 11.18, into four categories:

a_1, those having a good location for transport
a_2, those with little likely political interference
a_3, those with predicted high and steady demand
a_4, those with good raw material sources

These categories were thought by the company's analysts to be mutually exclusive in the sense that each investment alternative would fit in one such category only.

The analysts also worked out a set of four possible outcomes:

s_1, high profits but cyclical variations
s_2, steady but moderate profit
s_3, recurrent labor problems
s_4, high level of taxation, if profits are good

The cost of each alternative, subject to the range of possible outcomes, was

Table 11.18 ITADCO: Cost matrix of alternative investments*

		Possible outcomes			
Alternatives		High sales potential, s_1	Steady, moderate profit, s_2	Likely labor problems, s_3	Basis for expansion, s_4
Good location	a_1	15	20	24	20
Little political interference	a_2	12	13	30	17
High and steady demand	a_3	21	25	28	20
Good raw material sources	a_4	19	16	25	18

*Cell entries are in multiples of $10,000.

worked out. That cost was expressed as the uniform equivalent annual cost of each alternative at the cost of money, assumed to be 15 percent. The following matrix collects all the relevant information by investment alternative categories and by outcome categories. The cells show the cost estimates of the alternative investment possible-outcome combinations.

If there were no uncertainty about the possible outcomes, then alternative category a_2 should be selected since it will result in the lowest uniform equivalent annual cost. But, should there be a rash of strikes, alternative a_2 is clearly the most expensive. However, if management has no information which would permit an assessment of the probability of any particular outcome, how should it make a decision about investment alternatives?

Minimax Principle

One principle or set of rules for making an investment choice is minimax. This principle is very pessimistic for it assumes that in each case the worst possible outcome is the most likely. The rule tells management to determine for each alternative the maximum cost and then to select that alternative which minimizes maximum cost. For example,

	Maximum cost
a_1	$240,000
a_2	$300,000
a_3	$280,000
a_4	$250,000

If this conservative rule is adopted, a_1 is the alternative to select since it minimizes costs under the worst possible outcome.

Minimin Principle

The minimin principle or rule is, in contrast, very optimistic. It calls for selecting that alternative which minimizes the minimum cost. Thus, from the cost matrix, management can select for each alternative the minimum cost. For example,

	Minimum cost
a_1	$150,000
a_2	$120,000
a_3	$200,000
a_4	$180,000

Using this rule, a_2 is the appropriate alternative.

Regret Principle

The regret principle is a selection rule that assumes that a decision-maker is most concerned with the difference between the actual outcome and that which would have occurred if she had been able to predict correctly the future outcome. These differences are called regrets and, given these regrets, the decision-maker should adopt a conservative position such that she will select that alternative which will minimize her maximum potential regret for each alternative.

Table 11.19   Regret matrix

	s_1	s_2	s_3	s_4
a_1	15 − 12 = 3	20 − 13 = 7	24 − 24 = 0	20 − 17 = 3
a_2	12 − 12 = 0	13 − 13 = 0	30 − 24 = 6	17 − 17 = 0
a_3	21 − 12 = 9	25 − 13 = 12	28 − 24 = 4	20 − 17 = 3
a_4	19 − 12 = 7	16 − 13 = 3	25 − 24 = 1	18 − 17 = 1

Table 11.19 shows a regret matrix put together by subtracting from each cell value the minimum value in each s column. Then, using this matrix, that alternative is selected which minimizes maximum regret as

	Maximum regret
a_1	$ 7,000
a_2	$ 6,000
a_3	$12,000
a_4	$ 7,000

Thus, according to the regret principle, alternative a_2 would be selected.

Chapter Summary

This chapter has presented an analysis of capital budgeting in a context that is, by implication, the management of the American, Western European, or Japanese corporation. Corporate capital budgeting makes three key assumptions:

1. That corporation management is continually engaged in planning for the future
2. That corporate planning involves taking all possible actions to ensure the survival of the corporation
3. That corporate management is able to obtain by good forecasting, including technological forecasting as well as market and product research, not only adequate information about capital decisions but a rather complete set of viable investment alternatives

These assumptions imply that the market competitive structure for the industry of which the corporation is a part is oligopolistic. There would be little place for capital budgeting, at least in the form we have presented in this chapter, in a purely competitive industry. Further, an alert management facing a wide choice of investment alternatives might well choose conglomerate status. It may be more than just coincidental that, with the increase in use and improvements in techniques for capital budgeting, major conglomerates—some of them international in scope—have been growing fast. In simple terms, capital budgeting is a study in corporate survival and growth.

If you have read this chapter carefully, you must have been struck by the fact that, after a careful argument for the correctness of NPW as a choice criterion had been presented, references to uncertainty and to capital rationing made that argument less valid and less applicable. But that is the way things really are. As with the $MR = MC$ rule, management cannot ultimately be concerned with correctness but with practical application. Increasing evidence about corporate management's capital budgeting procedures, however, does show that NPW or something very akin to it is growing in acceptance. Of course, the very fact that choice criteria of any kind are used is itself an indication of management rationality. NPW is, of course, an application of $MR = MC$ rule in the long run, but so is each of the other criteria. In the light of uncertainty and the prevalence of capital rationing, perhaps the best that can be said is that for many corporations long-run rational behavior is not easy to define. NPW is a solid step in the direction of rationality but hardly enough.

Since the real world is uncertain, why did we bother with the fiction of certainty? First of all, uncertainty is a matter of degree. If the uncertainty is small, little is gained by abandoning the assumption of certainty. More important, the techniques for capital budgeting in this chapter provide a framework and a foundation on which all rules for capital budgeting under uncertainty are built. Most corporations play the deadly serious game of capital budgeting, the game of survival planning, on the sandlots of certainty. Uncertainty introduces the chance of adversity.

The essence of uncertainty's impact on capital budgeting rules is that corporations are forced to move from a one-at-a-time consideration of each investment to an evaluation of a total capital budget, a complete portfolio of investment. Portfolio analysis basically implies zero-based capital budgeting. And that means that, when uncertainty arises, it is the firm itself that becomes the capital budget. The firm is the portfolio of assets. The choice is between continuing the firm as is or beginning again. In that context, once uncertainty has been properly handled, NPW and $MR = MC$ become the names of the game again. In short, most cases reduce to extensions on themes carefully outlined here.

Selected Readings

Arrow, K. J.: "Optimal Capital Policy with Irreversible Investment," in J. N. Wolfe (ed.), *Value, Capital and Growth*, Chicago, Aldine, 1968.

Barges, A.: *The Effect of Capital Structure on the Cost of Capital*, Englewood Cliffs, N.J., Prentice-Hall, 1964.

Baumol, William, and Richard E. Quandt: "Investment and Discount Rates Under Capital Rationing: A Programming Approach," *Economic Journal*, 75:317–329, June 1965.

Boness, A. J.: *Capital Budgeting: The Public and Private Sectors*, New York, Praeger, 1972.

Box, George E. P., and Gwilym M. Jenkins: *Time Series Analysis Forecasting and Control*, San Francisco, Holden-Day, 1976.

Carleton, Willard J.: "Linear Programming and Capital Budgeting Models: A New Interpretation," *Journal of Finance*, 24:825–833, December 1969.

Dudley, C. L.: "Note on Reinvestment Assumptions in Choosing Between Net Present Value and Internal Rate of Return," *Journal of Finance*, 27:907–915, September 1972.

Fremgen, J. M.: "Capital Budgeting Practices: A Survey," *Management Accounting*, 54:10–25, May 1973.

Grossack, I. M., and D. D. Martin: *Managerial Economics*, Boston, Little, Brown, 1973.

Hanssman, F.: *Operations Research Techniques for Capital Investment*, New York, Wiley, 1968 (especially chap. 3).

Hicks, John: *Capital and Growth*, New York, Oxford University Press, 1965.

Hirschman, Albert O.: *The Strategy of Economic Development*, New Haven, Conn., Yale University Press, 1958.

Hirshleifer, J.: "Efficient Allocation of Capital in an Uncertain World," *American Economic Review*, 54:77–85, May 1964.

Kantorovich, L. V.: *The Best Uses of Economic Resources*, Cambridge, Mass., Harvard University Press, 1965.

Klammer, T.: "Association of Capital Budgeting Techniques with Firm Performance," *Accounting Review*, 48:353–364, April 1973.

Klammer, T.: "Empirical Evidence of the Adoption of Sophisticated Capital Budgeting Techniques," *Journal of Business*, 45:387–397, July 1972.

Mitchell, G. B.: "Break-even Analysis and Capital Budgeting," *Journal of Accounting*, 7:332–338, Autumn 1969.

Modigliani, F., and M. H. Miller: "The Cost of Capital, Corporation Finance and the Theory of Investment," *American Economic Review*, 48:261–297, June 1958.

Myers, S. C.: "Note on Linear Programming and Capital Budgeting," *Journal of Finance*, 27:89–92, March 1972.

Parkison, P. W.: "Investment Decision Making: Conventional Methods vs. Game Theory," *Management Accounting*, 53:13–15, September 1971.

Theil, Henri: *Optimal Decision Rules for Government and Industry*, Chicago, Rand McNally, 1964.

Weingartner, H. Martin: *Mathematical Programming and the Analysis of Capital Budgeting Problems*, Englewood Cliffs, N.J., Prentice-Hall, 1963.

Questions, Problems, and Projects

1. Life-cycle costing (LCC) is a technique for estimating the total cost of a product over its useful life. LCC includes the expected cost of acquiring the item as well as the ownership costs. Ownership costs include spare parts, training, fuel, allowable overhead, and the pay and allowance system for personnel who operate and maintain the system in which the item is to be used. Generally, Department of Defense procurement is based on the lowest acquisition cost. If LCC were used rather than acquisition cost alone, what difference might this make in, say, major weapons systems? Compare LCC with cash-flow analysis. What do you suppose it would mean in LCC terms for a weapons system to be cost-effective?

2. MASS (Miller Assembled Stereophonic Sound) is a leading producer of high-fidelity equipment. MASS, after a marketing survey, has begun entry into the tape recorder field. In order to begin production, MASS has to choose between two machine systems, each of which will cost $150,000. The expected life of both machine systems is ten years. The MASS engineering department has projected the annual cash flows as

Machine system A: $30,000 a year for ten years
Machine system B: $50,000, first two years; $30,000, secondtwoyears; $25,000, third two years; $15,000, seventh year; $10,000, for each remaining year

The cost of funds is 12 percent. After serious appraisal of marketing alternatives in line with production possibilities, MASS management set up three planning periods, in the first of which an adequate market penetration should be attained in five years. The second planning period is seven and a half years. In it, tape recorder production must have become profitable. Within the third planning period, ten years, tape recorder profits must equal profits in other lines. These planning periods overlap. Sales goals for each planning period are

Year	Goal
5	$140,000
7½	210,000
10	280,000

Give an analysis of the alternatives for MASS.

3. What is the approximate NPW of each of the following proposals, using 10 percent as the hurdle rate (after taxes):

Year	Project A	Project B	Project C
0	$-5,000	$-5,000	$-5,000
1			
2			12,100
3		13,310	
4	14,640		

Which project would you select? Why? Would these projects have approximately similar IRRs?

4. Atlas Chemical Industries has extensively used the concept of long-range economic price (LREP) to evaluate capital investment projects. Long-range economic price is defined as the average price that, if received throughout the economic life of a product, will cover all direct and indirect costs and still yield an acceptance rate of return on all facilities used in production. The basic rule at Atlas is that if a product's long-range economic price is equal to or less than the forecast price, then a project to build a plant to produce it (or to divert existing production facilities) should be accepted. The equation for LREP is

$$\text{LREP} = a\,\frac{F}{A} + b\,\frac{FC}{A} + c\,(R) + d\,(VC)$$

where

F = amount of proposed investment

A = capacity of proposed plant in production units per year

FC = fixed costs in dollars per year

VC = variable costs in dollars per year

R = raw material costs in dollars per year

a, b, c, d = uniform discount rates, which could be equal

Implicit in the equation is the number of years over which these production amounts and costs must be discounted. Given the production and cost data, the solution depends on economic life estimates and discount rates.

Suppose plant capacity for product X is 5 million pounds per year, fixed operating costs are $210,000 per year, variable operating costs are 11 cents per pound, and the amount of the proposed fixed investment is $2 million. Raw material costs are 10 cents a pound. Estimated economic life of the plant is eight years. Atlas engineers have estimated that in order to yield 15 percent on the proposed investment, the discount factor would have to be 25 percent.

If Atlas enters into production of product X, at what price should X be sold? (Hint: Use uniform series present worth since each of the cash flows is constant over the eight-year horizon.)

5. Contrast and compare:

(a) Linear programming and integer programming in capital budgeting.

(b) Cost of capital and a management target rate of return.

(c) Economic life and depreciation accounting.

(d) Capital rationing and capital budgeting.

6. Since payback continues to be used widely, even by firms with sophisticated management tools available, what possible defense can you find for this practice?

Case 11.1   The Federal Executive Institute and Managerial Training Center at Charlottesville, Virginia

On November 22, 1974, the General Services Administration (GSA) sent a prospectus (a proposed document containing information about the needs for a project, estimated cost or rental information, and other data) to the Congress proposing the acquisition by lease of 196,000 net square feet of occupiable space in a complex of buildings for use as the Civil Service Commission's Federal Executive Institute and Managerial Training Center. The buildings were to be constructed to GSA specifications and requirements on a 25-acre site on the grounds of the University of Virginia in Charlottesville. The lease was to be for 20 years at an estimated annual rental of $2.4 million, starting in 1978. The university plans to provide financing for this project by selling tax-exempt bonds, contingent upon authorization of the Virginia legislature.

The present value analysis of alternative methods, included in the prospectus, indicated that leasing from the university would cost about $10 million less than Federal construction and ownership, $12.7 million less than leasing from a private developer, and $7.2 million less than acquisition by purchase contract. The analysis was for a 30-year period using the OMB-prescribed discount rates of 7 percent for construction and ownership and about 9 percent for future lease payments.

In the analysis, GSA included $7.1 million for imputed property taxes under the federal construction and ownership alternative. Real estate taxes are included as an imputed cost for taxes that would have been paid to the state and local governments if the property were privately owned. In this case, however, the property would be owned by a tax-exempt organization.

The United States General Accounting Office (GAO) found that its evaluation of the construction costs of the Federal Executive Institute building at Charlottesville, Virginia, differed significantly from those of the General Services Administration. The GSA contracts for the construction of government buildings across the United States and administers the buildings when built.

In defending its procedures and assumptions in making present worth cost comparisons of alternative methods of acquiring federal buildings, GSA leaned heavily on Office of Management and Budget (OMB) Circular A-104, dated June 14, 1972 (see Appendix I).

GAO in a November 4, 1975 Report of the Comptroller General to the Congress of the United States, made the following comparisons (see Appendix I) between its evaluation of the Federal Executive Institute project and that of GSA. Using OMB's prescribed discount rate, GAO found leasing less advantageous to the government than GSA had. And using the Treasury's borrowing costs, GAO found that it would have recommended construction and ownership as less costly than leasing.

APPENDIX I

Procedures and assumptions used in making present-value cost comparisons for alternative methods of acquiring federal buildings
The Office of Management and Budget (OMB) Circular A-104, dated June 14, 1972, prescribes the overall procedures, assumptions, and format to be used in a comparative cost analysis to support decisions to lease or purchase general-purpose real property. In making the analyses, the General Services Administration (GSA) follows the criteria in the OMB circular.

Specific assumptions Since June 1972 GSA's present-value cost comparisons in connection with facilities' acquisition have usually been based on projected costs over a thirty-year period. The comparisons include the following costs and related assumptions.

   A. *Federal Construction and Ownership Alternative*
      1. Construction costs (improvements) are assumed to be paid in a lump sum as of the present-value date and are therefore not discounted.
      2. Site, design, and other preparatory construction costs are assumed to be paid in a lump sum as of the present-value date and are therefore not discounted.
      3. Repair and improvement costs are assumed to begin as of the present-value date and continue over the period covered by the cost comparison. These costs are discounted.
      4. Real estate taxes are included as an imputed cost for taxes that would have been paid to state and local governments if the property were privately owned. Although the government pays no real estate taxes, the cost is imputed on the rationale that other federal support may be required to compensate the state and/or local governments for real estate tax revenues lost. (However, under the purchase contract alternative,[1] real estate taxes reflect an actual cost rather than an imputed cost because the trustee pays these taxes until the construction loan is liquidated. At this time, the government becomes the owner.) GSA believes that the imputed cost for real estate taxes represents an opportunity cost for tax revenue forgone by the local taxing authority. Real estate tax outlays are assumed to begin as of the present-value date and continue over the period covered by the cost comparison. These costs are discounted.
      5. Residual value is a cost offset representing the remaining market value that the property will have at the end of the period covered by the cost comparison. It is, therefore, a deduction from the stream of costs associated with the federal construction and ownership alternative. The residual value of the property is obtained by assuming that the value of the building declines 1.7 percent per year and the value of the site appreciates 1.5 percent per year. The residual value is discounted in the present-value cost comparison.
   B. *Leasing Alternatives*
      Annual lease payments are assumed to begin as of the present-value date and continue over the period covered by the comparison. Lease payments are discounted in the present-value comparison.

[1]Under this method of acquisition, GSA makes periodic payments of principal, interest, and taxes. Title to the facility is vested in the government when payments are completed.

GSA uses an OMB-prescribed 7 percent discount rate. Circular A-104 states that this rate represents an estimate of the internal rate of return on general-purpose real property leased from the private sector, exclusive of property taxes and expected inflation. In other words, the rate is based on the concept of opportunity cost forgone in the private sector.

APPENDIX II
Present-value analysis of federal construction compared with leasing
Federal Executive Institute and Managerial Training Center,
Charlottesville, Virginia
Revised by GAO, using OMB's prescribed discount rate over a 30-year period

	Per GSA's prospectus[a]	Revised by GAO[b]	Difference
Construction and ownership costs:			
Improvements	$17,775,000[c]	$14,149,000	$ 3,626,000
Site, design, etc.	2,696,000[c]	2,374,000	322,000
Repair and improvements	1,351,000	447,000	904,000
Real estate taxes	7,107,000	[d]	7,107,000
Less residual value	−1,772,000	−1,323,000	−449,000
Present value	$27,157,000	$15,647,000	$11,510,000
Lease payments:			
Total outlay, undiscounted	43,995,000	43,995,000	
Present value	17,159,000	12,560,000[e]	$ 4,599,000
Leasing less costly	$ 9,998,000	$ 3,087,000	

[a]GSA used the OMB rate of 7 percent for discounting future ownership outlays and about 9 percent for future lease outlays.

[b]Costs were adjusted to consider differences in the timing of cash outlays as discussed in our prior report (LCD-74-334, Feb. 13, 1975). The residual value was adjusted to recognize that the analysis period was extended from 30 to 34 years because occupancy under either the leasing or construction alternative would take place 4 years after the analysis was prepared.

[c]These costs were not discounted by GSA.

[d]Since the proposed lessor, the University of Virginia, does not pay property taxes as a private lessor would, we eliminated the imputed cost of property taxes.

[e]Total lease costs are reduced by an OMB-prescribed inflation deflator before the application of the 7 percent rate in order to put leasing costs on a constant dollar basis. This results in about a 9 percent discount rate for analysis purposes.

APPENDIX III

Present-value analysis of federal construction compared with leasing Federal Executive Institute and Managerial Training Center, Charlottesville, Virginia

Revised by GAO, using a discount rate based on Treasury's borrowing cost over a 30-year period

	Per GSA prospectus*	Revised by GAO†	Difference
Construction and ownership costs:			
Improvements	$17,775,000	$14,149,000	$ 3,626,000
Site, design, etc.	2,696,000	2,374,000	322,000
Repair and improvements	1,351,000	447,000	904,000
Real estate taxes	7,107,000		7,107,000
Less residual value	−1,772,000	−1,323,000	−449,000
Present value	$27,157,000	$15,647,000	$11,510,000

Present-value analysis of federal construction compared with leasing Federal Executive Institute and Managerial Training Center, Charlottesville, Virginia

Revised by GAO, using a discount rate based on Treasury's borrowing cost over a 30-year period

	Per GSA prospectus*	Revised by GAO†	Difference
Lease payments:			
Total outlay, undiscounted	43,995,000	43,995,000	
Present value	17,159,000	15,952,000	$ 1,207,000
Leasing less costly, present value	$ 9,998,000		
Construction and ownership less costly, present value		$ 305,000	

*GSA used the OMB rate of 7 percent for discounting future ownership outlays and about 9 percent for future lease outlays.

†Costs were adjusted to consider differences in the timing of cash outlays as discussed in our prior report (LCD-74-334, Feb. 13, 1975), using a discount rate based on the cost of Treasury borrowing (7 percent) for both the leasing and federal construction and ownership alternatives. The residual value was adjusted to recognize that the analysis period was extended.

DISCUSSION QUESTIONS 11.1

1. What is the "proper" discount rate for determining net present worth? Why?
2. Examine GAO's presentation and arguments. Do they convince you? In what way is the GAO argument different from that of GSA and OMB? Are there any other elements which you would add to these arguments?
3. Outline various other possible methods of comparing the cost of leasing with that of construction and ownership.
4. Could payback methods have been used in this context? If so, how?

Case 11.2 The 1976 Capital Budget for Moore McCormack Resources, Inc.

The 1975 annual report of Moore McCormack Resources (MMR) emphasized the future growth of the company's earning power. James R. Barker, chairman, president and chief executive officer, and Paul R. Tregurtha, executive vice president and chief financial officer, stressed that the nature of the markets MMR served required that the company's earning power be viewed in a long-term framework. In that context, they told MMR stockholders that "your company should be able to meet its stated objectives of a 15 percent annual average increase in earnings. MMR's prospects for 1976 and beyond are encouraging."

LONG-TERM STABILITY

The high degree of security in MMR's new projects can be illustrated by a review of some of their major characteristics. Most of the projects are based on medium- to long-term contractual obligations of others to Moore McCormack. Such arrangements help to input stable, predictable revenue flows into the company's earnings base. This is exemplified, in some situations, by term charters, contracts of affreightment which obligate shippers to use Moore McCormack vessels for shipment of bulk cargoes, and long-term management contracts. The objective of such arrangements is to assure asset utilization so that capital costs associated with substantial investments in fixed assets can be serviced without difficulty.

The size and relative financial strength of companies with which Moore McCormack has such contracts also gives additional assurance of stability which, in turn, will assist in financing the projects (see Table 1). Examples are tanker charters to a member of the Royal Dutch/Shell group, the presence of major American, Canadian, and international iron and steel companies as project partners in iron ore development and property interests, and the association of large steel, iron, automotive, and utility companies as partners in coal projects.

ATTRACTIVE FINANCING OPTIONS

Because of the high quality and comparatively low risk of its capital-intensive operations, as well as governmental aids, Moore McCormack Resources is able to meet its external funds requirements through varying methods.

Leveraged lease financing of the three product carrier tankers, which Moore McCormack Bulk Transport will operate for Shell International Petroleum Company, Ltd., eliminates the necessity for a capital contribution by Moore McCormack Resources.

In some situations, major participants in a project may offer completion guarantees and/or serve as guarantors for debt issued by the project itself.

Under Title XI provisions of the Merchant Marine Act, Moore McCormack can obtain government guarantees for financing up to $87\frac{1}{2}$ percent of the

Table 1   Financing Phase One projects
In thousands of dollars

Project	MMR participation	Debt	Equity	Debt	Equity
Hibbing Taconite	36,000 (15%)	26,000	10,000	Bank term loan	Internal funds
Moore McCormack Bulk Transport, three Coronado-class, 39,700 DWT tankers	49,000	49,000, leveraged lease	0	Leveraged lease	0
Scotts Branch Coal	10,000 (20%)	10,000	0	20% of 50,000 Private place-ment	0
Moore McCormack Lines, midbody conversion of two Constellation-class vessels	15,000	11,000	4,000	Title XI bonds (75%)	CCF (25%) (Capital Construc-tion Fund)
The Interlake Steamship Company, two 59,000-ton bulk carriers	88,500	76,800	11,700	Title XI bonds ($87^{1}/_{2}$%)	CCF ($12^{1}/_{2}$%)
Leslie Coal Mining Company	9,000 (20%)	9,000	0	20% of an affiliate with a term loan and leveraged leases	0
The Interlake Steamship Company, conversion of *Herbert C. Jackson*	6,000	0	6,000	0	CCF

cost of vessels to be used in domestic operations, such as the Interlake ore carriers now under construction, and up to 75 percent of the cost of American flag vessels to be employed in foreign trade, such as the Constellation-class cargo liners which have been enlarged with midbodies. It should be noted that Title XI guarantees lower effective borrowing costs to the level available to highest-rated corporate issuers.

Under the provisions of the Merchant Marine Act of 1970, tax-free deposits of vessel operating earnings which can be made to the Capital Construction Fund (CCF) may later be withdrawn on a tax-free basis if the funds are to be used for qualified purposes, such as acquiring vessels to be employed in the Great Lakes or foreign trades or retiring principal debt incurred in acquiring or modifying such ships.

The depreciable cost basis of any vessels acquired with CCF funds, however, must be lowered by the amount of funds used. The effect is to lower future depreciation expense, and, consequently, increase future tax payments and provisions if there is no continued building program. Accordingly, over the long term, judicious utilization of CCF demands the deposit and subsequent commitment of funds only in amounts that are likely to be required for vessels whose feasibility and profit potential are sound and attractive. That is Moore McCormack's policy.

PRUDENT LEVERAGE

The effect of the large proportion of the financing that will be committed in debt form will be to increase, over time, Moore McCormack's debt to capitalization ratio, which averaged 33 percent during 1975. The company's long-term debt used in this calculation does not include borrowings made to finance the construction of capital assets until such assets are actually in operation.

Although the company has not yet defined an ideal target mix of debt and equity in its capital structure, management feels that continued involvement in projects of the quality under current development, requiring heavy capital investment, warrants a debt capitalization of 50 percent or more.

However, as each of the capital projects comes on-stream, it will generate a new package of earnings. The proportion of such earnings and of profits that will continue to be generated by the company's present basic activities flowing ultimately to retained earnings, together with amortization of debt, will allow Moore McCormack Resources to continue to employ a debt-oriented financing strategy within acceptable limits.

It should be noted that, in January of this year, the company retired the last third of the $30 million in 9 percent preferred shares issued in connection with the acquisition of Pickands Mather.

An indication of the company's ability at present levels of earnings to handle large amounts of debt without impinging on liquidity is seen in the consolidated statement of changes in financial position (see Table 2). At the close of 1975, the working capital ratio was 2.2.

An analysis of Note 13 to the financial statements will indicate that the amount of present and prospective lease rentals and other commitments is not inordinate when related to current and prospective levels of earning power.

Table 2   Consolidated statement of changes in financial position
For the year ending December 31

	1975	1974
Funds provided from:		
Operations:		
Income before extraordinary item	$ 30,652,000	$24,749,000
Charges (credits) not affecting working capital:		
Depreciation, amortization, and depletion	5,488,000	5,309,000
Increase (decrease) in deferred Federal income taxes, net of extraordinary tax credit	11,587,000	(258,000)
Net increase in estimated liability for claims	2,029,000	4,080,000
Equity in undistributed earnings of affiliates	(3,721,000)	(1,476,000)
Total funds from operations	$ 46,035,000	$32,404,000
Other sources:		
Long-term debt and construction borrowings, less proceeds held in restricted funds	93,639,000	48,415,000
Proceeds on sale and leaseback of vessel	16,841,000	
Decrease in restricted funds, net	6,436,000	7,168,000
Reissuance of treasury shares	6,298,000	
Total funds provided	$169,249,000	$87,987,000
Funds used for:		
Additions to capital assets	107,909,000	24,858,000
Dividends	2,589,000	654,000
Reduction of long-term debt and preferred stock of subsidiary	26,744,000	43,698,000
Net increase in Capital Construction Fund	7,216,000	765,000
Decrease (increase) in net unterminated voyage revenue	5,081,000	(7,285,000)
Purchase of treasury shares		16,603,000
Other, net	578,000	(772,000)
Total funds used	150,117,000	78,521,000
Net increase in working capital	$ 19,132,000	$ 9,466,000
Analysis of changes in working capital:		
Cash and short-term investments	$ 10,125,000	$15,843,000
Receivables	(11,797,000)	16,532,000
Inventories and other current assets	5,185,000	(1,085,000)
Estimated deposits to Capital Construction Fund	7,377,000	(2,661,000)
Accounts payable and accrued liabilities	1,503,000	(9,253,000)
Long-term debt due within one year		(1,600,000)
Federal income taxes payable	6,739,000	(8,310,000)
Net increase in working capital	$ 19,132,000	$ 9,466,000

NOTE 13   LEASES AND COMMITMENTS

Total lease rental expense (net of subleases) was approximately $4,956,000 in 1975 and $4,807,000 in 1974, including rentals on noncapitalized financing leases of $1,382,000 and $2,044,000, respectively. As of December 31, 1975, future lease obligations are

	Total lease rentals payable	Portion representing financing leases payable
1976	$ 6,570,000	$2,997,000
1977	5,406,000	2,224,000
1978	4,707,000	2,064,000
1979	4,378,000	2,011,000
1980	3,813,000	2,011,000
1981–1985	15,007,000	8,933,000
1986–1990	12,302,000	8,503,000
1991–1995	9,970,000	8,468,000
After 1995	1,551,000	1,551,000

As of December 31, 1975, the capitalized present value of the financing leases referred to above was $19,623,000, including $16,807,000 for the first of three 39,700-deadweight-ton (DWT) tankers, delivered in December 1975. The balance of the leases, the present value of which was $6,075,000 as of December 31, 1974, is principally for containers. If these financing leases had been capitalized and the related assets amortized on a straight-line basis (with interest cost accrued on the basis of the outstanding lease liability), the effect on net income would have been insignificant.

DISCUSSION QUESTIONS 11.2

1. Examine the performance of MMR's stock over recent years and assess the impact of the 1976 capital budget on earnings per share, stock price, and yield on stockholders' equity.
2. Is there enough information in these excerpts from MMR's 1975 annual report to permit an effective evaluation of the 1976 capital budget?
3. It is rare for major corporations to disclose their capital budgets and proposals for financing. Why do you suppose that MMR did so in 1976? What advantages were there in this disclosure? To whom? When?
4. What implicit and explicit evaluation criteria were used by MMR in the determination of its 1976 capital budget? How can you tell? Would it have made a difference had NPW, IRR, or payback been used exclusively?

12

BENEFIT/COST ANALYSIS

Key Concepts

benefit
construction efficiency
cost
efficiency
equity
horizontal equity
indirect effects
production efficiency

program efficiency
program evaluation
social accounting prices
social efficiency
transfer efficiency
transfer price
vertical equity

What Is Ahead in This Chapter

Like the chapter on capital budgeting, this is another chapter on project appraisal. The tool applied to project evaluation in this chapter is benefit/cost (B/C) analysis. A series of case studies is used to show how benefit/cost analysis has been and can be used in a variety of situations. The cases vary from a flood prevention project in Indiana, to a toll road in Mexico, to a cement block factory. Each case takes a particular aspect of benefit/cost analysis, examines its meaning, and illustrates its application.

Essentially, benefit/cost analysis will be employed under those conditions where nonfinancial and nonproduction data have to be used for evaluation purposes. Other names for this kind of project evaluation include cost effectiveness, systems analysis, program budgeting, and cost-utility analysis. Each of these, along with benefit/cost, is an example of applying economic analysis to situations where, in the past, decisions were largely based on noneconomic criteria and were often ad hoc. The use of economic criteria, whatever their form, leads to an assessment of the value received (or to be received) by the members of society in return for the use of society's resources.

While benefit/cost analysis is an extension of profit measurement to take account of all social revenues and costs, it is also a way of extending the logic of management-effectiveness measurement to those areas and projects where the rule has been: "If we have the money, let's do it." But money and economic resources have opportunity costs. Benefit/cost analysis is a way of capturing and evaluating those costs.

While benefit/cost analysis tends to be most widely used where market criteria are weak, it is not the presence or absence of a marketplace, market prices, or market organization that makes benefit/cost applicable. Rather it is the need to evaluate all sectors of the economy, not just the business sector, since nonprofit and service enterprises continue to grow in relative size in an economy where more people are employed in nongoods than in goods production.

Why Benefit/Cost Analysis Is Used

Benefit/cost analysis is often used in investment-project evaluation because there is a basic skepticism about internal cost and profit measures. Nothing should be taken for granted when large sums are to be committed to a project, whether in private industry or in the public sector. This skepticism really should be applied to the economic, technical, institutional, and financial aspects of project appraisal. No matter how correct capital budgeting evaluation techniques are, they tend to be limited to the firm itself, but, in many cases, that is not enough.

The bigger an investment, the more likely it is that it will have an impact far beyond a company. In that light, there are three key questions that need to be answered for every large project, public or private:

1. What is to be the impact of the project on the local, regional, or national economy?
2. Is the project likely to contribute significantly and positively to the development of the local, regional, or national economy?
3. Is that contribution large enough and positive enough to justify the use of scarce resources needed not only to build and install the project but also to staff and manage it?

Internal criteria don't always answer these questions. There is even some doubt whether market criteria can answer these questions, especially if there is reason to think that market-price signals are not correct because of monopoly control, tariffs, subsidies, government regulation, and the impact of current fiscal and monetary policies.

Benefit/Cost Analysis and Optimization

Jacques Lesourne[1] has pointed out that some of the problems in developing and using benefit/cost measures arise from failure to recognize that benefit/cost analysis is not a method of overall optimization. Benefit/cost belongs to that family of measures where one investment is more profitable than another, where a new product meets some minimum profit criterion, or where situation A is better than situation B.

Economists have developed a theory of economic welfare to encompass that area of project analysis in which the objective is to maximize net social benefits or consumer surplus. In Fig. 12.1, the difference between economic welfare theory and benefit/cost analysis is made clear. Given the resources available, the price structure, and the known methods of production, TS is a transformation surface between the set of situations facing individual X and that set facing individual Y. TS is the focus of all those trade-off positions between X and Y from which it is impossible to benefit the welfare of X (a firm, a nation, a group of people, or a sector of the national economy) without hurting some other individual Y (firm, nation, group of people, or sector of the national economy). Within TS lie all the feasible trade-offs; beyond TS, to the right, lie unattainable trade-offs.

Any welfare optimum trade-off lies on TS. But suppose that we wished to compare situation A with situation B. A is clearly better than B, because at A both individuals are better off than at B. The benefits to X and to Y at A are greater than the costs of getting from B to A. Benefit/cost analysis helps

[1]Jacques Lesourne, *Cost-Benefit Analysis and Economic Theory*, Amsterdam, North-Holland, 1975.

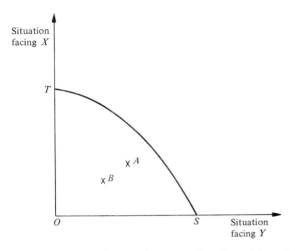

Figure 12.1. Welfare optimum trade-offs and benefit/cost analysis.

establish that A is better than B. It is not necessarily a good tool for determining how to arrive at *TS*.

Is an Economic Activity Worth Doing?

Benefit/cost analysis is a way of determining whether an economic activity is or has been worth doing. Profit measurement is a limited form of benefit/cost analysis based on the assumption that by measuring both costs and revenues or benefits internal to a firm, we can work out an effective indication of the worth of a project, an activity, or a production process. In the broadest sense, the essence of benefit/cost analysis is that society cannot always accept internal costs and corporate profits as adequate measures of social worth.

Since benefit/cost analysis must begin somewhere, however, it is customary to assume that actual recorded internal costs and revenues can be adjusted to reflect all relevant elements both within and outside the firm or the project. There are two steps in the adjustment of internal cost and revenue information to reflect all such relevant elements. One involves the use of social accounting prices to change the internal costs and revenues. The other involves extending the analysis beyond the firm or the project to cover all relevant indirect effects.

In the past, many applications of benefit/cost analysis have taken place in not-for-profit enterprises, in large government projects for which no or low fees will be charged to potential beneficiaries, and in public or semipublic corporations such as hospitals, educational television, the Tennessee Valley Authority, or the Seattle Power and Light Department. In these and similar instances, benefit/cost analysis has been used to provide an analog to enterprise profit, that is, to provide a measure which like profit would show what kind of return the investors, the direct intended beneficiaries, the public in general, or society as a whole was receiving on the capital and other resources employed in the economic activity or the project. But more and more corporate uses of benefit/cost analysis are being reported.

Social Accounting Prices

Social accounting prices are shadow prices. They indicate the full value to society of any resource in use in an enterprise. Since the prices a firm actually pays for labor, raw materials, land, money, or other production factors may reflect specially advantageous market situations, the use of social accounting prices provides a way to adjust the actual price. For example, in a multidivisional firm, many parts, assemblies, and materials are transferred from one division to another for use in production. There is the possibility that the transfer price—the price paid by one division for another division's sales—is not made at arm's length. In this instance, the market price would become the social accounting price which would be substituted for the transfer price to adjust internal costs.

Another example would be the effect of a tariff. A tariff is a sales tax imposed at the border on imported goods. It raises prices to reduce effective competition by a foreign-based firm. A tariff might account for the level of sales or competitive advantage attained by a domestic firm. Domestic profits generated by the protection provided by the tariff could not be assigned entirely to internal cost advantages. What would sales have been in the absence of the tariff?

Wherever there is reason to believe that internal prices, costs, revenues, or income flows are distorted by special situations, subsidies, tariffs, agreements, protected markets, transport charges, tax laws, lower rates than market interest rates for financing, or even weak competitive markets, there is a need to use social accounting prices to make internal cost and revenue adjustments. In every case, the reason for the adjustment is to permit an analysis and a comparison based on what would or could have happened under market conditions that are expected under competition.

Indirect Effects

Any economic activity is likely to have effects on members of society beyond the direct purchasers, employees, stockholders, or management. For example, a factory which, because of the nature of its market and the effectiveness of its management, maintains a consistently high level of employment does more than render a profit to its investors. It does more than pay wages, or salaries, or prices (however calculated) to its employees, management, suppliers, and contractors. That high and consistent level of employment provides the basis for the building of a prosperous community with schools, public services, a good-quality environment, and a sense of security for the families in the area.

The indirect effects of a new highway would include

1. Improvements in safety that reduce loss of life. The value of lives saved is thus an indirect benefit.
2. Reduction in migration costs of poorer people, thus inducing them to seek urban labor markets. Such movements might mean higher welfare expenses, perhaps even expansion of ghettos, or higher school costs in the cities along the highway routes.
3. Changes in land-use patterns as agricultural land is converted to factory, commercial, and residential use.
4. Improvements and cost reductions in goods movement with resultant lowering of consumer prices in particular places.

It is possible to distinguish between those indirect effects which have market consequences, that is, those which affect prices, costs, incomes, and market organization directly, and those which have extramarket consequences. The extramarket indirect effects are, of course, the hardest to identify and certainly to evaluate. But they are nonetheless of considerable significance. Indeed, in some contexts, they may be more important than all other of the impacts of a proposed investment taken together.

Benefit/Cost Analysis of the Lost River Project

The Lost River Project in southern Indiana was developed by the Soil Conservation Service in the late 1960s. Based on the Work Plan for Watershed Protection and Flood Prevention (dated February 1969), here is a detailed analysis of the benefits and costs of that project. This analysis, in the first column of Table 12.1, lists the direct or internal benefits and costs calculated by the Soil Conservation Service in its defense of the proposed Lost River project. The second column shows the social accounting prices, based upon a review of the project by Robert K. Davis, Barbara J. Ingle, and William J. Gillen in testimony before the Joint Economic Committee of the Congress of the United States in January 1973. The data in the third column are from the same testimony as well as from the Soil Conservation Service.

Social accounting prices are used to adjust both the benefits and the costs of the Lost River Project. These adjustments include, on the benefit side, an evaluation of the production to be derived from resources currently unemployed.

On the cost side, the interest rate is raised from 4.625 to 8 percent to account for the probable true cost of money to the federal government for use in this project. This increases the annual equivalent cost of construction by an additional $286,900. Account is also taken of the actual land treatment costs both for the federal government and for private landowners in the project area.

The indirect effects include additional estimates of benefits of flood control to areas beyond the impact area, as well as the value of production from new crop land likely to be put into production and the probable increase in production from land in and around the project area no longer subject to flood

Table 12.1   The Lost River Project (southern Indiana)
In thousands of dollars

	Internal or direct effects	Social accounting effects	Indirect effects	Summary
Benefits				
Flood damage reduction				
Agricultural production	150.1			150.1
Nonagricultural production	23.1			23.1
Erosion prevention	15.3			15.3
Indirect			21.0	21.0
Drainage improvement				
New crop land			35.0	35.0
Higher production			34.8	34.8
Recreation	252.5			252.5
Water supply	21.9			21.9
Use of unemployed resources		21.1		21.1
	462.9			574.8
Costs				
Annual equivalent cost of construction (at $4^5/8\%$)	398.2	286.9*		685.1
Annual maintenance and repair	57.5			57.5
Land treatment (private)		91.2		91.2
Land treatment (public)		22.5		22.5
Environmental losses			35.0	35.0
	455.7			891.3
Net benefits	7.2			−316.5

*At 8%.

damage. The environmental costs include the threatened loss of present tourist attractions in caves along the Lost River, as well as the likely destruction of blind fish and other cave life.

The result is that, while the Lost River Project appeared to be capable of producing a net benefit based on direct internal benefit/cost estimates, taking account of social accounting prices and indirect effects made it very apparent that the project would represent a poor investment for the state of Indiana and for the nation.

Comparisons of Benefits and Costs

Once the benefits and the costs of a proposed project have been measured in monetary terms and reasonable adjustments have been made for accounting or shadow prices and indirect effects, the results can be put into at least four different forms:

1. The internal rate of return on the investment
2. The benefit/cost ratio
3. Net present worth
4. Payback period

We have already examined three of these indicators of net benefit. The point to be made, however, is that their use need not imply the attainment of an optimum in a benefit/cost context.

Benefit/cost ratios can be presented in a variety of ways. Gross costs can be set off against gross benefits. Sometimes certain costs are netted out of benefits before the calculation of benefits. The more correct way is to determine the net benefit. In any case, it is important to know how any particular benefit/cost ratio was computed if the final result is to be correctly interpreted.

The basic ingredients of benefit/cost analysis are the same regardless of the final form of the evaluation measure. These basic ingredients are the values of the benefits and of the costs. Typically, any stream of benefits and/or costs will be discounted by some measure of the opportunity cost of capital. Thus, the discounted benefits will be divided by the discounted costs.

The acceptance criterion is that

$$\text{Benefits} - \text{costs} > 1$$

In IRR terms, the acceptance criterion is that the IRR of the project(s) must be equal to or greater than the opportunity cost of capital. And, in NPW terms, the NPW of the project at the opportunity cost of money must be positive. A payback criterion would, of course, have to be an arbitrary time limit within which the project would return the required outlay.

Mexican Road Projects

In 1962 the International Bank for Reconstruction and Development (the World Bank) lent the Mexican toll road authority $30.5 million. Mexico already had a well-established railroad and road transport network. The purpose of the World Bank loan was to relieve traffic overloads on key routes. The Mexican government had decided that, as a matter of public policy, high-traffic-density road projects should be financed outside the national budget, leaving the existing free roads available for local traffic and those who did not wish to pay tolls.

Table 12.2 shows a set of estimates of cost/benefit ratios and IRRs on the first phase of the Mexican program. The assumed cost of money is 12 percent. This rate is used to convert the original investment into a series of annual equivalent costs, as well as to convert the annual estimated road-user benefits into a present value of such benefits. The IRRs were calculated over an estimated economic life for the highways and bridges of thirty years.

Table 12.2 Estimates of cost/benefit ratios and IRRs: Mexican highways

Project	Original investment	Annual O&M*	Annual total equivalent cost	Annual benefits	B/C	IRR
Mexico-Orizaba						
Mexico-Puebla	276.1	3.3	4.44	41.8	9.4	19
Puebla-Orizaba	184.8	2.2	2.97	38.0	12.8	20
Mexico-Venta de Carpio	73.7	1.5	1.81	20.0	11.0	20
Tijuana-Ensenada	204.7	2.9	3.75	18.0	4.8	10
Bridges:						
Coatzocoalcos	73.7	0.4	0.43	6.5	15.1	12
Culiacan	16.8	0.1	0.19	1.5	7.9	12
Alvarado	25.7	0.2	0.26	3.5	13.5	15
Caracol	5.2	0.1	0.10	0.5	5.0	9
Papaloapan	7.0	0.1	0.11	0.8	7.3	12

*O&M = operation and maintenance expenses. Data are in Mexican pesos.
Source: Case 21, Part III, in John A. King, *Economic Development Projects and Their Appraisal*, Baltimore, Johns Hopkins, 1967.

In Table 12.2, all the individual projects except the Caracol Bridge are acceptable. However, the Caracol Bridge is not an independent project. It is contingently dependent on other elements of the proposed network. Therefore, it had to be accepted despite its lower IRR. The annual benefits were high, based on estimates of traffic to be diverted to toll highways. There was some reason to believe that the estimates were too high, but the values of the B/C ratios indicate that even a substantial reduction in benefits would still yield B/C ratios in excess of unity. Additionally, user benefits are a first estimate and do not take account of indirect effects that, given the stage of development of the Mexican economy, were likely to be quite large. In general, when highway projects are designed to relieve traffic, the known demand is almost always likely to make the project economically viable.

Transportation Planning in Ecuador: Calculating Payback

Ecuador is one of the least-developed nations in South America. In the 1960s, it had a per capita income range between $200 and $225 and a growth rate of about 2.7 percent. A Ten-Year Plan was adopted for the years 1964–1973 to transform the social structure of the country so that more Ecuadorians could share the benefits derived from foreign trade. Despite an enormous effort since 1947, large areas of Ecuador remained without access to markets because of the lack of roads. Thus, the Ten-Year Plan provided for 1050 kilometers of new highways and improvement of 2300 kilometers of existing highways, which would permit the completion of the Pacific Coast network. The Santo Domingo–Esmeraldas Highway, running from the northern part of the Guayas

River basin into Esmeraldas Province, links a new colonization area, which has been turning into one of the more prosperous regions, with a more tropical section in which is located Ecuador's third-largest banana-shipment port. The Santo Domingo-Esmeraldas road was to be upgraded to a paved all-weather highway, thus reducing losses of produce through bruising and rotting as well as delays and interruptions caused by bad weather. The 1960 traffic on the Santo Domingo–Esmeraldas road was estimated to have a weighted average-vehicle-operating cost of $.20 per kilometer. After improvement and paving, with the same composition of traffic, the weighted average-vehicle-operating costs should reduce to $.13 per kilometer. This saving of about $.07 a vehicle per kilometer amounts to a 36 percent reduction in operating costs.

The average 1960 traffic on the unimproved road was 200 vehicles a day. It is estimated that traffic on the unpaved road would increase by about ten vehicles a day each year. On this basis, the average daily traffic (ADT) would reach 420 vehicles by 1982 without improvement. If improved and paved, ADT would increase to 690 by 1982. The difference between ADT growth without improvement and that following improvement and pavement is called development traffic. Thus, by 1982, development traffic is estimated at 270, an amount in excess of that expected without change (see Table 12.3).

To assess benefits from the proposed improvement and paving of the Santo Domingo–Esmeraldas road, the planners assigned the full amount of the reduced vehicle operating costs to the normal traffic. Then, for the development traffic which would have been diverted and induced to use the improved road, benefits were calculated at half the reduction on the hypothesis that this new traffic would be induced proportionately to the amount of available vehicle operation savings (see Table 12.4).

Obviously, it was not likely that all traffic would use the entire length of the road; therefore, the planners estimated that of the total length of 174 kilometers, 115 would constitute an average trip. Thus, an equivalent ADT can be calculated by multiplying the qualifying ADT by 0.67. Annual savings in vehicle operating cost were calculated as follows:

Equivalent ADT × 365 days × 174 kilometer × $.07

so that, for 1967, this would be

(220) × 365 × 174 × $.07 = $978,054

Table 12.3 Projected ADT: Santo Domingo–Esmeraldas Road

	Unimproved	Improved and paved	Development
1960	200	200	0
1967	270	390	120
1972	320	490	170
1977	370	590	220
1982	420	690	270

Table 12.4 Calculation of payback: Santo Domingo–Esmeraldas Highway construction cost, $10,620,000

Year	(a) Normal ADT	(b) Development ADT × .5	(c) Total qualifying ADT × (a + b)	(d) Equivalent ADT (c × .67)	(e) Annual savings	(f) NPW discounted @ 8%	(g) NPW discounted @ 12%
1967	270	60	330	220	$ 978,054	$9,714,400	$9,746,760
1972	320	85	405	271	1,204,785	5,621,500	6,194,000
1977	370	110	480	372	1,431,515	2,265,600	3,764,100
1982	420	135	555	372	1,652,800	− 402,560	2,152,760
						NPW = 0 in 1981	NPW = 0 in 1986

Source: C. J. Stokes, *Transportation and Economic Development in Latin America*, New York, Praeger, 1969.

Discounted at 8 percent, the annual flow of savings would equal the construction cost of the new highway in 1981 so that payback would take place during approximately the fifteenth year of operation. At 12 percent, payback takes place in 1986. The IRR of the highway if economic life is assumed to be twenty years is about 12 percent. (See Table 12.4.)

The savings calculated did not include agricultural benefits. If these were combined with the vehicle-operation savings it is estimated that, over the economic life of the highway prior to any need for major repair or rebuilding, the internal rate of return on the highway (including any necessary capital investment for zone of highway influence) would come to 17 percent. However, since there was a net benefit over costs within the expected economic life of the highway, the more uncertain agricultural benefits did not have to be taken into consideration to establish the advantages of the Santo Domingo–Esmeraldas highway.

Systems Analysis of an Expansion Decision

Systems analysis is the application of methods of economic analysis and scientific method to problems of choice in business situations. It is a systematic attempt to provide decision-makers with full, accurate, and meaningful summaries of all the benefits and costs relevant to clearly defined issues and alternatives. Benefit/cost analysis is a tool in systems analysis. Here is an example of systems analysis in a business firm.

Kevin-Keith Corporation is a firm engaged in cement block manufacture. Cement block manufacture involves the risk of air pollution. To meet the growing demand for blocks, the firm has to increase and enlarge production facilities. The executives of Kevin-Keith have at least three objectives: to increase jobs, to increase community money flow, and to earn a profit on the operation.

There were several possible ways of measuring payoff on these objectives.

For example, if it were to cost $1.78 million a year to operate the cement block plant and if the plant employed 150 people, the benefit/cost measure would be the ratio between jobs and cost per year. In this instance, it would be .84 jobs per $1000 operating costs a year. Similarly, a dollar money flow per dollar operating-cost ratio could be worked out. In each case, the benefit to be achieved is compared with the corporate cost of implementing that objective.

Table 12.5 shows possible corporate strategies. These include not to expand (S_1), to expand the present manufacturing facility in the present location (S_2), or to replace the present facility with an entirely new and modern one in a different location (S_3). These strategies are affected by estimates of the firm's sales of products and services.

An evaluation of the demand conditions permits the derivation of the expected outcomes of each strategy. Management prepared a general statement of the attributes of each strategy (see Table 12.6). This statement made possible the costing of alternatives.

Kevin-Keith analysts assumed that the three demand levels most likely to be met were 9 million blocks (demand level I), 14 million blocks (demand level II), and 24 million blocks (demand level III). In Table 12.7, the revenues, costs, and profits at each demand level are calculated. Account is taken in each calculation of the relation between capacity costs and costs at the indicated production level. It is also assumed that the plant involved in S_1 cannot operate beyond 120 percent of its capacity. The same assumption is made for the plant involved in S_2.

In Table 12.8, the profit rates per dollar of sales revenue are worked out. In Table 12.9, the profit-rates matrix is then multiplied by the matrix of demand probabilities, yielding the expected values of the profit rates for each demand-level prediction.

In Table 12.10, the number of jobs per $1000 of manufacturing costs is calculated. This matrix, multiplied by the matrix of demand probabilities, gives the expected value of this benefit/cost ratio.

And, in Table 12.11, the additional money flow per $1000 of manufacturing costs is calculated. This matrix, multiplied by the matrix of demand probabilities, gives still another measure of the benefit/cost ratio, the additional money income to the community for each $1000 of manufacturing cost.

Table 12.5 Kevin-Keith Corporation: Statement of strategy attributes

Strategy	Additional investment	Labor force		Salaries
		Production workers	White collar	
S_1, no expansion	0	60	10	$460,000
S_2, expand in present location by 50%	$2,000,000	80	11	670,000
S_3, new plant in new location, two times current capacity	$4,500,000	100	15	850,000

Table 12.6 Kevin-Keith Corporation: Manufacturing costs for each strategic alternative

S_1

Depreciation	$ 160,000	(Assume 5-yr remaining life,
Executives	100,000	$800,000)
Direct labor	360,000	
Materials, etc.	180,000	
Total manufacturing cost	$ 800,000	Cost/100 $8.00
Revenue	$ 880,000	Price/100 $8.80
Profit	10%	

S_2

Depreciation	$ 200,000	(Assume 10-yr life)
Executives	110,000	
Direct labor	560,000	
Materials, etc.	210,000	
Total manufacturing cost	$1,080,000	Cost/100 $7.20
Revenue	$1,200,000	Price/100 $8.80
Profit	10%	

S_3

Depreciation	$ 450,000	(Assume 10-yr life)
Executives	150,000	
Direct labor	700,000	
Materials, etc.	360,000	
Total manufacturing cost	$1,660,000	Cost/100 $6.64
Revenue	$2,000,000	Price/100 $8.00
Profit	20.5%	

The final step in this analysis is the presentation and comparison of the three benefit/cost ratios used. In Table 12.12, it is apparent that to build a new plant (S_3) is preferable on a profit-ratio basis as well as on the basis of the number of jobs created. However, because of the relative efficiency of the new

Table 12.7 Kevin-Keith Corporation: Calculation of profit demand forecast level

Strategy	I 9 million blocks $R - C = P_r$	II 14 million blocks $R - C = P_r$
S_1	$ 792M − $ 720M = $72M	$1056M − $1000M = $56M
S_2	$ 720M − $ 720M = 0	$1120M − $1040M = $80M
S_3	$ 720M − $ 950M = −$230M	$1120M − $1150M = −$30M

Strategy	III 24 million blocks $R - C = P_r$
S_1	$1056M − $1000M = $56M
S_2	$1440M − $1440M = 0
S_3	$1920M − $1500M = $420M

Table 12.8 Expected profit rate, profit/sales revenue

Strategy/demand	I	II	III	Demand proba-bilities	Estimated profit rate
S_1	$\dfrac{72}{792} = .099$	$\dfrac{56}{1056} = .053$	$\dfrac{56}{1056} = .053$	.1	5.76%
S_2	$\dfrac{0}{720} = 0$	$\dfrac{80}{1120} = .072$	$\dfrac{0}{1440} = 0$	.4	2.98%
S_2	$\dfrac{-230}{720} = -.320$	$\dfrac{30}{1120} = -.027$	$\dfrac{420}{1920} = .22$	.5	6.72%

Table 12.9 Kevin-Keith Corporation: Calculation of expected outcome of alternate strategies

Strategy	Demand			Probability of demand	Expected outcome
	I	II	III		
	$10m$	$15m$	$15m$ up		
S_1, no expansion	a	b	c	I 0.1	S_1 $0.1a + 0.4b + 0.5c$
S_2, expand	d	e	f	II 0.4	S_2 $0.1d + 0.4e + 0.5f$
S_3, new plant	g	h	i	III 0.5	S_3 $0.1g + 0.4h + 0.5i$

Table 12.10 Kevin-Keith Corporation: Estimated number of jobs per $1000 of manufacturing cost

Strategy/demand	I	II	III	Demand probabilities	Estimated jobs/$1000
S_1	$\dfrac{60}{720} = 8.3$	$\dfrac{60}{1000} = 6.0$	$\dfrac{60}{1000} = 6.0$	.1	5.0
S_2	$\dfrac{80}{720} = 11.1$	$\dfrac{80}{1040} = 7.7$	$\dfrac{80}{1440} = 5.5$	.4	5.4
S_3	$\dfrac{100}{950} = 10.5$	$\dfrac{100}{1150} = 8.7$	$\dfrac{100}{1500} = 6.7$	.5	13.0

Table 12.11 Kevin-Keith Corporation: Estimated additional money flow per $1000 of manufacturing cost

Strategy/demand	I	II	III	Demand probabilities	Estimated value
S_1	$\dfrac{0}{720} = 0$	$\dfrac{137}{1000} = 13.70$	$\dfrac{137}{1000} = 13.70$	.1	$22.20
S_2	$\dfrac{-13}{720} = -1.81$	$\dfrac{210}{1040} = 20.19$	$\dfrac{389}{1440} = 27.01$	.4	$18.34
S_3	$\dfrac{-109}{950} = -11.47$	$\dfrac{61}{1150} = 5.30$	$\dfrac{401}{1500} = 26.73$	.5	$12.33

Table 12.12   Kevin-Keith Corporation: Benefit/cost ratios

Profits	Jobs/$1000 mfg. cost	Additional money flow/$1000 of mfg. cost
S_3 (6.72%)	S_3 (13.0)	S_1 ($22.20)
S_1 (5.76%)	S_2 (5.4)	S_2 ($18.34)
S_2 (2.98%)	S_1 (5.2)	S_3 ($12.33)

plant, it will yield fewer additional dollars to the money flow of the community than S_2, to enlarge the current facilities. Kevin-Keith management decided to move and enlarge the plant since this decision was the most profitable one and also increased total jobs in the community.

Assessment of Federal Housing Subsidy Programs

In October 1973, Secretary James T. Lynn of the United States Department of Housing and Urban Development issued the report of the National Housing Policy Review, *Housing in the Seventies*. This federal housing policy review thoroughly assessed the impact and effectiveness of subsidized housing programs. Included was a benefit/cost analysis that started by identifying those whom the programs served and determining how these programs affected these and other groups.

Three basic questions about federal housing policy were addressed in the policy review:

1. Are the subsidized housing programs serving the appropriate people? This is a matter of equity.
2. Are the programs having the desired effect on those served and on the community at large? This is a matter of impact.
3. How do the benefits compare with the costs incurred? This is a matter of efficiency.

Equity

Equity considers distinctions among income classes based on the presupposition that subsidized housing programs should treat people according to their income. This idea is called "vertical equity." These programs also provide equal housing to those who have approximately equal income, a dimension of the equity concept called "horizontal equity." In other words, programs should not provide extensive benefits to one family and no benefits to another family whose income is identical. One special case of horizontal equity, termed "geographical equity," concerns whether families in one section of the country have a higher probability of being served than families with identical income in other sections of the country.

Impact

Impact criteria measure whether the subsidized programs have the desired effect on those served and on the community at large. One impact measure is the *amount of "extra housing"* received by the beneficiary. The difference between the amount paid by a family for a subsidized unit and the market value of that unit (the price it would command on the open market) is the extra housing received by the subsidized family (see Table 12.13).

A second impact measure is the extent to which the beneficiaries of subsidy programs in fact live in better housing than they otherwise could

Table 12.13 Estimated impact of subsidized housing programs

Impact, average	Low-rent public housing*	236*	Rent supple- ment*	235*	502, interest credit*	502, non- interest credit*	504*
Percentage improve- ment in recipient's housing	75	51	NA	35	92	57	54
Percentage increase in expenditures on other goods	14	0	NA	8	−3	−7	−9
Annual benefit to each recipient household	$708	$526	$696	$857	$567	$30	NA
Annual direct subsidy to each recipient household	$702	$956	$1300	$948	$695	$92	$75
Annual total govern- ment cost for each recipient household	$1650	$1100	$1477	$1087	$813	$190	NA
Annual benefit as percentage of income	22	10	26	13	10	Less than $1/2$	NA
Annual direct subsidy as percentage of income	21	18	49	14	12	1	3

NA = Not available.
*236, rent supplement, and 235 data are for 1972. 502 and 504 data are for fiscal year 1972. Low-rent public housing data are for 1971 and include all methods of providing public housing.
Source: Department of Housing and Urban Development, National Housing Policy Review.

afford. This can be determined by relating the *market value of subsidized units* to the cost of housing the family would have occupied in the absence of the program. The percentage improvement in the quality of the subsidy-recipient's housing can be derived from this relationship. If one assumes that low-income households have little or nothing to put into savings, then the percentage change in expenditures on goods and services other than housing can also be derived.

Another impact issue concerns the extent to which the welfare of the average family is increased by participating in the subsidized housing programs. One way to measure this effect is to estimate the cash grant the family would accept in lieu of participation in the subsidy program. This cash grant represents the actual *dollar benefit to the recipient* of the subsidy received through the program.

Efficiency

Efficiency criteria measure the relationship of benefits to costs. If benefits are high relative to costs, the program is efficient, and vice versa. There are several possible efficiency measures, depending on the cost or benefit concepts utilized. In general, measurement of costs cannot be limited solely to the federal government's direct subsidy payments but must also include any other costs incurred by the government as a result of the program, for example, administrative costs, taxes forgone, default costs exceeding mortgage insurance premiums, and any special government interest rate subsidies.

One important efficiency measure is called "production efficiency," or the ratio at which the government transforms tax dollars into extra housing (see Table 12.14).

Production efficiency depends upon several factors. One is the cost of construction. If the prices paid for government-subsidized construction are higher than those paid by conventional builders, then production efficiency will be low. The relationship between the total development cost of a project built conventionally and an identical project built through government-subsidy programs is called "construction efficiency."

The price paid by occupants and all levels of government for construction, operation, and all other cost factors involved in a housing unit divided into the price of a similar unit in the private market is called "technical efficiency."

Tenants may not value extra housing as highly as its market price because the in-kind nature of the transfer restricts their flexibility in choosing among various housing options and other goods. The value to tenants can be measured by the size of unrestricted cash grants which they would accept in lieu of the subsidy. The ratio of this cash grant to the market value of the subsidy (the extra housing provided) is called "transfer efficiency."

Transfer efficiency is calculated by comparing how subsidy recipients spend their income after receipt of the subsidy with how they spent their income before they entered the program and then estimating, through statistical techniques, how much the subsidy added to their overall economic well-being.

Table 12.14   Measures of efficiency in government-subsidized housing programs*

Subsidy program	Production efficiency	Construction efficiency	Technical efficiency	Transfer efficiency	Program efficiency
Low-rent public housing	.74	NA	.85	.75	.55
236	.70	.83	NA	.71	.50
236, rent supplement	.84	.83	NA	.64	.54
Rent supplement	.75	.83	NA	NA	.48†
235	.87	1.00	.94	.90	.79
502, noninterest credit	.48	1.00	.94	.33	.16
502, interest credit	.85	1.00	.94	.82	.70
502	NA	NA	NA	NA	NA

NA = Not available.

*236, rent supplement, and 235 data are for 1972. 502 and 504 data are for fiscal year 1972. Low-rent public housing data are for 1971 and include all methods of providing public housing.

†Derived by assuming that transfer efficiency is the same as that found in the 236 rent-supplement program.

Source: Department of Housing and Urban Development, National Housing Policy Review.

The measure is based on observing consumer behavior rather than on a program participant's subjective evaluation of the cash value of the housing subsidy.

Transfer efficiency will almost always be less than 1 for programs that provide subsidies-in-kind instead of unrestricted cash grants.

An overall efficiency measure is the ratio of the increase in the occupant's welfare measured in terms of an unrestricted cash grant to the total costs incurred by government to achieve that increase in welfare. This measure is called "program efficiency."

If program efficiency is considerably less than 1, the program may still be a worthwhile government expenditure. Although program efficiency is determined from the viewpoint of subsidy recipients, taxpayers may have other reasons why they desire recipients to have better housing (e.g., new, subsidized housing may stabilize declining neighborhoods or some members of society may simply feel satisfaction because some low-income families are living in better housing than they would otherwise).

If one could measure all these costs and benefits, then total program benefits received by occupants and others could be compared with total program costs. This ultimate measure could be called "social efficiency." However, social efficiency is inherently unquantifiable. Nevertheless, if program efficiency has a value significantly less than 1.0, then to justify it, the social benefit of the program must be extensive or policy-makers should seek more efficient ways of achieving their objectives.

Findings and Conclusions about Federal Housing Programs

The following are what *Housing in the Seventies* listed as findings and conclusions:

1. Improvement in the housing of recipients ranged from a high of 92 percent for the beneficiaries of the Section 502 rural homeownership interest-credit program to 35 percent for the recipients of Section 235 homeownership dwellings. The improvement in housing is the difference between the value of housing occupied under the program and the value of housing that would have been occupied in the absence of the program.
2. Increased expenditures on nonhousing goods and services as a result of housing subsidies ranged from a high of 14 percent for recipients of public housing to a minus 9 percent for recipients of farm and rural homeownership repair programs.
3. The annual benefit measures the value in unrestricted cash of the extra housing which the subsidy has provided to the recipient.The annual benefit ranged from a high of $857 for the beneficiaries of the Section 235 homeownership program to $30 for those receiving a Section 502 noninterest credit subsidy.
4. The annual benefit as a percentage of income ranged from a high of 26 percent for beneficiaries of the rent-supplement program to little change for Section 502 noninterest credit participants.
5. About 60 percent of the subsidized units were provided to families having annual incomes of less than $5000. The low-rent public housing program served the great majority of these recipients.
6. Minority families were served by housing programs to a considerably greater degree, as a percentage of the total eligible, than other low- and moderate-income families.
7. There is some evidence that government subsidized housing programs increase opportunity for the geographical dispersion of central city inhabitants, particularly minorities, to suburban areas. There is also some evidence that the programs contribute to racial balance within some communities. However, the potential contribution of subsidized production is limited inasmuch as, even in the years of highest production, subsidized housing accounted for only about 5 percent of the total new and existing housing stock marketed.
8. Almost seven of every ten households in the public housing and rent-supplement programs are female-headed. Female-headed households are more likely than male-headed households to be poor and are generally subject to discrimination in the housing market.
9. Access to credit for housing purchases and home repair for many families in rural areas has improved the housing of low- and moderate-income households.
10. The Section 235 and Section 502 homeownership programs have enabled a number of low- to moderate-income families who desire to own homes to

achieve their objective. Nationally, only a third of homeowners have annual incomes below $7000; almost two of every three beneficiaries of these programs have incomes below that.

Chapter Summary

We have reviewed five examples of benefit/cost analysis: two highway projects, one in Ecuador and the other in Mexico; a watershed protection project in Indiana; a housing policy review by the Department of Housing and Urban Development (HUD); and a firm's manufacturing facility decision. These examples covered diverse kinds of benefit/cost evaluation, such as the benefit/cost ratio, NPW and IRR, payback, economic efficiency, production efficiency, systems analysis, shadow (or accounting) prices, direct and indirect effects, as well as the opportunity cost of money. This was a state-of-the-art review. Its purpose was to pose issues and questions in the context of real situations.

Most of the cases used involved government projects and government policy. This is because governmental capital budgeting practice typically cannot use internal profitability measures. However, the emphasis on governmental use of benefit/cost analysis should not leave the impression that this sort of analysis is not applicable in private industry. Quite the contrary.

However, the kinds of problems to which corporation management might apply benefit/cost analysis would probably differ from government examples. Major personnel policy changes including pensions, investments in antipollution devices, and location changes are projects where, unlike engineering-type projects, precise figures about benefits cannot normally be derived from an analysis of the machine or installation in production. Clearly, benefits and costs extend over wider areas of influence within and sometimes outside the corporation.

It must be added that there is still plenty of room for experimentation in the form of the benefit/cost analysis. That is another way of saying that no one, accepted approach is generally regarded as correct. It should be kept in mind that benefit/cost analysis is probably best used to determine project acceptability and that it is not a good tool for optimization. The question about how to do benefit/cost analysis can usually be answered in terms of company or project characteristics.

Selected Readings

Adler, Hans A.: *Sector and Project Planning in Transportation*, World Bank Staff, Occasional Papers no. 4, Baltimore, Md., The Johns Hopkins Press, 1967.

"Cost Effectiveness and Cost-Benefit Analysis Session Report," *Operations Research Quarterly Special Conference Issue, 21*:37–44, June 1970.

Fulmer, V. A.: "Cost/Benefit Analysis in Fund Raising," *Harvard Business Review, 51*: 103–110, March 1973.

Joskow, J.: "Cost-Benefit Analysis for Environmental Impact Statement," *Public Utilities Fortnightly, 91*: 21–25, January 18, 1973.

King, John A., Jr.: *Economic Development Projects and Their Appraisal*, Baltimore, Md., The Johns Hopkins Press, 1967.

Lee, Sang M., and Laurence J. Moore: *Introduction to Decision Science*, New York, Mason/Charter Publishers, 1975.

Little, I. M. D., and J. A. Mirrlees: *Project Appraisal and Planning for Developing Countries*, New York, Basic Books, 1974.

Lyden, F. J., and E. G. Miller (eds.): *Planning Programming, Budgeting*, Chicago, Markham, 1967.

McGuigan, J. R., and R. C. Moyer: *Managerial Economics*, Hinsdale, Ill., The Dryden Press, 1975.

Mehment, O.: "Benefit-Cost Analysis of Alternative Techniques of Production for Employment Creation," *International Labour Review*, vol. 104, July–August 1971.

Prest, A. R., and R. Turvey: "Cost-Benefit Analysis: A Survey," *Economic Journal, 75*: 731–735, December 1965.

Rowe, M. P.: "When the Employer Faces Day Care Decisions: Cost-Benefit Analysis and Other Decision Making Tools," *Sloan Management Review, 14*:1–11, Spring 1973.

Sastry, M. V. R.: "Systems Approach to Cost-Benefit Analysis of Urban Transportation," *Transportation Journal, 12*:39–45, Spring 1973.

Tabb, W. T.: "Cost-Benefit Analysis of Location Subsidies for Ghetto Neighborhoods," *Land Economics, 48*:45–52, February 1972.

United States General Accounting Office, *Evaluation and Analysis to Support Decision making*, Exposure Draft, Washington, D.C., December 9, 1975.

Questions, Problems, and Projects

1. Although a wide use of benefit/cost analysis was required under a 1974 act, GAO found in 1975 that little use was being made of this form of cost-effectiveness measure in budget preparation. The Associate Director of OMB, in response, said that although he agreed there was need for more of these studies, "experience had shown that simply requiring such studies was not sufficient and might prove counterproductive." He pointed to the limited resources available for such analyses and concluded that agencies could not be expected to use benefit/cost each year. Comment.

2. Nay, Scanlon, and Wholey, in reviewing the use of benefit/cost analysis in federal job-training programs, found that there was a wide and bewildering range of benefit/cost ratios. They thought the wide range of values stemmed from two problems:

(*a*) Uncertainty over what constitutes cost and benefit.

(*b*) Inadequate data.

In their examination of hundreds of benefit/cost analyses, they found basic methodological limitations which made it impossible to be sure that the true average results of the programs had been measured. What suggestions would you make for improving the use of benefit/cost analysis in programs like these?

3. In the analysis of federal housing programs, a distinction is made

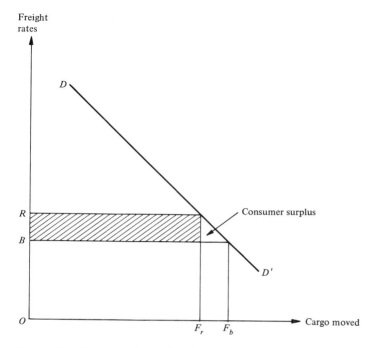

Figure P4. Consumer's surplus from a barge canal.

between impact, equity, and efficiency. Why is such a distinction of use in evaluating government programs? Of what use is this distinction in private industrial firms or in not-for-profit enterprises?

4. Do you see any possible use for the consumer surplus in benefit/cost analysis? For example, in Fig. P4, suppose that *DD'* is the demand for freight-cargo-movement use. This demand curve is a relation between possible freight rates and the amount of grain cargo moved. If *OR* is the current freight rate on a railroad serving the area, then *OF* is the current movement of grain cargoes by rail. If a barge canal were built, it is estimated that the barge freight rate for grain would be *OB* and that the bulk cargo movement of grain via the barge canal would be *OG*. Estimate, by changes in consumer surplus, what the saving would be from the construction of a barge canal. Is the shippers' gain, depending on how you measured it, equal to the public's gain? Should traffic diversion in areas beyond the direct impact area of the barge canal be taken into consideration? Are there conditions under which there might be little or no consumer surplus?

5. Table P5 is taken from a GAO report on the cost-effectiveness of two military physician-enlistment programs. One (scholarships) involved paying enlistees' upkeep and tuition during their medical education. The other (university) involved setting up a military medical school. There had been a debate from 1975 through 1976 over which of these two programs yielded the most benefit or output relative to cost. Cost-effectiveness techniques were used

Table P5 Comparative costs of two military physician-procurement programs, as of 1984

Retention rate, %	Cost per staff year of expected service		Education cost/ total cost		Increase in available staff years, %	
	Scholarship	University	Scholarship	University	Scholarship	University
10	$22,942		22.8			
20	22,277		22.4		8.0	
30	21,712		20.8		7.4	
40	21,206		19.9		7.0	
50	20,742	$28,382	19.1	42.1	6.6	
60	20,375	27,455	18.4	40.8	5.8	6.7
70		26,640		39.6		6.2
80		25,944		38.5		5.7
90		25,251		37.3		5.9

because many of the benefits could not be quantified. The analysis showed that, if 1984 were used as a base year for comparison, there were likely to be 988 graduates of a scholarship program in service costing $36,784 each. There would be 175 graduates of a military medical school in service costing $189,980 each. It was found that, as civilian medical tuition increases, the cost-effectiveness of the scholarship program decreases. The longer the required duty (number of staff years), the lower the cost of both programs. What recommendations would you make to the Congress in respect to the scholarship program? With respect to the university program? Under what conditions would you recommend one over the other?

6. Little and Mirrlees regard profit as a necessary but insufficient criterion for project selection. However, corporate profits do not always measure the relation between total benefits and total costs. What assumptions would you have to make about the real world if you wanted profits to measure actual net benefits to society?

Case 12.1 Comparisons of Estimated Costs of Motor Vehicle Accidents

The Safety Administration, the National Safety Council (NSC), and an Office of Science and Technology ad hoc committee each have estimated the annual costs of motor vehicle accidents. The Safety Administration's estimates were for use in benefit-cost analyses, NSC's estimates were for use by state highway officials in requesting appropriations and by research workers and others in the field of safety, and the committee's estimates were for a study of the

Table 1   Estimated costs of motor vehicle accidents
In millions of dollars

Type of cost	Safety administration	NSC	RECAT committee
Costs estimated by all:			
Future earnings lost	$18,100	$ 3,700	$ 7,700
Medical costs	1,950	1,100	6,100
Property damage	7,100	5,000	4,900
Total	$27,150	$ 9,800	$18,700
Costs not estimated by RECAT committee:			
Insurance administration	6,600	6,000	
	$ 6,600	$ 6,000	
Costs estimated only by Safety Administration:			
Home and family duties	4,500	. . .	. . .
Pain and suffering	3,800	. . .	. . .
Legal and court costs	1,050	. . .	. . .
Service to community	900	. . .	. . .
Time and money losses			
to others	800	. . .	. . .
Miscellaneous losses	800	. . .	. . .
Asset losses	300	. . .	. . .
Employer losses	50	. . .	. . .
Funeral costs	50	. . .	. . .
Total	$12,250	. . .	. . .
Total costs	$46,000	$15,800	$18,700

cumulative regulatory effects on the cost of automobile transportation (RE-CAT). The estimates shown in Table 1 vary widely because of differences in base years, data sources, statistical bases, assumptions, and calculations of future costs.

The Safety Administration and NSC estimates are based on 1971 data and are given in present-value terms. Under the present-value method, the current value of future costs is calculated by using a discount rate. Discounting future costs makes them comparable to present costs, that is, to the present value of costs. The higher the discount rate used, the lower the value that is placed on future costs. The Safety Administration used a 7 percent discount rate and NSC used a 3.5 percent discount rate. Costs were not discounted in the committee's estimate, which is based on 1970 data.

Congressional concern over the increasing number of motor vehicle deaths led to the enactment of the National Traffic and Motor Vehicle Safety Act of 1966 (15 U.S.C. 1381), the purpose of which was to reduce motor vehicle accidents and the deaths and injuries resulting from such accidents.

MOTOR VEHICLE SAFETY STANDARDS

As one means of reducing such deaths and injuries, the act directed the Department of Transportation to establish motor vehicle safety standards. The National Highway Traffic Safety Administration does this for the department. The act required that the standards be reasonable, practicable, and appropriate for the particular type of motor vehicle or item of equipment to which they applied.

In reporting on the proposed legislation which became the 1966 act, both the Senate Commerce Committee and the House Committee on Interstate and Foreign Commerce stated that safety was to be the overriding consideration in issuing a standard. Both committees pointed out, however, that the motoring public's cost of purchasing and maintaining safety equipment required by a standard also should be considered. In this regard, the Senate committee said that, in addition to the technical feasibility of the standard and adequate lead time for the industry to develop and produce safety equipment, reasonableness of equipment cost should be considered. The House committee said that all relevant factors, including economic ones, should be considered in determining practicality of a standard.

BENEFIT/COST ANALYSIS

The National Highway Traffic Safety Administration uses benefit/cost analyses primarily to establish an internal order of priorities among all safety standards. The analyses are an important factor to be considered in evaluating the merits of a proposed safety standard. Other factors are technical feasibility; research results; legislative mandates; congressional, public, and industry views; and legal considerations.

A benefit/cost analysis of a safety standard involves estimating, in dollars, the benefits from establishing the standard and the consumer costs to comply with the standard. Comparing these totals, usually by dividing dollar benefits by dollar costs, gives a benefit/cost ratio. A ratio greater than 1 indicates that the estimated dollar benefits from establishing a safety standard exceed the estimated cost to comply with the standard.

The Safety Administration measures benefits by estimating how much accidents, fatalities, injuries, and property damage cost society and by evaluating a standard's effectiveness in reducing such costs. Costs of complying with the standard include the consumer's cost for the safety equipment.

The Safety Administration does not generally publicize its estimates of the benefits and costs of a safety standard. The administration measured all costs which directly or indirectly caused a reduction in society's total welfare. The Safety Administration pointed out that each vehicle accident diminished individual and social welfare. It contended that society's welfare involved considerably more than its economic well-being and that money could be used only as a proxy measure for estimating changes in welfare. It further contended that, although the severe shortcomings of measuring welfare in terms of money were obvious, there was no better standard of value useful for public policy decision. Accordingly, the Safety Administration attempted to measure and to translate into dollar-and-cents equivalents identifiable inconvenience and hardship associated with motor vehicle accidents, such as pain and suffering, inability to perform home and family duties, loss of service to the community, and similar types of costs.

NSC and the RECAT committee tried to measure economic costs in what they considered to be the real dollars lost as a result of motor vehicle accidents. NSC did not include inconvenience and hardship costs in its estimates because it believed that such costs, although important to the individual who suffered as a result of an accident, did not represent a cost to the rest of society. RECAT believed that its estimate fully included all measurable economic losses.

The Safety Administration placed dollar values on some additional categories of costs, such as legal and court costs, loss of service to the community, time and money losses to others, and miscellaneous losses which in total amounted to about $4 billion. Legal and court costs were based on a study by the Travelers Research Corporation which showed that police and court costs associated with accidents amounted to about $1 billion annually. The cost of loss of service to the community amounted to about $900 million and was based on the Safety Administration's estimate that the average person spends about two hours a week for volunteer work in the community.

Time and money losses to others were estimated at about $800 million based on the belief that the family and friends of accident victims suffered large noncompensated time and money losses. The estimate included travel costs to visit accident victims and attend funerals, costs of time spent visiting and attending funerals, and costs of time spent by members of the family attending accident victims.

Estimated costs of motor vehicle accidents form the basis for determining the benefit to be derived from a proposed safety standard. Therefore, reasonable cost estimates must be used to show fairly whether a proposed safety standard is cost-effective. The foregoing estimates of the Safety Administration, NSC, and the RECAT committee varied widely for each motor vehicle accident, fatality, injury, or property damage. These estimates are as follows:

Average cost

	Safety Administration	NSC	RECAT committee
Each accident	$ 2,800	$ 960	$ 1,130
Each fatality	200,700	52,000	140,000
Each injury	7,300	3,100	2,750
Each property damage	300	440	178

The effect of these differences can be seen from the benefit/cost ratios which are obtained when NSC's and the committee's average costs for each fatality and injury are substituted for the costs for each fatality and injury used by the Safety Administration in its benefit/cost analyses for the following standards:

Benefit/cost ratio

Standard	Safety Administration	NSC	RECAT committee
Windshield zone intrusion	16:1	6:1	7:1
Bus passenger seating and crash protection	2.22:1	.88:1	.96:1

The Safety Administration recognized that including some cost categories in its estimates and the values placed on the categories were a matter of controversy. Also, in commenting on its estimate, the Safety Administration stated that:

> There are problems of comparability, reliability, and comprehensiveness with the studies that have produced data on the various components. Therefore, the estimates produced for this analysis should be viewed as interim measures and subject to revision as new data and methodology become available.

DISCUSSION QUESTIONS 12.1

1. GAO has found that, in many budget requests, there was much descriptive but limited analytical material and very few of what "could be considered benefit/cost analyses." Why should benefit/cost analysis be stressed in budget preparation?
2. Why have many agencies at all levels of government been reluctant to use benefit/cost analysis? Is it a matter of difficulty of technique, lack of data, or likelihood that budget decisions will be made for other than net benefit considerations?
3. Evaluate the differences between the Safety Administration and the Office of Science and Technology with respect to annual costs of motor vehicle accidents.
4. Why are there such wide differences in benefit/cost analysis results?

Case 12.2   Andrews University Elementary School

Andrews University is a church-supported school located at Berrien Springs, Michigan, a village some twenty miles north of South Bend, Indiana. As a part of its School of Education, it operates an elementary school for the community. This school is not financed by public funds but receives rather a subsidy from the Seventh Day Adventist Church and charges a nominal tuition. In recent years, however, financial problems have arisen out of the following circumstances:

1. The elementary school is used as a laboratory school for the university. Consequently, there is a need to be alert to new educational methods and techniques to maintain high standards. This aim entails the expenditure of more funds than would normally be expected.
2. A large proportion of the students are children of transients—people who are at Andrews for advanced studies and whose stay is thus limited. It is difficult, therefore, to predict enrollment from year to year and to maintain continuity in the student body and in the teaching staff.
3. Alternate school facilities are available.

Attendance record

1958–1959	220	1962–1963	320
1959–1960	285	1963–1964	350
1960–1961	310	1964–1965	368
1961–1962	305	1965–1966	375

The projection for 1966-1967 shows a decline of fifteen students; this prediction is based on experience which indicates that every four years attendance drops. However, since the university has just completed an apartment block for married students, the new Beechwood Apartments, the enrollment is likely to exceed the projected figure.

   Income   Tuition income has increased each year over the previous year for some time now (see Table 1). Moreover, the subsidies have also increased year by year. It is true that the subsidy for the 1965–1966 school year showed no percentage increase while the amount was going up. The decision of the Michigan Conference to increase its subsidy by $9601 and the Pioneer Memorial Church by $2232 has helped change the picture from one of a $19,938 loss for 1964–65 to a projected gain of $351 for the school year 1966–1967. Without this subsidy, a retrenchment in the program would have been necessary or tuition rates would have had to be raised substantially.

Income and cost per pupil

	1963–1964	1964–1965	1965–1966	1966–1967
Income per pupil	$227.01	$255.22	$299.40	$367.28
Cost per pupil	$263.01	$309.40	$321.90	$366.30
Difference	$−36.00	$−54.18	$−22.50	$0.98

Table 1 Andrews University Elementary School: Comparison of operating statements and budget
1963–1964 to 1966–1967

	1963–1964, actual, $	%	1964–1965, actual, $	%
Income				
Tuition	59,836.87	76.5	67,701.72	72.1
Internal transfers	6,143.00	7.8	11,982.00	12.7
Subsidy, Michigan Conference	3,660.30	4.6	5,047.81	5.4
Subsidy, Pioneer Memorial Church	8,755.00	11.0	9,190.00	9.8
Total Income	78,395.17	100.0	93,921.53	100.0
Expenses				
Salary and related expenses	65,933.83	71.6	74,559.38	65.5
Direct instructional expenses	6,621.42	7.2	9,091.26	8.0
Administrative and general expenses	5,509.07	6.0	10,472.63	9.2
Plant expense	13,998.34	15.2	19,736.22	17.3
Total expenses	92,053.66	100.0	113,859.49	100.0
Net gain (loss)	(13,658.49)		(19,937.96)*	

	1965–1966, actual and estimated, $*	%	1966–1967 budget, $	%
Income				
Tuition	84,465.36	75.2	88,560.00	67.7
Internal transfers	11,980.00	10.7	14,780.00	11.3
Subsidy, Michigan Conference	6,079.20	5.4	15,680.00	11.9
Subsidy, Pioneer Memorial Church	9,768.49	8.7	12,000.00	9.1
Total Income	112,293.05	100.0	131,020.00	100.0
Expenses				
Salary and related expenses	81,945.00	67.9	90,077.00	68.3
Direct instructional expenses	9,947.64	8.2	8,970.00	6.8
Administrative and general expenses	11,483.04	9.5	12,690.00	9.6
Plant expense	17,341.80	14.4	20,132.00	15.3
Total expenses	120,717.48	100.0	131,869.00	100.0
Net gain (loss)	(8,424.43)		(849.00)	

*Actual for eight months and estimated for four months.

Expenses The elementary school was first set up as a separate department, distinct from the School of Education, during the 1963–1964 school year. Whatever costs were incurred that year may be regarded as containing some elements of adjustment; therefore, attention is focused on the 1964–1965 operating statement.

Salaries and related expenses amounted to 65.5 percent of total expenses, exceeding tuition by $6857. The second largest item of expense was that for plant. However, the loss incurred may be explained as follows:

1. There was an increase in salary expense of some $6000 over budgeted expense. This was traceable to the hiring of additional teachers and resultant fringe benefit costs. Salaries and related expenses exceeded the budget by $14,448
2. Teaching supplies' budget overspent by   2,673
3. Scholarships for which no budget was provided   4,316
4. Excess of custodial expenses over budget   2,836
5. Overexpenditure on miscellaneous items   4,701

   Total amount overspent $28,974
   Amount received in excess of budgeted income   7,327

                       21,647
   Less budgeted gain   709
   Actual Loss $20,938

Tuition rates	*Semester, $*	*Year, $*
1966–1967 Grades 1–8	123	246
	135*	270
1965–1966 Grades 1–8	114	228
	123*	246
1964–1965 Grades 1–8	96	192
	105*	210
1963–1964 Grades 1–8	90	180
	100*	200
1962–1963 Grades 1–8	90	180

Tuition rate in Berrien Springs Village
1965–1966 Grades 1–8   160

Tuition rates for elementary schools in other unions
Atlantic: Grades 1–8   100–250
Columbia: Grades 1–8 $150
Northern: Any grade (minimum) $120
Pacific: Grades 1–8 $176
Southern: Grades 1–8 (minimum) $ 80
  *Tuition rates for nonstudent and nonfaculty families.

   The schedule of rates shows an increase of $12 for 1964–1965, $36 for 1965–1966, and $18 for 1966–1967.

THE SCHOOL DOLLAR

The school dollar: Where does it come from and where does it go? Tuition accounts for 72.1 cents; internal transfers, 12.7 cents; Pioneer Memorial Church, 9.8 cents; and Michigan Conference, 5.4 cents. The largest portion of expense, 65.5 cents, goes for salary and related expenses; followed by plant expenses, 17.3 cents; administrative and general expenses, 9.2 cents; and direct instructional expenses, 8 cents.

FIXED AND VARIABLE COSTS (TABLE 2)

Fixed expenses are those that are not controllable by the school administration, and variable expenses are those over which the administration has direct control.

Table 2 Andrews University Elementary School: Fixed and variable expenses, in dollars

Expenses	1963–1964	1964–1965	1965–1966*	1966–1967†
Fixed				
Salary and related expenses	60,473.32	70,431.37	79,977.72	86,477.00
Administrative and general	4,989.96	5,617.21	5,245.20	6,330.00
Plant expenses and depreciation	7,080.55	6,876.00	7,380.00	8,072.00
Total fixed costs	72,543.83	82,924.58	92,602.92	100,879.00
Variable				
Labor (students)	5,460.51	4,128.01	1,967.28	3,600.00
Direct instructional	6,621.42	9,091.26	9,947.64	8,970.00
Administrative and general	510.11	4,855.42	6,237.84	6,360.00
Plant expenses	6,917.79	12,860.22	9,961.80	12,060.00
Total variable costs	19,509.83	30,934.91	28,114.56	30,990.00
Total expenses	92,053.66	113,859.49	120,717.48	131,869.00

*Actual for eight months and estimated for four months.
†Based on budget.

DISCUSSION QUESTIONS 12.2

1. To what extent are there losses in the operation of the Andrews University Elementary School?
2. Are there costs and/or benefits accruing to the university which are not included in the statements presented in this case? What additional information might you like to have?
3. What product or service does an elementary school sell? How should that product or service be costed and priced?
4. The school administration feels that an increase in enrollment might reduce the losses they have sustained. Comment on this opinion.

13

LOCATION ANALYSIS

Key Concepts

area potential
basic/nonbasic ratio
central business district (CBD)
demand conditions
density gradient
economic base
economic zones
location quotient
market density

market organization
market share
minimum-requirements approach
nature of product
net revenue lines
von Thünen
warehouse-location problem
Weber

What Is Ahead in This Chapter

The emphasis of this chapter is on the business-location decision. The location decision, like that for capital budgeting, is often for keeps. It is less frequently made perhaps than any other major business decision, but it is vital, and indeed, it may well be the key decision for business survival.

The location decision comes about in a variety of ways. There is the "place-of-birth" decision. It is a part of enterprise start-up decisions. A great deal has been said after the fact in histories of firms about these place-of-birth decisions, but this is not a chapter on business history. Yet there is a pattern of location for the steel, the automobile, the rubber, the furniture, the communications industries, as examples, which suggests that the right location does make a difference. More often than not, the impact has been greatest on the city and its market area. In that context, we look at Philadelphia, America's fourth-largest city.

It is the relocation decision that is more important for us than the place-of-birth decision. That relocation decision takes two forms: One is the decision to move from a plant now in use to another and presumably better place. The other is the expansion decision where territorially larger markets are served by an expanding network of branches, warehouses, and production facilities. This chapter begins with a statement of the location decision in the expansion context. It also uses a linear programming transportation model to spell out how available information can be used to make and effectively evaluate location decisions. And the chapter ends with a strategy for location.

The use of quantitative tools in location analysis is still in a developmental state. Economic-base analysis, location quotients, and mathematical location models are, each of them, elements in the analysis this chapter undertakes. But, given the tentative nature of the art of location decision making, the chapter contains a review and critique of many actual location decisions.

The focus in the chapter is more on the industrial and manufacturing firm than on retail or service enterprises. Yet some of the same kinds of principles apply there, too. It is in the context of explaining the pattern of urban land use that some understanding of location problems and decision making in retailing, the central business district, suburban service areas, and similar locational development can be gained.

Basic Elements of the Location Decision

There are many separate elements that management must evaluate when it selects a site for location or relocation. Among these are market conditions.

Market conditions include market potential, market density, demand conditions, market organization, and the nature of the product.

Market Potential

Market potential is a way of judging the relative importance of different geographic regions. Measuring market potential rests upon the extent of market knowledge, availability of information, time, and cost factors. Most methods fall within one of the following classes: (1) statistical series method, (2) market survey method, (3) total market measure, and (4) census method.

The statistical series method develops an index of relative buying power for various industries. Such a statistical series is used to compare relative strengths of industries in particular locations.

One way to develop a statistical series is to

1. Identify purchasing or consuming industries by preparing a list of present customers and determining their Standard Industrial Classification (SIC) number from such published sources as Dun & Bradstreet.
2. Use census data to obtain complete statistics on the number, size, and location of firms in these SICs.
3. Select a relevant statistic for indicating relative purchasing power. The total of production employees is the one most often used on the assumption that a firm employing twice as many people as another firm in the same industry classification will have twice the requirement for the product.
4. Cumulate this statistic for the entire United States and for each market within it.
5. Convert this statistic to a percentage of total United States purchasing power for each market.
6. Compare markets on the basis of relative percentage potential.

Although in many cases market potential is only a rough-and-ready measure, it has considerable value. Relative market potentials remain fairly accurate because each is developed on a uniform basis. Although actual dollar projections may be wide of the mark, the percentage of error in each market is roughly the same. Consequently, on a relative basis (percentage of United States), this potential measuring method is sufficiently accurate for most purposes.

Further refinement is possible, of course. Rather than depend upon total employment, employment in a significant category can be determined. For example, the Census of Manufacturing has a table showing employment by type of operation for selected industries. Suppose we choose tool and die makers as our relevant employment category. For each industry, we can determine the proportion of tool and die workers to total industry employment. This weighting factor can then be applied to the gross employment statistics to determine an "equivalent employment" weight for that industry in each geographic region.

In the steam turbine industry there are 100 tool and die makers per 1000 production employees. In the automotive industry, there are 75 tool and die makers per 1000 employees. A firm classified in the automotive industry and employing 1000 employees will have an equivalent employment of 75. A steam turbine firm employing 1000 employees will have an equivalent employment weight of 100. From the point of view of potential, the steam turbine firm is thus a better prospect than the automotive firm. These weighted potentials are calculated for each market being evaluated and, on the basis of potential, one market is selected as the site for the proposed branch facility.

Market Density

Even if markets are of equal potential, there are significant differences in densities. Density is the degree of dispersion of potential buyers. Some markets, for example, may be geographically small because all the potential buyers are located relatively close to each other. In dispersed markets the buyers are spread over large areas. The degree of dispersion affects the costs of handling any given volume of most products. It also affects the quantity of service rendered potential customers.

If potential customers have no well-established preferences among suppliers, requiring only that each supplier be able to provide ordered goods within approximately similar delivery periods, the supplier closer to more potential customers than any other would have an advantage.

Other things being equal, the more dispersed the market, the larger the inventory that must be maintained, the more skilled the handling of orders, and the larger the production facilities that must be set up.

It follows, then, that if there are two possible market areas of equal potential, the more dispersed market is likely to be the more costly one. Providing the same standard of service in a less dispersed market would require fewer resources, lower costs, less space, and would more than likely yield more profit than in the more dispersed area.

Demand Conditions

If a firm seeks to enter a new market area with large potential sales, it must certainly consider the demand structure of that new market. The demand structure of the new market depends as much on the product itself as on its price or on the changing levels of income.

If the product demand is derived, that is, dependent not so much on product price as on the sales of another product, then it will be useful to know not only the identity of the current suppliers, their relation to each other in sales and marketing policies, and the existing price structure but also a good deal about the basic industry from whose sales the demand for this component is derived. An example may be taken from the sales of power-actuated tools

(PATs) to the construction industry. The sale of PATs, study has shown, depends not on local market prices or even on sales efforts of local suppliers but on conditions in the construction industry. Thus, a decision to establish a sales facility in a new market might be better based upon research into the potential market for the construction industry than that of the PAT industry.

If price is important, then the fact that changes in transport costs are equivalent to price changes must be taken into account, especially if prices are being quoted FOB factory or sales branch. Location nearer the market reduces the price, making the supplier that much more competitive. Even if the price is quoted FOB destination, which means that the shipper has been absorbing some of the freight costs, a move into a new territory at the very least increases the profit margin of the supplier and probably puts him in a position to use pricing policies more competitively.

Market Organization

Another factor in the selection of a market area as a location for a facility is the structure of the market. Area potential can be the result of the purchasing power of a limited number of large firms or of a much larger number of smaller firms. The particular condition prevailing will have important effects on the location decision.

The structural factors that management must take into account when selecting a site are

1. Number and size of buying points. The more points there are, the higher the costs of providing services will be but also the lower the risks of severe volume fluctuations.
2. Order size and frequency. Many small orders will require a processing system geared to high volume and low individual processing cost. As the number of buying points increases, a firm will observe the following effects: (a) a greater volume of individual shipments; (b) an increase in order-processing costs; and (c) the need for a bigger and more extensive inventory.

These factors exert their influence through their effect on the physical features of the proposed branch facility. Communication links, order-processing equipment, order-handling equipment, and similar elements in the order-filling function will change with the anticipated volume of transactions.

Nature of Product

The physical nature of the product that will affect location choices includes

1. Substitutability. Can the firm offer the buyer an alternative in the event that the exact item desired is out of stock?

2. Weight density, weight per cubic measure. As weight density increases, movement costs decline relatively so that inventory holding costs can be balanced against increased movement costs.
3. Dollar density, dollars per cubic measure. As this factor increases, inventory costs rise and movement costs decline. It is better (less costly) to maintain minimum local inventories of diamonds and pay the increased movement costs. Coal is an opposite example.

Decision Rules for Plant Location

Now that we have the elements of the location decision, we can determine where a plant should be located. Here is a simple algorithm for plant location. Start with the relationship between the price (or cost) of inputs and the price of the product. Table 13.1 sets forth at least four cost-price relationships.

If the price(s) of input(s) is(are) the same in all likely and possible locations and if the price(s) of the product(s) is(are) also the same in all locations, then the plant can be located anywhere in a cluster of likely and possible places. If the price of the input increases as the distance over which it must be transported increases, while the price at which the product sells does not vary with location, the plant location to be selected should be one with the lowest transport costs. By the same token, if input costs are the same everywhere, but sales prices of the product vary with location because of costs of transport, then the best place to locate the plant is where sales revenues would be highest. Finally, if both input costs and product prices vary with transport charges, the problem becomes one of selecting a plant location which maximizes the difference between revenue and costs, that is, one which maximizes profit.

This set of plant location solutions, however, does not include competition. The solutions more or less assume that a transport network has high connectivity, little built-in price discrimination, and equal efficiency in all directions. More important, there is no competition or choice among differing inputs. But suppose there were two or more possible inputs, each with different costs, different sources or locations of supply, and different transport tariffs, then the following model may be useful.

Table 13.1   Objectives in seeking optimum location

Price	Input	
	Constant	Varying
Constant	Locate anywhere	Select location maximizing revenue
Varying	Select location minimizing costs	Select location maximizing profit

Source: Adapted from M. Beckmann, *Location Theory*, New York. Random House, 1968, p. 11.

Optimal Plant Location with Infinite Transport Network

Here is a simple plant location model based on the steel industry. That industry, let us say, has two inputs, coal for coking and iron ore, and one product, pig iron (see Fig. 13.1). Coal deposits and iron ore deposits are to be found in known geographic locations. And there is one market to which the pig iron will be shipped.

A scheme for the problem solution would be

IO, iron ore deposit location: w_{io}, iron ore shipments
r_{io}, unit transport tariff for iron ore

C, coal deposit location: w_c, coal shipments
r_c, unit transport tariff for coal

M, market for rolled steel: r_m, unit transport cost for pig iron
L, optimal plant location

In general, if the pig iron plant is one of many users of the transportation system (so that there are no costs of back-hauling empty freight cars), the best plant location is where the total costs of transportation are minimized. That will be the inside of triangle *CIOM* at point *L*. The method of solution calls for the location analyst to minimize

$$w_{io}r_{io} + w_c r_c + r_m$$

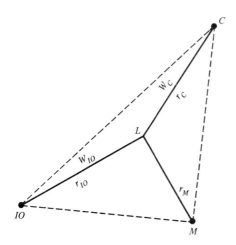

Figure 13.1. Where to locate a pig iron plant. *Solution:* Locate plant at *L* where all transport costs are minimized.

Linear Programming in Location Analysis

Linear programming can also be used in location analysis. The transportation method has a set of elements that both define the location problem and permit its solution. The first key element is "requirements," that is, the demand, or a forecast of sales, for each time period from each market segment. The market segment may be a list of individual customers, geographic territories, or industries in a specific location. The sales forecast reflects what the firm thinks it knows about the market. In addition to sales forecasts, the category of requirements may also include knowledge of marketing channels, market potentials, competitive effects, the locational effect of the facility, and all other variables that contribute to expected sales volume.

The second key element is "capacities." For the time period under consideration, the productive capacity of a firm is the amount it can produce at each locality. Anticipated changes in productive capacity, storage of finishing capacity of each facility, and all other known or estimated values must also be taken into account.

The final element is "costs." Although these figures usually refer only to transportation costs, costs can be adjusted to reflect inventory-carrying cost of material stored for an appreciable period of time, local handling costs, extent of manufacturing done at the branch, economies of scale, taxes, and amortization of equipment and facilities. In the single value given for the cost can be included all the variables having a cost effect. As a result, in a single linear programming array, economic, marketing, manufacturing, and accounting data can be gathered.

The transportation method provides a best answer in terms of some previously selected objective criterion. This objective must be quantifiable, that is, expressed in terms of magnitudes.

Fan Hill Distributors

Fan Hill is a nationwide wholesale service distributor with three supply points and seven major customers. The three supply points are located in New York, Atlanta, and Dallas. Capacities and customer requirements are given in Table 13.2 and transportation costs per unit shipment are shown in Table 13.3.

The minimum cost program to serve these customers from this net of supply points, and with the costs as given, is $1397.50 (see Fig. 13.2). Contrary to intuition, the lowest cost routing of each individual shipment is not the lowest cost routing for all shipments combined. For example, customer 6 receives ten units from New York at a shipping cost of $16 per unit and twenty from Dallas at $8.50 per unit. This occurs despite the fact that the cost from Atlanta to customer 6 is less than the cost from New York to 6. A similar situation occurs with respect to the shipments to customer 4 from New York.

A new branch with a capacity of twenty-five units is planned for San Francisco (see Fig. 13.3). Its proposed rate structure is shown in Table 13.4.

Table 13.2 Capacities and requirements: Location problem

Warehouse	Capacity	Customer	Requirements
New York	100	1	10
Atlanta	50	2	20
Dallas	55	3	25
Total	205	4	20
		5	50
		6	30
		7	35
		S*	15
Total			205†

*S is added as "slack" to make sure that requirements add up to capacities.

†Including S.

The building of this branch will add to total system capacity (no increase in total demand is assumed at this time). The least total cost solution will now be $1297.50, a saving of $100 over the previous best solution. Of greater significance, however, is the rearrangement of the optimum shipping pattern that will result from this new branch. Table 13.5 shows the differences that result from this change.

Surplus capacity would now exist in both New York and Dallas. Atlanta will continue to serve only a single customer. The Dallas pattern will change markedly.

If incremental costs associated with the San Francisco branch can be kept below $100 (for the time period included in the demands listed in the tables), then the new branch can be justified. If the diseconomies of small-scale operation exceed the transportation costs saved through a realignment of

Table 13.3 Unit transportation costs from warehouses to customers

Customer	Warehouses		
	New York	Atlanta	Dallas
1	$ 9.50	$16.00	$18.00
2	8.00	8.50	18.00
3	9.50	9.00	17.50
4	11.00	6.00	15.00
5	13.00	3.00	17.00
6	16.00	9.00	8.50
7	18.00	19.00	6.00
S*	0	0	0

*To the S(slack) customer is assigned the cost of surplus capacity to ensure that a least-cost solution results from the method. If this were not done, then the surplus capacity, being lower in cost than any real shipment, would be allocated first.

Warehouses Customer	New York	Atlanta	Dallas	Requirements
1	9.00 (10)	16.00	18.00	10
2	8.00 (20)	8.50	18.00	20
3	9.50 (25)	19.00	17.50	25
4	11.00 (20)	6.00	15.00	20
5	13.00	3.00 (50)	17.00	50
6	16.00 (10)	9.00	8.50 (20)	30
7	18.00	19.00	6.00 (35)	35
S	0 (15)	0	0	15
Capacity	100	50	55	205

Figure 13.2. First minimum-cost transportation program. *Note:* Total transportation cost is $1,397.50.

shipping patterns, however, then establishment of the branch cannot be defended.

One shortcoming of this method is that it produces a best solution within a rigidly defined framework. It takes the world as is and then makes the best of it. Only through repeated trials can better solutions be found as conditions change. This solution considered only the network of customers and supply points that would exist if the San Francisco facility were indeed established. Other alternative decisions were ignored.

To illustrate the potential savings that might be overlooked if the manufacturer accepts this solution as the best answer, let us re-solve the same problem, except that we expand the capacity of the Atlanta warehouse from fifty to a total of seventy-five units. This move will add the same capacity to the system as setting up the San Francisco branch with a capacity of twenty-five units.

Customer \ Warehouses	New York	Atlanta	Dallas	San Francisco	Requirements
1	9 (10)	16	18	21	10
2	8 (20)	8.50	18	2.50	20
3	9.50 (25)	9	17.50	21	25
4	11 (20)	6	15	20	20
5	13	3 (50)	17	21	50
6	16	9	8.50 (30)	13	30
7	18	19	6 (10)	5 (25)	35
S	0 (25)	0	0 (15)	0	40
Capacity	100	50	55	25	230

Figure 13.3. Second minimum-cost transportation program. *Note:* Total transportation cost is $1,297.50.

However, the results are entirely different. Figure 13.4 shows the solution for minimum cost transportation when the Atlanta warehouse is expanded in capacity and the San Francisco warehouse is left out of consideration.

Table 13.4

Customer	Transportation Rates
1	$21.00
2	21.50
3	21.00
4	20.00
5	21.00
6	13.00
7	5.00

Table 13.5 Changes in minimum-cost transportation program by addition of San Francisco warehouse

Shipments	Without San Francisco	With San Francisco
New York to 6	10	0
New York to S*	15	25
Dallas to 6	20	30
Dallas to 7	35	0
Dallas to S*	0	15
San Francisco to 7	0	25

*S(slack) customer.

Warehouses / Customer	New York	Atlanta	Dallas	Requirements
1	9 (10)	16	18	10
2	8 (20)	8.50	18	20
3	9.50 (25)	9	17.50	25
4	11 (5)	6 (15)	15	20
5	13	3 (50)	17	50
6	16	9 (10)	8.50 (20)	30
7	18	19	6 (35)	35
S	0 (40)	0	0	40
Capacity	100	75	55	230

Figure 13.4. Third minimum-cost transportation program. *Note:* Total transportation cost is $1,252.50.

Table 13.6 Summary of differences among three minimum-cost transportation programs

	Program 1, original network		Program 2, add San Francisco		Program 3, enlarge Atlanta	
	Source	Quantity	Source	Quantity	Source	Quantity
4	New York	20	New York	20	New York	5
					Atlanta	15
6	New York	10	Dallas	30	Atlanta	10
	Dallas	20			Dallas	20
7	Dallas	35	Dallas	10	Dallas	35
			San Francisco	25		
Excess	New York	15	New York	25	New York	40
			Dallas	15		

Table 13.6 summarizes the key differences among the three optimum solutions. The total cost of program 1 is $1397.50; program 2, $1297.50; and program 3, $1252.50.

Cost-Minimization Location Models

In general, economists have developed two kinds of economic location models. One is the cost-minimization model and the other is the market-area competition model. While we have already seen elements of both models, let us summarize their applications.

Cost-minimization models deal with the relation between where a firm buys its inputs and where it sells its output. Obviously, costs are minimized to the extent that the place of purchase of inputs is closer to the point of sale. Especially are transport costs minimized by any location decision having these characteristics. But the more advantages there are to a particular market area, the more firms will be bidding for a location in that market area. Land costs may rise to offset transport cost savings. It is the interaction between costs (rents) and transport costs that will determine how individual firms are scattered around a market area. Since land costs decline from the market center outward, those firms which do not have a strong attraction to the center will find the lower land costs of outlying locations offsetting transport costs to the market center. Firms with production functions requiring large land inputs will not locate at the market center. The advantage of a cost-minimization model is that it gives interesting insights into the location decision and the locational structure of many markets. But the model is not applicable to all location decisions.

Market-Area Competition Models

Market-area competition models differ from cost-minimization models in their assumptions about market dispersion, especially of customers. If customers are dispersed, there are transport costs for delivering the firm's output to them. Effectively, unless for competitive reasons a different price policy is used, each customer will be charged a different price. That price will be equal to production and sales costs plus transport costs. Generally, product transport costs in such a model are assumed to be large relative to production costs. To reach the largest number of customers, firms will spread out. In this way, they can be closer to more customers, avoid competition, and offer lower prices to more customers.

Pattern of Economic Activity in a City

The change in the pattern of economic activities in Philadelphia from 1954 to 1972 can be used as a test of which of these models best explains what has been happening in industrial and commercial locations in the United States. We can begin our analysis of Philadelphia with the use of an ancient form of the cost-minimization model, one developed by the early German economist J. H. von Thünen. In the 1820s he worked out an explanation of the way in which land used for the production of agricultural crops was patterned around a city located on a flat plain.

Suppose that in Philadelphia and its suburbs there are three major competing uses for land: commerce (stores, parking lots, warehouses, and office space), industry (factories, freight-handling facilities, and administrative offices), and residences. A von Thünen model explains how these different land uses patterned themselves in rings of development around a central business district (CBD).

In Fig. 13.5, along the horizontal axis are measured distances from *CBD*. Along the vertical axis, the net revenue per acre is measured. Net revenue means the revenue from the sales of the product or service of the economic activity that occupies a specific location less the production and transportation costs. Admittedly, net revenue measured in this way for some kinds of commercial, industrial, and residential uses is not always easy to calculate. We need to know product and service prices, input coefficients, and input prices as well as, in the case of residential use, estimates of benefits.

From *CBD* outward, the net revenue from any product or service per acre of space occupied will decrease as transportation costs rise. Thus, the slope of the net revenue curve is negative and equals the transportation cost per acre-product per mile. There are three net revenue curves, one each for each activity. The commerce net revenue curve runs from *RC* to *OC*, that is, from

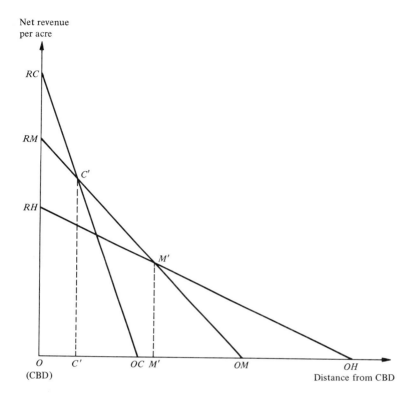

Figure 13.5. Economic land-use zones in Philadelphia.

RC-OC net revenue curve for commerce
RM-OM net revenue curve for manufacturing
RH-OH net revenue curve for residences

Zones: CBD Downtown
CBD-C' Commercial zone
C'M' Manufacturing zone
M'-OH Residential zone

the level of net revenue at the city center to that point *OC* at which net revenue from commerce drops to zero. The zone from *CBD* to *C'*, then, is the commercial zone. The maximum profits from the use of the land in this zone can be obtained by commercial activities, because only in that zone is net revenue from commerce higher than that for any other use.

The industrial net revenue curve runs from *RM* to *OM*. It will only pay to specialize in industrial land use, in the zone bounded by *C'* and *M'*. In that zone, industrial activities have a higher net revenue than any other economic

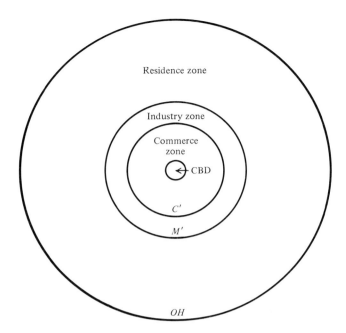

Figure 13.6. Von Thünen "map" of Philadelphia.

activities. And, by the same token, the residential zone begins at M' and runs out to OH, the city limits.

Note that the convex curve or density gradient connecting points RC, C', M', and OH is a maximum rent or net revenue curve for Philadelphia. This convex curve traces the net benefits from the current pattern of land use of the city. This curve can be used to develop a map something like Fig. 13.6 to show the zones of preferential development.

The position of the density gradient for any economic activity is dependent on the demand for the product or service of that activity. And the slope of the density gradient will depend on transportation costs. As competition changes with demand shifts, price increases or decreases, and changes in the methods and costs of transportation, the zone borders would also change. Perhaps more important, the sequence of zones might also change. Of course, the number of competing economic activities would also change.[1]

---

[1]By the way, the von Thünen land-use model is really a very early form of linear programming. Note that in it there is a limited number of possible economic activities (including activities in sequence), there are fixed technological coefficients (production functions), and there are fixed prices. In that sense, then, the determination of a zone for a particular economic activity is equivalent to a corner solution.

Employment Trends in Philadelphia

The Federal Reserve Bank of Philadelphia[2] worked out Figs. 13.7 through 13.18 to show how manufacturing employment was being distributed between the city of Philadelphia and its suburbs over the period from 1954 to 1972. In six of the eleven most important manufacturing industries—electrical machinery, nonelectrical machinery, fabricated metals, food, textiles, and chemicals (shown in Figs. 13.8 through 13.13)—there was an obvious shift from the city to the suburbs. Overall, as shown in Fig. 13.7, manufacturing shifted from a central city location outward to the suburbs. This kind of evidence casts doubt on the relevance of the cost-minimization model and seems to support the market-area competition model.

To be sure, not all the evidence was so clear-cut. In two industries, printing and publishing and apparel, the central city (Figs. 13.14 and 13.15) retained its dominance. In two other industries (Figs. 13.16 and 13.17), primary metals and petroleum, the suburbs retained their dominance. Only in transportation equipment (Fig. 13.18) was employment approximately equally divided between Philadelphia and its suburbs.

Philadelphia Fed Location Model

Economists at the Federal Reserve Bank of Philadelphia developed a regression model to determine why some firms and industries locate (and remain) in the central city and why others locate (or relocate) in the suburbs. The model was

$$\%CE_{ij} = a + b_1 K_i + b_2 K_i + b_3 D_i + b_4 A_j + e_{ij}$$

where

$\%CE_{ij}$ = percent of employment industry i in Standard Metropolitan Statistical Area (SMSA) j that is located in the central city

a = constant term

K_i = capital-output ratio for industry i

L_i = labor requirements for industry i

These requirements may take any of the following forms:

L_i^1 = labor-output ratio for industry i

$\sum_{k=1}^{8} L_{ik}^2$ = percentage of industry i's employment in each of eight major occupations, k

L_i^3 = average wage in the United States in industry i

---

[2] *Jobs in Philadelphia: Experience and Prospect,* Federal Reserve Bank of Philadelphia, December 1975.

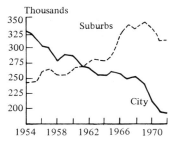

Figure 13.7. Manufacturing.

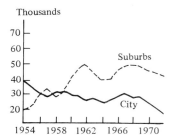

Figure 13.8. Electrical machinery.

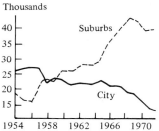

Figure 13.9. Nonelectrical machinery.

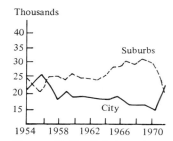

Figure 13.10. Fabricated metals.

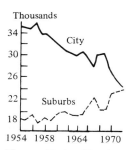

Figure 13.11. Food.

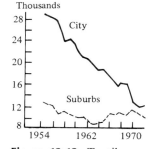

Figure 13.12. Textiles.

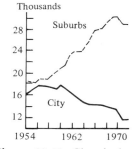

Figure 13.13. Chemicals.

Figures 13.7 through 13.18. Distribution of manufacturing employment between the City of Philadelphia and its suburbs, 1954–1972.

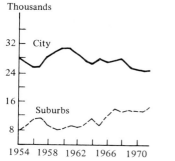

Figure 13.14. Printing and publishing.

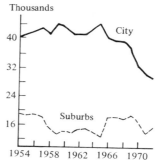

Figure 13.15. Apparel.

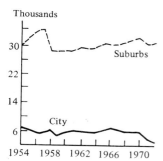

Figure 13.16. Primary metals.

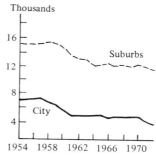

Figure 13.17. Petroleum.

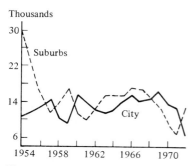

Figure 13.18. Transportation equipment.

Sources for Figures 13.7 through 13.18:
Suburban series are the difference between the regional series and city series; data for the region are from U.S. Department of Labor, Bureau of Labor Statistics, *Employment and Earnings, States and Areas, 1939-72, Bulletin 1370-10,* and Commonwealth of Pennsylvania, Department of Labor and Industry, Bureau of Employment Security, *Total Civilian Work Force, Unemployment and Employment by Industry: Annual Average, 1964-1973, Philadelphia Labor Market Area* (June 1974); data for the city are from Philadelphia Region Econometric Model Databank (February 21, 1975), Economics Research Unit of the University of Pennsylvania, and *Jobs in Philadelphia,* Technical Supplement B, Federal Reserve Bank of Philadelphia (December 1975).

D_i = dummy variable which takes the value of 1 if industry i produces durable goods and 0 otherwise

A_j = average percentage of manufacturing employment located in the central city of SMSA j

e_{ij} = random error term

b_1, b_2, b_3, b_4 = estimated coefficients

i = subscript indicating individual industry

j = subscript indicating individual SMSA

The basic assumptions of the model are the following:

1. The regional level of employment is assumed to be determined by exogenous forces (not examined in the model).
2. The current pattern of employment across the metropolitan landscape is assumed to reflect a stable adjustment to underlying supply and demand forces.
3. The prices of inputs and outputs facing firms are assumed to be essentially equal at all locations within the city and equal at all locations in the suburbs. Citywide prices, of course, differ from suburban prices.
4. Each firm in each industry is assumed to select a site where its profits are maximized.
5. Production processes and functions are assumed to be the same for all firms in a given industry.

While the Philadelphia Fed began its model building with observations about the Philadelphia Standard Metropolitan Statistical Area (SMSA), later data from Denver, Baltimore, St. Louis, and New York SMSAs were added.

Results of the Philadelphia Fed Location Model

Table 13.7 shows the regression coefficients that were obtained for the Philadelphia Fed location model. To interpret these results, here are the basic hypotheses being tested.

1. Hypothesis A—Industries requiring relatively more labor in their production processes will tend to locate in the central city. Thus the sign on the labor-output ratio would be positive.
2. Hypothesis B—Industries requiring extensive investment in plant and machinery per dollar of output would prefer a suburban location where land would be less expensive. The coefficient on the capital-output ratio should have a negative sign.
3. Hypothesis C—Durable goods firms that require less ready access to consumer markets will not compete vigorously for central city locations. The coefficient on the durable goods' dummy should be negative.

Table 13.7 Central city–suburban employment location hypothesis
Dependent variable: Central city employment as a percentage of SMSA employment in the industry

Hypothesis	Expected sign	Independent variable	Regression coefficients* Philadelphia SMSA only	Five SMSAs
		Constant (a)	0.2111 (1.333)*	1.235 (5.06)*
A	+	Labor-output ratio (L_i^1)	+1.775† (2.84)	—
B	−	Capital-output ratio (K_i)	−0.003 (−0.111)	0.071† (3.10)
C	−	Durable-goods dummy (D_i)	−0.122 (−1.51)	−0.345‡ (−4.41)
D	+	Average industry wage (L_i^3)		−0.011‡ (−4.42)
E	+	% employees craftsmen ($\Sigma L_{ik}^2; k = 1$)		+0.042‡ (4.35)
	+	% employees managers ($\Sigma L_{ik}^2; k = 1$)		+0.065‡ (2.85)
	+	% employees professionals ($\Sigma L_{ik}^2; k = 1$)		+0.011 (2.85)
F	0	% employees salespersons ($\Sigma L_{ik}^2; k = 1$)		−0.007 (−0.27)
G	+	% employees clerical workers ($\Sigma L_{ik}^2; k = 1$)		+0.044† (−2.41)
H	−	% employees laborers ($\Sigma L_{ik}^2; k = 1$)		−0.014† (−2.58)
	−	% employees service persons ($\Sigma L_{ik}^2; k = 1$)		+0.015 (0.26)
I	+	Average of dependent variable by city (A_i)		+0.616 (1.98)
		Adjusted R^2	.47	.51

*t statistics in parentheses.
†Coefficient significant at the 5 percent level.
‡Coefficient significant at the 1 percent level.
Source: Jobs in Philadelphia: Experience and Prospects, Federal Reserve Bank of Philadelphia, December 1975, p. 37.

4. Hypothesis D—Wages should decline with increasing distance from the central city since workers' housing and commutation costs will also decline. Therefore, the sign on the wage variable should be positive.
5. Hypothesis E—A high percentage of craftsmen, managers, or professionals implies less standardization of procedures and more interaction with other firms. This should make central location more attractive and means a positive sign on these coefficients.

6. Hypothesis F—A high percentage of sales workers would indicate orientation toward the consumer and, therefore, no direct pull either out or toward the city. The coefficients on these variables should not differ significantly from zero.
7. Hypothesis G—A high percentage of clerical workers is usually associated with management functions, thus leading to a central city location. A positive coefficient is expected.
8. Hypothesis H—High percentage of laborers or operatives implies standardized output and routine processes. Thus, a suburban location might be expected as well as negative coefficients.
9. Hypothesis I—The average percentage of regional manufacturing in the given central city is a coefficient hypothesized to be positive. If the concentration of employment in a city relative to SMSA is high, any industry in that city can be expected to reflect this aggregate concentration.

Labor-output ratios have positive coefficients that are statistically significant. Hypothesis A tests well. Capital-output ratio coefficients displayed erratic behavior both in the sign and in statistical significance of the variable. At best, this was not a good test of hypothesis B. For hypothesis C, the results consistently suggested that producers of durable goods tended toward the suburbs. There was a negative sign both for Philadelphia and the five SMSAs, though the variable was statistically significant only for the five SMSAs.

As to hypotheses D, E, F, G, and H, results were generally statistically significant. There were problems with hypothesis F and with service employees in hypothesis H. Yet the positive sign for hypothesis H in the case of service workers (groundskeepers and gardeners compared with other laborers) was an indication of suburban location preference.

While the coefficient in hypothesis D was statistically significant, the sign was negative. The hypothesis that central city wages are higher than suburban wages does not test out. In hypothesis I, accounting for the average dominance of the city over the suburb in a region's manufacturing employment made only a small contribution to explaining the share of employment in the city for individual industries. The regression coefficient was not statistically significant but it was positive.

Conclusions about the Philadelphia Model

A firm's input characteristics and market orientation seem to explain a large amount of the locational variation among individual industries. Industries that were labor-intensive, had high skill composition in the labor force they used and lower wage rates, and produced nondurable goods as services tended to be located in the city. Other kinds of industries—capital-intensive, high-wage, durable-goods plants—tended to locate in the suburbs. However, the regression model did not explain basic demand and supply factors. Therefore, its results, while interesting, should be used with some caution.

Yet, it would appear that there is support for both models. Some kinds of industries apparently do use cost-minimizing procedures in selecting or retaining their locations. Location decisions of other kinds of industries can be explained by market-area competition analysis. One thing seems sure: It is hard to assert that central city locations are losing their appeal under all circumstances. This means that the von Thünen model and the negative gradient to the net revenue curve are still pretty good hypotheses to explain some forms of urban land use and location decisions.

Economic-Base Analysis

Economic-base analysis is another location decision algorithm. The employment and income-generating activities of a city are its economic base.

Economic-base analysis distinguishes between those activities that export their products and their services to other places outside the city and those that serve the people and the industries of the city itself. Export activities are basic. The other activities are nonbasic. Once the technical problem of separating the basic from the nonbasic activities has been solved, then a nonbasic/basic ratio (N/B) can be worked out. This ratio varies, with larger cities having lower values. The larger the city, the more likely it is to be a market for a large share of what it produces because larger cities are generally more self-sufficient than smaller places.

The N/B ratio provides a good description of market potential. Ullman and Dacey have pointed out that there is a minimum entrance requirement for every industry or economic activity for each market of a given size range.

Minimum or Threshold Requirements

Ullman and Dacey[3] analyzed fourteen different industries in the United States in six size classes of cities. By comparing the labor forces of each of the six class sizes, they found the lowest proportion of participation in each of the fourteen industries. This lowest proportion they called the "minimum requirement," the minimum level for that industry which a city of a given size could support.

Figure 13.19 illustrates their findings. They found that for professional services 5 percent was the minimum proportion of the workforce in places of 10,000. It was about 4 for places of 1000. Each of the minimum-requirements lines was derived by regression and each is a threshold. Figure 13.19 shows different thresholds or minimum requirements for each size class of city for a variety of industries.

Applying their research to various cities, Ullman and Dacey calculated actual industry employment in 1950 and compared it with estimated minimum

[3]E. L. Ullman and M. F. Dacey, "The Minimum Requirements Approach to the Urban Economic Base," *Lund Studies in Geography*, Series B, Sweden, Lund, 1962.

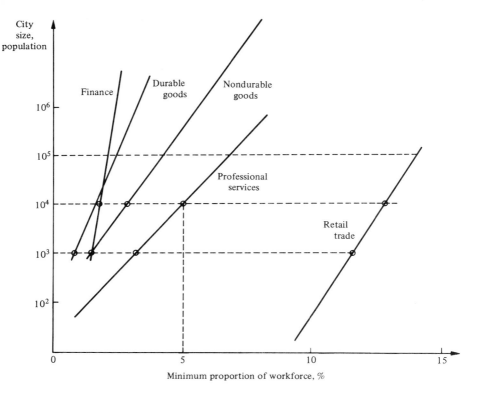

Figure 13.19. Industrial threshold requirements.

requirements. They combined the deviations between the expected and observed values for each industry in each city to get an index of specialization,

$$S = \frac{\sum_i [(P_i - M_i)^2/M_i]}{[(\Sigma_i P_i - \Sigma_i M_i)^2/\Sigma_i M_i]}$$

where

S = index of specialization
i = any given industry
P_i = observed percentage of labor force employed in ith industry
M_i = expected percentage of labor force employed in ith industry

They found a strong negative relationship between the size of a city and the index of specialization. The smaller the city, the higher the index of specialization.

Location Quotients

Location quotient LQ is another measure of the extent to which a given industry or economic activity is concentrated in a given market. The location quotient for any industry i is given by

$$\frac{e_i/e}{E_i/E}$$

where

e_i = local employment in the ith industry
e = total local employment
E_i = national or regional employment in the ith industry
E = total national employment

LQs are used to identify basic activities or industries. If an industry has an LQ with a value exceeding unity for that market, the industry is basic. It is a net exporter of products or services to other areas.

Table 13.8 Location quotients for certain industries in the greater Bridgeport planning region, Connecticut, 1970

(1) Industry	(2) Total industry employment as percent of all industry employment	(3) Local industry employment as percent of regional employment	(4) Location quotient (3) ÷ (2)
Transportation equipment	.0254	.0930	3.66
Fabricated metals and ordnance	.0224	.0678	3.03
Electrical machinery	.0256	.0706	2.76
Primary metals	.0174	.0394	2.26
Machinery	.0264	.0531	2.01
Stone, clay, glass	.0086	.0168	1.95
Government	.0567	.0987	1.74
All manufacturing	.2616	.4464	1.71
Rubber and plastics	.0077	.0097	1.26
Instruments	.0060	.0072	1.20
Apparel	.0185	.0196	1.06
Printing and publishing	.0155	.0156	1.01
Trade	.2180	.1848	0.85
Communications and utilities	.0287	.0210	0.73
Construction	.0623	.0433	0.70
Finance, insurance, and real estate	.0509	.0346	0.68
Food	.0238	.0152	0.64
Transportation	.0382	.0219	0.57
Services	.2751	.1474	0.54

Source: Status of Economic Growth, Plan Report no. 3, Greater Bridgeport Regional Planning Agency, November 1976.

Table 13.8 shows calculations of LQs for the Bridgeport (Connecticut) Planning Region based on 1970 data. In column (2) are the ratios of percentages between employment in each of the listed industries nationwide and total national wage employment. In column (3) is the ratio or percentage between employment by industry in the Bridgeport Planning Region and total wage employment in that region. Column (4), the LQ, is obtained by dividing column (3) by column (2). These LQs for the Bridgeport region indicate not only which are the basic industries but also give ranking of their relative importance to the Bridgeport market area.

LQs do not necessarily provide good indicators for plant location. Because they do tell the degree of concentration in any market for any given industry, management might well have some doubts about wanting to increase the degree of concentration by moving into that market. On the other hand, to the extent that there are positive external economies traceable to high LQs, these indicators may serve as the basis for a decision to move into the market area.

Strategy of Location

The essence of a strategy of location is that it depends on progressive market development from the time the initial opportunity is recognized until the market reaches maturity. There is a threshold at which the location decision is timely and likely to be successful. Location decisions taken prior to this threshold cannot be justified.

The strategic plan involves four phases. At the conclusion of each phase, a decision not to continue with the location decision can be made. The strategy applies to a manufacturer.

PHASE I: ANALYSIS
Step 1 The market or area potential is determined. This potential is an independent function of the prevailing economic and industrial environment in the proposed area for location.

Step 2 The potential determined is compared to the minimum potential set by the firm's management. There are certain minimum costs involved in taking this step, and depending on assessment of the excess, if any, of marginal revenue over marginal cost, the decision to proceed can be made. The profitability of the proposed move will signal whether to proceed or to hold up.

PHASE II: MARKET RECONNAISSANCE
Step 1 At this stage, the manufacturer will select a manufacturer's representative or distributor to open sales channels in the proposed area.

Step 2 The sales channel will, of course, involve additional costs in order processing, inventory management, transportation, and freight handling. There must be some minimum expected sales volume to cover these costs.

Step 3 As the sales volume increases to and beyond the threshold level of profitability set by management, the stage is set for phase III.

PHASE III: MARKET DEVELOPMENT

Step 1   The initial step is to measure and forecast market penetration. This is the manufacturer's share of the market in relation to market or area potential. There is some level of penetration, some share of the market, above which it is feasible to proceed.

Step 2   Assuming that this threshold is achieved, the next step will probably involve selecting a dealer who will stock the manufacturer's production for sale in the area.

Step 3   Concurrently with step 2, promotional efforts will be intensified to achieve a higher level of identification and recognition. These efforts, too, will involve additional costs so that some minimum acceptable profit criterion will be used to establish a minimum acceptable sales volume for this phase.

PHASE IV: MARKET SOLIDIFICATION

Step 1   This phase begins with another but more intensive market study. The purpose of the market study is to determine if market penetration exceeds the level required to justify the location and building of a new facility to serve the market area.

Step 2   Assuming that indications are favorable, the firm now proceeds to establish the facility, taking care to arrange for all channels of inflow of necessary input as well as channels of distribution and sales.

The progressive development of the strategy is illustrated in Figs. 13.20 and 13.21. Figure 13.20 shows the relationship between market or area potential and a selected market-potential criterion. Although a straight line is used for the location indicator, the actual situation facing the firm in the location decision will determine the general form of the location entrance indicator. In

Figure 13.20 The market potential criterion.

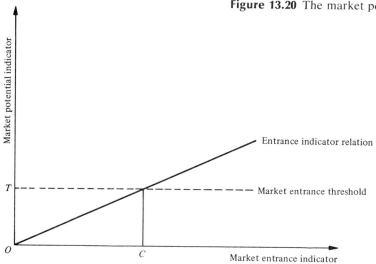

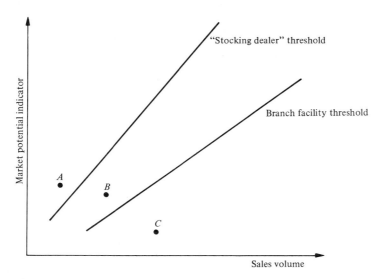

Figure 13.21. Development of market entrance strategy.

essence, the rule is that whenever the criterion of market potential exceeds the threshold level, a location decision should be made.

Figure 13.21 shows the relationship between market potential, sales volume, and the threshold shares of the market as found in phases III and IV. Point A represents the sales volume generated by the channel used during phase II (market reconnaissance). Point A is below the threshold for proceeding to phase III and no action is taken as a result.

Point B represents a sales volume generated by a different, more successful reconnaissance effort. Volume at point B exceeds the threshold for a move from phase II to phase III. When this indication is received, management will take the necessary steps to expand marketing effort to the stocking dealer stage.

Point C represents sales volume exceeding the threshold level for establishing a branch or new location. This is the trigger to make the move, assuming all other factors have been taken into consideration in the planning for the location decision.

Critique on Location and Relocation

No matter how well thought out the location decision and no matter how well executed, there is, of course, no assurance that a move will be successful. A survey[4] of more than 1000 moves found these results:

1. Some firms relied on average hourly wage rates instead of those appropriate to their own industries. Others failed to take account of local fringe benefits

[4]"Why Moves Go Wrong," *Industry Week*, p. 39, December 2, 1974.

in the new location. Still others did not account for regional differences in overtime, workweeks, productivity, and turnover differences in the new location compared with the old location.

2. Many firms did not acquire enough land for plant development. Others did not allow for residential and commercial encroachment on their sites nor did they consider problems with limited gas, electric, sewerage, and water resources.

3. A number of firms counted on transport and freight-handling facilities that turned out not to be available. Others assumed that freight rates available at nearby locations would also be available at their new locations.

4. At least 10 percent of the companies relocating did not have an adequate understanding of their own distribution and production cost relationships. They really didn't know what their most important costs were as they made their relocation decision.

5. A good many firms failed to estimate properly the impact of their activities on the new location in terms of traffic, fire protection, ecological factors, or even housing, school facilities, and medical resources.

6. Some locations were more than adequate in primary factors but, for example, metalworking firms often found no facilities for forging and plating. Other firms found they had to stockpile spare and assembly parts.

Chapter Summary

The economic landscape of a city, a region, or a nation became what it is through a complex system of location decisions. The economic landscape is a map, a record of decisions, a visible outline of how it all came about and of what is now in progress. In this chapter, we have looked at the location decisions of manufacturers, wholesalers, and retailers. By implication, we have seen the role of the "shakers and the movers"—the banks, the governments, the developers, the innovators, and the dreamers. Yet it was the business-owner who made the decision that the plant or the store or the office building be where it is.

We concentrated on three aspects of location decision making. The major emphasis was on the expansion decisions necessary to meet the requirements and challenges of a growing market. There also was an examination of threshold concepts. These serve as triggers for land-use change. Finally, we tried to put the whole ball of wax together by looking at specific places, especially the Philadelphia Standard Metropolitan Statistical Areas. There we examined the central city-suburb interaction so characteristic of North America.

And we finished with a look at a survey of hundreds of location decisions. If that look does nothing else, it serves to make us humble about our assertions concerning good location-decision making.

Selected Readings

Airov, Joseph:*The Location of the Synthetic-Fiber Industry*, New York, Wiley, 1959.

Alonso, William: *Location and Land Use*, Cambridge, Harvard University Press, 1964.

Beckmann, M.: *Location Theory*, New York, Random House, 1968.

Cliff, Andrew D., et al.: *Elements of Spatial Structure*, New York, Cambridge University Press, 1975.

Cutler, A. T.: "Changing Economic Profiles of Selected U.S. Cities," Federal Reserve Bank of Cleveland, 1962.

Fellner, David, et al.: "Jobs in Philadelphia: Experience and Prospects," *Business Review of the Federal Reserve Bank of Philadelphia*, December 1975.

Greenhut, M. L.: "When Is the Demand Factor of Location Important?" *Land Economics, 40:*175–184, May 1964.

Haggett, Peter: *Locational Analysis in Human Geography*, New York, St. Martin's, 1966.

Webber, M. J.: *Impact of Uncertainty on Location*, Cambridge, M.I.T., 1972.

Yeates, M. H.: "Some Factors Affecting the Spatial Distribution of Chicago Land Values, 1910–1960," *Economic Geography, 41*(1):57–70, 1965.

Questions, Problems, and Projects

1. Botsford Corporation's executive and administrative functions were all located in New York City, occupying ten floors of a high-rise office building in the East 50s, plus additional floor space in several other buildings. While Botsford had installed extensive computerization, the annual growth of its business still required sizable increases in the clerical staff. The quality of the available labor force was declining and the competitive pressures of other expanding employers were reflected in higher turnover, higher wage costs, and reduced productivity.

Botsford's management had become seriously concerned about the company's inability to attract bright, young executive trainees. Those who turned down Botsford's offers cited the high cost of living as the primary deterrent. Further adding to Botsford's problems, its landlord was negotiating for a substantial increase in rent upon lease expiration.

A consultant was engaged to review feasible alternatives, identified as

(*a*) Consolidation of offices within the East 50s area

(*b*) Partial or complete relocation to Connecticut or New Jersey

(*c*) Partial or complete relocation to a Southern or Southwestern city

The consultant found that beyond a possible estimated $425,000 reduction in rents through consolidation, there were no substantial advantages to seeking a different location in the East 50s in New York City.

Complete relocation to the Connecticut or New Jersey suburbs of a 750,000-square-foot facility could provide savings of $1.5 million annually on gross rental payments. Before adjusting for transferees, the suburban clerical wage cost differential could yield another $780,000 and some improvement in productivity. Nonrecurring costs (including severance pay, personnel replacement, and transfer costs) for this relocation were estimated at $5.9 million.

The economics of the suburban relocation were acceptable. Executive disruption would be minimal. However, a fifteen-year projection in both New Jersey and Connecticut locations by the consultant revealed that it was likely that many other corporations would also be moving to those areas, putting pressure on the suburban labor force. Moreover, there was some evidence that many portions of these nearby suburbs were becoming vulnerable to the spillover of environmental, tax and financial, and social problems.

A carefully selected moderate-sized Southern or Southwestern city with a self-contained labor force could offer at least comparable operating economies and a higher degree of stability. Rental savings might be as much as $2.25 million, the consultant reported, and payroll reductions might exceed $4.1 million annually. There would be other economies on corporate taxes, lower energy costs, and reduced employee turnover. However, the costs of the move, including all nonrecurring costs, would come to $9.1 million. Of course, state income taxes were lower as were real estate taxes and housing costs in the available locations.

What do you suggest that Botsford do? Spell out your arguments in detail.

2. Pequonnock Machine Works is a manufacturer of industrial machinery in the Northwest. Recently, management found that it was necessary to achieve a sharp reduction in fixed overhead. The recommendation of a consultant was that production facilities be consolidated. The key questions among a deeply divided production executive staff were: Which? And where?

The consultant gathered from each of Pequonnock's six plants such pertinent internal statistics as size of each facility, age, production capacity, expansion potentials, operating expenses, wages and fringe benefits, and labor-management relations. Careful consideration was also given to transportation services, characteristics of the local labor markets, tax trends, utility rates, and living conditions (especially for transferees).

Plants no. 1 and no. 2 were located in Tacoma in a mature industrial complex; they produced heavy machinery lines. Facilities were getting old and crowded and were designed for handling large units. Wage patterns reflected the dominant lumber economy and workers tended to be militant.

Plant no. 3 was in the Willamette Valley, south of Portland, of relatively modern construction; it had ample room for expansion. Operating expenses reflected higher amortization costs and an expensive labor contract.

Plant no. 4 was in central Seattle. It was an inefficient, older facility with limited expansion potential but the workers had good skills and long seniority.

Plant no. 5 was in Boise, in a converted old mill. It was designed for the production of heavy and moderately heavy machinery. The location was poor for transportation to national markets, but wage rates were favorable.

Plant no. 6, Pequonnock's newest facility, was in Everett. Production was concentrated in controls and primarily involved female workers.

The consultant provided three practical plans that combined relative economies; they are shown in Table 1.

Table 1 Pequonnock Machine Works, Inc.: Plans for cost reductions

Plan	Initial outlay	Annual opera- ting cost savings (or loss)	Simple payback, yr
A: Close and sell plant 6; relocate production to new lower-wage location	$ 464,000	$433,000 (Sales of real estate will offset relocation costs. Lower wages will add to savings.)	1.1
B: Close plant 4 and con- solidate with plant 6 and plant 3	$2,861,000	$712,000	4.0
C: Close plants 1 and 2; consolidate opera- tions at plant 5. Build new facility at plant 5	$3,064,400	$385,000	8.0

What is your recommendation? Why?

3. Attempt to apply economic zoning to a city with which you are familiar. How would you modify von Thünen? Why?

4. The Federal Reserve Bank of Dallas reported in 1975 that "the first shift away from (the) dependence (by the Texas apparel industry) on local markets came in the 1930s with the introduction of ready-made dresses . . . With this single item, Dallas emerged as a major apparel market. And Texas apparel makers, freed of the constraints of local demand for fairly standard items . . . were able to compete over broader areas. As they went into new markets, the competition was based not only on price but also on such things as workmanship, styling and fabric . . . The ability of even very small plants to operate profitably accounts for their dispersion across the state . . . Given the ready access to markets in Texas . . . and prospects for continued availability of labor, the outlook (for the apparel industry) is for still more growth . . . " Take this statement and develop a general-location decision matrix for the apparel industry.

5. "Until now, labor costs have been a primary determinant in the location of textile mills . . . But the introduction of equipment that makes the industry less labor-intensive offers new opportunities for growth . . . One new plant in Texas uses only eight employees a shift. With older machines, seven times that many workers would be needed to turn out the same volume of goods." If labor is less important in the location decision for the textile industry, suggest and analyze some of the other factors that become important as labor intensity declines.

6. Footloose manufacturing firms are those not dependent on proximity to raw materials, water, or power; they generally produce goods that are of high value per weight so that proximity to markets is not a major location factor.

Take the research-and-development–based manufacturer and try to work out the parameters of location decisions. What is causing the trend to Boston, Boulder, San Francisco, and Washington-Virginia-Maryland?

Case 13.1 Federal Assistance to Economically Distressed Areas[1]

This digest of a General Accounting Office (GAO) report to the Congress of the United States outlines a familiar problem in location analysis, the lack of adequate statistical resources.

WHY THE REVIEW WAS MADE

The Economic Development Administration of the Department of Commerce provides financial, technical, and planning assistance to aid long-range economic development of distressed areas. As authorized by law, the Secretary of Commerce designates areas eligible for assistance on the basis of statistical data developed by the Departments of Labor and the Interior and the Bureau of the Census.

For the most part, the Economic Development Administration's ability to identify properly areas eligible for assistance hinges on the soundness of unemployment and income data. The designations of economic distress may influence the distribution of monies and benefits from other federal agencies. For example, firms located in areas of high unemployment are eligible for federal procurement preference. Therefore, the General Accounting Office reviewed the currentness and accuracy of the statistical data used for determining an area's eligibility for assistance.

Findings and Conclusions

Unemployment and income data used by the Economic Development Administration in determining the eligibility of local areas are not current and are of questionable accuracy. The data should be improved to ensure realistic economic appraisals of those areas. GAO questions whether the areas of the United States experiencing economic distress, as indicated by high unemployment and/or low-income levels, are, in all instances, being properly identified. GAO did not attempt to evaluate the appropriateness of unemployment and income levels as criteria for eligibility.

---

[1]GAO, Comptroller General's Report to the Congress, *More Reliable Data Needed as a Basis for Providing Federal Assistance to Economically Distressed Areas*, Department of Commerce, Department of Labor B-133182, May 10, 1971.

UNEMPLOYMENT DATA

The questionable reliability of the unemployment data is attributable to conceptual weaknesses in the methodology for estimating unemployment as well as to problems in developing unemployment rates for small areas. This report discusses these weaknesses, which raise considerable doubt as to the accuracy and reliability of unemployment estimates for small and rural areas.

The many problems associated with the development of current and reliable statistical data are not subject to ready solution. This is especially true of small areas—characteristically redevelopment areas—where statistical data normally are not gathered on a continuing basis and where the costs of developing meaningful statistical data are significantly higher than those connected with developing data on a national or regional basis.

Within recent years the Department of Labor has initiated and sponsored studies designed to produce information which could be used to improve the methodology established for estimating unemployment in state and local areas. Except for a modification with respect to one major element of this methodology, however, the studies have not resulted in an improved methodology, and it remains basically the same as that introduced in 1960.

GAO evaluated the unemployment-estimating practices in two states. In both states the prescribed methodology was subjected to varied degrees of modification and was not applied uniformly. State agencies are severely handicapped in their attempts to develop reliable unemployment rates using this methodology by the lack of current labor market data for local areas.

Further study is required to determine the extent to which the practices and experiences of the states included in GAO's review are indicative of those in other states. GAO believes, however, that, although they may vary in degree, the problems experienced by the two states are characteristic of those in many other states, because of the general lack of labor market data for small and rural areas.

INCOME DATA

Family income data for states and local areas are available only from census information gathered once every ten years. There are two pronounced drawbacks to the use of these data in determining current eligibility:

1. They do not provide a reasonably current measure of income.
2. The preciseness and reliability of the data developed for small areas is questionable.

Because current family income data are not available, the Economic Development Administration is not able to make the annual review of area eligibility based on income that is required by the Public Works and Economic Development Act of 1965, as amended (42 U.S.C. 3121), or to base its determinations of maximum grant rates on recent data.

GAO believes that the Economic Development Administration should consider the feasibility of using per capita income data (developed by the Office of Business Economics, Department of Commerce) as one means by which income levels could be measured more frequently than every ten years. Any departure from using median family income criteria, however, will require a change in legislation. The preciseness and reliability of the per capita income data has not been fully tested. GAO is not necessarily advocating the use of these data in their present form.

RECOMMENDATIONS OR SUGGESTIONS

GAO is making several recommendations designed to improve the system. For example,

1. The Secretary of Labor should ascertain changes needed to improve unemployment estimates and to monitor state unemployment-estimating practices.
2. The Secretary of Commerce should study the problems associated with developing current unemployment and income data, consider the use of the more current per capita income data, and recommend changes in legislation as warranted.

AGENCY ACTIONS AND UNRESOLVED ISSUES

The Department of Labor said that, in line with GAO's recommendations and within the constraints of budget resources and staffing ceilings, it would take steps to ensure uniformity in the application of the prescribed estimating techniques and to improve the accuracy and comparability of data. The department said also that it would consider the GAO report as part of the department's evaluation of the unemployment-estimating procedures that currently was being made.

The Department of Labor agreed with GAO's recommendations that the findings of research studies on estimating unemployment should be converted into timely and meaningful action, where practicable and feasible, and that the department should improve the review and monitoring procedures of the unemployment-estimating practices of the state employment security agencies.

The Department of Labor said further that the improvements necessary in the methodology would be made by the end of fiscal year 1971 and would take account of GAO's findings as well as the findings of research studies sponsored by the department and by the affiliated state employment security agencies.

The Department of Labor noted that the reliability of estimating unemployment by using the prescribed estimating techniques tended to decrease for small areas. For many small, predominantly rural areas, the major problem is one of underemployment of available worker-power rather than unemployment which the methodology is intended to measure. Because of this, the department suggested that alternative approaches to measuring economic distress might be needed.

The Department of Commerce agreed, in principle, that it would be desirable to have more recent income information on a regular basis but stated that the costs of securing such information by duplicating Bureau of the Census procedures and techniques appeared prohibitive. By using other data sources, such as Office of Business Economics per capita income, however, the

Economic Development Administration hopes to develop reasonably accurate income estimates.

Further, a work group is studying per capita income data, but much remains to be done before they can be used to measure area economic distress.

MATTERS FOR CONSIDERATION BY THE CONGRESS

Titles I through IV of the Public Works and Economic Development Act of 1965 expire at the close of fiscal year 1971. The House Committee on Public Works plans to conduct extensive hearings on the Economic Development Administration and its programs in mid-1971.

Also the Secretary of Commerce may seek changes in legislation on the basis of the review recommendation by GAO of the problems associated with developing unemployment and income data.

GAO believes that this report will be useful to the Congress in considering these matters.

DISCUSSION QUESTIONS 13.1

1. How are income and employment data used to determine market potential?
2. What is the meaning of "economic distress" and how should it be measured? Is economic distress location- or time-oriented?
3. Are there certain kinds of industries which would find it advantageous to locate in areas of economic distress?
4. How would you evaluate the data available from the Departments of Commerce and Labor? How do they compare with data generated by states, local communities, and private agencies? Distinguish between accuracy and reliability in data for location decisions.

Case 13.2   Huyck: A Company That Moved South[1]

As a Northern-based manufacturer, Huyck Corporation faced a special problem in the early 1970s when it decided to find a new headquarters location. Earlier management decisions had actually split the home base between two communities 120 miles apart. Top officers worked in Stamford, Connecticut, while major staff executives, chiefly those in finance, operated out of Rensselaer, New York. "As our business grew and became more complex, the disadvantages of operating on that basis became acute," says Donald H. Grubb, president and chief executive of Huyck. "Clearly we had to combine them. The question was where."

Because of high local operating costs, neither Stamford nor Rensselaer was considered. Instead, Huyck, a $120 million manufacturer of belting products for the pulp and paper industry, ended up on a rolling, 85-acre site near Wake Forest, North Carolina, just north of Raleigh. There, in 1973, Huyck moved into a headquarters building of 8500 square feet and a second plant for Huyck's Formex Division, based in Greenville, Tennessee. "Our distribution pattern dictated a site east of the Mississippi River," says Grubb. "Beyond that, we looked at everything from northern New Jersey on down."

[1]See *Business Week*, May 17, 1976.

One key deciding factor was a Huyck study indicating that North Carolina's building costs ran about 24 percent lower than those in the New York–Connecticut area. In the early 1970s, Huyck's leased office space in Stamford cost just over $7 per square foot per year, while space in the Raleigh area averaged $4.50. "The cost of our headquarters building came to $265,000, and the cost of relocating our employees was $375,000," says Grubb. "We figure our operating savings on taxes, utilities, and such will pay back the one-time cost of the move in just under nine years."

JOB TURNOVER IS HIGH

Huyck finds that the average payroll for manufacturing employees runs 10 percent less in the Southeast than in the New York metropolitan area. But the company has not discovered any wonderland of cheap labor. "Had we been looking for a strictly manufacturing site," says Grubb, "we'd probably have gone to a smaller town without all the amenities we needed for our corporate managers. But we realized we were making a compromise. Manufacturing unemployment in the Raleigh area is only about 2.5 percent. So labor turnover tends to be high." In Huyck's first six months, in fact, labor turnover averaged 44 percent, which obviously cut into productivity and profits, though Huyck cannot put an exact figure on the cost. "Part of this was due to the normal problems of starting up a new plant in an area where you are not known," Grubb says. "In the last six months, the rate has stabilized at 17 percent."

Grubb claims that Huyck's current clerical help costs 10 to 15 percent less than in Stamford, "and we feel we get a better grade of employee," he adds. "A young girl who was doing some typing for me recently changed a percentage figure I had used in a letter. I changed it back, and she said, 'That's wrong.' I checked and found she was correct. In Stamford, that kind of thing just wouldn't happen."

For the benefit of employees who moved South with the company, Huyck paid special attention to the local tax bite on transferees. Connecticut has no state income tax, only a capital gains tax and a fairly stiff property tax. New York's state income tax runs to a maximum 14 percent on $14,000. The North Carolina rate is 7 percent on a maximum $10,000. However, North Carolina collects an "intangibles tax," computed at 10 cents per $100 of average quarterly cash on hand and 25 cents per $100 of securities owned at year-end.

On the basis of income tax alone, the move's impact on lower- to middle-level executives, most of whom were based in New York, proved negligible. An employee with a $20,000 salary, $1500 in cash on hand, $25,000 in securities, and $2000 in dividend and interest income or capital gains would pay $1023 in New York compared with $985 in North Carolina.

The tax bite on upper management, which had been based mostly in Stamford, was higher in the North. While Connecticut has no income tax, a Huyck study showed that a manager with a $50,000 salary, $3000 in cash on hand, an unusually large securities portfolio worth $400,000, and $18,000 in dividend or interest income and capital gains would pay Connecticut $1048 in capital gains taxes. Income and intangibles taxes in North Carolina would run $4637; in New York, income and capital gains taxes would run $6250.

HIGHER TAXES, CHEAPER SERVICES

North Carolina's high income taxes, however, are offset by savings in other areas. Smaller real and personal property taxes in North Carolina eliminate about two-thirds of the difference between the Northern and Southern locations. In the Raleigh area, for instance, the rate on property taxes averages $1.89 per $100 of property value. In Stamford, property taxes average roughly $4.60 per $100, while in Rensselaer, they go up to a startling $17.50 per $100. In Huyck's North Carolina location, savings on housing and transportation more than make up the rest of the difference. Thomas M. McCrary, senior vice president, says: "In buying a house in Raleigh, I doubled my floor space and went from pine siding to brick at about the same monthly payment."

In the same way, Grubb notes of his Stamford days, an evening out in New York was a major undertaking. "Here," he says, "you can be downtown in 15 minutes—and find a parking place."

"We found little difference in food costs, but car insurance is considerably cheaper down here," says Frederick A. Ferraro, vice president for finances. "Clothing is not as expensive, and you don't need as many heavy clothes. Compared to what we were used to, the winters down here are quite mild and a lot shorter." Services, ranging from orthodontists to bricklayers, painters, or auto mechanics, are also cheaper in price. "And they come when you call them, instead of maybe six or eight weeks later," says Ferraro.

He is equally enthusiastic about local financial services. For most routine corporate services, he turns to North Carolina banks. But he maintains his relationship with New York banks. "We actually find our New York banks call on us more frequently down here than they did when we were in Stamford," he says. "I guess they just like to come to this area." Johnson & Higgins, a New York company that handles most of Huyck's international insurance, now has a branch in Charlotte, 100 miles away.

As proof of the move's success, Grubb notes, all but one of the thirty-five executives who were originally asked to relocate accepted. Of those thirty-four executives, only one has since returned to the North. "Today if we were making the same decision on whether or not to move, there is no question that the decision would be the same as our previous decision," says Grubb. "We have no regrets. In fact, if we build another plant, I'd be very surprised if we didn't build it somewhere in the South."

DISCUSSION QUESTIONS 13.2

1. Enumerate the factors that made Huyck seek a new headquarters location. Would there be a different set of factors if the choice had been a plant location?
2. Why, if many other companies have found Stamford, Connecticut, a good location, did Huyck reject it? To what extent is there a noneconomic orientation in Huyck's location decision, if any?
3. How does a company location change affect the national economy, the regional economy, the local economy? How would you measure net benefits from a move?
4. What theory of location would you use to explain the Huyck move? Why?

INDEX